Lecture Notes in Computer

T0238253

Commenced Publication in 1973
Founding and Former Series Editors:
Gerhard Goos, Juris Hartmanis, and Jan van Leeuwen

Editorial Board

David Hutchison
  Lancaster University, UK
Takeo Kanade
  Carnegie Mellon University, Pittsburgh, PA, USA
Josef Kittler
  University of Surrey, Guildford, UK
Jon M. Kleinberg
  Cornell University, Ithaca, NY, USA
Alfred Kobsa
  University of California, Irvine, CA, USA
Friedemann Mattern
  ETH Zurich, Switzerland
John C. Mitchell
  Stanford University, CA, USA
Moni Naor
  Weizmann Institute of Science, Rehovot, Israel
Oscar Nierstrasz
  University of Bern, Switzerland
C. Pandu Rangan
  Indian Institute of Technology, Madras, India
Bernhard Steffen
  University of Dortmund, Germany
Madhu Sudan
  Massachusetts Institute of Technology, MA, USA
Demetri Terzopoulos
  University of California, Los Angeles, CA, USA
Doug Tygar
  University of California, Berkeley, CA, USA
Gerhard Weikum
  Max-Planck Institute of Computer Science, Saarbruecken, Germany

Mitsu Okada   Ichiro Satoh (Eds.)

Advances in Computer Science - ASIAN 2006

Secure Software and Related Issues

11th Asian Computing Science Conference
Tokyo, Japan, December 6-8, 2006
Revised Selected Papers

 Springer

Volume Editors

Mitsu Okada
Keio University
Japan
E-mail: mitsu@abelard.flet.keio.ac.jp

Ichiro Satoh
National Institute of Informatics
Japan
E-mail: ichiro@nii.ac.jp

Library of Congress Control Number: 2007943082

CR Subject Classification (1998): F.3, E.3, D.2.4, D.4.6-7, K.6.5, C.2

LNCS Sublibrary: SL 1 – Theoretical Computer Science and General Issues

ISSN   0302-9743
ISBN-10   3-540-77504-8 Springer Berlin Heidelberg New York
ISBN-13   978-3-540-77504-1 Springer Berlin Heidelberg New York

This work is subject to copyright. All rights are reserved, whether the whole or part of the material is concerned, specifically the rights of translation, reprinting, re-use of illustrations, recitation, broadcasting, reproduction on microfilms or in any other way, and storage in data banks. Duplication of this publication or parts thereof is permitted only under the provisions of the German Copyright Law of September 9, 1965, in its current version, and permission for use must always be obtained from Springer. Violations are liable to prosecution under the German Copyright Law.

Springer is a part of Springer Science+Business Media

springer.com

© Springer-Verlag Berlin Heidelberg 2007
Printed in Germany

Typesetting: Camera-ready by author, data conversion by Scientific Publishing Services, Chennai, India
Printed on acid-free paper   SPIN: 12210770   06/3180   5 4 3 2 1 0

Gilles Kahn: A Humble Tribute

Gilles Kahn was one of the visionary leaders whose accomplishments will be remembered for generations. In fact, the ASIAN series of conferences owes a great deal to him. He saw long ago the need to harness Southeast Asia for the next generation. He kindly accepted to be on our Steering Committee and indeed took personal interest and physically participated in the 1995 and 2002 conferences. His sharp criticisms, suggestions and support helped nurture the ASIAN conference from its birth.

Two of his distinct fundamental contributions in computer science that have had a big impact are: natural semantics and a framework for distributed asynchronous computation (often referred to as Kahn's networks of processes). The first one provides a theory that allows computation of properties of programs. This has had a big impact on the development of programming environments from specifications. The latter has had tremendous impact on the specification of asynchronous computation and contributed in many ways to early UNIX development and to formal theories of concurrent processes including communicating sequential processes. Not only did he pioneer the foundational area of computer science or formal methods through his personal contributions, but he also enriched his involvement in the measures of commissioning reliable software for space rocket missions.

He was one of the early members of IRIA (INRIA's name then) and the architect of the INRIA Sophia Antipolis Center. His leadership vision can be seen in the way INRIA has grown in the areas of science and technology, industry cooperations and international relations.

Above all he was always a simple, accessible, charismatic person who was easy to talk to. The ASIAN series owes its growth to his support. It was a great privilege for us to have an opportunity to learn from his visionary leadership through this series of conferences.

Asian Computing Science Conference
Steering Committee

Preface

The series of annual Asian Computing Science Conferences (ASIAN) was initiated in 1995 by AIT, INRIA and UNU/IIST to provide a forum for researchers in computer science from the Asian region and to promote interaction with researchers from other regions. The first ten conferences were held, respectively, in Bangkok, Singapore, Katmandu, Manila, Phuket, Penang, Hanoi, Mumbai, Chiang Mai, and Kunming. The 11th ASIAN conference was held in Tokyo, Japan, December 6-8, 2006. Each year, the conference focuses on a different theme at the cutting edge of computer science research. The theme of ASIAN 2006 was secure software. Three distinguished speakers were invited to the conference:

- Li Gong (Windows Live China, Microsoft Corporation, China)
- John Mitchell (Stanford University, USA)
- Patrick Cousot (Ecole Normale Supérieure-Paris, France)

We had 115 submission papers. The Program Committee reviewed all the papers carefully and then selected 17 regular papers and 10 short papers. After the conference, 1 invited paper, 17 regular papers and 8 short papers were selected for this post-conference formal proceedings volume. We wish to thank the Program Committee members and the external referees for their work in selecting the contributed papers. The conference was sponsored by the National Institute of Informatics, the Embassy of France in Japan, INRIA, and Keio University. We thank the Steering Committee for inviting us to organize the 11th ASIAN conference in Japan. Finally, many thanks to S. Nakajima and his Local Organizing Committee, for their sustained efforts in the organization of the conference.

March 2007

Mitsuhiro Okada
Ichiro Satoh

Organization

ASIAN 2006 was sponsored by the National Institute of Informatics, the Embassy of France in Japan, INRIA, and Keio University.

Executive Committee

General Chairs   Aki Yonezawa (University of Tokyo, Japan)
Philippe Codognet (Embassy of France in Japan)

Program Chairs   Mitsuhiro Okada (Keio University, Japan)
Ichiro Satoh (National Institute of Informatics, Japan)

Organization Chair   Shin Nakajima (National Institute of Informatics, Japan)

Organization   Kensuke Fukuda (National Institute of Informatics, Japan)
Soichiro Hidaka (National Institute of Informatics, Japan)
Hiroshi Hosobe (National Institute of Informatics, Japan)
Hiroyuki Kato (National Institute of Informatics, Japan)
Michihiro Koibuchi (National Institute of Informatics, Japan)

Steering Committee Stephane Grumbach (INRIA, France)
Joxan Jaffar (NUS, Singapore)
Gilles Kahn (INRIA, France)
Kanchana Kanchanasut (AIT, Thailand)
R.K. Shyamasundar (TIFR, India)
Kazunori Ueda (Waseda University, Japan)

Program Committee

Iliano Cervesato (Carnegie Mellon University, Qatar)
Shigeru Chiba (Tokyo Institute of Technology, Japan)
Patrick Cousot (Ecole Normale Supérieure-Paris, France)
Anupam Datta (Stanford University, USA)
Yuxi Fu (Shanghai Jiaotong University, China)
Sumanta Guha (AIT, Thailand)
Masami Hagiya (University of Tokyo)
Joxan Jaffar (National University of Singapore, Singapore)

Kanchana Kanchanasut (AIT, Thailand)
Kenji Kono (Keio University, Japan)
Ching-Laung Lei (Taiwan National University, Taiwan)
Xavier Leroy (INRIA, France)
Ninghui Li (Purdue University, USA)
John Mitchell (Stanford University, USA)
Atsushi Ohori (Tohoku University, Japan)
Mitsuhiro Okada(Keio University, Japan)
Andreas Podelski (Freiburg University, Germany)
Michael Rusinowitch (INRIA-Lorraine/University of Nancy/CNRS, France)
Ichiro Satoh (National Institute of Informatics, Japan)
Etsuya Shibayama (Tokyo Insitute of Technology, Japan)
L. Yohanes Stefanus (University of Indonesia, Indonesia)
Kazushige Terui (National Institute of Informatics, Japan)
Kazunori Ueda (Waseda University, Japan)

Sponsoring Institutions

National Institute of Informatics, Japan
The Embassy of France in Japan
INRIA, France
Keio University, Japan

The program committee thanks the following people for their assistance on the refereeing process.

Siva Anantharaman
Stephan Arlt
Anindya Banerjee
Adam Barth
Julien Bertrane
Frédéric Besson
Bruno Blanchet
Mun Choon Chan
Wei Ngan Chin
Samarjit Chakraborty
Hong Chen
Kuan-Ta Chen
Yu-Shian Chen
Shigeru Chiba
Chansophea Chuon
Veronique Cortier
Véronique Cortier
Jin Song Dong
Yuxin Deng
Ling Dong
Chun-I Fan
Jérôme Feret
Benjamin Gregoire
Yonggen Gu
Sumanta Guha
Masami Hagiya
Goichiro Hanaoka
Koji Hasebe
Chaodong He
Chun-Ying Huang
Run-Junn Hwang
Samuel Hym
Katsuyoshi Iida

Mastroeni Isabella
Florent Jacquemard
Joxan Jaffar
Bertrand Jeannet
Wen-Shenq Juang
Shin-ya Katsumata
Nguyen Tan Khoa
Kazukuni Kobara
Kenji Kono
Kenichi Kourai
Steve Kremer
Ralf Kuesters
Donggang Liu
Francesco Logozzo
Ken Mano
Ziqing Mao
Yutaka Matsuno
Antoine Miné
Mitchell
Ian Molloy
David Monniaux
Francesco Zappa Nardelli
Huu-Duc Nguyen
Qun Ni
Shin-ya Nishizaki
Yutaka Oiwa
Mitsuhiro Okada
Olivier Perrin
Tamara Rezk
Xavier Rival
Arnab Roy
Abhik Roychoudhury
Takamichi Saito

Isao Sasano
Ichiro Satoh
Etsuya Shibayama
Rie Shigetomi
Junji Shikata
SeongHan Shin
Yutaro Sugimoto
Martin Sulzmann
Yunfeng Tao
Yasuyuki Tsukada
Mathieu Turuani
Kazunori Ueda
Masashi Une
Daniele Varacca
Laurent Vigneron
Razvan Voicu
Tep Vuthy
Qihua Wang
Bogdan Warinschi
Martijn Warnier
Takuo Watanabe
Hajime Watanabe
Xian Xu
Mitsuharu Yamamoto
Yoshisato Yanagisawa
Roland Yap
Eugene Zalinescu
Steve Zdancewic
Han Zhu
Hengming Zou

Table of Contents

ASIAN'2006

Security Evaluation of a Type of
Table-Network Implementation of Block Ciphers

Akira Matsunaga and Tsutomu Matsumoto

Graduate School of Environment and Information Sciences,
Yokohama National University,
79-7 Tokiwadai, Hodogaya-ku, Yokohama, Kanagawa 240-8501, Japan
{matunaga, tsutomu}@mlab.jks.ynu.ac.jp

Abstract. Tamper-resistant software which implements a block cipher
with a fixed embedded cryptographic key is important for securing embedded systems for digital rights management, access control, and other
applications. The security of such software is measured by its ability
to hide the embedded key against numerous known attacks. A class of
methods for constructing tamper-resistant software by using a number of
look-up tables is called a white-box implementation or table-network implementation. We developed a method of evaluating the security of table-
network implementations of the Data Encryption Standard (DES). Link
and Neumann proposed a table-network implementation of DES that is
claimed to be resistant against all known attacks, which are effective for
table-network implementations of DES proposed by Chow, Eisen, Johnson, and van Oorschot. In this paper, we point out the existence of a
new attack, which allows efficient extraction of the hidden key in the
Link-Newman table-network implementation of DES. Our result should
contribute in completing the list of attacking methodologies and thus
help the design of better tamper-resistant software.

1 Introduction

Software implementation of cryptography plays an important role in many applications. Cryptographic software may be reverse engineered or analyzed by
malicious users or attackers. Thus, the software implementing the cryptographic
algorithms must be tamper resistant. Software implementation of a block cipher
with a fixed embedded cryptographic key is important for securing embedded
systems for digital rights management, access control, and other applications.
Tamper resistance with respect to the secrecy of such software is measured as
the ability to hide an embedded key against numerous known attacks. A class
of methods for making such tamper-resistant software that uses a large number
of look-up tables is called a white-box implementation or table-network implementation. We prefer to use the latter expression since white-box implementation does not imply the software structure of the implementation. Examples of
table-network implementations for the Data Encryption Standard (DES) and

M. Okada and I. Satoh (Eds.): ASIAN 2006, LNCS 4435, pp. 1–12, 2007.
© Springer-Verlag Berlin Heidelberg 2007

the Advanced Encryption Standard (AES) have been proposed by Chow, Eisen, Johnson, and van Oorschot [1, 5].

We developed a method of evaluating the security of table-network implementations of DES. In the table-network implementation proposed by Chow et al., the hidden key is efficiently extracted by the known attacks [1, 2, 3]. These researchers also demonstrated a modified block cipher that is a composite of an input-hidden bijection, DES, and an output-hidden bijection, and has a table-network implementation resistant against known attacks. However, in our view, such a non-standard cipher can be applied only in limited fields. There is a strong demand for better solutions. Link and Neumann [3, 4] proposed a table-network implementation of DES, claimed to be resistant against all known attacks which are effective for the table-network implementation proposed by Chow et al.

In this paper, we point out the existence of a new attack, which efficiently extracts the hidden key in the Link-Newman table-network implementation of DES.

The rest of this paper is organized as follows. In Section 2, we define the table-network implementation and describe the table-network implementation of DES proposed by [1]. In Section 3, we introduce the attacks and the improvements on table-network implementation of DES. In Section 4, we describe our proposal in detail and evaluate the table-network implementation proposed by [3, 4]. Section 5 concludes this paper.

2   Table-Network Implementation of DES

In this section we describe details of the table-network implementation of DES [1]. DES consists of permutations, S-boxes, and xor operations on bit vectors. In a table-network implementation, all these operations are represented with look-up tables. An $m \times n$-bit table is an m-bit to n-bit mapping, which is implemented as an array of 2^m entries, each of n-bits. The values between look-up tables are encoded by random bijections. A table-network implementation is roughly divided into two parts: T-boxes and tree-structure table networks.

In round r of DES operations, xor with a round key, transformation by S-boxes, and carrying L_r and R_r are represented by twelve 8×8-bit tables, named T-box $^r T_j$ for $r = 1, \ldots, 16$, $j = 1, \ldots, 12$. We denote T-boxes containing each S-box $S_1, \ldots, S_8$ as $^r T_1, \ldots, ^r T_8$, and T-boxes carrying only bits of L_r and R_r as $^r T_9, \ldots, ^r T_{12}$. However, T-boxes do not necessarily queue up in order from 1 to 12 in program code.

The operations, other than being composed as T-boxes, are linear transformations (e.g., permutation, xor operation). These are brought together in one function, and converted into networks of small look-up tables, named tree-structure table networks. This function is represented with an Affine Transformation (AT) over GF(2). An AT is a transformation from vector x to vector y, which is defined by $y = Mx + d$, where M is a constant matrix and d is a constant vector. Here, we define the size of x and y as $4b$ and $4a$ bits, respectively. Therefore, M is a $4a \times 4b$-bit matrix and d is $4a$-bit vector. M is then divided into a 4×4-bit sub-matrix $m_{k,l}$ and x, y, d are divided into 4-bit sub-vectors x_l, y_k, d_k for $k = 1, \ldots, a$, $l = 1, \ldots, b$. At this time, y_k denotes

$$y_k = m_{k,1}x_1 \oplus m_{k,2}x_2 \oplus \cdots \oplus m_{k,b}x_b \oplus d_k.$$

The above formula comprises one tree. The sub-matrices are transformed to 4×4-bit vector-multiply tables, and the xor operations are transformed to 8×4-bit vector-add tables.

In the above manner, all these operations are represented by look-up tables (See Figure 1). At this point, each look-up table still leak useful information for an attacker. So, the values appear between look-up tables are encoded by composing random bijections. Along with composing a bijection, the table is converted into a different one, making it difficult to decompose. This is because, given an encoded table, there are many possible (original table, composed bijection) combinations from which the same composed function could arise. Consequently, all the steps of DES can be obscured, and it is difficult for an attacker to extract the embedded key from the software by static or dynamic analyses.

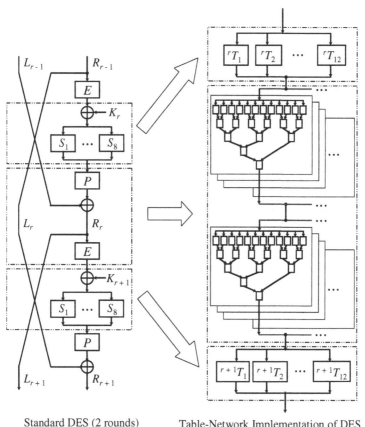

Standard DES (2 rounds)   Table-Network Implementation of DES

Fig. 1. Standard and Table-Networked Algorithms

3   Attacks and Improvements on the Implementation

Discussions have been done on the security of the table-network implementations of DES. We summarize in Table 1 the relationship between implementations and attacks considered so far. In Table 1, *secure* means the implementation is resistant against the corresponding attack, and *insecure* means the key embedded in the implementation can be efficiently extracted by the corresponding attack.

Let *CEJvO-DES* denote the table-network implementation proposed by Chow et al. [1] and let *LN-DES* denote that by Link et al. [3, 4]. Implementation CEJvO-DES cannot be resistant against the three attacks shown in Table 1. Chow et al. have proposed a *Recommended Variant*, which can be resistant against all existing attacks as seen from Table 1. However, since the recommended variant is no longer DES such a cipher's usage has limitations. For applications where only standardized block ciphers shall be adopted, the tamper resistance of the original DES should be investigated and improved.

In the following subsection we describe details of the Statistical Bucketing Attack, Recommended Variants, and LN-DES.

Table 1. Relationship between implementations and attacks

attack implementation	Statistical Bucketing Attack [1]	Improved Statistical Bucketing Attack [3]	Fault Injection Attack [2]
CEJvO-DES [1]	insecure	insecure	insecure
CEJvO-DES [1] (Recommended Variant)	secure	secure	secure
LN-DES [3, 4]	secure (?)	secure	secure

3.1   Statistical Bucketing Attack

Because random bijections were composed, an individual table is converted into one that does not directly relate to the original one. Therefore, it is difficult for an attacker to obtain useful information from a single table, such as a T-box. Attacks must be global in the sense that the attacker must look at multiple tables and correlate the knowledge of DES algorithm. The statistical bucketing attack extracts the round key of the first round (or final round) of the DES. We only describe attacks on the first round of encryption.

In preparation, the attacker searches for twelve tables that are the T-boxes of round 2 from among a large number of tables in CEJvO-DES. If the attacker knows the structure of CEJvO-DES, the T-boxes are easily discovered by tracking the data-flow. Afterwards, the attacker should identify which T-box corresponds to which S-box. Each of some eight of the twelve T-boxes should correspond to one of the eight S-boxes $S_1, \ldots, S_8$. The remaining four T-boxes only pass the information to the next round.

After identifying the relationship between T-boxes and S-boxes, the attacker tries to extract the key. For explanation, the i-th S-box in round r is denoted by ^rS_i. The attacker focuses on one bit of ^1S_i's output, which is denoted b. ^2S_j is defined by one of the S-boxes in round 2, which is affected by b. First, the attacker makes a guess on the 6-bit portion of the round key affecting ^1S_i and generates 64 plaintexts that correspond to the entire input pattern of ^1S_i. Then, the attacker inputs this plaintext to a standard DES implementation, which uses a portion of the key that is only a guess and focuses on the value of b. If $b = 0$, that plaintext belongs to the set I_0. Similarly, if $b = 1$, it belongs to the set I_1. Next, the attacker inputs the plaintext belonging to the set I_0 to the target CEJvO-DES, and then examines the input to ^2T_j involving ^2S_j. This value belongs to the set I_0'. The set I_1 similarly leads the set I_1'. Here, if I_0' and I_1' are disjoint sets, the key guess is almost correct. Any overlap indicates that the key guess is wrong.

To extract a 48-bit round key, the attacker tries the above operation for 8 S-boxes in round 1. The remaining 8 bits of the full DES key can be found by a brute-force search using a standard DES implementation. This gives a cracking complexity of about 2^{13} encryptions.

3.2   Recommended Variant

Chow et al. admit that CEJvO-DES is vulnerable to the statistical bucketing attack. However, they have proposed the recommended variant of the White-Box DES Implementation. This variant encodes the input and output of the whole DES implementation. That is, the recommended variant of the White-Box DES is a composite of an input hidden bijection, CEJvO-DES, and an output hidden bijection. They assume that there is no effective attack on the recommended variant.

Clearly, this modified implementation is not a standard DES cipher. They explain that this technique is useful because de-encodings can be done somewhere. Cryptography is often built in a large software like a software content player, thereby the input and output encodings can be canceled with pre- and post-process of an encryption or a decryption.

3.3   Modifications on LN-DES

Link et al. improved the resistance of CEJvO-DES against the known attacks without using the recommended variant. This implementation offers two modifications to prevent the statistical bucketing attack.

- Mix the certain 16 bits of R_r with L_r by including a random bijective AT.
- Encode a T-box input as a single 8×8-bit bijection.

In the T-box part, R_r and L_r $(32 + 32 = 64$ bits) must be carried to the next round (See Figure 1). In one round, the certain 16 bits of R_r that are duplicated by expansion parmutation E (i.e., 1, 4, 5, 8, 9, 12, 13, 16, 17, 20, 21, 24, 25, 28,

29, and 32nd bit of R_r) must pass to make T-box a bijection. The remaining 48 bits that we call *bypass only bits*, only pass through. These bits are mixed by a random bijective AT to diffuse information. In the next round, these bits are recovered by the inversion of the AT.

In CEJvO-DES, T-box input and output are encoded by two 4×4-bit bijections, which leads to biased data. Therefore, they encode a T-box input as a single 8×8-bit bijection.

As a result, an attacker has difficulty identifying which T-box corresponds to which S-box in round 2. These ideas are expected to be resistant against the statistical bucketing attack.

4   Evaluating Tamper Resistance of the Table-Network Implementation of DES

As mentioned above, the preparation for the statistical bucketing attack requires two steps. First, search out twelve tables that are T-boxes in round 2. Second, identify which T-box corresponds to which S-box in these tables. LN-DES focuses on the latter step.

According to Link et al., LN-DES makes it more difficult to identify which T-box corresponds to which S-box in round 2, and thus prevents the statistical bucketing attack. However, a method that identifies which T-box corresponds to which S-box in round 2 has not been described [1, 3, 4]. Now, we discuss the identification method. Subsection 4.1 introduces our basic idea, which is an effective method for CEJvO-DES, but not suitable for LN-DES due to the modifications shown in Subsection 3.3. Therefore, in Subsections 4.2 and 4.3, we propose two identification methods that are applicable to LN-DES.

Once the attacker identifies which T-box corresponds to which S-box, the statistical bucketing attack is possible on LN-DES. Both CEJvO-DES and LN-DES have the property that if the key is guessed correctly, I'_0 and I'_1 are disjoint sets; if the guess is wrong, I'_0 and I'_1 are almost overlapped.

Here, we assume that the attacker is able to input arbitrary value to the table-network implementation, observe outputs and any intermediate values during computation, and refer to the implemented cryptographic algorithm and correlate it with those intermediate values to find out the key.

4.1   Basic Idea

In the DES algorithm, 32 bits of L_0 correspond directly to 48 bits of the S-box input in round 2. Thus, it is already known which bit in L_0 affects which S-box in round 2. Figure 2 shows, for example that the first bit of L_0 affects $^2S_1$ and $^2S_8$. In order to identify which T-box corresponds to which S-box in round 2, we observe the changes of the T-box input in round 2 when one bit of L_0 is changed.

To be more specific, in the DES algorithm, we define $^r s_i(m)$ as a 6-bit value that is input to the i-th S-box (for $i = 1, \ldots, 8$) in round r (for $r = 1, \ldots, 16$) when a plaintext m is encrypted. Here, we select the base plaintext m_{base} and

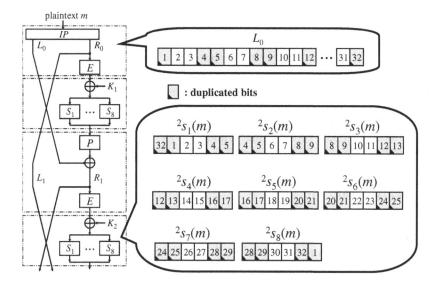

Fig. 2. Correspondence between L_0 and $^2s_i(m)$

the plaintext m_n of which the n-th bit in L_0 is changed compared with m_{base}. When m_{base} and m_n are encrypted, the value of R_0 remains the same. So the outputs from permutation P in round 1 are the same, too. The changed bit is input to one of the S-boxes in round 2 (according to the circumstances; this is input to two of the S-boxes by the effect of Expansion Permutation E). Thus in these one or two S-boxes, $^2s_i(m_n)$ differs from $^2s_i(m_{base})$. At the other S-box, $^2s_i(m_n)$ is equal to $^2s_i(m_{base})$. For example, we set m_{base} to all 0, and m_2 to all 0, excluding the 2nd bit. Then, we encrypt m_{base} and m_2 to observe $^2s_i(m_{base})$ and $^2s_i(m_2)$ for all i. Comparing these two values, we obtain the result that $^2s_1(m_2)$ differs from $^2s_1(m_{base})$ and $^2s_2(m_2), \ldots, ^2s_8(m_2)$ are equal to $^2s_2(m_{base}), \ldots, ^2s_8(m_{base})$ respectively.

In CEJvO-DES, we define $^rt_j(m)$ as an 8-bit value that inputs to the j-th T-box (for $j = 1, \ldots, 12$) in round r (for $r = 1, \ldots, 16$) when m is encrypted. $^rt_j(m)$ are given by

$$^rt_j(m) = \begin{cases} ^r\phi_j\left(^rs_j(m) \,||\, ^rb_j(m)\right) & (j = 1, \ldots, 8) \\ ^r\phi_j\left(^rb_j(m)\right) & (j = 9, \ldots, 12) \end{cases}$$

where we define $^r\phi_j$ as a bijection (or bijections), which are converted to the input to j-th T-box in round r, and $^rb_j(m)$ as bypass only bits of j-th T-box in round r. Thereby, $^rb_j(m)$ is a 2-bit value for $j = 1, \ldots, 8$, and an 8-bit value for $j = 9, \ldots, 12$. Moreover, let $||$ denote vector concatenation. For ease of explanation, we ignore the xor operation with a round key. This is not affect the outcome of our idea because a round key is a constant value. When m_{base} and m_n are encrypted, in the construction of CEJvO-DES, $^2b_1(m_n), \ldots, ^2b_8(m_n)$

are equal to $^2b_1(m_{base}), \ldots, {}^2b_8(m_{base})$ respectively because these are the bits of L_1 (i.e. R_0). So, only at the T-box containing the S-box affected by the changed bit, $^2t_j(m_{base}) \neq {}^2t_j(m_n)$. At the T-box containing the other S-box, $^2t_j(m_{base}) = {}^2t_j(m_n)$. Other results are brought about by $^2t_9(m), \ldots, {}^2t_{12}(m)$. These might or might not contain some bits of L_0. Therefore, these values change irregularly, and we can distinguish them from $^2t_1(m), \ldots, {}^2t_8(m)$ easily.

For CEJvO-DES, we can identify which T-box corresponds to which S-box in round 2 in this manner. However, this does not work for LN-DES because the bypass only bits are mixed by including a random bijective AT. As a result, $^2t_j(m_n)$ changes for many values of j because all the T-boxes contain bypass only bits.

4.2   Identification Method I

For LN-DES, the basic idea is not applicable as it is. So, we notice the existence of bits that do not change the bypass only bits in round 2. Choosing these bits and setting m_n, we can identify which T-box corresponds to which S-box in round 2 for LN-DES.

We focus on the 16 bits of R_1, which are duplicated by E. In round 2 of LN-DES, these duplicated bits do not affect bypass only bits, because these bits are carried as the S-box inputs and passed to the next round to make T-box a bijection. Figure 3 shows the internal structure of T-boxes. In this figure, an arrow means 1 bit. The important point is 2 of 6 bits which are input to S-box, bold arrows in this figure, are duplicated and passed to the next round. As mentioned, R_1 is determined by only L_0 between m_{base} and m_n. Therefore, even if the certain 16 bits of L_0 are changed in m_n, the bypass only bits of round 2 are not changed. In other words, $^2b_j(m_{base}) = {}^2b_j(m_n)$ for all j and $n = 1, 4, 5, 8,$ 9, 12, 13, 16, 17, 20, 21, 24, 25, 28, 29, and 32. The procedure for identification method I is described as follows, and an example is shown in Figure 4.

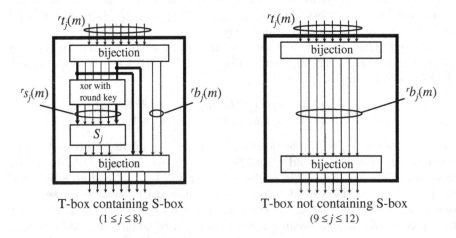

Fig. 3. Structure of T-boxes

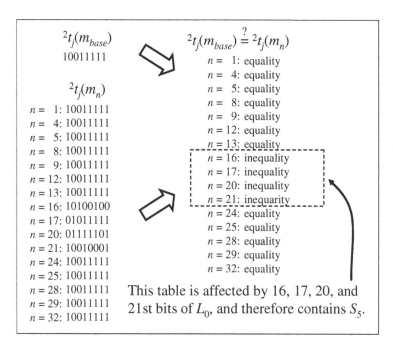

Fig. 4. An example of identification method I

STEP 1: An arbitrary m_{base} is generated.
STEP 2: 16 kinds of m_n are generated for $n = 1, 4, 5, 8, 9, 12, 13, 16, 17, 20,$ 21, 24, 25, 28, 29, and 32.
STEP 3: While encrypting m_{base} by LN-DES, $^2t_j(m_{base})$ are observed for all j. Similarly, while encrypting 16 kinds of m_n, 16 kinds of $^2t_j(m_n)$ are observed for all j.
STEP 4: The following STEP 5 is repeated for all j.
STEP 5: For all n, we check the combination such that $^2t_j(m_{base}) \neq {}^2t_j(m_n)$. If specific 4 patterns shown in Figure 2 are checked, the S-box that the T-box contains is identified.

4.3   Identification Method II

There are two reasons why $^2t_j(m_n)$ is changed compared with $^2t_j(m_{base})$:

(1) $^2s_j(m_n)$ (and $^2b_j(m_n)$) is changed.
(2) $^2s_j(m_n)$ is not changed but $^2b_j(m_n)$ is changed.

Focusing on the T-boxes that contain S-boxes ($^2T_1, \ldots, {}^2T_8$), we generate m_{base} and 32 patterns of m_n. Encrypting these plaintexts, $^2t_j(m_{base})$ and 32 $^2t_j(m_n)$ are obtained. There are only six of 32 $^2t_j(m_n)$ in which $^2s_j(m_n)$ is changed compared with $^2s_j(m_{base})$ (i.e. case (1)). Moreover, these necessarily have different values each other. In the remaining 26 $^2t_j(m_n)$, $^2s_j(m_n)$ are not changed, but $^2b_j(m_n)$ are changed because of the random bijective AT (i.e. case (2)). In this case, $^2b_j(m)$ afford only four patterns because $^2b_j(m)$ are 2 bits. It is clear that $^2t_j(m)$ also has only four patterns in case (2), and therefore these have a high probability of overlapping. Exploiting the above property, we exclude the patterns that overlap each other from 33 $^2t_j(m)$. As a result, Case (1) and (2) can be distinguished (See Figure 5).

In $^2T_9, \ldots, {}^2T_{12}$, the patterns of $^2t_j(m_n)$ are unpredictable. However, we easily observe these T-boxes do not contain S-boxes, so that we cannot reduce them to specific six patterns. The procedure for identification method II is described as follows, and an example of this method is shown in Figure 6.

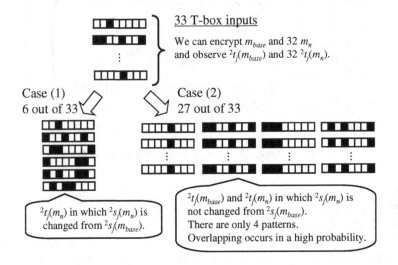

Fig. 5. Distinction of T-box inputs

STEP 1: An arbitrary m_{base} is generated.

STEP 2: 32 kinds of m_n are generated for all n.

STEP 3: While encrypting m_{base} by LN-DES, $^2t_j(m_{base})$ are observed for all j. Similarly, while encrypting 32 kinds of m_n, 32 kinds of $^2t_j(m_n)$ are observed for all j.

STEP 4: The following STEP 5 is repeated for all j.

STEP 5: For all n, we exclude overlapping patterns. If the six specific patterns shown in Figure 2 remain, the S-box that the T-box contains is identified.

4.4 Computational Costs

In this subsection, we estimate the computational costs of our proposal. Identification method I encrypts a base plaintext m_{base} and 16 kinds of m_n. Therefore,

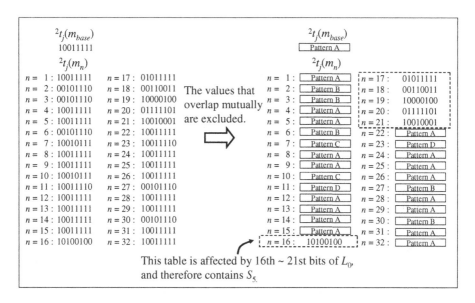

Fig. 6. An example of identification method II

the computational costs of this are 17 encryptions. Identification method II also encrypts m_{base} and 32 kinds of m_n. Hence, this method requires 33 encryptions. Considering that the computational costs of the Statistical Bucketing Attack are about 2^{13} encryptions, these costs are relatively less. It follows from this that we can easily identify which T-box corresponds to which S-box in round 2 in LN-DES.

5 Conclusions

We have pointed out the existence of a new attack, which can efficiently extract the hidden key in LN-DES, and thus we have evaluated the tamper-resistance of LN-DES. We have focused on the statistical bucketing attack. We have proposed the attack's specific pre-computation methods that can identify which T-box corresponds to which S-box in round 2. The T-boxes in LN-DES, which improves CEJvO-DES, can be identified by our methods. As a result, the hidden key of LN-DES can be extracted effectively by the statistical bucketing attack.

This study demonstrates that LN-DES does not have sufficient resistance against the statistical bucketing attack. In other words, when designing a table-network implementation of DES or Triple DES, it must have sufficient tamper-resistance, at least, against our methods. We need novel techniques to guarantee such resistance.

References

1. Chow, S., Eisen, P., Johnson, H., van Oorschot, P.C.: A White-Box DES Implementation for DRM applications, Security and Privacy in Digital Rights Management. In: Feigenbaum, J. (ed.) DRM 2002. LNCS, vol. 2696, pp. 1–15. Springer, Heidelberg (2003)
2. Jacob, M., Boneh, D., Felten, E.: Attacking an obfuscated cipher by injecting faults. In: Feigenbaum, J. (ed.) DRM 2002. LNCS, vol. 2696, pp. 16–31. Springer, Heidelberg (2003)
3. Link, H., Neumann, W.: Clarifying Obfuscation: Improving the Security of White-Box Encoding, Cryptology ePrint Archive (2004), `http://eprint.iacr.org/2004/025.pdf`
4. Link, H., Neumann, W.: Clarifying Obfuscation: Improving the Security of White-Box DES. In: ITCC 2005. International Conference on Information Technology: Coding and Computing, vol. 01(1), pp. 679–684. IEEE Computer Society Press, Los Alamitos (2005)
5. Chow, S., Eisen, P., Johnson, H., van Oorschot, P.C.: White-Box Cryptography and an AES Implementation. In: Nyberg, K., Heys, H.M. (eds.) SAC 2002. LNCS, vol. 2595, pp. 250–270. Springer, Heidelberg (2003)
6. FIPS 46-3 Data Encryption Standard (DES), `http://csrc.nist.gov/publications/fips/fips46-3/fips46-3.pdf`

A Symbolic Intruder Model for Hash-Collision Attacks[*]

Yannick Chevalier and Mounira Kourjieh

IRIT Université Paul Sabatier, France
{ychevali,kourjieh}@irit.fr

Abstract. In the recent years, several practical methods have been published to compute collisions on some commonly used hash functions. Starting from two messages m_1 and m_2 these methods permit to compute m_1' and m_2' *similar* to the former such that they have the same image for a given hash function. In this paper we present a method to take into account, at the symbolic level, that an intruder actively attacking a protocol execution may use these collision algorithms in reasonable time during the attack. This decision procedure relies on the reduction of constraint solving for an intruder exploiting the collision properties of hash functions to constraint solving for an intruder operating on words, that is with an associative symbol of concatenation. The decidability of the latter is interesting in its own right as it is the first decidability result that we are aware of for an intruder system for which unification is infinitary, and permits to consider in other contexts an associative concatenation of messages instead of their pairing.

1 Introduction

Hash functions. Cryptographic hash functions play a fundamental role in modern cryptography. While related to conventional hash functions commonly used in non-cryptographic computer applications - in both cases, larger domains are mapped to smaller ranges - they have some additional properties. Our focus is restricted to cryptographic hash functions (hereafter, simply hash functions), and in particular to their use as cryptographic primitive for data integrity, authentication, key agreement, e-cash and many other cryptographic schemes and protocols. Hash functions take a message as input and produce an output referred to as a *hash-value*, or simply *hash*.

Collisions. A hash function is many-to-one, implying that the existence of collisions (pairs of inputs with the identical output) is unavoidable. However, only a few years ago, it was intractable to compute collisions on hash functions, so they were considered to be collision-free by cryptographers, and protocols were built upon this assumption. From the nineties on, several authors have proved the tractability of finding pseudo-collision and collision attacks over several hash

---

[*] Supported by ARA-SSIA Cops and ACI JC 9005.

M. Okada and I. Satoh (Eds.): ASIAN 2006, LNCS 4435, pp. 13–27, 2007.
© Springer-Verlag Berlin Heidelberg 2007

functions. Taking this into account, we consider that cryptographic hash functions have the following properties:

- the input can be of any length, the output has a fixed length, $h(x)$ is relatively easy to compute for any given x;
- pre-image resistance: for essentially all pre-specified outputs, it is computationally infeasible to find any input which hashes to that outputs, i.e., to find any x such that $y = h(x)$ when given y;
- 2nd-pre-image resistance: it is computationally infeasible to find any second input which has the same output as any specified input, i.e., given x , to find x' different from x such that $h(x) = h(x')$;
- hash collision: it is computationally feasible to compute two distinct inputs x and x' which hash to the same output, i.e, $h(x) = h(x')$ provided that x and x' are created at the same time and independently one of the other.

In other words, a collision-vulnerable hash function h is one for which an intruder can find two different messages x and x' with the same hash value. To mount a collision attack, an adversary would typically begin by constructing two messages with the same hash where one message appears legitimate or innocuous while the other serves the intruder's purposes. For example, consider the *story of Alice and her boss* [8]. Alice has been working for some time in the office of Julius Caesar. On her last day of work, Caesar gives her a letter of recommendation on paper. Alice decides to take advantage of this opportunity to gain access to Caesar's secret documents. Caesar uses MD5 hash function which is collision−vulnerable for his digital signature algorithm DSA. When she receives her letter of recommendation on paper, Alice prepares two postcripts files with the same MD5 hash: one is the letter given by Caesar and the other is an order from Caesar to grant Alice some kind of security clearance. She asks Caesar to digitally sign the letter and due to the hash collision, Caesar's signature for the letter of recommendation is valid for the order. She then presents the order and the digital signature to the person in charge of Caesar's files and finally gains access to Caesar's secret documents.

Collisions in practise. MD5 Hash function is one of the most widely used cryptographic hash functions nowadays. It was designed in 1992 as an improvement on MD4, and its security was widely studied since then by several authors. The first result was a pseudo-collision for MD5 [9]. Recently, a real collision involving two 1024-bits messages was found with the standard value [18]. This first weakness was extended into a differential-like attack [21] and tools were developed [10] for finding the collisions which work for any initialisation value and which are quicker than methods presented in [18]. Finally, other methods have been developed for finding new MD5 collisions [22]. The development of collision-finding algorithms is not restricted to MD5 hash function. Several methods for MD4 research attack have been developed [19]. In [19] a method to search RIPE-MD collision attacks was also developed, and in [3], a collision on SHA-0 has been presented. Finally, Wang *et al.* have developed in [20] another method to search for collisions for the SHA-1 hash function.

Goal of this paper. This development of methods at the cryptographic level to built collisions in a reasonable time have until now not been taken into account in a symbolic model of cryptographic protocols. We also note that the inherent complexity of these attacks make them not representable in any computational model that we are aware of. In this paper we propose a decision procedure to decide insecurity of cryptographic protocols when a hash function for which collisions may be found is employed. Relying on the result [5] we do not consider here other cryptographic primitives such as public key encryption, signature or symmetric key encryption, and assume that a protocol execution has already been split into the views of the different equational theories. The decidability proof presented here heavily relies on a recent result [6] that permits to reduce constraint solving problems with respect to a given intruder to constraint solving problems for a simpler one. This result relies on a new notion of *mode*. This notion aims at exhibiting a modular structure in an equational theory but has no simple intuitive meaning. In the case of an exponential operator as treated in [6] the separation was between an exponential symbol and the abelian group operations on its exponents, whereas here the separation is introduced between the application of the hash function and the functions employed by the intruder to find collisions.

Outline. We first give in Section 2 the definitions relating to terms and equational theories. We then present in Section 3 our model of an attacker against a protocol, and how we reduce the search for flaws to reachability problems with respect to an intruder theory. In Section 4 we describe in detail how we model the fact that an intruder may construct colliding messages, and how this intruder theory can be decomposed into simpler intruder theories. We give proof sketch of these reductions in Section 5 and conclude in Section 6.

2   Formal Setting

2.1   Basic Notions

We consider an infinite set of free constants C and an infinite set of variables $\mathcal{X}$. For any signature $\mathcal{G}$ (*i.e.* sets of function symbols not in C with arities) we denote $\mathrm{T}(\mathcal{G})$ (resp. $\mathrm{T}(\mathcal{G}, \mathcal{X})$) the set of terms over $\mathcal{G} \cup \mathrm{C}$ (resp. $\mathcal{G} \cup \mathrm{C} \cup \mathcal{X}$). The former is called the set of ground terms over $\mathcal{G}$, while the latter is simply called the set of terms over $\mathcal{G}$. The arity of a function symbol f is denoted by $\mathrm{ar}(f)$. Variables are denoted by x, y, terms are denoted by s, t, u, v, and finite sets of terms are written $E, F, ...$, and decorations thereof, respectively. We abbreviate $E \cup F$ by E, F, the union $E \cup \{t\}$ by E, t and $E \setminus \{t\}$ by $E \setminus t$.

Given a signature $\mathcal{G}$, a *constant* is either a free constant or a function symbol of arity 0 in $\mathcal{G}$. We define the set of atoms Atoms to be the union of $\mathcal{X}$ and the set of constants. Given a term t we denote by $\mathrm{Var}(t)$ the set of variables occurring in t and by $\mathrm{Cons}(t)$ the set of constants occurring in t. We denote by $\mathrm{Atoms}(t)$ the set $\mathrm{Var}(t) \cup \mathrm{Cons}(t)$. A substitution σ is an involutive mapping from $\mathcal{X}$ to $\mathrm{T}(\mathcal{G}, \mathcal{X})$ such that $\mathrm{Supp}(\sigma) = \{x | \sigma(x) \neq x\}$, the *support* of σ, is a finite set. The application of a substitution σ to a term t (resp. a set of terms E) is denoted $t\sigma$ (resp. $E\sigma$) and is equal to the term t (resp. E) where all variables x have been replaced by the term $\sigma(x)$. A substitution σ is *ground* w.r.t. $\mathcal{G}$ if the image of $\mathrm{Supp}(\sigma)$ is included in $\mathrm{T}(\mathcal{G})$.

An *equational presentation* $\mathcal{H} = (\mathcal{G}, A)$ is defined by a set A of equations $u = v$ with $u, v \in \mathrm{T}(\mathcal{G}, \mathcal{X})$ and u, v without free constants. For any equational presentation $\mathcal{H}$ the relation $=_{\mathcal{H}}$ denotes the equational theory generated by $(\mathcal{G}, A)$ on $\mathrm{T}(\mathcal{G}, \mathcal{X})$, that is the smallest congruence containing all instances of axioms of A. Abusively we shall not distinguish between an equational presentation $\mathcal{H}$ over a signature $\mathcal{G}$ and a set A of equations presenting it and we denote both by $\mathcal{H}$. We will also often refer to $\mathcal{H}$ as an equational theory (meaning the equational theory presented by $\mathcal{H}$). An equational theory $\mathcal{H}$ is said to be *consistent* if two free constants are not equal modulo $\mathcal{H}$ or, equivalently, if it has a model with more than one element modulo $\mathcal{H}$.

For all signature $\mathcal{G}$ that we consider, we assume that $<_{\mathcal{G}}$ is a total simplification ordering on $\mathrm{T}(\mathcal{G})$ for which the minimal element is a free constant $c_{\min}$. *Unfailing completion* permits, given an equational theory $\mathcal{H}$ defined by a set A of equations, to build from A a (possibly infinite) set $R(A)$ of equations $l = r$ such that the ordered rewriting relation between terms defined by $t \rightarrow_{R(A)} t'$ if:

- There exists $l = r \in R(A)$ and a ground substitution σ such that $l\sigma = s$ and $r\sigma = s'$, $t = t[s]$ and $t' = t[s \leftarrow s']$;
- We have $t' <_{\mathcal{G}} t$.

This ordered rewriting relation is convergent, that is for all terms t, all ordered rewriting sequences starting from t are finite, and they all have the same limit, called the *normal form* of t. We denote this term $(t)\downarrow_{R(A)}$, or $(t)\downarrow$ when the equational theory considered is clear from the context. In the sequel we denote C_{spe} the set consisting of $c_{\min}$ and of all symbols in $\mathcal{G}$ of arity 0.

The *syntactic subterms* of a term t are denoted $\mathrm{Sub}_{\mathrm{syn}}(t)$ and are defined recursively as follows. If t is an atom then $\mathrm{Sub}_{\mathrm{syn}}(t) = \{t\}$. If $t = f(t_1, \ldots, t_n)$ then $\mathrm{Sub}_{\mathrm{syn}}(t) = \{t\} \cup \bigcup_{i=1}^{n} \mathrm{Sub}_{\mathrm{syn}}(t_i)$. The *positions* in a term t are sequences of integers defined recursively as follows, ε being the empty sequence. The term t is at position ε in t. We also say that ε is the root position. We write $p \leq q$ to denote that the position p is a prefix of position q. If u is a syntactic subterm of t at position p and if $u = f(u_1, \ldots, u_n)$ then u_i is at position $p \cdot i$ in t for $i \in \{1, \ldots, n\}$. We write $t_{|p}$ the subterm of t at position p. We denote $t[s]$ a term t that admits s as syntactic subterm. We denote by $\mathrm{top}(\_)$ the function that associates to each term t its root symbol.

2.2   Mode in an Equational Theory

We recall here the notion of *mode* on a signature, which is defined in [6]. Assume $\mathcal{H}$ is an equational theory over a signature $\mathcal{G}$, and let $\mathcal{G}_0$ be a subset of $\mathcal{G}$. Assume also that the set of variables is partitioned into two sets $\mathcal{X}_0$ and $\mathcal{X}_1$. We first define a signature function Sign(_) on $\mathcal{G} \cup$ Atoms in the following way:

$$\text{Sign}(\_) : \mathcal{G} \cup \text{Atoms} \rightarrow \{0, 1, 2\}$$
$$\text{Sign}(f) = \begin{cases} 0 \text{ if } f \in \mathcal{G}_0 \cup \mathcal{X}_0 \\ 1 \text{ if } f \in (\mathcal{G} \setminus \mathcal{G}_0) \cup \mathcal{X}_1 \\ 2 \text{ otherwise, i.e. when } f \text{ is a free constant} \end{cases}$$

The function Sign(_) is extended to terms by taking $\text{Sign}(t) = \text{Sign}(\text{top}(t))$.

We also assume that there exists a *mode* function $\text{m}(\cdot, \cdot)$ such that $\text{m}(f, i)$ is defined for every symbol $f \in \mathcal{G}$ and every integer i such that $1 \leq i \leq \text{ar}(f)$. For all valid f, i we have $\text{m}(f, i) \in \{0, 1\}$ and $\text{m}(f, i) \leq \text{Sign}(f)$. Thus for all $f \in \mathcal{G}_0$ and for all i we have $\text{m}(f, i) = 0$.

Well-Moded Equational Theories. A position different from ε in a term t is *well-moded* if it can be written $p \cdot i$ (where p is a position and i a nonnegative integer) such that $\text{Sign}(t_{|p \cdot i}) = \text{m}(\text{top}(t_{|p}), i)$. In other words the position in a term is well-moded if the subterm at that position is of the expected type w.r.t. the function symbol immediately above it. A term is *well-moded* if all its *non root* positions are well-moded. Note in particular that a well-moded term does not contain free constants. If a position of t is not well-moded we say it is *ill-moded* in t. A term is *pure* if its only ill-moded subterms are atoms. An equational presentation $\mathcal{H} = (\mathcal{G}, A)$ is well-moded if for all equations $u = v$ in A the terms u and v are well-moded and $\text{Sign}(u) = \text{Sign}(v)$. One can prove that if an equational theory is well-moded then its completion is also well-moded [6].

Note that if $\mathcal{H}$ is the union of two equational theories $\mathcal{H}_0$ and $\mathcal{H}_1$ over two disjoint signatures $\mathcal{G}_0$ and $\mathcal{G}_1$, the theory $\mathcal{H}$ is well-moded when assigning mode i to each argument of each operator $g \in \mathcal{G}_i$, for $i \in \{0, 1\}$.

Subterm Values. The notion of mode also permits to define a new subterm relation in $\text{T}(\mathcal{G}, \mathcal{X})$.

We call a *subterm value* of a term t a syntactic subterm of t that is either atomic or occurs at an ill-moded position of t^1. We denote Sub(t) the set of subterm values of t. By extension, for a set of terms E, the set Sub(E) is defined as the union of the subterm values of the elements of E. The subset of the maximal and strict subterm values of a term t plays an important role in the sequel. We call these subterm values the *factors* of t, and denote this set Factors(t).

Example 1. Consider two binary symbols f and g with $\text{Sign}(f) = \text{Sign}(g) = \text{m}(f, 1) = \text{m}(g, 1) = 1$ and $\text{m}(f, 2) = \text{m}(g, 2) = 0$, and $t = f(f(g(a, b), f(c, c)), d)$. Its subterm values are a, b, $f(c, c)$, c, d, and its factors are a, b, $f(c, c)$ and d.

In the rest of this paper and unless otherwise indicated, *the notion of subterm will refer to subterm values.*

---
[1] Note that the root position of a term is *always* ill-moded.

Unification systems. We review here properties of well-moded theories with respect to unification that are addressed in [6].

Assume $\mathcal{H}$ is a well-moded equational theory over a signature $\mathcal{G}$, and let $\mathcal{H}_0$ be its projection over the signature $\mathcal{G}_0$ of symbols of signature 0. Let us first define unification systems with ordering constraints.

Definition 1. *(Unification systems) Let $\mathcal{H}$ be a set of equational axioms on* $\mathrm{T}(\mathcal{G}, \mathcal{X})$. *An $\mathcal{H}$-unification system $\mathcal{S}$ is a finite set of couples of terms in* $\mathrm{T}(\mathcal{G}, \mathcal{X})$ *denoted by $\{u_i \overset{?}{=} v_i\}_{i \in \{1,\dots,n\}}$. It is satisfied by a ground substitution σ, and we note $\sigma \models_{\mathcal{H}} \mathcal{S}$, if for all $i \in \{1,\dots,n\}$ we have $u_i\sigma =_{\mathcal{H}} v_i\sigma$.*

We will consider only satisfiability of unification systems with ordering constraints. That is, we consider the following decision problem:

Ordered Unifiability

Input:	A $\mathcal{H}$-unification system $\mathcal{S}$ and an ordering $\prec$ on the variables X and constants C of $\mathcal{S}$.
Output:	SAT iff there exists a substitution σ such that $\sigma \models_{\mathcal{H}} \mathcal{S}$ and for all $x \in X$ and $c \in C$, $x \prec c$ implies $c \notin \mathrm{Sub}_{\mathrm{syn}}(x\sigma)$

3   Analysis of Reachability Properties of Cryptographic Protocols

We recall in this section the definitions of [5] concerning our model of an intruder attacking actively a protocol, and of the simultaneous constraint satisfaction problems employed to model a finite execution of a protocol.

3.1   Intruder Deduction Systems

We first give here the general definition of intruder systems, as is given in [5]. We then give the definition of a *well-moded intruder* that we will use in this paper. In the context of a security protocol (see *e.g.* [13] for a brief overview), we model messages as ground terms and intruder deduction rules as rewrite rules on sets of messages representing the knowledge of an intruder. The intruder derives new messages from a given (finite) set of messages by applying intruder rules. Since we assume some equational axioms $\mathcal{H}$ are satisfied by the function symbols in the signature, all these derivations have to be considered *modulo* the equational congruence $=_{\mathcal{H}}$ generated by these axioms. In our setting an intruder deduction rule is specified by a term t in some signature $\mathcal{G}$. Given values for the variables of t the intruder is able to generate the corresponding instance of t.

Definition 2. *An intruder system $\mathcal{I}$ is given by a triple $\langle \mathcal{G}, S, \mathcal{H} \rangle$ where $\mathcal{G}$ is a signature, $S \subseteq \mathrm{T}(\mathcal{G}, \mathcal{X})$ and $\mathcal{H}$ is a set of equations between terms in $\mathrm{T}(\mathcal{G}, \mathcal{X})$. To each $t \in S$ we associate a deduction rule $\mathrm{L}^t : \mathrm{Var}(t) \to t$ and $\mathrm{L}^{t,g}$ denotes the set of ground instances of the rule L^t modulo $\mathcal{H}$:*

$$\mathrm{L}^{t,g} = \{l \to r \mid \exists \sigma, \text{ground substitution on } \mathcal{G},\ l = \mathrm{Var}(t)\sigma \text{ and } r =_{\mathcal{H}} t\sigma\}$$

The set of rules $\mathrm{L}_{\mathcal{I}}$ is defined as the union of the sets $\mathrm{L}^{t,g}$ for all $t \in \mathcal{S}$.

Each rule $l \to r$ in $L_{\mathcal{I}}$ defines an intruder deduction relation $\to_{l \to r}$ between finite sets of terms. Given two finite sets of terms E and F we define $E \to_{l \to r} F$ if and only if $l \subseteq E$ and $F = E \cup \{r\}$. We denote $\to_{\mathcal{I}}$ the union of the relations $\to_{l \to r}$ for all $l \to r$ in $L_{\mathcal{I}}$ and by $\to_{\mathcal{I}}^{*}$ the transitive closure of $\to_{\mathcal{I}}$. Note that by definition, given sets of terms E, E', F and F' such that $E =_{\mathcal{H}} E'$ and $F =_{\mathcal{H}} F'$ we have $E \to_{\mathcal{I}} F$ iff $E' \to_{\mathcal{I}} F'$. We simply denote by $\to$ the relation $\to_{\mathcal{I}}$ when there is no ambiguity about $\mathcal{I}$.

A *derivation* D of length n, $n \geq 0$, is a sequence of steps of the form $E_0 \to_{\mathcal{I}} E_0, t_1 \to_{\mathcal{I}} \cdots \to_{\mathcal{I}} E_n$ with finite sets of ground terms $E_0, \ldots E_n$, and ground terms $t_1, \ldots, t_n$, such that $E_i = E_{i-1} \cup \{t_i\}$ for every $i \in \{1, \ldots, n\}$. The term t_n is called the *goal* of the derivation. We define $\overline{E}^{\mathcal{I}}$ to be equal to the set $\{t \mid \exists F \text{ s.t. } E \to_{\mathcal{I}}^{*} F \text{ and } t \in F\}$ *i.e.* the set of terms that can be derived from E. If there is no ambiguity on the deduction system $\mathcal{I}$ we write $\overline{E}$ instead of $\overline{E}^{\mathcal{I}}$.

We now define well-moded intruder systems and their properties.

Definition 3. *Given a well-moded equational theory $\mathcal{H}$, an intruder system $\mathcal{I} = \langle \mathcal{G}, S, \mathcal{H} \rangle$ is* well-moded *if all terms in S are well-moded.*

3.2 Simultaneous Constraint Satisfaction Problems

We introduce now the constraint systems to be solved for checking protocols. It is shown in [5] how these constraint systems permit to express the reachability of a state in a protocol execution.

Definition 4. *(Constraint systems) Let $\mathcal{I} = \langle \mathcal{G}, S, \mathcal{H} \rangle$ be an intruder system. An $\mathcal{I}$-Constraint system $\mathcal{C}$ is denoted: $((E_i \triangleright v_i)_{i \in \{1, \ldots, n\}}, S)$ and it is defined by a sequence of couples $(E_i, v_i)_{i \in \{1, \ldots, n\}}$ with $v_i \in \mathcal{X}$ and $E_i \subseteq \mathrm{T}(\mathcal{G}, \mathcal{X})$ for $i \in \{1, \ldots, n\}$, and $E_{i-1} \subseteq E_i$ for $i \in \{2, \ldots, n\}$ and by an $\mathcal{H}$-unification system S.*

An $\mathcal{I}$-Constraint system $\mathcal{C}$ is satisfied by a ground substitution σ if for all $i \in \{1, \ldots, n\}$ we have $v_i \sigma \in \overline{E_i \sigma}$ and if $\sigma \models_{\mathcal{H}} S$. If a ground substitution σ satisfies a constraint system $\mathcal{C}$ we denote it by $\sigma \models_{\mathcal{I}} \mathcal{C}$.

Constraint systems are denoted by $\mathcal{C}$ and decorations thereof. Note that if a substitution σ is a solution of a constraint system $\mathcal{C}$, by definition of constraint and unification systems the substitution $(\sigma) \downarrow$ is also a solution of $\mathcal{C}$. In the context of cryptographic protocols the inclusion $E_{i-1} \subseteq E_i$ means that the knowledge of an intruder does not decrease as the protocol progresses: after receiving a message a honest agent will respond to it. This response can be added to the knowledge of an intruder who listens to all communications.

We are not interested in general constraint systems but only in those related to protocols. In particular we need to express that a message to be sent at some step i should be built from previously received messages recorded in the variables $v_j, j < i$, and from the initial knowledge. To this end we define:

Definition 5. *(Deterministic Constraint Systems) We say that an $\mathcal{I}$-constraint system $((E_i \triangleright v_i)_{i \in \{1, \ldots, n\}}, S)$ is* deterministic *if for all i in $\{1, \ldots, n\}$ we have $\mathrm{Var}(E_i) \subseteq \{v_1, \ldots, v_{i-1}\}$*

In order to be able to combine solutions of constraints for the intruder theory $\mathcal{I}$ with solutions of constraint systems for intruders defined on a disjoint signature we have, as for unification, to introduce some ordering constraints to be satisfied by the solution (see [5] for details on this construction). Intuitively, these ordering constraints prevent from introducing cycle when building a global solution. This motivates us to define the *Ordered Satisfiability* problem:

Ordered Satisfiability

Input:	an $\mathcal{I}$-constraint system $\mathcal{C}$, $X = \text{Var}(\mathcal{C})$, $C = \text{Const}(\mathcal{C})$ and a linear ordering $\prec$ on $X \cup C$.
Output:	SAT iff there exists a substitution σ such that $\sigma \models_{\mathcal{I}} \mathcal{C}$ and for all $x \in X$ and $c \in C$, $x \prec c$ implies $c \notin \text{Sub}_{\text{syn}}(x\sigma)$

4   Model of a Collision-Aware Intruder

We define in this section intruder systems to model the way an active intruder may deliberately create collisions for the application of hash functions. Note that our model doesn't take into account the time for finding collisions, which is significantly greater than the time necessary for other operations. The results that we can obtain can therefore be seen as worst-case results, and should be assessed with respect to the possible time deadline in the actual specification of a protocol under analysis. Further works will also be concerned with the fact that given a bound on intruder's deduction capabilities, a collision may be found only with a probability p, $0 \leq p \leq 1$.

We consider in this paper five different intruder models. We will reduce in two steps the most complex one to a simpler one, relying on the notion of well-moded theories and on the results in [6]. We then prove decidability of ordered reachability for this simpler intruder system.

4.1   Intruder on Words

We first define our goal intruder, that is an intruder only able to concatenate messages and extract *prefixes* and *suffixes*. We denote $\mathcal{I}_{\text{AU}} = \langle \mathcal{F}_{AU}, S_{AU}, \mathcal{E}_{AU} \rangle$ an intruder system that operates on words, such that, if $\_ \cdot \_$ denotes the concatenation and ϵ denotes the empty word, the intruder has at its disposal all ground instances of the following deduction rules:

$$\left\{ \begin{array}{ll} x, y \to x \cdot y & \to \epsilon \\ x \cdot y \to x & x \cdot y \to y \end{array} \right.$$

We moreover assume that the concatenation and empty word operations satisfy the following equations:

$$\left\{ \begin{array}{ll} x \cdot (y \cdot z) = (x \cdot y) \cdot z \\ \quad x \cdot \epsilon = x & \epsilon \cdot x = x \end{array} \right.$$

Given these definitions, we can see terms over $T(\mathcal{F}_{AU}, \mathcal{X})$ as *words* over the alphabet $\mathcal{X} \cup C$, and we denote letters(w) the set of atoms (either variable or free constants) occurring in w. As usual, we extend letters(_) to set of terms in $T(\mathcal{F}_{AU}, \mathcal{X})$ by taking the union of letters occurring in each term.

Pitfall. Note that this intruder model does not fit into the intruder systems definition of [5,6]. The rationale for this is that, in the notation given here, the application of the rules is non-deterministic, and thus cannot be modelled easily into our "deduction by normalisation" model. We however believe that a deterministic and still associative model of message concatenation by means of an "element" unary operator, associative operator "·", and Head and Tail operations may be introduced. This means that we also assume that unification problems are only among words of this underlying theory, disregarding equations that may involve these extra operators. We leave the exact soundness of our model for further analysis and concentrate on the treatment of collisions discovery for hash functions.

4.2   Intruder on Words with Free Function Symbols

We extend the $\mathcal{I}_{AU}$ intruder with two free function symbols g and f. We first define an intruder able to compose messages using a free function symbol g of arity 4. We denote $\mathcal{I}_g = \langle \{g\}, \{g(x_1, x_2, y_1, y_2)\}, \emptyset \rangle$ this intruder. It has at its disposal all ground instances of the following rule:

$$x_1, x_2, y_1, y_2 \rightarrow g(x_1, x_2, y_1, y_2)$$

We define a similar intruder with function symbol f. We denote $\mathcal{I}_f = \langle \{f\}, \{f(x_1, x_2, y_1, y_2)\}, \emptyset \rangle$ this intruder which has at its disposal all ground instances of the following rule:

$$x_1, x_2, y_1, y_2 \rightarrow f(x_1, x_2, y_1, y_2)$$

Finally, we define $\mathcal{I}_{free}$ intruder as the disjoint union of $\mathcal{I}_{AU}$, $\mathcal{I}_f$ and $\mathcal{I}_g$, and we have:

$$\mathcal{I}_{free} = \langle \mathcal{F}_{AU} \cup \{g, f\}, S_{AU} \cup \{f(x_1, x_2, y_1, y_2), g(x_1, x_2, y_1, y_2)\}, \mathcal{E}_{AU} \rangle.$$

4.3   Hash-Colliding Intruder

We consider a signature modelling the following different operations:

- The *concatenation* of two messages, the extraction of a suffix or a prefix of a concatenated message and the production of an empty message, as in the case of the $\mathcal{I}_{AU}$ intruder system;
- The application of a hash function h for which it is possible to find collisions, the hash-value of a message m denoted $h(m)$;
- Two function symbols f and g denoting the (complex) algorithm being used to find collisions starting from two different messages m and m'.

We assume that the algorithm employed by the intruder to find collisions starting from two messages m and m' proceeds as follows:

1. First the intruder splits both messages into two parts, thus choosing m_1, m_2, m_1', m_2' such that $m = m_1 \cdot m_2$ and $m' = m_1' \cdot m_2'$;
2. Then, in order to find collisions, the intruder computes two messages $g(m_1, m_2, m_1', m_2')$ and $f(m_1, m_2, m_1', m_2')$ such that:

$$(HC) \quad h(m_1 \cdot g(m_1, m_2, m_1', m_2') \cdot m_2) = h(m_1' \cdot f(m_1, m_2, m_1', m_2') \cdot m_2')$$

A consequence of our model is that in order to build collisions starting from two messages m and m' the intruder must know (*i.e.* have in its knowledge set) these two messages. A side effect is that it is not possible to build three (or more) different messages with the same hash value by iterating the research for collisions. Formally, the core of the proof of this assertion is the following lemma that permits to prove that in an equivalence class of $\mathcal{E}_h$ containing pure terms there exists only two different members modulo $\mathcal{E}_{AU}$. The proof is in [4]. In the following lemma, $t =^1_{HC} t'$ denotes that there exists a one step rewriting between t and t' using (HC) rule.

Lemma 1. *Let* $t_0, t, t' \in T(\mathcal{F}_h, \mathcal{X})$ *such that* $t_0 =_{\mathcal{E}_{AU}} t =^1_{HC} t'$ *and* $t_0 = h(t_1 \cdot f(t_1, t_2, t_3, t_4) \cdot t_2)$. *We have:* $t' =_{\mathcal{E}_{AU}} h(t_3 \cdot g(t_1, t_2, t_3, t_4) \cdot t_4)$.

In a more comprehensive model we might moreover want to model that collisions cannot always be found using attacks published in the literature, but instead that given a deadline, the probability p of success of an attack is strictly below 1. This would imply that the application of this rule by the intruder would, assuming independence of collision attacks, reduce the likelihood of the symbolic attack found. In this setting our model would account for attacks with a non-negligible probability of success as is shown in [2].

Leaving probabilities aside, we express intruder's deductions in our setting by adding the rule $x \to h(x)$ to the deduction rules of the $\mathcal{I}_{\text{free}}$ intruder. As a consequence, the previous description of the $\mathcal{I}_{\text{free}}$ intruder enables us to model a collision-capable intruder

$$\mathcal{I}_h = \langle \mathcal{F}_h, S_h, \mathcal{E}_h \rangle$$

with:
$$\begin{cases} \mathcal{F}_h = \mathcal{F}_{AU} \cup \{f, g, h\} \\ S_h = S_{AU} \cup \{f(x_1, x_2, y_1, y_2), g(x_1, x_2, y_1, y_2), h(x)\} \\ \mathcal{E}_h = \mathcal{E}_{AU} \cup \{(HC)\} \end{cases}$$

For the following mode and signature functions the theory $\mathcal{E}_{AU} \cup \{(HC)\}$ is a well-moded theory.

$$\text{mode:} \quad \begin{cases} m(.,1) = m(.,2) = m(g,i) = m(f,i) = 0 \; \forall i \in \{1, \ldots, 4\} \\ m(h,1) = 0 \end{cases}$$

$$\text{Signature:} \quad \begin{cases} \text{Sign}(\cdot) = \text{Sign}(\epsilon) = \text{Sign}(f) = \text{Sign}(g) = 0 \\ \text{Sign}(h) = 1 \end{cases}$$

Notice that in this case, every well-moded syntactic subterm of a term t is of signature 0, and that every ill-moded strict syntactic subterm is of signature 1 [4]. The main result of this paper is the following decidability result.

Theorem 1. *Ordered satisfiability for the $\mathcal{I}_h$ intruder is decidable.*

The rest of this paper is dedicated to the proof of this theorem. The technique employed consists in successive reductions to simpler problems and in finally proving that all simpler problems are decidable. These reductions are summarised in Figure 1. A proof sketch for the decidability of the $\mathcal{I}_g$, $\mathcal{I}_f$ and $\mathcal{I}_{AU}$ is given in Section 5.2. Algorithm 1, that permits the first re-

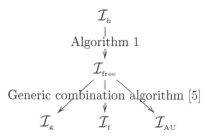

Fig. 1. Reduction strategy

duction, is based on the facts that the $\mathcal{I}_h$ intruder is well-moded (as seen above) and that we can apply a reduction according to the criterion of [6] for well-moded intruder systems.

CRITERION: If $E \to_{\mathcal{S}_1} E, r \to_{\mathcal{S}_1} E, r, t$ and $r \notin \mathrm{Sub}(E, t) \cup C_{\mathrm{spe}}$ then there is a set of terms F such that $E \to_{\mathcal{S}_0}^* F \to_{\mathcal{S}_1} F, t$.

If a well-moded intruder system system satisfies this criterion, then the following proposition holds. It is a cornerstone for the proof of completeness of Algorithm 1.

Proposition 1. *Let $\mathcal{I}$ be a well-moded intruder that satisfies criterion, and let $\mathcal{C}$ be a deterministic $\mathcal{I}$-constraint system. If $\mathcal{C}$ is satisfiable, there exists a substitution σ such that $\sigma \models_{\mathcal{I}} \mathcal{C}$ and:*

$$\{t \in \mathrm{Sub}((\mathrm{Sub}(\mathcal{C})\sigma)\downarrow) | \mathrm{Sign}(t) = 1\} \subseteq \{(t\sigma)\downarrow | \ (t \in \mathrm{Sub}(\mathcal{C}) \ and \ \mathrm{Sign}(t) = 1) \ or \ t \in \mathcal{X}\}$$

5 Decidability of Reachability

We present here a decision procedure for *Ordered Satisfiability Problem* for $\mathcal{I}_h$ intruder system. Our technique consists in simplifying the intruder system $\mathcal{I}_h$ to $\mathcal{I}_{\mathrm{free}}$. We then reduce the decidability problems of ordered reachability for deterministic constraint problems for $\mathcal{I}_{\mathrm{free}}$ to the decidability problems of ordered reachability for deterministic constraint problems for $\mathcal{I}_g$, $\mathcal{I}_f$ and $\mathcal{I}_{AU}$. We finally prove the decidability for these intruder systems.

5.1 Reduction to $\mathcal{I}_{\mathrm{free}}$-intruder

Algorithm. We present here a procedure for reducing $\mathcal{I}_h$ intruder system to $\mathcal{I}_{\mathrm{free}}$ intruder system that takes as input a deterministic constraint system $\mathcal{C}$ $= ((E_i \triangleright v_i)_{i \in \{1, \dots, n\}}, \mathcal{S})$ and a linear ordering $\prec_i$ on atoms of $\mathcal{C}$. Let $m = |\mathrm{Sub}(\mathcal{C})|$ be the number of subterms in $\mathcal{C}$.

Algorithm 1

Step 1. Choose a number $k \leq m$ and add k equations $h_j \stackrel{?}{=} \mathrm{h}(c_j)$ to $\mathcal{S}$ where the h_j, c_j are new variables.

Step 2. For each $t \in \mathrm{Sub}(\mathcal{C}) \cup \{c_1, \ldots, c_k\}$ choose a *type* 0 or 1. If t is of type 1, choose $j_t \in \{1, \ldots, k\}$ and add an equation $t \stackrel{?}{=} h_{j_t}$ to $\mathcal{S}$.

Step 3. For all $t, t' \in \mathrm{Sub}(\mathcal{C})$, if there exists $h \in \{h_1, \ldots, h_k\}$ such that $t \stackrel{?}{=} h$ and $t' \stackrel{?}{=} h$ are in $\mathcal{S}$, add to $\mathcal{S}$ an equation $t \stackrel{?}{=} t'$ to $\mathcal{S}$.

Step 4. Choose a subset H of $\{c_1, \ldots, c_k\} \cup \{h_1, \ldots, h_k\}$ and guess a total order $<_d$ on $L = H \cup \{v_1, \ldots, v_n\}$ such that $v_i <_d v_j$ iff $i < j$. Write the obtained list $w_1, \ldots, w_l$. Let $\mathcal{S}'$ be the unification system obtained so far, and form: $\mathcal{C}' = ((F_i \rhd w_i)_{1 \leq i \leq l}, \mathcal{S}')$ with:

$$\begin{cases} F_1 = E_1 \\ F_{i+1} = F_i \cup (E_{j+1} \setminus E_j) & \text{if } w_i = v_j \\ F_{i+1} = F_i, w_i & \text{Otherwise} \end{cases}$$

Step 5. For all $t \in \mathrm{Sub}(\mathcal{C})$ chosen of type 1, replace all occurrences of t in the F_i and all occurrence occurrences of t *as a strict subterm* in $\mathcal{S}'$ by the representant of its class h_{j_t}. Let F_i' be the set F_i once this abstraction has been applied

Step 6. Non-deterministically reduce $\mathcal{S}'$ to a unification system $\mathcal{S}''$ free of h symbols, and form the satisfiable $\mathcal{I}_{\mathrm{free}}$ constraint system:

$$\mathcal{C}'' = ((F_i' \rhd w_i)_{1 \leq i \leq l}, \mathcal{S}'')$$

Sketch of the Completeness Proof. Assume that the initial deterministic constraint system is satisfiable. By Proposition 1, there exists a bound substitution σ satisfying $\mathcal{C}$.

- Let the number k chosen at Step 1 be the number of subterms whose top symbol is h in $\mathrm{Sub}((\mathrm{Sub}(\mathcal{C})\sigma)\!\downarrow)$. The h_j represent the different values of the terms of signature 1. In the sequel we assume that σ is extended to the h_j such that all $h_j \sigma$ have a different value and are of signature 1.
- In Step 2, if $\mathrm{Sign}((t\sigma)\!\downarrow) = 1$ we choose the j such that $(t\sigma)\!\downarrow = h_j \sigma$ and add the corresponding equation to $\mathcal{S}$.
- In Step 3, we add equations between terms whose normal form by σ are equals in order to simplify the reduction to $\mathcal{I}_{\mathrm{free}}$.
- Step 4 is slightly more intricate. It relies on the fact that a rule in $\mathcal{S}_1$ may only yield a term whose normal form by σ is of signature 1.

   The subset H correspond to the subterms of signature 1 of $\mathrm{Sub}((\mathrm{Sub}(\mathcal{C}\sigma))\!\downarrow)$ that are deduced by the intruder using a rule in $\mathcal{S}_1$. We then anticipate the construction of $h_j \sigma$ with the application of a rule in $\mathcal{S}_1$ by requiring that the corresponding $c_j \sigma$ has to be build just before. Given the bound on k, this means that all remaining deductions performed by the intruder are now instances of rules in $\mathcal{S}_0$. Since $\mathcal{C}$ is satisfied by σ there exists a choice corresponding to *quasi well-formed* derivations such that all remaining reachability constraints are satisfiable by instances of rules in $\mathcal{S}_0$.

- At Step 5 we "purify" almost all the constraint system by removing all occurrences of a symbol h but the ones that are on the top of an equality. By the choice of the equivalence classes it is clear that this purification does not loose the satisfiability by the substitution σ.
- The non-deterministic reduction is performed by guessing whether the equality of two hashes is the consequence of a collision set up by the intruder or of the equality of the hashed messages, and will produce a constraint system $\mathcal{C}$" without h symbol and also satisfiable by σ.

5.2   Decidability of Reachability for the $\mathcal{I}_{\text{free}}$-intruder

We first reduce the $\mathcal{I}_{\text{free}}$ intruder system to simpler intruder systems using the combination result of [5]. We will consider the decidability of these subsystems in the remainder of this section.

Theorem 2. *Ordered satisfiability for the $\mathcal{I}_{\text{free}}$ intruder system is decidable.*

Decidability of reachability for the $\mathcal{I}_{\text{g}}$-intruder. In this subsection, we consider an $\mathcal{I}_{\text{g}}$ intruder system with $\mathcal{I}_{\text{g}} = \langle \text{g}, \text{g}(x_1, x_2, x_1', x_2'), \emptyset \rangle$. This intruder has at its disposal all ground instances of the following deduction rule:

$$x_1, x_2, y_1, y_2 \rightarrow \text{g}(x_1, x_2, y_1, y_2)$$

Theorem 3. *Ordered satisfiability for the $\mathcal{I}_{\text{g}}$ intruder system is decidable.*

The proof of the above theorem is in [4]. Since the $\mathcal{I}_{\text{g}}$ and $\mathcal{I}_{\text{f}}$ intruder are isomorphic the result also applies to $\mathcal{I}_{\text{f}}$ after renaming of the symbol g into f.

Decidability of reachability for the AU-intruder. We now give a proof sketch for the decidability of ordered satisfiability for the $\mathcal{I}_{\text{AU}}$ intruder since the procedure is new.

Theorem 4. *Ordered satisfiability for the $\mathcal{I}_{\text{AU}}$ intruder system is decidable.*

PROOF. The algorithm proceeds as follows:

- Transform the deduction constraints $E \rhd v$ into an ordering constraint $<_d$;
- Check that $< = <_d \cup <_i$ is still a partial order on atoms of $\mathcal{C}$;
- Solve the unification problem with linear constant restriction $<$.

Let $\mathcal{C} = ((E_i \rhd v_i)_{0 \leq i \leq n}, \mathcal{S})$ be a deterministic constraint system for the $\mathcal{I}_{\text{AU}}$ intruder, $<_i$ be a (partial) order on $\text{Cons}(\mathcal{C}) \cup \text{Var}(\mathcal{C})$, and let σ be a solution of the $(\mathcal{C}, <_i)$ ordered satisfiability problem.

Given a set of terms $E \subseteq \text{T}(\mathcal{F}_{\text{AU}}, \mathcal{X})$, let us denote $\text{K}_{\mathcal{C}} = (\text{Cons}(\mathcal{C}) \setminus \text{letters}(E)) \setminus \mathcal{X}$. In plain words, $\text{K}_{\mathcal{C}}(E)$ is the set of constants in $\mathcal{C}$ **not** occurring in E. We are now ready to define $<_d$ as a partial order on $\text{Cons}(\mathcal{C}) \cup \{v_0, \dots, v_n\}$: We set $v_i <_d c$ for all constants c in $\text{K}_{\mathcal{C}}(E_i)$.

Claim. For all σ, we have $\sigma \models (\mathcal{C}, <_i)$ if, and only if, $\sigma \models (\mathcal{S}, <_i \cup <_d)$

PROOF OF THE CLAIM. Let us first prove the direct implication. Let σ be a ground solution of the $(\mathcal{C}, <_i)$ ordered satisfiability problem. By definition we have that σ is a solution of $(\mathcal{S}, <_i)$ ordered unifiability problem. Since for all $0 \leq i \leq n$ we have $\sigma \models E_i \triangleright v_i$, we easily see that letters$((v_i\sigma)\!\downarrow) \subseteq \mathrm{Cons}(E_i)$, and therefore letters$((v_i\sigma)\!\downarrow) \cap \mathrm{K}_{\mathcal{C}}(E_i) = \emptyset$. Thus σ is also a solution of $(\mathcal{S}, <_d \cup <_i)$. Conversely, assume now that σ is a ground solution of $(\mathcal{S}, <_d \cup <_i)$. By definition for all $0 \leq i \leq n$ we have letters$((v_i\sigma)\!\downarrow) \cap \mathrm{K}_{\mathcal{C}}(E_i) = \emptyset$, and thus letters$((v_i\sigma)\!\downarrow) \subseteq$ letters$(E_i) \setminus \mathcal{X}$. Thus we have $(v_i\sigma)\!\downarrow \in \overline{(E_i\sigma)\!\downarrow}$ for all $0 \leq i \leq n$, and thus $\sigma \models (\mathcal{C}, <_i)$ $\Diamond$

Since unifiability with linear constant restriction is decidable for the *AU* equational theory [17], this finishes the proof of the theorem. Note that the exact complexity is not known, but the problem is NP-hard and solvable in PSPACE [14,15], and it is conjectured to be in NP [16,11].   □

6   Conclusion

We have presented here a novel decision procedure for the search for attacks on protocols employing hash functions subject to collision attacks. Since this procedure is of practical interest for the analysis of the already normalised protocols relying on these weak functions, we plan to implement it into an already existing tool, CL-Atse [12]. Alternatively an implementation may be done in OFMC [1], though the support of associative operators is still partial. We also plan to formalise according to the model of [5] the underlying *AU* intruder system. In order to model hash functions we have introduced new symbols to denote the ability to create messages with the same hash value. This introduction amounts to the skolemisation of the equational property describing the existence of collisions. We believe that this construction can be extended to model the more complex and game-based properties that appear when relating a symbolic and a concrete model of cryptographic primitives.

References

1. Basin, D.A., Mödersheim, S., Viganò, L.: Ofmc: A symbolic model checker for security protocols. Int. J. Inf. Sec. 4(3), 181–208 (2005)
2. Baudet, M.: Random polynomial-time attacks and Dolev-Yao models. In: Anantharaman, S. (ed.) SASYFT 2004. Proceedings of the Workshop on Security of Systems: Formalism and Tools, Orléans, France (June 2004)
3. Biham, E., Chen, R.: Near-collisions of sha-0. In: Frankli, M.K. (ed.) CRYPTO 2004. LNCS, vol. 3152, pp. 290–305. Springer, Heidelberg (2004)
4. Chevalier, Y., Kourjieh, M.: A symbolic intruder model for hash-collision attacks. Technical report, IRIT (to appear)
5. Chevalier, Y., Rusinowitch, M.: Combining intruder theories. In: Caires, L., Italiano, G.F., Monteiro, L., Palamidessi, C., Yung, M. (eds.) ICALP 2005. LNCS, vol. 3580, pp. 639–651. Springer, Heidelberg (2005)

6. Chevalier, Y., Rusinowitch, M.: Hierarchical combination of intruder theories. In: Giesl, J. (ed.) RTA 2005. LNCS, vol. 3467, Springer, Heidelberg (2005)
7. Cramer, R.J.F. (ed.): EUROCRYPT 2005. LNCS, vol. 3494, pp. 22–26. Springer, Heidelberg (2005)
8. Daum, M., Lucks, S.: Attacking hash functions by poisoned messages. In: Cramer, R.J.F. (ed.) EUROCRYPT 2005. LNCS, vol. 3494, Springer, Heidelberg (2005), http://www.cits.rub.de/MD5Collisions
9. den Boer, B., Bosselaers, A.: Collisions for the compressin function of md5. In: Helleseth, T. (ed.) EUROCRYPT 1993. LNCS, vol. 765, pp. 293–304. Springer, Heidelberg (1994)
10. Klìma, V.: Finding md5 collisions on a notebook pc using multi-message modificatons, Cryptology ePrint Archive, Report 2005/102 (2005), http://eprint.iacr.org/
11. Larsen, K.G., Skyum, S., Winskel, G.: Automata, languages and programming. In: Larsen, K.G., Skyum, S., Winskel, G. (eds.) ICALP 1998. LNCS, vol. 1443, pp. 13–17. Springer, Heidelberg (1998)
12. Turuani, M.: The cl-atse protocol analyser, 17th international conference on term rewriting and applications - rta 2006, seattle, wa/usa (July 12 2006) 4098, 277–286 (2006)
13. Meadows, C.: The NRL protocol analyzer: an overview. Journal of Logic Programming 26(2), 113–131 (1996)
14. Plandowski, W.: Satisfiability of word equations with constants is in pspace. In: FOCS, pp. 495–500 (1999)
15. Plandowski, W.: Satisfiability of word equations with constants is in pspace. J. ACM, 483–496 (2004)
16. Plandowski, W., Rytter, W.: Application of lempel-ziv encodings to the solution of words equations. In: Larsen, K.G., Skyum, S., Winskel, G. (eds.) ICALP 1998. LNCS, vol. 1443, pp. 731–742. Springer, Heidelberg (1998)
17. Schulz, K.U.: Makanin's algorithm for word equations - two improvements and a generalization. In: Schulz, K.U. (ed.) IWWERT 1990. LNCS, vol. 572, pp. 85–150. Springer, Heidelberg (1992)
18. Wang, X., Feng, D., Lai, X., Yu, H.: Collisions for hash functions md4, md5, haval-128 and ripemd (2004), http://eprint.iacr.org/
19. Wang, X., Lai, X., Feng, D., Chen, H., Yu, X.: Cryptanalysis of the hash functions md4 and ripemd. In: Cramer [7], pp. 1–18
20. Wang, X., Yin, Y.L., Yu, H.: Finding collisions in the full sha-1. In: Shoup, V. (ed.) CRYPTO 2005. LNCS, vol. 3621, pp. 17–36. Springer, Heidelberg (2005)
21. Wang, X., Yu, H.: How to break md5 and other hash functions. In: Cramer [7], pp. 19–35
22. Yajima, J., Shimoyama, T.: Wang's sufficient conditions of md5 are not sufficient (2005), http://eprint.iacr.org/

A Denotational Approach to Scope-Based Compensable Flow Language for Web Service[*]

Huibiao Zhu, Geguang Pu, and Jifeng He

Software Engineering Institute, East China Normal University
3663 Zhongshan Road (North), Shanghai, China 200062
{hbzhu,ggpu,jifeng}@sei.ecnu.edu.cn

Abstract. Web Services have become more and more important in these years, and BPEL4WS is a de facto standard for the web service composition and orchestration. We have proposed a language *BPEL0* to capture the important features of BPEL4WS, with the scope-based compensation and fault handling mechanism. In this paper we formalize the denotational semantics for *BPEL0*, which can support the refinement calculus and the verification of program equivalence. A set of algebraic laws is investigated within the denotational framework. The distinct features of *BPEL0* make the investigation of the denotational semantics and algebraic laws more challenging.

1 Introduction

Web services and other web-based applications have been becoming more and more important in practice. In this blooming field, various web-based business process languages have been introduced, such as XLANG, WSFL, BPEL4WS (BPEL) and StAC [2,3,7,8]. BPEL has become the de facto standard for specifying and executing workflow specification for web service composition. It contains several interesting features, including the scope-based compensation and fault handling mechanism.

In [4], we have focused on the theoretical foundations of scope-based flow language and proposed a language *BPEL0*. We have formalized its operational semantics. For the aim of exploring program equivalence, we have also introduced the concept of bisimulation in a hierarchy structure.

Compared with operational semantics, denotational semantics provides more abstract meanings to programs. The distinct features of *BPEL0* make the study of the denotational semantics more challenging. Our approach for the formalization of the denotational semantics for *BPEL0* is under *Unifying Theories of programming* (abbreviated as *UTP*) [5]. Denotational semantics can be used to deduce the interesting properties of programs. These properties are most elegantly expressed as algebraic laws [5], which can be verified in our denotational framework.

---

[*] Partially supported by National Basic Research Program of China (No. 2002CB312001 and No. 2005CB321904) and the 211 project of The Ministry of Education of China.

M. Okada and I. Satoh (Eds.): ASIAN 2006, LNCS 4435, pp. 28–36, 2007.
© Springer-Verlag Berlin Heidelberg 2007

This paper is organised as follows. Section 2 introduces the language *BPEL0* and explores its semantic model. The behaviour of a statement is expressed in a form consisting of four parts: divergent, waiting, fault and terminating part. In order to deal with the compensation feature, two semantic variables are introduced, which store the programs for compensation in nested stack structures. Section 3 formalises the denotational semantics of each statement. Algebraic laws have also been studied, including the BPEL featured laws. Section 4 concludes the paper.

2   The Semantic Model for *BPEL0*

2.1   The Syntax of *BPEL0*

BPEL0 is a subset of BPEL, where its syntax is designed in the style of traditional programming languages instead of complicated XML style. Its syntax is described as follows:

$$BA ::= \mathsf{skip} \mid x := e \mid \mathsf{wait}\ n \mid \mathsf{rec}\ a\ x \mid \mathsf{inv}\ a\ x\ y \mid \mathsf{throw}$$
$$A \quad ::= BA \mid A;\ A \mid \mathbf{if}\ b\ \mathbf{then}\ A\ \mathbf{else}\ A \mid \mathbf{while\ do}\ P \mid$$
$$\qquad A \parallel A \mid A \sqcap A \mid \{A\,?\,C\!:\!F\}_n$$
$$C, F ::= \urcorner n \mid \ldots \quad \text{(similar to } A)$$
$$BP \quad ::= \{\!|A : F|\!\}$$

where:

"$x := e$" is the assignment, which is considered as an atomic action in our language. "skip" behaves the same as "$x := x$". "wait n" let time advance n time units, where n is considered as a positive integer. "rec $a\ x$" models a process calling a web service, named a. As a result, it receives a value storing in variable x. Similarly, "inv $a\ x\ y$" models calling a web service (named a) with y as its parameter. However, for a service call, a fault may be encountered.

$P \parallel Q$ is the parallel composition. Our parallel mechanism is a shared-variable interleaving model. For a parallel process, if one component enters into a fault state after performing a sequence of actions, the whole process also enters into the fault state.

$\{A\,?\,C : F\}_n$ stands for a scope-based compensation statement, where n is the scope name, and A, C and F stand for the primary activity, compensation handler and fault handler respectively. The execution of a scope is the execution of its primary activity. The compensation handler is installed with its scope name when the primary activity completes its execution. During the execution of the primary activity, if a fault is encountered, the corresponding fault handler will be triggered for further execution. An installed compensation handler with the scope name n can be invoked by activity $\urcorner n$.

$\{\!|A : F|\!\}$ stands for the business process. It is at the outmost level of the scope-based compensation process, where it does not have the compensation part. Here A and F stand for the primary activity and fault handler respectively.

In order to consider the compensation mechanism, we first give the definition of the concept of *compensation sequence*:

(1) $\langle \; \rangle$ is a compensation sequence;

(2) $((C_1, n_1) : \alpha_1)\widehat{\;}\ldots\widehat{\;}((C_m, n_m) : \alpha_m)$ is a compensation sequence if $\alpha_1, \ldots, \alpha_m$ are also compensation sequences.

For the aim of installing the compensation handler in the execution of a scope, we introduce two variables $s1$ and $s2$. Both of them are compensation sequences. Variable $s1$ records the accumulated compensation handlers installed in the immediately enclosing scope before the current scope starts. It is called as the *static* compensation text. On the other hand, $s2$ is used to record the accumulated compensation closures during the execution of the current scope, which can be changed within the execution of the current scope. We regard $s2$ as the *active* compensation text.

2.2   The Semantic Model

This section considers the denotational model for *BPEL0*. Our approach is based on the relational calculus [5]. In order to deal with the shared-variable parallel model for *BPEL0*, we introduce a trace variable tr into our semantic framework, which consists of a sequence of *snapshots*. A snapshot is used to record the contribution of an atomic action, which can be expressed as a pair (t, σ), where: (1) t indicates the time when the atomic action happens; (2) σ stores the contribution of the atomic action. For the elements selection from a snapshot, we can define:

$$\pi_1((t, \sigma)) =_{df} t \qquad \text{and} \qquad \pi_2((t, \sigma)) =_{df} \sigma$$

For the aim of describing the timed feature of *BPEL0*, we introduce two variables *time* and *time'* to model the observation interval. In our model *time* and *time'* stand for the starting point and ending point of an observation interval correspondingly. We use $\delta(time)$ to represent the length of the time interval, which is defined as $\delta(time) =_{df} (time' - time)$, and is abbreviated as δ.

In order to deal with the compensation feature, we introduce two pairs of variables $s1$ and $s1'$, as well as $s2$ and $s2'$. Here, (1) $s1$ and $s1'$ stand for the initial and final static compensation behaviour respectively; (2) $s2$ and $s2'$ stand for the initial and final active compensation behaviour correspondingly.

A process may perform an infinite computation and enter into a *divergent* state. To distinguish its chaotic behaviour from the stable ones we introduce the variables $ok, ok' : Bool$ into the semantic model, where "$ok = true$" indicates the process has been started, and "$ok' = true$" states the process has become *stable*. A service call may wait for the remote process to transfer a message back to the program. For dealing with the waiting behaviour, we introduce another pair of variables $wait, wait' : Bool$. "$wait = true$" indicates that the process starts in an intermediate state, and "$wait' = true$" means the process is waiting.

For the aim of dealing with the fault handling, we introduce two Boolean variables $fault$ and $fault'$. "$fault = true$" indicates that the prior process has encountered a fault, whereas "$fault = false$" indicates that the prior process has successfully terminated.

The execution of a program can never undo an atomic action performed already. A formula P which identifies a program must therefore imply this fact; i.e., it has to meet the following healthiness condition:

$(H1)$ $P = P \wedge Inv(tr)$,   where $Inv(tr) =_{df} tr \preceq tr'$

Here $Inv(tr)$ indicates that tr is a prefix of tr', which indicates that trace can only get longer. Here, $s \preceq t$ indicates that s is a prefix of t.

Now we consider the healthiness conditions that a program should satisfy. For sequential composition "$R \; ; \; P$", it is defined as the relational composition [5]; i.e., $R \; ; \; P =_{df} \exists S \bullet R[S/X'] \wedge P[S/X]$, where X stands for all the free variables of R and P.

The introduction of intermediate waiting state has implications for sequential composition "$R; P$": if P is asked to start in a waiting state of R, it leaves the state unchanged; i.e., it satisfies the following healthiness condition.

$(H2)$ $P = II \lhd wait \rhd P$,   where, $P \lhd b \rhd Q =_{df} (b \wedge P) \vee (\neg b \wedge Q)$

We leave the definition of II direct after the healthiness condition $(H3)$.

Similarly, for process "$R; P$", if process R has encountered a fault, P cannot have the chance to be scheduled. Therefore, it should satisfy the following healthiness condition:

$(H3)$ $P = II \lhd fault \rhd P$

where: $II =_{df} \mathbf{true} \vdash (\delta = 0) \wedge (tr' = tr) \wedge (\bigwedge_{x \in \{s1, s2, wait, fault\}} x' = x)$
$P \vdash Q =_{df} \neg ok \wedge Inv(tr) \vee \neg P \vee (ok' \wedge Q)$

Definition 2.1 A formula is healthy if and only if it can be expressed as the form below:

$$\mathbf{H}(Q \vdash W \lhd wait' \rhd (F \lhd fault' \rhd T))$$

where, $\mathbf{H}(X) =_{df} (II \lhd wait \rhd (II \lhd fault \rhd (X \wedge Inv(tr))))$ □

Theorem 2.2 A healthy formula satisfies healthiness conditions $(H1)$, $(H2)$ and $(H3)$.   □

Theorem 2.3 If P_1 and P_2 are healthy formulae, so are $P_1 \vee P_2$, $P_1 \wedge P_2$, $P_1 \lhd b \rhd P_2$ and $P_1 \; ; \; P_2$.   □

Let $P_i = \mathbf{H}(Q_i \vdash W_i \lhd wait' \rhd (F_i \lhd fault' \rhd T_i))$, where $\neg Q_i = \neg Q_i \wedge Inv(tr)$, $W_i = W_i \wedge Inv(tr)$, $F_i = F_i \wedge Inv(tr)$, $T_i = T_i \wedge Inv(tr)$ for $i = 1, 2$, then we can have:

$$P_1 \; ; \; P_2 = \mathbf{H}(\neg(\neg Q_1 \; ; \; Inv(tr)) \wedge \neg(T_1 \; ; \; \neg Q_2) \vdash (W_1 \vee (T_1 \; ; \; W_2)) \lhd wait' \rhd$$
$$((F_1 \vee (T_1 \; ; \; F_2)) \lhd fault' \rhd (T_1 \; ; \; T_2)))$$

This theorem shows that healthy formulae are closed under sequential composition, conditional choice, disjunction and conjunction.

In what follows, the denotational semantics of a program can be expressed in the form:

$$\mathbf{H}(\neg D \vdash W \lhd wait' \rhd (F \lhd fault' \rhd T))$$

where, (1) D stands for the divergent behaviour of the process. (2) W stands for the waiting behaviour of the process. (3) F stands for the behaviour the process has been performed before it encounters a fault. (4) T stands for the terminating behaviour of the process.

For simplicity, for a healthy formula P, we use $div(P)$, $wait(P)$, $fau(P)$ and $ter(P)$ to represent its divergent, waiting, fault and terminating behaviours respectively. For a program P, we use $\llbracket P \rrbracket$ to represent its denotational semantics. Now we consider the refinement of two programs.

Definition 2.4 (Refinement) $P \sqsubseteq Q =_{df} \llbracket P \rrbracket \Rightarrow \llbracket Q \rrbracket$

3   The Denotational Semantics of *BPEL0*

3.1   Primitive Statement

P ; Q behaves like P before P terminates, then behaves like Q afterwards.

$$\llbracket P ; Q \rrbracket =_{df} \llbracket P \rrbracket ; \llbracket Q \rrbracket$$

The execution of assignment is instantaneous, which indicates that the length of the corresponding observation interval is 0 (i.e., $\delta = 0$). Further, the execution does not cause any faults and is not in the waiting state.

$\llbracket x := e \rrbracket$

$$=_{df} \mathbf{H} \left(\mathbf{true} \vdash \neg wait' \land \neg fault' \land \left(\begin{array}{c} \delta = 0 \land stable \land \\ (\ tr' = tr \lhd \pi_2(last(tr))(x) = e \rhd \\ tr' = tr\,\hat{}\,(time, \pi_2(last(tr))[e/x]) \ ) \end{array} \right) \right)$$

where: (1) $stable =_{df} (s1' = s1) \land (s2' = s2 = \langle\rangle)$. (2) $last(s)$ denotes the last element of sequence s.

skip behaves the same as $x := x$. It is the unit of sequential composition.

(skip-1)   skip ; P = skip = P ; skip

The *BPEL0* assignment obeys the same set of algebraic laws as its counterpart in conventional programming languages.

(assign-1) $x := x$ = skip,   (assign-2) $(x := e)$ = $(x, y := e, y)$

(assign-3) $(x, y, z := e, f, g)$ = $(y, x, z := f, e, g)$

throw encounters a fault immediately. All the variables remain unchanged.

$\llbracket throw \rrbracket =_{df} \mathbf{H}(\mathbf{true} \vdash \neg wait' \land fault \land stable \land (tr' = tr) \land (\delta = 0))$

where, *stable* has been defined as shown above.

throw is the left unit of sequential composition.

(throw-1)   throw ; P = throw

Proof. Here we only give the consider the fault part. The proof for other parts is similar.

$$fau(\llbracket throw \rrbracket \; ; \; \llbracket P \rrbracket) \qquad\qquad \{\text{Def of throw, Th 2.3}\}$$
$$= fau(\llbracket throw \rrbracket) \vee (\textbf{false} \; ; \; fau(\llbracket P \rrbracket)) \qquad \{\textbf{false} \; ; \; X = \textbf{false}\}$$
$$= fau(\llbracket throw \rrbracket) \qquad\qquad\qquad\qquad\qquad\qquad \square$$

"wait n" let time advance n time units. Its meaning can be expressed as:

$\llbracket wait\ n \rrbracket$

$=_{df} \textbf{H}(\textbf{true} \vdash ((\delta < n) \lhd wait' \rhd \neg fault' \wedge (\delta = n)) \wedge stable \wedge (tr' = tr))$

The delay command satisfies the law below.

(delay-1) wait n ; wait m = wait $(n+m)$

For nondeterministic choice, conditional, iteration and service call, their semantics can be found in [6].

3.2 Scope Activity

$\{A?C:Y\}_n$ models the scope-based compensation and fault handling behaviour.

Let $\llbracket A \rrbracket = \textbf{H}(\neg D_1 \vdash W_1 \lhd wait' \rhd (F_1 \lhd fault' \rhd T_1))$
       $\llbracket Y \rrbracket = \textbf{H}(\neg D_2 \vdash W_2 \lhd wait' \rhd (F_2 \lhd fault' \rhd T_2))$

Then, $div(\llbracket\{A?C:Y\}_n\rrbracket) =_{df} D_1 \vee (F_1 \; ; \; D_2)$
         $wait(\llbracket\{A?C:Y\}_n\rrbracket) =_{df} W_1 \vee (F_1 \; ; \; W_2)$
         $fau(\llbracket\{A?C:Y\}_n\rrbracket) =_{df} F_1 \; ; \; F_2$
         $ter(\llbracket\{A?C:Y\}_n\rrbracket) =_{df} (T_1 \; ; \; Comp(C,n)) \vee (F_1 \; ; \; T_2)$

where, $Comp(C,n) =_{df} \delta = 0 \wedge s1' = ((P,n):s2)\hat{\ }s1 \wedge (\llbracket P \rrbracket \Rightarrow \llbracket C \rrbracket) \wedge s2' = \langle\rangle$.

For the terminating behaviour of $\{A?C:Y\}_n$, if process A terminates successfully, the whole process also terminates successfully. In this case, program C will be installed for the later compensation use, which has been expressed using the behaviour $Comp(C,n)$ shown above. Further, if process A encounters a fault which activates the execution of process Y, and the execution of Y terminates successfully, the whole process also terminates successfully.

The scope activity satisfies the following algebraic laws.

(scope-1) If A_1 does not have rec, inv and throw statements,

then $A_1 \; ; \; \{A?C:F\}_n = \{(A_1;A)?C:F\}_n$

(scope-2) $\{(A_1 \sqcap A_2)?C:F\}_n = \{A_1?C:F\}_n \sqcap \{A_2?C:F\}_n$

(scope-3) $\{A?C:(F_1 \sqcap F_2)\}_n = \{A?C:F_1\}_n \sqcap \{A?C:F_2\}_n$

(scope-4) $\{(\textbf{if } b \textbf{ then } A_1 \textbf{ else } A_2)?C:F\}_n$
             $= \textbf{if } b \textbf{ then } \{A_1?C:F\}_n \textbf{ else } \{A_2?C:F\}_n$

(scope-5) $\{\textbf{while } b \textbf{ do } A?C:F\}_n$
             $= \textbf{if } b \textbf{ then } \{(A \; ; \; \textbf{while } b \textbf{ do } A)?C:F\}_n \textbf{ else } \{skip?C:F\}_n$

The business process $\{\!|P:F|\!\}$ is at the outmost level of the scope-based compensation process.

Let $P = \mathbf{H}(\neg D_1 \vdash W_1 \lhd wait' \rhd (F_1 \lhd fault' \rhd T_1))$

$\quad\quad F = \mathbf{H}(\neg D_2 \vdash W_2 \lhd wait' \rhd (F_2 \lhd fault' \rhd T_2))$

Then $div([\![\{\!|P:F|\!\}]\!]) =_{df} D_1 \vee (F_1; D_2), \quad wait([\![\{\!|P:F|\!\}]\!]) =_{df} W_1 \vee (F_1; W_2)$

$\quad\quad fau([\![\{\!|P:F|\!\}]\!]) =_{df} F_1; F_2, \quad\quad\quad ter([\![\{\!|P:F|\!\}]\!]) =_{df} T_1 \vee (F_1; T_2)$

The business process $\{\!|P:F|\!\}$ shares similar scope algebraic laws.

3.3 Looking Up

$\curvearrowright n$ looks up process with the scope name n from the static compensation sequence, and executes it when successfully finding it.

$$[\![\curvearrowright n]\!] =_{df} \exists x, x' \bullet \begin{pmatrix} x = ge(s1,n) \wedge (s2' = s2 =<>) \wedge \\ s1' = x' \wedge [\![gp(s1,n)]\!][x/s1, x'/s1'] \end{pmatrix}$$

Function $gp(s1,n)$ is used to find the corresponding process with the scope name n. After the successful finding, the corresponding process will be executed, where its initial value of $s1$ should be replaced with the rest corresponding subsequence expressed by $ge(s1,n)$. The detailed definition of $gp(s1,n)$ and $ge(s1,n)$ can be found in [6].

3.4 Parallel Composition

Firstly, we define a function $merge$, which can be used to merge two traces from different parallel components.

(1) $merge(\epsilon, \epsilon) =_{df} \{\epsilon\}, \quad merge(\epsilon, a\hat{\ }s) =_{df} \{a\hat{\ }s\}, \quad merge(a\hat{\ }s, \epsilon) =_{df} \{a\hat{\ }s\}$

(2) $merge(a\hat{\ }s, b\hat{\ }t) =_{df} \begin{cases} \{a\hat{\ }x | x \in merge(s, b\hat{\ }t)\} & \text{if } \pi_1(a) < \pi_1(b) \\ \{b\hat{\ }x | x \in merge(a\hat{\ }s, t)\} & \text{if } \pi_1(a) > \pi_1(b) \\ \{a\hat{\ }x | x \in merge(a, b\hat{\ }t)\} \cup & \text{if } \pi_1(a) = \pi_1(b) \\ \{b\hat{\ }x | x \in merge(a\hat{\ }s, t)\} \end{cases}$

Next we define the $\otimes$ operator for parallel composition, which can be used to define the combined behaviour for two parallel components.

$$X \otimes Y =_{df} \begin{pmatrix} \exists \, tr_1, tr_2, s11, s12, s21, s22, tr_1', tr_2', s11', s12', s21', s22' \bullet \\ tr_1 = tr_2 = tr \wedge s11 = s12 = s1 \wedge s21 = s22 = s2 \wedge \\ X[tr_1, s11, s21, tr_1', s11', s21'/tr, s1, s2, tr', s1', s2'] \wedge \\ Y[tr_2, s12, s22, tr_2', s12', s22'/tr, s1, s2, tr', s1', s2'] \wedge \\ tr' - tr \in merge(tr_1' - tr_1, tr_2' - tr_2) \wedge \\ (\ s1' - s1 \sqsubseteq (s11' - s11)\hat{\ }(s12' - s12) \vee \\ s1' - s1 \sqsubseteq s12' - s12)\hat{\ }(s11' - s11)\ ) \wedge \\ (\ s2' - s2 \sqsubseteq (s21' - s21)\hat{\ }(s22' - s22) \vee \\ s2' - s2 \sqsubseteq s22' - s22)\hat{\ }(s21' - s21)\ ) \end{pmatrix}$$

For the contributed static compensation sequence of $X \otimes Y$ (denoted as $s1' - s1$), it can either be the refinement of the contributed static compensation sequence for X followed by the contributed static compensation sequence for Y, or the refinement of the compensation sequence for Y followed by the sequence for X. This can be expressed via "$s1' - s1 \sqsubseteq (s11' - s11)^\frown(s12' - s12)$" or "$s1' - s1 \sqsubseteq s12' - s12)^\frown(s11' - s11)$". Here, $\sqsubseteq$ stands for the refinement for the compensation sequences, which is defined as: $((C, n) : s)^\frown t \sqsubseteq ((D, n) : u)^\frown v =_{df} (\llbracket C \rrbracket \Rightarrow \llbracket D \rrbracket) \wedge (s \sqsubseteq u) \wedge (t \sqsubseteq v) \wedge Cond(s, u) \wedge Cond(t, v)$, where $Cond(x, y) =_{df} x = \langle \rangle \Leftrightarrow y = \langle \rangle$. We also add $\langle \rangle \sqsubseteq \langle \rangle$ for the completion of the definition. Similar analysis also applies to the active compensation sequence.

Finally, we give the definition for parallel composition, which is based on the divergent, waiting, fault and terminating behaviours of two parallel components.

- It behaves chaotically if either component is divergent.

$$
\begin{aligned}
div(\llbracket P \parallel Q \rrbracket) =_{df}\ & div(\llbracket P \rrbracket) \otimes div(\llbracket Q \rrbracket) \ \vee\ div(\llbracket P \rrbracket) \otimes wait(\llbracket Q \rrbracket) \ \vee \\
& div(\llbracket P \rrbracket) \otimes fau(\llbracket Q \rrbracket) \ \vee\ div(\llbracket P \rrbracket) \otimes (ter(\llbracket Q \rrbracket); \Theta) \ \vee \\
& wait(\llbracket P \rrbracket) \otimes div(\llbracket Q \rrbracket) \ \vee\ fau(\llbracket P \rrbracket) \otimes div(\llbracket Q \rrbracket) \ \vee \\
& (ter(\llbracket P \rrbracket); \Theta) \otimes div(\llbracket Q \rrbracket)
\end{aligned}
$$

where, $\Theta =_{df} \exists n \bullet (s1' = s1) \wedge (s2' = s2) \wedge (tr' = tr) \wedge \delta(time) = n$. Here Θ is used to synchronize the behaviour of a process with its parallel partner.

- It stays in a waiting state if either component does so.

$$
\begin{aligned}
wait(\llbracket P \parallel Q \rrbracket) =_{df}\ & wait(\llbracket P \rrbracket) \otimes wait(\llbracket Q \rrbracket) \ \vee\ wait(\llbracket P \rrbracket) \otimes (ter(\llbracket Q \rrbracket); \Theta) \ \vee \\
& (ter(\llbracket P \rrbracket); \Theta) \otimes wait(\llbracket Q \rrbracket)
\end{aligned}
$$

- It is in the fault state if either component is at the fault state.

$$
\begin{aligned}
fau(\llbracket P \parallel Q \rrbracket) =_{df}\ & fau(\llbracket P \rrbracket) \otimes fau(\llbracket Q \rrbracket) \ \vee\ fau(\llbracket P \rrbracket) \otimes (ter(\llbracket Q \rrbracket); \Theta) \ \vee \\
& (ter(\llbracket P \rrbracket); \Theta) \otimes fau(\llbracket Q \rrbracket) \ \vee\ wait(\llbracket P \rrbracket) \otimes fau(\llbracket Q \rrbracket) \\
& fau(\llbracket P \rrbracket) \otimes wait(\llbracket Q \rrbracket)
\end{aligned}
$$

- It terminates when both components complete their execution.

$$
ter(\llbracket P \parallel Q \rrbracket) =_{df} ter(\llbracket P \rrbracket) \otimes (ter(\llbracket Q \rrbracket); \Theta) \ \vee\ (ter(\llbracket P \rrbracket); \Theta) \otimes ter(\llbracket Q \rrbracket)
$$

4   Conclusion

In this paper, we have formalized the denotational semantics for *BPEL0*, which is a kernel subset for BPEL. In order to formalize the fault handling mechanism, we have introduced fault behaviour in our denotational semantic framework. Meanwhile, aimed to deal with the scope-based compensation, two nested stack structured variables have been applied.

The formalized denotational semantics can help us to do refinement calculus and equivalence checking for processes. Based on the achieved semantics, a set of algebraic laws has been explored, also including the BPEL featured algebraic laws.

For the future, we are continuing to explore web service models with other different fundamental features [1]. Based on this, the exploration of their semantics is an interesting and immediate start.

References

1. Alonso, G., Kuno, H., Casati, F., Machiraju, V.: Web Services: Concepts, Architectures and Applications. Springer, Heidelberg (2003)
2. Butler, M.J., Ferreira, C.: An operational semantics for StAC, a language for modelling long-running business transactions. In: De Nicola, R., Ferrari, G.L., Meredith, G. (eds.) COORDINATION 2004. LNCS, vol. 2949, Springer, Heidelberg (2004)
3. Curbera, F., Goland, Y., Klein, J., Leymann, F., Roller, D., Satish Thatte, M., Weerawarana, S.: Business Process Execution Language for Web Service (2003), http://www.siebel.com/bpel
4. Pu, G., Zhu, H., Qiu, Z., Wang, S., Zhao, X., He, J.: Theoretical foundations of scope-based compensation flow language for web service. In: Gorrieri, R., Wehrheim, H. (eds.) FMOODS 2006. LNCS, vol. 4037, Springer, Heidelberg (2006)
5. Hoare, C.A.R., Jifeng, H.: Unifying Theories of Programming. Prentice Hall International Series in Computer Science (1998)
6. Zhu, H., Pu, G., He, J.: A denotational approach to scope-based compensable flow language for web service. Technical report, Software Engineering Institute, East China Normal University (2006)
7. Leymann, F.: Web Services Flow Language (WSFL 1.0). IBM (2001), http://www-3.ibm.com/software/solutions/webservices/pdf/WSDL.pdf
8. Thatte, S.: XLANG: Web Service for Business Process Design. Microsoft (2001), http://www.gotdotnet.com/team/xml_wsspecs/xlang-c/default.html

Certificateless Authenticated Two-Party Key Agreement Protocols

Tarjei K. Mandt and Chik How Tan

Norwegian Information Security Laboratory
Department of Computer Science and Media Technology
Gjøvik University College
P.O. Box 191, N-2802 Gjøvik, Norway
{tarjei.mandt,chik.tan}@hig.no

Abstract. In their seminal paper on certificateless public key cryptography, Al-Riyami and Paterson (AP) proposed a certificateless authenticated key agreement protocol. Key agreement protocols are one of the fundamental primitives of cryptography, and allow users to establish session keys securely in the presence of an active adversary. AP's protocol essentially requires each party to compute four bilinear pairings. Such operations can be computationally expensive, and should therefore be used moderately in key agreement. In this paper, we propose a new certificateless authenticated two-party key agreement protocol that only requires each party to compute two pairings. We analyze the security of the protocol and show that it achieves the desired security attributes. Furthermore, we show that our protocol can be used to establish keys between users of different key generation centers.

Keywords: Certificateless public key cryptography, authenticated key agreement, bilinear map.

1 Introduction

In the public key infrastructure (PKI), certificates are used to provide an assurance of the relationship between the public keys and the identities that hold the corresponding private keys. However, there are many problems associated with certificates such as revocation, storage, distribution, and cost of validation. In 1984, Shamir [7] proposed the notion of identity-based public key cryptography (ID-PKC) to simplify certificate management. The idea of ID-PKC is to let an entity's public key be directly derived from certain aspects of its identity, such as the IP address of the hostname or the e-mail address. Thus, ID-PKC also eliminates the need for certificates.

Unfortunately, ID-PKC is not without problems. Identity-based systems rely on a private key generator (PKG) that uses a system-wide master key in generating private keys. Thus, many identity-based schemes inevitably introduce *key escrow*: the PKG can recover the session key established by entities for which it has issued a private key. This property is either acceptable or unacceptable. For instance, in the health care profession it may be a legal requirement to provide

M. Okada and I. Satoh (Eds.): ASIAN 2006, LNCS 4435, pp. 37–44, 2007.
© Springer-Verlag Berlin Heidelberg 2007

an audit trail to every transaction. On the other hand, such invasion of privacy may cause ID-PKC to be unsuited in a variety of other applications, such as personal communications.

Certificateless public key cryptography (CL-PKC) [1] was proposed by Al-Riyami and Paterson to alleviate the problems associated with PKI and ID-PKC. It does not require the use of certificates and yet does not have the key escrow limitation of ID-PKC. For this reason, CL-PKC can be seen as a public key cryptography model intermediate between the two former paradigms.

In their seminal paper, Al-Riyami and Paterson (AP) proposed a certificateless authenticated two-party key agreement protocol. Key agreement protocols allow entities to establish session keys securely in the presence of an active adversary. AP's protocol essentially requires each party to compute four bilinear pairings. Such operations can be computationally expensive (for instance, on low-power devices) and should therefore be used moderately in key agreement. Moreover, AP's protocol also requires users to exchange public keys comprising two group elements. Ideally, public keys should only comprise one group element as in identity-based key agreement.

This paper proposes a new certificateless authenticated two-party key agreement protocol [5] that is more efficient than AP's protocol. Each entity involved in the protocol is only required to compute two pairings, and the public keys exchanged by the entities only comprise one group element. As public keys are not bound to a specific key generation center (KGC), the protocol can also be used to establish session keys between users of different KGCs. Furthermore, we show that the protocol achieves the security attributes that are desired in authenticated key agreement.

The rest of the paper is organized as follows. In Section 2 we give underlying definitions and define the security attributes of authenticated key agreement. In Section 3 we propose a new certificateless authenticated two-party key agreement protocol, and in Section 4 we show how the protocol can be used by entities of different KGCs. In Section 5 and 6 we analyze the security and the efficiency of the protocol respectively, and in Section 7 we provide a conclusion of the paper.

2   Preliminaries

2.1   Bilinear Pairings

Let $\mathbb{G}_1$ be an additive group with a large prime order q and let $\mathbb{G}_2$ be a multiplicative group of the same order. An *admissible pairing* e is then a function $e : \mathbb{G}_1 \times \mathbb{G}_1 \rightarrow \mathbb{G}_2$ that satisfies the following properties:

1. *Bilinearity*: For all $P, Q \in \mathbb{G}_1$ and $a, b \in \mathbb{Z}_q^*$, $e(aP, bQ) = e(P, Q)^{ab}$.
2. *Non-degeneracy*: There exists a $P \in \mathbb{G}_1$ such that $e(P, P) \neq 1$.
3. *Computability*: There is an efficient algorithm to compute $e(P, Q)$ for all $P, Q \in \mathbb{G}_1$.

The admissible pairing e can be derived from a Weil or Tate pairing on an elliptic curve over a finite field. For further details, see [3].

2.2   Diffie-Hellman Problems

The security of the proposed protocols is based on a set of well-studied problems that are assumed to be hard to compute efficiently. These problems are defined as follows:

Definition 1 (Discrete Logarithm Problem). *Given* $Q \in \mathbb{G}_1$ *where* P *is a generator of* $\mathbb{G}_1$, *find an element* $a \in \mathbb{Z}_q^*$ *such that* $aP = Q$.

Definition 2 (Computational Diffie-Hellman Problem). *Let* P *be a generator of* $\mathbb{G}_1$. *Given* $\langle P, aP, bP \rangle \in \mathbb{G}_1$ *where* $a, b \in \mathbb{Z}_q^*$, *compute* abP.

Definition 3 (Bilinear Diffie-Hellman Problem). *Let* e *be a bilinear pairing on* $(\mathbb{G}_1, \mathbb{G}_2)$ *and* P *be a generator of* $\mathbb{G}_1$. *Given* $\langle P, aP, bP, cP \rangle \in \mathbb{G}_1$ *where* $a, b, c \in \mathbb{Z}_q^*$, *compute* $e(P, P)^{abc} \in \mathbb{G}_2$.

We assume that the order q of the groups $\mathbb{G}_1$ and $\mathbb{G}_2$ is large enough to make solving the discrete logarithm problem computationally infeasible.

2.3   Security of Authenticated Key Agreement

A key agreement protocol is said to be *authenticated* (AK) if it ensures authenticity of the involved parties. Specifically, a party can only compute a shared key if it holds the claimed identity. Thus, by mutually proving possession of the shared key, each party may be assured that the peer is a legitimate entity. The proposed protocols of this paper will use cryptographic *message authentication codes* in providing such assurance.

Definition 4 (Message Authentication Code). *A message authentication code* MAC $= (\mathcal{K}_{\mathrm{mac}}, \mathcal{T}_{\mathrm{mac}}, \mathcal{V}_{\mathrm{mac}})$ *consists of three algorithms: key generation* $\mathcal{K}_{\mathrm{mac}}$, *message authentication* $\mathcal{T}_{\mathrm{mac}}$ *and verification* $\mathcal{V}_{\mathrm{mac}}$. *The key generation algorithm* $\mathcal{K}_{\mathrm{mac}}$ *generates a key* $k \leftarrow \mathcal{K}_{\mathrm{mac}}$. *The message authentication algorithm* $\mathcal{T}_{\mathrm{mac}}$ *returns an authentication tag* $\tau = \mathcal{T}_{\mathrm{mac}}(k, m)$ *for given a key* k *and a message* m. *The verification algorithm* $\mathcal{V}_{\mathrm{mac}}$ *returns 1 for "accept" and 0 for "reject", for given a key* k, *the message* m *and the authentication tag* τ.

Furthermore, it is desired that AK protocols possess a number of *security attributes* [2, 4]:

- **Known session key security**. Each run of the key agreement protocol should result in a unique secret session key. An adversary who learns a session key should not be able to recover data from past or future sessions.
- **Forward secrecy**. If long-term private keys of one or more entities are compromised, the secrecy of previous session keys established by these entities should not be affected. In the presence of a key generation center (KGC) with a system-wide master key, *KGC forward secrecy* implies that compromise of this key should not reveal previously established session keys.

- **Key-compromise impersonation.** If A's long-term private key is compromised, the adversary can impersonate A, but the adversary should not be able to impersonate other entities to A.
- **Unknown key-share.** Entity A should not be coerced into sharing a key with entity C when, in fact, A thinks she is sharing a key with entity B.
- **Key control.** Neither party involved in a protocol run should be able to control the outcome of the session key more than the other.
- **Known session-specific temporary information security.** Many protocols use some randomized private input to produce a unique session key in each run of a protocol. Exposure of such private temporary information should not compromise the secrecy of the generated session key.

3   Proposed Certificateless Authenticated Key Agreement

In this section, we will present a new certificateless authenticated two-party key agreement protocol based on pairings. As noted earlier, certificateless key agreement does not rely on certificates, nor does it employ a key generation center (KGC) that knows every user's private key.

Setup: Let H_1 and H_2 be two independent key derivation functions such that $H_1 : \mathbb{G}_2 \times \mathbb{G}_1 \times \mathbb{G}_1 \rightarrow \{0,1\}^k$ and $H_2 : \mathbb{G}_2 \times \mathbb{G}_1 \times \mathbb{G}_1 \rightarrow \{0,1\}^l$ for some integers $k, l > 0$. Let also H be a Map-To-Point [3] function such that $H : \{0,1\}^* \rightarrow \mathbb{G}_1$. The KGC randomly selects its secret master key $s \in \mathbb{Z}_q^*$ and computes the public key $P_0 = sP$ where $P \in \mathbb{G}_1$ is a public generator. The KGC then publishes the system parameters $\langle \mathbb{G}_1, \mathbb{G}_2, e, q, P, P_0, H, H_1, H_2 \rangle$.

Private Key Extraction: For any given entity A with identity $\text{ID}_A \in \{0,1\}^*$, the long-term private/public key pair is generated as follows:

1. A randomly selects a secret value $x_A \in \mathbb{Z}_q^*$.
2. The KGC generates A's *partial* private key $D_A = sQ_A$ where A's identifier $Q_A = H(\text{ID}_A) \in \mathbb{G}_1$. A may check the validity of D_A by verifying that $e(Q_A, P_0) = e(D_A, P)$.
3. A's (full) private key is given by $S_A = \langle D_A, x_A \rangle$. A's public key is computed as $P_A = x_A P$.

For entity B, the private key extraction is similar to A.

Key Agreement: In order to jointly establish a session key, entities A and B randomly select the short-term session-specific private keys $a, b \in \mathbb{Z}_q^*$ and compute the corresponding short-term public keys $T_A = aP$ and $T_B = bP$ respectively. They then exchange the following messages:

$$(1)\ A \rightarrow B : T_A, P_A$$

$$(2)\ B \rightarrow A : T_B, P_B, \mathcal{T}_{\text{mac}}(k', T_B, P_B)$$

$$(3)\ A \rightarrow B : \mathcal{T}_{\text{mac}}(k', T_A, P_A)$$

Both entities validate each other's public key by testing the group membership $P_A, P_B \in \mathbb{G}_1^*$. The MAC algorithm $\mathcal{T}_{\text{mac}}$ is used to generate an authentication tag τ of the shared key k' (defined below) and the transmitted message. If a party fails to verify a received authentication tag, then the protocol run is terminated. A and B compute the session key as follows:

$$K_A = e(Q_B, P_0 + P_B)^a \cdot e(D_A + x_A Q_A, T_B)$$
$$K_B = e(D_B + x_B Q_B, T_A) \cdot e(Q_A, P_0 + P_A)^b$$

The scheme is consistent because:

$$K = K_A = K_B = e(Q_B, P)^{a(s+x_B)} \cdot e(Q_A, P)^{b(s+x_A)}$$

In order to ensure that an attacker cannot gain any information from the session key, A and B use a key derivation function H on K, abP, and $x_A x_B P$. Thus, the final session key is given by $k = H_1(K\|abP\|x_A x_B P)$. The MAC key $k' = H_2(K\|abP\|x_A x_B P)$ is different from k in order to provide key indistinguishability [2].

Note that both parties are authenticated through the verification of an authentication tag τ (provided by the peer) when they successfully establish a shared key. Thus, both parties are assured that the peer holds the claimed identity. If no such assurance had been provided, an adversary could possibly engage in a key agreement with B, while impersonating A. This would lead B to falsely believe a session key is established with A.

Furthermore, note that the structure of the long-term private/public key pair differs from Al-Riyami and Paterson's protocol [1]. Specifically, the public key P_A only comprises one element of $\mathbb{G}_1$ and no longer binds an entity to a specific KGC, thus allowing protocol participants under different trusted authorities to establish keys. Also see that S_A separates D_A from x_A such that these values may be used independently (in [1], $S_A = x_A D_A$) in session key construction.

4   Certificateless Key Agreement Using Separate KGCs

It may in many cases be desired by users of different KGCs to establish shared keys. For example, in order for encrypted VoIP to be able to operate globally, key agreement and compatibility between networks become a necessary requirement. The following protocol enables session key establishment between users of different KGCs in the certificateless setting.

Setup: Let H, H_1, and H_2 be defined as in the previous protocol. Two different key generation centers, KGC$_1$ and KGC$_2$, then respectively generate a key pair $(P_1 = s_1 P \in \mathbb{G}_1, s_1 \in \mathbb{Z}_q^*)$ and $(P_2 = s_2 P \in \mathbb{G}_1, s_2 \in \mathbb{Z}_q^*)$ where P and $\mathbb{G}_1$ are globally agreed. Both KGCs publish their respective public parameters.

Private Key Extraction: This step is similar to the previous protocol, except that entities A and B have their partial private keys generated by different KGCs. Thus, A, under KGC$_1$, has the private key $S_A = \langle D_A = s_1 Q_A, x_A \rangle$, while B, under KGC$_2$, has the private key $S_B = \langle D_B = s_2 Q_B, x_B \rangle$.

Key Agreement: A and B generate short-term keys and exchange messages as in the previous protocol. In computing the session key, however, each entity uses the KGC public key of the peer. Thus, A uses $P_2 = s_2 P$ in computing the shared key, while B uses $P_1 = s_1 P$. A and B then compute respectively:

$$K_A = e(Q_B, P_2 + P_B)^a \cdot e(D_A + x_A Q_A, T_B)$$
$$K_B = e(D_B + x_B Q_B, T_A) \cdot e(Q_A, P_1 + P_A)^b$$

The scheme is consistent because:

$$K = K_A = K_B = e(Q_B, P)^{a(s_2 + x_B)} \cdot e(Q_A, P)^{b(s_1 + x_A)}$$

The final session key is given by $k = H_1(K \| abP \| x_A x_B P)$.

5   Security Attributes

In this section, we will show that the proposed protocol achieves the security attributes identified in Section 2.3. Note that we only consider the basic protocol of Section 3, as it is very similar to the multi-KGC protocol. Furthermore, we trust the KGC not to replace any long-term public keys as, in doing so, a man-in-the-middle attack is made possible (see [1, 5] for discussion).

- **Known session key security**. As short-term keys are used in generating session keys, a compromised session key does not compromise past or future sessions. All protocol runs, even when its participants remain the same, produce a different session key.
- **Forward secrecy**. We let this property constitute two separate parts; both to capture the forward secrecy against an adversary who holds both A and B's long-term private keys (*user forward secrecy*) and against an adversary who has the KGC master key (*KGC forward secrecy*).
  - *User forward secrecy.* Compromising the long-term private keys of entities A and B will not reveal previously established session keys. In order to compute abP of $H_1(K \| abP \| x_A x_B P)$, an adversary must know at least one short-term private key of a given session.
  - *KGC forward secrecy.* Compromise of the KGC master key s does not enable an adversary to reveal previously established session keys. Although the adversary may generate partial private keys, both a short-term private key and the long-term (full) private key of a party involved in a session must be obtained in order to compute the established key.
- **Key-compromise impersonation**. The proposed protocol is resistant to key-compromise impersonation. Assume that the adversary E knows A's private key $S_A = \langle D_A, x_A \rangle$. If E is to impersonate B in a protocol run with A, then E must be able to correctly compute $K = K_A = K_B$. E cannot compute $K_A = e(Q_B, P_B + P_0)^a \cdot e(D_A + x_A Q_A, T_B)$ where $P_0 = sP$ because she does not know the short-term key a. If E was to compute K_B, she would need to know B's long-term private key S_B. Although E could possibly replace B's public key P_B with a value of her choice, she would still need to know $D_B = sQ_B$ in order to successfully impersonate B to A.

- **Unknown key-share**. Suppose an adversary E attempts to make A believe a key is shared with B, while B instead believes the key is shared with E. For E to launch this attack successfully, she should force A and B to share the same secret $K = K_A = K_B$. However, A and B can never share the same key if they don't believe they are mutually communicating. This stems from the fact that both parties use the identifier of the intended peer (i.e. A uses Q_B, while B uses Q_E) in computing the session key. Thus, A cannot verify the authentication tag τ generated by B (passed on by E) and the attack fails.
- **Key control**. Neither party can control the outcome of the session key. However, if A sends her short-term key first, B may be able to predict some bits of the final key by trying different short-term keys before sending the key back to A. Precisely, in computing the shared session key $f(a, b)$ where a is known, B may compute 2^s variants of b and thus select approximately s bits of the joint key. This deficiency exists in all interactive key agreement protocols as pointed out by [6].
- **Known session-specific temporary information security**. Compromising the short-term private keys of a session does not reveal the established key. Specifically, obtaining the keys a and b in any session between entities A and B, allows the adversary to compute $K = (Q_B, P_B + P_0)^a \cdot (Q_A, P_A + P_0)^b$ and abP. However, in order to compute $x_A x_B P$, the adversary must also know at least one long-term private key (or solve the CDH problem). Note that an adversary who is able to obtain short-term private keys is considered very powerful and can break many existing protocols (see [4] for examples).

6   Efficiency

The efficiency of key agreement protocols is essentially measured by the computational and communication overhead. Communication overhead refers to the number of bits transmitted by each entity in a protocol run, while computational overhead refers to the cost of all arithmetic computations each entity must perform in order to carry out the key agreement. Table 1 compares the efficiency of the proposed protocol to the previously proposed protocol by Al-Riyami and Paterson. In evaluating the computational overhead, only heavy operations such as pairings, point multiplications, and pairing exponentiations are considered. Generally, point multiplications and pairing exponentiations are much faster to compute than pairings.

In AP's protocol, each entity is required to exchange three group elements, of which one element represents the short-term public key and the other elements represent the long-term public key. Each entity also must compute four pairings, perform two point multiplications, and make one pairing exponentiation. Note that an entity must still compute four pairings, even when values are *precomputed* (aspects of the session key is computed before a protocol run).

In the proposed protocol, each entity is only required to compute two pairings, perform three point multiplications, and make one pairing exponentiation.

Table 1. Efficiency of certificateless authenticated key agreement protocols

	Al-Riyami-Paterson[1]	Proposed protocol
Message	3 elements of $\mathbb{G}_1$	2 elements of $\mathbb{G}_1$
No precomputation	$4p + 2m + 1e$	$2p + 3m + 1e$
Precomputation	$4p + 1m$	$2p + 2m$

Notation: (p)airing, point (m)ultiplication, pairing (e)xponentiation

Moreover, the long-term public keys only comprise one group element, and thus, the protocol can be considered more efficient than AP's in terms of computation and message bandwidth. Although the proposed protocol introduces one additional pass and requires entities to compute MACs, AP's protocol should use a similar method in order to prevent an adversary from impersonating parties.

Once long-term public keys have been exchanged in both protocols, only a single pairing is required by the participating parties. Thus, certificateless protocols can be just as efficient as identity-based schemes.

7   Conclusion

This paper has proposed a certificateless authenticated two-party key agreement protocol that is more efficient than the previously proposed protocol by Al-Riyami and Paterson. The protocol is more efficient both in terms of computation and message bandwidth. The protocol also achieves the security attributes that are desired in authenticated key agreement. Furthermore, the proposed protocol can be used to establish keys between users of different key generation centers.

References

[1] Al-Riyami, S.S., Paterson, K.: Certificateless Public Key Cryptography. In: Laih, C.-S. (ed.) ASIACRYPT 2003. LNCS, vol. 2894, pp. 452–473. Springer, Heidelberg (2003)

[2] Blake-Wilson, S., Menezes, A.: Authenticated Diffie-Hellman Key Agreement Protocols. In: Tavares, S., Meijer, H. (eds.) SAC 1998. LNCS, vol. 1556, pp. 339–361. Springer, Heidelberg (1998)

[3] Boneh, D., Franklin, M.: Identity-Based Encryption from the Weil Pairing. In: Kilian, J. (ed.) CRYPTO 2001. LNCS, vol. 2139, pp. 213–229. Springer, Heidelberg (2001)

[4] Cheng, Z., Nistazakis, M., Comley, R., Vasiu, L.: On The Indistinguishability-Based Security Model of Key Agreement Protocols - Simple Cases. Technical Track Proceedings, Journal of China Information Security. ICISA Press (2004)

[5] Mandt, T.K.: Certificateless Authenticated Two-Party Key Agreement Protocols. Master's Thesis. Gjøvik University College (2006)

[6] Mitchell, C.J., Ward, M., Wilson, P.: Key Control in Key Agreement Protocols. Electronics Letters 34, 980–981 (1998)

[7] Shamir, A.: Identity-Based Cryptosystems and Signature Schemes. In: Blakely, G.R., Chaum, D. (eds.) CRYPTO 1984. LNCS, vol. 196, pp. 47–53. Springer, Heidelberg (1985)

FORM : A Federated Rights Expression Model for Open DRM Frameworks

Thierry Sans, Frédéric Cuppens, and Nora Cuppens-Boulahia

GET/ENST Bretagne,
2 rue de la Châtaigneraie, 35576 Cesson-Sévigné Cedex, France
{thierry.sans, frederic.cuppens, nora.cuppens}@enst-bretagne.fr

Abstract. Digital Rights Management frameworks (DRM) aim at protecting and controlling information contents widely distributed on client devices. Using a license, the content provider can decide which rights can be rendered and who are the authorized end-users (as identity holders) allowed to exercise those rights. Most of the time, it is hard to add new feature to the client application, it is even impossible when the new feature is not considered trustworthy by the corporation distributing the rendering application. In a same way, the rendering application identifies the end-user with a dedicated identity and it is impossible to take into account an identity provided by an external corporation. In this paper, we aim at providing a federated approach called FORM where a content provider can decide to trust external rendering rights and external identities. We even go further introducing identity providers, actions providers as we consider content providers. Thus, all kind of providers can define license specifying what can be done with the object they provide. FORM defines a new license model and a new license interpretation mechanism taking into account all licenses issued by a federation of object providers.

1 Introduction

In a corporate information system, the information remain on the trusted server side and only an extract or a computation of the information is given to the end-user. Nowadays with the development of Internet and better bandwidths, multimedia contents are more and more widely spread over the Internet. Obviously, with multimedia application it is impossible to keep the information on the server side and only send the result of the rendering to the client. So, the information and the corresponding rendering application must be sent to the client side. Then, the problem is how to keep the information under control whereas the information content itself and the rendering application do not remain on a safe domain of the information system. Digital Rights Management (DRM) frameworks [12,1] aim at providing security mechanisms in order to protect and keep sensitive information under control even if it is out of the scope of a corporate information system. Mainly, a DRM framework provides three essential components: 1) A content packager in charge of protecting digital documents in order to ensure information confidentiality [1]. 2) A license designer in charge

M. Okada and I. Satoh (Eds.): ASIAN 2006, LNCS 4435, pp. 45–59, 2007.
© Springer-Verlag Berlin Heidelberg 2007

of defining the license according to the Right Expression Language (REL) used by the given DRM framework [1,10]; the license specifies what could be done with the content (rights) and who are the authorized end-users (identity) having those rights. 3) A rendering application [1] in charge of interpreting licenses to decide if a right can be exercised or not, and possibly, render this right to the end-users. The decision mechanism is given by the semantics of the underlying license interpretation model defined by the Rights Expression Language. The rendering application is executed on the client side and is able to deal with the content protection. So, the rendering application must be trustworthy and tamper resistant [6,1].

If we focus on the rendering application we can see that there are three parts as well: 1) The user interface layer in charge of getting the request from the end-user and deliver the result of the content rendering. 2) The DRM controller in charge of evaluating the request according to the different licenses. 3) A rendering layer in charge of executing the rights requested by the end-user. The set of rights supported by the DRM application is defined by the Rights Data Dictionary (RDD). Existing DRM applications usually consider a certain type of content, and thus, consider a certain RDD as well. So, for each right in the RDD corresponds a rendering action in the rendering application. Usually, these actions are enclosed in the rendering application and are designed by the corporation delivering the rendering application. We clearly see here that a content provider, who wants to use a given DRM framework to protect his or her contents, must trust the corporation delivering the protection mechanism and the rendering actions. There is no way for him or her to redefine or extend the set of rendering actions. In this paper, we aim at providing a federated approach (FORM) to take into account external rendering actions. We specify a new license model where a content provider can decide which are the trusted rendering actions able to use his or her content. We even go further in FORM, we consider that the rendering action provider wants to restrict how end-users and content providers use their rendering actions. Using license, action providers can specify which end-users and which contents can be used with their rendering actions.

We can have the same approach with identities as well. In existing DRM applications, the way to define the user identity is specific to each DRM framework. Nowadays, an end-user has many identities over the Internet. The identity of a user is not unique but rather a collection of identities issued by different corporations. With FORM, the content provider can specify which user identity must be considered instead of using a new one for the DRM purpose. Using a license, the content provider can specify who are the authorized end-users according to one of their identities and who are the trusted corporation providing those identities. As well, we go further with FORM considering that the identity provider may want to restrict what action providers and content providers can do with their identities. Using license, identities providers can specify which rendering actions and which content can deal with their identities.

We claim that existing DRM frameworks are content centric. Content centric means that only content providers are involved. The way to define identities and rendering actions are specific to each DRM framework. In this paper we aim at providing a new model to move toward a federated approach to manage contents, identities and actions in a same way. With FORM, content providers, identity providers and actions providers can independently specify licenses restricting the usage of the object provided. In section 2, we deeper explain the content centric approach and we show how to move towards a federated approach. In sections 2.2 and 2.3, we investigate the advantages of a federated approach. With FORM, we provide a new decision mechanism to take all licenses into account when an end-user wants to use a given content with a given rendering action and using one of his or her identity. We formalize this decision mechanism in section 3.

2 From a Content Centric Approach to a Federated Approach

In this section, we first investigate the content centric approach to explain what we call the ownership principle in DRM. Then, we show how to move towards a federated approach studying separately the rendering actions and the identities. Finally, we introduce in details the Federated Rights Expression Model (FORM) and show that this approach preserves the ownership principle.

2.1 The Content Centric Approach

As we say in the introduction, there is mainly three components in a DRM framework : The content packager, the license designer and the rendering application. When a content provider wants to distribute a digital document through a DRM framework, he or she will first wrap the digital document into a secure content using the content packager. Only the given trustworthy rendering application is able to deal with this content protection. Secondly, he or she will design a license defining who can use the content (identity) and what are the rendering actions which can be applied (right). Then, the content and the license are distributed to the end-users. Through the rendering application, the end-user can then use the content. But, how to ensure that anyone cannot write a license about a content provided by someone else? This is what we call the *ownership principle*: a mechanism to ensure that only a license delivered by the same content owner can be used in the authorization mechanism[1]. Existing DRM standards [7,9] have the same approach to enforce the ownership principle. The content and the license are tight using hashing and cryptographic mechanisms. For example in Windows Media DRM framework (Microsoft Media Player) [3,2], the content is ciphered using a symmetric key. This key is distributed to the user through the license. Obviously, this key cannot be distributed in clear in the license. The license, or the part of the license with the key, is ciphered using a session key between the license server and the rendering application. Thus, only the license issued by the content provider can be used to deciphered the content. In OMA-DRM, this

---

[1] Notice that we do not consider super-distribution mechanism here.

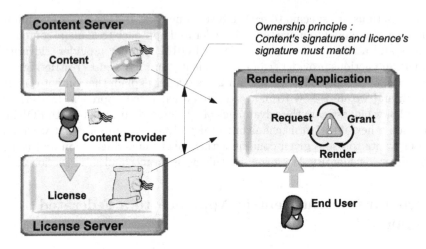

Fig. 1. The ownership principle in DRM

mechanism is strengthen using digital signatures to both identify the content provider and the license provider. If those two identities match, the corresponding license is then said to be valid and can be taken into account by the DRM controller as showed in the figure 1.

We claim that existing DRM frameworks enforce the content centric approach, and so, they verify the ownership principle. Obviously, we cannot cut with this principle. In the federated approach we keep the principle true but we extend it to identities and actions as well.

2.2 Considering External Rendering Actions

As Bill Rosenblatt says in [12], there is two kinds of rendering applications regarding existing DRM applications: Standalone application and Plugin-based application. In Standalone application, rendering actions are enclosed in the rendering application program. That kind of application appears more secure since external malicious codes cannot be added. But a standalone application is not flexible. First, because providing a new rendering action means upgrading and redistributing the application itself. Secondly, because the most rendering actions there are, the bigger the application is and most of the time, end-users only use few of them. Nevertheless, this kind of application can be adequate considering a specific content type with limited rendering actions like in Microsoft Media Player [3] dedicated to audio and video contents. For more flexibility, we can consider to distribute rendering actions as plugins. With a plugin based application, no update is needed since the root application does not change and only actions needed by the end-users can be installed. In order to counter rogue plugin, only "official" plugins are allowed to be installed, i.e. plugin certified by the same corporation distributing the rendering application. For instance, only plugins from Adobe can be added in the Adobe Acrobat Reader [12] enabling

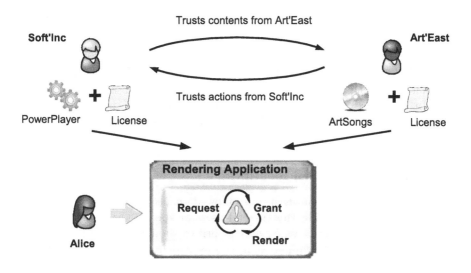

Fig. 2. Trust relationships between an action provider and a content provider

end-users to read specific protected content. Obviously, allowing anyone to write such plugins would lead to a security breach since everyone can access directly to the digital information. So, the corporation providing the DRM application is the only one who can judge if a plugin is trusted or not. We want to go further here, why do not let the content provider decide if a rendering action provided by someone else can be used or not? Why do not let the content provider decide if the corporation providing a plugin can be trusted or not? There are many consequences of such an approach. First, not only content providers decide what rights the end-user can get with the content but also which trusted code must be used to exercise these rights. Then, the content provider identifies in the license what piece of code must be used to render the content, or at least specify which corporation can be trusted. The following assertions are examples of a content provider policy:

– SoftInc is an action provider distributing a player plugin. The player plugin enables three new rendering actions: LitePlayer, PowerPlayer and Extract. Art'East is a content provider distributing audio contents over the Internet. Art'East allows any end-users to "play" an Art'East's content. The "play" right can be implemented by trusted rendering actions such as LitePlayer or PowerPlayer provided by SoftInc.

Why do not consider a plugin as a content also? Action providers could be able to decide which end-users can use the plugin, and what kind of content can be rendered with it. Action providers must be able to define licenses specifying who are the authorized end-users and the authorized contents. The following assertions are examples of a content provider policy:

– For SoftInc, end-users can only use LitePlayer freely. There is a partnership with Art'East, and anyone can use the PowerPlayer with an Art'East
  content.

Even if Art'East allows anyone to use the PowerPlayer, we see that SoftInc
might not agree with that and could have set that no one can use the PowerPlayer
freely. In the figure 2, we show how to enable a partnership between Art'East
and SoftInc with FORM. Soft'Inc allows anyone to use the PowerPlayer right
since the content is provided by Art'East.

2.3 Considering External Identities

In order to define which end-users are allowed to use a content, the content
provider must be able to identify the end-users or specify properties that end-
user's identities must have. Which user identities should the DRM framework
consider? In existing DRM application, the user identity is directly related to
the system under which the rendering application is executed. The identity is a
combination of hardware IDs (like mac address, chipset ID, . . .), cryptographic
keys and sometimes user information. That explains why, most of the time,
it is impossible to read a protected content on another system than the one
under which you have previously got the license. It is not really the user identity
which is used here but rather the system identity. Nevertheless, if we take a
look at Rights Expression Languages like MPEG-REL [7], we notice that the
standard gives the possibility to define user identity with X509 certificates but
the standard does not specify how to manage these certificates. Who issues these
certificates? Which identity provider to trust? Nowadays, Internet users have
many IDs over the Internet. Governmental organizations issue citizenship IDs
to grant access to on-line public services. Banks issue Credit Cards that can be
considered as another identity used over the Internet. Companies issue identities
to customers to give access to their services. The identity of a user is not unique
but rather a collection of identities issued by different corporations that we called
identity providers. So, rather than defining a new identity for the DRM purpose,
why do not we use IDs issued by external identity providers? Thus, a content
provider can decide 1) which end-users are allowed to use the content according
to one of their identities 2) which identity providers are trusted to issue these
identities. The following assertions are examples of a content provider policy:

– Pop'mag and Rock'mag are two on-line music magazines. Each of them re-
  spectively issues Pop'Member IDs and Rock'Member IDs to their readers.
  Art'East agrees that Pop'mag readers and Rock'Mag readers can play Art-
  Songs freely. So, Art'East allows any "Mag readers" to play the ArtSong
  content. A "Mag reader" is someone holding a trusted identity either from
  Pop'Mag or from Rock'Mag.

Our federated model allows a content provider to specify what are the authorized end-users according to one of their identities and according to who delivers
the identity (Identity Provider). Moreover, we aim at managing identities like we

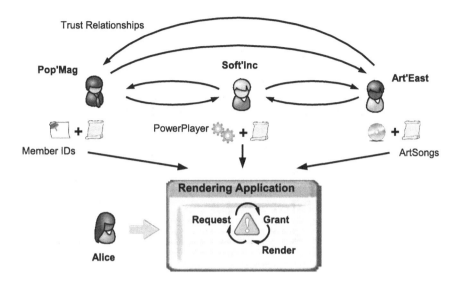

Fig. 3. Trust relationships between an identity provider, an action provider and a content provider

manage content. Identity provider may not allow anyone to use their identities in order to do anything. Identity provider may want to restrict which rendering actions and which contents are allowed to be used with identity information they provide. The following assertions are examples of an identity provider policy:

– In Rock'Mag Ids, there are private information that must not be disclosed. Rock'mag allows rendering actions like "read" and "print" only with the "RockMagazine" content. The "read" and "print" rights are provided by a trusted action provider. "RockMag" is also a content provider distributing the "Rock'Magazine" content.
– In Pop'Mag Ids, there are private information also. But, Pop'Mag knows that rendering actions provided by Soft'Inc do not reveal private information during the content rendering. Then anyone can use Pop'Mag Ids with any content since a "privacy compliant action" is used. A "privacy compliant action" is an action distributed by trusted action providers like Soft'Inc.

In this example, we see that, according to Art'East, an end-user like Alice needs an identity from Rock'Mag or Pop'Mag in order to read the ArtSong. But, even if Alice is a Rock'Mag reader, she will fail to read an Art'East content because Rock'Mag does not allow such a usage of its identities. Nevertheless, if Alice is also a Pop'Mag reader, she will be allowed to play the Art'East content using her Pop'Mag Id. Pop'Mag will allow her because she uses the LitePlayer from Soft'Inc which is privacy compliant. The figure 3 shows the trusted relationship existing between the identity provider "Pop'Mag", the action provider "Soft'Inc" and the content provider "Art'East".

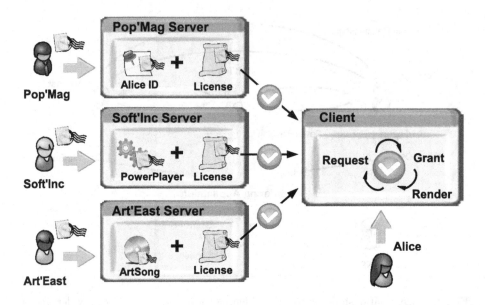

Fig. 4. Authorization process with FORM

2.4 FORM: The Federated Approach

The federated approach aims at managing external identities and external rendering actions in a same way than contents in the content centric approach. There are not only content providers but also action providers and identity providers. More generally, there are object providers distributing objects typed as either identity, action or content. All object providers define licenses for the object they provide independently from each other. With FORM, a content provider must define a license specifying who can use the content (identity + identity provider) and which are the trusted rendering actions (action + action provider). In a same way, an action provider must define a license specifying who can use the rendering action (identity + identity provider) and what kind of content can be rendered (content + content provider). In a same way, an identity provider must define a license specifying which rendering actions can be used (action + action provider) and what kind of content can be involved (content + content provider).

In 2.1, we introduced the ownership principle specifying that only a license issued by the content provider can be used by the DRM controller in order to decide whether someone can use a content or not. Obviously, we cannot cut with this ownership principle in FORM since we still want that only the object provider can decide what can be done with the object provided. So, with FORM, we extend the ownership principle to identities and rendering actions as well. Briefly, only a license issued by the object provider can be used by the DRM controller to decide whether or not the object can be used. When an end-user like Alice wants to use an object, she will perform a request to her rendering application. The request is a triple composed by one of her identities, a content and the rendering application she wants to use. In order to take the decision, the DRM controller must take into account all licenses from all object providers involved in the request. The figure 4 shows that all providers must agree in order to authorize the request to be rendered. Consequently, we must provide a new decision mechanism to support the FORM license model. In the next section, we formalize the FORM license model and we provide a new decision mechanism.

3   The Underlying Model

This section formalizes our approach using first order logic. We first introduce the content centric approach. We provide a license model and an interpretation mechanism taking into account the ownership principle. Then, we extend the model to enable the federated approach. We extend the license model introducing identity and action providers. We extend the interpretation mechanism to take into account the ownership principle applied to identity and actions as well.

3.1   The Content Centric Approach

We do not attempt to cover all the expressiveness of a complete Rights Expression Language but at least model main concepts needed to formalize the content centric approach.

A license is a set of grants where a grant is a triple composed of an identity, a right and a digital document. Most of existing RELs add a contextual condition to the grant. We do not need to take into account this condition parameter in order to formalize FORM. But obviously in practice, we must consider a REL including contextual conditions [4]. As required to enable the ownership principle, both content and license must contain the provider identity. So a provider parameter is associated both with the license and the content. The content $[ArtSong]_{Art'East}$ means that Art'East is the owner of the digital document ArtSong. The license $[< Alice, Play, ArtSong >]_{Art'East}$ means that Art'East allows Alice to play ArtSong. The language is then defined as follows:

$Identity, Right, Document$ are nominal types

$$
\begin{aligned}
Content &::= [Document]_{Provider} \\
License &::= [setOf(Grant)]_{Provider} \\
Grant   &::= < Identity, Right, Content > \\
Provider &::= Identity
\end{aligned}
$$

Once defined the basic license language, we need to formalize the license interpretation mechanism enforced by the DRM controller. The DRM controller is in charge of deciding if someone can use a right on a given content according to the corresponding license. The license interpretation mechanism must take into account the ownership principle introduced previously, i.e. only a license issued by the content owner can decide whether or not an access can be granted. We define the *isPermitted* predicate to decide whether or not a right can be used. This predicate checks if there is a corresponding grant in any licenses. The *isPermitted* predicate is true for a given provider if there is a license, issued by the content provider, with a grant matching the given identity, the given right and the given document. The isPermitted predicate can be formalized as follows:

$$isPermitted ::= [\ Provider \times Identity \times Right \times Content \rightarrow Boolean\ ]$$

$$\forall\ i : Identity,\ r : Right,\ [d : Document]_{p:Provider} : Content$$
$$\exists\ [s : SetOf(Grant)]_{p:Provider} : License,\ g : Grant \in s\ |$$
$$g = <i, r, d> \rightarrow isPermitted(p, i, r, [d]_p)$$

Then, we define a set of authorization predicates. These predicates are used to decide if a requested right (*request* predicate) can be allowed (*allow* predicate) or not (*deny* predicate). The authorization predicates (*allow* and *deny*) are defined as follows:

$$request ::= [Identity \times Right \times Content \rightarrow Boolean\ ]$$
$$allow\ \ ::= [Identity \times Right \times Content \rightarrow Boolean\ ]$$
$$deny\ \ \ ::= [Identity \times Right \times Content \rightarrow Boolean\ ]$$

$$\forall\ i : Identity,\ r : Right,\ [d : Document]_{p:Provider} : Content$$
$$request(i, r, [d]_p) \wedge\ isPermitted(p, i, r, [d]_p)\ \rightarrow allow(i, r, [d]_p)$$

$$\forall\ i : Identity,\ r : Right,\ [d : Document]_{p:Provider} : Content$$
$$request(i, r, [d]_p) \wedge\ \neg\ isPermitted(p, i, r, [d]_p)\ \rightarrow deny(i, r, [d]_p)$$

With the content centric approach, Art'East can allow Alice to read the Art-Song's content. Art'East issues a license $[< Alice, Play, ArtSong >]_{Art'East}$. Through her rendering application, Alice tries to play the ArtSong's content. A request such as $request(Alice, Play, [ArtSong]_{Art'East})$ is evaluated by the DRM controller. According to the license issued by Art'East, the predicate $isPermitted(Art'East, Alice, Play, [ArtSong]_{Art'East})$ is true. Therefore, the predicate $allow(Alice, Play, [ArtSong]_{Art'East})$ is true and the corresponding rendering action can be launched.

In order to define the "Alice identity", Art'East has to refer to the specific identity defined by the DRM application. Art'East cannot use a trusted external identity. In a same way, Art'East does not have any other choice than the rendering actions enclosed in the rendering application to implement the "play" right. Art'East cannot choose to trust an external rendering application. Using the Federated Rights Expression Model detailed in the next section, Art'East can define which are the trusted identities and which are the trusted rendering actions that can be involved with his content.

3.2   The Federated Approach

The federated approach introduces different improvements to the content centric license model introduced previously. Contrary to the content centric approach, not only contents have providers but identities and rendering actions have providers as well. The FORM approach introduces "action" and "ID" as new nominal types. An "action" corresponds to the piece of code used to render the content, the "right" is the corresponding rendering action tagged with the action provider signature. An "ID" corresponds to the piece of information related to a given end-user, the "identity" is the corresponding ID tagged with the identity provider signature. Therefore, in order to enable the federated approach the identity and the right are redefined as follows:

$ID, Action, Document$ are nominal types

$$Identity ::= [ID]_{Provider}$$
$$Right \quad ::= [Action]_{Provider}$$
$$Content ::= [Document]_{Provider}$$

In the example introduced previously in section 2.2, Soft'Inc, as a content provider, distributes pieces of code implementing three rendering actions $LitePlayer$, $PowerPlayer$ and $Extract$. Using a specific action packager, Soft'Inc creates three corresponding packages compatible with the FORM rendering application. These packages called "right" are the corresponding pieces of code all signed with the Soft'Inc's signature. In a same way, Pop'mag uses an identity packager to create compatible identities. These identities are signed with the Pop'Mag's signature. Once the identity, the right or the content packed, object providers must define a license specifying what can be done with their objects. Basically, the license defines a set of grants corresponding to the authorized request that can be executed through the rendering application. A grant explicitly identifies the identity, the right and the content. Doing that, object providers identify the authorized pieces of information and the trusted providers distributing these information as well. According to the previous definition of the $grant$ as triple Identity × Right × Content, we do not need to change the grant definition given in the previous section. But we need to change the definition of the $isPermitted$ predicate to take into account the new definition of $Right$ and $Identity$:

$$\forall \; [i : ID]_{p_i:Provider} : Identity, \; [a : Action]_{p_r:Provider} : Right,$$
$$[d : Document]_{p_c:Provider} : Content$$
$$\exists \; p \; \in \{p_i, p_r, p_c\}, \; [s : setOf(Grant)]_p : License, \; g : Grant \in s \;|$$
$$g =< [i]_{p_i}, [a]_{p_r}, [d]_{p_c} > \; \rightarrow isPermitted(p, [i]_{p_i}, [a]_{p_r}, [d]_{p_c})$$

With FORM, the DRM controller must check every license from every provider involved in the request, i.e. the identity provider, the action provider and the content provider. In our example, when Alice, as a Pop'Mag reader, tries to use the ArtSong with the PowerPlayer, the DRM will check the licenses from Pop'Mag, Soft'Inc and Art'East. All of them must agree that this request can be executed, i.e. the $isPermitted$ predicate with the corresponding objects must

be true for all providers. Finally, the *request*, the *allow* and the *deny* predicates
are redefined as follows:

$$\forall \ [i:ID]_{p_i:provider} : Identity, \ [a:Action]_{p_r:Provider} : Right,$$
$$[d:Document]_{p_c:Provider} : Content$$
$$\forall \ p \in \{p_i, p_r, p_c\} \ |$$
$$request([i]_{p_i}, [a]_{p_r}, [d]_{p_c}) \ \wedge \ isPermitted(p, [i]_{p_i}, [a]_{p_r}, [d]_{p_c})$$
$$\rightarrow allow([i]_{p_i}, [a]_{p_r}, [d]_{p_c})$$

$$\forall \ [i:ID]_{p_i:provider} : Identity, \ [a:Action]_{p_r:Provider} : Right,$$
$$[d:Document]_{p_c:Provider} : Content$$
$$\exists \ p \in \{p_i, p_r, p_c\} \ |$$
$$request([i]_{p_i}, [a]_{p_r}, [d]_{p_c}) \ \wedge \ \neg \ isPermitted(p, [i]_{p_i}, [a]_{p_r}, [d]_{p_c})$$
$$\rightarrow deny([i]_{p_i}, [a]_{p_r}, [d]_{p_c})$$

When Alice wants to use the PowerPlayer to play the ArtSong, she performs
a request through her rendering application. The DRM controller will evaluate
the three licenses from the objects providers involved in the request. According
to the FORM license interpretation mechanism, all licenses must define a specific grant $< [Alice]_{Pop'Mag}, [PowerPlayer]_{Soft'Inc}, [ArtSong]_{Art'East} >$. Until
here, an object provider must specify the objects that must be present in the
request to satisfy the isPermitted predicate. In practice, this would lead to a
great number of rules to be expressed in the different licenses. Most of the time,
the provider will better specify the trusted provider rather than identify the object. For instance, Art'East wants to allow anyone with a Pop'Mag identity but
does not want to specify that specifically Alice can do it. In the next section we
aim at providing facilities simplifying the license expression and then we aim at
reducing the number of rules and getting a user-friendly language.

3.3   Abstraction Layer

We add an abstraction layer to avoid defining a rule for each possible request.
In the literature, there are some access control models who enable abstraction
to simplify the definition of the access control policy. Role Based Access Control
(RBAC) [13] provides an abstraction of identities into roles. A given identities
can play several roles and access control rules are based on roles. The Organization Based Access Control model (OrBAC) [8] goes further by abstracting
identities in roles, actions in activities and contents in views. The notion of role,
activity and view are interesting here in order to lessen the number of rules to be
defined. Thus, rather than specifying a rule for each Pop'Mag reader, Art'East
would better define a rule for the role "PopReader" and define that anyone with
a Pop'Mag identity are assigned to that role. In a same way, we could imag-
ine that Soft'Inc allows only "All ArtSongs" to be render with his players, or
Pop'Mag allows only a "Privacy Compliant" action to be used with Pop'Mag
identities. The OrBAC model also introduces the main concept of organization
as the scope of the access control policy. According to the OrBAC model semantics, identities, rights and contents belong to a given organization and only

access control rules under this organization can be used by the controller. This concept of organization is actually close to the concept of provider and fits with the ownership principle. Thus, the OrBAC model provides interesting concepts that could be used to improve the expressiveness of our basic license model. So, we first redefine the license expression language introducing roles, activities and views and then we redefine the license interpretation mechanism to take into account these abstractions. Let us first redefine the language as follows:

$ID, Action, Document, Role, Activity, View$ are nominal types
any is a constant

$$Identity ::= [ID \mid any]_{Provider} \mid any$$
$$Right \quad ::= [Action \mid any]_{Provider} \mid any$$
$$Content ::= [Document \mid any]_{Provider} \mid any$$
$$Grant \quad ::= < Role, Activity, View > \mid < Identity, Empower, Role >$$
$$\mid < Right, Consider, Activity > \mid < Content, Use, View >$$

The constant any specifies that any value can match. When any takes place instead of an ID, an action or a document, it means that any object can match. When any takes place instead of an identity, a right or a content, it means that any objects from any providers can match. As showed in the figure 5, we can simplify the definition of the different licenses of our example.

Previously, a grant was a triple composed by an identity, a right and a content. Abstracting identities in roles, actions in activities and contents in views, a grant is now composed of a role, an activity and a view. We then define three specific grants: One with the *empower* right specifying that a given identity matches a role. One with the *consider* right specifying that a given action matches an activity. Another one with the *use* right to express that a given content matches a view. Consequently, we must redefine the license interpretation mechanism. In the formalism introduced previously, we need to modify the *isPermitted* predicate as follows:

$$\forall \ [i : ID]_{p_i:Provider} : Identity, \ [a : Action]_{p_r:Provider} : Right,$$
$$[d : Document]_{p_c:Provider} : Content$$
$$\exists \ p \in \{p_i, p_r, p_c\}, \ [s : setOf(Grant)]_p : License,$$
$$g, g_\alpha, g_\beta, g_\gamma \in s, \ \alpha : Role, \ \beta : Activity, \ \gamma : View \mid$$
$$g =< \alpha, \beta, \gamma > \ \wedge \ g_\alpha =< [i]_{p_i}, empower, \alpha >$$
$$\wedge \ g_\beta =< [a]_{p_r}, consider, \beta > \ \wedge \ g_\gamma =< [d]_{p_c}, use, \gamma >$$
$$\rightarrow isPermitted(p, [i]_{p_i}, [a]_{p_r}, [d]_{p_c})$$

We can go one step further by using role definition and view definition as proposed in [5] improving OrBAC expressiveness. With role definitions and view definitions, it is possible to define properties that identities or contents must have in order to match a role or a view. Using this kind of definition here, Art'East could define the property that a song must have to be in the view "ArtSongs" rather than explicitly define that a given song is in a given view.

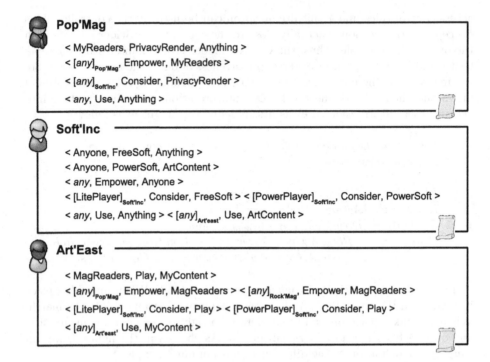

Pop'Mag

< MyReaders, PrivacyRender, Anything >
< [any]$_{Pop'Mag}$, Empower, MyReaders >
< [any]$_{Soft'Inc}$, Consider, PrivacyRender >
< *any*, Use, Anything >

Soft'Inc

< Anyone, FreeSoft, Anything >
< Anyone, PowerSoft, ArtContent >
< *any*, Empower, Anyone >
< [LitePlayer]$_{Soft'Inc}$, Consider, FreeSoft > < [PowerPlayer]$_{Soft'Inc}$, Consider, PowerSoft >
< *any*, Use, Anything > < [any]$_{Art'east}$, Use, ArtContent >

Art'East

< MagReaders, Play, MyContent >
< [any]$_{Pop'Mag}$, Empower, MagReaders > < [any]$_{Rock'Mag}$, Empower, MagReaders >
< [LitePlayer]$_{Soft'Inc}$, Consider, Play > < [PowerPlayer]$_{Soft'Inc}$, Consider, Play >
< [any]$_{Art'east}$, Use, MyContent >

Fig. 5. FORM licenses with abstract layer

4   Conclusion

This paper provides a new approach called FORM (Federated Organization based access control Model) to manage rights. We claim that existing DRM frameworks are content centric since only content providers are taken into account. A content provider distributes contents and defines the corresponding license. Such a license identifies: 1) which rights can be rendered with the content and 2) who are the authorized end-users (as identity holders) allowed to exercised these rights. Usually, each right corresponds to a rendering action. These rendering actions are usually enclosed into the rendering application on the client side. With FORM, we aim at taking into account external rendering actions. Rather than using proprietary actions, a content provider decides which external renderings actions can be used and which corporations, issuing these actions, can be trusted. We assume that the identity of the user is not unique but it is rather a collection of different identities issued by different corporations over the Internet. With FORM, we aim at taking into account external identities. Rather than using a proprietary identity for the DRM purpose, a content provider decides which external identities can be used and which corporation, issuing these identities, can be trusted.

We go further in FORM considering identity providers and action providers as first-class providers. Identity providers can define a license specifying which rights and which contents can be used with the identity they provide. In the same way, action providers can decide which contents can be rendered and who are allowed to use the actions they provide.

Finally, when an end-user requests for a content rendering, the DRM controller checks all licenses belonging to the different requested objects i.e. the identity license, the action license and the content license. According to the ownership principle, only a license issued by the object provider can be taken into account by the license interpretation mechanism. If all of the providers agree with the request, then the rendering can be performed.

We are currently working on a proof of concept of a DRM framework enabling FORM. We aim at enhancing the robustness of our application by considering trusted computing issues [6,1,11].

Acknowledgement. This work was supported by funding from the French ministry for research under "ACI Sécurité Informatique: CASC Project".

References

1. Becker, E., Buhse, W., Günnewig, D., Rump, N. (eds.): Digital Rights Management: Technological, Economic, Legal and Political Aspects. LNCS. Springer, Heidelberg (2003)
2. Microsoft Corporation. Using windows media encoder to protect content. Technical report (March 2003)
3. Microsoft Corporation. Architecture of windows media rights manager. Technical report (May 2004)
4. Cuppens, F., Miège, A.: Modelling Contexts in the Or-BAC Model. In: Omondi, A.R., Sedukhin, S. (eds.) ACSAC 2003. LNCS, vol. 2823, Springer, Heidelberg (2003)
5. Cuppens, F., Cuppens-Boulahia, N., Sans, T., Miège, A.: A formal approach to specify and deploy a network security policy, Toulouse, France (August 2004)
6. Erickson, J.S.: Fair Use, DRM and Trusted Computing. Communication of the ACM 46(4) (2003)
7. International Organization for Standardization (ISO). ISO/IEC 21000:2004 Information technology – Multimedia framework (MPEG-21) (2004)
8. Alexandre Miège. Definition of a formal framework for specifying security policies - The Or-BAC model and extensions. PhD thesis, Telecom Paris (Ecole Nationale Supérieure des Télécommunications) (2005)
9. Open Mobile Alliance (OMA). OMA Digital Rights Management V2.0 (2006), http://www.openmobilealliance.org/release_program/drm_v2_0.html
10. David P.: Requirements for a Rights Data Dictonary and Rights Expression Language. Technical report, Reuters (June 2001)
11. Siani Pearson. Trusted Computing Platforms: TCPA Technolog. In: Context. Prentice Hall PTR (July 2002)
12. Rosenblatt, B., Trippe, B., Mooney, S.: Digital Rights Management: Business and Technology. Wiley, Chichester, UK (2001)
13. Sandhu, R.S.: Role-Based Access Control. Advances in Computers 46 (1998)

A Method of Safety Analysis
for Runtime Code Update*

Masatomo Hashimoto

National Institute of Advanced Industrial Science and Technology,
1-18-13 Sotokanda, Chiyoda-ku, Tokyo 101-0021 Japan
m.hashimoto@aist.go.jp

Abstract. In this paper, we present a novel method of safety analysis
for *runtime code update*, i.e., updating a program at runtime without
terminating its execution. Runtime code update is an emerging technique
especially for increasing availability of the servers which should always be
in service and free of any known bugs or security flaws. However, it may
cause state inconsistency or unintended behaviors unless it is properly
restricted. Although too much restriction enables us to easily ensure
safety of updating code at runtime, it prevents us from coping with the
realistic updates. To reveal appropriate restriction, we first construct a
very precise model of safe runtime code update based on a framework
of explicit data/control flow and dependency. Then, a class of analyses
which statically estimates the set of *safe update points* is derived by
approximating the model. We restrict only the timing: behaviorally safe
runtime code update may occur only at safe update points. Moreover,
we can relax the restriction by explicitly specifying non-critical points.

1 Introduction

Updating software is one of the usual tasks for computer users or system administrators to enjoy kinds of system improvements such as bug fixes, stabilization,
or functional extensions. Above all, security related updates are mandatory especially for Internet applications; they should be applied as soon as possible
against possible malicious attacks. However, we tend to think too much trouble
to frequently update running systems because of unwanted downtime or interruption to continuous operations. In many cases, in order to complete update
tasks, we must first terminate the execution of the relevant programs and hence
the services they provide. For a certain kind of applications, downtime is even
critical for normal operations. Typical examples include telephone exchange or
financial transaction processing system. Those systems are also continuously un-
dergoing changes to take advantage of hardware and software improvements. As
of 1987, 422 exchanges utilizing AT&T's digital switching system, called 5ESS,
retrofitted to the newer version without a noticeable service interruption to sub-
scribers [1]. As of 2000, Visa's financial transaction processing system is kept

---

* This research was supported by PRESTO research program of Japan Science and
Technology Agency.

M. Okada and I. Satoh (Eds.): ASIAN 2006, LNCS 4435, pp. 60–74, 2007.
© Springer-Verlag Berlin Heidelberg 2007

99.5% available against average of 20,000 routine software updates per year [2]. In both cases, the system is updated without disrupting the users' experience. It is achieved by making use of specially configured redundant hardware primarily designed for fault-tolerance. Although it works quite well actually, application of such method is very limited.

We call updating programs at runtime without terminating their executions *runtime code update*. At least since 1970s, a number of software-based approaches to runtime code update have been developed [3,4,5]. Some systems are based on code fragment replacement at runtime, and others execution state transfer between processes. In general, simple replacement of code or state during execution of the code is not a safe operation in that it will easily cause state inconsistency and unintended system behaviors. Several systems ensure *type* safety that means no type error occurs after (well-formed) update. However, it may still allow unintended *behavior* after update. For example, updated BBS system may continue to accept connections from a site in a blacklist. Granularity of supported updates is another characteristic of runtime code update. In order to ensure safety, updates are usually restricted to pre-defined patterns: replacement of modules or abstract data types, etc. However, we cannot predict where bugs exist and how should they be fixed.

In this paper, we present a novel method of safety analysis for runtime code update which ensures behavioral safety. We first model safe runtime code update with a variant of higher-order call-by-value language. The model precisely tracks the effect of update by making use of explicit flow and dependency information. Roughly speaking, to avoid state inconsistency, we restrict the timing of runtime code update: it may occur only at *safe update points*, where no dependence on modified code exists and no reaching affected values have subsequent critical uses. In addition, one may specify non-critical uses for more safe update points. Then we derive a class of safety analyses from that model by way of abstract interpretation of the semantics [6]. The derived class of analyses estimates the set of safe update points statically. In our model, updates are not restricted to pre-defined patterns. Any modifications to abstract syntax tree of source code are allowed and recognized. It is even possible to safely update a part of the definition of an active function while it is active.

The rest of the paper is organized as follows. First, our model of runtime code update is introduced informally in Sect. 2. Then it is formally defined in Sect. 3. Section 4 describes the safety analysis derived from the model. After a brief review of related work in Sect. 5, we conclude the work in Sect. 6.

2   Runtime Code Update

In this section, we informally introduce our model of runtime code update. We consider minor updates including bug fixes and functional extensions. Note that safe runtime code update would be in principle impossible if a program changed drastically. The basic idea is to reuse a part of computation for the new version's execution as long as possible. Our model is based on state transfer between processes similar to the one of Gupta et al. [7] Suppose that applying a modification δ to a program P yields a new version P'. An execution of a program can be represented as a sequence of state transitions by some interpreter. Let initial states for P and P' be S_0 and S_0' respectively. Then the execution of P proceeds like $S_0 \longrightarrow S_1 \longrightarrow \ldots \longrightarrow S_n$. Suppose that δ is applied to P at some state S_i. Generally, it is not possible to continue the execution after δ is applied, as S_i is not always consistent with the new program P'. If the state S_i is properly transformed by some state transformer Δ, the execution will be able to continue. If $\Delta(S_i)$ is equivalent to some S_j' where initial state S_0' of P' reaches, we say that Δ is *valid* for P, δ, and S_i. We adopt the validity for our definition of safety.

$$
\begin{array}{ccccccc}
P & S_0 & \rightarrow & \cdots & \rightarrow & S_i & \rightarrow & \cdots \\
\delta\downarrow & & & & & \downarrow\Delta & \\
P' & S_0' & \rightarrow & \cdots & \rightarrow & S_j' & \rightarrow & \cdots
\end{array}
$$

However, we cannot construct valid state transformer for arbitrary P, δ, and S_i, since validity check is not decidable [7]. Gupta and others have attempted to construct valid state transformer by restricting the patterns of δ and implemented it for the C programming language. The restrictions include:

1. only values of global variables may change,
2. stack frames for the modified functions are not on the call stack, and
3. the values of all local variables and the program counter do not change.

Those restrictions, however, are not admissible for practical use, even if simple and efficient implementations are possible. For example, by the second restriction, we cannot update the functions whose stack frames stay on the call stack for a long time (e.g. `main` function) without restarting the program. Actually, `main` functions were modified in all of the downloadable 13 versions between 1.3.0 and 1.3.22 of the apache HTTP server (`www.apache.org`). Moreover, we have observed that 4 functions out of 54 modified or deleted functions between versions 1.3.20 and 1.3.22 have stayed on the call stack for many hours.

Our solution is to restrict the domain of valid state transformer to the set of *safe update points*. The purpose of our safety analysis is to estimate the set of safe update points. To obtain an algorithm which computes the set of safe update points, first we introduce a model called *exact model*. The exact model makes use of the program itself to obtain valid state transformer. In the exact model, all of the safe update points are computed exactly. Then we derive an *abstract model* from the exact model. In the abstract model, the set of safe update points are conservatively approximated.

Figure 1 illustrates the exact model. Two horizontal lines represent sequences of state transitions for two versions respectively. We assume that we can take snapshot of any state in the transition sequence and can restart the execution from the state. Suppose that the update starts at the state S. By analyzing the difference between old and new programs and exactly tracking control/data flow and dependency, we can enumerate the states affected by the change. If S is not affected at all and no affected states exist before S, we can simply derive

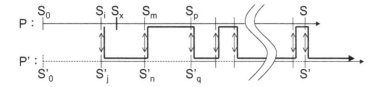

Fig. 1. Exact model

S' from S. Then we can safely start execution of P' from S'. If there exists some affected state S_x before S and there are no affected states before S_x, we start execution from S'_j derived from S_i just before S_x. The execution from S'_j proceeds with checking if some states after S_i and the current state match. If S_m and S_p match to S'_n and S'_q, respectively, and there is no influence of the version change between S_m and S_p, we can safely reuse the transition from S_m to S_p. By repeating the 'execute-and-reuse' process, we can finally derive S' form S if S matches to S'. A reusable state corresponds to a safe update point.

Although we can precisely compute the set of safe update points by the exact model, it seems almost impossible to implement state transformer or safe update point analyzer based on the exact model, since the exact model requires recording all of the states before S. Therefore we introduce an abstract model obtained from the exact model by employing the following:

- approximation of control/data flow and dependency by abstract interpretation of the semantics, and
- analysis to find the states affected by the computation which is not reusable (e.g. between S_i and S_m in Fig. 1).

Roughly speaking, approximated set of safe update points contains the states which is not affected by the version change. The abstract model enables us to statically analyze the programs to obtain the set of safe update points for runtime code update. The difference between two programs can be precisely analyzed by applying tree matching algorithms [8,9] to the abstract syntax trees. It is also possible to apply conventional techniques for control/data flow and dependency analyses [10] to implement the safety analysis. State transfer at a safe update point from the execution of the old program to that of the new program is safe if we construct a valid state transformer. Note that there exist no restriction on the *pattern of change* in our model. Even updates which modify the **main** function are allowed. However computed set of safe update points may be empty if given update radically changes the control/data flow of the original program.

3   Exact Model

3.1   Language

The target language is a variant of higher-order call-by-value language. It consists of *simple* expressions, call-by-value function applications, let-bindings, primitive

applications, first-class references, tuples, if-branches, and *markers*. A simple
expression is either a constant, variable, lambda expression, or recursive function.
We assume left-to-right evaluation order. The set of expressions is defined as
follows:

$$e ::= k \mid x \mid \lambda x.e \mid \mathsf{rec}\ f.\lambda x.e \mid e\ @e \mid \mathsf{let}\ x = @e\ \mathsf{in}\ e \mid p(e,\ldots,e) \mid \mathsf{ref}\ e \mid !e \mid e := e \mid$$
$$(e,\cdots,e) \mid e.i \mid \mathsf{if}\ e\ \mathsf{then}\ e\ \mathsf{else}\ e \mid @e$$

A marker $@e$ just behaves like e except that it is used to properly propagate
changes made to e to the surrounding expressions. All markers must appear in
applications and let-bindings as seen in the definition above. We assume that
a unique label $l \in Label$ is assigned to each of all the subexpressions. The set
of bound variables and free variables are defined conventionally. We sometimes
explicitly assign another label to a variable to indicate the binder of the variable.
A program is represented as a closed expression.

Example 1 (Program).

$$P = (\mathsf{let}\ f = \left(@(\lambda x.(x_{l_4}^{l_2} + 1_{l_5})_{l_3})_{l_2}\right)_{l_1}\ \mathsf{in}\ (f_{l_7}^{l_0}\ (@2_{l_9})_{l_8})_{l_6})_{l_0}$$

is a program.

We regard a labeled expression as a finite map from *Label* to expressions where
all subexpressions are represented as links (labels). For example, the program P
in Example 1 is equivalent to the following finite map.

$$\left\{ \begin{array}{llll} l_0 \mapsto \mathsf{let}\ f = l_1\ \mathsf{in}\ l_6\ , & l_1 \mapsto @l_2\ , & l_2 \mapsto \lambda x.l_3\ , & l_3 \mapsto l_4 + l_5\ , & l_4 \mapsto x, \\ l_5 \mapsto 1 & , & l_6 \mapsto l_7\ l_8\ , & l_7 \mapsto f & , & l_8 \mapsto @l_9 & , & l_9 \mapsto 2 \end{array} \right\}$$

A program is also regarded as an ordered labeled tree with the following scheme:
1) each label $l \in \mathrm{dom}(P)$ corresponds to a node which is labeled with a language
construct of $P(l)$, i.e., k, x, λx, $\mathsf{rec}\ f$, app, let x, p, ref, !, :=, tpl, prj, if, and @,
2) each of the children corresponds to the label which occurs in $P(l)$ preserving
the left-to-right order.

3.2 Exact Semantics

The operational semantics is defined based on the formulation by Jagannathan
et al. [11] The exact semantics of a program P is specified by a set of exact
states and a transition relation $\xrightarrow{I}$ between the states, where I denotes transition
information. Three kinds of information is recorded in I: $I.u$ holds the set of used
variables, $I.n$ the label of the subexpression to be evaluated next, and $I.c$ the
label of the innermost surrounding subexpression. The exact states are defined
in Fig. 2. For sets A and B, $A \to B$ denotes the set of partial functions. We
sometimes regard a partial function as a set. $A*$ denotes the set of finite sequences
of elements of A. We denote the empty sequence by $\langle \rangle$. $\mathcal{P}(A)$ denotes the power
set of A. The set of nodes is represented as a partial mapping from *NodeLabel* to
Value. There are two kinds of nodes: the *expression node* (l,b) and the *variable
node* (x, cn). An expression node (l,b) contains the value of e_l evaluated in the

$$State = Label \times BindEnv \times Contour \times Nodes \times Edges \times Edges$$
$$BindEnv = Var \rightarrow Contour \qquad Contour = Label*$$
$$Nodes = NodeLabel \rightarrow Value \qquad Value = ((Label \times BindEnv) \times CVal)$$
$$Edges = \mathcal{P}(Edge) \qquad Edge = NodeLabel \times NodeLabel$$
$$NodeLabel = (Label \times BindEnv) + (Var \times Contour)$$
$$CVal = Int + Bool + \{cls\} + \{cell\} + \{unit\} + (CVal \times \cdots \times CVal)$$

Fig. 2. Exact states

environment b. The value of free variable x will be found in $(x, b(x))$. $CVal$ denotes the set of concrete values. For $\langle l, b, cn, N, E, D \rangle \in State$, N, E, and D define a control/data flow and dependency graph. E and D correspond to flow and dependence edges, respectively. Intuitively, l corresponds to a program counter, b and $cn = l_1 : \cdots : l_n$ correspond to a current environment and a stack of activation frames, respectively. Some auxiliary functions for the definition of the operational semantics are defined. First one is the *first* function. $first(e)$ returns the label l of subexpression e' where the control reaches firstly when evaluating expression e. Note that the result of $first(e)$ is always an simple expression.

Definition 1 (first).

$$first(e_l) = l \text{ if } e \text{ is simple} \qquad first(e_1\ e_2) = first(e_1)$$
$$first(\text{let } x = e_1 \text{ in } e_2) = first(e_1) \qquad first(p(e_1, \ldots, e_n)) = first(e_1)$$
$$first(\text{ref } e) = first(e) \qquad first(!e) = first(e)$$
$$first(e_1 := e_2) = first(e_1) \qquad first((e_1, \ldots, e_n)) = first(e_1)$$
$$first(e.i) = first(e) \qquad first(\text{if } e_1 \text{ then } e_2 \text{ else } e_3) = first(e_1)$$
$$first(@e) = first(e)$$

We can get label component l of $S = \langle l, b, cn, N, E, D \rangle$ by $lab(S) = l$. There are also overloaded $labs(\_)$ functions: $labs(e) = \text{dom}(e)$ and $labs(E) = \{l_1, l_2 \mid (l_1, \_) \rightsquigarrow (l_2, \_) \in E\}$. The function $cval : Value \rightarrow CVal$ extracts concrete values from values. Thus $cval((l, b, cv)) = cv$. Equality test between values $(l_1, b_1, cv_1) = (l_2, b_2, cv_2)$ ignores l_1, b_1, l_2, and b_2 when cv_1 and cv_2 are constants. The initial state for P is denoted by $S_P^{\text{INI}} = \langle first(P), \emptyset, \langle \rangle, \emptyset, \emptyset, \emptyset \rangle$. The semantics of primitives is defined by the auxiliary function $papp(p, cv_1, \ldots, cv_n)$. By using those auxiliary functions, state transitions are defined as the set of transition rules. We show the rules only for the functional core in Fig. 3 for lack of space.

3.3 Code Mapping

In order to identify point-wise correspondence between programs, we define the notion of *code mapping*. Let P' be a revision of P. A code mapping $\mathcal{M}$ between P and P' is a one-to-one partial finite map from labels in $\text{dom}(P)$ to labels in $\text{dom}(P')$ which preserves the order of siblings and ancestor-descendant relations.

For a program P and its state $S = \langle l, b, cn, N, E, D \rangle$,

CONST If $occur_P(k_l)$ and $N(l, b) = \bot$, then
$$S \xrightarrow{I} \langle l, b, cn, N[(l, b) \mapsto (l, b, k)], E, D \rangle$$

VAR If $occur_P(x_l^{l'})$ and $N(l, b) = \bot$, then
$$S \rightarrow \langle l, b, cn, N[(l, b) \mapsto N((x^{l'}, b(x^{l'})))], E \cup \{(x^{l'}, b(x^{l'})) \rightsquigarrow (l, b)\}, D \rangle$$

LAM If $occur_P((\lambda x.e)_l)$ and $N(l, b) = \bot$, then
$$S \xrightarrow{I} \langle l, b, cn, N[(l, b) \mapsto (l, b, cls)], E, D \rangle$$

REC If $occur_P((\mathsf{rec}\, f.(\lambda x.e)_{l'})_l)$ and $N(l, b) = \bot$,
$$S \xrightarrow{I} \langle l, b, cn, N[(l, b), (f^l, cn) \mapsto (l', b[f^l \mapsto cn])], E, D \rangle$$

ARG If $occur_P(((e_1)_{l_1} (e_2)_{l_2})_{l_0})$ and $N(l, b) = v(\neq \bot)$,
$$S \xrightarrow{I} \langle first(e_2), b, cn, N, E, D \cup \{(l, b) \rightsquigarrow (l_0, b)\} \rangle$$
where $I.n = \{l_2\}$ and $I.c = \{l_0\}$

CALL If $occur_P(((e_1)_{l_1} (e_2)_l)_{l_0})$, $occur_P((\lambda x.e_{l''})_{l'})$, $N(l_1, b) = (l', b', cls)$, and $N(l, b) = v(\neq \bot)$, then
$$S \xrightarrow{I} \langle l''', b'', l_0\colon cn, N[(x^{l'}, l_0\colon cn) \mapsto v], E', D' \rangle$$
where $l''' = first(e_{l''})$, $b'' = b'[x^{l'} \mapsto l_0\colon cn]$,
$E' = E \cup \{(l, b) \rightsquigarrow (x^{l'}, l_0\colon cn), (l'', b'') \rightsquigarrow (l_0, b)\}$,
$D' = D \cup \{(l_1, b) \rightsquigarrow (labs(e), b''), (l', b') \rightsquigarrow (x^{l'}, l_0\colon cn), (l, b), (l_1, b) \rightsquigarrow (l_0, b)\}$,
$I.u = \{(l_1, b)\}$, $I.n = \{l''\}$, and $I.c = \{l_0\}$

RET If $occur_P((\lambda x.e_l)_{l_0})$, $N(l, b) = v(\neq \bot)$, $(l, b) \rightsquigarrow (l', b') \in E$, and $cn = l'\colon cn'$,
$$S \xrightarrow{I} \langle l', b', cn', N[(l', b') \mapsto v], E, D \rangle \text{ where } I.c = \{l_0\}$$

Fig. 3. Transition rules for functional core

Example 2 (Code Mapping). A code mapping between the program in Example 1 and

$$(\mathsf{let}\ f = (@(\lambda x.(x_{l_4'} + 1_{l_5'})_{l_3'})_{l_2'})_{l_1'} \text{ in}$$
$$(\mathsf{let}\ g = (@(\lambda y.((f_{l_9'} (@y_{l_{11}'})_{l_{12}'})_{l_{10}'} \times 3_{l_{14}'})_{l_9'})_{l_8'})_{l_7'} \text{ in}$$
$$(g_{l_{16}'} (@2_{l_{18}'})_{l_{17}'})_{l_{15}'})_{l_6'})_{l_0'}$$

is $\{l_0 \mapsto l_0', l_1 \mapsto l_1', l_2 \mapsto l_2', l_3 \mapsto l_3', l_4 \mapsto l_4', l_5 \mapsto l_5', l_6 \mapsto l_{10}', l_7 \mapsto l_9', l_8 \mapsto l_{12}', l_9 \mapsto l_{11}'\}$ depicted in Fig. 4. The code mapping is denoted by dashed lines. In addition, relabeled nodes are denoted by dashed ellipses, and inserted nodes are denoted by bold ellipses.

Note that multiple code mappings are possible for each pairs of programs in general. In order to choose better ones, we introduce a metric called *mapping cost* for code mappings. It corresponds to the number of operations which are used to transform P to P': deleting tree nodes in P which are not in $dom(\mathcal{M})$ inserting tree nodes in P' which are not in $cod(\mathcal{M})$, and changing the tree node label of mapped node. There exists several efficient algorithms [8,9] which computes code (tree) mapping which minimizes the mapping cost. For example, by applying one of the algorithms [9], we can obtain mapping cost 8 of the code mapping in Example 2 which is optimal. We will always choose code mappings of minimum cost since lower cost code mappings tend to provide more chances of runtime code update.

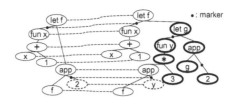

Fig. 4. Example of code mapping

Definition 2 (Modified Tree Nodes). *Let* $\mathcal{M}$ *be a code mapping between* P *and* P'. *The set of* modified tree nodes *with respect to* $\mathcal{M}$ *denoted by* $Mod_{\mathcal{M}}^{PP'}$ *is defined as* $\{l \,|\, P(l)$ *is deleted, or* $l \in \mathrm{dom}(\mathcal{M})$ *and tree node label of* $P(l)$ *is changed, new children are inserted to* $P(l)$, *or some of the children are deleted from* $P(l)\}$

Example 3. The set of modified tree nodes with respect to the code mapping in Example 2 is $\{l_0, l_8\}$.

3.4   Exact Update Model

We begin this section with a number of definitions. We sometimes omit some parameters when they are obvious by context. For some program P, if $S_0 (= S_P^{\mathrm{INI}}) \xrightarrow{I_0} S_1 \xrightarrow{I_1} \cdots \xrightarrow{I_{i-1}} S_i \xrightarrow{I_i} \cdots \xrightarrow{I_{n-1}} S_n$ $(0 \leq i \leq n)$ is a transition sequence derived from the transition rules, we say that the sequence $\langle S_i, \ldots, S_n \rangle$ is an *execution trace* of P. We say that S is a *valid* state for P if $\langle S \rangle$ is an execution trace of P. In the rest of this subsection, we let P' be a revision of P, $\mathcal{M}$ a code mapping between P and P', and $T = \langle S_0, \ldots, S_n \rangle$ an execution trace of P unless otherwise specified. The sequence which is obtained by filtering out $S_i (0 \leq i \leq n)$ such that

- $lab(S_i) \notin Mod_{\mathcal{M}}^{PP'}$, or
- $lab(S_{i-1}) \in Mod_{\mathcal{M}}^{PP'}$ and $P(lab(S_{i-1}))$ is simple

is called *sequence of directly affected points* of T with respect to $\mathcal{M}$, denoted by $DAP_{\mathcal{M}}^{PP'}(T)$. We also define the set of *directly affected nodes* denoted by $DAN_{\mathcal{M}}^{PP'}(T)$ as $\{(l_j, b_j) | 0 \leq j \leq m\}$ where $DAP_{\mathcal{M}}^{PP'}(T) = \langle \langle l_0, b_0, \_, \_, \_ \rangle, \ldots, \langle l_m, b_m, \_, \_, \_ \rangle \rangle$. For a valid state $S = \langle \_, \_, \_, N, E, D \rangle$ of P, the set of *affected nodes*, denoted by $AN_{\mathcal{M}}^{PP'}(S)$, is defined as the set of reachable nodes from $DAN_{\mathcal{M}}^{PP'}(\langle S_P^{\mathrm{INI}}, \ldots, S \rangle)$. Let $S_0 \xrightarrow{I_0} \cdots \xrightarrow{I_{n-1}} S_n$ be a transition sequence of P. The set of *essentially used values* denoted by $UseV(T)$, the set of *next labels* denoted by $NL(T)$, and the set of *context labels* denoted by $CL(T)$ are defined as $I_0.u \cup \cdots \cup I_{n-1}.u$, $I_0.n \cup \cdots \cup I_{n-1}.n$, and $I_0.c \cup \cdots \cup I_{n-1}.c$, respectively. The *sequence of resume points*, denoted by $RP_{\mathcal{M}}^{PP'}(T)$, is defined by filtering out all of the states from T except the states just before directly affected points. The leftmost state in $RP_{\mathcal{M}}^{PP'}(T)$ is called the *leftmost resume point* and denoted by

$LRP_{\mathcal{M}}^{PP'}(T)$. The *renaming map* α derived from P, P', and $\mathcal{M}$ is a finite map from tagged variables to tagged variables defined as follows: for any $l \mapsto l' \in \mathcal{M}$, $\alpha(x^l) = y^{l'}$ if and only if

- $occur_P((\lambda x.e_{l_0})_l)$, $occur_{P'}((\lambda y.e'_{l'_0})_{l'})$, and $\mathcal{M}(l_0) = l'_0$, or
- $occur_P((\mathrm{rec}\, x.e_{l_0})_l)$, $occur_{P'}((\mathrm{rec}\, y.e'_{l'_0})_{l'})$, and $\mathcal{M}(l_0) = l'_0$

$\alpha(x^l) = x^l$ otherwise. We extend the domain of expression label map to the set of states. The extended expression label map of $\mathcal{M}$, denoted by $\widetilde{\mathcal{M}}$, is defined by trivially extending the original domain to the set of states based on the following equations:

$$\widetilde{\mathcal{M}}(l) = \begin{cases} \mathcal{M}(l) & l \in \mathrm{dom}(\mathcal{M}) \\ \bot & l \notin \mathrm{dom}(\mathcal{M}) \end{cases} \qquad \widetilde{\mathcal{M}}(l_0 {:} \cdots {::} l_n) = \widetilde{\mathcal{M}}(l_0) {:} \cdots {::} \widetilde{\mathcal{M}}(l_n)$$

$$\widetilde{\mathcal{M}}([x_0^{l_0} \mapsto cn_0, \ldots, x_n^{l_n} \mapsto cn_n]) = [\alpha(x_0^{l_0}) \mapsto \widetilde{\mathcal{M}}(cn_0), \ldots, \alpha(x_n^{l_n}) \mapsto \widetilde{\mathcal{M}}(cn_n)]$$

For the rest of the paper, we use $\overline{X}$ for $\widetilde{\mathcal{M}}(X)$ when code mapping to be applied is determined by the context. Note that all of the valid states for P before any affected states become also valid for P' by applying the expression label map.

Definition 3 (State Match). *Let P' be a revision of P, $\mathcal{M}$ a code mapping between P and P', $S = \langle l, b, cn, N, E, D \rangle$ a valid state of P, and $S' = \langle l', b', cn', N', E', D' \rangle$ a valid state of P'. If $l' = \overline{l}$, for all $x \in \mathrm{dom}(b') \cap \mathrm{dom}(\overline{b})$, $b'(x) = \overline{b}(x)$, and $\overline{N((l,b))} = N'((l', b'))$, then we say that S' matches S denoted by $Match_{\mathcal{M}}(S, S')$.*

Let $S_i = \langle l_i, b_i, cn_i, N_i, E_i, D_i \rangle$. The partial function $dN(T)$ is defined as the sum of extensions made to N_0 in the transition from S_0 to S_n. Similarly $dE(T)$ and $dD(T)$ are defined. We denote the summary of contour operations applied to cn_0 by $dcn(T) = \langle l_0^+, \ldots, l_p^+ \wr l_0^-, \ldots, l_q^- \rangle$ where l_j^+ denote pushed labels to cn_0, and l_k^- denote popped labels from cn_0. The application of cn to $dcn(T)$ is defined as follows.

$$dcn(T)(cn) = \begin{cases} l_0^+ {:} \cdots {:} l_p^+ {:} cn' & \text{if } cn = l_0^- {:} \cdots {:} l_q^- {:} cn' \\ \bot & \text{otherwise} \end{cases}$$

Theorem 1 (Side-by-side). *Let P' be a revision of P, $\mathcal{M}$ a code mapping between P and P', $T = \langle S_0, \ldots, S_n \rangle$ an execution trace of P where $S_i = \langle l_i, b_i, cn_i, N_i, E_i, D_i \rangle (0 \leq i \leq n)$. If*

- *there exists a valid state $S' = \langle l', b', cn', N', E', D' \rangle$ of P' which matches S_0,*
- $UseV(T) \cap DAN(S_0) = \emptyset$,
- $\overline{dcn(T)(cn')} \neq \bot$,
- *for all $l \in NL(T)$, $first(P(l)) = first(P'(\overline{l}))$,*
- $DAP(T) = \langle \rangle$, *and*
- $CL(T) \cap Mod_{\mathcal{M}}^{PP'} = \emptyset$,

then $\langle S_0^*, \ldots, S_n^* \rangle$ is an execution trace of P' where $T_i = \langle S_0, \ldots, S_i \rangle$ and $S_i^* = \langle \overline{l_i}, \overline{b_i}, \overline{dcn(T_i)}(cn'), N' \overline{dN(T_i)}, E' \cup \overline{dE(T_i)}, D' \cup \overline{dD(T_i)} \rangle$.

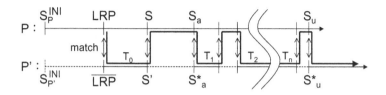

Fig. 5. Side-by-side execution

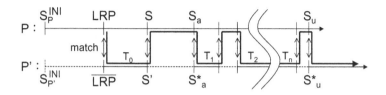

Fig. 6. Exact semantics of runtime code update

We now describe the exact semantics of runtime code update in terms of Theorem 1. Let $T = S_P^{INI}, S_1, \ldots, S_u$. Suppose that we are updating P at S_u.

1. Start the execution of P' from $\overline{LRP_{\mathcal{M}}^{PP'}(T)}$.
2. Whenever the control reaches $S' = \langle l', b', cn', N', E', D' \rangle$ such that $Match_{\mathcal{M}}(S, S')$ for some S in T, the following is repeated.
   (a) Let $T_0 = \langle S, \ldots, S_a \rangle$ where S_a is between S and the nearest resume point after S.
   (b) If $UseV(T_0) \cap DAN(S) = \emptyset$, $\overline{dcn(T_0)}(cn') \neq \bot$, for all $l \in NL(T_0)$, $first(P(l)) = first(P'(\bar{l}))$, $DAP(T_0) = \langle \rangle$, and $CL(T_0) \cap Mod_{\mathcal{M}}^{PP'} = \emptyset$, then the execution from S to S_a can be reused: the execution proceeds from S_a^*.
   (c) Otherwise, the execution proceeds from S'.

This model is illustrated in Fig. 6. In this model, the computation of P' is constructed by reusing the computation of P as much as possible by way of the execution trace. However recording whole of the execution trace is not feasible in most cases. We would like to construct S_u^* from S_u without any execution traces or rollback. It is only possible to construct some state S_u' equivalent to S_u^* in that the transition from S_u^* can be simulated by S_u'. The traces of updated program contains transitions which does not present in the original program:

- transitions for creation of nodes in $\overline{AN(S_u)}$ or $Added_{\mathcal{M}}(S_u^*)$
  where $Added_{\mathcal{M}}(S_u^*) = \{n \mid n \in N_u^*, l \text{ appears in } n, \text{and } l \in dom(P') \setminus cod(\mathcal{M})\}$,
- transitions for binding environment extensions(shortenings) by the rules LET(END) and CALL(RET), and
- transitions for contour changes by the rules CALL and RET.

If the transition from S_u^* is free from effects caused by the extra transitions above: $(l_u, b_u) \notin AN(S_u)$, no value of $\overline{AN(S_u)} \cup Added_{\mathcal{M}}(S_u^*)$ belongs to $UseV(\langle S_u^*, \ldots \rangle)$, and b_u and cn_u are not subject to change where $S_u = \langle l_u, b_u, cn_u, N_u, E_u, D_u \rangle$, then we call S_u *safe update point* and can construct

$$\widehat{State} = \widehat{Nodes} \times \widehat{Edges} \times \widehat{Edges} \qquad \widehat{Nodes} = NodeLabel \to \mathcal{P}(\widehat{Value})$$
$$\widehat{Value} = (Label \times \widehat{BindEnv} \times CVal) \quad \widehat{BindEnv} = Var \to \widehat{Contour}$$
$$\widehat{Edges} = \mathcal{P}(\widehat{Edge}) \qquad\qquad\qquad \widehat{Edge} = NodeLabel \times NodeLabel$$
$$NodeLabel = (Label \times \widehat{BindEnv}) + (Var \times \widehat{Contour})$$
$$\widehat{CVal} = Int + Bool + \{cls\} + \{cell\} + \{unit\} + \{?\} + (CVal \times \cdots \times CVal)$$

Fig. 7. Abstract states

S'_u only from S_u by providing some dummy values with $\overline{S_u}$, since the useless node values cannot interfere the transition. In addition, some values may be removed from $UseV(\langle S^*_u, \ldots \rangle)$ if it is of no importance what the values are for the user. For example, consider the following program fragment.

$$\textsf{let } loop = \textsf{rec } f.\lambda c. \cdots \underline{print\ c} \cdots f\ (c+1) \cdots \textsf{ in } loop\ 0$$

Suppose that 0 is changed by some update. Since affected values reach the occurrences of c in the body of λc and are used there, it is possible to update the code nowhere in the body. However, for instance, if the user permits c's values at the underlined part inaccurate and the values do not reach other important parts, all the points in the body become safe. Note that the user must provide appropriate values (some integer values) for affected and used values at the time of runtime code update. We call nodes whose value is permitted to be inaccurate *user specified non-critical nodes*.

4   Abstract Model

In this section, we describe a method of safe runtime code update based on a static analysis. The analysis is derived from the abstract version of the semantics introduced in the previous section.

4.1   Abstract Semantics

We define the abstract semantics following Jagannathan et al. [11] The abstract semantics for a program P is given by a set of abstract states $\widehat{State}$ and an abstract transition function $\widehat{T} : \widehat{State} \to \widehat{State}$. The definition of abstract states appears in Fig. 7 The abstraction is parameterized by the following:

- a finite set of abstract contour $\widehat{Contour}$,
- an abstraction function $\mathcal{A}_{cn}$ from $Contour$ to $\widehat{Contour}$,
- a mapping $\widehat{\cdot}$ from $Label \times \widehat{Contour}$ to $\widehat{Contour}$ which satisfies $\mathcal{A}_{cn}(l : cn) = l\widehat{\cdot}\mathcal{A}_{cn}(cn)$,
- an abstraction function $\mathcal{A}_b$ which maps $BindEnv$ to $\widehat{BindEnv}$. It must satisfy $\mathcal{A}_{cn}(cur(b)) = \widehat{cur}(\mathcal{A}_b(b))$, where cur maps a binding environment to the contour of its lexically deepest variable and $\widehat{cur}$ maps an abstract binding environment to the abstract contour of its lexically deepest variable.

$$\tilde{N}(\widehat{nl}) = \begin{cases} \{(l,\widehat{b},cv)\} & \text{if } \widehat{nl} = (l,\widehat{b}), \ reach_P(\widehat{nl}), \text{ and } cv = cvalof_P(l) \\ \{(l',\widehat{b},cls)\} & \text{if } \widehat{nl} = (l,\widehat{b}), \ reach_P(\widehat{nl}), \text{ and } occur_P\left((\operatorname{rec} f.(\lambda x.e)_{l'})_l\right) \\ \bigcup\{\widehat{N}(\widehat{nl'}) \mid \widehat{nl'} \rightsquigarrow \widehat{nl} \in \widehat{E}\} & \text{otherwise} \end{cases}$$

Fig. 8. Definition of $\tilde{N}$ for functional core

– an abstract binding environment extension function $\widehat{extend}$. It must satisfy $\mathcal{A}_b(b[x \mapsto cn]) = \widehat{extend}(\mathcal{A}_b(b), x, \mathcal{A}_{cn}(cn))$.

A collection of abstract functions is obtained by extending $\mathcal{A}_{cn}$ and $\mathcal{A}_b$ as follows.

$$\begin{array}{ll} \mathcal{A}(\langle l, b, cn, N, E, D\rangle) = \langle \mathcal{A}(N), \mathcal{A}(E), \mathcal{A}(D)\rangle & \mathcal{A}((l,b)) = (l, \mathcal{A}_b(b)) \\ \mathcal{A}(N) = \lambda \widehat{nl}.\{\mathcal{A}(N(nl)) \mid \mathcal{A}(nl) = \widehat{nl}\} & \mathcal{A}(x, cn) = (x, \mathcal{A}_{cn})(cn) \\ \mathcal{A}(E) = \{\mathcal{A}(nl_1) \rightsquigarrow \mathcal{A}(nl_2) \mid nl_1 \rightsquigarrow nl_2 \in E\} & \\ \mathcal{A}(D) = \{\mathcal{A}(nl_1) \rightsquigarrow \mathcal{A}(nl_2) \mid nl_1 \rightsquigarrow nl_2 \in D\} & \end{array}$$

Abstract transition function builds a control/data flow and dependency graph. The source of data flow is created by self-evaluating expressions such as constants, lambdas, and recursive expressions. Abstract values are propagated through the control/data flow edges, possibly causing the creation of new sources of data flow or new edges. The abstract transition function $\widehat{\mathcal{T}}$ is defined by $\widehat{\mathcal{T}}(\langle \widehat{N}, \widehat{E}, \widehat{D}\rangle) = \langle \tilde{N}, \tilde{E}, \tilde{D}\rangle$. The definition of $\tilde{N}$ for the functional core is given in Fig. 8 where $cvalof_P$ denotes the function from $Label$ to $CVal$ which is defined by

$$cvalof_P(l) = \begin{cases} k & \text{if } P(l) = k \\ cls & \text{if } P(l) = \lambda x.e_l \\ ? & otherwise. \end{cases}$$

The first two cases in Fig. 8 assign the abstract values in nodes corresponding to expressions where the control may reach from the entry node $nl_P^{\text{INI}} = (first(P), \emptyset)$. Reachability of control is represented as the sets of *control flow edges* denoted by $\widehat{nl_1} \xrightarrow{I} \widehat{nl_2} \in CFlowEdge = \widehat{NodeLabel} \times \mathcal{P}(\widehat{NodeLabel}) \times \widehat{NodeLabel}$. A control flow edge is labeled with transition information I. We only use $I.u$. For a program P, $CFlow(P) \in CFlowEdges = \mathcal{P}(CFlowEdge)$ and the predicate $\widehat{reach_P} \subseteq \widehat{NodeLabel}$ are computed by the rules (again only for the functional core) in Fig. 9. The third case in the definition of $\tilde{N}$ propagates abstract values along data flow edges in the graph. The definition of $\tilde{E}$ appears in Fig. 10. The definition of $\tilde{D}$ is easily derived from the exact transition rules. Let P' be a revision of P, $\mathcal{M}$ a code mapping between P and P', and S is a valid state of P. The set of *abstract affected nodes* of $\widehat{S}$ is defined by $\widehat{AN_{\mathcal{M}}^{PP'}}(\widehat{S}) = \mathcal{A}(AN_{\mathcal{M}}^{PP'}(S))$.

Definition 4 (Abstract Match). *Let P' be a revision of P and $\mathcal{M}$ a code mapping between P and P'. Let $\widehat{N}$ and $\widehat{N'}$ be components of abstract graphs of P and P', respectively. Suppose that $(l,\widehat{b})$ and $(l',\widehat{b'})$ are in $CFlow(P)$ and $CFlow(P')$, respectively. We say $(l,\widehat{b})$ has* abstract match $(l',\widehat{b'})$, *denoted by $\widehat{Match_{\mathcal{M}}}((l,\widehat{b}),(l',\widehat{b'}))$ if $l' = \bar{l}$.*

1. $reach_P(nl_P^{\text{INI}})$
2. For all l such that $occur_P(((e_1)_{l_1} (e_2)_{l_2})_l)$,
   (a) If $\widehat{N}((l_1,\widehat{b})) \neq \{\}$, then $reach_P((l'_2,\widehat{b}))$ and $(l_1,\widehat{b}) \xrightarrow{I} (l'_2,\widehat{b}) \in CFlow(P)$ where $l'_2 = first(e_2)$, $I.n = \{l_2\}$, and $I.c = \{l\}$.
   (b) If $(l',\widehat{b'}) \in \widehat{N}((l_1,\widehat{b}))$, $occur_P((\lambda x.e_{l''})_{l'})$, and $\widehat{N}((l_2,\widehat{b})) \neq \{\}$, then $reach_P((l''',\widehat{b''}))$ and $(l_2,\widehat{b}) \xrightarrow{I} (l''',\widehat{b''}) \in CFlow(P)$ where $l''' = first\,e$, $\widehat{b''} = \widehat{extend}(\widehat{b'},x,l\widehat{:cur}(\widehat{b}))$, $I.u = \{(l_1,\widehat{b})\}$, $I.n = \{l''\}$, and $I.c = \{l\}$.

Fig. 9. Definition of $reach_P$ and $CFlow(P)$ for functional core

$$\tilde{E} = \bigcup_{l \in \text{dom}(P),(l,\widehat{b}) \in \text{dom}(\widehat{N})} \tilde{E}_{l\widehat{b}}$$

where

if $occur_P(x_l)$, $\tilde{E}_{l\widehat{b}} = \{(x,\widehat{b}(x)) \rightsquigarrow (l,\widehat{b}) \mid reach_P((l,\widehat{b}))\}$

if $occur_P((\text{rec}\,f.\lambda x.e)_l)$, $\tilde{E}_{l\widehat{b}} = \{(l,\widehat{b}) \rightsquigarrow (f,\widehat{cur}(\widehat{b})) \mid reach_P((l,\widehat{b}))\}$

if $occur_P(((e_1)_{l_1} (e_2)_{l_2})_l)$,

$$\tilde{E}_{l\widehat{b}} = \left\{ \begin{array}{l} (l_1,\widehat{b}) \rightsquigarrow (x,l\widehat{:cur}(\widehat{b})), \\ (l'',\widehat{b''}) \rightsquigarrow (l,\widehat{b}), \\ (y,\widehat{b'}) \rightsquigarrow (y,\widehat{b''}) \end{array} \middle| \begin{array}{l} (l',\widehat{b'}) \in \widehat{N}((l_1,\widehat{b})), occur_P((\lambda x.e_{l''})_{l'}) \\ \widehat{b''} = \widehat{extend}(\widehat{b'},x,l\widehat{:cur}(\widehat{b})), \\ y \in \text{dom}(\widehat{b'}) \end{array} \right\}$$

Fig. 10. Definition of $\tilde{E}$ for functional core

Now we can statically estimate safe update points. We denote the set of all possible uses from $\widehat{nl_0}$ in $CFlow(P)$ by $\widehat{UseV}(CFlow(P),\widehat{nl_0})$: for all possible path $\widehat{nl_0} \xrightarrow{I_0} \cdots \xrightarrow{I_{n-1}} \widehat{nl_n}$ in $CFlow(P)$, $\widehat{UseV}(CFlow(P),\widehat{nl_0}) = \bigcup\bigcup_{0 \leq i \leq n} I_i.u$. By NCL, we denote the set of *user specified non-critical labels* which corresponds to the set of user specified non-critical nodes appeared in the last of Sect. 3. Then we define the notion of *safe update points* as follows.

1. Build abstract states $\widehat{S} = \langle \widehat{N}, \widehat{E}, \widehat{D} \rangle$ and $\widehat{S'} = \langle \widehat{N'}, \widehat{E'}, \widehat{D'} \rangle$ for P and P', respectively.
2. Let $NCN = \{(l',\widehat{b'}) \mid (l',\widehat{b'}) \in CFlow(P')$ and $l \in \overline{NCL}\}$.
3. Let $Added = \{(l',\widehat{b'}) \mid (l',\widehat{b'}) \in CFlow(P')$ and $l' \in \text{dom}(P') \setminus \text{cod}(\mathcal{M})\}$.
4. For all $\widehat{nl} \in CFlow(P)$, $\widehat{nl}$ is a safe update point if the following conditions hold.
   (a) $\widehat{nl} \notin \widehat{AN}_{\mathcal{M}}^{PP'}(\widehat{S})$
   (b) $\widehat{Match}_{\mathcal{M}}(\widehat{nl},\widehat{nl'})$ for some $\widehat{nl'}$ in $\widehat{N'}$. We let $\widehat{nl'}$ be the matched point.
   (c) Let $KN = (\widehat{AN}_{\mathcal{M}}^{PP'}(\widehat{S}) \setminus NCN) \cup Added$ and $KV = \{(l'_1,\widehat{b'_1}) \mid (l'_1,\widehat{b'_1}) \in KN$, $(l'_1,\widehat{b'_1},?) \in \widehat{N'}(\widehat{nl'_0})$, and $\widehat{nl'_0}$ is reachable from $\widehat{nl'}\}$.
       Then $KV \cap \widehat{UseV}(CFlow(P'),\widehat{nl'}) = \emptyset$.

We can instantiate the abstract update model to obtain nCFA [12] based analyses. For example, by setting $\widehat{Contour} = \{0\}$, $\mathcal{A}_{cn}(cn) = 0$, $l\widehat{:cn} = 0$, $\mathcal{A}_b(b) = \lambda x.0$, and $\widehat{extend}(\widehat{b},x,\widehat{cn}) = \lambda x.0$, we obtain a 0CFA based analysis.

5   Related Work

There exist several works which formalized termination-avoiding update [7,13,14,15]. Some are based on code replacement technique(e.g., dynamic load/link), and the others are based on state transfer between old and new versions. Gilmore and others [13] and Duggan [15] have modeled the type-safe dynamic replacement of ML modules. In Dynamic ML, Update occurs when the garbage collector is activated. Bierman and others [14] extended a simply typed first-order lambda calculus with a notion of modules, then defined a model of type-safe dynamic module update. Stoyle and others [5] developed an analysis to determine *con-free* program points where type-safe dynamic update can be performed for a type safe variant of C-like language. Though their work is very similar in spirit to ours, they ensure only type safety. Suppose that we are updating the following program fragment by changing underlined *true* is changed to *false*.

$$\cdots \mathsf{let}\ a = \underline{true}\ \mathsf{in}\ \mathsf{if}\ a\ \mathsf{then}\ e_1\ \mathsf{else}\ e_2 \cdots$$

If e_1 does not contain any concrete access to a, update is allowed at any point in e_1. However, executing the changed program from its initial state never reaches e_1. Such inconsistency should be at least warned. Gupta and others [7] proposed a formal model for on-the-fly program modification based on state transfer between processes. They defined validity of updates and have shown that validity check for all of the possible programs is not decidable. Therefore they put some restrictions on available updates as mentioned in Sect. 2. Although their notion of validity is strictly stronger than type safety, their restrictions are too restrictive.

6   Conclusion

We have developed a method of ensuring safety of updating programs at runtime. Safe runtime code update never causes state inconsistency and unintended behavior. Our safety is strictly stronger property than type safety. In order to ensure the safety, applicable updates must be properly restricted. We constructed a very precise (but infeasible) model to reveal appropriate restriction and derived a class of safety analysis from the model. The resulting restriction is only on the update timing: runtime code update may occur only at safe update points where no data and control dependence on modified code exists and no reaching affected values have subsequent critical uses. The set of safe update points is statically estimated by analyzing the old and new programs.

To apply our method to a large number of realistic updates, a lot of further work is required. First, we have to develop update models and analyses for commonly used programming languages other than higher-order functional languages. We are developing an experimental difference analyzer called ASTDiff. Currently, it can convert source code written in Java, Python, or C to the abstract syntax tree and compare the trees by means of an applied tree matching algorithm. Most of our analysis except the difference analysis can be implemented by utilizing existing frameworks for data flow and dependency analyses.

Second, some mechanism for code replacement or state transfer must be implemented. Although our method is in principle applicable to both mechanisms, it complicates the implementation. At least, we have to precisely track heap objects without sacrificing efficiency which is itself a hard problem.

Acknowledgment

The author would like to thank anonymous referees for their suggestions on further investigation and helpful comments.

References

1. Toy, L.: Large-Scale Real-Time Program Retrofit Methodology in AT&T 5ESS Switch. In: Reliable computer systems, 3rd edn. design and evaluation, pp. 574–586. A K Peters (1998)
2. Pescovitz, D.: Monsters in a box. Wired 8(12), 341–347 (2000)
3. Fabry, R.: How to design A system in which modules can be changed on the fly. In: Proceedings of the Second International Conference on Software Engineering, IEEE, Los Alamitos (1976)
4. Frieder, O., Segal, M.E.: On Dynamically Updating a Computer Program: From Concept to Prototype. Journal of Systems and Software 14(2), 111–128 (1991)
5. Stoyle, G., Hicks, M.W., Bierman, G.M., Sewell, P., Neamtiu, I.: Mutatis mutandis: safe and predictable dynamic software updating. In: POPL, pp. 183–194 (2005)
6. Cousot, P., Cousot, R.: Abstract interpretation: A unified lattice model for static analysis of programs by construction or approximation of fixpoints. In: Conference Record of the Fourth Annual ACM SIGPLAN-SIGACT Symposium on Principles of Programming Languages, pp. 238–252. ACM Press, New York (1977)
7. Gupta, D., Jalote, P., Barua, G.: A formal framework for on-line software version change. IEEE Transactions on Software Engineering 22(2), 120–131 (1996)
8. Tai, K.-C.: The tree-to-tree correction problem. J. ACM 26(3), 422–433 (1979)
9. Zhang, K., Shasha, D.: Simple fast algorithms for the editing distance between trees and related problems. SIAM J. Comput. 18(6), 1245–1262 (1989)
10. Tip, F.: A survey of program slicing techniques. Journal of programming languages 3, 121–189 (1995)
11. Jagannathan, S., Weeks, S.: A unified treatment of flow analysis. In: Conference Record of 22nd Annual Symposium on Principles of Programming Languages, pp. 393–407 (1995)
12. Shivers, O.: Control-Flow Analysis of Higer-Order Languages. PhD thesis, Carnegie Mellon University (May 1991)
13. Gilmore, S., Kirli, D., Walon, C.: Dynamic ML without dynamic types. Technical Report ECS-LFCS-97-378, Laboratory for the Foundations of Computer Science, The University of Edinburgh (December 1997)
14. Bierman, G., Hicks, M., Sewell, P., Stoyle, G.: Formalizing dynamic software updating. In: Proceedings of the Second International Workshop on Unanticipated Software Evolution (USE), April 2003 (2003)
15. Duggan, D.: Type-based hot swapping of running modules. In: Proc. International Conference on Functional Programming, pp. 62–73 (2001)

Automata-Based Confidentiality Monitoring*

Gurvan Le Guernic[1,2], Anindya Banerjee[2],
Thomas Jensen[1], and David A. Schmidt[2]

[1] IRISA - Campus universitaire de Beaulieu, 35042 Rennes - France
{Gurvan.Le_Guernic, jensen}@irisa.fr
[2] Kansas State University - Manhattan, KS 66506 - USA
{ab,schmidt}@cis.ksu.edu

Abstract. Non-interference is typically used as a baseline security policy to formalize confidentiality of secret information manipulated by a program. In contrast to static checking of non-interference, this paper considers dynamic, automaton-based, monitoring of information flow for a single execution of a sequential program. The monitoring mechanism is based on a combination of dynamic and static analyses. During program execution, abstractions of program events are sent to the automaton, which uses the abstractions to track information flows and to control the execution by forbidding or editing dangerous actions. The mechanism proposed is proved to be sound, to preserve executions of well-typed programs (in the security type system of Volpano, Smith and Irvine), and to preserve some *safe* executions of ill-typed programs.

1 Introduction

With the intensification of communication in information systems, interest in security has increased. This paper deals with the problem of confidentiality, more precisely with *non-interference* in sequential programs. This notion has first been introduced by Goguen and Meseguer [1] as the absence of *strong dependency* [2].

A sequential program, P, is said to be *non-interfering* if the values of its public (or low) outputs do not depend on the values of its secret (or high) inputs. Formally, non-interference of P is expressed as follows: given any two initial input states σ_1 and σ_2 that are indistinguishable with respect to low inputs, the executions of P started in states σ_1 and σ_2 are *low-indistinguishable*; i.e. there is no observable difference in the public outputs. In the simplest form of the *low-indistinguishable* definition, public outputs include only the final values of low variables. In a more general setting, the definition may additionally involve intentional aspects such as power consumption, computation times, etc.

Static analyses for non-interference have been studied extensively and are well surveyed by Sabelfeld and Myers [3]. The *novelty* of the approach developed in this paper lies in:

* Banerjee and Le Guernic were partially supported by NSF grants CNS-0627748, CNS-0209205, CCF-0296182 and ITR-0326577. Schmidt was partially supported by NSF grants ITR-0326577 and ITR-0086154. Le Guernic was also partially supported by the *PoTestAT* project (*ACI Sécurité*).

M. Okada and I. Satoh (Eds.): ASIAN 2006, LNCS 4435, pp. 75–89, 2007.
© Springer-Verlag Berlin Heidelberg 2007

1. its ability to give a judgment for a *single execution alone* and not only for *all the executions of a program as a whole*,
2. the monitoring mechanism used to ensure the confidentiality of secret data.

The bulk of previous research [4, 5, 6, 7, 8, 9, 10, 11] associates the notion of non-interference to a program and develops static analyses that accept a *program* only if *all its executions* ensure the confidentiality of secrets. In contrast, this paper presents a *dynamic analysis that uses the results of a static analysis*: the dynamic analysis accepts or rejects a *single execution* of a program without necessarily doing the same for all other executions. The monitoring mechanism introduced guarantees confidentiality of secret data: either the monitor deduces that the current execution is non-interfering or it alters the behavior of the execution to obtain a non-interfering execution. The feasibility of this approach is shown by Hamlen et al. [12] who prove that any policy that can be statically asserted is enforceable using monitors which have access to the program's source.

There are three main benefits to using a monitoring mechanism rather than a static analysis. First, the security levels of inputs and outputs may be different from one execution to another; and a monitoring mechanism lets the security levels vary before each execution while still enforcing non-interference. For example, consider the effect of monitoring the Unix command **more** that takes as input a file divided into blocks and displays the blocks sequentially while waiting for the user to press a key between each block. A monitor for **more** would display a block only if the security level of the block is lower than the security level of the user; otherwise a default security message will be displayed. The monitor behavior depends on the particular file given as input, *not on all possible inputs*. This feature makes the monitoring mechanism a "lazy" polyvariant static analysis. A second benefit of monitors is their ability to safely use a program which has not been proved to respect a given property — maybe because one of its executions does not respect it; the monitor can run the *safe executions* — i.e. non-interferent executions — of an *unsafe program*. Finally, a monitoring mechanism follows the precise control flow of a program and thus calculation of control dependences (as might be performed in static analyses) can be more accurate. Section 5 contains an example showing how the work presented in this paper benefits from this improved accuracy.

A distinguishing feature of this dynamic analysis, compared to other program monitors, lies in the property overseen. Monitoring information flow is more complicated than, *e.g.*, monitoring divisions by zero, since it must take into account not only the current state of the program but also the execution paths *not taken* during execution. For example, executions of the following programs (a) **if** h **then** x :=1 **else** **skip** and (b) **if** h **then** **skip** **else** **skip** in an initial state where h is **false** are equivalent concerning executed commands. In contrast, (b) is obviously a non-interfering program, while (a) is not. The execution of (a), with a low-equivalent initial state where h is **true** and x is 0, does not give the same final value for the low output x.

This paper presents the semantics of a confidentiality monitoring mechanism which is proved to be sound. This mechanism is useful, for example, for the execution of programs downloaded from untrusted sources. Based on the semantics presented here, the monitoring mechanism can be implemented as a program transformation or as a virtual machine. To the best of our knowledge, this work is the first that presents a non-interference monitoring mechanism supported by formal proofs of soundness. Because of its dynamic nature, the mechanism is more expressive than the non-interference type system of Volpano et al. [11]. The next section defines terminology and introduces the scope of the work. Section 3 defines the monitoring semantics, which is automata-based. The properties of monitored executions and a comparison with type systems are contained in Sect. 4. Section 5 discusses related work and concludes. Proofs of theorems in this paper can be found in the companion technical report [13].

2   Language and Non-interference Monitoring Principles

The work presented aims at monitoring executions in order to enforce *non-interference*. The novelty and difficulty of this objective, compared to standard works on monitoring, lies in the monitoring mechanism. Monitors which see executions as a sequence of executed actions, like standard execution monitors [14], are not sufficient to enforce non-interference. This particular point is supported by works of McLean and Schneider. McLean [15] proved that information flow policies equivalent to non-interference are not *properties*; and Schneider [14] concluded that execution monitors are limited to the enforcement of *properties*. An information theoretic viewpoint why this is the case is given by Ashby:

> "the information carried by a particular message depends on the set it comes from. The information conveyed is not an intrinsic property of the individual message." [16, § 7/5 page 124].

In order to enforce strong constraints on the information flow (like non-interference), the monitoring mechanism must be aware of the commands that are *not* evaluated by a given execution [17, Sect. 4.2.2]. This is part of the approach taken in the work presented in this paper. Conceptually, the monitor has a partial access to the target program's source code.

The notion of non-interference is intrinsically linked to the notion of information flow. This paper distinguishes three types of information flows: *direct flows* from the right part to the left part (or target) of assignments, *explicit indirect flows* from the *context* of execution to targets of *executed* assignments and *implicit indirect flows* from the *context* of execution to targets of *un-executed* assignments. The *context* of execution of a command is the set of entities that influence whether this command is executed or not.

The language: syntax and semantics. We study a simple imperative sequential language with loops and outputs. The work proposed in this paper can be extended to more complex languages. The main requirement is to have a precise knowledge of the control flow. The grammar of the studied language follows:

$$A ::= x := e \mid \textbf{skip} \mid \textbf{output } e$$
$$B ::= \textbf{if } e \textbf{ then } S \textbf{ else } S \textbf{ end} \mid \textbf{while } e \textbf{ do } S \textbf{ done}$$
$$S ::= S \; ; \; S \mid B \mid A$$

The only constraints put on expressions (e) are that their evaluation must be deterministic and without side effects. Statements (S) are either sequences ($S \; ; \; S$), conditionals and while loops (B), or atomic actions (A). The output statement, "$\textbf{output } e$", is a generic statement used to represent any kind of public (or low) output, e.g., the action of printing the value of expression e on the terminal, producing a sound, or laying out a new window on the desktop. Only public outputs (i.e. outputs that are visible by standard users) are coded with the output statement; secret outputs are simply ignored. For example, sending a message m on a public network is represented by "$\textbf{output } m$," but sending an encrypted message n on a public network is abstracted by "$\textbf{output } c$", where c is a constant which emphasizes the fact that the content of an encrypted message cannot be revealed. Finally, sending a message on a private network, to which standard users do not have access, does not appear in the code of the programs studied.

Non-terminating executions leaks information through timing channels; such channels are not in the scope of this work. Consequently, the paper focuses on terminating executions, which allows the use of big-step operational semantics (also called *natural semantics* [18]). The standard semantics of the language (Fig. 2) is described using evaluation rules, written $\sigma \vdash S \xrightarrow{o} \sigma'$. This reads as follows: statement S executed in state σ yields state σ' and *output sequence o*. Let $\mathbb{D}$ be the semantic domain of values, and $\mathbb{X}$ the domain of variables. The definition of program states ($\mathbb{X} \to \mathbb{D}$) is extended to expressions, so that $\sigma(e)$ is the value of the expression e in state σ. An output sequence is a word in $\mathbb{D}^\star$.

$$\sigma \vdash x := e \xrightarrow{\epsilon} \sigma[x \mapsto \sigma(e)] \qquad \sigma \vdash \textbf{output } e \xrightarrow{\sigma(e)} \sigma \qquad \sigma \vdash \textbf{skip} \xrightarrow{\epsilon} \sigma$$

$$\frac{\sigma \vdash S_1 \xrightarrow{o_1} \sigma' \quad \sigma' \vdash S_2 \xrightarrow{o_2} \sigma''}{\sigma \vdash S_1 \; ; \; S_2 \xrightarrow{o_1 \, o_2} \sigma''} \qquad \frac{\sigma(e) = v \quad \sigma \vdash S_v \xrightarrow{o} \sigma'}{\sigma \vdash \textbf{if } e \textbf{ then } S_{\text{true}} \textbf{ else } S_{\text{false}} \textbf{ end} \xrightarrow{o} \sigma'}$$

$$\frac{\sigma(e) = \textbf{true}}{\sigma \vdash S \; ; \; \textbf{while } e \textbf{ do } S \textbf{ done} \xrightarrow{o} \sigma'} \qquad \frac{\sigma(e) = \textbf{false}}{\sigma \vdash \textbf{while } e \textbf{ do } S \textbf{ done} \xrightarrow{\epsilon} \sigma}$$

Fig. 1. Semantics outputting the values of low-outputs

The monitoring principles. Non-interference formalizes that there is no information flow from secret (or high) inputs to public (or low) outputs. For any program P, let $\mathcal{S}(\text{P}) \subseteq \mathbb{X}$ be the set of variables whose initial values are the secret inputs. The only public output is the output sequence resulting from the execution. Contrary to the majority of works on non-interference, the values of the variables in the program state are never *directly* accessible (even at the end of the execution). Consequently, the values of the variables in the program state are never considered public outputs. We made this choice in order to be more flexible with regard to what is considered as publicly accessible. All, and only, the values which are visible to low users must be displayed using an output statement at the position inside the program where they are visible. If the desired behavior is that low users have access to the values of low variables at the end of the execution, those values must be output at the end of the program.

The main monitoring mechanism principle is based on information transmission notions of classical information theory [16]. Cohen states it as follows:

"information can be transmitted from a to b over execution of H [(a sequence of actions)] if, by suitably varying the initial value of a (exploring the variety in a), the resulting value in b after H's execution will also vary (showing that the variety is conveyed to b)." [2, Sect. 3].

Hence, for preventing information flows from secret inputs to public outputs, the monitoring mechanism must ensure that variety — which can be seen as the property of variability or mutability — of the initial values of the variables in the set $\mathcal{S}(P)$ is not conveyed to the output sequence. This means that the monitoring mechanism, which works on a single execution, must ensure that even if the initial values of the variables belonging to $\mathcal{S}(P)$ were different, the output sequence would be identical.

The monitoring automaton has two jobs. The first is to track "variety," that is, to track entities (program variables, program counter, ...) having different values when the initial values of variables in $\mathcal{S}(P)$ are different. Its second job is to prevent conveying of variety to the output sequence, that is, to ensure that the output sequence would be identical for any execution having the same public inputs (the initial values of the variables not in $\mathcal{S}(P)$). To complete the first job, the states of the monitoring automaton are pairs. The first element of this pair is a set of variables. At any step of the computation, it contains all the variables that have "variety" (i.e., have a different value if the initial values of the variables belonging to $\mathcal{S}(P)$ are different). The second element of the pair is a word in $\{\top, \bot\}^\star$. This word tracks "variety" in the context of the execution (the value of the program counter). The second job (avoiding transfer of variety to the output sequence) is accomplished by authorizing, denying, or editing output statements depending on the current state of the monitoring automaton.

3   Definition of the Monitoring Mechanism

The monitoring mechanism is divided into two main elements. The first is an automaton similar to *edit automata* [19]. Inputs to the automaton are abstractions of the actions accomplished during an execution. The automaton tracks information flow and authorizes, forbids or edits the actions of the monitored execution to enforce non-interference. The second element of the monitoring mechanism is a semantics of monitored executions that merges together the behavior of the monitoring automaton and that of the standard output semantics in Fig. 2.

3.1 The Automaton

The automaton's transition function is independent of the monitored program, but the initial automaton's state is not. The automaton enforcing non-interference is the tuple $\mathcal{A}(P) = (Q, \Phi, \Psi, \delta, q_0)$ where: Q is a set of states $(Q = 2^X \times \{\top, \bot\}^*)$, Φ is the input alphabet, Ψ is the output alphabet, δ is a transition function $(Q \times \Phi) \longrightarrow (\Psi \times Q)$, and $q_0 \in Q$ is the start state $(q_0 = (\mathcal{S}(P), \epsilon))$.

An automaton state is a pair (V, w). $V \subseteq X$ contains all the variables whose current value *may* have been influenced by the initial values of the variables in $\mathcal{S}(P)$; w, which belongs to $\{\top, \bot\}^*$, can be seen as a stack that tracks variety in the context of the execution. In our approach, the context consists of only the program counter's value. If $\top$ occurs in w, then the statement executed belongs to a conditional whose test may have been influenced by the initial values of $\mathcal{S}(P)$. Hence the statement may not have been executed for a different choice of initial values of $\mathcal{S}(P)$. The input alphabet of the automaton (Φ) consists of abstractions of events that occur during an execution. It is defined below. The output alphabet (Ψ) is composed of the following: ACK, OK, NO, and atomic actions of the language. An atomic action is the answer of the monitoring automaton whenever an action other than the current one has to be executed.

Figure 2 specifies the transition function of the automaton. A transition is written $(q, \phi) \xrightarrow{\psi} q'$. It reads as follows: in the state q, on reception of the input ϕ, the automaton moves to state q' and outputs ψ. Let $\mathcal{V}(e)$ be the set of variables occurring in e and *modified*(S) be the set of all variables whose value may be modified by an execution of S.

Figure 2 shows that the automaton forbids (NO) or edits (**output** θ) only executions of output statements. For other inputs, it merely tracks, in the set V, the variables that may contain secret information (have *variety*), and it tracks, in w, the *variety* of the branching conditions.

Inputs "**branch** e" are generated at exit point of conditionals. On reception of such inputs in state (V, w), the automaton checks if the value of the branching condition (e) might be influenced by the initial values of $\mathcal{S}(P)$: only if some variable occurring in e belongs to V. If this is the case then the automaton pushes $\top$ at the end of w; otherwise it pushes $\bot$. In either case, the automaton acknowledges the reception of the input by outputting ACK.

Whenever execution exits a branch — which is a member of a conditional c — the input "**exit**" is sent to the automaton. The last letter of w is then removed. As any such input matches a previous input "**branch** e" — generated by the same conditional c — which adds a letter to the end of w, the effect of "**exit**" is to restore the context to its state before the conditional was processed.

Inputs "**not** S" are generated at exit point of conditionals. It means that, due to the value of a previous branching condition, statement S has not been executed. This detects *implicit indirect flows*. On input "**not** S" in state (V, w),

$$modified(x := e) = \{x\}$$
$$modified(\textbf{output } e) = modified(\textbf{skip}) = \emptyset$$
$$modified(S_1 \ ; \ S_2) = modified(S_1) \cup modified(S_2)$$
$$modified(\textbf{if } e \textbf{ then } S_1 \textbf{ else } S_2 \textbf{ end}) = modified(S_1) \cup modified(S_2)$$
$$modified(\textbf{while } e \textbf{ do } S \textbf{ done}) = modified(S)$$

$$((V,w), \textbf{branch } e) \xrightarrow{ACK} (V, w\top) \qquad \text{iff } \mathcal{V}(e) \cap V \neq \emptyset$$
$$((V,w), \textbf{branch } e) \xrightarrow{ACK} (V, w\bot) \qquad \text{iff } \mathcal{V}(e) \cap V = \emptyset$$
$$((V,wa), \textbf{exit}) \xrightarrow{ACK} (V, w)$$
$$((V,w), \textbf{not } S) \xrightarrow{ACK} (V \cup modified(S), w) \qquad \text{iff } w \notin \{\bot\}^\star$$
$$((V,w), \textbf{not } S) \xrightarrow{ACK} (V, w) \qquad \text{iff } w \in \{\bot\}^\star$$
$$((V,w), \textbf{skip}) \xrightarrow{OK} (V, w)$$
$$((V,w), x := e) \xrightarrow{OK} (V \cup \{x\}, w) \qquad \text{iff } w \notin \{\bot\}^\star \text{ or } \mathcal{V}(e) \cap V \neq \emptyset$$
$$((V,w), x := e) \xrightarrow{OK} (V \setminus \{x\}, w) \qquad \text{iff } w \in \{\bot\}^\star \text{ and } \mathcal{V}(e) \cap V = \emptyset$$
$$((V,w), \textbf{output } e) \xrightarrow{OK} (V, w) \qquad \text{iff } w \in \{\bot\}^\star \text{ and } \mathcal{V}(e) \cap V = \emptyset$$
$$((V,w), \textbf{output } e) \xrightarrow{\text{output } \theta} (V, w) \qquad \text{iff } w \in \{\bot\}^\star \text{ and } \mathcal{V}(e) \cap V \neq \emptyset$$
$$((V,w), \textbf{output } e) \xrightarrow{NO} (V, w) \qquad \text{iff } w \notin \{\bot\}^\star$$

Fig. 2. Transition function of monitoring automata

the automaton verifies whether S may have been executed with differing values for $\mathcal{S}(P)$. This is the case if the context of execution carries *variety* (i.e. if w does not belong to $\{\bot\}^\star$). Let (V', w') be the new state of the automaton. If the context carries *variety* then V' is the union of V with the set of variables whose values may be modified by an execution of S. Otherwise, nothing is done.

Atomic actions (assignment, skip or output) are sent to the automaton for validation before their execution. The atomic action **skip** is considered safe because the non-interference definition considered in this work is not time sensitive. Hence the automaton always authorizes its execution by outputting OK.

When executing an assignment $(x := e)$, two types of flows are created. The first is a direct flow from e to x. The second flow is an explicit indirect flow from the context of execution to x. For example, the execution of the assignment in "**if** b **then** $x := y$ **else skip end**" creates such a flow from b to x. Both forms of flows are *always* created when an assignment is executed. What is important is to check if secret information is carried by one of the flows (i.e., if variety in $\mathcal{S}(P)$ is conveyed by one of the flows). Hence, on input $x := e$, the automaton checks if the value of the *origin* of one of those two flows is influenced by the initial values of $\mathcal{S}(P)$. For instance, if b is true in "**if** b **then** $x := y$ **else skip end**", y is the origin of a direct flow to x and b is the origin of an explicit indirect flow to x. The origin of the explicit indirect flow is influenced by $\mathcal{S}(P)$ only if w contains $\top$, meaning that the condition of a previous (but still active) conditional was potentially influenced by the initial values of $\mathcal{S}(P)$. The origin of the direct flow is influenced by $\mathcal{S}(P)$ only if $\mathcal{V}(e)$ and V are not disjoint. If the value of e is influenced by the initial values of $\mathcal{S}(P)$ then at least one of the variables appearing in e has been influenced by $\mathcal{S}(\mathtt{P})$. Such variables are members of V. Let (V', w') be the new automaton state after the transition. If the origin of either the direct flow or the explicit indirect flow is influenced by the initial values of $\mathcal{S}(\mathtt{P})$, then x (the variable modified) is added to V: $V' = V \cup \{x\}$. On the other hand, if none of the origins are influenced by the initial values of $\mathcal{S}(\mathtt{P})$, then x receives a new value which is not influenced by $\mathcal{S}(\mathtt{P})$. In that case, V' equals $V \setminus \{x\}$. This makes the mechanism flow-sensitive.

The rules for the automata input, "**output** e," prevent bad flows through two different channels. The first one is the actual content of what is output. In a public context, $(w \in \{\bot\}^\star)$, if the program tries to output a secret (i.e., the intersection of V and the variables in e is not empty), then the value of the output is replaced by a default value. This value can be a message informing the user that, for security reasons, the output has been denied. To do so, the automaton outputs a new output statement to execute in place of the current one. The second channel is the behavior of the program itself. This channel exists because, depending on the path followed, some outputs may or may not be executed. Hence, if the automaton detects that this output may not be executed with different values for $\mathcal{S}(\mathtt{P})$ (the context carries *variety*) then *any* output must be forbidden; and the automaton outputs NO.

3.2   The Semantics

The semantics merging the standard output semantics in Fig. 2 with the monitoring automaton is given in Fig. 3. The semantics is described using evaluation rules written: $(q, \sigma) \Vdash S \overset{o}{\Rightarrow} (q', \sigma')$. This reads: statement S executed in automaton state q and program state σ yields automaton state q', program state σ', and output sequence o. There are three rules for atomic actions: **skip**, $x := e$ and **output** e. There is one rule for each possible automaton answer to the action executed. Either the automaton authorizes the execution (OK), denies the execution (NO), or replaces the action by another one. The rules use the standard semantics (Fig. 2) when an action must be executed. In the case where the execution is denied, the evaluation omits the current action (as if the action was "skip"). For the case where, on reception of input A, the monitoring automaton returns A', the monitoring semantics executes A' instead of A. Note from Fig. 2, that A' can only be the action that outputs the default value (**output** θ).

For conditionals, the evaluation begins by sending to the automaton the input "**branch** e" where e is the test of the conditional. Then, the branch designated by e is executed (in the case of a while statement whose test is **false**, the branch executed is "**skip**"). The execution follows by sending the automaton input "**not** S" where S is the branch not executed (in case of a while statement whose test is **true**, what happens is equivalent to sending the automaton input "**not skip**"). Finally, the input "**exit**" is sent to the automaton and the execution proceeds as usual. In the case of a while statement with a condition equals to **true**, the execution proceeds by executing the while statement once again.

$$\frac{(q, A) \xrightarrow{OK} q' \qquad \sigma \vdash A \xRightarrow{o} \sigma'}{(q, \sigma) \Vdash A \xRightarrow{o} (q', \sigma')} \qquad \frac{(q, A) \xrightarrow{A'} q' \qquad \sigma \vdash A' \xRightarrow{o} \sigma'}{(q, \sigma) \Vdash A \xRightarrow{o} (q', \sigma')} \qquad \frac{(q, A) \xrightarrow{NO} q}{(q, \sigma) \Vdash A \xRightarrow{\epsilon} (q, \sigma)}$$

$$\frac{(q, \sigma) \Vdash S_1 \xRightarrow{o_1} (q_1, \sigma_1) \qquad (q_1, \sigma_1) \Vdash S_2 \xRightarrow{o_2} (q_2, \sigma_2)}{(q, \sigma) \Vdash S_1 \, ; \, S_2 \xRightarrow{o_1 \, o_2} (q_2, \sigma_2)}$$

$$\frac{\sigma(e) = v \quad (q, \text{branch } e) \xrightarrow{ACK} q_1 \quad (q_1, \sigma) \Vdash S_v \xRightarrow{o} (q_2, \sigma_1) \quad (q_2, \text{not } S_{\neg v}) \xrightarrow{ACK} q_3 \quad (q_3, \text{exit}) \xrightarrow{ACK} q_4}{(q, \sigma) \Vdash \text{if } e \text{ then } S_{\text{true}} \text{ else } S_{\text{false}} \text{ end} \xRightarrow{o} (q_4, \sigma_1)}$$

$$\frac{\sigma(e) = \text{true} \quad (q, \text{branch } e) \xrightarrow{ACK} q_1 \quad (q_1, \sigma) \Vdash S \xRightarrow{o_l} (q_2, \sigma_1) \quad (q_2, \text{exit}) \xrightarrow{ACK} q_3 \quad (q_3, \sigma_1) \Vdash \text{while } e \text{ do } S \text{ done} \xRightarrow{o_w} (q_4, \sigma_2)}{(q, \sigma) \Vdash \text{while } e \text{ do } S \text{ done} \xRightarrow{o_l \, o_w} (q_4, \sigma_2)}$$

$$\frac{\sigma(e) = \text{false} \quad (q, \text{branch } e) \xrightarrow{ACK} q_1 \quad (q_1, \text{not } S) \xrightarrow{ACK} q_2 \quad (q_2, \text{exit}) \xrightarrow{ACK} q_3}{(q, \sigma) \Vdash \text{while } e \text{ do } S \text{ done} \xRightarrow{\epsilon} (q_3, \sigma)}$$

Fig. 3. Semantics of monitored executions

3.3 Example of Monitored Execution

Table 1 is an example of monitored execution. The monitored program is given in column "Program P". Its inputs are h and l. The execution monitored is the one for which h equals true and l equals 22. $\mathcal{S}(P)$, the set of secret inputs of P, is $\{h\}$. So the initial state of the automaton is $(\{h\}, \epsilon)$. Column "input" contains the inputs which are sent to the automaton, "output" contains the output sent back to the semantics, and "new state" shows the *new* internal state of the automaton *after* the transition. Finally, the last column shows the actions which are really fulfilled by the monitored execution.

Table 1. Example of the automaton evolution during an execution

Program P	Automaton: input	output	new state	Actions executed
1 x := l + 3;	x := l + 3	OK	$(\{h\}, \epsilon)$	x := l + 3
2 if (x > 10) then	branch x > 10	ACK	$(\{h\}, \bot)$	
3 y := h;	y := h	OK	$(\{h,y\}, \bot)$	y := h
4 output x;	output x	OK	$(\{h,y\}, \bot)$	output x
5 output y;	output y	output θ	$(\{h,y\}, \bot)$	output θ
6 if (h) then	branch h	ACK	$(\{h,y\}, \bot\top)$	
7 z := 0;	z := 0	OK	$(\{h,y,z\}, \bot\top)$	z := 0
8 output x	output x	NO	$(\{h,y,z\}, \bot\top)$	
9 else x := 1	not x := 1	ACK	$(\{h,y,z,x\}, \bot\top)$	
10 end	exit	ACK	$(\{h,y,z,x\}, \bot)$	
11 else skip	not skip	ACK	$(\{h,y,z,x\}, \bot)$	
12 end	exit	ACK	$(\{h,y,z,x\}, \epsilon)$	

In this example, there are only two alterations of the execution (on lines 5 and 8). The first occurs when the program attempts to output a value influenced by $\mathcal{S}(\mathsf{P})$ – **output** y. At this point of the execution, the value contained in y has been influenced by the initial values of the variables belonging to $\mathcal{S}(\mathsf{P})$. This is known because y belongs to the first element of the automaton state *before* execution of line 5. Consequently, the automaton disallows the output of this value. However, the fact of outputting something in itself is safe because the context of execution (the program counter) has not been influenced by $\mathcal{S}(\mathsf{P})$ (the second element of the automaton state belongs to $\{\perp\}^\star$). Hence, the automaton replaces the current action by an output action whose value is a default one (therefore not influenced by $\mathcal{S}(\mathsf{P})$). This value lets the user know that an output action has been denied for security reasons.

On line 8, the program tries to output something while the current context of execution has been influenced by $\mathcal{S}(\mathsf{P})$. Hence, if the output occurs, the sequence generated by the execution is influenced by some secret values. Therefore the automaton denies any output; it does not even give another action to execute in place of the current one. The semantics does as if the action was "**skip**".

4   Properties of the Monitoring Mechanism

A first theorem states soundness: any monitored execution is a non-interfering execution. A second one states "pseudo-completeness": the monitor does not alter observable behavior of a non-trivial set of non-interfering executions. Complete proofs of these theorems can be found in the companion technical report [13].

Soundness. The soundness property is based on the notion of non-interference between the secret inputs and the output sequence of an execution. An execution is considered *safe* — knowing that the program's source is public — if and only if it does not convey the variety in its secret inputs to the sequence output, that is, if the secret inputs have no influence on the execution's outputs.

For all programs P, with set of secret inputs $\mathcal{S}(\mathsf{P})$, and value store σ, let $[\![\mathsf{P}]\!]\sigma$ be the output sequence obtained via the monitored execution of P in the initial state $((\mathcal{S}(\mathsf{P}), \epsilon), \sigma)$. This definition is formally stated as follows:

$$[\![\mathsf{P}]\!]\sigma = o \text{ if and only if } \exists\, q', \sigma' : ((\mathcal{S}(\mathsf{P}), \epsilon), \sigma) \Vdash \mathsf{P} \overset{o}{\Rightarrow} (q', \sigma')$$

The following theorem states that every monitored execution is *safe*, i.e. it is non-interfering. Let $\overset{X}{=}$ be an equivalence relation between value stores. Let $\sigma_1 \overset{X}{=} \sigma_2$ assert that σ_1 and σ_2 are indistinguishable for X, i.e., σ_1 and σ_2 associate the same value to every variable in X. Let X^c be the complement of set X in $\mathbb{X}$.

Theorem 1 (Soundness: monitored executions are non-interfering).
For all programs P, whose set of secret inputs is $\mathcal{S}(P)$, and value stores σ_1 and σ_2,

$$\sigma_1 \overset{\mathcal{S}(P)^c}{=} \sigma_2 \;\Rightarrow\; [\![P]\!]\sigma_1 = [\![P]\!]\sigma_2$$

Proof (sketch). The proof — which can be found in [13] — goes by induction on the derivation tree of $[\![P]\!]\sigma_1$. It relies on the fact that, after any "step" in the evaluation of $[\![P]\!]\sigma_1$ and "equivalent step" in the evaluation of $[\![P]\!]\sigma_2$, the automaton states of both executions are equal and the value stores are indistinguishable for the complement of the first element of the automaton states.

Pseudo-completeness. Thus any terminating monitored execution is non-interfering. However, to achieve this goal, the monitor sometimes modifies the output sequence of the execution. The sequence of outputs resulting from the execution of program P with initial state σ might differ according to the semantics used, the standard one (Fig. 2) or the monitoring semantics (Fig. 3). The sequel gives a lower bound on the set of non-interfering executions on which the monitoring mechanism has no impact. It shows that the mechanism proposed in this paper preserves the output sequence of any execution of a program which is well-typed under a security type system similar to the one of Volpano et al. [11].

Figure 4 shows the security type system. It is the same one as that of Volpano et al. [11] except for a small modification of the typing environment and the addition of a rule for output statements (which are not in the language of [11]). The typing environment, γ, prescribes types for identifiers and is extended to handle expressions. $\gamma(e)$ is the type of the expression e in the typing environment γ. The lattice of types used has only two elements and is defined using the reflexive relation $\leq$ $(L \leq H)$. L is the type for public data and H the type for secrets. A program P is well-typed if it can be typed under a typing environment γ in which every secret input is typed secret (i.e. $\forall x \in \mathcal{S}(P), \gamma(x) = H$).

$$\frac{\gamma(e) = \tau' \quad \tau' \leq \tau}{\gamma \vdash e : \tau} \qquad \frac{\gamma(x) = \tau' \quad \gamma \vdash e : \tau' \quad \tau \leq \tau'}{\gamma \vdash x := e : \tau \text{ cmd}} \qquad \frac{\tau \leq H}{\gamma \vdash \textbf{skip} : \tau \text{ cmd}}$$

$$\frac{\gamma \vdash e : L}{\gamma \vdash \textbf{output } e : L \text{ cmd}} \qquad \frac{\gamma \vdash S_1 : \tau \text{ cmd} \quad \gamma \vdash S_2 : \tau \text{ cmd}}{\gamma \vdash S_1 ; S_2 : \tau \text{ cmd}}$$

$$\frac{\gamma \vdash e : \tau' \quad \gamma \vdash S_1 : \tau' \text{ cmd} \quad \gamma \vdash S_2 : \tau' \text{ cmd} \quad \tau \leq \tau'}{\gamma \vdash \textbf{if } e \textbf{ then } S_1 \textbf{ else } S_2 \textbf{ end } : \tau \text{ cmd}} \qquad \frac{\gamma \vdash e : \tau' \quad \gamma \vdash S : \tau' \text{ cmd} \quad \tau \leq \tau'}{\gamma \vdash \textbf{while } e \textbf{ do } S \textbf{ done } : \tau \text{ cmd}}$$

Fig. 4. The type system used for comparison

The problem of non-interference is neither dynamically nor statically decidable. Consequently, the monitoring mechanism proposed in this paper is not complete or transparent. However, Theorem 2 states that the monitoring mechanism does not alter executions of well-typed programs. To show that the inclusion is strict, consider the following program: $x := h$; $x := 0$; **output** x. h is the only secret input. Every execution is non-interfering. But as the type system is flow insensitive, this program is ill-typed. However, the monitoring mechanism does not interfere with the outputs of this program while still guaranteeing that any monitored execution is non-interfering.

Theorem 2 (Monitoring preserves *type-safe* programs).
For all programs P with secret inputs $S(P)$, typing environments γ with variables belonging to $S(P)$ typed secret, types τ, and value stores σ and σ',

$$\left. \begin{array}{c} \gamma \vdash P : \tau\ cmd \\ \sigma \vdash P \overset{o}{\Rightarrow} \sigma' \end{array} \right\} \ \Rightarrow\ [\![P]\!]\sigma = o$$

Proof (sketch). The proof goes by induction on the derivation tree of the unmonitored evaluation of P. It relies on the fact that the unmonitored evaluation of any well-typed command is matched by an equivalent monitored evaluation.

5   Conclusion

This paper addresses the security problem of confidentiality from the point of view of non-interference. It presents a monitoring mechanism enforcing non-interference of any execution. This monitoring mechanism is based on a semantics that communicates with a security automaton. During the execution, the semantics generates automaton inputs abstracting the events occurring. The automaton tracks the flows of information between the secret inputs and the current value of the program's variables. It also validates the execution of atomic actions (mainly outputs) to ensure confidentiality of the secret inputs.

Because the monitoring mechanism enforces non-interference, it significantly differs from standard monitors [20,14]. Usually, monitors are only aware of statements which *are* really executed. With the mechanism proposed, when exiting a conditional, the branch which has *not* been executed is analyzed. This takes into account implicit indirect flows between the test of a conditional and those variables whose values would be modified by the execution of the branch which is not executed. As noticed — but not elaborated on — by Vachharajani et al. [17, Sect. 4.2.2], this feature is required in order to enforce non-interference.

Section 4 shows that any monitored execution is non-interfering. Thus a user having access to the low outputs of a monitored execution is unable to deduce anything about the values of the secret inputs. In addition, the monitoring mechanism is proved not to alter executions of a program which is well-typed under a type system similar to the one of Volpano, Smith and Irvine [11].

Future work, which is under way, addresses the extension of the monitoring mechanism to a concurrent setting that includes a synchronization command. The goal is to achieve more precision than a type system equivalent to, e.g., the concurrent one due to Smith and Volpano [21].

Related work. Reference monitors is a widely studied area [22, 23]. The use of automata to monitor "good behaviors" led Schneider to formalize reference monitors as *truncation automata* that enforce safety properties [14]; and develop, with Erlingsson, a monitoring tool called *SASI* [24]. Among other works on the subject, Hamlen et al. worked on an extension to the .NET Common Intermediate Language called *Mobile* [25]. Their extension supports a type system that certifies in-lined reference monitors. In a successful attempt to increase the power of monitors, Ligatti et al. [19] introduced monitors, based on *edit automata*, able to modify the sequence of actions executed and to enforce *infinite renewal properties* [26]. Such properties include every safety property, some liveness properties and some properties that are neither. Because such monitors are limited to the enforcement of *trace* properties, it is not immediately obvious that they can handle non-interference (which is not a *trace* property).

The vast majority of research on non-interference concerns static analyses and involves type systems [27, 3]. Some "real size" languages together with security type system have been developed (for example, JFlow/JIF [5] and FlowCaml [6]).

Information flow monitoring is not as popular as static analyses for information flow, but there has been interesting research. For example, RIFLE [17] is a complete runtime information flow security system; which however lacks formal analysis and proofs. The majority of those works, including RIFLE, does not take into consideration flows created by un-executed commands. It has been shown [28] that this feature can be used to gain information about secrets in some cases. The only exception known by the authors – in the domain of information flow monitoring – is the work by Masri et al. [29] which presents a dynamic information flow analysis for structured or unstructured languages. However, their work does not study deeply the dynamic correction of "bad" flows and lacks formal statements and proofs of the correctness of the correction mechanism. The solution proposed is to stop the execution as soon as a potential flow from a secret data to a public *sink* is detected. In some cases, this can create a new covert channel revealing secret information — see, e.g., [28].

Benefits of monitoring compared to static analyses. Monitoring an execution has a cost. So, what are the main benefits of non-interference monitoring compared to static analyses? The first concerns the possibility that a monitoring mechanism can be used to change the security policy for each execution. In the majority of cases, running a static analysis before every execution would be more costly than using a monitor. The second reason is that non-interference is a rather strong property. Many programs are rejected by static analyses of non-interference. In such cases it is still possible to use a monitoring mechanism with the possibility that some executions will be altered by the monitoring mechanism. However behavior alteration is an intrinsic feature of any monitoring mechanism. Monitoring non-interference ensures confidentiality while still allowing testing with regard to other specifications using unmonitored executions as perfect oracle — at least as perfect as the original program.

There are two main reasons why it is interesting to use a non-interference monitor on a program rejected by a static analysis. The first one lies in the granularity of the non-interference property. Static analyses have to take into consideration all possible executions of the program analyzed. This implies that if a single execution is unsafe then the program (thus all its executions) is rejected. Whereas, even if some executions of a program are unsafe, a monitor still allows this program to be used. The unsafe executions, which are not useful, are altered to respect the desired property while the safe executions are still usable.

The second one is that a monitoring mechanism may be more precise than static analyses because during execution the monitoring mechanism gets some accurate information about the "path behavior" of the program. As an example, let us consider the following program where h is the only secret input and l the only other input (a public one).

```
if ( test1(l) ) then tmp := h else skip end;
if ( test2(l) ) then x := tmp else skip end;
output x
```

Without information on $test1$ and $test2$ (and often, even with), a static analysis would conclude that this program is unsafe because the secret input information could be carried to x through tmp and then to the output. However, if $test1$ and $test2$ are such that no value of l makes both predicates true, then any execution of the program is perfectly safe. In that case, the monitoring mechanism would allow any execution of this program. The reason is that, l being a public input, only executions following the same path as the current execution are taken care of by the monitoring mechanism. So, for such configurations where the branching conditions are not influenced by the secret inputs, a monitoring mechanism is at least as precise as any static analysis — and often more precise.

Acknowledgments. The authors are grateful to the reviewers for their remarks; and to Jay Ligatti, David Naumann and Andrei Sabelfeld for insightful and helpful comments on an earlier version of this paper.

References

1. Goguen, J.A., Meseguer, J.: Security Policies and Security Models. In: Proc. Symp. Security and Privacy, pp. 11–20 (1982)
2. Cohen, E.S.: Information Transmission in Computational Systems. ACM SIGOPS Operating Systems Review 11(5), 133–139 (1977)
3. Sabelfeld, A., Myers, A.C.: Language-Based Information-Flow Security. IEEE J. Selected Areas in Communications 21(1), 5–19 (2003)
4. Banerjee, A., Naumann, D.A.: Stack-based Access Control and Secure Information Flow. Journal of Functional Programming 15(2), 131–177 (2005)
5. Myers, A.C.: JFlow: Practical Mostly-Static Information Flow Control. In: Proc. ACM Symp. Principles of Programming Languages, pp. 228–241 (1999)
6. Pottier, F., Simonet, V.: Information flow inference for ML. ACM Trans. on Programming Languages and Systems 25(1), 117–158 (2003)
7. Abadi, M., Banerjee, A., Heintze, N., Riecke, J.G.: A Core calculus of Dependency. In: Proc. ACM Symp. Principles of Programming Languages, pp. 147–160 (1999)
8. Barthe, G., Serpette, B.: Partial evaluation and non-interference for object calculi. In: Middeldorp, A. (ed.) FLOPS 1999. LNCS, vol. 1722, pp. 53–67. Springer, Heidelberg (1999)
9. Sabelfeld, A., Sands, D.: A Per Model of Secure Information Flow in Sequential Programs. Higher Order and Symbolic Computation 14(1), 59–91 (2001)

10. Mizuno, M., Schmidt, D.: A Security Flow Control Algorithm and Its Denotational Semantics Correctness Proof. J. Formal Aspects of Comp. 4(6A), 727–754 (1992)
11. Volpano, D., Smith, G., Irvine, C.: A Sound Type System for Secure Flow Analysis. J. Computer Security 4(3), 167–187 (1996)
12. Hamlen, K.W., Morrisett, G., Schneider, F.B.: Computability classes for enforcement mechanisms. ACM Trans. Program. Lang. Syst. 28(1), 175–205 (2006)
13. Le Guernic, G., Banerjee, A., Schmidt, D.: Automaton-based Non-interference Monitoring. Technical Report, -1, Kansas State University, Manhattan, KS, USA (April 2006) (2006), http://www.cis.ksu.edu/schmidt/techreport/2006.list.html
14. Schneider, F.B.: Enforceable security policies. ACM Trans. Inf. Syst. Secur. 3(1), 30–50 (2000)
15. McLean, J.: A General Theory of Composition for Trace Sets Closed Under Selective Interleaving Functions. In: Proc. Symp. Security and Privacy, pp. 79–93 (1994)
16. Ashby, W.R.: An Introduction to Cybernetics. Chapman & Hall, London (1956)
17. Vachharajani, N., Bridges, M.J., Chang, J., Rangan, R., Ottoni, G., Blome, J.A., Reis, G.A., Vachharajani, M., August, D.I.: RIFLE: An Architectural Framework for User-Centric Information-Flow Security. In: Proc. Symp. Microarchitecture (2004)
18. Kahn, G.: Natural Semantics. In: Brandenburg, F.J., Wirsing, M., Vidal-Naquet, G. (eds.) STACS 87. LNCS, vol. 247, pp. 22–39. Springer, Heidelberg (1987)
19. Ligatti, J., Bauer, L., Walker, D.: Edit automata: enforcement mechanisms for run-time security policies. Int. J. Inf. Sec 4(1-2), 2–16 (2005)
20. Viswanathan, M.: Foundations for the Run-time Analysis of Software Systems. PhD thesis, University of Pennsylvania (December 2000)
21. Smith, G., Volpano, D.: Secure Information Flow in a Multi-threaded Imperative Language. In: Proc. ACM Symp. on Principles of Programming Languages (January 1998), pp. 355–364 (1998)
22. Schneider, F.B., Morrisett, G., Harper, R.: A Language-Based Approach to Security. In: Wilhelm, R. (ed.) Informatics. LNCS, vol. 2000, pp. 86–101. Springer, Heidelberg (2001)
23. Erlingsson, Ú.: The Inlined Reference Monitor Approach to Security Policy Enforcement. PhD thesis, Department of Computer Science, Cornell University (2003)
24. Erlingsson, Ú., Schneider, F.B.: SASI Enforcement of Security Policies: A Retrospective. In: Proc. New Security Paradigms Workshop, pp. 87–95. ACM Press, New York (1999)
25. Hamlen, K.W., Morrisett, G., Schneider, F.B.: Certified In-lined Reference Monitoring on .NET. In: ACM Workshop on Programming Languages and Analysis for Security, ACM Press, New York (2006)
26. Ligatti, J., Bauer, L., Walker, D.: Enforcing Non-safety Security Policies with Program Monitors. In: di Vimercati, S.d.C., Syverson, P.F., Gollmann, D. (eds.) ESORICS 2005. LNCS, vol. 3679, pp. 355–373. Springer, Heidelberg (2005)
27. Pottier, F.c., Conchon, S.: Information flow inference for free. In: Proc. ACM International Conf. on Functional Programming, pp. 46–57 (2000)
28. Le Guernic, G., Jensen, T.: Monitoring Information Flow. In: Proceedings of the Workshop on Foundations of Computer Security (June 2005), pp. 19–30. DePaul University (2005)
29. Masri, W., Podgurski, A., Leon, D.: Detecting and Debugging Insecure Information Flows. In: Symp. on Software Reliability Engineering, pp. 198–209 (2004)

Efficient and Practical Control Flow Monitoring for Program Security

Nai Xia, Bing Mao, Qingkai Zeng, and Li Xie

State Key Laboratory for Novel Software Technology
Nanjing University, 210093, Nanjing, China
{xianai, maobing, zqk, xieli}@nju.edu.cn

Abstract. Control-hijacking attacks are known as critical threats to software security. Control flow monitoring is a kind of important method to mitigate this problem. In this paper, we present a new method for program control flow monitoring. Based on the static analysis of a program, we apply very simple instrumentation of a program's source code to encode its runtime function level control flow traces and check the correctness of the traces in the OS kernel. Experiments show that this method has a tiny performance impact and is still highly effective in detecting control-hijacking attacks. We also propose to automatically handle non-standard control flow by learning programs' dynamic profiling data. Our method is hopeful to be enforceable in different environments because it does not depend closely on specific platform features and the underlying techniques can be easily found in many platforms.

Keywords: Control Flow, Dynamic Profiling, Program Vulnerability, Source Code Instrumentation, Static Analysis.

1 Introduction

Modern software trends to be inevitably embedded with vulnerabilities (e.g. buffer overflows [1], format string bugs [2]). An attacker exploits a program's vulnerabilities and hijacks the control flow by corrupting its control-sensitive data. Control-hijacking attacks have become one of the most critical security threats.

Over the years, many ingenious approaches have been proposed to mitigate control-hijacking attacks from different aspects. One kind of important method is control flow monitoring, such as Program Shepherding[3], Control Flow Integrity[4] (CFI) and some host-based intrusion detection techniques[5-12]. The basic idea behind the control flow monitoring methods is that the control flow of a program should obey some pre-determined rules, which are usually extracted either statically from the source/binary code or from the statistical results of the program's representative runs.

In this paper, we propose that the verification of function level control flow can be further simplified. Our key observation is that nearly all control-hijacking attacks eventually make use of system calls (either through shellcode or code in victim program) to achieve their ultimate goals. So if we could properly *encode* the control

M. Okada and I. Satoh (Eds.): ASIAN 2006, LNCS 4435, pp. 90–104, 2007.
© Springer-Verlag Berlin Heidelberg 2007

flow description between system calls, it is enough to verify the control flow just before any harmful system call is made. In this way, we do not need to make the time consuming control verification at every indirect control flow transfer. Besides the performance gain, the simplified instrumentation also brings about the benefit of applicability because the simplification makes the instrumentation code much less complex and platform dependent. As a proof of concept, we build our prototype using source code analysis. Meanwhile, when dealing with the implementation issue of non-standard control flow, we try to avoid exploiting too many platform dependent features by using dynamic profiling to achieve the automatic discovery of non-standard control flow. In short, we think our work has two major contributions:

1) We simplify the way of control flow verification with control flow encoding.
2) With dynamic profiling, we quantitively analyze the behavior of non-standard control flow for popular programs and achieve the automatic discovery of it.

The rest of the paper is organized as follows. In Section 2, we summarize the work related to ours. Section 3 presents our approach to monitor program control flow and the implementation details. Section 4 presents the experimental results and evaluation. And section 5 is our conclusion and discussion for future work.

2 Related Work

Our work is related to a broad range of approaches aiming to mitigate control-hijacking attacks. As the amount of the related work is rather huge, we decide to focus on the work using control flow monitoring.

Control flow monitoring for purpose of software security actually started in the form of intrusion detection. The control flow in those techniques is usually called as "application behavior". Dean and Wagner [5] firstly used static analysis of program source code to achieve "a high degree of automation, protection against a broad class of attacks based on corrupted code and the elimination of false alarms". In their method, the CFG of a program is extracted from a program source code and used to build the models for system calls, which are actually sets of pre-determined rules to be verified at runtime through system call interception. They also discuss about the non-standard control flow, which cannot be directly inferred from a program's CFG. Although they claimed that "some program properties that are difficult to infer statically may become easier to model satisfactorily when the burden is offloaded to a runtime agent, where available", the problem of non-standard control flow remains an ugly issue because it's less automatically solved and it may vary from implementation to implementation and platform to platform. More work in this area following this one incorporates additional program properties to improve the precision [6-10, 12] at the possible cost of performance or model complexity.

Program Shepherding [3] lowers the granularity of control flow description to function level and tries to verify the statically extracted CFG directly during the execution of a program. Its implementation is based on a program interpreter (translator) called Dynamo. A hash table is maintained to explicitly list the valid targets for an indirect control flow transfer. Extra checkpoints are added to handle non-standard control flow. The main limitation of this approach is its huge performance overhead (up to 660%). However, Program Shepherding supports other security policies (e.g. sandboxing) besides control flow monitoring.

Control-Flow Integrity [4] also defines the control flow at function level. Different from Program Shepherding, CFI extracts a program's CFG from the binary code and uses binary rewriting to inject x86 assembly instructions to the program for control flow verification. The verification mechanism is formally proved to never let one instruction of malicious code be executed. It is transparent because binary instrumentation does not need source code. It is also efficient because the instrumentation code size is relatively small (its measured overhead ranges from zero to 45%, at average of 16%). Our work is similar with CFI in that we also use code instrumentation to depict the control flow of a program at runtime and we also construct equivalence sets for the relation of indirect control transfer. However, our work differs from CFI in three important aspects:

- We do not verify the control flow of a program using instrumentation code. Instead, the instrumentation code is only used for the encoding of control flow. The work of verification is elevated to the place of system call entry.
- In order to make the model consistent with non-standard control flows, CFI (and many other approaches) exploits system specific features. While in our work, we learn the cases of non-standard control flow through program profiling.
- CFI does not rely on dynamic secrets. While in our work runtime randomization is needed to ensure security. Although the trick of runtime randomization was found vulnerable in some circumstances [13, 14], we make the secrets of our system easy to be re-randomized. As suggested by Sovarel et al., the enhancement of re-randomization can make secret based system insusceptible to incremental key breaking attacks.

There are other approaches trying to achieve software security by restricting program control flow, for example, IRM and SFI [15, 16] apply restrictions to control flow to ensure the proper enforcement of fine-grained security policies. And some approaches in area of fault-tolerance also verify the control flow of a program to detect transient or permanent faults in computer systems that can lead to incorrect sequence of instruction execution. As the aims of these methods deviate from the control-hijacking attacks, we do not consider them as closely related.

3 Efficient and Practical Control Flow Monitoring

3.1 Extraction of Static Control Flow Information

We use static analysis of program source code to determine the valid targets for each indirect control flow transfer. Due to the extensive use of pointers in real world C programs, the technique of point-to analysis (alias analysis) [17] is needed to narrow the range of each valid target set. We choose Steensgaard Analysis [18], which is common and scales well to large programs. The control flow that cannot be decided in program source code should be considered as non-standard control flow (e.g. an external function invoking a call back function). We will discuss about the handling of non-standard control flow later.

Note that binary analysis is another good alternative for extracting static control flow information with advantages of transparency. We choose source code analysis and instrumentation for ease of implementation.

3.2 Control Flow Encoding and Verification

3.2.1 Basic Description of Control Flow

If the execution of a program conforms to its static CFG, then at every point of indirect control flow transfer, the target should fall into a valid target set. Commonly, indirect control flow transfer refers to indirect function call or function return.

```
int  foo1()  /* ID = 1*/         int (*fptr)();
{                                int main(int argc)
  CAL_ACTUAL_CALL(1);            {
  CAL_EXPECTED_CALL(2);            if(argc < 2) fptr=foo1;
  foo2();                          else fptr=foo2;
  CAL_EXPECTED_RETURN(2);          /* some code */
  /* some code */                  CAL_EXPECTED_CALL(1|2);
  CAL_ACTUAL_RETURN(1);            (*fptr)();
  return 0;                        CAL_EXPECTED_RETURN(1|2);
}                                  return 0;
int foo2()   /* ID=2 */          }
{
  CAL_ACTUAL_CALL(2);            int foo3() /* ID =3 */
  CAL_EXPECTED_CALL(3);          {
  foo3();                          CAL_ACTUAL_CALL(3);
  CAL_EXPECTED_RETURN(3);          CAL_ACTUAL_RETURN(3);
  CAL_ACTUAL_RETURN(2);            return 0;
  return 0;                      }
}
```

Fig. 1. Example calculation for expected/actual call/return sequences

We view the control flow of a program as two sequences: *function call sequence*, which is the ordering of the functions called and *function return sequence*, which is the ordering of functions that have returned. So to verify the validness of a program execution is to verify the validness of these two sequences because it's trivial to see that attacks change at least one of these two sequences. We further introduced *expected call/return sequences* and *actual call/return sequences* to help the verification. The expected call/return sequences are calculated at every function call site and function return site respectively. Each item of an expected call sequences represents the possible targets of an indirect call, each item of expected return sequences represents the possible functions that may return to a return site. Each item of actual sequences is generated at function entry points and before functions' return to indicate respectively the actual function called and the function which is actually returning. In this paper, we denote the expected call sequence, expected return sequence, actual call sequence, actual return sequence as *expected_callseq*, *expected_returnseq*, *actual_callseq*, *actual_returnseq* respectively. The code in Figure.1 illustrates this idea. We define an execution sequence *seq* as follows:

$$seq = \{id_1 \mid ... \mid id_n\}, seq. \tag{1}$$

In the formula, *id* is a function's integral identification and the notion of $id_i \mid id_{i+1}$ means that there are several possible directions for one control flow transfer. If we assign each function an unique id value and assume that argc < 2, the execution sequences of the program in Figure.1 would be: expected_callseq={1|2;2;3}, actual_callseq={1;2;3}, expected_returnseq={3;2;1|2}, actual_returnseq={3;2;1}. We construct equivalence sets for functions and call/return sites. Thus we need to do only equality test for equivalence set *id* instead of doing "belongs to" test over all possible expected values. The rules for constructing equivalence sets are listed below and can be efficiently implemented with *Union-Find* algorithm:

- If two functions may be pointed to by the same function pointer, they are put into a same equivalence function set.
- If two equivalence function sets have intersection they are merged to one.
- If two functions that may be called by (or may return to) two different call sites (or return sites) belong to the same equivalence function set, these two call sites (return sites) should belong to the same equivalence call (return) set. The id of the corresponding equivalent function set is also assigned to the equivalent call (return) set.

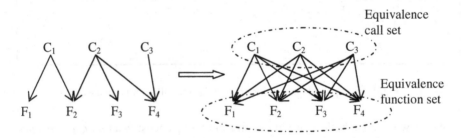

Fig. 2. Construction of equivalence sets

Figure 2 illustrates the construction of equivalence call sets and equivalence function sets, where C_x (x=1, 2, 3) represents call sites and F_x (x=1, ..., 4) represents functions. Each directed edge in this figure represents a "may call" relation between a call site and a function.

It is worthy to note that constructing equivalence sets brings about precision loss because of two cases:

- The merge of direct calls into equivalence call sets containing indirect calls (e.g. In Figure 2, the added edge from C_3 to F_3). Theoretically, there is no need to verify direct calls. The merge operation is only to keep direct calls compatible with indirect calls, because each function that may be called by indirect calls contains the calculation for actual call sequences and so needs a corresponding calculation for expected call sequences.
- The union of two equivalent sets having intersection but not identical (e.g. In Figure 2, the added edge from C_2 to F_1). It's trivial to see this is a precision loss because that makes more functions share the same id.

Table 1 presents the precision loss for several popular UNIX programs. The loss is measured by the percentage of the calls merged to other equivalence call sets. The result shows that it is reasonable to ignore this tiny precision loss. However, improving the precision of the alias analysis itself or using code duplication as proposed in CFI, may be two promising ways to further reduce the loss.

Table 1. Precision loss caused by construction of equivalence sets

	bash	ctags	gzip	jed	mc	opensshd	tar	vsftpd
LOC	104981	26654	7379	32735	73288	34815	16812	13145
DC	9633	2277	365	3323	8968	5465	1630	2206
MDC	572	0	0	5	112	274	0	0
M/D	5.93%	0	0	0.15%	1.24%	5.01%	0	0
IDC	77	1	4	58	53	103	11	2
MIDC	24	0	0	3	29	17	1	0
M/I	31.17%	0	0	5.17%	54.71%	16.50%	9.09%	0
AM/AC	6.13%	0	0	0.23%	1.56%	5.22%	0.06%	0

LOC: Lines of Code   DC: Direct Calls   MDC: Merged Direct Calls
M/D: MDC/DC   IDC: Indirect Calls   MIDC: Merged Indirect Calls
M/I: MIDC/IDC   AM/AC: All Merged calls /All calls

Another precision loss in our current work comes from the fact that it is valid for a function to return to any possible return sites. The precision loss could be reduced by enhancing our method with shadow call stack or similar techniques. We decide not to implement this enhancement at this moment until any practical attack exploiting this case is found in real world.

3.2.2 Control Flow Encoding and Verification

As we have mentioned in the introduction, we decide to do the verification job at the entry point of system calls. Since too many function calls may happen between two consecutive system calls, we encode the control flow by hashing the expected/actual call/return sequences into 4 integer values and then make the verification as simple as equality test of corresponding hash values. Suppose a control flow sequence is $X_n = \{x_1; x_2 \ldots x_n\}$, its hash value Y_n is computed as follows (where f is the hash function):

$$Y_n = \begin{cases} x_1 & n = 1 \\ f(Y_{n-1}, x_n) & n > 1 \end{cases}. \tag{2}$$

In order to achieve both good security and good performance, we must make sure that:

- The possibility of hash *collision* (i.e. different sequences hashing to same value) must be reasonably small.
- The hash algorithm must be simple enough to be easily inserted to programs with minimum cost.

We use rather simple approach to meet these requirements. We choose the function $f(x,y) = x+y$ as the hash function because in many platforms it is implemented as one machine instruction. Regarding the security requirement, we map at runtime the equivalence set *ids* sparsely to a very large space with randomization (same randomization is done for the addresses of hash variables). This trick is much less possible to be circumvented by "derandomization attack" [13, 14] than Address Space Layout Randomization[19] or instruction randomization[20] does. Because in their cases, one fundamental weakness is that a parent process and its child process may share the same secret key. This feature may enable the incremental guess of the secret key. While in our approach it is very easy to re-randomize the *ids* any time a program is running. So when an attack fails a guess, the *ids* could get *re-randomized* at once, eliminating the possibility of incremental brute-force attack.

We consider it enough hard to deduce all the randomized *ids* and the current hash values unless one can analyze the runtime image of a program, which is not a privilege acquired by most attackers (e.g. A normal user cannot use gdb to attach a privileged process). Even if an attacker can successfully get all the randomized information and hash collision does exist, it is still hard for him to exploit the collision because he has to exploit enough indirect control flows to construct a collision. And when his malicious system call happens and he must ensure there is no other system call in the way.

Note that since we take the system call entry as the verification point, this verification granularity makes it possible for the execution of system-call-free injected code. So there are two more cases we need to address:

1) It is possible for shellcode to jump back to the correct control flow after it finishes its execution. In this way, the execution of injected code is not detectable.

2) Just before an attacker triggers his malicious system call to change the system's state, it is theoretically possible that the injected code can analyze the process memory to "learn" and "mimic" the correct calculation of the hash values.

We do not consider them as severe problems because for case 1), neither the shellcode can achieve its aim though direct system call nor can it change the following control flow. Actually it is a case faced by all methods that do verification at system call entry points such as intrusion detection. None of the other methods even point it out as a consideration.

For case 2), it adds to the burden of any attacker to embed in injected code complex binary analyzing code. Given that usually the space for code injection is limited, it is not an easy job. Simple code obfuscation techniques [21] could be applied to further increase the difficulty.

Many modern platforms (e.g. SPARC, Alpha, PowerPC, IA-64, x86) support the feature of Non-Executable Data (NXD) which prevents the execution of injected shellcode [22] and thus remove the consideration of both case 1) and 2). So before we adopt further techniques to defeat the code analysis, the using of NXD depends on the choice of more security or more compatibility.

3.3 Handling of Non-standard Control Flow

Some control flow does not follow static program CFG. It's mainly because not all function calls are triggered at analyzable function call sites (e.g. signals handlers can be triggered by code other than the functions within a program). Every method using control flow monitoring needs to consider non-standard control flow. Although addressed in previous work, no automatic ways have been found to properly deal with this problem. In this paper, we take the first step to automatic handling of non-standard control flow. We discover the non-control flow of a program from its dynamic profiling data, and then use the result to re-instrument the program.

There are basically four kinds of non-standard control flow in our approach:

1) *Setjmp/longjmp. Longjmp* never returns to the next statement after its call sites. It returns to the next statement after a *setjmp* call site. So the expected return id after a *setjmp* call site should also be the id of *longjmp*.

2) *External library routines.* For pre-compiled external library functions, which are not analyzable in our approach, we create wrapper functions to do actual sequence calculation.

3) *Signal/exception handlers.* Functions acting as signal/exception handlers may either be called directly/indirectly in the program or be triggered by some non-function-call statement. So when they execute, there may be no calculation of expected call/return sequences that corresponds to the calculation of actual call/return sequences within the handler function.

4) Hook/callback functions. Hook or callback functions may be called either by the function within the same program source or by library routines. These functions bring about inconsistency of control flow sequences because of the similar reason in case 3).

Case 1) and case 2) can be automatically handled. Case 3) and case 4) present the challenge, because it is traditionally difficult to identify these cases by static analysis. We decide to discover non-standard control flow from representative runs of a program. So before a final instrumented program is generated, it is firstly instrumented to spill log data for non-standard control flow discovery. We call this instrumented version the program's *profiling version* while the final instrumented version its *detecting version*.

Observed that for standard control flow, one expected call sequence calculation is always followed by one actual call sequence calculation. So if there is no standard control flow violation, the hash value for expected call sequence should equal to that of actual call sequence just *before* any calculation of expected call sequence or *after* any calculation of actual call sequence. Similar feature holds when expected/actual return sequences get calculated. So the instrumentation for profiling version is straightforward: log all the difference between corresponding expected hash values and actual hash values. Then we apply enumeration analysis to the logged values because each difference represents a case of non-standard control.

In order to evaluate the effectiveness of our approach for discovering non-standard control flow and also quantify the precision loss, we experimented with a group of real world applications. To have a good coverage of different application types, these applications were classified by functionality as file utilities (gzip-1.3.5, tar-1.13), remote server programs (ghttpd-1.4, openssh-3.6, vsftpd-2.0.1), interactive programs (bash-3.1, mc-4.6.1, jed-0.99) and program syntax analyzer (ctags-5.5.4). These applications were run on representative inputs (e.g. using their test suit).

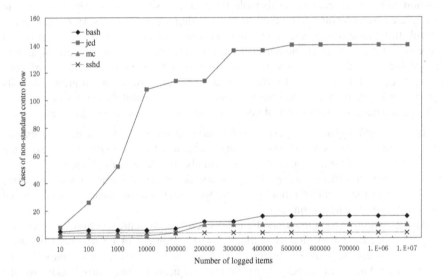

Fig. 3. Cases of non-standard control flow in real world application

The result shows that there is zero case of non-standard control flows detected in gzip, tar, vsftpd and ghttpd only because there are no direct/indirect call sites of signal handler and hook function in their source code. Figure 3 shows how the number of discovered cases of non-standard control flow increases in the other programs. We draw the following conclusions from the experiment results:

1) The number of the cases of non-standard control flow is directly related to an application's programming style. For example, the extensive use of hook functions in *jed* increases the number dramatically. Normally, the cases of non-standard control flow are rare and therefore the precision loss caused is very small compared with total calls.

2) The cases of non-standard control flow trend to repeat themselves but in a rather frequent way, so they should not be overlooked.

3)   The number of the cases of non-standard control flow converges at reasonable speed, so it can be considered that the time for the discovery of non-standard control flow is relatively small.

After the cases of non-standard control are lined out, a program is re-instrumented to final detecting version: the calculation code for expected/actual call sequences pairs which may correspond to a case of non-standard control flow is omitted to ensure non-standard control flow does not bring inconsistency.

Note that although the convergence of the non-standard control flow indicates that the cases that are not discovered by profiling trend to be rare, there can be time when some non-standard control flow function call is not triggered in the representative runs. So it is possible that new non-standard control flow cases emerge after the detecting version is created. We incorporate newly discovered cases of non-standard control flow by replacing the corresponding instrumented machine code with "NOP" instructions (thus there is no need for users to re-instrument the program and compile it). Just like software debugging, it may be hard to theoretically prove that all the ugly cases have been removed, but it is easy to satisfy users.

3.4   Implementation on x86 Linux

In this sub-section, we explain how we implement our first prototype on top of x86 Debian Linux sid.

Platform features required. As we use instrumentation code to encode a program's control flow, we must ensure that the encoding mechanism cannot be altered by an attacker. So the feature of non-writeable code is needed to ensure the integrity of program code. Non-writeable code is a popular and default setting on many platforms. In our work, we only temporarily *mmap* the code pages as writeable during initialization and when we need to re-randomize or to incorporate new cases of non-standard control flow. The encoding mechanism is under total protection of non-writeable code. Moreover, as we mentioned in previous sections, NXD is an optional platform feature that can strengthen our approach. Our current prototype makes use of NXD to maximize the security.

Analysis tool and code instrumentation. We build our source code analysis and instrumentation tool using the freely available C language transforming tool CIL [23]. CIL is directed to compute the point-to information, construct the equivalence sets and then generate instrumentation code either for profiling version or for detecting version. For profiling version, the code for expected/actual sequence calculation is generated as calls to a library function for profiling. While for detecting version, the corresponding code is generated as one-instruction inline assembly. Additional function call is also generated at the entry of *main* function for initialization whose job focuses mainly on the generation of address-randomized hash variables, randomizing equivalence set id values, rewriting of the instrumentation code and the initialization for the program's kernel *task_struct*.

Kernel patch. We patch the Linux kernel 2.4.32 for control flow verification. The algorithm is trivial — if two corresponding hash values are not equal, an attack must have happened. The addresses of hash variables are maintained in the program's kernel *task_struct* and a new system call *svmon_submit* is added to let a program submit the randomized addresses to kernel at initialization.

Dynamic re-randomization. The dynamic re-randomization is actually the same process with the randomization in the initialization phase. It is designed as a special routine and executed by kernel just like a *fake* signal handler (i.e. in the context of current process) whenever needed (e.g if a process forks). Note that this routine may reset all the hash values but is not vulnerable for malicious use, because any execution of it begins with a system call and so applies control-flow verification.

Incorporation of new cases of non-standard control flow. An external helper program is designed to remove the calculation of newly discovered unwanted expected/actual sequences (fill the code area with one-byte "nop" instructions) using the *ptrace* in Linux. It does not require the restart of a program.

Every protected program is instrumented to two versions: profiling version and detecting version. After that, they are compiled with native compiler and linked with the utility functions we mentioned above. The profiling version is only used for the discovery of non-standard control flow; the detecting version is the final version that may be released to end users.

4 Evaluation

4.1 Performance Overhead

We applied micro-benchmarks and macro-benchmarks to give a performance overview.

4.1.1 Micro Benchmarks

The overhead of our approach comes from kernel space and user space. So we did experiments to evaluate the overhead in both spaces.

The first experiment aimed to find out the overhead caused by the kernel verification. We wrote a C program that invoked 100,000,000 times the Linux system call of *sys_ni_syscall*. A *sys_ni_syscall* is just an empty system call that returns directly. The program was run under the standard kernel and our patched kernel. We logged the system time used by the program under these two kernels to get the results. The results indicate that the worst kernel overhead (since *sys_ni_syscall* can be considered as the smallest system call) was about 2.1%. For real world programs that often use *big* system calls, the overhead is hardly observable.

The second experiment designed to get the worst user space overhead was a program calling 50,000,000 times an empty function whose body contained only a "return" statement. The program was compiled by a native compiler (GCC) and then was run 50 times to get the average execution time of the empty function. After that, the program was transformed to detecting version by our instrumentation tool and compiled and run 50 times to get the average execution time of an instrumented empty function. The inferred worst case overhead in user space was 3.3%. For real world programs that seldom have any empty function call, this overhead trends to decrease.

4.1.2 Macro Benchmarks

We used the same set of application used in section 3.3 to give a good overview of performance overhead for different types of application. In addition, we used the benchmark of SciMark2 [24] to evaluate the overhead for CPU-bound programs. The hardware was two Xeon x86 processors at 2.4GHZ with 1GMB of RAM. The overhead was evaluated as average execution time measured through bash built-in command of *time*. Since for interactive programs like text editors, most of the application time is used waiting for human input, we did not evaluate their performance. The experiments included: "ctags –R linux-2.6.16.9"; "tar cf linux.tar linux-2.6.16.9"; "gzip linux.tar"; transmission of linux.tar using ghttpd, sshd and vsftpd. Where the size of linux.tar was 224M. Each experiment was carried out 10 times to get average results. Figure 4 gives the normalized results. For profiling version, the measured overhead ranged from 0.27% to 189% at average of 35%, program size was increased at average of 25%. While for detecting version, average increase of program size was 13%, and the performance overhead was almost unnoticeable at average of 2.76%. Note that CFI achieved an average overhead of 16% by exploiting many platform features (e.g. making use of specific CPU registers).

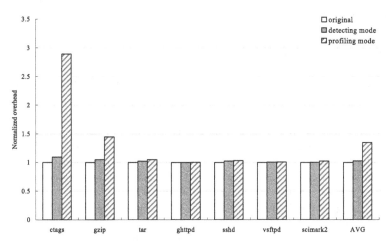

Fig. 4. Performance overhead on real world applications

4.2 Security-Related Experiments

In order to assess the effectiveness of our approach, we found from the Internet several vulnerable programs and tried to exploit them. The vulnerabilities in our experiments included format string vulnerability in ghttpd-1.4, buffer overflow in lhttpd-0.1 and zawhttpd-0.8.23. All the compromising attempts were correctly detected because they all made the control flow deviate from the normal path.

As a concrete example, the Log() function in *util.c* from ghttpd-1.4 at line 219 is vulnerable because of improper use of limited local buffer. When the function returns, it is possible that the return address has been maliciously overwritten, in our experiment, to be the address of an injected shellcode. The computed equivalence function set containing the Log() function has the return ID of 14 (before ID randomization). Before the Log() returns , the hash variable for the actual return sequence is added 14. However, there is no corresponding expected return sequence calculation in the shellcode. So when the shellcode tries to make a *socket* system call, the inequality between hash variables for expected and actual return sequences is detected by kernel. Attacks using *return-to-libc* instead of shellcode can also be detected because they will cause the incorrect calculation of expected return hash variable.

In order to make a good coverage of more attack types, we also applied our approach on Wilander's test bed [25]. None of the attacks escaped the detection, because all of the attacks, regardless of which vulnerability they exploit, were control-hijacking attacks.

Like many others, we did not prove formally that our method cannot be circumvented. But the analysis in section 3.2 gives us confidence that our system has enough strength.

4.3 Applicability

We argue that our approach can be easily implemented in many other platforms by summing up the following facts:

- The underlying techniques of our work are easily obtained in many platforms. The code instrumentation is based on alias analysis, which nearly any modern compiler or analyzer has as a basic utility. CIL itself is "able to process not only ANSI-C programs but also those using Microsoft C or GNU C extensions".
- Each platform specific features we use have direct correspondences in other platforms. The instructions used for detecting version are the *add* instruction and *nop* instruction — basic instructions for CPU of nearly any architecture. The memory management unit of modern operating systems provides the functions needed at initialization phase. And the verification of control flow could be carried out whenever a program from user land issues a call to OS kernel API, which is also a common OS facility.
- Although non-standard control may be platform and application dependent, in our method it is discovered uniformly though representative runs of programs. So no special consideration for non-standard control is needed when our method gets adopted in other platforms.

Compared with the most related work —CFI on applicability, our method is more platform independent but currently does not take advantage of the binary rewriting and requires program profiling.

5   Conclusion

In this paper, we present an efficient and practical method for control flow monitoring. Our method verifies the control flow of a program by inserting into it simple instrumentation code. We simplify the verification of program control flow by control flow encoding and at the same time provide enough guarantees for security. Also we propose using program profiling to automatically discover non-standard control flow. We have shown that our method has good applicability because of the simplicity of the underlying techniques and the platform specific features used.

There are a number of ways in which our method can be improved. We aim to improve the verification strength of our methods by employing more techniques such as code obfuscation and provide more formal argument for security. We will explore ways to improve the precision of control flow description and keep the implementation as simple as possible to achieve high performance.

References

1. One, A.: Smashing The Stack For Fun And Profit. Phrack 7(49) (1996)
2. Lamagra Argamal.Ftpd: the advisory version. bugtraq mailing list (23 June, 2000) http://www.securityfocus.com/archive/1/66544
3. Kiriansky, V., Bruening, D., Amarasinghe, S.: Secure execution via program shepherding. In: Proc of the Usenix Security Symposium (2002)
4. Abadi, M., Budiu, M., Erlingsson, ú., Ligatti, J.: Control-flow integrity. ACM Conference on Computer and Communications Security (2005)
5. Wagner, D., Dean, D.: Intrusion detection via static analysis. In: Proc of the IEEE Symposium on Security and Privacy, IEEE Computer Society Press, Los Alamitos (2001)
6. Sekar, R., Bendre, M., Dhurjati, D., Bollineni, P.: A fast automaton-based method for detecting anomalous program behaviors. In: Proc. of the IEEE Symposium on Security and Privacy, pp. 144–155. IEEE Computer Society Press, Los Alamitos (2001)
7. Feng, H., Kolesnikov, O., Fogla, P., Lee, W., Gong, W.: Anomaly detection using call stack information. In: Proc. of the IEEE Symposium on Security and Privacy, pp. 62–77. IEEE Computer Society Press, Los Alamitos (2003)
8. Basu, S., Uppuluri, P.: Proxy-annotated control flow graphs: Deterministic context-sensitive monitoring for intrusion detection. In: Ghosh, R.K., Mohanty, H. (eds.) ICDCIT 2004. LNCS, vol. 3347, pp. 353–362. Springer, Heidelberg (2004)
9. Feng, H., Giffin, J., Huang, Y., Jha, S., Lee, W., Miller, B.: Formalizing sensitivity in static analysis for intrusion detection. In: Proc. of the IEEE Symposium on Security and Privacy, pp. 194–210. IEEE Computer Society Press, Los Alamitos (2004)
10. Giffin, J., Jha, S., Miller, B.: Efficient context-sensitive intrusion detection. In: NDSS 2004. Proc. of the Network and Distributed System Security Symposium (2004)
11. Lam, L., Chiueh, T.: Automatic extraction of accurate application-specific sandboxing policy. In: Jonsson, E., Valdes, A., Almgren, M. (eds.) RAID 2004. LNCS, vol. 3224, pp. 1–20. Springer, Heidelberg (2004)
12. Gopalakrishna, R., Spafford, E., Vitek, J.: Efficient intrusion detection using automaton inlining. In: Proc. of the IEEE Symposium on Security and Privacy, IEEE Computer Society Press, Los Alamitos (2005)
13. Shacham, H., Page, M., Pfaff, B., Goh, E.-J., Modadugu, N., Boneh, D.: On the Effectiveness of Address Space Randomization. In: ACM Conference on Computer Security 2004, ACM Press, New York (2004)
14. Sovarel, A.N., Evans, D., Paul, N.: Where's the FEEB? The Effectiveness of Instruction Set Randomization. In: Proc. of the 14th USENIX Security Symposium (July 31–August 5) Baltimore, MD (2005)
15. Erlingsson, Ú., Schneider, F.: IRM enforcement of java stack inspection. In: Proc. of the IEEE Symposium on Security and Privacy, pp. 246–255 (2000)

16. McCamant, S., Morrisett, G.: Efficient, verifiable binary sandboxing for a CISC architecture. Technical Report MIT-LCS-TR-988, MIT Laboratory for Computer Science (2005)
17. Hind, M., Pioli, A.: Which pointer analysis should I use? In: Proc. of the International Symposium on Software Testing and Analysis (2000)
18. Steensgaard, B.: Points-to Analysis in Almost Linear Time. In: Proc. Symposium on Principles of Programming Languages (1996)
19. PaX Team. PaX address space layout randomiza-tion(ASLR), http://pax.grsecurity. net/docs/aslr.txt
20. Kc, G.S., Keromytis, A.D., Prevelakis, V.: Countering code-injection attacks with instruction-set randomization. In: CCS. Proc of the 10th ACM Conference on Computer and Communications Security, ACM Press, New York (2003)
21. Linn, C., Debray, S.: Obfuscation of Executable Code to Improve Resistance to Static Disassembly. In: Proc. of the 10th ACM Conference on Computer and Communications Security (2003)
22. "Solar Designer". Non-Executable User Stack, http://www.false.com/security/linux-stack/
23. Necula, G.C., McPeak, S., Rahul, S.P., et al.: CIL: Intermediate Language and Tools for Analysis and Transformation of C Programs. In: Horspool, R.N. (ed.) CC 2002 and ETAPS 2002. LNCS, vol. 2304, Springer, Heidelberg (2002)
24. Pozo, R., Miller, B.: SciMark 2.0. (June 20, 2000), http://math.nist.gov/scimark
25. Wilander, J., Kamkar, M.: A Comparison of Publicly Available Tools for Dynamic Buffer Overflow Prevention. In: NDSS 2003. Proc of the 10th Network and Distrib-uted System Security Symposium, San Diego, California (2003)

Modular Formalization of Reactive Modules in COQ*

Ming-Hsien Tsai[1,2] and Bow-Yaw Wang[1,**]

[1] Institute of Information Science
Academia Sinica, Taiwan
[2] Department of Information Management
National Taiwan University

Abstract. We present modular formalizations of the model specification language Reactive Modules and the temporal logic CTL* in the proof assistant COQ. In our formalizations, both shallow and deep embeddings of each language are given. The modularity of our formalizations allows proofs and theorems to be reused across different embeddings. We illustrate the advantages of our modular formalizations by proving the mutual exclusion property of the Bakery algorithm in different embeddings.

1 Introduction

Verifying systems in proof assistants consists of several tedious tasks. Firstly, system behavior has to be specified. Issues such as finite versus infinite states, deterministic versus non-deterministic computation, interleaving versus concurrent semantics need be resolved in behavioral specification. Secondly, system requirements are needed. Formalisms featuring linear- or branching-time semantics, logical or algebraic descriptions are available. Finally, the verification need be carried out in proof assistants to show that system behavior is indeed expected.

Since describing system behavior and requirements is very tedious and error-prone, model and requirement specification languages are hence developed to help verifiers specify system behavior and requirements. Several specification languages have also been formalized in proof assistants. Roughly, two kinds of formalizations are possible. A shallow embedding defines the semantics of specification languages in logics of proof assistants. Alternatively, a deep embedding additionally encodes syntactic representations of specification languages in proof assistants. They have consequently different characteristics.

Shallow embeddings are easier to carry out since syntactic representations are not defined. But structural induction on specification languages is not possible due to the lack of syntactic representations. Deep embedding, on the other hand, are more complicated. Nevertheless, their syntactic representations allow

---

* The work is partly supported by NSC grands 95-3114-P-001-002-Y02, 95-2221-E-001-024-MY3, and the project SISARL of Academia Sinica.
** Part of the the work was done during the second author visited to the project ProVal supported by INRIA Futurs.

to analyze properties about encoded languages. In practice, objectives of formalizations determine which embedding is used. If a specific requirement is to be verified on a particular system, shallow embeddings of both model and requirement specification languages are preferred, for instance.

For some applications, switching between different embeddings may be necessary. If a verifier is developing a new model specification language, she may try some examples in shallow embedding at early stages of the development. When the language is more mature, deep embedding will be necessary to prove properties about the language itself. Ideally, the theorems and proofs in different embeddings should be reused. But it is not clear how the migration can be done easily.

In this paper, we present modular formalizations of model and requirement specification languages in the proof assistant CoQ [4]. We give the shallow and deep embeddings of both specification languages and compare their formalizations in different embeddings. More importantly, our modular formalizations allow to share theorems and proofs between embeddings. We have developed tactics for different embeddings to reduce the migration cost. As an example, we prove the mutual exclusion of the Bakery algorithm with indefinite number of processes in both embeddings.

We formalize Reactive Modules [1] for system descriptions. Reactive Modules is a model specification language for synchronous, shared-memory, and concurrent processes. Multiple processes may update different variables simultaneously. The temporal logic CTL* is used for requirement specifications. Unlike linear-time temporal logic (LTL) and computation tree logic (CTL), CTL* admits both path and state formulae and is therefore more expressive than LTL and CTL. Purely path- or state-based semantics would not suffice for CTL*. Our formalization integrates both semantics seamlessly.

The branching-time temporal logic μ-calculus has been formalized in CoQ [10,16], LEGO [18], and ACL2 [8] with different intentions. A formalization of LTL can be found in CoQ [3]. The temporal logic of actions TLA [5] has been formalized in Isabelle [9]. A shallow embedding of CTL can be found in [2]. Since CTL* is an accessible generalization of LTL and CTL, our formalization subsumes prior formalizations of LTL and CTL. Furthermore, verifiers are more familiar with CTL* than μ-calculus. Our formalization would be more useful to them.

In [14,13,11,12], I/O automata [6] and (extensions to) linear-time temporal logic [7] are formalized in Isabelle [15]. An I/O automaton is formalized as the set of admissible paths. A path in turn is formalized as a lazy list or a function on natural numbers. The authors are able to prove meta-theorems about I/O automata in their framework. Our formalization of Reactive Modules is more syntactic. We provide constants to help verifiers define their models and give corresponding syntactic representation. Verifiers will find it more accessible than pure semantic-based formalizations.

The paper is organized as follows. Section 2 gives the preliminaries. Both the shallow and deep embeddings of Reactive Modules are presented in Section 3.

The embeddings of CTL* are shown in Section 4. The verification of the Bakery algorithm is discussed in Section 5. Finally, Section 6 discusses possible future work and concludes the paper.

2 Preliminaries

Let AP be the set of atomic propositions. A *Kripke structure* K is a 4-tuple (S, S_0, δ, L) where S is the set of *states*, $S_0 \subseteq S$ the set of *initial states*, $\delta \subseteq S \times S$ the total *transition relation*, and $L : S \to 2^{AP}$ the *labeling function* which assigns atomic propositions to each state.

Given a set of atomic propositions AP, a *state formula* f is defined inductively as follows.

- If $p \in AP$, then p is a state formula;
- If f and f' are state formulae, then $\neg f$, $f \vee f'$, and $f \wedge f'$ are state formulae;
- If g is a path formula, then $\mathbf{E}g$ and $\mathbf{A}g$ are state formulae.

A *path formula* g, on the other hand, is constructed by the following rules.

- If f is a state formula, then f is also a path formula;
- If g and g' are path formulae, then $\neg g$, $g \vee g'$, $g \wedge g'$, $\mathbf{X}g$, $\mathbf{F}g$, $\mathbf{G}g$, $g\mathbf{U}g'$, and $g\mathbf{W}g'$ are path formulae.

A *formula* in the full branching-time temporal logic CTL* is either a state or a path formula.

Let $K = (S, S_0, \delta, L)$ be a Kripke structure. A *path* is an infinite sequence of states $\pi = s_0 s_1 \cdots s_n \cdots$ such that $(s_i, s_{i+1}) \in \delta$ for $i \geq 0$. We define $\pi(i) = s_i$ and the *i-th suffix* $\pi_i = s_i s_{i+1} \cdots s_n \cdots$ for any natural number i. Let $s \in S$. Define the relations $K, s \models f$ and $K, \pi \models g$ as follows.

$$
\begin{aligned}
&K, s \models p && \text{if } p \in L(s) \\
&K, s \models \neg f && \text{if } K, s \not\models f \\
&K, s \models f \vee f' && \text{if } K, s \models f \text{ or } K, s \models f' \\
&K, s \models \mathbf{E}g && \text{if there is a path } \pi \text{ with } \pi(0) = s \text{ such that } K, \pi \models g \\
&K, \pi \models f && \text{if } K, \pi(0) \models f \\
&K, \pi \models \neg g && \text{if } K, \pi \not\models g \\
&K, \pi \models g \vee g' && \text{if } K, \pi \models g \text{ or } K, \pi \models g' \\
&K, \pi \models \mathbf{X}g && \text{if } K, \pi_1 \models g \\
&K, \pi \models g\mathbf{U}g' && \text{if there exists an } i \geq 0 \text{ such that } K, \pi_i \models g' \text{ and} \\
&&& \quad K, \pi_j \models g \text{ for all } 0 \leq j < i
\end{aligned}
$$

The semantics of other operators is obtained by $\phi \wedge \phi' \equiv \neg(\neg \phi \vee \neg \phi')$, $\mathbf{A}f \equiv \neg\mathbf{E}\neg f$, $\mathbf{F}g \equiv true\mathbf{U}g$, $\mathbf{G}g \equiv \neg\mathbf{F}\neg g$, and $g\mathbf{W}g' \equiv g\mathbf{U}g' \vee \mathbf{G}g$. Moreover, we say the state s in K *satisfies* the state formula f if $K, s \models f$. Similarly, the path π *satisfies* the path formula g if $K, \pi \models g$.

A *reactive module* consists of a set of atoms that define how variables are updated. Both the old and new values of a variable can be referred in atoms.

If a variable x is updated by an atom A, we say x is *controlled* by A. If its old value is referred in A, we say it is *read* by A. If its new value is referred, we say x is *awaited* by A. An *atom* is a 5-tuple $A = (V_c^A, V_r^A, V_a^A, C_i^A, C_u^A)$ where V_c^A is the set of variables controlled by A, V_r^A the set of variables read by A, V_a^A the set of variables awaited by A, C_i^A the set of *initial guarded commands*, and C_u^A the set of *updating guarded commands*.

Variables are updated by their controlling atoms in each step. In the beginning of each step, external and uncontrolled variables are assigned to arbitrary values nondeterministically. An atom updates its controlled variables only after all its awaited variables have been updated in the same step.

We write x and x' for the old and new values of the variable x respectively. For example, consider the following textual representation of an atom $A = (V_c^A, V_r^A, V_a^A, C_i^A, C_u^A)$ where $V_c^A = \{x, y\}$, $V_r^A = \{x, y, z\}$, and $V_a^A = \{z\}$.

```
atom A  controls x y  reads x y z  awaits z
inits
    [] true → x := 1; y := 2
    [] true → x := 2; y := 1
updates
    [] x = 1 → x' := y; y' := z'
    [] ¬(x = 1) → x' := z; y' := x
```

There are two initial guarded commands in C_i^A and two updating guarded commands in C_u^A. One of the updating guarded command, for example, assigns the old value of y to x and the new value of z to y when the old value of x is 1.

3   Reactive Modules

Our formalization differs from other formalizations in its modularity. Instead of formalizing the requirement specification language on top of the model specification language, an abstraction of Kripke structures is introduced as the interfaces in our formalization. Any formalization of Reactive Modules must conform to the abstract Kripke interface. In particular, both the shallow and deep embeddings share the same interface so that they can be used in our CTL* formalization interchangeably.

We formalize the abstraction as a COQ module type. The following fragment shows the abstract Kripke interface.

```
Module Type KRIPKE .
  Parameters Var St : Set .
  Parameter Val : St -> Var -> nat .
  Parameter Init : St -> Prop .
  Parameter Succ : St -> St -> Prop .
End KRIPKE .
```

In the module type KRIPKE, the variable set Var and the state set St are declared. The valuation of each variable x on a given state s is obtained by Val s x. A state s is an initial state if Init s holds. Similarly, the state t is a successor of s if Succ s t holds. The labeling function L is not declared for it is formalized as state predicates of type St -> Prop.

In the shallow embedding, only the semantics of Reactive Modules is encoded. Constants are provided to help verifiers construct reactive modules. New constructs can be formalized by adding new constants. On the other hand, both the syntax and semantics are encoded in the deep embedding. Each syntactic class of Reactive Modules corresponds to an inductive type in COQ. A semantic function is defined to give the meaning of constructs in each syntactic class. Adding a new construct requires modifying the inductive type and the semantic function of its syntactic class.

3.1   Shallow Embedding

In the shallow embedding SRM, variables in reactive modules are of type Var. A state is a function which maps variables to values. For simplicity, all variables in our formalization have values in natural numbers (nat).

```
Variable Var : Set .
Definition St : Set := Var -> nat .
```

Since both the old and new values of variables may be referred in reactive modules, an expression is formalized as a function of type St -> St -> nat where the arguments are the current and the next state respectively. It returns a nat term as its semantic value. A Boolean expression, on the other hand, is a predicate on the current and next states.

```
Definition Exp : Set := St -> St -> nat .
Definition BExp : Type := St -> St -> Prop .
```

It is easy to encode constructs in SRM. For instance, the following definition defines the constant add for the arithmetic addition operator.

```
Definition add (e1 e2 : Exp) : Exp := fun s s' : St => e1 s s' + e2 s s' .
```

The constant add passes the current and next states to its parameters, evaluates the subexpressions, and finally returns the sum as its result. Other constants for expressions are defined similarly.

Likewise, constants for Boolean expressions are given. For example, the following constants define the truth value *true* and the negation.

```
Definition wahr : BExp := fun s s' : St => True .
Definition nicht (be : BExp) : BExp := fun s s' : St => ~ be s s' .
```

Another constant which is handy in the specification of mutual exclusion is forall_nat. It checks whether the operand f of type nat -> BExp holds for all nat.

```
Definition forall_nat (f : nat -> BExp) : BExp :=
  fun s s' : St => forall n : nat, f n s s' .
```

A command in C_u^A is a predicate over the current and next states while an initial command in C_i^A a predicate over states.

```
Definition Command : Type := St -> St -> Prop .
Definition ICommand : Type := St -> Prop .
```

Predefined constants are available for commands. For example, `Assign` assigns an expression to a variable, and `Comp` makes a new command out of two. Similar constants in `ICommand` can be defined as well.

```
Definition Assign (v : Var) (exp : Exp) : Command :=
  fun s s' : St => s' v = exp s s' .
Definition Comp (c c' : Command) : Command :=
  fun s s' : St => c s s' /\ c' s s' .
```

Note that the composition of commands is formalized as conjunction. It conforms to the semantics defined in [1].

3.2   Deep Embedding

The syntax and semantics are defined explicitly in the deep embedding DRM. For each syntactic class, we define an inductive type for its terms and a semantic function for its semantics.

Syntax. For expressions, we define the inductive type Exp as follows.

```
Inductive Exp : Set :=
  | add : Exp -> Exp -> Exp
  ...
```

The inductive type BExp for Boolean expressions is defined similarly.

```
Inductive BExp : Set :=
  | wahr : BExp
  | nicht : BExp -> BExp
  | forall_nat : (nat -> BExp) -> BExp
  ...
```

In DRM, elements of Exp and BExp are constructed inductively. Subsequently, properties about expressions or Boolean expressions can be proved by induction. On the other hand, Exp and BExp are of functional types in the shallow embedding. Inductive reasoning about these expressions would not work in SRM.

A command can be an assignment or a composition of commands. A guarded command is a record which contains a Boolean expression and a command. Finally, an atom is a record of a list of controlled variables, a list of initial guarded commands, and a list of updating guarded commands.

```
Inductive Command : Set :=
  | assign (v : Var) (exp : Exp) | comp (c c' : Command) .
Record GuardedCommand : Set := mkGuardedCommand
  { guard : BExp; command : Command } .
Record Atom : Set := mkAtom
  { controls : list Var; inits : list GuardedCommand;
    updates : list GuardedCommand } .
```

Semantics. To give a term its meaning, a semantic function for its syntactic class is defined. The semantic functions `eval` and `beval` compute the semantic value of any `Exp` and `BExp` term respectively based on the current and next states.

```
Fixpoint eval (exp : Exp) (s s' : St) { struct exp } : nat :=
  match exp with
    | add exp' exp'' => (eval exp' s s') + (eval exp'' s s')
    ...
  end .
Fixpoint beval (bexp : BExp) (s s' : St) { struct bexp } : Prop :=
  match bexp with
    | wahr => True
    | nicht bexp' => ~ (beval bexp' s s')
    | forall_nat F => forall n : nat, beval (F n) s s'
    ...
  end .
```

Compare the definition of `Exp` in SRM and the type of the semantic function `eval` in DRM.

```
Exp := St -> St -> nat        (* in SRM *)
eval : Exp -> St -> St -> nat  (* in DRM *)
```

The type of the term `eval add` in DRM corresponds to the type of the constant `add` in SRM. Indeed, the semantic function `eval` collects the corresponding definitions of `Exp` constants in the shallow embedding. The correspondence will be observed throughout the formalizations. It helps us differentiate embeddings systematically.

The semantic function `Exec` for commands can be defined easily.

```
Fixpoint Exec (c : Command) (s s' : St) { struct c } : Prop :=
  match c with
    | assign v exp => s' v = (eval exp s s')
    | comp c' c'' => Exec c' s s' /\ Exec c'' s s'
  end .
```

In order to define the parameter `Succ` in the module type `KRIPKE`, several auxiliary definitions are needed. Given a term of `Atom` and two states `s`, `s'`, `SuccAtom` holds if `s'` can be obtained from `s` by executing an enabled guarded command. Hence, the state `s'` is a successor of `s` if `s'` can be obtained from `s` by executing enabled guarded commands of all atoms simultaneously.

```
Definition SuccAtom (atom : Atom) (s s' : St) : Prop :=
  exists gcmd : GuardedCommand, In gcmd (updates atom) /\
    beval (guard gcmd) s s' /\ Exec (command gcmd) s s' .
Definition Succ (atoms : Ensemble Atom) (s s' : St) : Prop :=
  forall atom : Atom, In Atom atoms atom -> SuccAtom atom s s' .
```

4 CTL*

As in the formalizations of Reactive Modules, the shallow and deep embeddings of CTL* must conform to the same interface. Moreover, we would like to maximize the applicability of our CTL* formalization, and therefore would not commit to particular model specification languages. CTL* is therefore formalized as a functor on modules of type KRIPKE.

In the abstract interface of CTL*, the formalization of paths is required. Standard functions such as hd, tl, and cons are declared.

```
Module Type CTLS (K : KRIPKE) .
  Parameter Path : Set .
  Parameter hd : Path -> K.St .
  Parameter tl : Path -> Path .
  Parameter cons : forall (s : K.St) (pi : Path),
      K.Succ s (hd pi) -> Path .
  Parameter suffix : nat -> Path -> Path .
  ...
```

The function suffix i pi returns the i-th suffix of the path pi. It is used in the formalizations of various temporal operators.

The declarations of state and path formulae follows those of paths. The satisfaction relations $K, s \models f$ and $K, \pi \models g$ will be formalized by model_s and model_p respectively.

```
  Parameters state_formula path_formula : Type .
  Parameter model_s : state_formula -> K.St -> Prop .
  Parameter model_p : path_formula -> Path -> Prop .
  Parameter A : path_formula -> state_formula .
  Parameter G : path_formula -> path_formula .
  Axiom def_A : forall (s : K.St) (f : path_formula),
      model_s s (A f) <-> forall pi : Path, s = hd pi -> model_p pi f .
  ...
End CTLS .
```

The types of path quantifiers and temporal operators are defined. For instance, the path quantifier A must be of type path_formula -> state_formula. Finally, semantic constraints on temporal operators are explicated.

4.1   Paths

Paths are formalized by imposing constraints on streams. A *stream* is an infinite sequence of states. A stream of states $\sigma = s_0 s_1 \cdots s_n \cdots$ is a path if and only if s_{i+1} is a successor of s_i for all $i \geq 0$. For simplicity, we formalize streams as functions from natural numbers to states in both embeddings of CTL*. Other formalizations via domain theory [13] or coinductive types [17] are possible.

```
Definition stream : Set := nat -> K.St .
Definition is_path (str : stream) : Prop :=
  forall i : nat, K.Succ (str i) (str (i + 1)) .
Definition Path : Set := { pi : stream | is_path pi } .
```

The predicate is_path checks whether successive states in the given stream satisfy the transition relation K.Succ. Path is hence a set of streams satisfying the predicate is_path. Auxiliary functions such as hd, tl, and cons can be defined easily and are skipped here.

4.2   Shallow Embedding

State and path formulae are formalized as predicates over states and paths in the shallow embedding SCTLS respectively.

```
Definition path_formula : Type := Path -> Prop .
Definition state_formula : Type := St -> Prop .
```

Consider, for example, the path quantifier **A**. It makes a state formula out of a path formula. In our formalization, it transforms a path predicate to a state predicate.

```
Definition A (P : path_formula) : state_formula :=
  fun s : St => forall pi : Path, s = hd pi -> P pi .
```

Similarly, the temporal operator **G** checks whether all suffixes (suffix i pi) of the input path (pi) satisfy the given path predicate.

```
Definition G (P : path_formula) : path_formula :=
  fun pi : Path => forall i : nat, P (suffix i pi) .
```

4.3   Deep Embedding

The deep embedding DCTLS follows a similar style in Reactive Modules. We define two inductive types for the syntactic classes of path and state formulae respectively. Semantic functions for the syntactic classes are defined accordingly.

Syntax. The syntactic classes of state and path formulae correspond to the mutually inductive types state_formula and path_formula respectively.

```
Inductive state_formula : Type :=
  | A : path_formula -> state_formula
  ...
with path_formula : Type :=
  | X : path_formula -> path_formula
  | G : path_formula -> path_formula
  ...
```

Semantics. The semantics of state and path formulae are defined mutually recursively by the functions model_s and model_p respectively.

```
Fixpoint model_s (f : state_formula) (s : St) {struct f} : Prop :=
  match f with
  | A g => forall pi : Path, s = hd pi -> model_p g pi
  ...
  end
with model_p (g : path_formula) (pi : Path) {struct g} : Prop :=
  match g with
  | X g' => model_p g' (tl pi)
  | G g' => forall k : nat, model_p g' (suffix k pi)
  ...
  end .
```

The correspondence of both embeddings can be re-illustrated.

```
(* in SCTLS *)
state_formula := St -> Prop
path_formula := Path -> Prop
(* in DCTLS *)
model_s : state_formula -> St -> Prop
model_p : path_formula -> Path -> Prop
```

The semantic functions `model_s` and `model_p` in DCTLS collect the definitions of corresponding operators in SCTLS. As in the formalization of Reactive Modules, it is easy to add new operators in the shallow embedding. But DCTLS allows verifiers to analyze CTL* formulae inductively.

5   The Bakery Algorithm

In this section, we demonstrate the ease of proof sharing in our modular formalization. The mutual exclusion of the Bakery algorithm will be used as the example. More precisely, three versions of the property are proved in different embeddings. We first specify the Bakery algorithm with the shallow and deep embeddings of Reactive Modules and obtain the modules SBakery and DBakery respectively. Two versions of mutual exclusion are specified by the shallow and deep embeddings of CTL* as SMUTEX and DMUTEX respectively. The similarity between the proofs of SMUTEX in SBakery and DBakery will be illustrated. Finally, the theorem SMUTEX is reused to prove DMUTEX in DBakery (Figure 1).

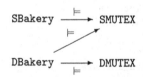

Fig. 1. Different Versions of Mutual Exclusion

We deliberately use the same notation in both embeddings to demonstrate the similarity of proofs. Hence some functions and constructors may have different types in different embeddings. For example, the term or is a function in SBakery but a constructor in DBakery. The following constants are used in both encodings.

```
Definition reqCS := 1 .
Definition inCS := 2 .
Definition outCS := 3 .
Parameter n : nat .
Axiom n_gt_0 : n > 0 .
Parameters pc y : nat -> Var .
```

Intuitively, n denotes the number of processes. `pc i` is the control location of the process `i`, which can be `reqCS`, `inCS`, or `outCS`. `y i` is the ticket number of the process `i`. Then the condition that process `i` can enter the critical section is as follows.

```
Definition cond (i : nat) : BExp :=
  let cond_i_j (i : nat) (j : nat) : BExp :=
    y j = 0 \/ y i < y j \/ (y i = y j /\ i < j) in
  forall_nat j, i <> j --> cond_i_j i j .
```

It states that if all other process `j` has ticket number 0, a larger ticket number (`y i < y j`), or the index `j` greater than `i` when both have the same ticket number, then the process `i` may go into the critical section. Note that `cond` has different types in different embeddings.

5.1   Shallow Modeling

In the shallow modeling, the initial and updating commands are defined as predicates. To mimic the textual representation of Reactive Modules, several notations are defined. For instance, $x' := e$ stands for `Assign` x e; `Updates [] gcmd`$_0$ `[] gcmd`$_1$ $\cdots$ stands for `fun s s' : St =>` `gcmd`$_0$ `s s'` $\backslash/$ `gcmd`$_1$ `s s'` $\backslash/ \cdots$, and so on.

```
Definition atom_inits (i : nat) : ICommand :=
  (Inits
    [] wahr -> (pc i) := outCS; (y i) := 0) .
Definition atom_updates (i : nat) : Command :=
  (Updates
    [] pc i = outCS -> (pc i)' := reqCS; (y i)' := max_y + 1
    [] pc i = reqCS /\ cond i -> (pc i)' := inCS; (y i)' := y i
    [] pc i = reqCS /\ ~ cond i -> (pc i)' := reqCS; (y i)' := y i
    [] pc i = inCS -> (pc i)' := outCS; (y i)' := 0) .
Definition sys_inits (s : St) : Prop :=
  forall (i : nat), i < n -> atom_inits i s .
Definition sys_updates (s s' : St) : Prop :=
  forall (i : nat), i < n -> atom_updates i s s' .
```

The concrete module `SBakery` of type `KRIPKE` is created as follows.

```
Module SBakery <: KRIPKE .
  Definition Var := SRM.Var .
  Definition St := SRM.St .
  Definition Val (s : St) (v : Var) := s v .
  Definition Init := sys_inits .
  Definition Succ := sys_updates .
End SBakery .
```

With the module `SBakery` in place, we can instantiate the module `SBakerySCTL` as follows.

```
Module SBakerySCTL := SCTLS SBakery .
```

Mutual exclusion is expressed as a state formula smutex.

```
Definition smutex : state_formula :=
  fun s : St => forall i j : nat, i < n -> j < n -> i <> j ->
    s (pc i) <> inCS \/ s (pc j) <> inCS .
```

It is now straightforward to prove the following lemma in SBakerySCTL.

```
Lemma SMUTEX : forall s : St, Init s -> model_s (A (G smutex)) s .
```

5.2 Deep Modeling

To model the Bakery algorithm in the deep embedding, we define the Atom term atom i for each natural number i. The notations $x' := e$ and Updates [] gcmd$_0$ [] gcmd$_1$ $\cdots$ stand for assign x e and [gcmd$_0$; gcmd$_1$; $\cdots$] respectively.

```
Definition atom (i : nat) : Atom := mkAtom (pc i::y i::nil)
  (Inits
    [] wahr -> (pc i) := outCS; (y i) := 0)
  (Updates
    [] pc i = outCS -> (pc i)' := reqCS; (y i)' := max_y + 1
    [] pc i = reqCS /\ cond i -> (pc i)' := inCS; (y i)' := y i
    [] pc i = reqCS /\ ~ cond i -> (pc i)' := reqCS; (y i)' := y i
    [] pc i = inCS -> (pc i)' := outCS; (y i)' := 0) .
```

The system with n atoms is defined as an ensemble of atoms (Ensemble Atom).

```
Definition sys : Ensemble Atom :=
  fun a : Atom => exists i : nat, i < n /\ a = atom i .
```

The concrete model of type KRIPKE is defined as follows.

```
Module DBakery <: KRIPKE .
  Definition Var := DRM.Var .
  Definition St := DRM.St .
  Definition Val (s : St) (v : Var) := s v .
  Definition Init := DRM.Init sys .
  Definition Succ := DRM.Succ sys .
End DBakery .
```

Similar to using shallow embedding, we instantiate the module DBakerySCTL.

```
Module DBakerySCTL := SCTLS DBakery .
```

The following lemma shows the mutual exclusion in DBakerySCTL.

```
Lemma SMUTEX : forall s : St, Init s -> model_s (A (G smutex)) s .
```

Recall that both SBakerySCTL.SMUTEX and DBakerySCTL.SMUTEX specify the mutual exclusion property in the shallow embedding of CTL*. Further, SBakery and DBakery are merely two encodings of the Bakery algorithm in different embeddings. Intuitively, the proofs of SBakerySCTL.SMUTEX and DBakerySCTL.SMUTEX should be similar. If so, one may establish DBakerySCTL.SMUTEX by adopting the

in SBakerySCTL.SMUTEX   in DBakerySCTL.SMUTEX

gen_cmd Hsucc i Hi unfold cond_i_j;   gen_cmd Hsucc (atom i);
  gen_cmd Hsucc j Hj unfold cond_i_j;   gen_cmd Hsucc (atom j);
  clear Hsucc.   clear Hsucc.
  . . .   . . .
case (eq_nat_dec (s (pc j)) inCS); intro . case (eq_nat_dec (s (pc j)) inCS); intro .
  generalize (Hin j Hj e); clear Hin; intro .   generalize (Hin j Hj e); clear Hin; intro .
  generalize (Hreq i Hi H0); clear Hreq;   generalize (Hreq i Hi H0); clear Hreq;
  intro .   intro .
  generalize   generalize
    (Hin' j Hj e i Hi (sym_not_eq Hij));   (Hin' j Hj e i Hi (sym_not_eq Hij));
  clear Hin'; intro .   clear Hin'; intro .
  generalize (H1 j Hij); clear H1 .   generalize (H1 j Hij); clear H1 .
  intros; elim_all_or; elim_all_and;   intros; elim_all_or; elim_all_and;
  auto_contradict .   auto_contradict .

auto_replace H; auto .   auto_replace H4; auto .

Fig. 2. Proof Scripts

proof of SBakerySCTL.SMUTEX. The cost of migrating from SBakery to DBakery would be greatly reduced.

It is indeed the case in this example. Figure 2 shows fragments of the proofs of SBakerySCTL.SMUTEX and DBakerySCTL.SMUTEX, where differences are underlined. In the beginning of the proof, the tactic gen_cmd generates relations between the current and next states according to the transition relation Hsucc specified by the atoms. For example, for the guarded command [] pc i = inCS -> (pc i)' := outCS; (y i)' := 0 in atom i, gen_cmd would generate two assumptions H0 : s (pc i) = inCS and H1 : s' (pc i) = outCS /\ s' (y i) = 0 in the context where the guarded command is fired. We provide two versions of the tactic for different embeddings to help verifiers migrate their proofs. The remaining fragments analyze the scenario where process i enters the critical section and process j stutters. The only difference is due to the names generated during the case analysis. The tactics elim_all_or, elim_all_and, auto_contradict, and auto_replace simplify assumptions and look for contradiction. They are shared in both embeddings.

Figure 2 shows that the proofs of SBakerySCTL.SMUTEX and DBakerySCTL.SMUTEX are very similar despite using different encodings. In both proofs, the tactic gen_cmd translates the transition relation into logical relations between the current and next states. The proofs do not involve any encoding henceforth. If verifiers follow a similar proof strategy, the proof within the shallow embedding could be transformed to a proof within the deep embedding, and the migration cost is therefore reduced.

It is even simpler to prove the mutual exclusion property with the deep embedding of CTL* from DBakerySCTL.SMUTEX. We instantiate the module DBakeryDCTL of the deep embedding.

```
Module DBakeryDCTL := DCTLS DBakery .
```

The atomic proposition `smutex` in the shallow embedding becomes the following term in the deep embedding of CTL*.

```
Definition dmutex : AP :=
  forall_nat (fun i : nat => forall_nat (fun j : nat =>
    i < n --> j < n --> i <> j -->
      (pc i) <> inCS \/ (pc j) <> inCS)) .
```

The property can now be specified with the module `DBakeryDCTL` as follows.

```
Lemma DMUTEX : forall s : St, Init s -> model_s (A (G dmutex)) s .
```

To prove `DMUTEX`, note that both `DBakerySCTL.SMUTEX` and `DBakeryDCTL.DMUTEX` are of the same type in `CTLS`. A simple application of `DBakerySCTL.SMUTEX` proves `DBakeryDCTL.DMUTEX` trivially.

6   Future Work and Conclusion

Migration from one formalization to another requires effort, even for different embeddings of the same formalism. In this paper, we exploit the CoQ module system and give both the shallow and deep embeddings of two specification languages. We show how the Bakery algorithm is specified in both embeddings of Reactive Modules, as well as the mutual exclusion in both embeddings of CTL*. Three versions of the property are formally proved as examples. The examples suggest that the migration cost can be alleviated by the modular formalization presented in the paper.

Our formalization of the Reactive Modules could still be improved. In the future, we would also like to formalize other model specification languages within our framework. Moreover, the integration with different model checkers may be possible by formalizing model specification languages of different model checkers. Other formalizations of the requirement specification languages can also be done. In particular, we are working on a comparison of different formalizations of CTL*.

Acknowledgment. We would like to thank Yih-Kuen Tsay and anonymous reviewers for their constructive comments in improving the paper.

References

1. Alur, R., Henzinger, T.: Reactive modules. In: Proceedings of the 11th IEEE Symposium on Logic in Computer Science, pp. 207–218. IEEE Computer Society Press, Los Alamitos (1996)
2. Bauer, G.: Some properties of CTL. Technische Universität München, Isabelle/Isar document (2001)
3. Coupet-Grimal, S.: An axiomatization of linear temporal logic in the calculus of inductive constructions. Logic and Computation 13(6), 801–813 (2003)

4. Huet, G., Kahn, G.: Paulin-Mohring: The Coq proof assistant: a tutorial: version 6.1. Technical Report 204, Institut National de Recherche en Informatique et en Automatique (1997)
5. Lamport, L.: The temporal logic of actions. ACM Transactions on Programming Languages and Systems 16(3), 872–923 (1994)
6. Lynch, N.: Distributed algorithms. Morgan Kaufmann, San Francisco (1996)
7. Manna, Z., Pnueli, A.: The temporal framework for concurrent programs. In: Boyer, R., Moore, J. (eds.) The Correctness Problem in Computer Science, pp. 215–274. Academic Press, London (1981)
8. Manolios, P.: Mu-calculus model-checking. In: Computer-Aided Reasoning: ACL2 Case Studies, pp. 93–111. Kluwer Academic Publishers, Dordrecht (2000)
9. Merz, S.: Isabelle/TLA. Technische Universität München, Isabelle/Isar document (1998)
10. Miculan, M.: On the formalization of the modal μ-calculus in the calculus of inductive constructions. Information and Computation 164(1), 199–231 (2001)
11. Müller, O.: I/O automata and beyond - temporal logic and abstraction in Isabelle. In: Grundy, J., Newey, M. (eds.) Theorem Proving in Higher Order Logics. LNCS, vol. 1479, pp. 331–348. Springer, Heidelberg (1998)
12. Müller, O.: A Verification Environment for I/O Automata Based on Formalized Meta-Theory. PhD thesis, Technische Universität München (1998)
13. Müller, O., Nipkow, T.: Traces of I/O automata in Isabelle/HOLCF. In: Bidoit, M., Dauchet, M. (eds.) CAAP 1997, FASE 1997, and TAPSOFT 1997. LNCS, vol. 1214, pp. 580–595. Springer, Heidelberg (1997)
14. Nipkow, T., Slind, K.: I/O automata in Isabelle/HOL. In: Smith, J., Dybjer, P., Nordström, B. (eds.) TYPES 1994. LNCS, vol. 996, pp. 101–119. Springer, Heidelberg (1995)
15. Paulson, L.C., Nipkow, T.: Isabelle tutorial and user's manual. Technical Report TR-189, Computer Laboratory, University of Cambridge (1990)
16. Sprenger, C.: A verified model checker for the modal μ-calculus in Coq. In: Steffen, B. (ed.) ETAPS 1998 and TACAS 1998. LNCS, vol. 1384, pp. 167–183. Springer, Heidelberg (1998)
17. Tsai, M.H., Wang, B.Y.: Formalization of CTL* in calculus of inductive constructions. submitted for publication (2006)
18. Yu, S., Luo, Z.: Implementing a model checker for LEGO. In: Jones, C.B. (ed.) FME 1997. LNCS, vol. 1313, pp. 442–458. Springer, Heidelberg (1997)

Closing Internal Timing Channels by Transformation

Alejandro Russo[1], John Hughes[1], David Naumann[2], and Andrei Sabelfeld[1]

[1] Department of Computer Science and Engineering
Chalmers University of Technology, 412 96 Göteborg, Sweden Fax: +46 31 772 3663
[2] Department of Computer Science
Stevens Institute of Technology, Hoboken, New Jersey 07030, USA

Abstract. A major difficulty for tracking information flow in multithreaded programs is due to the *internal timing* covert channel. Information is leaked via this channel when secrets affect the timing behavior of a thread, which, via the scheduler, affects the interleaving of assignments to public variables. This channel is particularly dangerous because, in contrast to external timing, the attacker does not need to observe the actual execution time. This paper presents a compositional transformation that closes the internal timing channel for multithreaded programs (or rejects the program if there are symptoms of other flows). The transformation is based on spawning dedicated threads, whenever computation may affect secrets, and carefully synchronizing them. The target language features semaphores, which have not been previously considered in the context of termination-insensitive security.

1 Introduction

An active area of research is focused on information flow controls in multithreaded programs [21]. Multithreading opens new covert channels by which information can be leaked to an attacker. As a consequence, the machinery for enforcing secure information flow in sequential programs is not sufficient for multithreaded languages [25]. One particularly dangerous channel is the *internal timing* covert channel. Information is leaked via this channel when secrets affect the timing behavior of a thread, which, via the scheduler, affects the interleaving of assignments to public variables.

Suppose that h is a secret variable, and k and l are public ones. Assuming that $\|$ denotes parallel composition, consider a simple example of an internal timing leak:

$$
\begin{array}{l}
\text{if } h \geq k \text{ then skip; skip else skip;} \\
l := 1
\end{array}
\qquad \|
\qquad
\begin{array}{l}
\text{skip;} \\
\text{skip;} \\
l := 0
\end{array}
\quad \text{(Internal timing leak)}
$$

Under a one-step round-robin scheduler (and a wide class of other reasonable schedulers), if $h \geq k$ then by the time assignment $l := 1$ is reached in the first thread, the second thread has terminated. Therefore, the last assignment to execute is $l := 1$. On the other hand, if $h < k$ then by the time assignment $l := 0$ is reached in the second thread, the first thread has terminated. Therefore, the last assignment to execute is $l := 0$. Hence, the truth value of $h \geq k$ is leaked into l. Programs with dynamic thread creation are vulnerable to similar leaks. For example, a direct encoding of the example above is depicted in Fig. 1 (where $\texttt{fork}(c)$ spawns a new thread c).

M. Okada and I. Satoh (Eds.): ASIAN 2006, LNCS 4435, pp. 120–135, 2007.
© Springer-Verlag Berlin Heidelberg 2007

This program also leaks whether $h \geq k$ is true, under many schedulers. Internal timing leaks are particularly dangerous because, in contrast to *external* timing, the attacker does not need to observe the actual execution time. Moreover, leaks similar to those considered so far can be magnified via loops as shown in Fig. 2 (where k, l, n, and p are public; and h is an n-bit secret integer). Each iteration of the loop leaks one bit of h. As a result, the entire value of h is copied into p. Although this example assumes a round-robin scheduler, similar examples can be easily constructed where secrets are copied into public variables under any fair scheduler [25].

Existing proposals to tackling internal timing flows heavily rely on the modification of run-time environment. (A more detailed discussion of related work is deferred to Section 8.) A series of work by Volpano and Smith [25, 27, 23, 24] suggests a special $\text{protect}(c)$ state-

```
fork(skip; skip; l := 0);
if h ≥ k
  then skip; skip else skip;
l := 1
```

Fig. 1. Internal timing leak with fork

```
p := 0;
while n ≥ 0 do
  k := 2^{n-1};
  fork(skip; skip; l := 0);
  if h ≥ k
    then skip; skip else skip;
  l := 1;
  if l = 1
    then h := h - k; p := p + k
    else skip;
  n := n - 1
```

Fig. 2. Internal timing leak magnified

ment that, by definition, takes one atomic computation step with the effect of running command c to the end. Internal timing leaks are made invisible because $\text{protect}()$-based security typed systems ensure that computation that branches on secrets is wrapped by $\text{protect}()$ commands. However, implementing $\text{protect}()$ is a major challenge [22, 19, 16] because while a thread runs $\text{protect}()$, the other threads must be instantly blocked. Russo and Sabelfeld argue that standard synchronization primitives are not sufficient and resort to primitives for direct interaction with scheduler in order to enable instant blocking [16]. However, a drawback of this approach (and, arguably, any approach that implements $\text{protect}()$ by instant blocking) is that it relies on the modification of run-time environment: the scheduler must be able to immediately suspend all threads that might potentially assign to public variables while a protected segment of code is run, which limits concurrency in the program.

This paper eliminates the need for modifying the run-time environment for a class of round-robin schedulers. We give a transformation that closes internal timing leaks by spawning dedicated threads for segments of code that may affect secrets. There are no internal timing leaks in transformed programs because the timing for reaching assignments to public variables does not depend on secrets. The transformation carefully synchronizes the dedicated threads in order not to introduce undesired interleavings in the semantics of the original program. Despite the introduced synchronization, threads that operate on public data are not prevented from progress by threads that operate on secret data, which gives more concurrency than in [25, 27, 23, 24, 16].

For a program with internal timing leaks under a particular deterministic scheduler, the elimination of leaks necessarily changes the interleavings and so possibly the final result. What thread synchronization allows us to achieve is refinement of results under nondeterministic scheduling: the result of the transformed program (under round-robin) is a possible result of the source program under nondeterministic scheduling. Although an attacker would seek to exploit information about the specific scheduler in use, good software engineering practice suggests that a program's functional behavior should not be dependent on specific properties of a scheduler beyond such properties as fairness.

The transformation does not reject programs unless they have symptoms that would already reject sequential programs [5, 28]. The transformation ensures that the rest of insecurities (due to internal timing) are repaired.

It is seemingly possible to remove internal timing leaks by applying the following naive transformation. Suppose a command (program) c only has two variables h and l to store a secret and a public value, respectively. Assume that c does not have insecurities other than due to internal timing (this can be achieved by disallowing explicit and implicit flows, defined later in the paper). Then the following program does not leak any information about h, while it computes output as intended for c (or diverges):

$$h_i := h;\ l_i := l;\ h := 0;\ c;\ bar;\ l_o := l;\ h := h_i;\ l := l_i;\ c;\ bar;\ l := l_o$$

where bar is a barrier command that ensures that all other threads have terminated before proceeding. This transformation suffers from at least two drawbacks. Firstly, the program c is run twice, which is inefficient. Secondly, it is hard to ensure that any kind of nondeterminism (e.g., due to the scheduler, random number generator, or input channels) in c is resolved in the same way in both copies. For example, the transformation does not scale up naturally when c uses input channels. It is not obvious how to communicate inputs between the two copies of the program.

Another attempt to remove internal timing leaks could be done by applying slicing techniques, which can automatically split the original program into low and high parts. Unfortunately, these techniques in presence of concurrency are not enough to preserve the semantics of the original program. The reason for that is simple: public variables, which are updated by threads, might affect the computation of secrets. Therefore, an explicit communication of public values to the high part is required.

2 Language

Although our technique is applicable to fully-fledged programming languages, we use a simple imperative language to formalize the transformation. The language includes a command $\mathrm{fork}((\lambda \vec{x}.c)\,@\,\vec{e})$, which dynamically creates and runs a new thread with local variables $\vec{x}$ with initial values given by the expressions $\vec{e}$. When the list of local variables is empty, we sometimes use simpler notation: $\mathrm{fork}(c)$. The command c may also use the program's global variables. The transformation requires dynamically allocated semaphores, so these too are included in the language defined in this section.

Without making it precise, we assume that each variable is of type integer or type semaphore. There are no expressions of type semaphore other than semaphore variables. A main program is a single command c, in the grammar of Fig. 3. Its free variables comprise the *globals* of the program. The *source language* is the subset in which there are no stop commands, no semaphore variables and therefore no semaphore allocations or operations. Moreover, the list of local variables in every fork must be empty. Locals

$$c ::= \texttt{skip} \mid x := e \mid c; c \mid \texttt{if } e \texttt{ then } c \texttt{ else } c \mid \texttt{while } e \texttt{ do } c \mid \texttt{fork}((\lambda \vec{x}.c) @ \vec{e})$$
$$\mid \texttt{stop} \mid s := \texttt{newSem}(n) \mid \texttt{P}(s) \mid \texttt{V}(s)$$

Fig. 3. Command syntax (with x and s ranging over variables, and n over integer literals)

$$\frac{(\vec{e}, m) \downarrow \vec{v}}{\langle \texttt{fork}((\lambda \vec{x}.d) @ \vec{e}), m, h \rangle \overset{\lambda \vec{x}.d, \vec{v}}{\dashrightarrow} \langle \texttt{stop}, m, h \rangle} \qquad \frac{(s, m) \downarrow r \qquad h(r).cnt = 0}{\langle \texttt{P}(s), m, h \rangle \overset{\otimes r}{\dashrightarrow} \langle \texttt{stop}, m, h \rangle}$$

$$\frac{(s, m) \downarrow r \qquad h(r).cnt > 0 \qquad h' = h[r.cnt := r.cnt - 1]}{\langle \texttt{P}(s), m, h \rangle \dashrightarrow \langle \texttt{stop}, m, h' \rangle}$$

$$\frac{(s, m) \downarrow r}{\langle \texttt{V}(s), m, h \rangle \overset{\odot r}{\dashrightarrow} \langle \texttt{stop}, m, h \rangle}$$

$$\frac{i = max(dom(h)) + 1 \qquad h' = h \cup \{i \mapsto (cnt = n, que = \langle \rangle)\}}{\langle s := \texttt{newSem}(n), m, h \rangle \dashrightarrow \langle \texttt{stop}, m[s := i], h' \rangle}$$

Fig. 4. Commands semantics

are needed for the transformation, but locals in source code would complicate the transformation (because each source thread is split into multiple threads, and locals are not shared between threads).

3 Semantics

The formal semantics is defined in two levels: individual command and threadpool semantics. The small-step semantics for sequential commands is standard [29], and we thus omit these rules. The rules for concurrent commands are given in Fig. 4.

Configurations have the form $\langle c, m, h \rangle$, where c is a command, m is a memory (mapping variables to their values), and h is a heap for dynamically allocated semaphores. The expression language does not include dereferencing of semaphore references, so evaluation of expressions does not depend on the heap. We write $(e, m) \downarrow n$ to say that n is the value of e in memory m. A *heap* is a finite mapping from semaphore references (which we take to be naturals) to records of the form $(cnt = n, que = ws)$ where n is a natural number and ws is the list of blocked thread states.

Let α range over the following *events*, which label command transitions for use in the threadpool semantics: $\odot r$, to indicate the semaphore at reference r is signaled; $\otimes r$, to indicate it is waited; or a pair $\lambda \vec{x}.c, \vec{v}$ where $\vec{v}$ is a sequence of values that match $\vec{x}$.

Threadpool configurations have the form $\langle \langle (c_0, m_0) \dots (c_i, m_i) \dots (c_{n-1}, m_{n-1}) \rangle$ $g, h, j \rangle$, where each (c_i, m_i) is the state of thread i which is not blocked, g maps global variables to their values, h is the heap, $j \in 0 \dots n - 1$ is the index of the thread that will take the next step. For all i, $dom(m_i)$ is disjoint from $dom(g)$. Numbering threads $0 \dots n - 1$ slightly simplifies some definitions related to round-robin scheduling.

The threadpool semantics is defined for any scheduler relation SC. We interpret $(i, n, n', i') \in SC$ to mean that i is the current thread taking a step, n is the current pool size, n' is the size of the pool after that step, and i' is the next thread chosen by the scheduler. This model is adequate to define a round-robin scheduler for which thread activation, suspension, and termination do not affect the interleaving of other threads, and also to model full nondeterminism. The fully nondeterministic scheduler ND is defined by $(i, n, n', i') \in ND$ if and only if $0 \leq i < n$ and $0 \leq i' < n'$.

A little care is needed with round-robin to maintain the order when threads are blocked or terminated. The definition relies on some details of the threadpool semantics, e.g., when a step by thread i removes a thread from the pool (by termination or blocking), that thread is i itself. Define the round-robin scheduler RR by $(i, n, n', i') \in RR$ if and only if $0 \leq i < n$ and equation (1) holds.

The threadpool semantics is given in Fig. 5. Note that memories in command configurations are disjoint unions $m_i \cup g$, where m_i is the thread-local memory, and g is the global one. We write

$$
\begin{aligned}
i' &= i, && \text{if } n' < n \text{ and } i < n - 1 \\
&= 0, && \text{if } n' < n \text{ and } i = n - 1 \\
&= (i + 1) \bmod n', && \text{otherwise}
\end{aligned}
\tag{1}
$$

$h[r.\text{que} := (r.\text{que} :: (c, m))]$ to abbreviate an update of the record at r in h to change its que field by appending (c, m) at the tail. Although semaphores are stored in a heap, we streamline the semantics by not including a null reference. Thus, an initial heap is needed. It is defined to initialize semaphores to 1, which is an arbitrary choice. The security condition defined later refers to initial values for all global variables, for simplicity, but only integer inputs matter.

Definition 1. *The* initial heap of size k *is the mapping* h_k *with domain* $1 \ldots k$ *that maps each* i *to the semaphore state* $(cnt = 1, que = \langle\rangle)$. *Suppose that* k *of the globals have type semaphore. Given a global memory* g, *the* initial global memory g_k *agrees with* g *on integer variables, and the* ith *semaphore variable (under some enumeration) is mapped to* i ($i \in dom(h_k)$).

Define $(c, g) \Downarrow g'$ *if and only if* $\langle\langle (c, m)\rangle, g_k, h_k, 0\rangle \rightarrow^* \langle\langle\rangle, g', h', j\rangle$, *for some* h' *and* j, *where* $\rightarrow^*$ *is the reflexive and transitive closure of the transition relation* $\rightarrow$, *and* m *is the empty function (since the initial thread* c *has no local variables).*

Note that the definitions of $\rightarrow^*$ and $\Downarrow$ depend on the choice of scheduler, but this is elided in the notation.

4   Security Specification

Assume that all global non-semaphore variables are labeled with *low* or *high* security levels to represent public and secret data, respectively. We label all semaphore variables as high in the target code (recall that the source program has no semaphore variables). To define the security condition, it suffices to define *low equality* of global memories, written $g_1 =_L g_2$, to say that $g_1(x) = g_2(x)$ for all low variables x.

Definition 2. *Program* c *is secure if for all* g_1, g_2 *such that* $g_1 =_L g_2$, *if* $(c, g_1) \Downarrow g_1'$ *and* $(c, g_2) \Downarrow g_2'$ *then* $g_1' =_L g_2'$, *where* $\Downarrow$ *refers to the round-robin scheduler* RR.

$$\frac{\langle c_i, m_i \cup g, h \rangle \rightarrow \langle c_i', m_i' \cup g', h' \rangle \qquad (i, n, n, j) \in SC}{\langle\langle \ldots (c_i, m_i) \ldots \rangle, g, h, i \rangle \rightarrow \langle\langle \ldots (c_i', m_i') \ldots \rangle, g', h', j \rangle}$$

$$\frac{c_i = \texttt{stop} \qquad (i, n, n-1, j) \in SC}{\langle\langle \ldots (c_i, m_i) \ldots \rangle, g, h, i \rangle \rightarrow \langle\langle \ldots (c_{i-1}, m_{i-1})(c_{i+1}, m_{i+1}) \ldots \rangle, g, h, j \rangle}$$

$$\frac{\langle c_i, m_i \cup g, h \rangle \xrightarrow{\lambda \vec{x}.d, \vec{v}} \langle c_i', m_i' \cup g', h' \rangle \qquad m = \{\vec{x} \mapsto \vec{v}\} \qquad (i, n, n+1, j) \in SC}{\langle\langle \ldots (c_i, m_i) \ldots (c_{n-1}, m_{n-1}) \rangle, g, h, i \rangle \rightarrow \langle\langle \ldots (c_i', m_i') \ldots (c_{n-1}, m_{n-1})(d, m) \rangle, g', h', j \rangle}$$

$$\frac{\langle c_i, m_i \cup g, h \rangle \xrightarrow{\otimes r} \langle c_i', m_i' \cup g', h' \rangle \qquad h'' = h'[r.\text{que} := (r.\text{que} :: (c_i', m_i'))] \qquad (i, n, n-1, j) \in SC}{\langle\langle \ldots (c_i, m_i) \ldots \rangle, g, h, i \rangle \rightarrow \langle\langle \ldots (c_{i-1}, m_{i-1})(c_{i+1}, m_{i+1}) \ldots \rangle, g', h'', j \rangle}$$

$$\frac{\langle c_i, m_i \cup g, h \rangle \xrightarrow{\odot r} \langle c_i', m_i' \cup g', h' \rangle \qquad h''= h'[r.\text{que} := ws] \qquad (i, n, n+1, j) \in SC}{h'(r).\text{que} = (c, m) :: ws}{\langle\langle \ldots (c_i, m_i) \ldots (c_{n-1}, m_{n-1}) \rangle, g, h, i \rangle \rightarrow \langle\langle \ldots (c_i', m_i') \ldots (c_{n-1}, m_{n-1})(c, m) \rangle, g', h'', j \rangle}$$

$$\frac{\langle c_i, m_i \cup g, h \rangle \xrightarrow{\odot r} \langle c_i', m_i' \cup g', h' \rangle \qquad h'' = h'[r.\text{cnt} := r.\text{cnt} + 1] \qquad (i, n, n, j) \in SC}{h'(r).\text{que} = \langle\rangle}{\langle\langle \ldots (c_i, m_i) \ldots \rangle, g, h, i \rangle \rightarrow \langle\langle \ldots (c_i', m_i') \ldots \rangle, g', h'', j \rangle}$$

Fig. 5. Threadpool semantics (for scheduler SC)

The definition says that low equality of initial global memories implies low equality of final global memories. Note that this definition is termination-insensitive [21], in the sense that nonterminating runs are ignored.

Observe that the examples from the introduction are rejected by the above definition because the changes in the final values of low variables break low equality. Consider another example (where k and l are low; and h is high):

$$\texttt{if } (h \geq k) \texttt{ then skip; skip else skip} \parallel l := 0 \parallel l := 1$$

This program is secure because the timing of the first thread does not affect how the race between assignments in the second and third threads is resolved. This holds for round-robin schedulers that run each thread for a fixed number of steps (which covers the case of a one-step round-robin scheduler RR), machine instructions, or even calls to the `fork` primitive. Note, however, that schedulers that are able to change the order of scheduled threads depending on the number of live threads would not necessarily guarantee secure execution of the above program. For example, consider a scheduler that runs the first thread for two steps and then checks the number of live threads. If this number is two then the second thread is scheduled; otherwise the third thread is scheduled. This leaks the truth value of $h \geq k$ into l. Round-robin schedulers are not only practical but also in this sense more secure, which motivates our choice to adopt them in the semantics.

5   Transformation

In this section, we give a transformation that rules out *explicit* and *implicit* flows [5] and closes internal timing leaks under round-robin schedulers. The transformation rules have the form $\Gamma; w, s, a, b, m \vdash c \hookrightarrow c'$, where command c is transformed into c' under the security type environment Γ, which maps variables to their security levels, and special semaphore variables w, s, a, b, and m needed for synchronization. Moreover, a fresh high variable h_x is introduced for each low variable x in the source code. The transformation comprises the rules presented in Fig. 6 and the top-level rule:

$$\frac{\Gamma; w, s, a, b, m \vdash c \hookrightarrow c' \qquad w, s \text{ fresh}}{\Gamma \vdash c \hookrightarrow_t m := \texttt{newSem}(1); a := \texttt{newSem}(1); w := \texttt{newSem}(1); \vec{h_l} := \vec{l}; c'} \qquad (2)$$

where $\vec{h_l} := \vec{l}$ stands for copying all low variables l into fresh high variables h_l.

Define *low assignments* to be assignments to low variables. Explicit flows are prevented by not allowing high variables to occur in low assignments (see rule L-ASG). Define *high conditionals (loops)* to be conditionals (loops) that branch on expressions that contain high variables. Implicit flows for high conditionals and loops are prevented by rules of the form $\Gamma \vdash c \leftrightsquigarrow c'$, where command c is transformed into c' under Γ. These rules guarantee that high if's and while's do not have assignments to low variables in their bodies. These rules for tracking explicit and implicit flows are adopted from security-type systems for sequential programs [28].

As illustrated by previous examples, internal timing channels are introduced by low assignments after high conditionals and loops. To close these channels, the transformation introduces a `fork` whenever the source code branches on high data (see rules (H-IF) and (H-W)). Since such computations are now spawned in new threads, the number of executed instructions before low assignments does not depend on secrets. However, new threads open up possibilities for new races between high variables, which can unexpectedly change the semantics of the program. To ensure that such races are avoided (which we also prove in Section 7), the transformation spawns dedicated threads for all computations that might affect high data (see rules (H-ASG) and (L-ASG)) and carefully places synchronization primitives in the transformed program. We will illustrate this, and other interesting aspects of the transformation, through examples.

Consider the following simple program that suffers from an internal timing leak:

$$(\text{if } h_1 \text{ then skip; skip else skip}); l := 1 \parallel d \qquad (3)$$

where d abbreviates command skip; skip; $l := 0$. The assignment $l := 1$ may be reached in three or two steps depending on h_1. However, by spawning the high conditional in a new thread, the number of instructions to execute it will no longer affect when $l := 1$ is reached. More precisely, we can rewrite program (3) as `fork`(if h_1 then skip; skip; else skip); $l := 1 \parallel d$, where internal timing leaks are not possible. From now on, we assume that the initial values of l and h_2 are always 0. Suppose now that we modify program (3) by:

$$(\text{if } h_1 \text{ then } h_2 := 2 * h_2 + l; \text{skip else skip}); l := 1 \parallel d \qquad (4)$$

$$\frac{\forall v \in Vars(e).\, \Gamma(v) = low}{\Gamma \vdash e : low} \qquad \frac{\exists v \in Vars(e).\, \Gamma(v) = high}{\Gamma \vdash e : high}$$

$$\frac{}{\Gamma; w, s, a, b, m \vdash \texttt{skip} \hookrightarrow \texttt{skip}} \qquad \frac{(\Gamma; w, s, a, b, m \vdash c_i \hookrightarrow c'_i)_{i=1,2}}{\Gamma; w, s, a, b, m \vdash c_1; c_2 \hookrightarrow c'_1; c'_2}$$

$$\text{(H-ASG)} \frac{\Gamma \vdash e \rightsquigarrow e' \qquad \Gamma(x) = high}{\Gamma; w, s, a, b, m \vdash x := e \hookrightarrow \begin{array}{l} s := \texttt{newSem}(0); \\ \quad \texttt{fork}((\lambda \hat{w} \hat{s}.\texttt{P}(\hat{w}); x := e'; \texttt{V}(\hat{s})) @ ws); \\ w := s \end{array}}$$

$$\text{(L-ASG)} \frac{\Gamma \vdash e : low \qquad \Gamma(x) = low \qquad \Gamma \vdash e \rightsquigarrow e'}{\Gamma; w, s, a, b \vdash x := e \hookrightarrow \begin{array}{l} s := \texttt{newSem}(0); \\ \texttt{P}(m);\ x := e;\ b := \texttt{newSem}(0); \\ \texttt{fork}((\lambda \hat{w} \hat{s} \hat{a} \hat{b}.\texttt{P}(\hat{w}); \texttt{P}(\hat{a}); h_x := e'; \texttt{V}(\hat{b}); \texttt{V}(\hat{s})) @ wsab) \\ a := b; \texttt{V}(m); \\ w := s \end{array}}$$

$$\frac{\Gamma \vdash e : low \qquad \Gamma; w, s, a, b, m \vdash c \hookrightarrow c'}{\Gamma; w, s, a, b, m \vdash \texttt{while } e \texttt{ do } c \hookrightarrow \texttt{while } e \texttt{ do } c'}$$

$$\frac{\Gamma \vdash e : low \qquad (\Gamma; w, s, a, b, m \vdash c_i \hookrightarrow c'_i)_{i=1,2}}{\Gamma; w, s, a, b, m \vdash \texttt{if } e \texttt{ then } c_1 \texttt{ else } c_2 \hookrightarrow \texttt{if } e \texttt{ then } c'_1 \texttt{ else } c'_2}$$

$$\text{(H-IF)} \frac{\Gamma \vdash e : high \qquad \Gamma \vdash e \rightsquigarrow e' \qquad (\Gamma \vdash c_i \rightsquigarrow c'_i)_{i=1,2} \qquad c_t = \texttt{if } e' \texttt{ then } c'_1 \texttt{ else } c'_2}{\Gamma; w, s, a, b, m \vdash \texttt{if } e \texttt{ then } c_1 \texttt{ else } c_2 \hookrightarrow \begin{array}{l} s := \texttt{newSem}(0); \\ \quad \texttt{fork}((\lambda \hat{w} \hat{s}.\texttt{P}(\hat{w}); c_t; \texttt{V}(\hat{s})) @ ws); \\ w := s \end{array}}$$

$$\text{(H-W)} \frac{\Gamma \vdash e : high \qquad \Gamma \vdash e \rightsquigarrow e' \qquad \Gamma \vdash c \rightsquigarrow c' \qquad c_t = \texttt{while } e' \texttt{ do } c'}{\Gamma; w, s, a, b, m \vdash \texttt{while } e \texttt{ do } c \hookrightarrow \begin{array}{l} s := \texttt{newSem}(0); \\ \quad \texttt{fork}((\lambda \hat{w} \hat{s}.\texttt{P}(\hat{w}); c_t; \texttt{V}(\hat{s})) @ ws); \\ w := s \end{array}}$$

$$\frac{\Gamma; w', s', a, b, m \vdash d \hookrightarrow d' \qquad c_t = \texttt{fork}((\lambda \hat{w} \hat{s} \hat{w}'.\texttt{P}(\hat{w}); \texttt{V}(\hat{w}); \texttt{V}(\hat{s}); \texttt{V}(\hat{w}')) @ \hat{w} \hat{s} w') \qquad w', s' \text{ fresh}}{\Gamma; w, s, a, b, m \vdash \texttt{fork}(d) \hookrightarrow \begin{array}{l} s := \texttt{newSem}(0); \\ \quad \texttt{fork}((\lambda \hat{w} \hat{s}.w' := \texttt{newSem}(0); c_t; d') @ ws); \\ w := s \end{array}}$$

$$\frac{}{\Gamma \vdash e \rightsquigarrow e[h_x/x]_{\Gamma(x)=low}} \qquad \frac{}{\Gamma \vdash \texttt{skip} \rightsquigarrow \texttt{skip}} \qquad \frac{\Gamma(v) = high \qquad \Gamma \vdash e \rightsquigarrow e'}{\Gamma \vdash v := e \rightsquigarrow v := e'}$$

$$\frac{\Gamma \vdash e \rightsquigarrow e' \qquad (\Gamma \vdash c_i \rightsquigarrow c'_i)_{i=1,2}}{\Gamma \vdash \texttt{if } e \texttt{ then } c_1 \texttt{ else } c_2 \rightsquigarrow \texttt{if } e' \texttt{ then } c'_1 \texttt{ else } c'_2} \qquad \frac{\Gamma \vdash d \rightsquigarrow d'}{\Gamma \vdash \texttt{fork}(d) \rightsquigarrow \texttt{fork}(d')}$$

$$\frac{(\Gamma \vdash c_i \rightsquigarrow c'_i)_{i=1,2}}{\Gamma \vdash c_1; c_2 \rightsquigarrow c'_1; c'_2} \qquad \frac{\Gamma \vdash e \rightsquigarrow e' \qquad \Gamma \vdash c \rightsquigarrow c'}{\Gamma \vdash \texttt{while } e \texttt{ do } c \rightsquigarrow \texttt{while } e' \texttt{ do } c'}$$

Fig. 6. Transformation rules

where the final value of h_2 is always 0. This code still suffers from an internal timing leak. Unfortunately, by putting a `fork` around the `if` as before, we introduce 1 as a possible final value for h_2, which was not possible in the original code. This discrepancy originates from an undesired new interleaving of the rewritten program: $l := 1$ can be computed before $h_2 := 2 * h_2 + l$. To prevent such an interleaving, we introduce fresh high variables for every low variable in the code. We call this kind of new variables *high images* of low variables. Since low variables are only read, and not written, by high conditional and loops, it is possible to replace low variables inside of high contexts by their corresponding high images. Then, every time that low variables are updated, their corresponding images will do so but in due course.

To illustrate this, let us rewrite the left side of program (4) as in (5). Variable h_l is the corresponding high image of low variable l. Two dedicated threads are spawned with different local snapshots of w and s, written as $\hat{w}$ and $\hat{s}$, respectively. The second dedicated

$$
\begin{aligned}
&w := \texttt{newSem}(1); \quad //\text{initialization from top-level rule (2)}\\
&s := \texttt{newSem}(0);\\
&\texttt{fork}((\lambda\hat{w}\hat{s}.\texttt{P}(\hat{w}); \ (\texttt{if } h_1 \texttt{ then } h_2 := 2 * h_2 + h_l; \texttt{skip}\\
&\hspace{6.5cm}\texttt{else skip}); \texttt{V}(\hat{s}))\\
&\hspace{1cm}@ws)\\
&w := s\\
&l := 1; s := \texttt{newSem}(0);\\
&\texttt{fork}((\lambda\hat{w}\hat{s}.\texttt{P}(\hat{w}); h_l := 1; \texttt{V}(\hat{s})) @ ws)\\
&w := s
\end{aligned}
$$
(5)

thread, which updates the high image of l to 1, waits $(\texttt{P}(\hat{w}))$ for the first one to finish, and the first one indicates when the second one should start $(\texttt{V}(\hat{s}))$. By doing so, and by properly updating w and s in the main thread, the command $h_l := 1$ is never executed before the `if` statement. Note that the first dedicated thread does not need to synchronize with previous ones. Hence, the top-level transformation rule, presented at the beginning of the section, initializes the semaphore w to 1.

The thread d also needs to be modified to include an update to h_l. Let us rewrite d as in (6). Semaphore variables w_d and s_d do not play any important role here, since just one dedicated thread is spawned. Note that if we run programs (5) and (6) in parallel, it might be possible that the updates of low variables happen in a dif-

$$
\begin{aligned}
&w_d := \texttt{newSem}(1);\\
&\texttt{skip}; \texttt{skip};\\
&l := 0; s_d := \texttt{newSem}(0);\\
&\texttt{fork}((\lambda\hat{w}_d\hat{s}_d.\texttt{P}(\hat{w}_d); h_l := 0; \texttt{V}(\hat{s}_d))\\
&\hspace{2cm}@w_ds_d);\\
&w_d := s_d
\end{aligned}
$$
(6)

ferent order than the updates of their corresponding high images. In order to avoid this, we introduce three global semaphores, called a, b, and m. The final transformed code is shown in Fig. 7, where c'_1 runs in parallel with d'_1. Semaphore variables a and b ensure that the queuing processes update high images in the same order as the low assignments occur. Since a and b are globals, we protect their access with the global semaphore m. As in the original program, h_2 can only have the final value 0. From now on, we assume that the semaphore a is allocated and initialized with value 1 .

Let us modify program (4) by adding assignments to high and low variables:

$$(\texttt{if } h_1 \texttt{ then } h_2 := 2 * h_2 + l; \texttt{skip else skip}); l := 1; h_2 := h_2 + 1; l := 3 \parallel d \quad (7)$$

The final value of h_2 is 1. As before, this code still suffers from internal timing leaks. By putting `fork`'s around high conditionals and introducing updates for high images as

$$c_1' : w := \mathtt{newSem}(1);$$
$$\qquad s := \mathtt{newSem}(0);$$
$$\qquad \mathtt{fork}((\lambda \hat{w}\hat{s}.\mathtt{P}(\hat{w});$$
$$\qquad\qquad \mathtt{if}\ h_1\ \mathtt{then}\ h_2 := 2 * h_2 + h_l;$$
$$\qquad\qquad\qquad \mathtt{skip};$$
$$\qquad\qquad \mathtt{else\ skip};$$
$$\qquad\qquad \mathtt{V}(\hat{s}))@ws);$$
$$\qquad w := s$$
$$\qquad s := \mathtt{newSem}(0);$$
$$\qquad \mathtt{P}(m); l := 1; b := \mathtt{newSem}(0);$$
$$\qquad \mathtt{fork}((\lambda \hat{w}\hat{s}\hat{a}\hat{b}.\mathtt{P}(\hat{w});\mathtt{P}(\hat{a}); h_l := 1;$$
$$\qquad\qquad \mathtt{V}(\hat{b});\mathtt{V}(\hat{s}))@wsab);$$
$$\qquad a := b; \mathtt{V}(m);$$
$$\qquad w := s$$

$$d_1' : w_d := \mathtt{newSem}(1);$$
$$\qquad \mathtt{skip};\mathtt{skip};$$
$$\qquad s_d := \mathtt{newSem}(0);$$
$$\qquad \mathtt{P}(m); l := 0; b := \mathtt{newSem}(0);$$
$$\qquad \mathtt{fork}((\lambda \hat{w}_d\hat{s}_d\hat{a}\hat{b}.\mathtt{P}(\hat{w}_d);\mathtt{P}(\hat{a}); h_l := 0;$$
$$\qquad\qquad \mathtt{V}(\hat{b});\mathtt{V}(\hat{s}_d))@w_d s_d ab);$$
$$\qquad a := b; \mathtt{V}(m);$$
$$\qquad w_d := s_d$$

Fig. 7. Transformed code for program (4)

in program (5), we would introduce 2 as a new possible final value for h_2, when h_1 is positive. The new value arises from executing $h_2 := h_2 + 1$ before the if statement.

In order to remove this race, we use synchronization to guarantee that computations on high data are executed in the same order as they appear in the original code. However, this synchronization should not lead to recreating timing leaks: waiting for the if to finish before executing $h_2 := h_2 + 1; l := 3$ would imply that the timing of the low assignment $l := 3$ could depend on h_1. We resolve this problem by spawning dedicated threads for assignments to high variables and synchronizing, via semaphores, these threads with

$$c_2' : c_1'; s := \mathtt{newSem}(0);$$
$$\qquad \mathtt{fork}((\lambda \hat{w}\hat{s}.\mathtt{P}(\hat{w}); h_2 := h_2 + 1; \mathtt{V}(\hat{s}))@ws)$$
$$\qquad w := s;$$
$$\qquad \mathtt{P}(m); l := 3; b := \mathtt{newSem}(0);$$
$$\qquad \mathtt{fork}((\lambda \hat{w}\hat{s}\hat{a}\hat{b}.\mathtt{P}(\hat{w});\mathtt{P}(\hat{a}); h_l := 3; \mathtt{V}(\hat{b});$$
$$\qquad\qquad \mathtt{V}(\hat{s}))@wsab);$$
$$\qquad a := b; \mathtt{V}(m);$$
$$\qquad \| d_1'$$

$$(8)$$

other threads that either read from or write to high data. The dedicated thread to compute $h_2 := h_2 + 1$ will wait until the last dedicated thread in c_1' finishes. The transformed code is shown in (8). Note that spawned dedicated threads are executed in the same order as they appear in the main thread.

Let us modify program (7) to introduce a fork as in (9). The final value of h_2 is 5. However, the rewritten program will spawn several dedicated

$$\mathtt{if}\ h_1\ \mathtt{then}\ h_2 := 2 * h_2 + l; \mathtt{skip\ else\ skip};$$
$$l := 1; h_2 := h_2 + 1; l := 3;$$
$$\mathtt{fork}(h_2 := 5)\ \|\ d$$

$$(9)$$

threads: for the conditional, for updating high images, $h_2 := h_2 + 1$, and $h_2 := 5$, which need to be synchronized. In particular, $h_2 := 5$ cannot be executed before $h_2 := h_2 + 1$ finishes. Thus, we need to synchronize dedicated threads in the main thread with the dedicated threads from their children. This is addressed by the transformation in (10), where d^* spawns a new thread that waits on w' to perform $h_2 := 5$. In order to be able to receive a signal on w', it is necessary to firstly receive a signal on $\hat{w}$, which can be only done after computing $h_2 := h_2 + 1$. Note that the transformation spawns a new thread to wait on $\underline{\hat{w}}$ in order to avoid recreating timing leaks. When a fork occurs inside a loop in the source program, there is potentially a number of dynamic threads that need to wait for the previous computation on high data to finish. This is resolved by passing-the-baton technique: whichever thread receives a signal first ($P(\hat{\underline{w}})$) passes it to another thread ($V(\hat{\underline{w}})$).

The examples above show how to close internal timing leaks by spawning dedicated threads that perform computation on high data. We have seen that some synchronization is needed to avoid producing different outputs than intended in the original program. Transformed programs introduce performance overhead related to synchronization. This overhead comes as a price for not modifying the run-time environment when preventing internal timing leaks.

$$
\begin{aligned}
&c_2'; \\
&s := \texttt{newSem}(0); \\
&\texttt{fork}((\lambda \hat{w}\hat{s}.w' := \texttt{newSem}(0); \\
&\quad\quad \texttt{fork}((\lambda \hat{\underline{w}}\hat{s}\hat{w}'.P(\hat{\underline{w}}); V(\hat{\underline{w}}); \\
&\quad\quad\quad V(\hat{s}); V(\hat{w}'))@\hat{w}\hat{s}w'); d^*) \\
&\quad\quad @ws); \\
&w := s; \| \ d_1'
\end{aligned}
\tag{10}
$$

6   Geo-Localization Example

Inspired by a scenario from mobile computing [1], we give an example of closing timing leaks in a realistic setting. Modern mobile phones are able to compute their geographical positions. The widely used MIDP profile [10] for mobile devices includes API support for obtaining the current position of the handset [11]. Furthermore, geo-localization can be approximated by using the identity of the current base station and the power of its signal. It is desirable that such information can only be used by trusted parties.

Consider the code fragment in

```
hotel_l := nextHotel();
hotelLoc_l := getHotelLocation(hotel_l);
d_h := distance(hotelLoc_l, userLoc_h);
closest_h := hotel_l;
while (moreHotels?()) do
  hotel_l := nextHotel();
  hotelLoc_l := getHotelLocation(hotel_l);
  d'_h := distance(hotelLoc_l, userLoc_h);
  if (d'_h < d_h) then d_h := d'_h; closest_h := hotel_l
            else skip
i_h := 0;
while (moreTypeRooms?(closest_h)) do
  type_h := nextTypeRoom(closest_h);
  showTypeRoom(type_h, i_h);
  i_h := i_h + 1;
```

Fig. 8. Geo-localization example

Fig. 8. This fragment is part of a program that runs on a mobile phone. Such a program typically uses dynamic thread creation (which is supported by MIDP) to perform time-consuming computation (such as establishing network connections) in separate threads [12, 14].

The program searches for the closest hotel in the area where the handset is located. Once found, it displays the types of available rooms at that hotel. Variables have subscripts indicating their security levels (l for low and h for high). Suppose that $hotel_l$ and $hotelLoc_l$ contain the public name and location for a given hotel, respectively. The location of the mobile device is stored in the high variable $userLoc_h$. Variables d_h and d'_h are used to compute the distance to a given hotel. Variable $closest_h$ stores the location of the closest hotel in the area. Variable i_h is used to index the type of rooms at the closest hotel. Variable $type_h$ stores a room type, i.e., single, double, etc. Function $nextHotel()$ returns the next available hotel in the area (for simplicity, we assume there is always at least one). Function $getHotelLocation()$ provides the location of a given hotel, and function $distance()$ computes the distance between two locations. Function $moreHotels?()$ returns true if there are more hotels for $nextHotel()$ to retrieve. Function $moreTypeRooms?()$ returns true if there are more room types for $nextTypeRoom()$. Function $showTypeRoom()$ displays room types on the screen.

This code may leak information about the location of the mobile phone through the internal timing covert channel. The source of the problem is a conditional that branches on secret data, where the `then` branch performs two assignments while the `else` branch only `skip`. However, internal timing leaks can be closed by the transformation given in Section 5 (provided the transformed program runs under a round-robin scheduler). This example highlights the permissiveness of the transformation. For instance, the type systems by Boudol and Castellani [3, 4] reject the example because both high conditionals and low assignments appear in the body of a loop. Transformations in [22, 13] also reject the example due to the presence of a high loop in the code.

7   Soundness

This section shows that a transformed program is secure and refines the source program in a suitable sense. The details of the proofs for lemmas and theorems shown in this section are to appear in an accompanying technical report.

Security. We identify two kinds of threads. *High* threads are dedicated threads introduced by the transformation and threads in the source program spawned inside a high conditional or a high loop. Other threads are *low* threads. We designate high threads by arranging that they have a distinguished local variable called $\hbar$. It is not difficult to modify the transformation in Section 5 to guarantee this.

In order to prove non-interference under round-robin schedulers, we firstly need to exploit some properties of programs produced by the transformation.

Definition 3. *A command c is* syntactically secure *provided that (i) there are no explicit flows, i.e., assignments $x := e$ with high e and low x; (ii) each low thread, $\text{fork}((\lambda \vec{x}.c') @ \vec{e})$, in c satisfies the following: there are no high conditionals or high loops or $V()$ or $P()$ operations related to synchronize high threads, except inside high threads forked in c'; and (iii) in high threads, there are neither low assignments nor forks of low threads.*

Lemma 1. *If $\Gamma \vdash_t c \hookrightarrow c'$ then c' is syntactically secure.*

We let γ and δ range over threadpool configurations. We assume, for convenience in the notation, that $\gamma = \langle\!\langle (c_0, m_0) \ldots \rangle, g, h, j\rangle$. We also define $\gamma.pool = \langle (c_0, m_0) \ldots \rangle$, $\gamma.globals = g$, $\gamma.heap = h$, and $\gamma.next = j$. A program configuration γ is called *syntactically secure* if every command in $\gamma.pool$ and every command in a waiting queue of $\gamma.heap$ is syntactically secure.

A thread configuration (c, m) is low, noted $low?(m)$, if and only if $\hbar \notin dom(m)$. Define $low?(i, \gamma)$ if and only if the ith thread in $\gamma.pool$ is low. Define γ_L as the subsequence of thread configurations (c_i, m_i) in $\gamma.pool$ that are low. For each thread configuration $(c_i, m_i) \in \gamma$ that is low, define $lowpos(i, \gamma)$ (and, for simplicity in the notation, $lowpos(i, \gamma.pool)$) to be the index of the thread but in γ_L. The key property of a round-robin scheduler is that the next low thread to be scheduled is independent of the values of global or local variables, the states of high threads (running or blocked), and even the number of high threads in the configuration. We can formally capture this property as follows. Define $nextlow(\gamma) = j \bmod (\#\gamma.pool)$ where j is the least number such that $j \geq \gamma.next$ and $low?(j \bmod (\#\gamma.pool), \gamma)$.

Definition 4 (Low equality). *Define $P =_L P'$ for threadpools $P = \langle (c_1, m_1) \ldots \rangle$ and $P' = \langle (c'_1, m'_1) \ldots \rangle$ (not necessarily the same length) if and only if $c_i \equiv c'_j$ for all i, j such that $low?(m_i)$, $low?(m'_j)$, and $lowpos(i, P) = lowpos(j, P')$. Define $\gamma =_L \delta$ if and only if γ and δ are syntactically secure, $\gamma.globals =_L \delta.globals$, $\gamma.pool =_L \delta.pool$, $lowpos(nextlow(\gamma), \gamma) = lowpos(nextlow(\delta), \delta)$, and all threads blocked in $\gamma.heap$ and $\delta.heap$ are high.*

Theorem 1. *Let γ and δ be configurations such that $\gamma =_L \delta$. If $\gamma \rightarrow^* \gamma'$ and $\delta \rightarrow^* \delta'$ where γ', δ' are terminal configurations, then $\gamma' =_L \delta'$. Here $\rightarrow^*$ refers to the semantics using the round-robin scheduler RR.*

Corollary 1 (Security). *If $\Gamma \vdash c \hookrightarrow_t c'$ then c' is secure under round-robin scheduling.*

Refinement. For programs produced by our transformation, the result from a round-robin computation from any initial state is a result from the original program using the fully nondeterministic scheduler. In fact, any interleaving of the transformed program matches some interleaving of the original code.

Theorem 2. *Suppose $\Gamma \vdash c \hookrightarrow_t c'$ and g'_1 and g'_2 are global memories for c' such that $(c', g'_1) \Downarrow g'_2$ using the nondeterministic scheduler ND. Let g_1 and g_2 be the restrictions of g'_1 and g'_2 to the globals of c. Then $(c, g_1) \Downarrow g_2$ using ND.*

8   Related Work

Variants of possibilistic noninterference have been explored in process-calculus settings [7, 6, 18, 8, 15], but without considering the impact of scheduling.

As discussed in the introduction, a series of work by Volpano and Smith [25, 27, 23, 24] suggests a special `protect(c)` statement to hide the internal timing of command c in the semantics. In contrast to this work, we are not dependent on the randomization of the scheduler. To the best of our knowledge, no proposals for `protect()` implementation avoid significantly changing the scheduler (unless the scheduler is cooperative [17]).

Boudol and Castellani [3, 4] suggest explicit modeling of schedulers as programs. Their type systems, however, reject source programs where assignments to public variables follow computation that branches on secrets.

Smith and Thober [26] suggest a transformation to split a program into high and low components. Jif/split [31] partitions sequential programs into distributed code on different hosts. However, the main focus is on security when some trusted hosts are compromised. Neither approach provides any formal notion of security or refinement.

A possibility to resolve the internal timing problem is by considering external timing. Definitions sensitive to external timing consider stronger attackers, namely those that are able to observe the actual execution time. External timing-sensitive security definitions have been explored for multithreaded languages by Sabelfeld and Sands [22] as well as languages with synchronization [19] by Sabelfeld and message passing [20] by Sabelfeld and Mantel. Typically, padding techniques [2, 22, 13] are used to ensure that the timing behavior of a program is independent of secrets. Naturally, a stronger attacker model implies more restrictions on programs. For example, loops branching on secrets are disallowed in the above approaches. Further, padding might introduce slow-down and, in the worst case, nontermination.

Another possibility to prevent internal timing leaks in programs is by disallowing any races on public data, as pursued by Zdancewic and Myers [30] and improved by Huisman et al. [9]. However, such an approach rejects innocent programs such as $l :=$ $0 \parallel l := 1$ where l is a public variable.

9   Conclusion

We have presented a transformation that closes internal timing leaks in programs with dynamic thread creation. In contrast to existing approaches, we have not appealed to nonstandard semantics (cf. the discussion on protect()) or to modifying the run-time environment (cf. the discussion on interaction with schedulers). Importantly, the transformation is not overrestrictive: programs are not rejected unless they have symptoms of flows inherent to sequential programs. The transformation ensures that the rest of insecurities (due to internal timing) are repaired. Our target language includes semaphores, which have not been considered in the context of termination-insensitive security.

Future work includes introducing synchronization and declassification primitives into the source language and improving the efficiency of the transformation: instead of dynamically spawning dedicated threads, one could refactor the program into high and low parts and explicitly communicate low data to the high part, when needed (and high data to the low part, when prescribed by declassification).

Acknowledgments. This work was funded in part by the Swedish Emergency Management Agency and in part by the Information Society Technologies program of the European Commission, Future and Emerging Technologies under the IST-2005-015905 Mobius project.

References

[1] Report on resource and information flow security requirements, Deliverable D1.1 of the EU IST FET GC2 MOBIUS project, (March 2006), http://mobius.inria.fr/
[2] Agat, J.: Transforming out timing leaks. In: Proc. POPL 2002, pp. 40–53 (January 2000)
[3] Boudol, G., Castellani, I.: Noninterference for concurrent programs. In: Orejas, F., Spirakis, P.G., van Leeuwen, J. (eds.) ICALP 2001. LNCS, vol. 2076, pp. 382–395. Springer, Heidelberg (2001)

[4] Boudol, G., Castellani, I.: Non-interference for concurrent programs and thread systems. Theoretical Computer Science 281(1), 109–130 (2002)

[5] Denning, D.E., Denning, P.J.: Certification of programs for secure information flow. Comm. of the ACM 20(7), 504–513 (1977)

[6] Focardi, R., Gorrieri, R.: Classification of security properties (part I: Information flow). In: Focardi, R., Gorrieri, R. (eds.) Foundations of Security Analysis and Design. LNCS, vol. 2171, pp. 331–396. Springer, Heidelberg (2001)

[7] Honda, K., Vasconcelos, V., Yoshida, N.: Secure information flow as typed process behaviour. In: Smolka, G. (ed.) ESOP 2000 and ETAPS 2000. LNCS, vol. 1782, Springer, Heidelberg (2000)

[8] Honda, K., Yoshida, N.: A uniform type structure for secure information flow. In: Proc. ACM Symp. on Principles of Programming Languages, pp. 81–92. ACM Press, New York (2002)

[9] Huisman, M., Worah, P., Sunesen, K.: A temporal logic characterisation of observational determinism. In: Proc. IEEE Computer Security Foundations Workshop (July 2006)

[10] JSR 118 Expert Group. Mobile information device profile (MIDP), version 2.0. Java specification request, Java Community Process (November 2002)

[11] JSR 179 Expert Group. Location API for J2ME. Java specification request, Java Community Process (September 2003)

[12] Knudsen, J.: Networking, user experience, and threads. Sun Technical Articles and Tips, (2002), http://developers.sun.com/techtopics/ mobility/midp/ articles/threading/

[13] Köpf, B., Mantel, H.: Eliminating implicit information leaks by transformational typing and unification. In: Dimitrakos, T., Martinelli, F., Ryan, P.Y.A., Schneider, S. (eds.) FAST 2005. LNCS, vol. 3866, Springer, Heidelberg (2006)

[14] Mahmoud, Q.H.: Preventing screen lockups of blocking operations. Sun Technical Articles and Tips (2004), http://developers.sun.com/techtopics/mobility/ midp/ttips/screenlock/

[15] Pottier, F.: A simple view of type-secure information flow in the pi-calculus. In: Proc. IEEE Computer Security Foundations Workshop, pp. 320–330. IEEE Computer Society Press, Los Alamitos (2002)

[16] Russo, A., Sabelfeld, A.: Securing interaction between threads and the scheduler. In: Proc. IEEE Computer Security Foundations Workshop, pp. 177–189. IEEE Computer Society Press, Los Alamitos (2006)

[17] Russo, A., Sabelfeld, A.: Security for multithreaded programs under cooperative scheduling. In: Virbitskaite, I., Voronkov, A. (eds.) PSI 2006. LNCS, vol. 4378, Springer, Heidelberg (2007)

[18] Ryan, P.: Mathematical models of computer security—tutorial lectures. In: Focardi, R., Gorrieri, R. (eds.) FOSAD 2001. LNCS, vol. 2946, Springer, Heidelberg (2004)

[19] Sabelfeld, A.: The impact of synchronisation on secure information flow in concurrent programs. In: Bjørner, D., Broy, M., Zamulin, A.V. (eds.) PSI 2001. LNCS, vol. 2244, Springer, Heidelberg (2001)

[20] Sabelfeld, A., Mantel, H.: Static confidentiality enforcement for distributed programs. In: Hermenegildo, M.V., Puebla, G. (eds.) SAS 2002. LNCS, vol. 2477, Springer, Heidelberg (2002)

[21] Sabelfeld, A., Myers, A.C.: Language-based information-flow security. IEEE J. Selected Areas in Communications 21(1), 5–19 (2003)

[22] Sabelfeld, A., Sands, D.: Probabilistic noninterference for multi-threaded programs. In: Proc. IEEE Computer Security Foundations Workshop, pp. 200–214. IEEE Computer Society Press, Los Alamitos (2000)

[23] Smith, G.: A new type system for secure information flow. In: Proc. IEEE Computer Security Foundations Workshop, pp. 115–125. IEEE Computer Society Press, Los Alamitos (2001)

[24] Smith, G.: Probabilistic noninterference through weak probabilistic bisimulation. In: Proc. IEEE Computer Security Foundations Workshop, pp. 3–13. IEEE Computer Society Press, Los Alamitos (2003)

[25] Smith, G., Volpano, D.: Secure information flow in a multi-threaded imperative language. In: Proc. ACM Symp. on Principles of Programming Languages, pp. 355–364. ACM Press, New York (1998)

[26] Smith, S.F., Thober, M.: Refactoring programs to secure information flows. In: PLAS 2006, pp. 75–84. ACM Press, New York (2006)

[27] Volpano, D., Smith, G.: Probabilistic noninterference in a concurrent language. J. Computer Security 7(2–3), 231–253 (1999)

[28] Volpano, D., Smith, G., Irvine, C.: A sound type system for secure flow analysis. J. Computer Security 4(3), 167–187 (1996)

[29] Winskel, G.: The Formal Semantics of Programming Languages: An Introduction. MIT Press, Cambridge (1993)

[30] Zdancewic, S., Myers, A.C.: Observational determinism for concurrent program security. In: Proc. IEEE Computer Security Foundations Workshop, pp. 29–43. IEEE Computer Society Press, Los Alamitos (2003)

[31] Zheng, L., Chong, S., Myers, A.C., Zdancewic, S.: Using replication and partitioning to build secure distributed systems. In: Proc. IEEE Symp. on Security and Privacy, pp. 236–250. IEEE Computer Society Press, Los Alamitos (2003)

Responsiveness in Process Calculi[*]

Lucia Acciai[1] and Michele Boreale[2]

[1] Laboratoire d'Informatique Fondamentale de Marseille, Université de Provence.
[2] Dipartimento di Sistemi e Informatica, Università di Firenze
lucia.acciai@lif.univ-mrs.fr, boreale@dsi.unifi.it

Abstract. In a process calculus, an agent guarantees responsive usage of a channel name r if a communication along r is guaranteed to eventually take place.
Responsiveness is important, for instance, to ensure that any request to a service
be eventually replied. We propose two distinct type systems, each of which statically guarantees responsive usage of names in well-typed pi-calculus processes.
In the first system, we achieve responsiveness by combining techniques for deadlock and livelock avoidance with *linearity* and *receptiveness*. The latter is a guarantee that a name is ready to receive as soon as it is created. These conditions
imply relevant limitations on the nesting of actions and on multiple use of names
in processes. In the second system, we relax these requirements so as to permit
certain forms of nested inputs and multiple outputs.

1 Introduction

In a process calculus, an agent guarantees responsive usage of a channel name r if a
communication along r is guaranteed to eventually take place. That is, under a suitable
assumption of fairness, all computations contain at least one reduction with r as subject.
We christen this property *responsiveness* as we are particularly interested in the case
where r is a return channel passed to a service or function. As an example, a network
of processes S may contain a service $!a(x,r).P$ invocable in RPC style: the caller sends
at a an argument x and a return channel r. S's responsive usage of r implies that every
request at a will be eventually replied. This may be a critical property in domains of
applications such as service-oriented computing.

Our goal is to individuate substantial classes of pi-calculus processes that guarantee
responsiveness and that can be statically checkable. In the past decade, several type
systems for the pi-calculus have been proposed to analyze properties that share some
similarities with responsiveness, such as linearity [10], uniform receptiveness [13], lock
freedom [6,7] and termination [5]; they will be examined throughout the paper. However none of the above mentioned properties alone is sufficient, or even necessary, to
ensure the property we are after (Section 2), as we discuss below (further discussion is
found in the concluding section).

The first system we propose (Section 3) builds around Sangiorgi's system for uniform
receptiveness [13]. However, we discard uniformity and introduce other constraints, as

---

[*] The first author is supported by the French government research grant ACI TRALALA. The
second author is supported by the EU within the FET-GC2 initiative, project SENSORIA.

M. Okada and I. Satoh (Eds.): ASIAN 2006, LNCS 4435, pp. 136–150, 2007.
© Springer-Verlag Berlin Heidelberg 2007

explained below. As expected, most difficulties in achieving responsiveness originate from responsive names being passed around. If an intended receiver of a responsive name r, say $a(x).P$, is not available "on time", r might never be delivered, hence used. In this respect, receptiveness is useful, because it can be used to ensure that inputs on a and on r are available as soon as they are created.

Even when delivery of r is ensured, however, one should take care that r will be processed properly. Indeed, the recipient might "forget" about r, like in $(\nu a, r)(a(x).\mathbf{0} | \overline{a}\langle r \rangle)$; or r might be passed from one recipient to another, its use as a subject being delayed forever, like in

$$(\nu a, b, r)\big(!a(x).\overline{b}\langle x \rangle \mid !b(y).\overline{a}\langle y \rangle \mid \overline{a}\langle r \rangle \big). \tag{1}$$

The first situation can be avoided by imposing that in the receiver $a(x).P$, name x occurs at least once in the body P. In fact, as we shall discuss in the paper, it is necessary that any responsive name be used *linearly*, that is, it appears exactly once in input and once in output. Infinite delays like (1) can be avoided by using a stratification of names into *levels*, like in the type system for termination of Deng and Sangiorgi [5]. We will rule out divergent computations that involve responsive names infinitely often, but we'll do allow divergence in general.

Finally, even when a responsive name is eventually in place as subject of an output action, one has to make sure that such action becomes eventually available. In other words, one must avoid cyclic waiting like in

$$r(x).\overline{s}\langle x \rangle \mid s(y).\overline{r}\langle y \rangle. \tag{2}$$

This will be achieved by building a graph of the dependencies among responsive names and then checking for its acyclicity.

Receptiveness and linearity impose relevant limitations on the syntax of well-typed processes: nested free inputs are forbidden, as well as multiple outputs on the same name. On the other hand, the type system is expressive enough to enable a RPC programming style; in particular, we show that the usual CPS encoding of primitive recursive functions gives rise to well-typed processes (Section 5).

In the second system we propose (Section 6), the constraints on receptiveness and linearity are relaxed so as to allow certain forms of nested inputs and multiple outputs. For instance, the new system allows nondeterministic internal choice, which was forbidden in the first one. Relaxation of linearity and receptiveness raises new issues, though. As an example, responsiveness might fail due to "shortage" of inputs, like in (a, b and d responsive):

$$\overline{a}\langle b \rangle | \overline{a}\langle d \rangle | a(x).\overline{x} | b | d \xrightarrow{\tau} \xrightarrow{\tau} \overline{a}\langle d \rangle | d.$$

These issues must be dealt with by carefully "balancing" inputs and outputs in typing contexts and in processes. In a long version of this paper [1] we prove that this system is flexible enough to encode into well-typed processes all orchestration patterns of Cook and Misra's ORC language [4]. Due to a rather crude use of levels, however, only certain forms of (tail-)recursion are encodable. In fact, neither the first system is subsumed by the second one, nor vice versa.

2 Syntax and Operational Semantics

In this section we describe the syntax (processes and types) and the operational semantics of the calculus. On top of the operational semantics, we define the responsiveness property we are after.

Syntax. We focus on an asynchronous variant of the pi-calculus without nondeterministic choice. Indeed, asynchrony is a natural assumption in a distributed environment. Moreover, in the presence of a choice, it would be difficult to guarantee responsiveness of names that occur in branches that are discarded. A countable set of names $\mathcal{N}$, ranged over by $a, b, \ldots, x, y, \ldots$, is presupposed. The set $\mathcal{P}$ of *processes* $P, Q, \ldots$ is defined as the set of terms generated by the grammar $P ::= \mathbf{0} \mid \overline{a}\langle b \rangle \mid a(x).P \mid !a(x).P \mid P|Q \mid (\nu b)P$, with $x \notin \mathrm{in}(P)$ in $a(x).P$ and $!a(x).P$.

In a non blocking output action $\overline{a}\langle b \rangle$, name a is said to occur in *output subject position* and b in *output object position*. In an input prefix $a(x).P$, and in a replicated input prefix $!a(x).P$, name a is said to occur in *input subject position* and x in *input object position*. We denote by $\mathrm{in}(P)$ the set of names occurring free in input subject position in P. The condition $x \notin \mathrm{in}(P)$, for input and replicated input, means that names can be passed around with the output capability only. This assumption simplifies reasoning on types and does not significantly affect the expressiveness of the language (see e.g. [3,11]). As usual, parallel composition, $P|Q$, represents the concurrent execution of P and Q and restriction, $(\nu b)P$, creates a fresh name b with initial scope P. Notions of free and bound names ($\mathrm{fn}(\cdot)$ and $\mathrm{bn}(\cdot)$), and alpha-equivalence ($=_\alpha$) arise as expected. In the paper, we shall only consider *well-formed* processes, where all bound names are distinct from each other and from free names. Note that we do *not* identify processes up-to α-equivalence (this means that an explicit operational rule that equates transitions of α-equivalent processes will be needed).

Notationally, we shall often abbreviate $a(x).\mathbf{0}$ as $a(x)$, and $(\nu a_1)\ldots(\nu a_n)P$ as $(\nu \tilde{a})P$ or $(\nu a_1, \ldots, a_n)P$, where $\tilde{a} = a_1, \ldots, a_n$. Sometimes, the object part of an action may be omitted if not relevant for the discussion; e.g., $a(x).P$ may be shortened into $a.P$.

Sorts and types. The set of names $\mathcal{N}$ is partitioned into a family of countable *sorts* $S, S', \ldots$. A fixed sorting à la Milner [12] is presupposed: that is, any sort S has an associated object sort S', and a name of sort S can only carry names of sort S'. We only consider processes that are well-sorted in this system. Alpha-equivalence is assumed to be sort-respecting. Each sort is associated with a *type* T taken from the set $\mathcal{T}$ defined below. We write $a : \mathsf{T}$ if a belongs to a sort S with associated type T. The association between types and sorts is such that for each type there is at least one sort of that type.

Definition 1 (types). *The set $\mathcal{T}$ of types contains the constant $\bot$ and the set of terms generated by the grammar* $\mathsf{T} ::= \mathsf{I} \mid \mathsf{T}^U$ *and* $U ::= [\rho, k] \mid [\omega, k]$*, with* $k \geq 0$*. We use* $\mathsf{T}, \mathsf{S}, \ldots$ *to range over* $\mathcal{T}$*.*

A channel type $\mathsf{T}^{[u,k]}$ conveys three pieces of information: a type of carried objects T, a *usage* u, that can be *responsive* (ρ) or ω-*receptive* (ω), and an integer *level* $k \geq 0$. If $a : \mathsf{T}^{[u,k]}$ and $u = \rho$ (resp. $u = \omega$) we say that a is *responsive* (resp. ω-*receptive*). Informally, responsive names are guaranteed to be eventually used as subject in a communication, while ω-receptive names are guaranteed to be constantly ready to receive. Levels are used to bound the number of times a responsive name can be passed around, so to avoid infinite delay in their use as subject. We also consider a type I of *inert* names that cannot be used as subject of a communication – they just serve as tokens to be passed around. Finally, a type $\perp$ is introduced to collect those names that cannot be used at all: as we discuss below, $\perp$ is useful to formulate the subject reduction property while keeping the standard operational semantics.

Operational semantics. The semantics of processes is given by a labelled transition system in the early style, whose rules are presented in Table 1. An *action* μ can be of the following forms: free output, $\bar{a}\langle b\rangle$, bound output, $\bar{a}(b)$, input $a(b)$, or internal move τ. We define $n(a(b)) = n(\bar{a}\langle b\rangle) = n(\bar{a}(b)) = \{a,b\}$ and $n(\tau) = \emptyset$. A substitution σ is a finite partial map from names to names; for any term P, we write $P\sigma$ for the result of applying σ to P, with the usual renaming convention to avoid captures.

The rules are standard, with a difference that we discuss in the following. The notation $\xrightarrow{\tau\langle a,b\rangle}$ is used to denote a τ-transition where the – free or bound – names a and b are used as subject and object, respectively, of a communication (we omit the formal definition of this notation, that can be given by keeping track of subject and object names in derivation of transitions.) In Rule (RES-ρ), a bound responsive subject a is alpha-renamed to a $\perp$-name c (a sort of "casting" of a to type $\perp$.) Informally, this alpha-renaming is necessary because in a well-typed process, due to the linearity constraint on responsive names, name a must vanish after being used as subject. The rule (RES) deals with the remaining cases of restriction. Note that if type and sorting information is ignored, one gets back the standard operational semantics of pi-calculus.

Table 1. Rules for the labeled transition system

$$(\text{IN}) \; a(x).P \xrightarrow{a(b)} P[b/x] \qquad\qquad (\text{REP}) \; !a(x).P \xrightarrow{a(b)} !a(x).P|P[b/x]$$

$$(\text{OUT}) \; \bar{a}\langle b\rangle \xrightarrow{\bar{a}\langle b\rangle} \mathbf{0} \qquad\qquad (\text{COM}_1) \; \frac{P \xrightarrow{\bar{a}\langle b\rangle} P' \quad Q \xrightarrow{a(b)} Q'}{P|Q \xrightarrow{\tau} P'|Q'}$$

$$(\text{OPEN}) \; \frac{P \xrightarrow{\bar{a}\langle b\rangle} P' \quad a \neq b}{(\nu b)P \xrightarrow{\bar{a}(b)} P'} \qquad (\text{CLOSE}_1) \; \frac{P \xrightarrow{\bar{a}(b)} P' \quad Q \xrightarrow{a(b)} Q' \quad b \notin \text{fn}(Q)}{P|Q \xrightarrow{\tau} (\nu b)(P'|Q')}$$

$$(\text{ALPHA}) \; \frac{P =_\alpha Q \quad Q \xrightarrow{\mu} Q' \quad Q' =_\alpha P'}{P \xrightarrow{\mu} P'} \qquad (\text{RES}) \; \frac{P \xrightarrow{\mu} P' \quad a \notin n(\mu)}{\mu = \tau\langle a,b\rangle \text{ implies } a \text{ not responsive}}{(\nu a)P \xrightarrow{\mu} (\nu a)P'}$$

$$(\text{PAR}_1) \; \frac{P \xrightarrow{\mu} P' \quad \text{bn}(\mu) \cap \text{fn}(Q) = \emptyset}{P|Q \xrightarrow{\mu} P'|Q} \qquad (\text{RES-}\rho) \; \frac{P \xrightarrow{\tau\langle a,b\rangle} P' \quad a \text{ responsive} \quad c:\perp \quad c \text{ fresh}}{(\nu a)P \xrightarrow{\tau\langle a,b\rangle} (\nu c)P'[c/a]}$$

Symmetric rules not shown.

Notation. We shall often refer to a silent move $P \xrightarrow{\tau} P'$ as a *reduction*. $P \xrightarrow{[a]} P'$ means $P \xrightarrow{\tau\langle a,b\rangle} P'$ for some free or bound name b. For a string $s = a_1 \cdots a_n \in \mathcal{N}^*$, $P \xrightarrow{[s]} P'$ means $P \xrightarrow{[a_1]} \cdots \xrightarrow{[a_n]} P'$, while $P \xRightarrow{[c]} P'$ means $P \xrightarrow{\tau}^* \xrightarrow{[c]} \xrightarrow{\tau}^* P'$. We use such abbreviations as $P \xRightarrow{[c]}$ to mean that there exists P' such that $P \xRightarrow{[c]} P'$.

We can now introduce the responsiveness property we are after. Informally, we think of a fair computation as a sequence of communications where for no name a a transition $\xrightarrow{[a]}$ is enabled infinitely often without ever taking place. Then a process uses a name in a responsive way if that name is eventually, that is, in all fair computations, used as subject of a communication. We then have the following definition. Below, we assume that any bound name occurring in P and s is distinct from any free name in P.

Definition 2 (responsiveness). *Let P be a process and $c \in \mathrm{fn}(P)$. We say that P guarantees responsiveness of c if whenever $P \xrightarrow{[s]} P'$ ($s \in \mathcal{N}^*$) and c does not occur in s then $P' \xRightarrow{[c]}$.*

3   The Type System $\vdash_1$

The type system consists of judgments of the form $\Gamma; \Delta \vdash_1 P$, where Γ and Δ are sets of names.

Overview of the system. Informally, names in Γ are those used by P in input, while in Δ are those used by P in output actions. There are several constraints on the usage of these names by P. A name in Γ must occur *immediately* (at top level) in input subject position, exactly once if it is responsive and replicated if it is ω-receptive. A responsive name in Δ must occur in P exactly once either in subject or in object output position, although not necessarily at top level, that is, occurrences in output actions underneath prefixes are allowed. There are no constraints on the use in output actions of ω-receptive names: they may be used an unbounded number of times, including zero. Linearity ("exactly once" usage) on responsive names is useful to avoid dealing with "dangling" responsive names, that might arise after a communication, like in (r responsive, object parts ignored):

$$(\nu r)(r.\mathbf{0}|\bar{r}|\bar{r}) \xrightarrow{\tau} (\nu r)(\mathbf{0}|\mathbf{0}|\bar{r}).$$

If the process on the LHS above were declared well-typed, this transition would violate the subject reduction property, as the process on the RHS above cannot be well-typed.

Linearity and receptiveness alone are not sufficient to guarantee a responsive usage of names. As discussed in the Introduction, we have also to avoid deadlock situations involving responsive names, like (2). This is simply achieved by building a *graph of dependencies* among responsive names of P (defined in the sequel) and checking for its acyclicity. We have also to avoid those situations described in the Introduction by which a responsive name is indefinitely "ping-pong"-ed among a group of replicated processes, like in (1). To this purpose, levels in types are introduced and the typing rules stipulate that sending a responsive name to a replicated input of level k may only trigger output of level less than k. This is similar to the use of levels in [5] to ensure termination. In our case, we just avoid divergent computations that involve responsive names infinitely often.

There is one more condition necessary for responsiveness, that is, the sets of input and output names must be "balanced", so as to ban situations like an output with no input counterpart. This constraint, however, is most easily formulated "on top" of well-typed-ness, and will be discussed later on.

Preliminary definitions. Formulation of the actual typing rules requires a few preliminary definitions. *Structural equivalence* is necessary in order to correctly formulate the absence of cyclic waiting on responsive names. We define structural equivalence $\equiv$ as the least equivalence relation satisfying the axioms below and closed under restriction and parallel composition. Let us point out a couple of differences from the standard notion [12]. First, there is no rule for replication ($!P \equiv P|!P$), as its right-hand side would not be well-typed. For a similar reason, in the rule $(\nu a)\mathbf{0} \equiv \mathbf{0}$ we require $a : \bot$ or $a : \mathsf{I}$.

$$(\nu a)(P|Q) \equiv (\nu a)P|Q \quad \text{if } a \notin \mathrm{fn}(Q) \qquad (\nu a)(\nu b)P \equiv (\nu b)(\nu a)P \qquad P|Q \equiv Q|P$$

$$(P|Q)|R \equiv P|(Q|R) \quad P \equiv Q \quad \text{if } P =_\alpha Q \qquad (\nu a)\mathbf{0} \equiv \mathbf{0} \quad \text{if } a : \bot \text{ or } a : \mathsf{I} \qquad P|\mathbf{0} \equiv P$$

Let us call a process P *prime* if either $P = \bar{a}\langle b \rangle$, or $P = a(x).P'$ or $P = !a(x).P'$. A process P is in *normal form* if $P = (\nu \tilde{d})(P_1|\cdots|P_n)$ ($n \geq 0$), every P_i is prime and $\tilde{d} \subseteq \mathrm{fn}(P_1,...,P_n)$. Every process is easily seen to be structurally equivalent to a process in normal form.

In the dependency graph, defined below, nodes are responsive names of typing contexts and there is an arc from a to b exactly when an output action that involves a depends on an input action on b. Although the following definition does not mention processes, one should think of the pairs (Γ_i, Δ_i) below as typing contexts – limited to responsive names – for the P_i's in $P_1|\cdots|P_n$.

Definition 3 (dependency graph). *Let* $\{(\Gamma_i, \Delta_i) : i = 1,...,n\}$ *be a set of context pairs. The* dependency graph $\mathrm{DG}(\Gamma_i, \Delta_i)_{i=1,...,n}$ *is a graph* (V, T) *where:* $V = \bigcup_{i=1,...,n}(\Gamma_i \cup \Delta_i)$ *is the set of nodes and* $T = \bigcup_{i=1,...,n}(\Gamma_i \times \Delta_i)$ *is the set of arcs.*

We will have more to say on both structural equivalence and dependency graphs in Remark 1 at the end of the section. Like in [5], we will use a function $\mathrm{os}(P)$, defined below, that collects all – either free or bound – names in P that occur as subject of an *active* output action, that is, an output not underneath a replication (!).

$$\mathrm{os}(\mathbf{0}) = \emptyset \qquad \mathrm{os}(!a(b).P) = \emptyset \qquad \mathrm{os}((\nu a)P) = \mathrm{os}(P)$$

$$\mathrm{os}(\bar{a}\langle b \rangle) = \{a\} \qquad \mathrm{os}(a(b).P) = \mathrm{os}(P) \qquad \mathrm{os}(P|Q) = \mathrm{os}(P) \cup \mathrm{os}(Q)$$

Finally, some notation for contexts and types. For any name a, we set $\mathrm{lev}(a) = k$ if $a : \mathsf{T}^{[\mathsf{u},k]}$ for some T and u, otherwise $\mathrm{lev}(a)$ is undefined. Given a set of names V, define $V^\mathsf{p} \triangleq \{x \in V \mid x \text{ is responsive }\}$ and $V^\omega \triangleq \{x \in V \mid x \text{ is } \omega\text{-receptive }\}$. For V and W sets of names, we define $V \ominus W \triangleq V \setminus W^\mathsf{p}$. If $\Delta \cap \Delta' = \emptyset$, we abbreviate $\Delta \cup \Delta'$ as Δ, Δ' and if $a \notin \Delta$, we abbreviate $\Delta \cup \{a\}$ as Δ, a; similarly for Γ.

The typing rules. The type system is displayed in Table 2. Recall that each sort has an associated type. Linear usage of responsive names is ensured by rules (T-NIL) and (T-OUT), by the disjointness conditions in (T-PAR) and by forbidding responsive names to occur free underneath replication (T-REP). Absence of cyclic waiting involving responsive names is checked in (T-PAR). Finally, note the use of levels in rule (T-REP): communication involving a replicated input subject a and a responsive object can only trigger outputs of level less than $\mathrm{lev}(a)$. We say that a process P is *well-typed* if there are Γ and Δ such that $\Gamma; \Delta \vdash_1 P$ holds.

Table 2. Typing rules of $\vdash_1$

$$(\text{T-NIL})\ \frac{\Gamma = \Delta^\rho = \emptyset}{\Gamma; \Delta \vdash_1 \mathbf{0}} \qquad (\text{T-OUT})\ \frac{\Gamma = \emptyset \quad a,b \in \Delta \quad a : \mathsf{T}^\mathsf{U} \quad b : \mathsf{T} \quad \Delta^\rho - \{a,b\} = \emptyset}{\Gamma; \Delta \vdash_1 \overline{a}\langle b \rangle}$$

$$(\text{T-STR})\ \frac{P \equiv Q \quad \Gamma; \Delta \vdash_1 Q}{\Gamma; \Delta \vdash_1 P} \qquad (\text{T-INP})\ \frac{a : \mathsf{T}^{[\rho,k]} \quad b : \mathsf{T} \quad a \notin \Delta \quad \emptyset; \Delta, b \vdash_1 P}{a; \Delta \vdash_1 a(b).P}$$

$$(\text{T-RES-T})\ \frac{a : \bot \quad \Gamma; \Delta \vdash_1 P}{\Gamma; \Delta \vdash_1 (va)P} \qquad (\text{T-RES})\ \frac{a : \mathsf{T}^\mathsf{U} \quad \Gamma, a; \Delta, a \vdash_1 P}{\Gamma; \Delta \vdash_1 (va)P}$$

$$(\text{T-RES-I})\ \frac{a : \mathsf{I} \quad \Gamma; \Delta, a \vdash_1 P}{\Gamma; \Delta \vdash_1 (va)P} \qquad (\text{T-REP})\ \frac{\begin{array}{c} a : \mathsf{T}^{[\omega,k]} \quad b : \mathsf{T} \quad \Delta^\rho = \emptyset \quad \emptyset; \Delta, b \vdash_1 P \\ (\,b \text{ responsive implies } \forall c \in \mathrm{os}(P) : \mathrm{lev}(c) < k\,) \end{array}}{a; \Delta \vdash_1 !a(b).P}$$

$$(\text{T-PAR})\ \frac{\begin{array}{c} P = P_1 | \cdots | P_n \ (n>1) \quad \forall i : P_i \text{ is prime and } \Gamma_i; \Delta_i \vdash_1 P_i \\ \forall i \neq j : \Gamma_i^\rho \cap \Gamma_j^\rho = \emptyset \text{ and } \Delta_i^\rho \cap \Delta_j^\rho = \emptyset \quad DG(\Gamma_i^\rho, \Delta_i^\rho)_{i=1,\ldots,n} \text{ is acyclic} \end{array}}{\bigcup_{i=1,\ldots,n} \Gamma_i \ ; \ \bigcup_{i=1,\ldots,n} \Delta_i \ \vdash_1 P}$$

Remark 1. (1) Avoiding deadlock on responsive names might be achieved by using levels in rule (T-INP), in the same fashion as in rule (T-REP), rather than using graphs. In fact, this would rule out cyclic waiting such as the one in (2) in the Introduction. We shall pursue this approach in the system of Section 6, where there is no way of defining a meaningful notion of dependency graph. However, in the present system this way of dealing with cyclic waiting would be unnecessarily restrictive, in particular it would ban as ill-typed the usual encoding of recursive functions into processes (see also Section 6).

(2) We note that, despite the presence of a rule for structural equivalence, the type system may be viewed as essentially syntax driven, in the following sense. Given P in normal form, $P = (v\tilde{d})(P_1 | \cdots | P_n)$, and ignoring structural equalities that just rearrange the $\tilde{d}$ or the P_i's, there is at most one rule one can apply with P in the conclusion.

4   Subject Reduction and Responsiveness for System $\vdash_1$

Subject reduction states that well-typedness is preserved through reductions, and it is our first step towards proving responsiveness.

Theorem 1 (subject reduction). *Suppose* $\Gamma; \Delta \vdash_1 P$ *and* $P \xrightarrow{[a]} P'$. *Then* $\Gamma \ominus \{a\}; \Delta \ominus \{a\} \vdash_1 P'$.

Our task is proving that any "balanced" well-typed process guarantees responsiveness (Definition 2) for all responsive names it contains.

Definition 4 (balanced processes). *A process P is* $(\Gamma; \Delta)$-*balanced if* $\Gamma; \Delta \vdash_1 P$, $\Gamma^\rho = \Delta^\rho$ *and* $\Delta^\omega \subseteq \Gamma^\omega$. *It is* balanced *if it is* $(\Gamma; \Delta)$-*balanced for some* Γ *and* Δ.

We need two main ingredients for the proof. The first one is given by the following proposition, stating that if the dependency graph of a process P is acyclic, then P always offers at least one output action involving a responsive name.

Proposition 1. *Suppose that* $\Gamma; \Delta \vdash_1 P$, *with* Γ, Δ *and P satisfying the conditions in the premise of rule* (T-PAR) *and* $\Gamma^\rho = \Delta^\rho$. *Then for some* $j \in \{1, \ldots, n\}$ *we have* $P_j = \overline{a}\langle b \rangle$ *with either a or b responsive.*

Next, we need a measure of processes that is decreased by reductions involving responsive names. We borrow from [5] the definition of *weight* of P, written $\mathrm{wt}(P)$: this is defined as a vector $\langle w_k, w_{k-1}, \ldots, w_0 \rangle$, where $k \geq 0$ is the highest level of names in $\mathrm{os}(P)$, and w_i is the number of occurrences in output subject position of names of level i in P. A formal definition can be found in [5]. We denote by $\prec$ the lexicographic ordering on vectors. This order is total and well-founded, that is, there are no infinite descending chains of vectors.

Proposition 2. *Suppose* $\Gamma; \Delta \vdash_1 P$ *and* $P \xrightarrow{\tau\langle a,b \rangle} P'$, *with either a or b responsive. Then* $\mathrm{wt}(P') \prec \mathrm{wt}(P)$.

We can now introduce the main result of the section. The proof relies on the well-foundness of the ordering on vectors, on the fact that a reduction involving a responsive name is always enabled (Proposition 1) and that such a reduction decreases the weight of processes (Proposition 2).

Theorem 2 (responsiveness). *Let P be* $(\Gamma; \Delta)$-*balanced and* $r \in \Delta^\rho$. *Then P guarantees responsiveness of r.*

In [1], we also establish that $|P|^{k+1}$ steps are always sufficient for a given responsive name to be used as subject, where $|P|$ represents the syntactic size of P and k is the maximal level of names used in output in P.

5 Recursion on Well-Founded Data Values

The system presented in Section 3 bans as ill-typed processes implementing recursive functions. As an example, consider the classical implementation of the factorial function, the process P below. For the purpose of illustration, we consider a polyadic version of the calculus enriched with if...then...else, natural numbers, variables $(x, y, \ldots)$

and predicates/functions as expected. These extensions are straightforward to accommodate in the type system.

$$P \stackrel{\triangle}{=} !f(n,r).\text{if } n = 0 \text{ then } \bar{r}\langle 1 \rangle \text{ else } (\nu r')(\bar{f}\langle n-1,r' \rangle \mid r'(m).\bar{r}\langle m*n \rangle). \qquad (3)$$

It would be natural to see f as ω-receptive and r and r' as responsive, but under these assumptions P would not be well-typed: the recursive call $\bar{f}\langle n-1,r' \rangle$ violates the constraint on levels of output actions under replication (rule (T-REP).) Nevertheless, it is natural to see an output $\bar{f}\langle n-1,r' \rangle$ triggered by a recursive call at f as "smaller" than the output $\bar{f}\langle n,r \rangle$ that has triggered it: at least, this is true if one takes into account the ordering relation on natural numbers. This means that the "weight" of the process decreases after each recursive call, and since natural numbers are well-founded, after some reductions no further recursive call will be possible, and a communication on r must take place. This idea from [5] is adapted here to our type system. For simplicity, we only consider the domain of natural values Nat. However, the results may be extended to any data type on which a well-founded ordering relation can be defined. We define an ordering relation "<" between (possibly open) integer expressions and variables as follows: $e < x$ if for each evaluation ρ under which e is defined, $e\rho < \rho(x)$. E.g., $x - 1 < x$. In the case of the monadic calculus, this relation is lifted to a "smaller than" relation $\lhd$ between output and input actions as follows. Below, d, d' denote either names or (open) expressions.

Definition 5 (ordering on actions). *We write $\bar{c}\langle d \rangle \lhd a(d')$ if either $\text{lev}(c) < \text{lev}(a)$ or $\text{lev}(c) = \text{lev}(a)$ and $d = e < x = d'$.*

The $\lhd$ relation is used in the typing rule below, that replaces rule (T-REP). We denote by $O(P)$ the set of all output actions of P that are active, that is, not underneath a replication.

$$\text{(T-REP')} \quad \frac{a : \mathsf{T}^{[\omega,k]} \quad b : \mathsf{T} \quad \Delta^\rho = \emptyset \quad 0;\Delta,b \vdash_1 P}{a;\Delta \vdash_1 !a(b).P}$$
$$(b : \mathsf{Nat} \text{ or } b \text{ responsive}) \quad \text{implies} \quad \forall \bar{c}\langle d \rangle \in O(P) : \bar{c}\langle d \rangle \lhd a(b)$$

In the polyadic case, $\lhd$ compares first the subject and then the object parts of two actions lexicographically (a different ordering is considered in [5].) As an example, it is easy to see that the process P in (3) is well-typed if $f : (\mathsf{Nat}, \mathsf{Nat}^{[\rho,0]})^{[\omega,1]}$ and $r, r' : \mathsf{Nat}^{[\rho,0]}$. The proof of responsiveness remains the same, modulo a change in function $\text{wt}(\cdot)$ that takes into account contribution to weight given by the object part of active outputs. We omit the details of this definition.

Primitive Recursive Functions can be encoded into well-typed processes. The scheme of the encoding is an easy generalization of that seen above in (3) for the factorial function. More precisely, we have:

Proposition 3. *For every n-ary primitive recursive function f there is a well-typed process $\langle f \rangle_b$ such that: for each $(v_1,\ldots,v_n)$ in Nat^n the process $G \stackrel{\triangle}{=} (\nu b)(\langle f \rangle_b | \bar{b}\langle v_1,\ldots,v_n,r \rangle \mid r(x).\mathbf{0})$, with b ω-receptive and $r : (\mathsf{Nat})^{[\rho,k]}$ ($k \geq 0$), is balanced. Moreover, $f(v_1,\ldots,v_n) = m$ if and only if $G \stackrel{\tau}{\rightarrow}^* \stackrel{\bar{r}\langle m \rangle}{\longrightarrow}$.*

6   Nested Inputs, Multiple Outputs: The Type System $\vdash_2$

The type system presented in Section 3 puts rather severe limitations on nesting of input actions and multiple use of names. These limitations stem from the "immediate receptiveness" and linearity conditions imposed on responsive names. For instance, the following encoding of internal choice $\bar{r}\langle a\rangle \oplus \bar{r}\langle b\rangle$, where r is responsive and a,b inert, is not well-typed

$$(\nu c)(\bar{c}\langle a\rangle|\bar{c}\langle b\rangle \,|\, c(x).\bar{r}\langle x\rangle). \tag{4}$$

Limitations are also built-in in process syntax, as for example replicated outputs, that clearly violate linearity, are absent. These might be useful to encode situations like a process receiving from r a value y and storing it into a variable a, where reading from a means doing an input on a:

$$(\nu a)(r(x).!\bar{a}\langle x\rangle|a(y).P). \tag{5}$$

For another example, a process that receives two values in a fixed order from two return channels, r_1 and r_2, and then outputs the max along s, may not be well-typed

$$r_1(x_1).r_2(x_2).\mathtt{if}\ x_1 \geq x_2\ \mathtt{then}\ \bar{s}\langle x_1\rangle\ \mathtt{else}\ \bar{s}\langle x_2\rangle. \tag{6}$$

We present below a new type system $\vdash_2$ that overcomes the limitations discussed above. In fact, we will trade off flexibility for expressiveness in terms of encodable functions, as only certain patterns of (tail-)recursion will be well-typed in system $\vdash_2$.

Overview of the system. We extend the syntax of processes by introducing replicated output and the syntax of types by introducing a new responsive usage of names, ρ^+, as follows: $P ::= \cdots | !\bar{a}\langle b\rangle$ and $U ::= \cdots | [\rho^+,k]$. A name $a : \mathsf{T}^{[\rho^+,k]}$ is called +-*responsive*, as it is meant to be used *at least once* as subject of a communication. Therefore now we consider three different usages: ρ (for names used once), ρ^+ (for names used at least once) and ω (for names used an undefined number of times.) We point out that responsive names are not subsumed by +-responsive: in particular, as we shall see, the conditions on the type of carried objects are more liberal for responsive names. Operational semantics is enriched by adding the obvious rule for replicated output.

We give here an informal overview of the system. Judgements are of the form $\Gamma;\Delta \vdash_2 P$ where in Γ and Δ each +-responsive name a is annotated with a *capability* t, written a^t. A capability t can be one of four kinds: n (*null*), s (*simple*), m (*multiple*), p (*persistent*). Informally, capabilities have the following meaning (in the examples below, we ignore object parts of some actions and assume b is a (+-)responsive name):

- a^{n} indicates that a cannot be used at all. This capability has been introduced to uniformly account for +-responsive names that disappear after being used as subjects.
- a^{s} indicates that a appears at least once, but never under a replication. Examples: $a.P, b.a.P, \bar{a}$ and $b.\bar{a}$.
- a^{m} indicates that a appears at least once, even under replication, but never as a subject of a replicated action. Examples: $a.P|a.Q, !b.a.P$ and $!b.\bar{a}$.
- a^{p} indicates that a only appears as a subject of a replicated action. Examples: $!a.P, !\bar{a}, b.!\bar{a}$ and $!b.!\bar{a}$.

Note that a name a may be given distinct capabilities in input (Γ) and output (Δ). E.g. one may have, again ignoring the object parts, $\Gamma; \Delta \vdash_2 !a.P|\bar{a}$, where $a^p \in \Gamma$ and $a^s \in \Delta$. Next we illustrate and motivate the constraints on names usage realized by the typing rules and by the balancing conditions discussed later on. There are essentially three of them:

1. If $a^m \in \Gamma$ then $a^p \in \Delta$. This is to avoid deadlocks arising from not having enough output actions of subject a, like in (a and b +-responsive): $a|a.b|\bar{a}|\bar{b} \xrightarrow{\tau} a.b|\bar{b} \not\rightarrow$. This situation is in fact avoided if a appears in replicated output subject, like in $a|a.b|!\bar{a}|\bar{b}$.

2. If $a^t \in \Gamma$ and a carries (+-)responsive names, then $t = p$. This is to avoid deadlocks arising from having too many outputs of subject a that carry (+-)responsive names, like in (a +-responsive, b and d (+-)responsive): $\bar{a}\langle b \rangle|\bar{a}\langle d \rangle|a(x).\bar{x}|b|d \xrightarrow{\tau}\xrightarrow{\tau} \bar{a}\langle d \rangle|d$.

3. Names occurring under an (either simple or replicated) input must be of smaller level than the input subject. The role of this condition is twofold, now. Under replicated inputs, it avoids infinite delays, like in the first system. Under simple inputs, it serves to avoid cyclic waiting, like in (a,b (+-)responsive): $a.\bar{b}|b.\bar{a}$. This was achieved by the use of dependency graphs in the first system. As announced in Remark 1, however, there appear to be no meaningful extension of this notion of graph in the present system. In particular, acyclicity of the graph might not be preserved by reductions. E.g. consider the reduction on c of the process $b(x).\bar{a}\langle x \rangle|c(x).a(y).\bar{x}\langle y \rangle|\bar{c}\langle b \rangle$.

There are other constraints, often met in applications, that have been introduced also for technical convenience (essentially, to avoid divergences and deadlocks difficult to control in the proof of responsiveness) and that shall not be discussed further:

(a) names with input capability s (simple) occur exactly once in input subject position;
(b) names with capability p (persistent) occur exactly once in subject position, either in input or in output, but not in both; this also implies that persistent names cannot be passed around. Moreover, free replicated inputs cannot be guarded.

Typing rules, subject reduction and responsiveness We first introduce some additional notations. Contexts Γ and Δ are sets of annotated names of the form a^t, where t is a capability. Each name occurs at most once in a context. +-responsive names are annotated with one of the four capabilities n, s, m or p, while non-+-responsive names are always annotated with a default "$-$" capability; when convenient a^- is abbreviated simply as a. Union and intersection of two contexts, written $\Gamma_1 \cup \Gamma_2$ and $\Gamma_1 \cap \Gamma_2$, are defined only if the contexts agree on capabilities of common names, that is whenever $a^{t_i} \in \Gamma_i$ for $i = 1,2$ then $t_1 = t_2$. We write Γ_1, Γ_2 in place of $\Gamma_1 \cup \Gamma_2$ if $\Gamma_1 \cap \Gamma_2 = \emptyset$; while Γ_1, a^t abbreviates $\Gamma_1, \{a^t\}$. For any context Γ and capability t, we define $\Gamma^t \stackrel{\Delta}{=} \{a|a^t \in \Gamma\}$. The set of names $\Gamma^{p^+} \stackrel{\Delta}{=} \{a| a$ is +-responsive and $a^t \in \Gamma$ for some $t \neq n\}$ and Γ^p, Γ^ω (defined similarly) will also be useful. The typing rules are presented in Table 3.

Subject reduction carries over to the new system, modulo a small notational change. For Γ a typing context and V a set of names let us denote by $\Gamma \ominus^+ V$ the typing context obtained by removing from Γ each a^t such that $a \in V$. Let us denote by on(P) the set of names occurring free in output position in P.

Table 3. Typing rules of $\vdash_2$

$$(\text{T}_+\text{-OUT}) \quad \frac{a:\text{T}^\text{U} \quad b:\text{T} \quad \Delta^\rho = \Delta^{\rho^+} = \emptyset \quad t' \neq \text{n},\text{p} \quad t \neq \text{n},\text{p}}{\emptyset; \Delta, a^t, b^{t'} \vdash_2 \overline{a}\langle b \rangle}$$

$$(\text{T}_+\text{-NIL}) \quad \frac{\Delta^\rho = \Delta^{\rho^+} = \emptyset}{\emptyset; \Delta \vdash_2 \mathbf{0}} \qquad (\text{T}_+\text{-OUT}^\text{P}) \quad \frac{\begin{array}{c} a:\text{T}^{[\rho^+,k]} \quad b:\text{T} \quad \Delta^\rho = \Delta^{\rho^+} = \emptyset \\ b \text{ not } (\text{+-})\text{responsive} \end{array}}{\emptyset; \Delta, a^\text{p}, b^- \vdash_2 !\overline{a}\langle b \rangle}$$

$$(\text{T}_+\text{-INP}) \quad \frac{\begin{array}{c} a:\text{T}^{[u,k]} \text{ with } u \neq \omega \quad b:\text{T} \quad \forall c \in \text{os}(P) \cup \text{in}(P): \text{lev}(c) < k \\ \Gamma^\text{p} = \Gamma^\omega = \emptyset \quad a \text{ +-responsive implies } b \text{ not } (\text{+-})\text{responsive} \\ \Gamma; \Delta, b^{t'} \vdash_2 P \quad t \neq \text{n},\text{p} \quad t' \neq \text{n},\text{p} \end{array}}{\Gamma, a^t; \Delta \vdash_2 a(b).P}$$

$$(\text{T}_+\text{-REP}) \quad \frac{\begin{array}{c} a:\text{T}^{[\omega,k]} \quad b:\text{T} \quad \Delta^\rho = \Delta^{\rho^+} = \emptyset \quad \emptyset; \Delta, b^{t'} \vdash_2 P \quad t' \neq \text{n},\text{p} \\ b \ (\text{+-})\text{responsive implies } \forall c \in \text{os}(P): \text{lev}(c) < k \end{array}}{a^-; \Delta \vdash_2 !a(b).P}$$

$$(\text{T}_+\text{-REP}^\text{P}) \quad \frac{\begin{array}{c} a:\text{T}^{[\rho^+,k]} \quad b:\text{T} \quad \Gamma^\ell = \emptyset \text{ for } \ell \in \{\rho,\omega,\text{s},\text{p}\} \quad \Delta^\ell = \emptyset \text{ for } \ell \in \{\text{s},\text{p},\rho\} \\ \Gamma; \Delta, b^t \vdash_2 P \quad t \neq \text{n},\text{p} \quad \forall c \in \text{os}(P) \cup \text{in}(P): \text{lev}(c) < k \end{array}}{\Gamma, a^\text{p}; \Delta \vdash_2 !a(b).P}$$

$$(\text{T}_+\text{-RES-}\bot) \quad \frac{a:\bot \quad \Gamma; \Delta \vdash_2 P}{\Gamma; \Delta \vdash_2 (va)P} \qquad (\text{T}_+\text{-RES}) \quad \frac{a:\text{T}^\text{U} \quad \Gamma, a^t; \Delta, a^{t'} \vdash_2 P}{\Gamma; \Delta \vdash_2 (va)P}$$

$$(\text{T}_+\text{-RES-I}) \quad \frac{a:\text{I} \quad \Gamma; \Delta, a^- \vdash_2 P}{\Gamma; \Delta \vdash_2 (va)P} \qquad (\text{T}_+\text{-w-}\Gamma) \quad \frac{\Gamma; \Delta \vdash_2 P}{\Gamma, a^\text{n}; \Delta \vdash_2 P} \qquad (\text{T}_+\text{-w-}\Delta) \quad \frac{\Gamma; \Delta \vdash_2 P}{\Gamma; \Delta, a^\text{n} \vdash_2 P}$$

$$(\text{T}_+\text{-PAR}) \quad \frac{\begin{array}{c} \Gamma = \Gamma_1 \cup \Gamma_2 \quad \Delta = \Delta_1 \cup \Delta_2 \quad \Gamma_i; \Delta_i \vdash_2 P_i \quad (i = 1,2) \\ \Gamma_1^\ell \cap \Gamma_2^\ell = \emptyset \text{ for } \ell \in \{\rho,\text{s},\text{p}\} \quad \Delta_1^{\ell'} \cap \Delta_2^{\ell'} = \emptyset \text{ for } \ell' \in \{\rho,\text{p}\} \\ \Gamma^\text{p} \cap \Delta^\text{p} = \emptyset \quad \Gamma^\text{m} \cap (\Delta^\text{s} \cup \Delta^\text{m}) = \emptyset \end{array}}{\Gamma; \Delta \vdash_2 P_1 | P_2}$$

Theorem 3 (subject reduction for system $\vdash_2$). $\Gamma; \Delta \vdash_2 P$ and $P \xrightarrow{[a]} P'$ imply $\Gamma'; \Delta' \vdash_2 P'$, with $\Gamma' = \Gamma \ominus^+ (\{a\} \setminus \text{in}(P'))$ and $\Delta' = \Delta \ominus^+ (\{a\} \setminus \text{on}(P'))$.

The balancing requirements are now more stringent. They include those for responsive and ω-receptive names necessary in the first system (condition 1 below). Concerning +-responsive names, "perfect balancing" between input and output is required only for those names that carry (+-)responsive names (condition 2). Moreover, the same requirements apply also to restricted +-responsive names (condition 3).

Given a set of names V let us define $V^+ = \{a \in V \mid a: \text{T and T is of the form } (\text{S}^{[u,k]})^{[u',h]}$ with $u \in \{\rho, \rho^+\}$ }. Define $\text{r}_i^+(P)$ (resp. $\text{r}_o^+(P)$) as the set of restricted +-responsive names in P occurring in an input (resp. output) action in P, even underneath a replication. We have the following definition and result.

Definition 6 (strongly balanced processes). *A process P is $(\Gamma;\Delta)$-strongly balanced if $\Gamma;\Delta \vdash_2 P$ and the following conditions hold: (1) $\Gamma^\rho = \Delta^\rho$ and $\Delta^\omega \subseteq \Gamma^\omega$; (2) $\Gamma^{\rho^+} \subseteq \Delta^{\rho^+}$ and $(\Delta^{\rho^+})^\dagger \subseteq (\Gamma^{\rho^+})^\dagger$; (3) $r_i^+(P) \subseteq r_o^+(P)$ and $(r_o^+(P))^\dagger \subseteq (r_i^+(P))^\dagger$.*

The proof of the following theorem is non-trivial, as strong balancing is preserved through reductions only up to certain transformations on processes.

Theorem 4 (responsiveness for system $\vdash_2$). *Suppose P is $(\Gamma;\Delta)$-strongly balanced and $r \in \Delta^\rho \cup \Gamma^{\rho^+}$. Then P guarantees responsiveness of r.*

Examples. Let us now examine a few examples. In what follows, unless otherwise stated we assume that x, y are of type inert, that a, b, c are +-responsive and that r, s are responsive. Conditions on levels are ignored when obvious. Process (4) at the beginning of the section is well-typed with c of capability multiple in output and simple in input; it is strongly balanced if put in parallel with an appropriate context of the form $r(x).P$. Process (5) is well-typed with a of capability persistent in output and simple in input (also, P must be assumed strongly balanced, and not containing free persistent inputs or names of level greater than a's); it is strongly balanced if put in parallel with $\bar{r}\langle x\rangle$. Process (6) is well-typed assuming r_1 and r_2 of capability simple in input and x_1, x_2 natural number variables (the obvious extension of the system with conditionals and naturals is assumed); again, it is strongly balanced if put in parallel with an appropriate context.

The next two examples involve non-linear usages of +-responsive names arising from replication and reference passing. We mention these examples also because they will help us to compare our system to existing type systems that enforce lock freedom, a property related to responsiveness (see the concluding section). The first example involves only replication, object parts play no role:

$$!a.\bar{b} \mid \bar{a} \mid b. \tag{7}$$

The above process is strongly balanced under the assumption that a has capability persistent in input and simple/multiple in output, and b has capability simple in input and multiple in output; also, the level of b must be less than a's. In the next example, an agent sort of "looks up" a directory a to get the address of a service b, and then calls this service:

$$!a(z).\bar{z}\langle b\rangle \mid (\nu r)(\bar{a}\langle r\rangle \mid r(w).\bar{w}) \mid b. \tag{8}$$

This process is strongly balanced under the assumption that: a is persistent in input and simple or multiple in output; b is simple in input and multiple in output; also, the level of b must be smaller than r's and the level of r must be smaller than a's (the variant where b is replaced by $!b$ is also strongly balanced; in this case b is persistent in input.)

The type system $\vdash_2$ can be extended to the polyadic version of the calculus with naturals and variables exactly as seen in Section 5, i.e. by using the "$\lhd$" relation over actions in rules $(\text{T}_+\text{-INP})$, $(\text{T}_+\text{-REP})$ and $(\text{T}_+\text{-REP}^P)$. Now, consider the factorial function in (3) and assume r, r' are (+-)responsive. It is easily seen that (3) is not well-typed in the present system: in fact, because of the recursive call at f, it cannot be $\text{lev}(r) < \text{lev}(r')$. In general, the type system bans as ill-typed recursive calls of the form $g(h(g(i),i))$, thus ruling out the usual encoding of primitive recursion. Certain forms of recursion, like the tail-recursive version of factorial below, are however still well-typed

$$!f(x,a,r).\texttt{if } x = 0 \texttt{ then } \bar{r}\langle a\rangle \texttt{ else } \bar{f}\langle x-1, a*x, r\rangle.$$

7 Conclusions and Related Works

Both systems are syntax driven, so that type checking should be straightforward and efficient to implement. Extensions with type inference and subtyping deserve further investigation, mainly due to the presence of levels.

Beside the works, already discussed, on receptiveness [13] and termination [5], there are a few more works related to ours and that are discussed below.

Closely related to our system one are a series of papers by Berger, Honda and Yoshida on linearity-based type systems. In [17], they introduce a type system that guarantees termination and determinacy of pi-calculus processes, i.e. *Strong Normalization* (SN). Our techniques of system one are actually close to theirs, as far as the linearity conditions and cycle-detection graphs are concerned (see also the type system in [15]). However SN is stronger than responsiveness, in particular SN implies responsiveness on all linear names under a balancing condition. In fact, the system in [17] is stricter than our system one, e.g. it does not allow linear subjects to carry linear objects, and bans ω-names, hence any form of nondeterminism and divergence, as these features would obviously violate SN. Yoshida's type system in [16], in turn a refinement of the systems in [17] and [2], is meant to ensure a *Linear Liveness* property, meaning that the considered process eventually prompts for a free output at a given channel. This property is related to responsiveness, the difference being that Linear Liveness does not imply synchronization, hence the corresponding input might not become available. Two kinds of names are considered in [16]: linear (used exactly once) and *affine* (used at most once). Linear subjects carrying linear objects are forbidden and internal mobility is assumed – only restricted names can be passed around.

Closely related to our system two are a series of papers by Kobayashi and collaborators. A type system for linearity in the pi-calculus was first introduced in [10]. This system can be used to ensure that any linear name in a process occurs exactly once in input and once in output; however, it cannot ensure that a linear name will be eventually used as a subject of a synchronization. Kobayashi's type systems in [6,7] can be used to guarantee that, under suitable fairness assumptions, certain actions are lock free, i.e. are deemed to succeed in synchronization, if they become available ([8] is a further refinement, but the resulting system cannot be used to enforce responsiveness.) Channel types are defined in terms of *usages*: roughly, CCS-like expressions on the alphabet $\{I, O\}$, that define the order in which each channel must be used in input (I) and in output (O). Each I/O action is annotated with an *obligation* level, related to when the action must become available, and a *capability* level, related to when the action must succeed in synchronization if it becomes available. A level can be a natural number or infinity, the latter used to annotate actions that are not guaranteed to become available/succeed in synchronization. This scheme is fairly general, allowing e.g. for typing of shared-memory structures such as locks and semaphores, which are outside the scope of our systems. Concerning responsiveness, on the other hand, it appears that our +-responsive types cannot in general be encoded into lock-freedom types. More precisely, one can exhibit processes well-typed in our system two and containing +-responsive names that cannot be assigned a finite capability in Kobayashi's systems. For example, both the process (7) and the "service-lookup" (8) are well-typed (in fact, strongly balanced) in our system two, under a typing context where b is +-responsive.

They are not in the systems of [6,7], under any type context that assigns to b a finite capability: the reason is that a finite-capability input on b is required to be balanced by an instance of a finite-obligation output $\bar{b}$, that cannot be statically determined in the given processes (although, after the submission of the present paper, the TyPiCal tool [9] has been modified to handle also processes of this form.) Another difference from [6,7] is that these systems partly rely on a form of dynamic analysis which is performed on types: the *reliability* condition on usages, which roughly plays the same role played in our systems by balancing, is checked via a reduction to the reachability problem for Petri Nets. As previously remarked, our systems are entirely static.

Acknowledgments. We wish to thank Davide Sangiorgi and Naoki Kobayashi for stimulating discussions on the topics of the paper.

References

1. Acciai, L., Boreale, M.: Responsiveness in Process Calculi. Long version, available at http://www.cmi.univ-mrs.fr/~lucia/PAPIERS/respFull.pdf
2. Berger, M., Honda, K., Yoshida, N.: Sequentiality and the π-calculus. In: Abramsky, S. (ed.) TLCA 2001. LNCS, vol. 2044, pp. 29–45. Springer, Heidelberg (2001)
3. Boreale, M.: On the Expressiveness of Internal Mobility in Name-Passing Calculi. Theoretical Computer Science 195(2), 205–226 (1998)
4. Cook, W.R., Misra, J.: Computation Orchestration: A Basis for Wide-Area Computing. Journal of Software and Systems Modeling (2006), http://www.cs.utexas.edu/wcook/projects/orc/
5. Deng, Y., Sangiorgi, D.: Ensuring Termination by Typability. In: Proc. of IFIP TCS, pp.619–632, 2004. Full version in Information and Computation, 204(7), 1045–1082 (2006)
6. Kobayashi, N.: A type system for lock-free processes. Information and Computation 177(2), 122–159 (2002)
7. Kobayashi, N.: Type-Based Information Flow Analysis for the Pi-Calculus. Acta Informartica 42(4-5), 291–347 (2005)
8. Kobayashi, N.: A New Type System for deadlock-Free Processes. In: Baier, C., Hermanns, H. (eds.) CONCUR 2006. LNCS, vol. 4137, Springer, Heidelberg (2006)
9. Kobayashi, N.: The verb TyPiCal tool, http://www.kb.ecei.tohoku.ac.jp/ koba/typical/
10. Kobayashi, N., Pierce, B.C., Turner, D.N.: Linearity and the Pi-Calculus. ACM Transactions on Programming Languages and Systems 21(5), 914–947 (1999)
11. Merro, M., Sangiorgi, D.: On asynchrony in name-passing calculi (Full version in). Mathematical Structures in Computer Science 14(5), 715–767 (2004)
12. Milner, R.: The polyadic π-calculus: a tutorial. Tec.Rep. LFCS report ECS-LFCS-91-180, 1991. Also in Logic and Algebra of Specification, Springer-Verlag, pp.203-246 (1993)
13. Sangiorgi, D.: The name discipline of uniform receptiveness. In: Proc. of ICALP, 1997. TCS, 221(1-2), 457-493 (1999)
14. Sangiorgi, D., Walker, D.: The π-calculus: a Theory of Mobile Processes. Cambridge University Press, Cambridge (2001)
15. Yoshida, N.: Graph Types for Monadic Mobile Processes. In: Chandru, V., Vinay, V. (eds.) Foundations of Software Technology and Theoretical Computer Science. LNCS, vol. 1180, pp. 371–386. Springer, Heidelberg (1996)
16. Yoshida, N.: Type-Based Liveness in the Presence of Nontermination and Nondeterminism. MCS Technical Report, 2002-20, University of Leicester (2002)
17. Yoshida, N., Berger, M., Honda, K.: Strong Normalisation in the π-calculus. In: Proc. of LICS, pp. 311–322. IEEE Computer Society Press, Los Alamitos (2001)

Normal Proofs in Intruder Theories

Vincent Bernat and Hubert Comon-Lundh

LSV, Ecole Normale Supérieure de Cachan
94235 Cachan cedex, France
{bernat,comon}@lsv.ens-cachan.fr

Abstract. Given an arbitrary intruder deduction capability, modeled as an inference system S and a protocol, we show how to compute an inference system $\hat{S}$ such that the security problem for an unbounded number of sessions is equivalent to the deducibility of some message in $\hat{S}$. Then, assuming that S has some subformula property, we lift such a property to $\hat{S}$, thanks to a proof normalisation theorem. In general, for an unbounded number of sessions, this provides with a complete deduction strategy. In case of a bounded number of sessions, our theorem implies that the security problem is co-NP-complete. As an instance of our result we get a decision algorithm for the theory of blind-signatures, which, to our knowledge, was not known before.

1 Introduction

Cryptographic protocols aim at achieving some security goal, while relying on a public network. Several such protocols have been designed and used in various applications. Many of them appeared to be flawed, not because of the weakness of cryptographic primitives, but simply because of the logical structure of the protocol (see the protocols repository [20] for examples). That is why several teams started to work on the formal verification of security protocols.

Though there are not so many different protocol designs, if one wants, say, to set a shared secret between two agents using a public key infrastructure, there are many small variants, which depend on the application domain. For instance, if a server has to manage thousands of users, it is mandatory to reduce both the time and space resources on its side and let the client do the job. Also, the companies (e.g. telecommunication companies) not only want to reduce the cost, but also to get robust protocols: if a key is compromised, this should not compromise the whole infrastructure. If possible, be resistant to guessing attacks on weak passwords... That is the reason why we need to *automate* the protocol verification: we can check many small variants of a same protocol.

Formally, what we need to achieve depends on several inputs: the protocol itself, but also what are the intruder capabilities, what are the known properties of cryptographic primitives and which property we want to prove. In the present paper, we only consider reachability properties: is some message deducible by the intruder after message exchanges that follow the protocol rules ?

Fixing an a priori bound on the number of messages which are sent through the network, several decision procedures have been designed, depending on the

M. Okada and I. Satoh (Eds.): ASIAN 2006, LNCS 4435, pp. 151–166, 2007.
© Springer-Verlag Berlin Heidelberg 2007

intruder capabilities and the algebraic properties. Let us cite our main source: in [18] the authors prove that the security problem is co-NP complete for the so-called "Dolev-Yao" intruder, assuming no equational property (the message algebra is free). The proof in this paper relies on two properties: first the intruder deduction rules are *local* (according to [17]), meaning some sub-formula property: to prove s from hypotheses T, we only need intermediate formulas in the subterms of s, T^1. The other ingredient is similar: if there is an attack, there is one which binds variables to subterms of messages already sent at this point.

We aim at viewing these two ingredients as a single subformula property. In other words, we want to design a proof system and a normalisation theorem such that all formulas occurring in the proof are subterms of the protocol rules, the hypotheses and the conclusion, and variable substitutions are also bound in a similar way. In addition, we would like to abstract from the particular intruder capabilities, relying only on the good properties of the inference systems which allow to derive the normalisation theorem.

To achieve these goals, we show first in section 3 that, given any inference system S describing intruder capabilities, an equational theory E and a protocol P, we can compute a proof system $\widehat{S}$, such that the protocol P is insecure if and only if some term is deducible in $\widehat{S}$. For further strategies design, formulas $\widehat{S}$ will be constrained by equations representing possible bindings of the free variables.

Then, our main result in section 4 is a proof normalisation result, which assumes additional hypotheses on the intruder capabilities and no equational properties. Normal proofs only involve terms that can be computed from the hypotheses, the conclusion and (instances of) the protocol rules. This result does not assume that the number of sessions is bounded. Hence we can use it as a proof search strategy. Moreover, if we fix the number of sessions, our main theorem shows that protocol security is then decidable, and co-NP-complete for intruder deduction systems that are in PTIME. As an example of application, we show in section 4.4 that, for the deduction system corresponding to blind signatures, the security problem is co-NP-complete. Security of protocols with blind signatures were also studied in [10], for an unbounded number of sessions, as an application of more general completeness results. In [10] the protocols are however approximated using a clausal formalism.

We also show in section 4.1 that our additional hypotheses on S are necessary: dropping them yields undecidability, even for a fixed number of sessions. We also briefly compare in section 5 our result, when restricted to a bounded number of sessions to [21] and the so-called "oracle rules" (see also [3] for oracle rules in presence of exclusive or).

Our ultimate hope is to generalize the proof normalisation result to associative and commutative symbols. This would be a major step, since it is shown in [7] that many relevant equational theories can be reduced to associativy and commutativity. The price to pay is a modification of the inference system S (and the protocol P). However, this transformation preserves the locality of S. And that is what we need in our theorem.

---

[1] A similar property was observed in [5] in the particular case of atomic keys.

2   Models of Security Protocols

We recall here a possible model of security protocols, which we use for proving the adequacy of our proof system in the next section. This model is close to many existing ones (e.g. [11,2,13]).

2.1   Messages

Messages are terms of an algebra, generated by a finite set of function symbols $\mathcal{F}$. Typically, $\mathcal{F}$ contains (a)symetric encryption (a binary symbol used in infix notation: $\{\_\}\_$), pairing (a binary symbol used in infix notation $< \_, \_ >$) and constants. It may also contain symbols for public keys, decryption functions, exclusive or, etc... If X is a set of (first-order) variable symbols, $T(\mathcal{F}, X)$ is the set of terms built over $\mathcal{F}$ and X. $T(\mathcal{F})$ is an abbreviation for $T(\mathcal{F}, \emptyset)$. A *substitution* σ is a mapping from a finite subset of X, called its *domain*, into $T(\mathcal{F}, X)$. As usual, such mappings are confused with their (unique) extension as an endomorphism of $T(\mathcal{F}, X)$. Substitutions are used in postfix notation. If σ, τ are substitutions, which coincide on $Dom(\sigma) \cap Dom(\tau)$, then $\sigma \uplus \theta$ is the substitution whose domain is $Dom(\sigma) \cup Dom(\theta)$ and coincides respectively with σ and θ on their domains. Terms can also be seen as trees, i.e. mappings t from a finite prefix-closed domain $Dom(t)$ to $\mathcal{F}$ (or $\mathcal{F} \cup X$). If $p \in Dom(t)$, $t|_p$ is the subterm of t at position p, $t[u]_p$ is the term obtained by replacing $t|_p$ with u in t. The *depth* of t is the maximal length of a position in $Dom(t)$. Finally, for any expression e, $Var(e)$ is the set of variables occurring in e.

In addition, we consider an equational theory $\mathcal{E}$ defined by a finite set of equations over the alphabet $\mathcal{F}$ and variables. Some typical examples are studied in [8,3,19,4]. We assume that $\mathcal{E}$ is given by a convergent rewrite system, possibly modulo the axioms of associativity and commutativity, in which case it is supposed to be coherent as well (see e.g. [12] for definitions concerning rewrite systems). This is the case in all relevant examples. For any message $m \in T(\mathcal{F}, X)$, $m \downarrow$ will denote the (unique up to associativity communativity) normal form of m. Substitutions are assumed to be normalized: the image of every variable is a term in normal form. We let Σ be the set of normalized substitutions.

2.2   Protocols

Protocols consist in a finite set of roles $R_1, \ldots R_m$, each of which consists in

- agent generations of the form λa: these agent names are the parameters of the role. For each role there is a distinguished agent name: the *main actor*.
- nonce generations of the form νN
- a finite sequence of rules $u_i \Rightarrow v_i$, where u_i, v_i are either empty or a term in normal form in the algebra $T(\mathcal{F}, X)$.

Example 1. Consider the following protocol (inspired by Denning and Sacco):

$$A \to B : < A, \{\{K_{ab}\}_{\mathsf{priv}(A)}\}_{\mathsf{pub}(B)} >$$
$$B \to A : \{s_b\}_{K_{ab}}$$

The agent playing the role A sends a new key, signed by her private key and encrypted with the public key of an agent playing the role B. Then he replies, sending a confidential text s_b encrypted with the newly generated key. (We overload symmetric and asymmetric encryption). This may be compiled into two roles:

A role: $\left\{ \begin{array}{l} \lambda a, \lambda b, \nu K_{ab}. \qquad\qquad \Rightarrow\; < a, \{\{K_{ab}\}_{\mathsf{priv}(a)}\}_{\mathsf{pub}(b)} > \\ \qquad\qquad \{x\}_{K_{ab}} \Rightarrow \end{array} \right.$

A generates a key K_{ab}, sends a message (no premisse) and receives a message (without reply): u_1, v_2 are empty.

B role: $\{ \lambda b, \nu s_b.\; < y, \{\{z\}_{\mathsf{priv}(y)}\}_{\mathsf{pub}(b)} > \Rightarrow \{s_b\}_z$

For this protocol, the equational theory $\mathcal{E}$ is defined by the two rewrite rules:

$$\{\{x\}_{\mathsf{pub}(y)}\}_{\mathsf{priv}(y)} \rightarrow x \quad \{\{x\}_{\mathsf{priv}(y)}\}_{\mathsf{pub}(y)} \rightarrow x$$

which express that decryption of a message encrypted with a key is the same as encryption of the message with the inverse key.

The λ, ν statements for parameters and nonces can be removed in the case of a finite number of sessions, duplicating and instantiating the roles as many times as necessary.

We assume that, in any protocol rule $u_i \Rightarrow v_i$, the variables of v_i are contained in the parameters, the nonces, and the variables of $u_j, j \leq i$. In other words, the action of sending v_i is determined by the actual values of the parameters and the messages which have been received so far.

2.3   Offline Intruder Theories

We consider sequents $T \vdash u$ where $u \in T(\mathcal{F}, X)$ and $T \subseteq T(\mathcal{F}, X)$ is finite. The intended meaning is "from a knowledge T, it is possible to deduce u".

The *offline intruder theory* $\mathcal{S}$ is defined by a (recursive) set of inference rules

$$\frac{T \vdash u_1 \;\cdots\; T \vdash u_n}{T \vdash u} \text{ If } C$$

where C is a recursive predicate on instances of $u_1, \ldots, u_n, u$, which is invariant by $\mathcal{E}$. $\mathcal{S}$ contains for instance the *composition rules*:

$$\frac{T \vdash u_1 \;\cdots\; T \vdash u_n}{T \vdash f(u_1, \ldots, u_n) \downarrow}$$

for a subset C of $\mathcal{F}$. This states the ability of an intruder to apply f to known terms. There is no side condition here. We also consider the axiom $T, u \vdash u$ as a composition rule. Examples of composition rules are $(E), (S), (B)$ in figure 1.

We write $T \vdash_{\mathcal{S}} u$ when $T \vdash u$ is derivable in $\mathcal{S}$. We will assume in the following that the deduction system $\mathcal{S}$ has some kind of subformula property. For any set of terms T let $\mathsf{St}(T)$ be the set of strict subterms of terms in T (for instance $\mathsf{St}(\{f(g(a), b), g(a), f(b, g(c))\}) = \{a, b, c, g(a), g(c)\}$), then:

Definition 1. *Let F be a computable mapping from sets of terms to sets of terms such that for every set of terms T, $T \cup St(T) \subseteq F(T)$ and $F(F(T)) \subseteq F(T)$. We say that the inference system S is F-local, if, for every proof $T \vdash_S s$,*
- *Either the last inference rule is a composition and there is a proof in which all nodes belong to $F(T \cup \{s\})$*
- *Or all nodes of the proof belong to $F(T)$*

Example 2. The Dolev-Yao intruder theory is F-local, $F(T)$ being the set of subterms of terms in T. We will later consider another example: the *blind signatures*. They are used in electronic vote protocols such as [14]and have been formalised in [16]. Following [16] and using a result of [7], the intruder deduction capabilities can be described by the inference rules of figure 1. Let F be the

$$\frac{T \vdash m \quad T \vdash r}{T \vdash \{m\}_r} (E) \qquad \frac{T \vdash \mathsf{sign}(m, sk) \quad T \vdash \mathsf{pub}(sk)}{T \vdash m} (V) \qquad \frac{T \vdash m \quad T \vdash r}{T \vdash \mathsf{blind}(m, r)} (B)$$

$$\frac{T \vdash \{m\}_r \quad T \vdash r}{T \vdash m} (D) \qquad \frac{T \vdash \mathsf{blind}(m, k) \quad T \vdash k}{T \vdash m} (UB_1) \qquad \frac{T \vdash m \quad T \vdash sk}{T \vdash \mathsf{sign}(m, sk)} (S)$$

$$\frac{T \vdash \mathsf{sign}(\mathsf{blind}(m, r), sk) \quad T \vdash r}{T \vdash \mathsf{sign}(m, sk)} (UB_2)$$

Fig. 1. Intruder deduction rules for blind signatures

function, mapping a set of terms T to the least set S containing T, such that $\forall t \in S, \mathsf{St}(t) \subseteq S$ and

1. If $\mathsf{sign}(m, sk) \in S$ then $\mathsf{pub}(sk) \in S$
2. If $\mathsf{sign}(\mathsf{blind}(m, r), sk) \in S$ then $\mathsf{sign}(m, sk) \in S$

$F(T)$ is finite and polynomially computable, $F(F(T)) \subseteq F(T)$ and the inference system of figure 1 is F-local.

2.4 Transition Systems

We shortly describe a standard semantics of security protocols, which is compatible with, e.g., [2,9,6]. We assume that $\mathcal{A}$ is a (infinite) set of agent names, some of which are honest and others are dishonest (or compromised). Nonces are modeled as terms $N_1(s), \ldots, N_k(s)$ where $s \in \mathbb{N}$ is a *session number*.

A *state* q consists in a set $\mathcal{I}_q$ of terms (the *intruder knowledge*) and, for each agent name a, a *local state*. A local state is a partial mapping $M_{q,a}$ from non-negative integers (session numbers) to tuples containing at least a role, a step number and a list of bindings (for roles or protocol variables). The initial state q_0 consists in a set $\mathcal{I}_0$ of terms representing the initial intruder knowledge. The mapping $M_{q_0,a}$ is empty for all a.

There is a transition from state q to a state q' if q and q' only differ in their intruder knowledge component and in the local state of an agent a and there is a role R such that one of the following holds:

session opening: let $u \Rightarrow v$ be the first rule of R, σ be a binding of the session parameters such that the main actor is bound to a. Either u must be empty or $\mathcal{I}_q \vdash_S u\theta \downarrow$ for some θ such that $x\sigma = x\theta$ for variables on which they are both defined. Then the local state of a is changed by adding an integer s, which does not occur in any (sub)term of q, to the domain of $M_{q,a}$ and letting $M_{q',a}(s)$ be $(R, 1, \sigma \uplus \theta)$.
The intruder knowledge is increased by adding $v\theta \downarrow$ and, if a is dishonest, also adding $N_1(s), \ldots, N_k(s)$: $\mathcal{I}_{q'} = \mathcal{I}_q \cup \{v\theta \downarrow\}$ or $\mathcal{I}_{q'} = \mathcal{I}_q \cup \{v\theta \downarrow , N_1(s), \ldots, N_k(s)\}$.

session progression: Let $u \Rightarrow v$ be the rule k of R, $M_{q,a}(s) = (R, k-1, \sigma)$. There must be a substitution θ such that $\mathcal{I}_q \vdash_S u\theta \downarrow$ and $x\sigma = x\theta$ for variables on which they are both defined. Then $M_{q',a}(s) = (R, k, \sigma \uplus \theta)$. The intruder knowledge is increased by adding $v\theta \downarrow$: $\mathcal{I}_{q'} = \mathcal{I}_q \cup \{v\theta \downarrow\}$.

We assume that the variables are renamed in such a way that two distinct role instances do not share variables. Then, for every state q, there is a unique substitution σ_q such that, for every a, s and every variable x, if $M_{q,a}(s) = (R, k, \theta)$ and x is in the domain of θ, then $x\theta = x\sigma_q$.

For any session number s, the role R_s and the parameters $a_s^1, \ldots, a_s^m$ are entirely determined by s, by uniqueness of session numbers.

Definition 2. *There is an attack on the secrecy of some term $t \in T(\mathcal{F}, X)$ if there is a substitution σ and a reachable state q such that $\mathcal{I}_q \vdash_S t\sigma \downarrow$ and all session variables occurring in t are substituted with integers s such that $a_s^1, \ldots, a_s^m$ are honest identities.*

Example 3. We continue example 1: Assume there are two honest agents a_1, a_2 The initial knowledge of the intruder consists of the names a_1, a_2 and their public keys $\mathsf{pub}(a_1), \mathsf{pub}(a_2)$. The initial state q_0 is defined by this knowledge $\mathcal{I}_0$.

Consider an instance of the B-role, in which b is bound to a_1. There is a transition step from q_0 to the state q_1 such that $M_{q_1,a_1}(1) = (B, 1, \theta)$, with $\theta = \{b \mapsto a_1; y \mapsto a_1; z \mapsto a_2\}$ since

$$\mathcal{I}_0 \vdash_S < a_1, a_2 >=< y\theta, \{\{z\theta\}_{\mathsf{priv}(y\theta)}\}_{\mathsf{pub}(y\theta)} > \downarrow$$

$\mathcal{I}_{q_1} = \mathcal{I}_{q_0} \cup \{\{s_b\}_{a_2}\}$ and s_b is deducible in this state: the protocol is insecure.

3   Online Deductions

Now, our goal is to enrich the intruder theory, so as to capture *online deduction*, i.e. deductions which use the protocol as an oracle. Moreover, as explained in the introduction, we want to keep the attack (substitution) apart from the deduction itself and that is why we use constrained sequents. The syntax of such formulas is $T \vdash u[\![E]\!]_\varepsilon$ where u is a term containing possibly variables, T is a finite set of ground terms, E is a conjunction of equations and ε is a finite set of equations. The idea is to lift the offline intruder deduction rules to terms with variables, recording in E the variable bindings, introduced by some inference rule.

Equations in the constraint part are interpreted modulo ε: σ is a ε-*solution of* E if, for every equation $u = v \in E$, $\varepsilon \models u\sigma = v\sigma$, which we also write $\sigma \models_\varepsilon u = v$. More generally, given two formulas ϕ_1, ϕ_2, we write $\phi_1 \models_\varepsilon \phi_2$ instead of $\varepsilon, \phi_1 \models \phi_2$ (the usual logical consequence of first-order logic) and $\phi_1 \dashv\vdash_\varepsilon \phi_2$ if $\phi_1 \models_\varepsilon \phi_2$ and $\phi_2 \models_\varepsilon \phi_1$. We omit the subscript ε when it is irrelevant.

Finally, we also record in the constraints the control points of the various instances of the roles; we use variables $x_{R,k,s}$ ranging over $\{0, 1\}$ and which, when raised, mean that the session s of role R reached stage k.

Given an inference system $\mathcal{S}$, we compute an inference system $\widehat{\mathcal{S}}$, which acts on constrained sequents and extends $\mathcal{S}$ with the use of protocol rules as oracles. First, every rule of $\mathcal{S}$:

$$\frac{T \vdash u_1 \ldots T \vdash u_k}{T \vdash u} \text{ If } C$$

is replaced with the rule

$$\frac{T \vdash u_1'[\![E_1]\!] \ldots T \vdash u_k'[\![E_k]\!]}{T \vdash u \downarrow[\![E_1 \wedge \ldots \wedge E_k]\!]} \text{ If } C \wedge R$$

$u_1', \ldots, u_k'$ are the result of linearizing $u_1, \ldots, u_k$. R is the set co-references: $\forall i. u_i' \sigma_R = u_i$. As an example:

$$\frac{T \vdash \{x\}_y \ T \vdash y}{T \vdash x} \quad \text{becomes} \quad \frac{T \vdash \{x\}_y[\![E_1]\!] \quad T \vdash y'[\![E_2]\!]}{T \vdash x \downarrow[\![E_1 \wedge E_2]\!]} \text{ If } y = y'$$

In addition to the extensions of rules of $\mathcal{S}$, we add the following inference rules:

Instantiation Rule:

$$\frac{T \vdash u[\![E]\!]}{T \vdash u\sigma \downarrow[\![\sigma]\!]} \text{ If } \sigma \models_\varepsilon E \text{ and } \mathcal{X}_c \cap Var(\sigma) \subseteq Var(E)$$

σ is meant to be any solution of E: this reflects the semantics of the constraints. Moreover, σ should not bind any control variable, which was unbounded before.

Weakening Rule:

$$\frac{T \vdash u_1[\![E_1]\!] \quad T \vdash u_2[\![E_2]\!]}{T \vdash u_1 \downarrow[\![E_1 \wedge E_2]\!]} \text{ W}$$

Such a rule is useful when deducing u_2 is irrelevant: only deducing *some* term with constraint E_2 is used later in the proof. This happens when the intruder needs to use the second rule of a role, but not the first one. Then he must be able to force the agents to play the first rule, regardless to the result, moving on the control point to the second rule.

The protocol rule for session progression

$$\frac{T \vdash u[\![E]\!]}{T \vdash w \downarrow [\![u = v \land E \land x_{R,k,s} = 1]\!]} \, P \qquad \text{If} \begin{cases} 1. \ v \Rightarrow w \text{ is the rule } k > 1 \text{ of} \\ \quad \text{role } R, \text{ session } s \\ 2. \ E \not\models_{\mathcal{E}} x_{R,k,s} = 1 \text{ and } E \models_{\mathcal{E}} \\ \quad x_{R,k-1,s} = 1 \end{cases}$$

The rule expresses that, whenever some (instance of) v has been deduced and the protocol as reached stage $k-1$ of session s of role R, then the intruder may use the kth rule of R as an oracle: he gets the corresponding instance w and the control point moves to k for that session. In addition, we impose $u = v$ in the constraint, meaning that the corresponding instance of u matches (modulo $\mathcal{E}$) the left side of the protocol rule.

Note that the rules of R are assumed to be renamed in such a way that the variables have different names in different sessions.

There is a similar rule for session opening: the only difference is that we do not require having reached the stage $k-1$ of session s, but we require s to be a new session number instead. Moreover, parameters of the new sessions are bound and their values are recorded in the constraint for further compatibility check.

Compromised agents

$$\frac{T \vdash u[\![E]\!]}{T \vdash N_i(s)[\![E]\!]} \quad \text{If} \begin{cases} 1. \ E \models_{\mathcal{E}} x_{R,1,s} = 1 \\ 2. \ \text{The main actor of session } s \text{ is compromised} \\ 3. \ N_i(s) \text{ is one of the nonces generated in session} \\ \quad s. \end{cases}$$

This expresses that all data generated by compromised (or dishonest) agents are available to the intruder. We only require that the session s has been opened. With such a rule, we do not need to give the intruder the ability to generate new data, as soon as there is at least one compromised agent.

Example 4. We continue example 3, restating the attack as a deduction in $\widehat{\mathcal{S}}$.

$$\frac{\dfrac{\dfrac{a_1, a_2 \vdash a_2[\![]\!] \qquad a_1, a_2 \vdash a_2[\![]\!]}{a_1, a_2 \vdash\, < a_2, a_2 >[\![]\!]}}{\dfrac{a_1, a_2 \vdash \{s_b(1)\}_z[\![y = a_2 \land z = a_2 \land b = a_1 \land x_{B,1,1} = 1]\!]}{a_1, a_2 \vdash \{s_b(1)\}_{a_2}[\![y = a_2 \land z = a_2 \land b = a_1 \land x_{B,1,1} = 1]\!]} \, \mathcal{I} \qquad a_1, a_2 \vdash a_2[\![]\!]}}{a_1, a_2 \vdash s_b(1)[\![y = a_2 \land z = a_2 \land b = a_1 \land x_{B,1,1} = 1]\!]} \, P$$

The next lemmas show that our inference rules are adequate with the transition system: the model in which we view the protocol rules as oracles can safely be used in place of the transition system.

Lemma 1 (Completeness of $\widehat{S}$). *For any reachable state q and any term t, if $\mathcal{I}_q \vdash_S t$, then we can build a proof Π in $\widehat{S}$ of $\mathcal{I}_0 \vdash t \downarrow [\![E]\!]$ such that $\sigma_q \models_\varepsilon E$.*

Conversely, the proof system $\widehat{S}$ is correct w.r.t. the trace semantics:

Lemma 2 (Correctness of $\widehat{S}$). *Let Π be a proof of $\mathcal{I}_0 \vdash t[\![E]\!]$. Then, for every substitution σ such that $\sigma \models_\varepsilon E$, there is a reachable state q such that $\mathcal{I}_q \vdash_S t\sigma \downarrow$.*

Therefore, we claim that the existence of an attack can be restated in this setting:

Theorem 1. *There is an attack on the secrecy of s iff there is a proof of some $T \vdash s'[\![E]\!]$ such that $s =_\varepsilon s'\sigma \downarrow$ and $\sigma \models_\varepsilon E$.*

4 A Normal Proof Result

From now on, we assume that $\mathcal{E}$ is empty. We also assume that T (in the left of sequents) always contains a constant 0 as well as terms $f(0, \ldots, 0)$ for (public) constructor symbols $f \in \mathcal{C}$. Moreover, we need some hypotheses on the inference system $\mathcal{S}$, beyond F-locality, as shown by lemma 3.

4.1 Additional Hypotheses on the Offline Deduction System

We assume that decomposition rules (i.e. those which are not composition rules):

$$(\mathcal{D}) \quad \frac{t_1 \quad \cdots \quad t_n}{t} \text{ IF } C$$

are such that each t_i is at most of depth 2 and for each t_i whose depth is 2, one of the following holds:

1. t is a subterm of t_i and t is a variable or a term of depth 1.
2. $t_i = C[f(u_1, \ldots, u_m)]$ and $t = C[u_i]$, where C is any context and $f \in \mathcal{C}$. Moreover f cannot occur at depth 1 in another decomposition rule.

And the side condition C is a conjunction of equations between variables such that, if $x = y \in C$ and x occurs at depth 2 and y occurs at depth at least one, then x occurs below a unary symbol and y occurs below a unary symbol.

Example 5. The decomposition rules of the blind signature theory satisfy these conditions, as well as classical Dolev-Yao rules or deduction rules for Cipher Block Chaining, for instance.

The conditions on C might be not necessary for our main result, but the other conditions are necessary as shown by the following lemma, obtained by reduction of the Post Correspondance Problem:

Lemma 3. *There is a local intruder inference system (decidable in PTIME) such that every decomposition rule has a single hypothesis of depth 2 and a conclusion of depth 1 and such that the insecurity problem for one session of a protocol containing one rule is undecidable.*

4.2   Modifying the Instanciation Rule

Since constraints are now interpreted in the free algebra, following standard concepts in unification theory, we can keep a satisfiable constraint in *solved form*, i.e. a conjunction of equations $x_1 = t_1 \wedge \ldots \wedge x_n = t_n$ where $x_1, \ldots, x_n$ are distinct variables and $x_i \notin Var(t_i, \ldots, t_n)$. Such a solved form defines an *occurrence ordering* $\geq_{occ}$ by $x_i \geq_{occ} y$ for every $y \in Var(t_i)$. E also defines a congruence $=_E$ on the set of terms: the least congruence containing E.

Our instanciation rule is currently too coarse. We want to use it more carefully, and keep the terms as small as possible. That is why we replace it with:

$$\frac{T \vdash u[x]_p [\![E \wedge x = t]\!]}{T \vdash u[t]_p [\![E \wedge x = t]\!]} \ (I)$$

in other words, we only replace one occurrence of one variable with its current binding in the equality constraint, which is assumed to be in solved form. The original instanciation rule can be simulated iterating the new one.

4.3   The Normal Proof Theorem

We want to show that, if there is a proof of $T \vdash s [\![E]\!]$, then there is a proof, which only uses particular sequents, which depend on the protocol rules P, T and s, E. In order to state the result, we need the notion of admissible sequent. Intuitively, the substitution defined by the final constraint E should be a stack of elementary assignments, each of which to a subterm of a term in T, s, P.

Definition 3. *For any set of terms S and constraints E, G in solved form, a sequent $T \vdash s [\![G]\!]$ is S, E-admissible iff*

1. *for all $x = t \in G$, if x is maximal (w.r.t. $\geq_{occ}$), then $T \vdash t [\![G \setminus \{x = t\}]\!]$ is S, E-admissible*
2. *$s \in S$ or else there is a t such that $s =_E t$ and $t \in S$.*

Example 6. Assume $S = \{\{x_1\}_{k_1}, k_2, x_3\}$, $E = [\![x_1 = \{x_2\}_{k_2}]\!]$ The following sequents are S, E-admissible:

$$T \vdash \{\{x_2\}_{k_2}\}_{k_1} [\![\,]\!] \, , \, T \vdash x_3 [\![x_3 = \{\{x_2\}_{k_2}\}_{k_1} \wedge x_2 = k_2]\!]$$

while the following are not S, G-admissible:

$$T \vdash \{x_3\}_{k_2} [\![\,]\!] \, , \, T \vdash x_3 [\![x_3 = \{x_2\}_{k_2} \wedge x_2 = \{x_1\}_{k_2}]\!]$$

If Π is a proof in $\widehat{S}$ we write $V(\Pi)$ the union, for all roles R and all sessions s of R opened in Π of

1. The control variables $x_{R,i,s}$ (i smaller than the number of rules in R)
2. The nonces $N_i(s)$ generated in this instance of role R
3. The parameter bindings for session s
4. The terms $\{u_i, v_i\}$ for every (renamed) protocol rule $u_i \Rightarrow v_i$ in R

Using for instance results in [6], the parameter bindings can actually be restricted to a finite fixed set, hence the size of each $V(\Pi)$ is $O(|R|)$.

Theorem 2. *Assume the hypotheses of the previous section on $\mathcal{S}$, in particular its F-locality. Assume that there is a proof Π of $T \vdash s[\![E]\!]$ in $\widehat{\mathcal{S}}$, with a satisfiable E then there is a proof Π' of a sequent $T \vdash s'[\![E']\!]$ in $\widehat{\mathcal{S}}$ such that:*

1. *$s\sigma_E = s'\sigma_{E'}$*
2. *$T \vdash s'[\![E']\!]$ is $F(V(\Pi) \cup T \cup \{s\sigma_E\}), \emptyset$-admissible*
3. *every sequent $T \vdash t[\![E'']\!]$ in Π' is $F(V(\Pi) \cup T \cup \{s\}), E'$-admissible*

The full proof of this theorem can be found in [1] (in French). We will try now to sketch it and convince the reader that it works.

The first step consists in performing several proof rewritings, such as:

Lemma 4. *If there is a proof Π of $T \vdash s[\![E]\!]$, then there is a proof of the same sequent in which no weakening precedes an $\mathcal{S}$-rule.*

Slighty more complex is the control of instanciations, whose delay is necessary if we want to keep the sequents small:

Lemma 5. *If there is a proof Π of $T \vdash s[\![E]\!]$ and E is satisfiable, then there is a proof Π' of $T \vdash s'[\![E]\!]$ such that $s\sigma_E = s'\sigma_E$ and any application of an instanciation rule in Π' replaces occurrences of variables at depth at most one. Moreover, this instanciation must be followed by a decomposition rule which would not be applicable before.*

To prove this, we simply swicth instanciations with other rules when it is possible and rely on the hypotheses on the depth of the premises of decomposition rules.

We may also rely on F-locality for the normalization of pure $\mathcal{S}$-parts of the proof. Then, it is not easy to perform further proof transformations: we would need contextual rewriting rules; it may be the case that a proof Π satisfies the conditions of the theorem, while some of its subproofs do not. Also, conversely, every subproof of Π may satisfy the theorem while Π does not. Let us show an example of the first case, which illustrates the need of contextual rewriting (or more complicated inductive hypotheses).

Example 7. Consider a toy deduction system $\mathcal{S}$, with the deduction rules $\dfrac{x}{a(x)}$, $\dfrac{x}{f(x)}$, $\dfrac{b_0(x)}{c_1}$, $\dfrac{b_n(0)}{c_2}$ and $\dfrac{x \quad y}{<x, y>}$. And protocol rules $r_0 : f(x_0) \to b_0(x_0)$ and, for every $i \le n - 1$, $r_{i+1} : b_i(a(x_{i+1})) \to b_{i+1}(x_{i+1})$. The proof of $< c_1, c_2 >$ is displayed in figure 2 (we omit control variables for simplicity) The proof satisfies the hypotheses of the theorem: $a(x_i)$ is a subterm of some protocol rule, hence

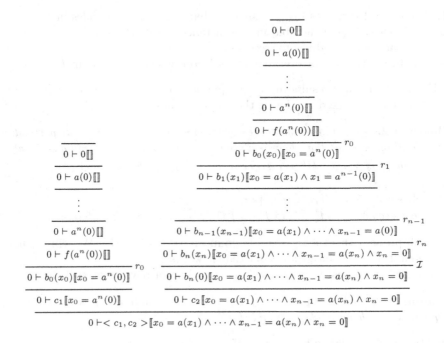

Fig. 2. An example of a proof

the final constraint is admissible. Other constraints, such as $x_0 = a^n(0)$ are also E-admissible since $a^n(0) =_E a(x_1)$ for instance.

However, the left part of the proof does not satisfy the theorem as, in this subproof, $a^n(0)$ is not admissible if $n \geq 1$. And, indeed, there is a much simpler proof, with $x_0 = 0$, while there is no simpler proof of the right branch. We must bind x_0 to $a^n(0)$ for compatibility between the two branches. This shows that the simplification of the left part proof depends on contextual informations.

The idea is to keep in a box the terms which are superfluously large (such as $a^n(0)$ in the example) and open the box only when necessary (at the last step in the above example). If a box is not opened, then it can be replaced by an arbitrary term, which can be deduced by the intruder. Now, the invariant in our proof transformations is that an expression $\Box_t$ can be replaced by an arbitrary deducible term in the current proof, but we remember that t is also deducible at this stage. Let us now skecth how these boxes are introduced and opened. The core of the result is that we only need to replace $\Box_{C[t]}$ with $C[\Box_t]$ when C is a piece of a protocol rule.

Assume the last rule of the proof is a protocol rule (we omit the control points here) and that (by an induction hypothesis) there is a proof of $T \vdash u[\![E]\!]$ which has the desired properties:

$$\cfrac{\cfrac{\Pi}{T \vdash u[\![E]\!]}}{T \vdash w[\![E \wedge u = v \wedge \ldots]\!]}$$

if $v \Rightarrow w$ is a protocol rule. Let also E_1 be a solved form of $E \wedge u = v$. Now, by definition $w \in F(V(\Pi) \cup T)$, but there might be a variable x of v such that $x = t \in E_1$ and t is not in $F(V(\Pi) \cup T)$. We have then to transform the proof.

Let $t = f(t_1, \ldots, t_n)$. By properties of the classical matching algorithm, t is a subterm of u. Moreover, $t \notin F(V(\Pi) \cup T)$ implies that any inference rule in Π yielding a superterm of t is a construction rule. By a simple induction, there must be in Π a rule $\cfrac{T \vdash t_1[\![C_1]\!] \cdots T \vdash t_n[\![C_n]\!]}{T \vdash f(t_1, \ldots, t_n)[\![C_1 \wedge \ldots \wedge C_n]\!]}$. Now, we can replace $t_1, \ldots, t_n$ with arbitrary terms, which are deducible by the intruder: the proof will still be valid. Le $\Box_{t_i}$ be such a replacement. We now have a proof of $T \vdash w[\![x = f(\Box_{t_1}, \ldots, \Box_{t_n}) \wedge \ldots]\!]$, which satisfies the requirements.

Now, if, later in the proof, we use an instantiation of x, our tranformation yields

$$\cfrac{\cfrac{\cfrac{\Pi_1}{T \vdash C[x]_p[\![x = f(\Box_{t_1}, \ldots, \Box_{t_n}) \wedge \ldots]\!]}}{T \vdash C[f(\Box_{t_1}, \ldots, \Box_{t_n})]_p[\![x = f(\Box_{t_1}, \ldots, \Box_{t_n}) \wedge \ldots]\!]} \quad T \vdash u_1[\![D_1]\!] \cdots T \vdash u_n[\![D_n]\!]}{T \vdash u[\![D]\!]} \mathcal{I}$$

which might no longer be a proof in $\widehat{\mathcal{S}}$.

By lemma 5, the last rule must be a decomposition rule and, thanks to our hypotheses on $\mathcal{S}$, p has a length 0 or 1. u cannot be $\Box_{t_i}$ or $f(\Box_{t_1}, \ldots, \Box_{t_n})$, otherwise we would have a much simpler proof of the same sequent using a subproof of Π_1 yielding u, and weakenings. Similarly, p must be of length 1, otherwise we have a shorter proof. According to our conditions on $\mathcal{S}$, we are in one of the following cases:

1. $u = \Box_{t_i}$
2. u is a subterm of u_i at depth 1
3. u is a subterm of $C[f(\Box_{t_1}, \ldots, \Box_{t_n})]_p$ at depth 1
4. $u = C[\Box_{t_i}]_p$ and f cannot occur at depth 1 in another decomposition rule

The first case has already been ruled out. In the second case we still get a proof in $\widehat{\mathcal{S}}$. In the third case, either the position of u is p and we have seen already that there is a simpler proof, or else we get a proof in $\widehat{\mathcal{S}}$. In the last case, the idea is to apply a proof transformation in the original proof, replacing $f(t_1, \ldots, t_n)$ with t_i. We then get again a shorter proof.

The last problem, which we do not want to address here, are the side conditions in the decomposition rules: it might be the case that the box-replacement sketched above yields a failure of an equality test in the side conditions.

Then we have to perform transformations on other branches of the proofs, and we will use the additional hypotheses on side conditions.

4.4   Consequences of the Normalisation Theorem

Corollary 1. *If the number of sessions is fixed and if F can be computed in PTIME, then the insecurity problem is in NP.*

Indeed, in this case, $P = V(\Pi)$ is fixed and E is empty. We can first guess s', E'; E' must bind each variable to a term in $F(P \cup T \cup \{s\})$. Then note that there are only a polynomial number of admissible sequents, up to E': at the possible price of initial weakenings, all constraints are identical to E', except for their control part. Then any sequent $T \vdash t[\![E'']\!]$ in the normal proof is such that $t = u\theta$ with $u \in F(P, T, s)$ and $E' \models \theta$. It is sufficient then to guess a subset S of $T(P, T, s)$ (the deducible terms) and an ordering on S (the ordering in which the terms are deduced), assign non-deterministically a control point to each of these terms and check that every term in S (or one of its instances by $\sigma_{E'}$) can be deduced in one step from smaller ones and their instances by $\sigma_{E'}$.

This is actually similar to NP membership proofs in the papers by Y. Chevalier, M. Rusinowitch and M. Turuani, such as [18].

Corollary 2. *For the theory of blind signatures, the insecurity problem in a fixed number of sessions is in NP.*

5   Discussion and Comparison with Related Work

Our starting point was the PhD thesis of M. Turuani [21]: we tried to formulate the results in terms of proof normalisations. We hoped first to better understand the reasons why we can get decidability results and, of course, derive more general results. We also planned to extend theorem 2 to equational theories, but it turns out to be quite technical and not very illuminating so far.

We partly succeeded to achieve our goals. The statement of our main theorem is satisfactory because the conditions on the inference system are straightforward to check and the normal proof results provides with a general (complete) proof strategy. Moreover, we cover some intruder theories, which are not in the scope of the "oracle rules" of [21]. We have seen blind signatures and there are other examples such as Dolev-Yao plus the rule $\dfrac{T \vdash g(x) \quad T \vdash f(g(x))}{T \vdash f(x)} \ldots$

This is only a partial success since first there are restrictions, which are probably not necessary. Second there are also intruder theories, which can be handled by oracle rules and do not satisfy our hypotheses. For instance, we cannot handle "shortcuts", which are rules obtained by composing other rules of the system.

The main remaining work, besides tuning our prototype implementation, is to extend the results to the associative-commutative case, which looks quite challenging.

References

1. Bernat, V.: Théories de l'intrus pour la vérification de protocoles cryptographiques. PhD thesis, École Normale Supérieure de Cachan (2006)
2. Cervesato, I., Durgin, N., Lincoln, P., Mitchell, J., Scedrov, A.: A meta-notation for protocol analysis. In: Syverson, P. (ed.) 12-th IEEE Computer Security Foundations Workshop, IEEE Computer Society Press, Los Alamitos (1999)
3. Chevalier, Y., Kuester, R., Rusinowitch, M., Turuani, M.: An NP decision procedure for protocol insecurity with xor. In: Kolaitis [15]
4. Chevalier, Y., Küsters, R., Rusinowitch, M., Turuani, M.: Deciding the security of protocols with Diffie-Hellman exponentiation and products in exponents. In: Pandya, P.K., Radhakrishnan, J. (eds.) FST TCS 2003: Foundations of Software Technology and Theoretical Computer Science. LNCS, vol. 2914, pp. 124–135. Springer, Heidelberg (2003)
5. Clarke, E., Jha, S., Marrero, W.: Using state space exploration and a natural deduction style message derivation engine to verify security protocols. In (PRO-COMET). Proceedings of the IFIP Working Conference on Programming Concepts and Methods (1998)
6. Comon-Lundh, H., Cortier, V.: Security properties: two agents are sufficient. Science of Computer Programming 50(1–3), 51–71 (2004)
7. Comon-Lundh, H., Delaune, S.: The finite variant property: How to get rid of some algebraic properties. In: Giesl, J. (ed.) RTA 2005. LNCS, vol. 3467, Springer, Heidelberg (2005)
8. Comon-Lundh, H., Shmatikov, V.: Intruder deductions, constraint solving and insecurity decision in preence of exclusive or. In: Kolaitis [15]
9. Cortier, V., Millen, J., Rueß, H.: Proving secrecy is easy enough. In: 14th IEEE Computer Security Foundations Workshop, pp. 97–108. IEEE Computer Society Press, Los Alamitos (2001)
10. Cortier, V., Rusinowitch, M., Zalinescu, E.: A resolution strategy for verifying cryptographic protocols with cbc encryption and blind signatures. In (PPDP 2005). Proc. 7th ACM-SIGPLAN Int. Conf. on Principles and Practice of Declarative Programming, pp. 12–22. ACM Press, New York (2005)
11. Denker, G., Millen, J., Rueß, H.: The CAPSL integrated protocol environment. Technical report, SRI International (October 2000)
12. Dershowitz, N., Jouannaud, J.-P.: Rewrite systems. In: van Leeuwen, J. (ed.) Handbook of Theoretical Computer Science, vol. B, pp. 243–309. North Holland, Amsterdam (1990)
13. Fabrega, F.T., Herzog, J., Guttman, J.: Strand spaces: Proving security protocol correct. Journal of Computer Security 7, 191–230 (1999)
14. Fujioka, A., Okamoto, T., Ohta, K.: A practical secret voting scheme for large scale elections. In: Proc. ASIACRYPT 1992. LNCS, vol. 718, pp. 244–251. Springer, Heidelberg (1993)
15. Kolaitis, P. (ed.): Eighteenth Annual IEEE Symposium on Logic in Computer Science. IEEE Computer Society Press, Los Alamitos (2003)
16. Kremer, S., Ryan, M.: Analysis of an electronic voting protocol in the applied pi-calculus. In: Sagiv, M. (ed.) ESOP 2005. LNCS, vol. 3444, Springer, Heidelberg (2005)
17. McAllester, D.: Automatic recognition of tractability in inference relations. J. ACM 40(2), 284–303 (1993)

18. Rusinowitch, M., Turuani, M.: Protocol insecurity with finite number of sessions is NP-complete. In: Proc.14th IEEE Computer Security Foundations Workshop, Cape Breton, Nova Scotia (June 2001)
19. Shmatikov, V.: Decidable analysis of cryptographic protocols with products and modular exponentiation. In: Schmidt, D. (ed.) ESOP 2004. LNCS, vol. 2986, Springer, Heidelberg (2004)
20. Security protocols open repository, http://www.lsv.ens-cachan.fr/spore/
21. Turuani, M.: Sécurité des protocoles cryptographiques: décidabilité et complexité. PhD thesis, Université Henri Poincaré- Nancy 1 (2003)

Breaking and Fixing Public-Key Kerberos*

I. Cervesato[1], A. D. Jaggard[2], A. Scedrov[3], J.-K. Tsay[3], and C. Walstad[3]

[1] Carnegie Mellon University — Qatar
`iliano@cmu.edu`
[2] Tulane University
`adj@math.tulane.edu`
[3] University of Pennsylvania
{`scedrov@math,jetsay@math,cwalstad@seas`}`.upenn.edu`

Abstract. We report on a man-in-the-middle attack on PKINIT, the public key extension of the widely deployed Kerberos 5 authentication protocol. This flaw allows an attacker to impersonate Kerberos administrative principals (KDC) and end-servers to a client, hence breaching the authentication guarantees of Kerberos. It also gives the attacker the keys that the KDC would normally generate to encrypt the service requests of this client, hence defeating confidentiality as well. The discovery of this attack caused the IETF to change the specification of PKINIT and Microsoft to release a security update for some Windows operating systems. We discovered this attack as part of an ongoing formal analysis of the Kerberos protocol suite, and we have formally verified several possible fixes to PKINIT—including the one adopted by the IETF—that prevent our attack.

1 Introduction

Kerberos [1] is a successful, widely deployed single sign-on protocol that is designed to authenticate clients to multiple networked services, *e.g.*, remote hosts, file servers, or print spoolers. Kerberos 5, the most recent version, is available for all major operating systems: Microsoft has included it in its Windows operating system, it is available for Linux under the name Heimdal, and commercial Unix variants as well as Apple's OS X use code from the MIT implementation of Kerberos 5. Furthermore, it is being used as a building block for higher-level protocols [2]. Introduced in the early 1990s, Kerberos 5 continues to evolve as new

---

* Cervesato was partially supported by the Qatar Foundation under grant number 930107, with early aspects of this work supported by ONR under Grant N00014-01-1-0795. Jaggard was partially supported by NSF Grants DMS-0239996 and CNS-0429689, and by ONR Grant N00014-05-1-0818. Scedrov was partially supported by OSD/ONR CIP/SW URI "Software Quality and Infrastructure Protection for Diffuse Computing" through ONR Grant N00014-01-1-0795 and OSD/ONR CIP/SW URI "Trustworthy Infrastructure, Mechanisms, and Experimentation for Diffuse Computing" through ONR Grant N00014-04-1-0725. Additional support from NSF Grants CNS-0429689 and CNS-0524059. Tsay was partially supported by ONR Grant N00014-01-1-0795 and NSF grant CNS-0429689.

M. Okada and I. Satoh (Eds.): ASIAN 2006, LNCS 4435, pp. 167–181, 2007.
© Springer-Verlag Berlin Heidelberg 2007

functionalities are added to the basic protocol. One of these extensions, known as PKINIT, modifies the basic protocol to allow public-key authentication. Here we report a protocol-level attack on PKINIT and discuss the constructive process of fixing it. We have verified a few defenses against our attack, including one we suggested, a different one proposed in the IETF Kerberos working group and included in recent drafts of PKINIT, and a generalization of these two approaches.

A Kerberos session generally starts with a user logging onto a system. This triggers the creation of a client process that will transparently handle all her authentication requests. The initial authentication between the client and the Kerberos administrative principals (altogether known as the KDC, for Key Distribution Center) is traditionally based on a shared key derived from a password chosen by the user. PKINIT is intended to add flexibility, security and administrative convenience by replacing this static shared secret with two pairs of public/private keys, one assigned to the KDC and one belonging to the user. PKINIT is supported by Kerberized versions of Microsoft Windows, typically for use with smartcard authentication, including Windows 2000 Professional and Server, Windows XP, and Windows Server 2003 [3]; it has also been included in Heimdal since 2002 [4]. The MIT reference implementation is being extended with PKINIT.

The flaw [5] we have uncovered in PKINIT allows an attacker to impersonate the KDC, and therefore all the Kerberized services, to a user, hence defeating authentication of the server to the client. The attackers also obtains all the keys that the KDC would normally generate for the client to encrypt her service requests, hence compromising confidentiality as well. This is a protocol-level attack and was a flaw in the then-current specification, not just a particular implementation. In contrast to recently reported attacks on Kerberos 4 [6], our attack does not use an oracle, but is efficiently mounted in constant time by simply decrypting a message with one key, changing one important value, and re-encrypting it with the victim's public key. The consequences of this attack are quite serious. For example, the attacker could monitor communication between an honest client and a Kerberized network file server. This would allow the attacker to read the files that the client believes are being securely transferred to the file server.

Our attack is possible because the two messages constituting PKINIT were insufficiently bound to each other.[1] More precisely, the second message of this exchange (the reply) can easily be modified as to appear to correspond to a request (the first message) issued by a client different from the one for which it was generated. Assumptions required for this attack are that the attacker is a legal user, that he can intercept other clients' requests, and that PKINIT is used in "public-key encryption mode". The alternative "Diffie-Hellman (DH) mode" does not appear vulnerable to this attack; we are in the process of proving its full security.

---

[1] The possibility of an 'identity misbinding' attack was independently hypothesized by Ran Canetti, whom we consulted on some details of the specification.

We discovered this attack as part of an ongoing formal analysis of the Kerberos 5 protocol suite. Our earlier work on Kerberos successfully employed formal methods for the verification of the authentication properties of basic intra-realm Kerberos 5 [7] and of cross-realm authentication [8]. Although our work is carried out by hand, automated approaches exist and have also been applied to deployed protocols [9,10,11]. In a recent collaboration with M. Backes, we have started extending our results from the abstract Dolev-Yao model examined here to the more concrete computational model [12]. Interestingly, the results described in more detail here served as a blueprint for the much more fine-grained proofs of [12].

After discovering the attack on PKINIT, we worked in close collaboration with the IETF Kerberos Working Group, in particular with the authors of the PKINIT specification documents, to correct the problem. Our contribution in this regard has been a formal analysis of a general countermeasure to this attack, as well as the particular instance proposed by the Working Group that has been adopted in the PKINIT specification [13]. Our attack led to an August 2005 Microsoft security patch and bulletin [3].

2   Kerberos 5 and Its Public-Key Extension

The Kerberos protocol [1] allows a legitimate user to log on to her terminal once a day (typically) and then transparently access all the networked resources she needs in her organization for the rest of that day. Each time she wants to retrieve a file from a remote server, for example, Kerberos securely handles the required authentication behind the scene, without any user intervention.

We will now briefly review how Kerberos achieves secure authentication based on a single logon. We will be particularly interested in the initial exchange, which happens when the user first logs on, and review the messages in this exchange both with and without PKINIT.

Kerberos Basics. The client process—usually acting for a human user—interacts with three other types of principals when using Kerberos 5 (with or without PKINIT). The client's goal is to be able to authenticate herself to various application servers (*e.g.*, email, file, and print servers). This is done by obtaining a "ticket-granting ticket" (TGT) from a "Kerberos Authentication Server" (KAS) and then presenting this to a "Ticket-Granting Server" (TGS) in order to obtain a "service ticket" (ST), the credential that the client uses to authenticate herself to the application server. A TGT might be valid for a day, and may be used to obtain several STs for many different application servers from the TGS, while a single ST might be valid for a few minutes (although it may be used repeatedly) and is used for a single application server. The KAS and the TGS are altogether known as the "Key Distribution Center" (KDC).

The client's interactions with the KAS, TGS, and application servers are called the Authentication Service (AS), Ticket-Granting (TG), and Client-Server (CS) exchanges, respectively. The focus of this work will be the AS exchange, as PKINIT does not alter the remaining parts of Kerberos.

The Traditional Authentication Service Exchange. The abstract structure of the traditional (non-PKINIT) AS exchange is given in Fig. 1 once we ignore the $\boxed{\text{boxed}}$ items. A client C generates a fresh nonce n_1 and sends it, together with her own name and the name T of the TGS for whom she desires a TGT, to some KAS. The KAS responds by generating a fresh key AK for use between the client and the TGS. This key is sent back to the client, along with the nonce from the request and other data, encrypted under a long-term key k_C shared between C and the KAS; this long-term key is usually derived from the user's password. This is the only time that this long-term key is used in a standard Kerberos run because later exchanges use freshly generated keys. AK is also included in the ticket-granting ticket, sent alongside the message encrypted for the client. The TGT is encrypted under a long-term key shared between the KAS and the TGS named in the request. These encrypted messages are accompanied by the client's name—and other data that we abstract away— sent in the clear. Once the client has received this reply, she may undertake the Ticket-Granting exchange.

It should be noted that the actual AS exchange, as well as the other exchanges in Kerberos, is more complex than the abstract view given here; the details we omit here do not affect our results and including them would obscure the exposition of our results. We refer the reader to [1] for the complete specification of Kerberos 5, and to [7] for a formalization at an intermediate level of detail.

Public-Key Kerberos. PKINIT [13] is an extension to Kerberos 5 that uses public key cryptography to avoid shared secrets between a client and KAS; it modifies the AS exchange but not other parts of the basic Kerberos 5 protocol. The long-term shared key (k_C) in the traditional AS exchange is typically derived from a password, which limits the strength of the authentication to the user's ability to choose and remember good passwords; PKINIT does not use k_C and thus avoids this problem. Furthermore, if a public key infrastructure (PKI) is already in place, PKINIT allows network administrators to use it rather than expending additional effort to manage users' long-term keys needed for traditional Kerberos. This protocol extension adds complexity to Kerberos as it retains symmetric encryption in the later rounds but relies on asymmetric encryption, digital signatures, and corresponding certificates in the first round.

In PKINIT, the client C and the KAS possess independent public/secret key pairs, (pk_C, sk_C) and (pk_K, sk_K), respectively. Certificate sets $Cert_C$ and $Cert_K$ issued by a PKI independent from Kerberos are used to testify of the binding between each principal and her purported public key. This simplifies administration as authentication decisions can now be made based on the trust the KDC holds in just a few known certification authorities within the PKI, rather than keys individually shared with each client (local policies can, however, still be installed for user-by-user authentication). Dictionary attacks are defeated as user-chosen passwords are replaced with automatically generated asymmetric keys. The login process changes as very few users would be able to remember a random public/secret key pair. In Microsoft Windows, keys and certificate chains are stored in a smartcard that the user swipes in a reader at login time.

A passphrase is generally required as an additional security measure [14]. Other possibilities include keeping these credentials on the user's hard drive, again protected by a passphrase.

The manner in which PKINIT works depends on both the protocol version and the mode invoked. As the PKINIT extension to Kerberos has recently been defined in RFC 4556 after a sequence of Internet Drafts [13], we use "PKINIT-n" to refer to the protocol as specified in the nth draft revision and "PKINIT" for the protocol more generally. These various drafts and the RFC can be found at [13]. We discovered the attack described in Sect. 3 when studying PKINIT-25; our description of the vulnerable protocol is based on PKINIT-26, which does not differ from PKINIT-25 in ways that affect the attack. In response to our work described here, PKINIT-27 included a defense against our attack; we discuss this fix in Sect. 4. The current version of the protocol is defined in RFC 4556 and does not differ from the parts of PKINIT-27 we discuss here.

PKINIT can operate in two modes. In *Diffie-Hellman (DH) mode*, the key pairs (pk_C, sk_C) and (pk_K, sk_K) are used to provide digital signature support for an authenticated Diffie-Hellman key agreement which is used to protect the fresh key AK shared between the client and KAS. A variant of this mode allows the reuse of previously generated shared secrets. In *public-key encryption mode*, the key pairs are used for both signature and encryption. The latter is designed to (indirectly) protect the confidentiality of AK, while the former ensures its integrity.

We will not discuss the DH mode any further as our preliminary investigation did not reveal any flaw in it; we are currently working on a complete analysis of this mode. Furthermore, it appears not to have yet been included in any of the major operating systems. The only support we are aware of is within the PacketCable system [15], developed by CableLabs, a cable television research consortium.

Figure 1, including $\boxed{\text{boxed}}$ terms, illustrates the AS exchange in PKINIT-26. In discussing this and other descriptions of the protocol, we write $[m]_{sk}$ for the digital signature of message m with secret key sk. (PKINIT realizes digital signatures by concatenating the message and a keyed hash for it, occasionally with other data in between.) In our analysis of PKINIT in Sect. 6, we assume that digital signatures are unforgeable [16]. The encryption of m with public key pk is denoted $\{\!|m|\!\}_{pk}$. As usual, we write $\{m\}_k$ for the encryption of m with symmetric key k.

The first line of Fig. 1 describes the relevant parts of the request that a client C sends to a KAS K using PKINIT-26. The last part of the message—C, T, n_1—is exactly as in basic Kerberos 5, containing the client's name, the name of the TGS for which she wants a TGT, and a nonce. The $\boxed{\text{boxed}}$ parts are added by PKINIT and contain the client's certificates $Cert_C$ and her signature (with her secret key sk_C) over a timestamp t_C and another nonce n_2. (The nonces and timestamp to the left of this line indicate that these are generated by C specifically for this request, with the box indicating data not included in our abstract formalization of basic Kerberos 5 [7].)

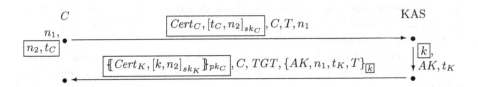

Fig. 1. Message Flow in the Traditional AS Exchange and in PKINIT-26, where $TGT = \{AK, C, t_K\}_{k_T}$

The second line in Fig. 1 shows our formalization of K's response, which is more complex than in basic Kerberos. The last part of the message—$C, TGT, \{AK, n_1, t_K, T\}_{\boxed{k}}$—is very similar to K's reply in basic Kerberos; the difference (boxed) is that the symmetric key k protecting AK is now freshly generated by K and not a long-term shared key. The ticket-granting ticket TGT and the message encrypted under k is as in traditional Kerberos. Because k is freshly generated for the reply, it must be communicated to C before she can learn AK. PKINIT does this by adding the (boxed) message $\{\!|\, Cert_K, [k, n_2]_{sk_K}\,|\!\}_{pk_C}$. This contains K's certificates and his signature, using his secret key sk_K, over k and the nonce n_2 from C's request; all of this is encrypted under C's public key pk_C.

This abstract description leaves out a number of fields which are of no significance with respect to the reported attack or its fix. We invite the interested reader to consult the specifications [13]. Also, recall that PKINIT leaves the subsequent exchanges of Kerberos unchanged.

3   The Attack

In this section, we report on a dangerous attack against PKINIT in public-key encryption mode. We discovered this attack as we were interpreting the specification documents of this protocol [13] in preparation for its formalization in MSR. We start with a detailed description of the attacker's actions in the AS exchange, the key to the attack. We then review the conditions required for the attack and close this section with a discussion of how the attacker may propagate the effects of her AS exchange actions throughout the rest of a protocol run.

Message Flow. Figure 2 shows the AS exchange message flow in the attack. The client C sends a request to the KAS K which is intercepted by the attacker I, who constructs his own request message using the parameters from C's message. All data signed by C are sent unencrypted—indeed $[msg]_{sk}$ can be understood as an abbreviation for the plaintext msg together with a keyed hash—so that I may generate his own signatures over data from C's request. The result is a well-formed request message from I, although constructed using some data originating with C. I's changes to the request message are boxed above the top-right arrow of Fig. 2. (We have omitted an unkeyed checksum taken over unencrypted data from these messages; I can regenerate this as needed to produce a valid request.)

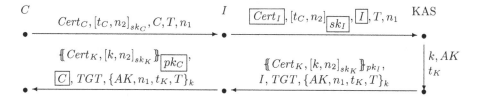

Fig. 2. Message Flow in the Man-In-The-Middle Attack on PKINIT-26, where $TGT = \{AK, I, t_K\}_{k_T}$

I forwards the fabricated request to the KAS K, who views it as a valid request for credentials if I is himself a legitimate client; there is nothing to indicate that some of the data originated with C. K responds with a reply containing credentials for I (the bottom-right arrow in Fig. 2). The ticket-granting ticket, denoted TGT, has the form $\{AK, I, t_K\}_{k_T}$; note that, since it is encrypted with the key k_T shared between K and the TGS T, it is opaque to C. Another part of the reply is encrypted using the public key of the client for whom the credentials are generated, in this case I. This allows the attacker to decrypt this part of the message using his public key, learn the key k, and use this to learn the key AK. An honest client would only use this information to send a request message to the TGS T. Instead, I uses C's public key to re-encrypt the data he decrypted using his private key (having learned pk_C, if necessary, from $Cert_C$ in the original request), replaces his name with C's, and forwards the result to C. To C this message appears to be a valid reply from K generated in response to C's initial request (recall that C cannot read I's name inside the TGT).

At this point, C believes she has authenticated herself to the KAS and that the credentials she has obtained—the key AK and the accompanying TGT—were generated for her. However, the KAS has completed the PKINIT exchange with I and has generated AK and the TGT for I. The attacker knows the key AK (as well as k, which is not used other than to encrypt AK) and can therefore decrypt any message that C would protect with it.

Protocol-level attacks in the same vein of the vulnerability we uncovered have been reported in the literature for other protocols. In 1992, Diffie, van Oorschot, and Wiener noted that a signature-based variant of the Station-to-Station protocol [17] could be defeated by a man-in-the-middle (MITM) attack which bears similarities to what we observed in the first half of our vulnerability; in 2003 Canetti and Krawczyk [18] observed that the "basic authenticated Diffie-Hellman" mode of the Internet Key Exchange protocol (IKE) had this very same vulnerability. In 1996, Lowe [19] found an attack on the Needham-Schroeder public key protocol which manipulates public key encryption essentially in the same way as what happens in the second half of our attack. Because it alters both signatures and asymmetric encryptions, our attack against PKINIT stems from both [19] and [17]. In 1995, Clark and Jacob [20] discovered a similar flaw on Hwang and Chen's corrected SPLICE/AS protocol.

Assumptions. In order for this attack to work, the attacker must be a legal Kerberos client so that the KAS will grant him credentials. In particular, he must possess a public/secret key pair (pk_I, sk_I) and valid certificates $Cert_I$ trusted by the KAS. The attacker must also be able to intercept messages, which is a standard assumption. Finally, PKINIT must be used in public-key encryption mode, which is commonly done as the alternative DH mode does not appear to be readily available, except for domain specific systems [14,15].

Effects of the Attack. Once the attacker learns AK in the AS exchange, he may either mediate C's interactions with the various servers (essentially logging in as I while leaking data to C so she believes she has logged in) or simply impersonate the later servers. In the first case, once C has AK and a TGT, she would normally contact the TGS to get a service ticket for some application server S. This request contains an *authenticator* of the form $\{C, t'_C\}_{AK}$ (*i.e.*, C's name and a timestamp, encrypted with AK). Because I knows AK, he may intercept the request and replace the authenticator with one that refers to himself: $\{I, t'_C\}_{AK}$. The reply from the TGS contains a freshly generated key SK; this is encrypted under AK, for C to read and thus accessible to I, and also included in a service ticket that is opaque to all but the TGS and application server. I may intercept this message and learn SK, replace an instance of his name with C's name, and forward the result to C. As I knows SK, he can carry out a similar MITM attack on the CS exchange, which ostensibly authenticates C to the application server; however, because the service ticket names I, this server would believe that he is interacting with I, not C.

Alternatively, the attacker may intercept C's requests in the TG and CS exchanges and impersonate the involved servers rather than forwarding altered messages to them. For the exchange with the TGS, I will ignore the TGT and only decrypt the portion of the request encrypted under AK (which he learned during the initial exchange). The attacker will then generate a bogus service ticket, which the client expects to be opaque, and a fresh key SK encrypted under AK, and send these to C in what appears to be a properly formatted reply from the TGS. This very same behavior can be perpetrated at the next phase, by which C requests service to the end-server S, for communicating with whom the key SK was purportedly generated. Note that the attacker may take the first approach in the TG exchange and then the second in the CS exchange. The reverse is not possible because I cannot forge a valid service ticket.

Regardless of which approach the attacker uses to propagate the attack throughout the protocol run, C finishes the CS exchange believing that she has done so with a server S and that T has generated a fresh key SK known only to C and S. Instead, I knows SK in addition to, or instead of, S (depending on how I propagated the attack). Thus I may learn any data that C attempts to send to S; depending on the type of server involved, such data could be quite sensitive. Note that this attack does not allow I to impersonate C to a TGS or an application server because all involved tickets name I. This also means that if C is in communication with an actual server (T or S), that server will view the client as I, not C.

4   Preventing the Attack

The attack outlined in the previous section was possible because the two messages constituting the then-current version of PKINIT were insufficiently bound to each other. More precisely, the attack shows that, although a client can link a received response to a previous request (thanks to the nonces n_1 and n_2, and to the timestamp t_C), she cannot be sure that the KAS generated the key AK and the ticket granting ticket TGT appearing in this response *for her*. Indeed, the only evidence of the principal for whom the KAS generated these credentials appears inside the ticket granting ticket TGT, which is opaque to her. This suggests one approach to making PKINIT immune to this attack, namely to require the KAS to include the identity of this principal in a component of the response that is integrity-protected and that the client can verify. An obvious target is the submessage signed by the KAS in the reply.

Following a methodology we successfully applied in previous work on Kerberos [7,8], we have constructed a formal model of both PKINIT-26 and various possible fixes to this protocol (including the one adopted in PKINIT-27). Details can be found in Sect. 6. Property 1 below shows the informal statement of the property that we saw violated in PKINIT-26 but that holds of subsequent revisions, hence demonstrating that this fix does indeed defend against our attack.

Property 1. *In PKINIT-27 (and subsequent versions), whenever a client C processes a message containing server-generated public-key credentials, the KAS previously produced such credentials for C.*

This property follows from a corollary to Thm. 2, which we prove in Sect. 6.

As we worked on our formal analysis, we solicited feedback from the IETF Kerberos Working Group, and in particular the authors of the PKINIT specifications, about possible fixes we were considering. We also analyzed the fix, proposed by the Working Group, that was included in PKINIT-27 and subsequent revisions of this specification [13].

Abstract Fix. Having traced the origin of the discovered attack to the fact that the client cannot verify that the received credentials (the TGT and the key AK) were generated for her, the problem can be fixed by having the KAS include the client's name, C, in the reply, in such a way that it cannot be modified *en route* and that the client can check it. Following well-established recommendations [21], we initially proposed a simple and minimally intrusive approach to doing so, which consists in mentioning C in the portion of the reply signed by the KAS (in PKINIT-26, this is $[k, n_2]_{sk_K}$). We then generalized it by observing that the KAS can sign k and any message fragment $F(C, n_i)$ built from C and at least one of the nonces n_1, n_2 from C's request for credentials. With this abstract fix in place, the PKINIT exchange in public-key encryption mode appears as follows, where we have used a box to highlight the modification with respect to PKINIT-26.

$$C \qquad\qquad\qquad\qquad\qquad\qquad\qquad\qquad\qquad\qquad \text{KAS}$$

$$\underset{\substack{n_1,\\ n_2, t_C}}{\bullet} \xrightarrow{\qquad\qquad Cert_C,\, [t_C, n_2]_{sk_C},\, C, T, n_1 \qquad\qquad} \bullet \;\downarrow\, \substack{k,\, AK \\ t_K}$$

$$\bullet \xleftarrow{\quad \{\!| Cert_K, [k, \boxed{F(C, n_i)}]_{sk_K} |\!\}_{pk_C},\, C,\, TGT,\, \{AK, n_1, t_K, T\}_k \quad} \bullet$$

Here, F represents any construction that involves C and n_1 or n_2, and is verifiable by the client. Integrity protection is guaranteed by the fact that it appears inside a component signed by the KAS, and therefore is non-malleable by the attacker (assuming that the KAS's signature keys are secure). This defends against the attack since the client C can now verify that the KAS generated the received credentials for her and not for another principal (such as I in our attack). Indeed, an honest KAS will produce the signature ($[k, F(C, n_i)]_{sk_K}$) only in response to a request by C. The presence of the nonces n_1 or n_2 uniquely identifies which of the (possibly several) requests of C this reply corresponds to. Note that the fact that we do not need F to mention both n_1 and n_2 entails that the nonce n_2 is superfluous as far as authentication is concerned.

A simple instance of this general schema consists in taking $F(C, n_i)$ to be (C, n_2), yielding the signed data $[k, C, n_2]_{sk_K}$, which corresponds to simply including C's name within the signed portion of the PKINIT-26 reply. This version is very similar to the initial target of our formal verification. We showed that indeed it defeats the reported attack and satisfied the formal authentication property violated in PKINIT-26. Only later did we generalize the proof to refer to the abstract construction F.

Solution Adopted in PKINIT-27. When we discussed our initial fix with the authors of the PKINIT document, we received the request to apply our methodology to verify a different solution: rather than simply including C's name in the signed portion of the reply, replace the nonce n_2 there with a keyed hash ("checksum" in Kerberos terminology) taken over the client's entire request. We did so and showed that this approach also defeats our attack. It is on the basis of this finding that we distilled the general fix discussed above, of which both solutions are instances.

The checksum-based approach was later included in PKINIT-27 and its revisions [13]. This version of PKINIT has the following intended message flow:

$$C \qquad\qquad\qquad\qquad\qquad\qquad\qquad\qquad\qquad\qquad \text{KAS}$$

$$\underset{\substack{n_1,\\ n_2, t_C}}{\bullet} \xrightarrow{\qquad\qquad Cert_C,\, [t_C, n_2]_{sk_C},\, C, T, n_1 \qquad\qquad} \bullet \;\downarrow\, \substack{k,\, AK \\ t_K}$$

$$\bullet \xleftarrow{\quad \{\!| Cert_K, [k, \boxed{ck}]_{sk_K} |\!\}_{pk_C},\, C,\, TGT,\, \{AK, n_1, t_K, T\}_k \quad} \bullet$$

Here, ck is a checksum of the client's request keyed with the key k, that ck has the form $H_k(CertC, [tC, n2]_{skC}, C, T, n_1)$ where H is a preimage-resistant MAC function H. This means that it is computationally infeasible for the attacker to find a message whose checksum matches that of a given message. Following the specifications in [22], which discusses cryptographic algorithms for use in the

Kerberos protocol suite, current candidates for H include hmac-sha1-96-aes128. New strong keyed checksums can be used for ck as they are developed.

5   Formalizing PKINIT in MSR

MSR [8,23,24] is a flexible framework for specifying complex cryptographic protocols, possibly structured as a collection of coordinated subprotocols. It uses strongly-typed multiset rewriting rules over first-order atomic formulas to express protocol actions and relies on a form of existential quantification to symbolically model the generation of fresh data (*e.g.*, nonces or short-term keys).

Terms and Types. MSR represents network messages and their components as first-order terms. Thus the TGT $\{AK, C, t_K\}_{k_T}$ sent from K to C is modeled as the term obtained by applying the binary encryption symbol $\{\_\}\_$ to the constant k_T and the subterm (AK, C, t_K). This subterm is built using atomic terms and two applications of the binary concatenation symbol ("$\_,\_$"). Terms are classified by types, which describe their intended meaning and restrict the set of terms that can be legally constructed. For example, $\{\_\}\_$ accepts a key (type key) and a message (type msg), producing a msg; using a nonce as the key yields an ill-formed message. Nonces, principal names, *etc.*, often appear within messages; MSR uses the subsort relation to facilitate this. For example, defining nonce to be a subsort of msg (written nonce <: msg) allows nonces to be treated as messages. Both term constructors and types are definable. This allows us to formalize the specialized principals of Kerberos 5 as subsorts of the generic principal type: we introduce types client, KAS, TGS and server, with the obvious meanings.

MSR supports more structured type definitions [23]. Dependent types allow capturing the binding between a key and the principals for whom it was created. For example, the fact that a short-term key k is shared between a particular client C and server S is expressed by declaring it of type shK C S. Because k is a key, shK C S is a subsort of key (for all C and S), and since k is short term this type is also a subsort of msg as k needs to be transmitted in a message. We similarly model the long-term keys that a principal A shares with the KAS as objects of type dbK A, again a subsort of key, but *not* of msg. Dependent types give us elegant means to describe the public-key machinery. If (pk, sk) is the public/secret key pair of principal A, we simply declare pk of type pubK A and sk of type secK pk. The constructors for encryption and digital signature are written $\{\!\{m\}\!\}_{pk}$ and $[m]_{sk}$, respectively.

Other types used in the formalization of PKINIT include time for timestamps, CertList for lists of digital certificates, and someSecK as an auxiliary type for working with digital signatures. We also use the constructor $H_k(m)$ to model the checksum (keyed hash) of message m keyed with symmetric key k.

States, Rules, and the Formalization of PKINIT-27. The *state* of a protocol execution is determined by the network messages in transit, the local knowledge of each principal, and other similar data. MSR formalizes individual bits

$\forall K : \mathsf{KAS}$

$$\left[\begin{array}{l} \forall C : \mathsf{client} \quad \forall T : \mathsf{TGS} \quad \forall n_1, n_2 : \mathsf{nonce} \quad \forall sk : \mathsf{someSecK} \quad \forall Cert_C, Cert_K : \mathsf{CertList} \\ \forall k_T : \mathsf{dbK}\ T \quad \forall t_C, t_K : \mathsf{time} \quad \forall pk_C : \mathsf{pubK}\ C \quad \forall pk_K : \mathsf{pubK}\ K \quad \forall sk_K : \mathsf{secK}\ pk_K \\[2mm] \qquad\qquad\qquad\qquad \exists AK : \mathsf{shK}\ C\,T, \ \exists k : \mathsf{shK}\ C\,K \\ \mathsf{N}(Cert_C, [t_C, n_2]_{sk}, \overset{\iota_{2.1}}{\Longrightarrow} \ \mathsf{N}(\{\!|Cert_K, [k, \boxed{H_k(Cert_C, [t_C, n_2]_{sk}, C, T, n_1)}]_{sk_K}\!\}_{pk_C}, \\ \quad C, T, n_1) \qquad\qquad\qquad\qquad C, \{AK, C, t_K\}_{k_T}, \{AK, n_1, t_K, T\}_k) \\[2mm] \mathsf{IF}\ \ VerifySig([t_C, n_2]_{sk}; (t_C, n_2); C, Cert_C),\ Valid_K(C, T, n_1),\ Clock_K(t_K) \end{array} \right]$$

Fig. 3. KAS's Role in the PKINIT-27 Version of the AS Exchange

of information in a state by means of *facts* consisting of *predicate name* and one or more terms. For example, the network fact $\mathsf{N}(\{AK, C, t_K\}_{k_T})$ indicates that the ticket granting ticket $\{AK, C, t_K\}_{k_T}$ is present on the network, and $\mathsf{I}(\{AK, C, t_K\}_{k_T})$ that it has been captured by the attacker.

A protocol consists of actions that transform the state. In MSR, this is modeled by the notion of *rule*: a description of the facts that an action removes from the current state and the facts it replaces them with to produce the next state. For example, Fig. 3 describes the actions of the KAS in PKINIT-27 (see Sect. 4). Ignoring for the moment the leading $\forall K : \mathsf{KAS}$ and the outermost brackets leaves us with a single MSR rule—labeled $\iota_{2.1}$ above the arrow—that we will use to illustrate characteristics of MSR rules in general.

Rules are parametric, as evidenced by the leading string of typed universal quantifiers: actual values need to be supplied before applying the rule. The middle portion $(\cdots \Longrightarrow \cdots)$ describes the transformation performed by the rule: it replaces states containing a fact of the form $\mathsf{N}(Cert_C, [t_C, n_2]_{sk}, C, T, n_1)$ with states that contain the fact on its right-hand side but which are otherwise identical. The existential marker "$\exists AK : \mathsf{shK}\ C\,T$" requires AK to be replaced with a newly generated symbol of type $\mathsf{shK}\ C\,T$, and similarly for "$\exists k : \mathsf{shK}\ C\,K$"; this is how freshness requirements are modeled in MSR. The last line, starting with the keyword IF, further constrains the applicability of the rule by requiring that certain predicates be present (differently from the left-hand side, they are not removed as a result of applying the rule). Here, we use the predicates *VerifySig* to verify that a digital signature is valid given a list of credentials (*VerifySig*$(s; m; P, Certs)$ holds if s is the signature, relative to certificates $Certs$, by principal P over the message m; we assume that this implies P has a key k such that the rank function $\rho_k(s; m) > 0$—see below). Additionally, we use *Valid*$_K$ to capture the local policy of K in issuing tickets, and *Clock*$_K$ to model the local clock of K. While the entities following 'IF' are logically facts, in practice they are often handled procedurally, outside of MSR.

Rule $\iota_{2.1}$ completely describes the behavior of the KAS; in general, multiple rules may be needed, as when modeling the actions of the client in the AS exchange. Coordinated rules describing the behavior of a principal are collected in a *role*. A role is just a sequence of rules, parameterized by the principal executing them (their *owner*)—the "∀K : KAS" above the brackets in Fig. 3. The two-rule role describing the client's actions in the AS exchange has been omitted here for space reasons. Formalizations of the TG and CS exchanges can be found in [7,8].

6   Formal Analysis of PKINIT

Our formal proofs rely on a double induction aimed at separating the confidentiality and authentication aspects of the analysis of Kerberos 5. They are supported by two classes of functions, rank and corank, defined recursively on MSR specifications [7]. In general, rank captures the amount of work done to generate a message and is connected to authentication, while corank captures the minimum effort needed to extract a secret and relates to confidentiality. Confidentiality and authentication can interact in complex ways, requiring both types of functions in a single proof. (This is not so much the case in the AS exchange, because it is the first exchange in Kerberos, but it is seen clearly in the later rounds as illustrated in [7].)

As a taste of our methodology, we present the theorem which establishes that PKINIT-27 and subsequent versions meet the expected authentication goals. It formalizes Prop. 1 in Sect. 4. We assume that digital signatures are unforgeable and we abstract collision resistance as the injectivity of H_-.

Theorem 2. *If (1) the fact* $\mathsf{N}(\{\!\{Cert_K, [k, ck]_{sk_K}\}\!\}_{pk_C}, C, X, \{AK, n_1, t_K, T\}_k)$ *appears in a trace[2]; (2)* $ck = H_k(Cert_C, [t_C, n_2]_{sk_C}, C, T, n_1)$[3]; *(3) the fact* $VerifySig([k, ck]_{sk_K}; (k, ck); K, Cert_K)$ *holds; and (4) for every* pk_K : pubK K *and* sk : secK pk_K, *the fact* $I(sk)$ *does not appear in the trace and no fact in the initial state of the trace contained a fact of positive* sk-*rank relative to* (k, ck), *then* K *fired rule* $\iota_{2.1}$, *consuming the fact* $\mathsf{N}(Cert_C, [t_C, n_2]_{sk_C}, C, T, n_1)$ *and creating the fact* $\mathsf{N}(\{\!\{Cert_K, [k, ck]_{sk_K}\}\!\}_{pk_C}, C, \{AK, C, t_K\}_{k_T}, \{AK, n_1, t_K, T\}_k)$.[4]

Proof. (Sketch)   Because $VerifySig([k, ck]_{sk_K}; (k, ck); K, Cert_K)$ holds, by assumption about the properties of $VerifySig$ there is some sk : secK pk_K such that $\rho_{sk}([k, ck]_{sk_K}; (k, ck)) > 0$ (where pk_K : pubK K). Thus the fact $\mathsf{N}(\{\!\{Cert_C, [k, ck]_{sk_K}\}\!\}_{pk_C}, C, X, \{AK, n_1, t_K, T\}_k)$ has positive sk-rank relative to (k, ck); by hypothesis, no such fact existed in the initial state of the trace, so some rule firing during the trace must have increased this rank.

In order for the intruder to perform cryptographic work using sk, she must have possession of this key; this is precluded by hypothesis, so some principal must have done cryptographic work using sk. The only principal rule which can use sk to do cryptographic work with respect to (k, ck) for some ck : msg is rule $\iota_{2.1}$. In order for this rule to do so, it must be: fired by the KAS K who owns sk, consume a network fact corresponding to a request message, and produce a

---

[2] For some C : client, K : KAS, k : shK C K, sk_K : someSecK, ck, X : msg, $Cert_K$: CertList, pk_C : pubK C, T : TGS, AK : shK C T, n_1 : nonce, and t_K : time.

[3] For some t_C : time, n_2 : nonce, sk_C : SecK pk_C, and $Cert_C$: CertList.

[4] For some k_T : dbK T, t_K : time.

reply message containing ck as the checksum over this request. By assumption about collision-freeness of checksums, the request that K processed must match the request described in the hypotheses.   □

As a corollary, if C processes a reply message containing the signed checksum of a request that C previously sent, then some KAS K fired rule $\iota_{2.1}$ as described by the theorem. This corresponds to Prop. 1.

7   Conclusions and Future Work

In this paper, we describe our discovery of a man-in-the-middle attack against PKINIT [13], the public key extension to the popular Kerberos 5 authentication protocol [1]. We found this attack as part of an ongoing formal analysis of Kerberos, which has previously yielded proofs of security for the core Kerberos 5 protocol [7] and its use for cross-realm authentication [8]. We have used formal methods approaches to prove that, at an abstract level, several possible defenses against our attack restore security properties of Kerberos 5 that are violated in PKINIT (as shown by the attack). The fixes we analyzed include the one proposed by the IETF Kerberos Working group, which included it in the specification of PKINIT starting with revision 27 [13]. Our attack was also addressed in a Microsoft security bulletin affecting several versions of Windows [3].

As a continuation of this research, we have carried over some of the results examined here to the computational model by expressing PKINIT and other aspects of Kerberos in the BPW model [25]. The main outcome of this effort was that the fixes examined here were proved to be correct at the cryptographic level [12]. There appears to be a strong relation between the symbolic proof technique used here and the verification steps in [12] and gaining a better understanding of how these two methods relate will be subject to future work. We are also in the process of extending our analysis to the Diffie-Hellman mode of PKINIT: our preliminary observations suggest that it is immune from the attack described in this paper, but we do not yet have definite results on other types of threats. Finally, we have started looking into automating the proof technique used here. This will have the effect of speeding up the analysis work, allowing us to tackle larger protocols, and, if a suitable connection to the BPW framework is discovered, contributing to the automation of proof in the cryptographic model [26].

References

1. Neuman, C., Yu, T., Hartman, S., Raeburn, K.: The Kerberos Network Authentication Service (V5) (2005), http://www.ietf.org/rfc/rfc4120
2. Thomas, M., Vilhuber, J.: Kerberized Internet Negotiation of Keys (KINK) (2003), http://ietfreport.isoc.org/all-ids/draft-ietf-kink-kink-06.txt
3. Microsoft: Security Bulletin MS05-042 (2005), http://www.microsoft.com/technet/security/bulletin/MS05-042.mspx
4. Strasser, M., Steffen, A.: Kerberos PKINIT Implementation for Unix Clients. Technical report, Zurich University of Applied Sciences Winterthur (2002)

5. CERT: Vulnerability Note 477341 (2005), `http://www.kb.cert.org/vuls/id/477341`
6. Yu, T., Hartman, S., Raeburn, K.: The perils of unauthenticated encryption: Kerberos version 4. In: Proc. NDSS 2004 (2004)
7. Butler, F., Cervesato, I., Jaggard, A.D., Scedrov, A., Walstad, C.: Formal Analysis of Kerberos 5. Theoretical Computer Science 367, 57–87 (2006)
8. Cervesato, I., Jaggard, A.D., Scedrov, A., Walstad, C.: Specifying Kerberos 5 Cross-Realm Authentication. In: Proc. WITS 2005, ACM Digital Lib. pp. 12–26 (2005)
9. Kemmerer, R., Meadows, C., Millen, J.: Three systems for cryptographic protocol analysis. J. Cryptology 7, 79–130 (1994)
10. Meadows, C.: Analysis of the internet key exchange protocol using the nrl protocol analyzer. In: Proc. IEEE Symp. Security and Privacy, pp. 216–231 (1999)
11. Mitchell, J.C., Shmatikov, V., Stern, U.: Finite-State Analysis of SSL 3.0. In: Proc. 7th USENIX Security Symp., pp. 201–216 (1998)
12. Backes, M., Cervesato, I., Jaggard, A.D., Scedrov, A., Tsay, J.K.: Cryptographically Sound Security Proofs for Basic and Public-key Kerberos. In: Gollmann, D., Meier, J., Sabelfeld, A. (eds.) ESORICS 2006. LNCS, vol. 4189, Springer, Heidelberg (2006)
13. IETF: Public Key Cryptography for Initial Authentication in Kerberos (1996–2006) RFC 4556. Preliminary versions available as a sequence of Internet Drafts at, `http://tools.ietf.org/wg/krb-wg/draft-ietf-cat-kerberos-pk-init/`
14. De Clercq, J., Balladelli, M.: Windows 2000 authentication, Digital Press (2001), `http://www.windowsitlibrary.com/Content/617/06/6.html`
15. Cable Television Laboratories, Inc.: PacketCable Security Specification Technical document PKT-SP-SEC-I11-040730 (2004)
16. Goldwasser, S., Micali, S., Rivest, R.L.: A Digital Signature Scheme Secure Against Adaptive Chosen Message Attacks. SIAM J. Computing 17, 281–308 (1988)
17. Diffie, W., van Oorschot, P.C., Wiener, M.J.: Authentication and authenticated key exchanges. Designs, Codes and Cryptography 2, 107–125 (1992)
18. Canetti, R., Krawczyk, H.: Security Analysis of IKE's Signature-Based Key-Exchange Protocol. In: Yung, M. (ed.) CRYPTO 2002. LNCS, vol. 2442, pp. 143–161. Springer, Heidelberg (2002)
19. Lowe, G.: Breaking and Fixing the Needham-Schroeder Public-Key Protocol using FDR. In: Margaria, T., Steffen, B. (eds.) TACAS 1996. LNCS, vol. 1055, pp. 147–166. Springer, Heidelberg (1996)
20. Clark, J., Jacob, J.: On the security of recent protocols. Information Processing Letters 56, 151–155 (1995)
21. Abadi, M., Needham, R.: Prudent Engineering Practice for Cryptographic Protocols. IEEE Trans. Software Eng. 22, 6–15 (1996)
22. Raeburn, K.: Encryption and Checksum Specifications for Kerberos 5 (2005), `http://www.ietf.org/rfc/rfc3961.txt`
23. Cervesato, I.: Typed MSR: Syntax and Examples. In: Gorodetski, V.I., Skormin, V.A., Popyack, L.J. (eds.) MMM-ACNS 2001. LNCS, vol. 2052, Springer, Heidelberg (2001)
24. Durgin, N.A., Lincoln, P., Mitchell, J., Scedrov, A.: Multiset Rewriting and the Complexity of Bounded Security Protocols. J. Comp. Security 12, 247–311 (2004)
25. Backes, M., Pfitzmann, B., Waidner, M.: A Composable Cryptographic Library with Nested Operations. In: Proc. CCS 2003, pp. 220–230. ACM, New York (2003)
26. Sprenger, C., Backes, M., Basin, D., Pfitzmann, B., Waidner, M.: Cryptographically sound theorem proving. In: Proc. CSFW 2006, pp. 153–166 (2006)

Computational Soundness of Formal Indistinguishability and Static Equivalence

Gergei Bana*, Payman Mohassel, and Till Stegers

Department of Computer Science
University of California at Davis, USA
gebana@cs.upenn.edu, mohassel@cs.ucdavis.edu, stegers@cs.ucdavis.edu

Abstract. In the investigation of the relationship between the formal and the computational view of cryptography, a recent approach, first proposed in [10], uses static equivalence from cryptographic pi calculi as a notion of formal indistinguishability. Previous work [10,1] has shown that this yields the soundness of natural interpretations of some interesting equational theories, such as certain cryptographic operations and a theory of XOR. In this paper however, we argue that static equivalence is too coarse to allow sound interpretations of many natural and useful equational theories. We illustrate this with several explicit examples in which static equivalence fails to work. To fix the problem, we propose a notion of formal indistinguishability that is more flexible than static equivalence. We provide a general framework along with general theorems, and then discuss how this new notion works for the explicit examples where static equivalence fails to ensure soundness.

1 Introduction

In the past few years, significant effort has been made to link formal and computational methods of cryptography. These directions had largely been developing independently; the first based on the seminal work of Dolev and Yao [15], and the second growing out of the work of Goldwasser and Micali [16]. While the computational method gives a more realistic and detailed description of an actual protocol, using probability theory and taking limited computational power into account, security proofs in this model are done by hand and are often notoriously hard to verify.

The formal method is a high-level treatment, amenable to automatization, but its reliability is sometimes questionable; namely, a protocol that is formally secure may not be so computationally, and, therefore, may be insecure in reality. It is therefore important how to translate one model into the other, and to characterize which security proofs in the simpler formal framework carry over to the computational setting.

The first paper to address this question was that of Abadi and Rogaway [4], which considered only passive adversaries. In their approach, the notion of

---

* Supported by a Packard Fellowship.

M. Okada and I. Satoh (Eds.): ASIAN 2006, LNCS 4435, pp. 182–196, 2007.
© Springer-Verlag Berlin Heidelberg 2007

security is formalized via equivalence relations on the formal and on the computational side that specify which messages look indistinguishable to an adversary of the corresponding view. Fixing an encryption scheme for the computational implementation of the formal operations, a natural *interpretation* assigns a computational object – an ensemble of probability distributions over bit strings – to each formal expression. The question then arises: Under which circumstances is the equivalence relation preserved by the interpretation? If the formal equivalence of any two expressions implies the computational equivalence of their interpretations, then we say the model is *sound*. This is the mathematical equivalent of saying that security in the formal model implies security in the computational model. Conversely, the model is *complete* if the computational equivalence of the interpretations of any two formal expressions implies that these expressions are equivalent. Completeness of a model indicates that the formal equivalence notion in question is not too fine, and helps in finding attacks: if completeness holds, the existence of a formal attack implies the existence of a computational one.

Abadi and Rogaway proved soundness for their language if the encryption scheme used in the interpretation is what they call type-0 secure (basically, it hides everything about the plaintext). A number of other papers followed, proving completeness as well [20,6], generalizing for weaker, more realistic encryptions schemes [6], considering purely probabilistic encryptions [17,6], including limited models for active adversaries [19], and addressing the issue of forbidding key-cycles [5]. Other approaches including active adversaries are considered by Backes et al. and Canetti in their *reactive simulatability* [8,7] and *universal composability* [11,12] frameworks, respectively. Using probabilistic polynomial-time semantics without explicit probabilistic reasoning in [14] is also notable.

1.1   Previous Work

Our paper addresses issues when the equivalence relation on the formal side is *static equivalence* (from cryptographic pi calculi [3,2]), induced by an *equational theory*. Equational theories model algebraic axioms in the formal world, such as axioms for groups, rings, XOR, etc. Once an equational theory is fixed, which means setting certain formal terms equal, static equivalence is uniquely determined. Roughly speaking, two n-tuples of formal terms are statically inequivalent, *i.e.* formally distinguishable, if an adversary is able to come up with two formal computations that, on one of the tuples yield two results that are identical according to the equational theory but yield different results on the other tuple. Baudet et al. [10] use this equivalence notion on the formal side, proving soundness of a theory of exclusive or as well as of certain symmetric encryptions that are deterministic and length-preserving. Abadi et al. [1] employ this framework to analyze a principled formal account of guessing attacks.

1.2   Our Contributions

In this paper, we show that even though static equivalence works well to obtain soundness results for the cases analyzed in [10,1], it does not work well in other important cases, and a more flexible notion is needed. For a brief exposition of why this is so, consider the Decisional Diffie-Hellman assumption. As Baudet et al. describe in [10], in an equational theory modeling group exponentiation without including logarithm, the 4-tuples (g, g^a, g^b, g^{ab}) and (g, g^a, g^b, g^c) are statically equivalent. Therefore, if the interpretation of the theory in a certain computational group scheme is sound, then this scheme satisfies the DDH assumption. However, formally much more is equivalent. For example, (g, g^a, g^b, ab) and (g, g^a, g^b, c) are also equivalent, and so on; an infinitude of statements *not necessarily implied* by the DDH assumption would be satisfied. There is no reason to think that such a computational group scheme exists at all. Moreover, the analysis often goes in the other direction: not a given formal model has to be interpreted in a sound manner, but for a given computational model we are looking for a formal theory that is simplifying, yet sound. A computational scheme that satisfies the DDH assumption may not satisfy the condition above (not to mention the infinitely many more that follow from static equivalence), so static equivalence cannot be used with such a group scheme to achieve soundness. Of course, if we *know* that the interpretations of two formal n-tuples are computationally distinguishable, then we may be able to incorporate the distinguisher into the formal theory, forcing those two n-tuples to be formally inequivalent. However, in many cases, we do not know whether the interpretations are inequivalent, so we have no explicit distinguishers. In such a case, to play it safe, it is better to assume that they are distinguishable, and that is how the formal theory should be constructed.

We argue that an equivalence relation finer than static equivalence is necessary to fit a number of interesting cases for which static equivalence is not suitable. We will call this type of equivalence relation a *formal indistinguishability relation* (FIR). We require four properties from any FIR, and through these properties an initial set of relations will generate a FIR. Each pair that is statically inequivalent is also inequivalent with respect to a formal indistinguishability relation. Moreover, static equivalence is one instance of a FIR. In order to test soundness with respect to a computational interpretation, it is enough to check soundness on a set of relations that generate the FIR in question. If soundness holds on the generating set of relations, then soundness holds in total.

Besides introducing the above equivalence notion, we also make some other improvements in the theory. Baudet et al. require the interpretations to be such that if a distribution is sampled twice, the probability of collision is negligible. We will not assume this because it would exclude the formal representation of interesting functions such as the least significant bit. We also use ordered sorts, allowing names to have multiple sorts.

After introducing the basic framework and proving some general propositions about FIRs, we discuss three examples. The first is the above-mentioned DDH assumption: We discuss how to introduce a FIR such that soundness is *equivalent* to the DDH assumption. Our second example considers the case of key-cycles and Laud's solution to them [18]. Laud proposed that if we do not want to exclude key-cycles from our theory and we do not want to assume that the encryption scheme is stronger than the usual assumptions (CPA, CCA-2, etc.), then we can simply assume that the formal adversary can decrypt all ciphertexts that were encrypted with keys that are in a key-cycle. We show how this assumption corresponds to a formal indistinguishability relation. Finally, the third example describes an embedding of Boolean propositional logic which fails to be sound with respect to static equivalence because two formal terms that are computationally distinguishable turn out to be statically equivalent.

We would like to thank Jonathan Herzog, Phillip Rogaway, and Andre Scedrov for valuable discussions on the topic. We would also like to express our special thanks to Matthew Franklin and Phillip Rogaway for their support.

2   Formal Model

2.1   Signatures, Terms, and Frames

A *signature* is a pair $(\mathfrak{S}, \mathcal{F})$, with $\mathfrak{S} = (\mathcal{S}, \mathcal{S}', \leq_{\mathcal{S}})$, $\mathcal{S}$ being a countably infinite set of *sorts* with partial order $\leq_{\mathcal{S}}$, $\mathcal{S}' \subseteq \mathcal{S}$, and $\mathcal{F}$ a finite set of *function symbols*. We use the notation $s, s_1, s_2, \ldots$ for sorts, and $f, f_1, f_2, \ldots$ for symbols. We assume that every $f \in \mathcal{F}$ has a unique *arity* $s_1 \times \cdots \times s_k \to s$ for some $s_1, \ldots, s_k, s \in \mathcal{S}$. If $k = 0$, then f is a *constant*, and we denote this as $f : s$.

Furthermore, let $\mathcal{X}$, $\mathcal{N}$ be countably infinite sets such that $\mathcal{S}$, $\mathcal{F}$, $\mathcal{X}$, $\mathcal{N}$ are pairwise disjoint. The elements of $\mathcal{X}$ are called *variables*, the elements of $\mathcal{N}$ *names*. We assume that both names and variables are sorted, that is, to each name or variable u, a subset $\mathcal{S}_u$ is assigned; we write $u : s$ and say u is of sort s whenever $s \in \mathcal{S}_u$. We require that $u : s_1$ and $s_1 \leq_{\mathcal{S}} s_2$ implies $u : s_2$, and that the set $\mathcal{S}_u$ has a minimum, which we denote by $\mathfrak{s}(u)$. For any subset U of the set of names or of the set of variables, let $[U]_s = \{u \in U \mid \mathfrak{s}(u) = s\}$. Finally, we require that for each sort s, $[\mathcal{X}]_s$ is infinite, and $[\mathcal{N}]_s$ is infinite whenever $s \in \mathcal{S}'$ and empty whenever $s \notin \mathcal{S}'$. A *renaming* is a bijection $\tau : \mathcal{N} \to \mathcal{N}$ such that $\mathfrak{s}(a) = \mathfrak{s}(\tau(a))$ for each name a. The terms of our language are sorted by elements of $\mathcal{S}$. As usual, if a term T has sort s, we write $T : s$. Terms of sort s are defined as follows:

$$T : s ::= x : s \mid a : s \mid f(T_1, \ldots, T_k)$$

where x is a variable, a is a name, and f is a function symbol of arity $s_1 \times \cdots \times s_k \to s'$ for some $s_1, \ldots, s_k \in \mathcal{S}$, $s' \leq_{\mathcal{S}} s$, and each term T_i is of sort s_i for $i = 1, \ldots, k$. The set of all terms will be denoted by $\mathcal{T}$. For a term T, we use $\mathrm{var}(T)$ for the set of variables occurring in T, and $\mathrm{names}(T)$ for the set of names occurring in T. A term T is said to be *closed* if $\mathrm{var}(T) = \emptyset$.

Let $x_1, \ldots, x_n$ be distinct variables, and let $T_1, \ldots, T_n$ be terms so that $\mathfrak{s}(T_i) \leq_{\mathcal{S}} \mathfrak{s}(x_i)$. A well-sorted *substitution* σ is written as $\sigma = \{x_1 = T_1, \ldots, x_n = T_n\}$. Since in this paper we will only have well-sorted substitutions, we will omit the term "well-sorted". The image of T under the substitution $\sigma = \{x_i = T_i\}_{i=1}^n$ is written as $T\sigma$, and is obtained by replacing every occurrence of x_i in T by T_i for each x_i. If all T_i are closed, σ is said to be *closed*; the *domain* of σ is $\mathrm{dom}(\sigma) = \{x_1, \ldots, x_n\}$

and the set of variables of σ is $\mathrm{var}(\sigma) = \bigcup_{i=1}^{n} \mathrm{var}(T_i)$. Similarly, we write $\mathrm{names}(\sigma)$ for the union of all sets $\mathrm{names}(T_i)$. As examples, we refer to the first paragraph of Subsection 5.1 or the second paragraph of 5.2.

Now we can define how to postulate axioms. In short, an *equational theory* is an equivalence relation on terms that is stable under (well-sorted) substitution of terms for variables, application of contexts, and renaming.

Definition 1. *An* equational theory *for a given signature is an equivalence relation $E \subseteq T \times T$ (written $=_E$ in infix notation) on the set of terms such that (i) $T =_E T'$ implies $T\sigma =_E T'\sigma$ for every substitution σ; (ii) $T_1 =_E T_2$ implies $T\{x = T_1\} =_E T\{x = T_2\}$ for every term T and every variable x with $\mathfrak{s}(x) \geq_S \mathfrak{s}(T_i)$; (iii) $T_1 =_E T_2$ implies $\tau(T_1) =_E \tau(T_2)$ for every renaming τ.*

If R is a relation on T, then the intersection $\langle R \rangle$ of all equational theories containing R is the smallest equational theory containing R. We say $\langle R \rangle$ is the equational theory *generated* by R. For examples, we refer to the second paragraph of Subsection 5.1 and the third paragraph of Subsection 5.2.

A *frame* φ is an expression $\nu \tilde{a}.\sigma$, where σ is a substitution and $\tilde{a} = \mathrm{names}(\sigma)$. Since $\tilde{a}$ is uniquely determined by its *underlying substitution* σ, we may sometimes only write the substitution for a frame to save space. We say that φ is *closed* if σ is closed. The set of all frames (with respect to an understood signature) is denoted by $\mathfrak{F}$, the set of closed frames are denoted by $\mathfrak{F}_c$.

If E is an equational theory and $\varphi = \nu \tilde{a}.\sigma$ is a frame, we say that a term T is *deducible from* φ with respect to E, written $\varphi \vdash_E T$, if there is a term M with $\mathrm{var}(M) \subseteq \mathrm{dom}(\varphi)$ and $\mathrm{names}(M) \cap (\mathrm{names}(\varphi) \cup \mathrm{names}(T)) = \emptyset$ such that $M\varphi =_E T$, where $M\varphi = M\sigma$.

Suppose that for closed frames φ_1, φ_2 with $\mathrm{dom}(\varphi_1) = \mathrm{dom}(\varphi_2)$, there are two terms M, N sharing no names with φ_1 and φ_2, $\mathrm{var}(M) \cup \mathrm{var}(N) \subseteq \mathrm{var}(\varphi_i)$, such that $M\varphi_1 =_E N\varphi_1$, but $M\varphi_2 \neq_E N\varphi_2$. Intuitively, this means that carrying out two computations – permitted by the model and determined by M and N – on the inputs provided by φ_1, we get identical results, whereas carrying out the same computations on the input provided by φ_2 produces distinct results. If the distinction of two closed frames is not possible this way, then we say that these two frames are *statically equivalent*.

Definition 2. *Two closed frames φ_1, φ_2 of the same domain are* statically equivalent *with respect to an equational theory E, written $\varphi_1 \approx_E \varphi_2$, if for all terms M, N with $\mathrm{var}(M) \cup \mathrm{var}(N) \subseteq \mathrm{var}(\varphi_i)$ and using no names occurring in φ_1 or φ_2, we have $M\varphi_1 =_E N\varphi_1 \iff M\varphi_2 =_E N\varphi_2$. Let $\tilde{E}$ denote static equivalence as a subset of $\mathfrak{F}_c \times \mathfrak{F}_c$.*

2.2   Formal Indistinguishability

For a frame $\varphi = \nu \bigcup_{i=1}^{n} \mathrm{names}(T_i).\{x_i = T_i\}_{i=1}^{n}$, if φ' is another frame, let $\varphi\varphi'$ denote the frame $\nu \bigcup_{i=1}^{n} \mathrm{names}(T_i) \cup \mathrm{names}(\varphi').\{x_i = T_i\varphi'\}_{i=1}^{n}$. For frames $\varphi_1, \ldots, \varphi_n$ with disjoint domains, let $\{\varphi_1 | \varphi_2 | \ldots | \varphi_n\}$ be the frame corresponding to the combination of all substitutions of $\varphi_1, \ldots, \varphi_n$.

Definition 3. *A formal indistinguishability relation* with respect to an equational theory E *is an equivalence relation* $\cong$ *on the set of closed frames such
that*

(i) $\varphi_1 \cong \varphi_2$ *only if* $\mathrm{dom}(\varphi_1) = \mathrm{dom}(\varphi_2)$;
(ii) for any frame φ, *if* φ_1 *and* φ_2 *are closed frames such that* $\mathrm{var}(\varphi) \subseteq \mathrm{dom}(\varphi_i)$,
    $\mathrm{names}(\varphi) \cap \mathrm{names}(\varphi_i) = \emptyset$ *and* $\varphi_1 \cong \varphi_2$ *then* $\varphi\varphi_1 \cong \varphi\varphi_2$;
(iii) for any two frames $\varphi' = \{x_i = T'_i\}_{i=1}^n$ *and* $\varphi'' = \{x_i = T''_i\}_{i=1}^n$, *if* $T'_i =_E T''_i$
    for all i, *then* $\varphi' \cong \varphi''$; *moreover,* $\varphi' \not\approx_E \varphi''$ *implies* $\varphi' \not\cong \varphi''$;
(iv) for any renaming τ, $\tau(\varphi) \cong \varphi$.

Remark 1. Corresponding sections of equivalent frames are equivalent. That is,
for example, if $\varphi_1 = \{x_i = T_i\}_{i=1}^4 \cong \varphi_2 = \{x_i = T'_i\}_{i=1}^4$, then $\{x_2 = T_2, x_4 = T_4\} \cong \{x_2 = T'_2, x_4 = T'_4\}$. This follows from (ii) by setting $\varphi = \nu\emptyset.\{x_2 = x_2, x_4 = x_4\}$.

If φ_1, φ_2, φ'_1, φ'_2 are frames such that $\mathrm{dom}(\varphi_1) \cap \mathrm{dom}(\varphi_2) = \emptyset$, $\mathrm{dom}(\varphi'_1) \cap \mathrm{dom}(\varphi'_2) = \emptyset$, $\mathrm{names}(\varphi_1) \cap \mathrm{names}(\varphi_2) = \emptyset$, $\mathrm{names}(\varphi'_1) \cap \mathrm{names}(\varphi'_2) = \emptyset$, and $\varphi_i \cong \varphi'_i$, then $\{\varphi_1|\varphi_2\} \cong \{\varphi'_1|\varphi'_2\}$. The reason is the following. Choose a renaming τ such that $\tau(\varphi_1) = \varphi_1$, $\tau(\varphi'_1) = \varphi'_1$, $\tau(\varphi'_2) = \varphi'_2$, and $\mathrm{names}(\tau(\varphi_2)) \cap \mathrm{names}(\varphi_1) = \mathrm{names}(\tau(\varphi_2)) \cap \mathrm{names}(\varphi'_1) = \emptyset$. This can be done because we assumed that there are infinitely many names of each sort. Using (iv), we see that $\{\varphi_1|\varphi_2\} \cong \tau(\{\varphi_1|\varphi_2\}) = \{\varphi_1|\tau(\varphi_2)\}$. If $\mathrm{dom}(\varphi_1) = \mathrm{dom}(\varphi'_1) = \{x_1, \ldots, x_k\}$, then let $\psi = \{x_1 = x_1, \ldots, x_k = x_k | \tau(\varphi_2)\}$. Using (ii), it follows that $\{\varphi_1|\tau(\varphi_2)\} = \psi\varphi_1 \cong \psi\varphi'_1 = \{\varphi'_1|\tau(\varphi_2)\}$. Since by (iv) again, $\tau(\varphi_2) \cong \varphi_2$, and $\varphi_2 \cong \varphi'_2$ by assumption, $\tau(\varphi_2) \cong \varphi'_2$ holds, and applying (ii) in a similar fashion as before, we obtain $\{\varphi'_1|\tau(\varphi_2)\} \cong \{\varphi'_1|\varphi'_2\}$. Putting all these together, $\{\varphi_1|\varphi_2\} \cong \{\varphi'_1|\varphi'_2\}$.

The following useful propositions are proved in the full version [9] of this paper.

Proposition 1. *Static equivalence* $\approx_E$ *is a formal indistinguishability relation
with respect to the equational theory* E.

Proposition 2. *The intersection of an arbitrary number of formal indistinguishability relations (with respect to the same equational theory* E*) is a formal
indistinguishability relation.*

Proposition 3. *Consider static equivalence as a subset* $\tilde{E} \subseteq \mathfrak{F}_c \times \mathfrak{F}_c$. *If* $S \subseteq \tilde{E}$,
then there is a unique smallest subset $\langle S \rangle \subseteq \tilde{E}$ *containing* S, *such that* $\langle S \rangle$ $(\cong_S$
in infix notation) is a formal indistinguishability relation with respect to E. $\langle S \rangle$
can be generated in the following way: Let

$$S' := \left\{ \begin{array}{l|l} (\varphi', \varphi'') & \varphi' = \varphi\{\varphi'_1| \ldots |\varphi'_n\} \text{ and } \varphi'' = \varphi\{\varphi''_1| \ldots |\varphi''_n\} \text{ such that} \\ \in & \mathrm{names}(\varphi) = \emptyset \text{ and for all } i = 1, \ldots, n, \ (\varphi'_i, \varphi''_i) \in S, \text{ or} \\ \mathfrak{F}_c \times \mathfrak{F}_c & (\varphi''_i, \varphi'_i) \in S, \text{ or } \varphi''_i =_E \tau_i(\varphi'_i) \text{ for some renaming } \tau_i. \end{array} \right\}.$$

Then $\langle S \rangle$ *is the transitive closure of* S'.

3   Relating Formal and Computational Models

We now present the computational interpretation of the formal model. Our definition is equivalent to the one given by Baudet et al. [10]; the only difference is that we allow probabilistic as opposed to only deterministic interpretations for the symbols in $\mathcal{F}$, and that we have ordered sorts. To each closed term, the interpretation assigns an ensemble of probability distributions on bit strings. This is a generalization of Abadi and Rogaway's definition in [4].

Given a signature $(\mathfrak{S}, \mathcal{F})$, where $\mathfrak{S} = (\mathcal{S}, \mathcal{S}', \leq_{\mathcal{S}})$, an $(\mathfrak{S}, \mathcal{F})$-*computational algebra* $\mathfrak{A}$ is a triple $\mathfrak{A} = (\{[\![s]\!]_{\mathfrak{A}}\}_{s \in \mathcal{S}}, \{[\![s]\!]_{\mathfrak{A}}\}_{s \in \mathcal{S}'}, \{f_{\mathfrak{A}}\}_{f \in \mathcal{F}})$ as follows: For each sort s in $\mathcal{S}$, $\overline{[\![s]\!]}_{\mathfrak{A}} = \{[\![s]\!]_{\mathfrak{A}_\eta}\}_\eta$ where $[\![s]\!]_{\mathfrak{A}_\eta} \subseteq \{0,1\}^*$ such that checking whether a bit string is in $\overline{[\![s]\!]}_{\mathfrak{A}}$ is computable in polynomial-time; for each s in $\mathcal{S}'$, $[\![s]\!]_{\mathfrak{A}} = \{[\![s]\!]_{\mathfrak{A}_\eta}\}_\eta$, each $[\![s]\!]_{\mathfrak{A}_\eta}$ being a probability distribution on $\{0,1\}^*$ with $\mathrm{supp}([\![s]\!]_{\mathfrak{A}_\eta}) = \overline{[\![s]\!]}_{\mathfrak{A}}$ such that there is a polynomial time algorithm to draw random elements from $[\![s]\!]_{\mathfrak{A}_\eta}$; for each $f \in \mathcal{F}$, with arity $s_1 \times \cdots \times s_k \to s$, $f_{\mathfrak{A}} = \{f_{\mathfrak{A}_\eta}\}_\eta$, where $f_{\mathfrak{A}_\eta} : \overline{[\![s_1]\!]}_{\mathfrak{A}_\eta} \times \cdots \times \overline{[\![s_k]\!]}_{\mathfrak{A}_\eta} \to \overline{[\![s]\!]}_{\mathfrak{A}_\eta}$ is a probabilistic function computable in polynomial time. Here, supp denotes the support of a probability distribution, which is the set where the distribution gives non-zero probability.

Once a computational algebra is fixed, we can associate a probability distribution to each closed term M through the following two algorithms. The interpretation of M is $\mathrm{INTERPRET}_\eta(M)$, which makes use of the algorithm $\mathrm{CONVERT}_\eta^\lambda(M)$ converting M to a tuple of values in $\mathfrak{A}_\eta$ whenever a function $\lambda \colon \mathrm{names}(M) \to \mathrm{supp}([\![\mathfrak{s}(a)]\!]_{\mathfrak{A}_\eta})$ is given:

algorithm $\mathrm{INTERPRET}_\eta(M)$
  for $a \in \mathrm{names}(M)$ **do**
    $\lambda(a) \xleftarrow{R} [\![\mathfrak{s}(a)]\!]_{\mathfrak{A}_\eta}$
    $v \xleftarrow{R} \mathrm{CONVERT}_\eta^\lambda(M)$
  return v

algorithm $\mathrm{CONVERT}_\eta^\lambda(M)$
  if $M = a$ with name a **then**
    return $\lambda(a)$
  if $M = f(M_1, \ldots, M_k)$ **then**
    for $i = 1, \ldots, k$ **do**
      $e_i \xleftarrow{R} \mathrm{CONVERT}_\eta^\lambda(M_i)$
    $v \xleftarrow{R} f_{\mathfrak{A}_\eta}(e_1, \ldots, e_k)$
    return v

algorithm $\mathrm{INTERPRET}_\eta'(\varphi)$
  for $a \in \mathrm{names}(\varphi)$ **do** $\lambda(a) \xleftarrow{R} [\![\mathfrak{s}(a)]\!]_{\mathfrak{A}_\eta}$
  if $\varphi = \{x_1 = T_1, \ldots, x_n = T_n\}$ **then**
    $e_i \xleftarrow{R} \mathrm{CONVERT}_\eta^\lambda(T_i)$ $i = 1, \ldots, n$
    $v \longleftarrow \{x_1 = e_1, \ldots, x_n = e_n\}$
    return v

For each η, the probability distribution of $v \xleftarrow{R} \mathrm{CONVERT}_\eta(M)$ is denoted by $[\![M]\!]_{\mathfrak{A}_\eta}$. The ensemble $\{[\![M]\!]_{\mathfrak{A}_\eta}\}_\eta$ is denoted by $[\![M]\!]_{\mathfrak{A}}$. We call $[\![M]\!]_{\mathfrak{A}}$ the *computational interpretation* of the term M. For any name $a \colon s$ with $s \in \mathcal{S}'$, $[\![s]\!]_{\mathfrak{A}} = [\![\mathfrak{s}(a)]\!]_{\mathfrak{A}} = [\![a]\!]_{\mathfrak{A}}$. We define the interpretation of a closed frame $\varphi = \{x_1 = T_1, \ldots, x_n = T_n\}$ via the algorithm $\mathrm{INTERPRET}_\eta'(\varphi)$. We use $[\![\varphi]\!]_{\mathfrak{A}_\eta}$ for the probability distribution given by $\mathrm{INTERPRET}_\eta'(\varphi)$ and $[\![\varphi]\!]_{\mathfrak{A}}$ for the ensemble of these distributions, which we call the *computational interpretation* of the frame φ in the model $\mathfrak{A}$.

Two ensembles of probability distributions are said to be *computationally indistinguishable*, if no probabilistic polynomial time algorithm can distinguish them. Once the formal expressions are interpreted, then we can consider the computational indistinguishability of interpretations of two closed terms or two closed frames. We will use the notation $[\![M_1]\!]_{\mathfrak{A}} \approx [\![M_2]\!]_{\mathfrak{A}}$ and $[\![\varphi_1]\!]_{\mathfrak{A}} \approx [\![\varphi_2]\!]_{\mathfrak{A}}$, respectively. Explicitly, this latter means that for any PPT algorithm $\mathcal{A}$,

$$\left| \Pr[\widehat{\varphi_1} \xleftarrow{R} [\![\varphi_1]\!]_{\mathfrak{A}_\eta} : \mathcal{A}(\eta, \widehat{\varphi_1}) = 1] - \Pr[\widehat{\varphi_2} \xleftarrow{R} [\![\varphi_2]\!]_{\mathfrak{A}_\eta} : \mathcal{A}(\eta, \widehat{\varphi_2}) = 1] \right|,$$

denoted by $\mathrm{Adv}_\eta^{\mathcal{A}}([\![\varphi_1]\!]_{\mathfrak{A}}, [\![\varphi_2]\!]_{\mathfrak{A}})$, is a negligible function; that is, for each $n \in \mathbb{N}$ and all sufficiently large η, $\mathrm{Adv}_\eta^{\mathcal{A}}([\![\varphi_1]\!]_{\mathfrak{A}}, [\![\varphi_2]\!]_{\mathfrak{A}}) < \eta^{-n}$.

4   Soundness, Completeness and Faithfulness

The computational model of a cryptographic scheme is in a sense closer to reality than its formal representation by being a more detailed description. Therefore, the accuracy of a formal model can be characterized based on how close it is to the computational model; more specifically, how formal and computational indistinguishability relate to each other via the interpretation. The most important concepts to describe this are given in the following definition.

Definition 4. *Let $\mathfrak{A}$ be an $(\mathfrak{S}, \mathcal{F})$-computational algebra, and let $\cong$ be a formal indistinguishability relation on the set of frames, and let $F \subseteq \mathfrak{F}_{\mathrm{c}}$. We say that the computational algebra $\mathfrak{A}$ is $\cong$-sound on F if for every closed pair of frames $\varphi_1, \varphi_2 \in F$, $\varphi_1 \cong \varphi_2$ implies that $[\![\varphi_1]\!]_{\mathfrak{A}} \approx [\![\varphi_2]\!]_{\mathfrak{A}}$. $\mathfrak{A}$ is $\cong$-complete on F if for every closed pair of frames $\varphi_1, \varphi_2 \in F$, $\varphi_1 \not\cong \varphi_2$ implies that $[\![\varphi_1]\!]_{\mathfrak{A}} \not\approx [\![\varphi_2]\!]_{\mathfrak{A}}$. $\mathfrak{A}$ is $\cong$-faithful on F if for every closed pair of frames $\varphi_1, \varphi_2 \in F$, $\varphi_1 \not\cong \varphi_2$ implies that the statistical distance $\Delta([\![\varphi_1]\!]_{\mathfrak{A}_\eta}, [\![\varphi_2]\!]_{\mathfrak{A}_\eta})$ is not negligible and there is a PPT algorithm $\mathcal{A}$ such that $|\mathrm{Adv}_\eta^{\mathcal{A}}([\![\varphi_1]\!]_{\mathfrak{A}_\eta}, [\![\varphi_2]\!]_{\mathfrak{A}_\eta}) - \Delta([\![\varphi_1]\!]_{\mathfrak{A}_\eta}, [\![\varphi_2]\!]_{\mathfrak{A}_\eta})|$ is negligible. For all three notions, we adopt the convention that if no such set F is mentioned, it is assumed that $F = \mathfrak{F}_{\mathrm{c}}$.*

It is well known that the advantage of an adversary trying to distinguish two distributions is less than or equal to the statistical distance between the two distributions. Faithfulness therefore means that if two frames are formally distinguishable, then there is an algorithm that distinguishes their interpretations almost optimally.

Remark 2. If a model is sound, then formal proofs of indistinguishability are valid proofs of computational indistinguishability.

Our faithfulness definition is different from the one by Baudet et al. given in [10]. They require the existence of an adversary whose advantage is negligibly close to 1. However, there are interesting cases where their requirement is too strong, as the following example shows. Nevertheless, we will not discuss faithfulness in this paper beyond this example.

Example 1. Suppose that we add a function symbol LSB: *Data* → *Data* to our theory, where *Data* is a sort. We think of this as the least significant bit, and accordingly, we define the interpretation for the LSB function such that $\text{LSB}_{\mathfrak{A}_\eta}(x)$ is the least significant bit of x. Suppose that names of sort *Data* get interpreted as bit strings with a certain maximum length with uniform distribution. Now, consider the two frames $\nu ab.\{x_1 = \text{LSB}(a), x_2 = \text{LSB}(b)\}$ and $\nu a.\{x_1 = \text{LSB}(a), x_2 = \text{LSB}(a)\}$. After interpretation, for each security parameter, the first frame will result in two independent bits of uniform distribution, whereas the interpretation of the second frame will contain two completely correlated bits of uniform distribution. No adversary can distinguish these two distributions with advantage greater than $1/2$, which is the statistical distance. However, the adversary that outputs 1 if the two bits are identical and 0 if they are different is clearly the best possible.

Remark 3. Completeness can be rewritten in the form that for every closed pair of frames φ_1, φ_2, $[\![\varphi_1]\!]_{\mathfrak{A}} \approx [\![\varphi_2]\!]_{\mathfrak{A}}$ implies $\varphi_1 \cong \varphi_2$. This notion is weaker then faithfulness, i.e., a faithful interpretation is also complete.

Let us introduce some notation. Let $\mathfrak{A}$ be an $(\mathfrak{S}, \mathcal{F})$-computational algebra, and let $\{x_1 = T_1, x_2 = T_2\}$ be a closed frame in this setting. Then by $e_1, e_2 \xleftarrow{R} [\![T_1, T_2]\!]_{\mathfrak{A}_\eta}$, we will denote the random sampling $\{x_1 = e_1, x_2 = e_1\} \xleftarrow{R} \text{INTERPRET}'_\eta(\{x_1 = T_1, x_2 = T_2\})$.

Definition 5. *Let $\mathfrak{A}$ be a $(\mathfrak{S}, \mathcal{F})$-computational algebra, and let E be an equational theory. We say that $\mathfrak{A}$ is $=_E$-sound if for each pair of closed terms T_1 and T_2, $T_1 =_E T_2$ implies that $\Pr[e_1, e_2 \xleftarrow{R} [\![T_1, T_2]\!]_{\mathfrak{A}_\eta} : e_1 \neq e_2]$ is negligible. It is $=_E$-complete if for each pair of closed terms T_1 and T_2, $T_1 \neq_E T_2$ implies that $\Pr[e_1, e_2 \xleftarrow{R} [\![T_1, T_2]\!]_{\mathfrak{A}_\eta} : e_1 \neq e_2]$ is not negligible.*

Remark 4. The reader may ask why no adversaries are used in this definition. For example, would it not make more sense to define $=_E$-soundness so that for each pair of closed terms T_1 and T_2 if $T_1 =_E T_2$ holds, then $[\![T_1, T_2]\!]_{\mathfrak{A}} \approx [\![T_1, T_1]\!]_{\mathfrak{A}}$? However, using the fact that the advantage of an adversary trying to distinguish the two distributions cannot exceed the statistical distance, it is easy to show that this definition would be equivalent to what is given above.

The following proposition shows that if a FIR $\cong$ is generated by a set $S \subseteq \mathfrak{F}_c \times \mathfrak{F}_c$, then it suffices to check soundness for pairs of frames in S to see that $\langle S \rangle$ is sound. The proof is included in the full version [9] of this paper.

Proposition 4. *Let $\mathfrak{A}$ be an $(\mathfrak{S}, \mathcal{F})$-computational algebra that is $=_E$-sound. Suppose $S \subseteq \tilde{E}$ is a binary relation on closed frames such that $(\varphi, \psi) \in S$ implies $[\![\varphi]\!]_{\mathfrak{A}_\eta} \approx [\![\psi]\!]_{\mathfrak{A}_\eta}$. Then $[\![\varphi]\!]_{\mathfrak{A}_\eta} \approx [\![\psi]\!]_{\mathfrak{A}_\eta}$ whenever $\varphi \cong_S \psi$. That is, $\mathfrak{A}$ is $\cong_S$-sound.*

Corollary 1. *Let $\mathfrak{A}$ be a $(\mathfrak{S}, \mathcal{F})$-computational algebra with $S \subseteq \mathfrak{F}_c \times \mathfrak{F}_c$ such that $\mathfrak{A}$ is $\cong_S$-sound on F. Let $S' := S \cap (F \times F)$. Then $\mathfrak{A}$ is $\cong_{S'}$-sound.*

5   Applications

In this section, we exemplify the utility of formal indistinguishability relations that refine static equivalence. In the theory of groups with exponentiation, we obtain an FIR such that soundness is equivalent to the Decisional Diffie-Hellman Assumption. Next, we show how to handle key-cycles by encoding Laud's approach in a formal indistinguishability relation. Finally, we give an example from propositional Boolean logic whose natural model would not be sound with respect to static equivalence, but is sound with respect to a particular FIR.

5.1   Decisional Diffie-Hellman Assumption

Consider the following equational theory to model a commutative group with exponentiation (as in [10]). Let A and G be sorts, $\mathcal{S} = \mathcal{S}'$ with the trivial ordering, and let $\mathcal{F}$ contain the following function symbols: $*: G \times G \rightarrow G$; $1_G: G$; $\cdot: A \times A \rightarrow A$; $+: A \times A \rightarrow A$; $-: A \rightarrow A$; $1_A: A$; $0: A$; $\exp: G \times A \rightarrow G$. To simplify our notation, we write U^V for $\exp(U, V)$.

Let the equational theory E be generated by the following equations:

$$
\begin{array}{lll}
x * 1_G = x & x + (-x) = 0 & (x + y) \cdot z = x \cdot z + y \cdot z \\
1_G * x = x & x + (y + z) = (x + y) + z & (x^a)^b = x^{(a \cdot b)} \\
x * (y * z) = (x * y) * z & x \cdot 1_A = x & x^a * x^b = x^{a+b} \\
x + 0 = x & x \cdot y = y \cdot x & x^{1_A} = x \\
x + y = y + x & x \cdot (y \cdot z) = (x \cdot y) \cdot z & x^0 = 1_G
\end{array}
$$

Observe that we did not include a symbol for the discrete logarithm in the language. The reason is that we want to assume that computing a from g^a is not feasible for an adversary.

Once a computational group scheme is set (for computational group schemes see for example the full version of [13]), the computational interpretation of this signature is straightforward. Names of sort G will be mapped to the ensemble of distributions corresponding to the generation of random group elements whereas names of sort A will correspond to the generation of ring elements. Addition, multiplication etc. will be translated to addition, multiplication etc. of ring or group elements, respectively. As Baudet et al. point out in their paper, in this theory, the frames $\nu g, a, b.\{x_1 = g, x_2 = g^a, x_3 = g^b, x_4 = g^{ab}\}$ and $\nu g, a, b, c.\{x_1 = g, x_2 = g^a, x_3 = g^b, x_4 = g^c\}$ are statically equivalent. Distinguishing the interpretations of these two frames is the Decisional Diffie-Hellman problem. So, a computational implementation that is sound with respect to static equivalence will imply that the DDH assumption holds for the given group scheme. Unfortunately, soundness would imply much more than the DDH assumption. For example, $\nu gab.\{x_1 = g, x_2 = g^a, x_3 = g^b, x_4 = g^{a^n b^m}\} \approx_E$ $\nu gabc.\{x_1 = g, x_2 = g^a, x_3 = g^b, x_4 = g^c\}$ for some naturals $n, m \geq 1$, and therefore $\approx_E$-soundness would imply that the computational interpretations of these are indistinguishable as well. Moreover, even $\nu gab.\{x_1 = g, x_2 = g^a, x_3 = g^b, x_4 = ab\} \approx_E \nu gabc.\{x_1 = g, x_2 = g^a, x_3 = g^b, x_4 = c\}$. It is unreasonable to require that all these hold for a computational implementation.

We therefore suggest to use a formal indistinguishability relation instead. Since we only want to assume that the DDH assumption holds and nothing more, simply let S be the set consisting of the pair

$$\left(\nu gab.\{x_1 = g, x_2 = g^a, x_3 = g^b, x_4 = g^{ab}\}, \nu gabc.\{x_1 = g, x_2 = g^a, x_3 = g^b, x_4 = g^c\}\right).$$

Then, by Proposition 4, a computational interpretation is $\cong_S$-sound if and only if the DDH assumption holds. In this model, $\cong_S$ will make exactly those frames equivalent for which equivalence necessarily follows from the DDH assumption and the algebraic identities that we included in the model. Hence, for example, $\nu gab.\{x_1 = g, x_2 = g^a, x_3 = g^b, x_4 = ab\} \not\approx_E \nu gabc.\{x_1 = g, x_2 = g^a, x_3 = g^b, x_4 = c\}$, but $\nu gg'ab.\{x_1 = gg', x_2 = (gg')^a, x_3 = (gg')^b, x_4 = (gg')^{ab}\} \cong_S \nu gg'c.\{x_1 = gg', x_2 = (gg')^a, x_3 = (gg')^b, x_4 = (gg')^c\}$. This follows from the commutativity of the group operation, from property (ii) and (iv) of the formal indistinguishability relation, and the definition of S.

Often (for example in the case of uniform distributions), $[\![\{x_1 = g, x_2 = g'\}]\!]_{\mathfrak{A}}$ and $[\![\{x_1 = g, x_2 = gg'\}]\!]_{\mathfrak{A}}$ are computationally indistinguishable. In this case, we can include the pair of frames $(\nu gg'.\{x_1 = g, x_2 = g'\}, \nu gg'.\{x_1 = g, x_2 = gg'\})$ in S, and then the above equivalence will follow without the use of commutativity. Alternatively, if we include $(\nu ab.\{x_1 = a, x_2 = b\}, \nu ab.\{x_1 = a, x_2 = ab\})$ in S, then it follows that $\nu gg'adf.\{x_1 = g, x_2 = g^{ad}, x_3 = g^f, x_4 = g'g^{adf}\} \cong_S \nu gg'df.\{x_1 = g, x_2 = g^{ad}, x_3 = g^f, x_4 = g'g^c\}$.

5.2   Key-Cycles

In their paper, Baudet et al. [10] also consider an equational theory for encryption schemes, and prove the soundness of static equivalence when key-cycles are excluded. Another such example in the framework of static equivalence can be found in the paper of Abadi et al. [1], where key-cycles are excluded as well. The problem of key-cycles is not specific to static equivalence. It necessarily comes up in the investigation of the relationship of formal and computational models; already Abadi and Rogaway in [4] had to exclude key-cycles. There are two ways to include them: Either the encryption scheme used for the interpretation has to be secure even in the presence of key-cycles, or the formal indistinguishability notion has to be relaxed. The problem with the former is that no realistic encryption scheme is known to be secure for key-cycles. Laud proposed a simple solution pursuing the second approach in [18]: Simply assume that the formal adversary can decrypt all the ciphertexts that were encrypted by keys that are part of a key-cycle. In the present formalism this means switching from static equivalence to another indistinguishability relation. We illustrate this by first recasting the original Abadi-Rogaway treatment into the present formalism and then showing how Laud's solution provides a special FIR.

The Abadi-Rogaway formal language of [4] gives a signature $(\mathfrak{S}_{\text{senc}}, \mathcal{F}_{\text{senc}})$, where $\mathfrak{S}_{\text{senc}} = (\mathcal{S}_{\text{senc}}, \mathcal{S}'_{\text{senc}}, \leq_S)$, with $\mathcal{S}_{\text{senc}} = \{Key, Data, Cipher, Pair\}$, $\mathcal{S}'_{\text{senc}} = \{Key\}$, $Key \leq_S Data$, $Cipher \leq_S Data$, $Pair \leq_S Data$. The following function symbols are in $\mathcal{F}_{\text{senc}}$:

enc	:	$Data \times Key \to Cipher$	symmetric encryption
dec	:	$Data \times Data \to Data$	symmetric decryption
pair	:	$Data \times Data \to Pair$	pairing
fst	:	$Data \to Data$	first projection
snd	:	$Data \to Data$	second projection
$0, 1, \text{error}$	:	$Data$	constants

Let the equational theory E_{senc} be generated by the following equations: $\mathbf{dec}(\mathbf{enc}(x, y), y) = x$, $\mathbf{fst}(\mathbf{pair}(x, y)) = x$, $\mathbf{snd}(\mathbf{pair}(x, y)) = y$, $\mathbf{pair}(\mathbf{fst}(x), \mathbf{snd}(x)) = x$, and furthermore, $\mathbf{dec}(x, y) = \text{error}$ whenever the sort $\mathfrak{s}(x)$ is $\leq_S$-incomparable with $Cipher$ or $\mathfrak{s}(y)$ is incomparable with Key, and $\mathbf{fst}(x) = \mathbf{snd}(x) = \text{error}$ whenever $\mathfrak{s}(x)$ is incomparable with $Pair$.

Given a computational encryption scheme $(\mathcal{E}, \mathcal{D}, \mathcal{K})$, along with a computational way of pairing, it is straightforward how to assign a computational algebra $\mathfrak{A}_{senc}$ to this signature: Simply interpret the formal function symbols as their computational counterpart, and let $[\![Key]\!]_{\mathfrak{A}_{senc}}$ be the distribution of key generation.

Definition 6. *A frame φ is* well-formed *if φ does not contain the symbols* dec, fst, snd, error. *For a well-formed frame φ, the set of* recoverable keys *of φ are those keys that are deducible from φ, i.e., R-Keys(φ) = $\{k \mid k \in$ names(φ), k: Key, $\varphi \vdash_{E_{senc}} k\}$. The set B-Keys($\varphi$) consists of those keys that encrypt the outermost undecryptable terms in φ, namely, those undecryptable terms that are deducible from φ:*

$$B\text{-}Keys(\varphi) = \{k \in \text{names}(\varphi) \mid \varphi \vdash_{E_{senc}} \mathbf{enc}(T, k) \text{ for some } T, \text{ and } k \notin R\text{-}Keys(\varphi)\}$$

We say that B-Keys(φ) is cyclic *in φ, if for some keys $k_1, k_2, \ldots, k_m \in$ B-Keys(φ) with $k_1 = k_m$, there are terms $M_1, \ldots, M_m$ with $M_1 = M_m$ such that k_i occurs in M_i in positions other than in the second argument of* enc *and $\varphi \vdash_{E_{senc}} \mathbf{enc}(M_i, k_{i+1})$.*

The reason for excluding some symbols from well-formed frames is that Abadi and Rogaway only considered expressions built via encryption and pairing. But these symbols of course can be used in the distinguishers M and N in the definition of static equivalence! The result of Abadi and Rogaway then says that if the encryption scheme is type-0 secure (as defined in [4]), then for two *well-formed* frames, $\varphi \approx_{E_{senc}} \psi$ implies $[\![\varphi]\!]_{\mathfrak{A}_{senc}} \approx [\![\psi]\!]_{\mathfrak{A}_{senc}}$ whenever neither B-Keys(φ) nor B-Keys(ψ) are cyclic in the corresponding frames..

The exclusion of key-cycles is necessary if the encryption scheme is just type-0 secure. In fact, all standard computational notions of security make it necessary to exclude key-cycles. If the encryption scheme satisfies stronger security definitions, for instance if it is KDM-secure (see [5]), then key-cycles do not cause problems, but no realistic KDM-secure encryptions are known at this time.

As we mentioned, following Laud's method, we can keep the computational algebra $\mathfrak{A}_{senc}$ but switch from static equivalence to another formal indistinguishability relation on the formal side which is sound even in the presence of key-cycles. Define S as static equivalence $\tilde{E}_{senc}$ minus pairs that contain key-cycles on at least one side. Then $\cong_S$-soundness including key-cycles will hold. More precisely, the following proposition is true:

Proposition 5. *Let $\mathfrak{A}_{senc}$ be the above $(\mathfrak{S}_{senc}, \mathcal{F}_{senc})$-computational algebra. Let $S \subseteq \mathfrak{F}_c \times \mathfrak{F}_c$ be the following set:*

$$S := \Big\{ (\varphi_1, \varphi_2) \,\Big|\, (\varphi_1, \varphi_2) \in \tilde{E}_{senc} \text{ and, if } \varphi_i \text{ is well-formed, } B\text{-}Keys(\varphi_i) \text{ is not cyclic} \Big\}.$$

Let $\cong_S$ be the formal indistinguishability relation generated by S. Then, for all well-formed frames φ_1 and φ_2, $\varphi_1 \cong_S \varphi_2$ implies $[\![\varphi_1]\!]_{\mathfrak{A}_{senc}} \approx [\![\varphi_2]\!]_{\mathfrak{A}_{senc}}$.

The proposition clearly holds on S, because from there we removed the the key-cycles. Then the proof is similar to that of Proposition 4.

5.3   Boolean Algebra

We give an example where static equivalence identifies frames that are computationally clearly distinguishable, whereas a more fine-grained formal indistinguishability relation can do better.

Consider a signature $(\mathfrak{S}, \mathcal{F})$, where $\mathfrak{S} = (\{B, S\}, \{B, S\}, =)$, and $\mathcal{F}$ contains the symbols $\wedge, \vee \colon B \to B$, constants $0, 1 \colon B$, as well as $\mathrm{LSB} \colon S \to B$. Let E be the equational theory generated by the set $\{(M, N) \mid M, N \colon B,\ M \leftrightarrow N$ is a tautology of propositional Boolean algebra$\}$.

Let $\mathfrak{A}$ denote the following $(\mathfrak{S}, \mathcal{F})$-computational algebra: $\mathrm{supp}([\![S]\!]_{\mathfrak{A}_\eta}) = \{0, 1\}^\eta \subset \{0, 1\}^*$, $\mathrm{supp}([\![B]\!]_{\mathfrak{A}_\eta}) = \{0, 1\} \subset \{0, 1\}^*$, where both spaces are equipped with the uniform distribution over their support. The operations 0, 1, $\wedge$, $\vee$ are interpreted as the obvious operations on the Boolean algebra $\{0, 1\}$, and $\mathrm{LSB}_{\mathfrak{A}_\eta}$ is defined by $\mathrm{LSB}_{\mathfrak{A}_\eta}(b_1 \ldots b_\eta) = b_\eta$. It is clear that $\mathfrak{A}$ is $=_E$-sound. However, it is not $\approx_E$-sound because

$$\nu ab.\{x = \mathrm{LSB}(a) \wedge \mathrm{LSB}(b)\} \approx_E \nu cd.\{x = \mathrm{LSB}(c) \vee \mathrm{LSB}(d)\}$$

if $a, b : S$, or, even more simply, $\nu ab.\{x = a \wedge b\} \approx_E \nu cd.\{x = c \vee d\}$ for $a, b : B$, whereas the interpretation of the left-hand side is distributed so that $\Pr[\{x = 1\}] = 1/4$, and for the right-hand side $\Pr[\{x = 1\}] = 3/4$, which are clearly distinguishable. (We remark that while $\mathfrak{A}$ does not satisfy a requirement of Baudet et al. that, for two names $a, b \colon B$, $\Pr[e_1, e_2 \leftarrow [\![a, b]\!]_{\mathfrak{A}_\eta}; e_1 = e_2]$ be negligible, this can also be satisfied by making minor changes to the model.)

To remedy the problem, we can use instead of static equivalence a custom formal indistinguishability relation. For a frame which has only sort B in its domain, it is easy to compute explicitly the probability distribution of its interpretation using only the formal expressions. Without writing down the explicit recursive formula, just consider for example that for $\nu ab.\{x_1 = a \wedge b, x_2 = a\}$, $\Pr[\{x_1 = 1, x_2 = 1\}] = 1/4$, $\Pr[\{x_1 = 1, x_2 = 0\}] = 0$, $\Pr[\{x_1 = 0, x_2 = 1\}] = 1/4$, $\Pr[\{x_1 = 0, x_2 = 0\}] = 1/2$. We can therefore define the binary relation S generating the FIR so that S contains those pairs for which the domains only have variables of sort B, and have identical probability distributions. This definition gives a formal indistinguishability relation that is both sound and faithful.

6   Conclusion

We suggested a generalized notion of formal indistinguishability which provides greater flexibility than static equivalence. This is needed because computational distinguishability is much more than just trying to distinguish with the algebraic manipulations allowed by the formal model. It is unrealistic to expect that an indistinguishability relation defined in a purely algebraic manner in a relatively simple formal model will cover all subtleties of computational indistinguishability. However, even though computational indistinguishability is a complex notion, in many cases it is possible to distill a simple formal indistinguishability relation, impose it on the formal model, and get a sound, meaningful theory. The utility of this new definition was demonstrated in Section 5: We pointed out natural models of certain equational theories in which static equivalence seems to be an insufficiently coarse notion of formal indistinguishability, and showed how to come up with different indistinguishability relations that do not identify more expressions than needed.

References

1. Abadi, M., Baudet, M., Warinschi, B.: Guessing attacks and the computational soundness of static equivalence. In: Aceto, L., Ingólfsdóttir, A. (eds.) FOSSACS 2006 and ETAPS 2006. LNCS, vol. 3921, pp. 398–412. Springer, Heidelberg (2006)
2. Abadi, M., Fournet, C.: Mobile values, new names, and secure communication. In: POPL 2001. Proceedings of the 28th ACM SIGPLAN-SIGACT symposium on Principles of programming languages, pp. 104–115. ACM Press, New York (2001)
3. Abadi, M., Gordon, A.D.: A calculus for cryptographic protocols: The Spi Calculus. Information and Computation, 148(1), 1–70 (1999)
4. Abadi, M., Rogaway, P.: Reconciling two views of cryptography (the computational soundness of formal encryption). Journal of Cryptology 15(2), 103–127 (2002)
5. Adão, P., Bana, G., Herzog, J., Scedrov, A.: Soundness of formal encryption in the presence of key-cycles. In: di Vimercati, S.D.C., Syverson, P.F., Gollmann, D. (eds.) ESORICS 2005. LNCS, vol. 3679, pp. 12–14. Springer, Heidelberg (2005)
6. Adão, P., Bana, G., Scedrov, A.: Computational and information-theoretic soundness and completeness of formal encryption. In: CSFW. Proceedings of the 18th IEEE Computer Security Foundations Workshop, pp. 170–184. IEEE Computer Society Press, Los Alamitos (2005)
7. Backes, M., Pfitzmann, B.: Symmetric encryption in a simulatable Dolev-Yao style cryptographic library. In: Proceedings of the 17th IEEE Computer Security Foundations Workshop, vol. 59, pp. 204–218. IEEE Computer Society Press, Los Alamitos (2004)
8. Backes, M., Pfitzmann, B., Waidner, M.: A composable cryptographic library with nested operations. In: Jajodia, S., Atluri, V., Jaeger, T. (eds.) CCS. Proceedings of the 10th ACM Conference on Computer and Communications Security, pp. 27–30. ACM Press, New York (2003)
9. Bana, G., Mohassel, P., Stegers, T.: Computational soundness of formal indistinguishability and static equivalence. Cryptology ePrint Archive, Report 2006/323, 2006, http://eprint.iacr.org/

10. Baudet, M., Cortier, V., Kremer, S.: Computationally sound implementations of equational theories against passive adversaries. In: Caires, L., Italiano, G.F., Monteiro, L., Palamidessi, C., Yung, M. (eds.) ICALP 2005. LNCS, vol. 3580, pp. 652–663. Springer, Heidelberg (2005)
11. Canetti, R.: Universally composable security: A new paradigm for cryptographic protocols. In: FOCS. 42nd IEEE Symposium on Foundations of Computer Science, October 14–17 2001, pp. 136–145. IEEE Computer Society Press, Los Alamitos (2001)
12. Canetti, R., Herzog, J.: Universally composable symbolic analysis of mutual authentication and key exchange protocols. In: Halevi, S., Rabin, T. (eds.) TCC 2006. LNCS, vol. 3876, Springer, Heidelberg (2006)
13. Cramer, R., Shoup, V.: A practical public key cryptosystem provably secure against adaptive chosen ciphertext attack. In: Krawczyk, H. (ed.) CRYPTO 1998. LNCS, vol. 1462, pp. 23–27. Springer, Heidelberg (1998)
14. Datta, A., Derek, A., Mitchell, J.C., Shmatikov, V., Turuani, M.: Probabilistic polynomial-time semantics for a protocol security logic. In: Caires, L., Italiano, G.F., Monteiro, L., Palamidessi, C., Yung, M. (eds.) ICALP 2005. LNCS, vol. 3580, pp. 11–15. Springer, Heidelberg (2005)
15. Dolev, D., Yao, A.C.: On the security of public-key protocols. IEEE Transactions on Information Theory 29(2), 198–208 (1983)
16. Goldwasser, S., Micali, S.: Probabilistic encryption. Journal of Computer and Systems Sciences 28(2), 270–299 (1982)
17. Guttman, J.D., Thayer, F.J., Zuck, L.D.: The faithfulness of abstract protocol analysis: Message authentication. In: Samarati, P. (ed.) CCS. Proceedings of the 8th ACM Conference on Computer and Communications Security, pp. 186–195. ACM Press, New York (2001)
18. Laud, P.: Encryption cycles and two views of cryptography. In (NORDSEC). Proceedings of the 7th Nordic Workshop on Secure IT Systems, Karlstad, Sweden, vol. 31, Karlstad University Studies (November 7–8 2002)
19. Laud, P.: Symmetric encryption in automatic analyses for confidentiality against active adversaries. In: Proceedings of the 2004 IEEE Symposium on Security and Privacy, May 9–12 2004, pp. 9–12. IEEE Computer Society Press, Los Alamitos (2004)
20. Micciancio, D., Warinschi, B.: Completeness theorems for the Abadi-Rogaway logic of encrypted expressions. Journal of Computer Security 12(1), 99–130 (2004)

Secrecy Analysis in Protocol Composition Logic[*]

Arnab Roy[1], Anupam Datta[1], Ante Derek[1], John C. Mitchell[1],
and Jean-Pierre Seifert[2]

[1] Department of Computer Science, Stanford University, Stanford, CA 94305, USA
[2] Institute for Computer Science, University of Innsbruck, 6020 Innsbruck, Austria

Abstract. Extending a compositional protocol logic with an induction
rule for secrecy, we prove soundness for a conventional symbolic protocol
execution model, adapt and extend previous composition theorems, and
illustrate the logic by proving properties of two key agreement protocols. The first example is a variant of the Needham-Schroeder protocol
that illustrates the ability to reason about temporary secrets. The second
example is Kerberos V5. The modular nature of the secrecy and authentication proofs for Kerberos makes it possible to reuse proofs about the
basic version of the protocol for the PKINIT version that uses public-key
infrastructure instead of shared secret keys in the initial steps.

1 Introduction

Two important security properties for key exchange and related protocols are
authentication and secrecy. Intuitively, authentication holds between two parties
if each is assured that the other has participated in the same session of the same
protocol. A secrecy property asserts that some data that is used in the protocol
is not revealed to others. If a protocol generates a fresh value, called a *nonce*, and
sends it in an encrypted message, then under ordinary circumstances the nonce
remains secret in the sense that only agents that have the decryption key can
obtain the nonce. However, many protocols have steps that receive a message
encrypted with one key, and send some of its parts out encrypted with a different
key. Since network protocols are executed asynchronously by independent agents,
some potentially malicious, it is non-trivial to prove that even after arbitrarily
many steps of independent protocol sessions, secrets remain inaccessible to an
attacker.

Our general approach involves showing that every protocol agent that receives
data protected by one of a chosen set of encryption keys only sends sensitive data
out under encryption by another key in the set. This reduces a potentially complicated proof about arbitrary runs involving a malicious attacker to a case-by-case
analysis of how each protocol step might save and send data. We formalize this
form of inductive reasoning about secrecy in a set of new axioms and inference

---

[*] This work was partially supported by the NSF TRUST Science and Technology
Center. The first author was partially supported by a Siebel Fellowship. Part of the
work was done when the first and fifth authors were at Intel Corporation.

M. Okada and I. Satoh (Eds.): ASIAN 2006, LNCS 4435, pp. 197–213, 2007.
© Springer-Verlag Berlin Heidelberg 2007

rules that are added to Protocol Composition Logic (PCL) [14,9,8,10,11], prove soundness of the system over a conventional symbolic protocol execution model, and illustrate its use with two protocol examples. The extended logic may be used to prove authentication or secrecy, independently and in situations where one property may depend upon the other. Among other challenges, the inductive secrecy rule presented here is carefully designed to be sound for reasoning about arbitrarily many simultaneous protocol sessions, and powerful enough to prove meaningful properties about complex protocols used in practice. While the underlying principles are similar to the "rank function method" [18] and work using the strand space execution model [19], our system provides precise formal proof rules that are amenable to automation. In addition, casting secrecy induction in the framework of Protocol Composition Logic avoids limitations of some forms of rank function arguments and eliminates the need to reason explicitly about possible actions of a malicious attacker. Compositional secrecy proofs are made possible by theorems developed in this paper, extending previous composition theorems for a simpler proof system [11,15].

Our first protocol example is a variant of the Needham-Schroeder protocol, used in [16] to illustrate a limitation of the original rank function method and motivate an extension for reasoning about temporary secrets. The straightforward formal proof in section 4 therefore shows that our method does not suffer from the limitations identified in [16]. Intuitively, the advantage of our setting lies in the way that modal formulas of PCL state properties about specific points in protocol execution, rather than only properties that must be true at all points in all runs.

Our second protocol example is Kerberos [17], which is widely used for authenticated client-server interaction in local area networks. The basic protocol has three sections, each involving an exchange between the client and a different service. We develop a formal proof that is modular, with the proof for each section assuming a precondition and establishing a postcondition that implies the precondition of the following section. One advantage of this modular structure is illustrated by our proof for the PKINIT [7] version that uses public-key infrastructure instead of shared secret keys in the initial steps. Since only the first section of PKINIT is different, the proofs for the second and third sections of the protocol remain unchanged. In previous work, Bella and Paulson use theorem proving techniques to reason about properties of Kerberos that hold in all traces containing actions of honest parties and a malicious attacker [3]. Our high-level axiomatic proofs are significantly more concise since we do not require explicit reasoning about attacker actions. Another line of work uses a multiset rewriting model to develop proofs in the symbolic and computational model [4,2]. However, proofs in these papers use unformalized (though rigorous) mathematical arguments and are not modular.

The rest of the paper is organized as follows. Some background on PCL is given in section 2, followed by the secrecy-related axioms and proof rules in section 3. The first protocol example is presented in section 4. Composition theorems are developed in section 5, and applied in the proofs for Kerberos in section 6. Finally, we conclude in section 7.

2   Background

Protocol Composition Logic (PCL) is developed in [14,9,8,10], with [11] providing a relatively succinct presentation of the most current form. A simple protocol programming language is used to represent a *protocol* by a set of *roles*, such as "Initiator", "Responder" or "Server", each specifying a sequence of actions to be executed by an honest participant. Protocol actions include nonce generation, encryption, decryption and communication steps (sending and receiving). Every principal can be executing one or more copies of each role at the same time. We use the word *thread* to refer to a principal executing one particular instance of a role. Each *thread* X is a pair $(\hat{X}, \eta)$ where $\hat{X}$ is a principal and η is a unique session id. A *run* is a record of all actions executed by honest principals and the attacker during protocol execution. The set of runs of a protocol is determined by the operational semantics of the protocol programming language.

Table 1 summarizes the syntax of the logic used in this paper. Protocol proofs usually use modal formulas of the form $\psi[P]_X\varphi$. The informal reading of the modal formula is that if X starts from a state in which ψ holds, and executes the program P, then in the resulting state the security property φ is guaranteed to hold irrespective of the actions of an attacker and other honest principals. The formulas of the logic are interpreted over protocol runs. We say that protocol $\mathcal{Q}$ satisfies formula φ, denoted $\mathcal{Q} \vDash \varphi$, if in all runs R of $\mathcal{Q}$ the formula φ holds, *i.e.*, $\mathcal{Q}, R \vDash \varphi$. For example, $\mathsf{Send}(X, t)$ holds in a run where the thread X has sent the term t. For every protocol action, there is a corresponding action predicate which asserts that the action has occurred in the run. Action predicates are useful for capturing authentication properties of protocols since they can be used to assert which principals sent and received certain messages. $\mathsf{Encrypt}(X, t)$ means that X computes the encrypted term t, while $\mathsf{New}(X, n)$ means X generates fresh nonce n. $\mathsf{Honest}(\hat{X})$ means that $\hat{X}$ is acting honestly, *i.e.*, the actions of every thread of $\hat{X}$ precisely follows some role of the protocol. $\mathsf{Start}(X)$ means that the thread X did not execute any actions in the past. $\mathsf{Has}(X, t)$ means X can compute the term t using symbolic Dolev-Yao rules, *e.g.* receiving it in the clear or receiving it under encryption where the decryption key is known.

To illustrate the terminology used in this section we describe the formalization of Kerberos V5, which is a protocol used to establish mutual authentication and a shared session key between a client and an application server [17]. It involves

Table 1. Syntax of the logic

Action formulas
$\mathsf{a} ::= \mathsf{Send}(X, t) \mid \mathsf{Receive}(X, t) \mid \mathsf{New}(X, t) \mid \mathsf{Encrypt}(X, t) \mid \mathsf{Start}(X)$
Formulas
$\varphi ::= \mathsf{a} \mid \mathsf{Has}(X, t) \mid \mathsf{Honest}(\hat{X}) \mid \varphi \wedge \varphi \mid \neg\varphi \mid \exists V.\ \varphi$
Modal form
$\Psi ::= \varphi\ [Actions]_X\ \varphi$

---

trusted principals known as the Kerberos Authentication Server (KAS) and the Ticket Granting Server (TGS). There are pre-shared long term keys between the client and the KAS, the KAS and the TGS, and the TGS and the application server. Typically, the KAS shares long-term keys with a number of clients and the TGS with a number of application servers. However, there is no pre-shared long term secret between a given client and an application server. Kerberos achieves establishment of mutual authentication and a shared session key between the client and the application server using the chain of trust leading from the client to the KAS and the TGS to the application server.

Kerberos has four roles, one for each kind of participant - **Client, KAS, TGS** and **Server**. The long-term shared keys are written here in the form $k_{X,Y}^{type}$ where X and Y are the principals sharing the key. The *type* appearing in the superscript indicates the relationship between X and Y in the transactions involving the use of the key. There are three *types* required in Kerberos: $c \to k$ indicates that X is acting as a client and Y is acting as a KAS, $t \to k$ is for TGS and KAS and $s \to t$ is for application server and TGS. Kerberos runs in three stages with the client role participating in all three. The description of the roles is based on the A level formalization of Kerberos V5 in [5]. We describe the formalization of the first stage in some detail so that the rest is easy to follow.

In the first stage, shown below, the client thread (C) generates a nonce (n_1) and sends it to the KAS ($\hat{K}$) along with the identities of the TGS ($\hat{T}$) and itself. The KAS generates a new nonce ($AKey$ - Authentication Key) to be used as a session key between the client and the TGS. It then sends this key along with some other fields to the client encrypted (represented by the match actions) under two different keys - one it shares with the client ($k_{C,K}^{c \to k}$) and one it shares with the TGS ($k_{T,K}^{t \to k}$). The encryption with $k_{T,K}^{t \to k}$ is called the *ticket granting ticket* (*tgt*). The client extracts $AKey$ by decrypting the component encrypted with $k_{C,K}^{c \to k}$.

Client $= (C, \hat{K}, \hat{T}, \hat{S}, t)$ [	**KAS** $= (K)$ [
new n_1;	receive $\hat{C}.\hat{T}.n_1$;
send $\hat{C}.\hat{T}.n_1$;	new $AKey$;
	match $E_{sym}[k_{T,K}^{t \to k}](AKey.\hat{C})$ as tgt;
receive $\hat{C}.tgt.enc_{kc}$;	match $E_{sym}[k_{C,K}^{c \to k}](AKey.n_1.\hat{T})$
match enc_{kc}	as enc_{kc};
as $E_{sym}[k_{C,K}^{c \to k}](AKey.n_1.\hat{T})$;	send $\hat{C}.tgt.enc_{kc}$;
......	$]_K$

In the second stage (not shown), the client uses the session key $AKey$ and the *ticket granting ticket* to interact with the TGS and gets a new session key $SKey$ and a *service ticket* (*st*). In the third stage, the client encrypts its identity and a timestamp with $SKey$ and sends it to the application server along with the service ticket. The server decrypts *st* and extracts the $SKey$. It then uses the session key to decrypt the client's encryption, matches the first component of the decryption with the identity of the client and extracts the timestamp. It then encrypts the timestamp with the session key and sends it back to the client. The client decrypts the message and matches it against the timestamp it used. The control flow of Kerberos exhibits a staged architecture where once one stage has been completed successfully, the subsequent stages can be performed multiple times or aborted and started over for handling errors.

3   Proof System for Secrecy Analysis

In this section, we extend PCL with new axioms and rules for establishing secrecy. Secrecy properties are formalized using the $\mathsf{Has}(X, s)$ predicate and requiring that $\hat{X}$ refer only to honest principals who share the secret s. In a typical two party protocol, $\hat{X}$ is one of two honest agents and s is a nonce generated by one of them. As an intermediate step, we establish that all occurrences of the secret on the network are protected by keys. This property can be proved by induction over possible actions by honest principals and reasoning that no action leaks the secret if it was not compromised already.

We introduce the predicate $\mathsf{SafeMsg}(M, s, \mathcal{K})$ to assert that every occurrence of s in message M is protected by a key in the set $\mathcal{K}$. Technically speaking, for each $n > 0$, there is an $(n + 2)$-ary predicate $\mathsf{SafeMsg}^n(M, s, \mathcal{K})$, with n corresponding to the size of set $\mathcal{K}$. However, we suppress this syntactic detail in this paper. The semantic interpretation of this predicate is defined by induction on the structure of messages. It is actually independent of the protocol and the run.

Definition 1 (SafeMsg). *Given a run R of a protocol $\mathcal{Q}$, we say $\mathcal{Q}, R \models \mathsf{SafeMsg}(M, s, \mathcal{K})$ if there exists an i such that $\mathsf{SafeMsg}_i(M, s, \mathcal{K})$ where $\mathsf{SafeMsg}_i$ is defined as follows:*

$\mathsf{SafeMsg}_0(M, s, \mathcal{K})$	*if M is an atomic term different from s*
$\mathsf{SafeMsg}_0(HASH(M), s, \mathcal{K})$	*for any M*
$\mathsf{SafeMsg}_{i+1}(M_0.M_1, s, \mathcal{K})$	*if $\mathsf{SafeMsg}_i(M_0, s, \mathcal{K})$ and $\mathsf{SafeMsg}_i(M_1, s, \mathcal{K})$*
$\mathsf{SafeMsg}_{i+1}(E_{sym}[k](M), s, \mathcal{K})$	*if $\mathsf{SafeMsg}_i(M, s, \mathcal{K})$ or $k \in \mathcal{K}$*
$\mathsf{SafeMsg}_{i+1}(E_{pk}[k](M), s, \mathcal{K})$	*if $\mathsf{SafeMsg}_i(M, s, \mathcal{K})$ or $\bar{k} \in \mathcal{K}$*

The axioms **SAF0** to **SAF5** below parallel the semantic clauses and follow immediately from them. Equivalences follow as the term algebra is free.

SAF0 $\neg\mathsf{SafeMsg}(s, s, \mathcal{K}) \wedge \mathsf{SafeMsg}(x, s, \mathcal{K})$,

where x is an atomic term different from s

SAF1 $\mathsf{SafeMsg}(M_0.M_1, s, \mathcal{K}) \equiv \mathsf{SafeMsg}(M_0, s, \mathcal{K}) \wedge \mathsf{SafeMsg}(M_1, s, \mathcal{K})$

SAF2 $\mathsf{SafeMsg}(E_{sym}[k](M), s, \mathcal{K}) \equiv \mathsf{SafeMsg}(M, s, \mathcal{K}) \vee k \in \mathcal{K}$

SAF3 $\mathsf{SafeMsg}(E_{pk}[k](M), s, \mathcal{K}) \equiv \mathsf{SafeMsg}(M, s, \mathcal{K}) \vee \bar{k} \in \mathcal{K}$

SAF4 $\mathsf{SafeMsg}(HASH(M), s, \mathcal{K})$

The formula $\mathsf{SendsSafeMsg}(X, s, \mathcal{K})$ states that all messages sent by thread X are "safe" while $\mathsf{SafeNet}(s, \mathcal{K})$ asserts the same property for all threads. These formulas may be written as $\mathsf{SendsSafeMsg}(X, s, \mathcal{K}) \equiv \forall M. (\mathsf{Send}(X, M) \supset \mathsf{SafeMsg}(M, s, \mathcal{K}))$ and $\mathsf{SafeNet}(s, \mathcal{K}) \equiv \forall X. \mathsf{SendsSafeMsg}(X, s, \mathcal{K})$.

In secrecy proofs, we will explicitly assume that the thread generating the secret and all threads with access to a relevant key belong to honest principals. This is semantically necessary since a dishonest principal may reveal its key, destroying secrecy of any data encrypted with it. These honesty assumptions are expressed by the formulas KeyHonest and OrigHonest respectively. KOHonest is the conjunction of the two.

- $\mathsf{KeyHonest}(\mathcal{K}) \equiv \forall X. \forall k \in \mathcal{K}. (\mathsf{Has}(X, k) \supset \mathsf{Honest}(\hat{X}))$
- $\mathsf{OrigHonest}(s) \equiv \forall X. (\mathsf{New}(X, s) \supset \mathsf{Honest}(\hat{X}))$.
- $\mathsf{KOHonest}(s, \mathcal{K}) \equiv \mathsf{KeyHonest}(\mathcal{K}) \wedge \mathsf{OrigHonest}(s)$

We now have the necessary technical machinery to state the induction rule. At a high-level, the **NET** rule states that if each "possible protocol step" P locally sends out safe messages, assuming all messages in the network were safe prior to that step, then all messages on the network are safe. A possible protocol step P is drawn from the set of basic sequences BS for all roles of the protocol. A set of basic sequences of a role is any partition of the sequence of actions in the role such that if any element sequence has a `receive` action then it is only at the beginning.

$$\mathbf{NET} \quad \forall \rho \in \mathcal{Q}. \forall P \in BS(\rho).$$

$$\frac{\mathsf{SafeNet}(s, \mathcal{K}) \, [P]_X \, \mathsf{Honest}(\hat{X}) \wedge \Phi \supset \mathsf{SendsSafeMsg}(X, s, \mathcal{K})}{\mathcal{Q} \vdash \mathsf{KOHonest}(s, \mathcal{K}) \wedge \Phi \supset \mathsf{SafeNet}(s, \mathcal{K})} \, (*)$$

$(*)$: $[P]_A$ does not capture free variables in Φ and $\mathcal{K}$ and the variable s. Φ should be prefix closed .

The axioms **NET0** to **NET3** below are used to establish the antecedent of the **NET** rule. Many practical security protocols consist of steps that each receive a message, perform some operations, and then send a resulting message. The proof strategy in such cases is to use **NET1** to reason that messages received from a safe network are safe and then use this information and the **SAF** axioms to prove that the output message is also safe.

NET0 $\mathsf{SafeNet}(s, \mathcal{K}) \, [\,]_X \, \mathsf{SendsSafeMsg}(X, s, \mathcal{K})$

NET1 $\mathsf{SafeNet}(s, \mathcal{K}) \, [\mathtt{receive} \ M]_X \, \mathsf{SafeMsg}(M, s, \mathcal{K})$

NET2 $\mathsf{SendsSafeMsg}(X, s, \mathcal{K}) \, [\mathtt{a}]_X \, \mathsf{SendsSafeMsg}(X, s, \mathcal{K})$, where a is not a send.

NET3 $\mathsf{SendsSafeMsg}(X, s, \mathcal{K}) \, [\mathtt{send} \ M]_X \, \mathsf{SafeMsg}(M, s, \mathcal{K}) \supset \mathsf{SendsSafeMsg}(X, s, \mathcal{K})$

Finally, **POS** and **POSL** are used to infer secrecy properties expressed using the Has predicate. The axiom **POS** states that if we have a safe network with respect to s and key-set $\mathcal{K}$ then the only principals who can possess an unsafe message are the generator of s or possessor of a key in $\mathcal{K}$. The **POSL** rule lets a thread use a similar reasoning locally.

POS $\mathsf{SafeNet}(s, \mathcal{K}) \wedge \mathsf{Has}(X, M) \wedge \neg \mathsf{SafeMsg}(M, s, \mathcal{K})$

$\qquad \supset \exists k \in \mathcal{K}. \mathsf{Has}(X, k) \vee \mathsf{New}(X, s)$

POSL $\dfrac{\psi \wedge \mathsf{SafeNet}(s, \mathcal{K}) \, [S]_X \, \mathsf{SendsSafeMsg}(X, s, \mathcal{K}) \wedge \mathsf{Has}(Y, M) \wedge \neg \mathsf{SafeMsg}(M, s, \mathcal{K})}{\psi \wedge \mathsf{SafeNet}(s, \mathcal{K}) \, [S]_X \, \exists k \in \mathcal{K}. \mathsf{Has}(Y, k) \vee \mathsf{New}(Y, s)}$,

where S is any basic sequence of actions.

Following are useful theorems which follow easily from the axioms.

SREC $\mathsf{SafeNet}(s, \mathcal{K}) \wedge \mathsf{Receive}(X, M) \supset \mathsf{SafeMsg}(M, s, \mathcal{K})$

SSND $\mathsf{SafeNet}(s, \mathcal{K}) \wedge \mathsf{Send}(X, M) \supset \mathsf{SafeMsg}(M, s, \mathcal{K})$

We write $\Gamma \vdash \gamma$ if γ is provable from the formulas in Γ and any axiom or inference rule of the proof system except the honesty rule **HON** from previous formulations of PCL and the secrecy rule **NET**. We write $\mathcal{Q} \vdash \gamma$ if γ is provable from the axioms and inference rules of the proof system including the rules **HON** and **NET** for protocol $\mathcal{Q}$.

Given a set of messages $\mathcal{M}$, let us denote by $\tilde{\mathcal{M}}$ to be the minimal set containing $\mathcal{M}$ and closed under pairing, unpairing, encryption with any public key or symmetric key, decryption with a private key or a symmetric key not in $\mathcal{K}$ and hashing.

Theorem 1. *If $\mathcal{M}$ is a set of messages, all safe with respect to secret s and key-set $\mathcal{K}$, then $\tilde{\mathcal{M}}$ also contains only safe messages.*

Proof. Any element $m \in \tilde{\mathcal{M}}$ can be constructed from elements in $\mathcal{M}$ using a finite sequence of the operations enumerated. From the semantics of $\mathsf{SafeMsg}$ it is easily seen that all the operations preserve safeness. Hence by induction, all the elements of $\tilde{\mathcal{M}}$ will be safe. $\square$

Lemma 1. *If a thread X, at any point in any protocol, possesses an unsafe message with respect to secret s and key-set $\mathcal{K}$ then either X received an unsafe message earlier, or X generated s, or X possesses a key in $\mathcal{K}$.*

Proof. Suppose thread X does not satisfy any of the conditions enumerated. Then the set of messages $\mathcal{M}$ it initially knows and has received are safe messages. Since it does not have a key in $\mathcal{K}$, $\tilde{\mathcal{M}}$ is a superset of all the messages it can construct from $\mathcal{M}$ (in the Dolev-Yao model). Hence, by theorem 1, X cannot compute any unsafe message. So it cannot possess an unsafe message – a contradiction. $\square$

Theorem 2 (Soundness). *If $\mathcal{Q} \vdash \gamma$, then $\mathcal{Q} \vDash \gamma$. Furthermore, if $\Gamma \vdash \gamma$, then $\Gamma \vDash \gamma$.*

Proof. Soundness for this proof system is proved, by induction on the length of proofs of the axioms and rules, the most interesting of which are sketched below.

NET: Consider a run R of protocol $\mathcal{Q}$ such that the consequent of **NET** is false. We will show that the antecedent is false too. We have $\mathcal{Q}, R \vDash$

KOHonest$(s, \mathcal{K}) \wedge \Phi$, but $\mathcal{Q}, R \nvDash$ SafeNet$(s, \mathcal{K})$. This implies that $\mathcal{Q}, R \vDash$ $\exists m, X.$ Send$(X, m) \wedge \neg$SafeMsg$(m, s, \mathcal{K})$. Note that there must be a first instance when an unsafe message is sent out - let $\tilde{m}$ be the first such message. Hence, we can split R into $R_0.R_1.R_2$ such that $\mathcal{Q}, R_0 \vDash$ SafeNet$(s, \mathcal{K})$ and $R_1 = \langle X \text{ sends } \tilde{m}; Y \text{ receives } \tilde{m} \rangle$, for some Y.

Since this is the first send of an unsafe message, therefore X could not have received an unsafe message earlier. Therefore, by the lemma, either X generated s or, X has a key in $\mathcal{K}$. In both cases, KOHonest$(s, \mathcal{K})$ implies Honest$(\hat{X})$. Therefore the fragment [send $\tilde{m}$]$_X$ must be part of a sequence of actions $[P]_X$ such that P is a basic sequence of one of the roles in $\mathcal{Q}$ - but, this violates the premise of **NET**. Hence the theorem. The need for Φ to be prefix-closed comes from a more detailed version of this proof .

POS: SafeNet$(s, \mathcal{K})$ implies no thread sent out an unsafe message in the run. Hence no thread received an unsafe message. Therefore, by lemma 1, any thread X possessing an unsafe message must have either generated s or possesses a key in $\mathcal{K}$.

POSL: The premise of the rule informally states that starting from a "safe" network and additional constraints ψ thread X concludes that some thread Y possesses an unsafe message M in all possible runs of any protocol. Specifically this should be true for a run where thread X executes the basic sequence $[S]_X$ uninterspersed with the actions of any other thread except the receipt of messages sent by X. Now the premise implies that X only sends safe messages - also since S is a basic sequence, the only message that X can receive in $[S]_X$ will be only at its beginning, which, due to the starting "safe" network precondition will be a safe message. Hence we can conclude that thread Y possessed an unsafe message before X started executing $[S]_X$ i.e., when SafeNet$(s, \mathcal{K})$ was true. Therefore using axiom **POS** we derive that thread Y either generated s or possesses a key in $\mathcal{K}$, which establises the conclusion of **POSL**. $\square$

4   Analysis of a Variant of NSL

In this section we use the proof system developed in section 3 to prove a secrecy property of a simple variant $NSLVAR$ of the Needham-Schroeder-Lowe protocol, proposed in [16], in which parties A and B use an authenticated temporary secret n_a to establish a secret key k that is in turn used to protect the actual message m. The main difference from the original NSL protocol is that the initiator's nonce is leaked in the final message. Reasoning from A's point of view, nonce n_a should be secret between A and B at the point of the run in the protocol where A is just about to send the last message. This protocol was originally used to demonstrate a limitation of the original rank function method in reasoning about temporary secrets. Modal formulas in PCL allow us to naturally express and prove properties that hold at intermediate points of a protocol execution.

Formally, $NSLVAR$ is a protocol defined by roles $\{\textbf{Init}, \textbf{Resp}\}$, with the roles, written using the protocol program notation, given below.

$\textbf{Init} = (A, \hat{B}, m)\,[$ $\textbf{Resp} = (B)\,[$

    `new` n_a;   `receive` enc_{r1};

    `match` $E_{pk}[k_B](\hat{A}.n_a)$ `as` enc_{r1};   `match` enc_{r1} `as` $E_{pk}[k_B](\hat{A}.n_a)$;

    `send` enc_{r1};   `new` k;

                                        `match` $E_{pk}[k_A](n_a.\hat{B}.k)$ `as` enc_i;

    `receive` enc_i;   `send` enc_i;

    `match` enc_i `as` $E_{pk}[k_A](n_a.\hat{B}.k)$;

    `match` $E_{sym}[k](m)$ `as` enc_{r2};   `receive` $enc_{r2}.n_a$;

    `send` $enc_{r2}.n_a$;   `match` enc_{r2} `as` $E_{sym}[k](m)$;

$]_A$ $]_B$

Theorem 3. *Let* $\widetilde{\textbf{Init}}$ *denote the initial segment of the initiator's role ending just before the last send action. The nonce* n_a *is a shared secret between A and B in every state of the protocol where A has executed* $\widetilde{\textbf{Init}}$ *and no further actions, as long as both $\hat{A}$ and $\hat{B}$ are honest. Formally,*

$$NSLVAR \vdash [\widetilde{\textbf{Init}}]_A\ \textsf{Honest}(\hat{A}) \wedge \textsf{Honest}(\hat{B}) \supset (\textsf{Has}(X, n_a) \supset \hat{X} = \hat{A} \vee \hat{X} = \hat{B})$$

Proof Sketch. To prove the secrecy property, we start off by proving an authentication property $[\widetilde{\textbf{Init}}]_A\ \textsf{Honest}(\hat{A}) \wedge \textsf{Honest}(\hat{B}) \supset \Phi$, where Φ is the conjunction of the following formulas:

$$\Phi_1 : \forall X, \hat{Y}.\ \textsf{New}(X, n_a) \wedge \textsf{Send}(X, E_{pk}[k_Y](\hat{X}.n_a)) \supset \hat{Y} = \hat{B}$$
$$\Phi_2 : \forall X, \hat{Y}, n.\ \textsf{New}(X, n_a) \supset \neg\textsf{Send}(X, E_{pk}[k_Y](n.\hat{X}.n_a))$$
$$\Phi_3 : \forall X, e.\ \textsf{New}(X, n_a) \supset \neg\textsf{Send}(X, e.n_a)$$
$$\Phi_4 : \textsf{Honest}(\hat{X}) \wedge \textsf{Send}(X, E_{sym}[k_0](m_0).n) \supset \textsf{New}(X, n)$$
$$\Phi_5 : \textsf{Honest}(\hat{X}) \wedge \textsf{EncSend}(X, E_{pk}[k_Y](\hat{X}'.n)) \supset \hat{X}' = \hat{X}$$

Informally, Φ_1 and Φ_2 hold because from the thread A's point of view it is known that it itself generated the nonce n_a and did not send it out encrypted with any other principal's public key except $\hat{B}$'s and that too in a specific format described by the protocol. Φ_3 holds because we are considering a state in the protocol execution where A has not yet sent the last message - sending of the last message will make $\textsf{Send}(A, e.n_a)$ true with $e = E_{sym}[k](m)$. These intuitive explanations can be formalized using a previously developed fragment of PCL but we will omit those steps in this paper. Φ_4 and Φ_5 follow from a straightforward use of the honesty rule.

In the next step we prove the antecedents of the **NET** rule. We take $\mathcal{K} = \{\bar{k}_A, \bar{k}_B\}$ where the bar indicates private key which makes $\mathsf{KeyHon}(\mathcal{K}) \equiv \mathsf{Honest}(\hat{A}) \wedge \mathsf{Honest}(\hat{B})$. In addition, since thread A generates n_a, therefore $\mathsf{KOHonest}(n_a, \mathcal{K}) \equiv \mathsf{Honest}(\hat{A}) \wedge \mathsf{Honest}(\hat{B})$. We show that all basic sequence of the protocol send "safe" messages, assuming that formula Φ holds and that the predicate $\mathsf{SafeNet}$ holds at the beginning of that basic sequence. Formally, for every basic sequence $\mathbf{P} \in \{\mathbf{Init}_1, \mathbf{Init}_2, \mathbf{Resp}_1, \mathbf{Resp}_2\}$ we prove that: $\mathsf{SafeNet}(n_a, \mathcal{K})[\mathbf{P}]_{A'} \mathsf{Honest}(\hat{A}') \wedge \Phi \supset \mathsf{SendsSafeMsg}(A', n_a, \mathcal{K})$ $\square$

Some secrecy proofs using the CSP [18] or strand space [19] protocol execution model use inductive arguments that are similar to the form of inductive reasoning codified in our formal system. For example, within CSP, properties of messages that may appear on the network have been identified by defining a *rank function* [18,16], with an inductive proof used to show that rank is preserved by the attacker actions and all honest parties. In comparison, arguments in our formal logic use a conjunction involving the $\mathsf{SafeNet}$ predicate and protocol specific properties Φ in our inductive hypotheses. These two formulas together characterize the set of possible messages appearing on the network and can be viewed as a symbolic definition of a rank function. We believe that our method is as powerful as the rank function method for any property expressible in our logic. However, it is difficult to prove a precise connection without first casting the rank function method in a formal setting that relies on a specific class of message predicates.

One drawback of the rank function approach is that the induction is performed by "global" reasoning. While analyzing a protocol, all relevant properties of the system (such as authentication and secrecy, for example) are modelled using a single rank function and proved to hold simultaneously. This makes the method somewhat less applicable since it cannot handle protocols which deal with temporary secrets or use authentication to ensure secrecy properties. In contrast, PCL allows separation and incremental proofs of different properties. Although some of these issues can be resolved by extensions of the rank function method [13,12], the PCL approach seems more general and may be better suited for some applications.

5   Compositional Reasoning for Secrecy

In this section, we present composition theorems that allow secrecy proofs of compound protocols to be built up from proofs of their parts. An application of this method to the Kerberos protocol is given in the next section. We consider three kinds of composition operations on protocols—*parallel, sequential,* and *staged*—as in our earlier work [11,15]. However, adapting that approach for reasoning about secrecy requires some work. One central concept in our compositional proof methods is the notion of an *invariant*. An invariant for a protocol is a logical formula that characterizes the environment in which it retains its security properties. While in previous work we had one rule for establishing invariants (the **HON** rule [11]), reasoning about secrecy requires, in addition, the **NET** rule introduced in this paper. A second point of difference arises from the fact that reasoning about secrecy requires a certain degree of global knowledge. Specifically, while proving that a protocol step does not violate secrecy, it is sometimes necessary to use information from earlier steps. In the technical presentation, this history information shows up as preconditions in the secrecy induction of the sequential and staged composition theorems.

Definition 2 (Parallel Composition). *The parallel composition $\mathcal{Q}_1 \otimes \mathcal{Q}_2$ of protocols $\mathcal{Q}_1$ and $\mathcal{Q}_2$ is the union of the sets of roles of $\mathcal{Q}_1$ and $\mathcal{Q}_2$.*

The parallel composition operation allows modelling agents who simultaneously engage in sessions of multiple protocols. The parallel composition theorem provides a method for ensuring that security properties established independently for the constituent protocols are still preserved in such a situation.

Theorem 4 (Parallel Composition). *If $\mathcal{Q}_1 \vdash \Gamma$ and $\Gamma \vdash \Psi$ and $\mathcal{Q}_2 \vdash \Gamma$ then $\mathcal{Q}_1 \otimes \mathcal{Q}_2 \vdash \Psi$, where Γ denotes the set of invariants used in the proof of Ψ.*

One way to understand the parallel composition theorem is to visualize the proof tree for Ψ for protocol $\mathcal{Q}_1$ in red and green colors. The steps which use the invariant rules are colored red and correspond to the part $\mathcal{Q}_1 \vdash \Gamma$, while all other proof steps are colored green and correspond to the part $\Gamma \vdash \Psi$. While composing protocols, all green steps are obviously preserved since they involve proof rules which hold for all protocols. The red steps could possibly be violated because of $\mathcal{Q}_2$. For example, one invariant may state that honest principals only sign messages of a certain form, while $\mathcal{Q}_2$ may allow agents to sign other forms of messages. The condition $\mathcal{Q}_2 \vdash \Gamma$ ensures that this is not the case, i.e., the red steps still apply for the composed protocol.

Definition 3 (Sequential Composition). *A protocol $\mathcal{Q}$ is a sequential composition of two protocols $\mathcal{Q}_1$ and $\mathcal{Q}_2$, if each role of $\mathcal{Q}$ is obtained by the sequential composition of a role of $\mathcal{Q}_1$ with a role of $\mathcal{Q}_2$.*

In practice, key exchange is usually followed by a secure message transmission protocol which uses the resulting shared key to protect data. Sequential composition is used to model such compound protocols. Formally, the composed role $P_1; P_2$ is obtained by concatenating the actions of P_1 and P_2 with the output parameters of P_1 substituted for the input parameters of P_2 (cf. [11]).

Theorem 5 (Sequential Composition). *If $\mathcal{Q}$ is a sequential composition of protocols $\mathcal{Q}_1$ and $\mathcal{Q}_2$ then we can conclude $\mathcal{Q} \vdash$ KOHonest$(s, \mathcal{K}) \wedge \Phi \supset$ SafeNet$(s, \mathcal{K})$ if the following conditions hold for all $P_1; P_2$ in $\mathcal{Q}$, where $P_1 \in \mathcal{Q}_1$ and $P_2 \in \mathcal{Q}_2$:*

1. *(Secrecy induction)*
   - $\forall i. \forall S \in BS(P_i). \quad \theta_{P_i} \wedge$ SafeNet$(s, \mathcal{K})$ $[S]_X$ Honest$(\hat{X}) \wedge \Phi \supset$ SendsSafeMsg$(X, s, \mathcal{K})$
2. *(Precondition induction)*
   - $\mathcal{Q}_1 \otimes \mathcal{Q}_2 \vdash$ Start$(X) \supset \theta_{P_1}$ *and* $\mathcal{Q}_1 \otimes \mathcal{Q}_2 \vdash \theta_{P_1} [P_1]_X \theta_{P_2}$
   - $\forall i. \forall S \in BS(P_i). \theta_{P_i} [S]_X \theta_{P_i}.$

The final conclusion of the theorem is a statement that secrecy of s is preserved in the composed protocol. The secrecy induction is very similar to the **NET** rule. It states that all basic sequences of the two roles only send out safe messages. This step is compositional since the condition is proved independently for steps of the two protocols. One point of difference from the **NET** rule is the additional precondition θ_{P_i}. This formula usually carries some information about the history of the execution, which helps in deciding what messages are safe for A to send out. For example, if θ_{P_i} says that A received some message m, then it is easy to establish that m is a safe message for A to send out again. The precondition induction proves that the θ_{P_i}'s hold at each point where they are assumed in the secrecy induction. The first bullet states the base case of the induction: θ_{P_1} holds at the beginning of the execution and θ_{P_2} holds when P_1 completes. The second bullet states that the basic sequences of P_1 and P_2 preserve their respective preconditions. This theorem is existential in the preconditions, *i.e.*, the theorem holds if there exist any set of formulas θ_{P_i} satisfying the conditions.

Definition 4 (Staged Composition). *A protocol Q is a staged composition of protocols $Q_1, Q_2, \ldots, Q_n$ if each role of Q is of the form $RComp(\langle R_1, R_2, \ldots, R_n \rangle)$, where R_i is a role of protocol Q_i.*

Consider the representation of sequential composition of n protocols as a directed graph with edges from Q_i to Q_{i+1}. The staged composition operation extends sequential composition by allowing self loops and arbitrary backward arcs in this chain. This control flow structure is common in practice, e.g., Kerberos [17], IEEE 802.11i [1], and IKEv2 [6]. A role in this composition, denoted $RComp(\langle ... \rangle)$ corresponds to a possible execution path in the control flow graph by a single thread (cf. [15]). Note that the roles are built up from a finite number of basic sequences of the component protocol roles.

Theorem 6 (Staged Composition). *If Q is a staged composition of protocols $Q_1, Q_2, \cdots, Q_n$ then we can conclude $Q \vdash \mathsf{KOHonest}(s, \mathcal{K}) \wedge \Phi \supset \mathsf{SafeNet}(s, \mathcal{K})$ if for all $RComp(\langle P_1, P_2, \cdots, P_n \rangle) \in Q$:*

1. *(Secrecy induction)*
   - $\forall i. \forall S \in BS(P_i).\quad \theta_{P_i} \wedge \mathsf{SafeNet}(s, \mathcal{K})\ [S]_X\ \mathsf{Honest}(\hat{X}) \wedge \Phi \supset \mathsf{SendsSafeMsg}(X, s, \mathcal{K})$
2. *(Precondition induction)*
   - $Q_1 \otimes Q_2 \cdots \otimes Q_n \vdash \mathsf{Start}(X) \supset \theta_{P_1}$ *and* $Q_1 \otimes Q_2 \cdots \otimes Q_n \vdash \forall i.\ \theta_{P_i}\ [P_i]_X\ \theta_{P_{i+1}}$
   - $\forall i. \forall S \in \bigcup_{j \geq i} BS(P_j).\ \theta_{P_i}[S]_X\ \theta_{P_i}.$

The secrecy induction for staged composition is the same as for sequential composition. However, the precondition induction requires additional conditions to account for the control flows corresponding to backward arcs in the graph. The technical distinction surfaces in the second bullet of the precondition induction. It states that precondition θ_{P_i} should also be preserved by basic sequences of all higher numbered components, i.e., components from which there could be backward arcs to the beginning of P_i. Again, the theorem holds if there exist any set of formulas θ_{P_i} satisfying the conditions.

6   Analysis of Kerberos

In this section we analyze Kerberos V5, which was described in section 2. The security properties of Kerberos that we prove are listed in table 2. We abbreviate the honesty assumptions by defining $\mathsf{Hon}(\hat{X}_1, \cdots, \hat{X}_n) \equiv \mathsf{Honest}(\hat{X}_1) \wedge \cdots \mathsf{Honest}(\hat{X}_n)$. The security objectives are of two types: authentication and secrecy. The authentication objectives take the form that a message of a certain format was indeed sent by some thread of the expected principal. The secrecy objectives take the form that a putative secret is known only to certain principals. For example, $AUTH_{kas}^{client}$ states that when the thread C finishes executing the **Client** role, some thread of $\hat{K}$ (the KAS) indeed sent the expected message; SEC_{akey}^{client} states that the authorization key is secret after execution of the **Client** role by C; the other security properties are analogous.

Theorem 7 (KAS Authentication). *On execution of the* **Client** *role by a principal it is guaranteed that the intended KAS indeed sent expected response assuming that the both the client and the KAS are honest. Similar result holds for a principal executing the* **TGS** *role. Formally, $KERBEROS \vdash AUTH_{kas}^{client}, AUTH_{kas}^{tgs}$*

Proof Sketch.   At a high level, the authentication proofs start by reasoning that a ciphertext could have been produced only by one of the possessors of the corresponding key. As an example, observe that in the first stage of Kerberos (described in section 2), the client decrypts a ciphertext encrypted with a key shared only between itself and the KAS ($k_{C,K}^{c \to k}$). Hence we can infer that one of them did the encryption. However, it is still not obvious that the client

Table 2. Kerberos Security Properties

$SEC_{akey} : \mathsf{Hon}(\hat{C}, \hat{K}, \hat{T}) \supset (\mathsf{Has}(X, AKey) \supset \hat{X} \in \{\hat{C}, \hat{K}, \hat{T}\})$

$SEC_{skey} : \mathsf{Hon}(\hat{C}, \hat{K}, \hat{T}, \hat{S}) \supset (\mathsf{Has}(X, SKey) \supset \hat{X} \in \{\hat{C}, \hat{K}, \hat{T}, \hat{S}\})$

$AUTH_{kas} : \exists \eta. \ \mathsf{Send}((\hat{K}, \eta), \hat{C}.E_{sym}[k_{T,K}^{t \to k}](AKey.\hat{C}).E_{sym}[k_{C,K}^{c \to k}](AKey.n_1.\hat{T}))$

$AUTH_{tgs} : \exists \eta. \ \mathsf{Send}((\hat{T}, \eta), \hat{C}.E_{sym}[k_{S,T}^{s \to t}](SKey.\hat{C}).E_{sym}[AKey](SKey.n_2.\hat{S}))$

$SEC_{akey}^{client} : [\textbf{Client}]_C \ SEC_{akey}$ $AUTH_{kas}^{client} : [\textbf{Client}]_C \ \mathsf{Hon}(\hat{C}, \hat{K}) \supset AUTH_{kas}$

$SEC_{akey}^{kas} : [\textbf{KAS}]_K \ SEC_{akey}$ $AUTH_{kas}^{tgs} : [\textbf{TGS}]_T \ \mathsf{Hon}(\hat{T}, \hat{K}) \supset \exists n_1. AUTH_{kas}$

$SEC_{akey}^{tgs} : [\textbf{TGS}]_T \ SEC_{akey}$

$\qquad\qquad\qquad\qquad\qquad$ $AUTH_{tgs}^{client} : [\textbf{Client}]_C \ \mathsf{Hon}(\hat{C}, \hat{K}, \hat{T}) \supset AUTH_{tgs}$

$SEC_{skey}^{client} : [\textbf{Client}]_C \ SEC_{skey}$ $AUTH_{tgs}^{server} : [\textbf{Server}]_S \ \mathsf{Hon}(\hat{S}, \hat{T})$

$SEC_{skey}^{tgs} : [\textbf{TGS}]_T \ SEC_{skey}$ $\qquad\qquad\quad \supset \exists n_2, AKey. AUTH_{tgs}$

---

itself did not produce the ciphertext! Some other thread of the client could have potentially created the ciphertext which could have been fed back to the thread under consideration as a reflection attack. We discount this case by observing that the client role of Kerberos never encrypts with a key of type $c \to k$. This property is an *invariant* of Kerberos proved by induction over all the protocol role programs. The **HON** rule enables us to perform this induction in the proof system. Thus, so far, we have reasoned that the encryption was done by the KAS. We again observe that any role of Kerberos which does an encryption of the specific form as in stage one also sends out a message of the intended form ($AUTH_{kas}$ in table 2). This is also an invariant of Kerberos. This concludes the proof of $AUTH_{kas}^{client}$. The proof of $AUTH_{kas}^{tgs}$ follows the same high level reasoning.   □

Theorem 8 (Authentication Key Secrecy). *On execution of the* **Client** *role by a principal, secrecy of the Authentication Key is preserved assuming that the client, the KAS and the TGS are all honest. Similar results hold for principals executing the* **KAS** *and* **TGS** *roles. Formally, KERBEROS ⊢* $SEC_{akey}^{client}, SEC_{akey}^{kas}, SEC_{akey}^{tgs}$

Proof Sketch. This theorem states a secrecy property for the Authentication Key $AKey$. Observe that in the first stage, the KAS sends out $AKey$ encrypted under two different keys - $k_{C,K}^{c \to k}$ and $k_{T,K}^{t \to k}$, and the client uses $AKey$ as an encryption key. As a first approximation we conjecture that in the entire protocol execution, $AKey$ is either protected by encryption with either of the keys in $\mathcal{K} = \{k_{C,K}^{c \to k}, k_{T,K}^{t \to k}\}$ or else used as an encryption key in messages sent to the network by honest principals. This seems like a claim to be established by induction. As a base case, we establish that the generator of $AKey$ (some thread of the KAS) satisfies the conjecture. The induction case is: whenever an honest principal decrypts a ciphertext with one of the keys in $\mathcal{K}$, it ensures that new terms generated from the decryption are re-encrypted with some key in $\mathcal{K}$ in any message sent out.

When we are reasoning from the point of view of the KAS (as in SEC_{akey}^{kas}), we already know the initial condition - that the KAS sent out $AKey$ encrypted under only these keys. However, when arguing from the point of view of the client and the TGS (as in SEC_{akey}^{client} and SEC_{akey}^{tgs}), we need to have some authentication conditions established first. These conditions are generally of the form that the KAS indeed behaved in the expected manner. Reasoning from this premise, it turns out that our initial conjecture is correct.

In the formal proof, we show that Kerberos is safe with respect to the nonce $AKey$ and the set of keys $\mathcal{K}$. The induction idea is captured, in its simplest form, by the proof rule **NET**. However, as Kerberos has a staged structure we use the staged composition theorem (theorem 6) which builds upon the rule **NET**. The core of the proof is the *secrecy induction* which is an induction over all the basic sequences of all the protocol roles. The authentication condition Φ is easily derived from the KAS Authentication theorem (theorem 7). The staged composition theorem allows us to facilitate the secrecy induction by obtaining inferences from the information flow induced by the staged structure of Kerberos in a simple and effective way. The secrecy induction is modular as the individual basic sequences are small in themselves. Secrecy of $AKey$ now follows from by the axiom **POS**.   □

Theorem 9 (TGS Authentication). *On execution of the* **Client** *role by a principal it is guaranteed that the intended TGS indeed sent the expected response assuming that the client, the KAS and the TGS are all honest. Similar result holds for a principal executing the* **Server** *role. Formally, KERBEROS $\vdash$ $AUTH_{tgs}^{client}, AUTH_{tgs}^{server}$*

Proof Sketch. The proof of $AUTH_{tgs}^{server}$ is very similar to the proof for theorem 7. The proof of $AUTH_{tgs}^{client}$ uses the secrecy property SEC_{akey}^{client} established in theorem 8 . At a high level, the client reasons that since $AKey$ is known only to $\hat{C}, \hat{K}$ and $\hat{T}$, the term $E_{sym}[AKey](SKey.n_2.\hat{S})$ - which it receives during the protocol execution - could only have been computed by one of them. Some non-trivial technical effort is required to prove that this encryption was indeed done by a thread of $\hat{T}$ and not by any thread of $\hat{C}$ or $\hat{K}$, which could have been the case if *e.g.*, there existed a reflection attack. After showing that it was indeed a thread of $\hat{T}$ who encrypted the term, we use the honesty rule to show that it indeed sent the expected response to C's message.   □

Theorem 10 (Service Key Secrecy). *On execution of the* **Client** *role by a principal, secrecy of the Service Key is preserved assuming that the client, the KAS, the TGS and the application server are all honest. Similar result holds for a principal executing the* **TGS** *role. Formally, KERBEROS $\vdash$ $SEC_{skey}^{client}, SEC_{skey}^{tgs}$*

Proof Sketch. The idea here is that the Service Key $SKey$ is protected by the key-set $\{k_{S,T}^{s \to t}, AKey\}$. The proof of this theorem follows the same high level steps as the proof of theorem 8.   □

Kerberos with PKINIT. We prove theorems for Kerberos with PKINIT [20] that are analogous to theorems 7-10. In the first stage of Kerberos with PKINIT, the KAS establishes the authorization key encrypted with a symmetric key which in turn is sent to the client encrypted with its public key. For client $\hat{C}$ and KAS $\hat{K}$ let us denote this symmetric key by $k_{C,K}^{pkinit}$. Since the structure of the rest of the protocol remains the same with respect to the level of formalization in this paper [7], we can take advantage of the PCL proofs for the symmetric key version. In particular, the proofs for the properties of Kerberos with PKINIT analogous to $AUTH_{kas}^{tgs}, AUTH_{tgs}^{client}$ and $AUTH_{tgs}^{server}$ are identical in structure to the symmetric key version. The proof of the property corresponding to $AUTH_{kas}^{client}$ is different because of the differing message formats in the first stage. There is an additional step of proving the secrecy of $k_{C,K}^{pkinit}$, after which the secrecy proofs of $AKey$ and $SKey$ are reused with only the induction over the first stage of the client and the KAS being redone.

7   Conclusion

We present formal axioms and proof rules for inductive reasoning about secrecy and prove soundness of this system over a conventional symbolic model of protocol execution. The proof system uses a *safe message* predicate to express that any secret conveyed by the message is protected by a key from a chosen list. This predicate allows us to define two additional concepts: a principal *sends safe messages* if every message it sends is safe, and the *network is safe* if every message sent by every principal is safe. Our main inductive rule for secrecy, **NET**, states that if every honest principal preserves safety of the network, then the network is safe, assuming that only honest principals have access to keys in the chosen list. The remainder of the system makes it possible to discharge assumptions used in the proof, and prove (when appropriate) that only honest principals have the chosen keys. While it might initially seem that network safety depends on the actions of malicious agents, a fundamental advantage of Protocol Composition Logic is that proofs only involve induction over protocol steps executed by honest parties.

We illustrate the expressiveness of the logic by proving properties of two protocols: A variant of the Needham-Schroeder protocol that illustrates the ability to reason about temporary secrets, and Kerberos V5. The modular nature of the secrecy and authentication proofs for Kerberos makes it possible to reuse proofs about the basic version of the protocol for the PKINIT version that uses public-key infrastructure instead of shared secret keys in the initial steps. Compositional secrecy proofs are made possible by the composition theorems developed in this paper.

In an as-yet unpublished result, we have also developed a proof system for secrecy analysis that is sound over a computational cryptographic protocol execution model. While the Kerberos proofs are similar in that proof system, we have been unable to formulate computationally sound proofs of NSL and variants.

References

1. IEEE P802.11i/D10.0. Medium Access Control (MAC) security enhancements, amendment 6 to IEEE Standard for local and metropolitan area networks part 11: Wireless Medium Access Control (MAC) and Physical Layer (PHY) specifications (April 2004)
2. Backes, M., Cervesato, I., Jaggard, A.D., Scedrov, A., Tsay, J.-K.: Cryptographically sound security proofs for basic and public-key kerberos. In: Proceedings of 11th European Symposium on Research in Computer Security (2006)
3. Bella, G., Paulson, L.C.: Kerberos version IV: Inductive analysis of the secrecy goals. In: Quisquater, J.-J., Deswarte, Y., Meadows, C., Gollmann, D. (eds.) ESORICS 1998. LNCS, vol. 1485, pp. 361–375. Springer, Heidelberg (1998)
4. Butler, F., Cervesato, I., Jaggard, A.D., Scedrov, A.: A Formal Analysis of Some Properties of Kerberos 5 Using MSR. In: Fifteenth Computer Security Foundations Workshop — CSFW-15, Cape Breton, NS, Canada, 24–26 June 2002, pp. 175–190. IEEE Computer Society Press, Los Alamitos (2002)

5. Butler, F., Cervesato, I., Jaggard, A.D., Scedrov, A.: Verifying confidentiality and authentication in kerberos 5. In: ISSS, pp. 1–24 (2003)
6. Kaufman, E.C.: Internet Key Exchange (IKEv2) Protocol, RFC 4306 (2005)
7. Cervesato, I., Jaggard, A., Scedrov, A., Tsay, J.-K., Walstad, C.: Breaking and fixing public-key kerberos. Technical report
8. Datta, A., Derek, A., Mitchell, J.C., Pavlovic, D.: Secure protocol composition. In: Proceedings of ACM Workshop on Formal Methods in Security Engineering, October
9. Datta, A., Derek, A., Mitchell, J.C., Pavlovic, D.: A derivation system for security protocols and its logical formalization. In: Proceedings of 16th IEEE Computer Security Foundations Workshop, pp. 109–125. IEEE Computer Society Press, Los Alamitos (2003)
10. Datta, A., Derek, A., Mitchell, J.C., Pavlovic, D.: Secure protocol composition. In: Proceedings of 19th Annual Conference on Mathematical Foundations of Programming Semantics, vol. 83. Electronic Notes in Theoretical Computer Science (2004)
11. Datta, A., Derek, A., Mitchell, J.C., Pavlovic, D.: A derivation system and compositional logic for security protocols. Journal of Computer Security 13, 423–482 (2005)
12. Delicata, R., Schneider, S.: Temporal rank functions for forward secrecy. In: 18th IEEE Computer Security Foundations Workshop (CSFW-18 2005), pp. 126–139. IEEE Computer Society Press, Los Alamitos (2005)
13. Delicata, R., Schneider, S.A.: Towards the rank function verification of protocols that use temporary secrets. In: WITS 2004. Proceedings of the Workshop on Issues in the Theory of Security (2004)
14. Durgin, N., Mitchell, J.C., Pavlovic, D.: A compositional logic for protocol correctness. In: Proceedings of 14th IEEE Computer Security Foundations Workshop, pp. 241–255. IEEE Computer Society Press, Los Alamitos (2001)
15. He, C., Sundararajan, M., Datta, A., Derek, A., Mitchell, J.C.: A modular correctness proof of ieee 802.11i and tls. In: ACM Conference on Computer and Communications Security, pp. 2–15 (2005)
16. Heather, J.: Strand spaces and rank functions: More than distant cousins. In: CSFW 2002. Proceedings of the 15th IEEE Computer Security Foundations Workshop, p. 104 (2002)
17. Kohl, J., Neuman, B.: The kerberos network authentication service. RFC 1510 (1991)
18. Schneider, S.: Verifying authentication protocols with csp. IEEE Transactions on Software Engineering, pp. 741–758 (1998)
19. Thayer, F.J., Herzog, J.C., Guttman, J.D.: Strand spaces: Proving security protocols correct. Journal of Computer Security 7(1) (1999)
20. Zhu, L., Tung, B.: Public key cryptography for initial authentication in kerberos, Internet Draft (2006)

A Type-Theoretic Framework for Formal Reasoning with Different Logical Foundations

Zhaohui Luo*

Dept of Computer Science, Royal Holloway, Univ of London
Egham, Surrey TW20 0EX, U.K.
zhaohui@cs.rhul.ac.uk

Abstract. A type-theoretic framework for formal reasoning with different logical foundations is introduced and studied. With logic-enriched type theories formulated in a logical framework, it allows various logical systems such as classical logic as well as intuitionistic logic to be used effectively alongside inductive data types and type universes. This provides an adequate basis for wider applications of type theory based theorem proving technology. Two notions of set are introduced in the framework and used in two case studies of classical reasoning: a predicative one in the formalisation of Weyl's predicative mathematics and an impredicative one in the verification of security protocols.

1 Introduction

Dependent type theories, or type theories for short, are powerful calculi for logical reasoning that provide solid foundations for the associated theorem proving technology as implemented in various 'proof assistants'. These type theories include Martin-Löf's predicative type theory [NPS90, ML84], as implemented in ALF/Agda [MN94, Agd00] and NuPRL [C+86], and the impredicative type theories [CH88, Luo94], as implemented in Coq [Coq04] and Lego/Plastic [LP92, CL01]. The proof assistants have been successfully used in formalisation of mathematics (e.g., the formalisations in Coq of the four-colour theorem [Gon05]) and in reasoning about programs (e.g., the analysis of security protocols).

The current type theories as found in the proof assistants are all based on intuitionistic logic. As a consequence, the type theory based proof assistants are so far mainly used for constructive reasoning. Examples that require or use other methods of reasoning, say classical reasoning, would have to be done by 'extending' the underlying type theory with classical laws by brute force and praying for such an extension to be OK.

We believe that the type theory based theorem proving technology is not (and should not be) limited to constructive reasoning. In particular, it should adequately support classical reasoning as well as constructive reasoning. To this end, what one needs is a type-theoretic framework that supports the use of a

---

* This work is partially supported by the following research grants: UK EPSRC grant GR/R84092, Leverhulme Trust grant F/07 537/AA and EU TYPES grant 510996.

M. Okada and I. Satoh (Eds.): ASIAN 2006, LNCS 4435, pp. 214–222, 2007.
© Springer-Verlag Berlin Heidelberg 2007

wider class of logical systems and, at the same time, keeps the power of type theory in formal reasoning such as inductive reasoning based on inductive types.

In this paper, we introduce such a type-theoretic framework where logic-enriched type theories are formulated in a logical framework such as LF [Luo94] and PAL$^+$ [Luo03]. Logic-enriched type theories with intuitionistic logic have been proposed by Aczel and Gambino in studying type-theoretic interpretations of constructive set theory [AG02, GA06]. They are studied here from the angle of supporting formal reasoning with different logical foundations. We show that it is possible to provide a uniform framework so that type theories can be formulated properly to support different methods of reasoning. The structure of our framework promotes a complete separation between logical propositions and data types. It provides an adequate support to classical inference as well as intuitionistic inference, in the presence of inductive types and type universes.

Two notions of set are introduced in the type-theoretic framework: a predicative one and an impredicative one. They are used in two case studies: one in the formalisation of Weyl's predicative mathematics [Wey18, AL06] and the other in the formalisation and analysis of security protocols. Both case studies use classical reasoning – we have chosen to do so partly because how to use type theory in constructive reasoning has been extensively studied and partly because we want to show how classical logic can be employed in a type-theoretic setting.

The proof assistant Plastic [CL01] has been extended (in an easy and straightforward way) by Paul Callaghan to implement the type-theoretic framework as described in this paper. The case studies have been done in the extended Plastic and help to demonstrate that type theory and the associated proof assistants can be used to support formal reasoning with different logical foundations.

2 Logic-Enriched Type Theories in a Logical Framework

The type-theoretic framework formulates logic-enriched type theories (LTTs for short) in a logical framework. It consists of two parts, *the part of logical propositions* and *the part of data types*. Both parts are formulated in a logical framework and linked by the induction rules (see below).

We start with the logical framework LF [Luo94] or PAL$^+$ [Luo03], where the kind *Type* represents the world of types. Now, we extend the logical framework with a new kind *Prop* that stands for the world of logical propositions and, for every $P : Prop$, a kind $Prf(P)$ of proofs of P.

The logic of an LTT is specified in *Prop* by declaring constants for the logical operators and the associated rules (as logics are introduced in Edinburgh LF [HHP93]). The data types are introduced in *Type* as in type theories such as Martin-Löf's type theory [NPS90] and UTT [Luo94]. Different LTTs can be formulated in the framework for formal reasoning with different logical foundations. Instead of considering LTTs in general, we shall present and study a typical example – the LTT with the classical first-order logic, abbreviated as LTT_1, to illustrate how an LTT is formulated in our type-theoretic framework.

2.1   LTT$_1$: **An Example**

The system LTT$_1$ consists of the classical first-order logic, the inductive data types, and type universes. Each of the components is described below.

Logic of LTT$_1$. The logical operators such as $\supset$, $\neg$ and $\forall$ are introduced by declaring as constants the operators and the direct proofs of the associated inference rules. For instance, for universal quantification $\forall$, we declare (where we write '$f[a_1, ..., a_n]$' for applications and '$f[x_1, ..., x_n] : A$ where $x_i : A_i$' for $f : (x_1{:}A_1, ..., x_n{:}A_n)A$):

$$\forall[A, P] : Prop, \quad \forall_I[A, P, f] : Prf(\forall[A, P]) \quad \textbf{and} \quad \forall_E[A, P, a, p] : Prf(P[a])$$

where $A : Type$, $P[x{:}A] : Prop$, $f[x{:}A] : Prf(P[x])$ and $p : Prf(\forall[A, P])$.

Note that $\forall$ can only quantify over types; that is, for a formula $\forall[A, P]$, or $\forall x{:}A, P[x]$ in the usual notation, A must be a type (of kind $Type$). Since $Prop$ is not a type (it is a kind), one cannot form a proposition by quantifying over $Prop$. Higher-order logical quantifications such as $\forall X{:}Prop.X$, as found in impredicative type theories, are not allowed. Similarly, since propositions are not types ($Prf(P)$ is a kind, not a type), one cannot quantify over propositions, either.

As another example, we declare the classical negation operator $\neg P : Prop$ for $P : Prop$ and the corresponding double negation rule $DN[P, p] : Prf(P)$ where $P : Prop$ and $p : Prf(\neg\neg P)$]. Other logical operators can be introduced in a similar way or defined as usual. For instance, an equality operator can be introduced to form propositions $a =_A b$, for $A : Type$ and $a, b : A$.

Inductive data types in LTT$_1$. The system LTT$_1$ (and every LTT) contains (some or all of) the inductive types as found in Martin-Löf's type theory [NPS90] or UTT [Luo94], which include those of natural numbers, dependent pairs, lists, trees, ordinals, etc. For example, the type $N : Type$ of natural numbers can be introduced by first declaring its constructors $0 : N$ and $s[n] : N$ where $n : N$, and then its elimination operator $\mathcal{E}_T[C, c, f, n] : C[n]$, for $C[n] : Type$ with $n : N$, and the associated computation rules

$$\mathcal{E}_T[C, c, f, 0] = c \quad : \quad C[0]$$
$$\mathcal{E}_T[C, c, f, s[n]] = f[n, \mathcal{E}_T[C, c, f, n]] \quad : \quad C[s[n]]$$

For each inductive type, there is an associated *induction rule* for proving properties of the objects of that type. For example, the induction rule for N is

$$\mathcal{E}_P[P, c, f, n] : P[n] \quad for\ P[n] : Prop\ [n : N]$$

Note that the elimination operator over types, $\mathcal{E}_T$, has associated computational rules, while the elimination operator over propositions, $\mathcal{E}_P$, does not.

The induction rules are crucial in connecting the world of logical propositions (formally represented by $Prop$) and that of the data types (formally represented by $Type$). Quantifications over types allow one to form propositions to express logical properties of data and the induction rules to prove those properties.

Type universes in LTT_1. The system LTT_1 (and every LTT) may contain type universes, types consisting of (names of) types as objects. For example, a universe of 'small types' can be introduced as

$$type : Type \quad \text{and} \quad T[x] : Type \quad [x : type].$$

Some of the inductive types have names in a type universe. For example, we can have nat as a name of N in $type$ by declaring $nat : type$ and $T[nat] = N : Type$. The general way of introducing type universes can be found in [ML84] and see, e.g., [Luo94] for universes containing inductive types generated by schemata.

We remark that, if we have introduced a type universe that contains the names of N and $\emptyset$ (the empty type), we can prove Peano's fourth axiom for natural numbers $(\forall x{:}N.(s[x] \neq_N 0))$ internally in the type-theoretic framework. This is similar to Martin-Löf's type theory, where Peano's fourth axiom is not provable internally without a type universe [Smi88].

Logical consistency of LTT_1. The system LTT_1 is logically consistent in the sense that there are unprovable propositions. If one is not satisfied with the 'simple minded consistency' [ML84], a meta-mathematical consistency can be proved – it can be shown that LTT_1 is relatively consistent w.r.t. ZF.

Theorem 1 (consistency). *The type system* LTT_1 *is logically consistent.*

Proof sketch. Let T be Martin-Löf's intensional type theory extended with Excluded Middle (i.e., extending it with assumed proofs of $A + (A \to \emptyset)$ for all types A). Then T is logically consistent w.r.t. ZF. Now, consider the mapping $\sharp : \text{LTT}_1 \to T$ that maps the types and propositions of LTT_1 to types of T so that $A^\sharp = A$ for $A : Type$ and, e.g., $\forall[A, P]^\sharp = \Pi[A^\sharp, P^\sharp]$ and $(\neg P)^\sharp = P^\sharp \to \emptyset$. Then, by proving a more general lemma by induction, we can show that if $\Gamma \vdash a : A$ in LTT_1, then $\Gamma^\sharp \vdash a^\sharp : A^\sharp$ in T. The logical consistency follows. □

Although there are other ways to prove the meta-mathematical consistency, the above proof sketch raises an interesting question one may ask: if Martin-Löf's type theory extended with a classical law (say Excluded Middle) is consistent, why does one prefer to use LTT_1 rather than such an extension directly?

One of the reasons for such a preference is that the LTT approach preserves the meaning-theoretic understanding of types as consisting of their canonical objects (e.g., N consists of zero and the successors). Such an *adequacy property* would be destroyed by a direct extension of Martin-Löf's type theory with a classical law, where every inductive type contains (infinitely many) non-canonical objects. Therefore, in this sense, it is inadequate to introduce classical laws directly to Martin-Löf's type theory or other type theories.

In our type-theoretic framework, there is a clear distinction between logical propositions and data types. For example, the classical law in LTT_1 does not affect the data types such as N. It hence provides an adequate treatment of classical reasoning on the one hand and a clean meaning-theoretic understanding of the inductive types on the other.

This clear separation between logical propositions and data types is an important salient feature of the type-theoretic framework in general. In Martin-Löf's type theory, for example, types and propositions are identified. The author has argued, for instance in the development of ECC/UTT [Luo94] as implemented in Lego/Plastic and the current version of Coq[1], that it is unnatural to identify logical propositions with data types and there should be a clear distinction between the two. This philosophical idea was behind the development of ECC/UTT, where data types are not propositions, although logical propositions are types.

Logic-enriched type theories, and hence our framework as presented in this paper, have gone one step further – there is a complete separation between propositions and types. Logical propositions and their totality *Prop* are not regarded as types. This has led to a more flexible treatment of logics in our framework.

2.2   Implementation

The type-theoretic framework has been implemented by Callaghan by extending the proof assistant Plastic [CL01]. Plastic implements the logical framework LF. The extension is to add the kind *Prop* and the operator *Prf*, as described at the beginning of this section. Logical operators such as those of LTT_1 are introduced by the user. Plastic already supports the inductive types in the kind *Type*. However, it does not automatically generate the induction rules (represented above by $\mathcal{E}_P$ for N) which, at the moment, are entered by the user (this is possible because $\mathcal{E}_P$ does not have associated computation rules.) We should also mention that Plastic supports adding computation rules of certain form and this allows one to add universes and the associated computation rules. The system LTT_1 has been completely implemented in Plastic and so have the notions of set and the case studies to be described in the following two sections.

3   Typed Sets

When we consider sets in our type-theoretic framework, the objects of a set are all 'similar' in the sense that every set is a *typed set*. In other words, every set has a *base type* from which every element of the set comes. For instance, a set with N as base type contains only natural numbers as its elements. We believe that such a notion of typed set is natural and much closer to the practice of everyday mathematical reasoning than that in the traditional set theory where there is no distinction between types. Sometimes, mathematicians use the word 'category' for what we call types and consider sets with elements of the same category (see, e.g., [Wey18]). Here, types are formal representations of categories.

In the following, we consider two notions of (typed) set: an impredicative notion and a predicative notion.

---

[1] The current type structure of Coq (version 8.0) [Coq04], after the universe Set becomes predicative, is very similar to (if not exactly the same as) that of ECC/UTT.

Impredicative notion of set. Impredicative sets can be introduced as follows.

- $Set[A{:}Type] : Type$ ($Set[A]$ is the type of sets with base type A.)
- $set[A{:}Type, P[x{:}A]{:}Prop] : Set[A]$ (Informally, $set[A, P]$ is $\{\, x : A \mid P[x] \,\}$.)
- $in[A{:}Type, a{:}A, S{:}Set[A]] : Prop$ (Informally, $in[A, a, S]$ is $a \in S$.)
- $in[A, a, set[A, P]] = P[a] : Prop$ (Computational equality)

Note that this notion of set is impredicative. For example, the powerset of S : $Set[A]$ can be defined as $\{\, S'{:}Set[A] \mid \forall x{:}A.\, x \in S' \supset x \in S \,\}$ of type $Set[Set[A]]$.

Predicative notion of set. The notion of predicativity has been studied by many people, most notably by Feferman in a series of papers, including [Fef05]. Intuitively, the definition of a set $\{\, x \mid p(x) \,\}$ is predicative if the predicate $p(x)$ does not involve any quantification over the totality that contains the entity being defined. If the set-forming predicate p does not involve any quantification over sets at all, then the definition of the set is predicative.

In our type-theoretic framework, predicative sets can be introduced by first introducing a propositional universe of small propositions:

$$prop : Prop, \qquad V[p : prop] : Prop$$

Intuitively, a small proposition contains only quantifications over small types (with names in $type$). This can be seen from the quantifier rules for $prop$:

$$\bar{\forall}[a, p] : prop \quad [a{:}type,\ p[x{:}T[a]] : prop]$$
$$V[\bar{\forall}[a, p]] = \forall[T[a], [x{:}T[a]]V[p[x]]] : Prop$$

where $p[x]$ must be a small proposition for any object x in the small type a.

Formally, predicative sets can be introduced as follows:

- $Set[a{:}type] : Type$ ($Set[a]$ is a type if a is a small type in universe $type$.)
- $set[a{:}type, p[x{:}T[a]]{:}prop] : Set[a]$ (Informally, p in $\{\, x : A \mid p[x] \,\}$ must be a small propositional function.)
- $in[a{:}type, x{:}T[a], S{:}Set[a]] : prop$ (Informally, $x \in S$ is a small proposition.)
- $in[a, x, set[a, p]] = p[x] : prop$ (Computational equality)

Note that a type of sets is not a small type. Therefore, quantification over sets is not allowed when stating a set-forming condition.

Remark 1. Aczel and Gambino [AG02, GA06] have considered a type universe **P** of small propositions in the world of types (formally, **P** : $Type$). Such a universe has played an important role in their study of the type-theoretic interpretation of constructive set theory. However, it seems that this has the effect of putting logical propositions directly 'back' to the world of types. In our case, the propositional universe $prop$ is of kind $Prop$, not of kind $Type$. □

We argue that the notions of set introduced above are adequate in supporting '*mathematical pluralism*'.[2] With these notions, the type-theoretic framework can be used to formalise, in the classical setting, the ordinary (classical and impredicative) mathematics and Weyl's predicative mathematics and, in the intuitionistic setting, the predicative and impredicative constructive mathematics.

---

[2] The philosophical view of mathematical pluralism is to be elaborated elsewhere.

4   Case Studies

Formalisation of Weyl's predicative mathematics. As is known, the ordinary mathematics is *impredicative* in the sense that it allows impredicative
definitions that some people might regard as 'circular' and hence problematic.
Such people would believe that the so-called *predicative* mathematics is safer,
where impredicative or circular definitions are regarded as illegal. For instance,
in the early quarter of the last century, the mathematician Hermann Weyl has
developed a predicative treatment of the calculus (in classical logic) [Wey18],
which has been studied and further developed by Feferman and others [Fef05].

The formalisation of Weyl's work [Wey18] has been done in the type-theoretic
framework (more specifically, in LTT_1 with predicative sets) in Plastic [AL06].

Formalisation and analysis of security protocols. Security protocols have
been extensively studied in the last two to three decades. Besides other interesting research, theorem provers have been used to formalise security protocols and
prove their properties. For instance, Paulson has studied the 'inductive approach'
[Pau98] in Isabelle [Pau94] to verify properties of security protocols.

As a case study of classical impredicative reasoning in the type-theoretic
framework, we have formalised in Plastic several security protocols in LTT_1
with impredicative sets. The examples include simple protocols such as the
Needham-Schroeder public-key protocol [NS78, Low96] and the Yahalom protocol [BAN89, Pau99]. Our formalisation has followed Paulson's inductive approach closely, in order to examine how well the power of inductive reasoning
in the type-theoretic framework matches that in Isabelle. Our experience shows
that the answer is positive, although more automation in some cases would be
desirable. In our formalisation, agents, messages and events are all modelled as
inductive types (rather than as inductive sets as in Isabelle). The operations
such as *parts*, *analz* and *synth* are defined as maps between sets of messages. A
protocol is then modelled as a set of traces (a set of lists of events). One can then
show that various properties are satisfied by the protocol concerned, including
the secrecy properties such as the session key secrecy theorem.

5   Concluding Remarks on Future Work

Future work includes comparative studies with other existing logical systems and
the associated theorem proving technology. For example, it would be interesting
to compare the predicative notion of set with that studied by Feferman and
others [Fef00, Sim99] and to consider a comparison with that of Martin-Löf's
type theory [NPS90, ML84] to study the relationship between the notion of
predicative set and that of predicative type.

Acknowledgements. Thanks go to Peter Aczel for his comments during his
visit to Royal Holloway, Robin Adams for discussions during our joint work
on formalisation of Weyl's predicative mathematics and Paul Callaghan for his
efforts in extending Plastic to implement the type-theoretic framework.

References

[AG02]   Aczel, P., Gambino, N.: Collection principles in dependent type theory. In: Callaghan, P., Luo, Z., McKinna, J., Pollack, R. (eds.) TYPES 2000. LNCS, vol. 2277, Springer, Heidelberg (2002)

[Agd00]   Agda proof assistant (2000), http://www.cs.chalmers.se/~catarina/agda

[AL06]   Adams, R., Luo, Z.: Weyl's predicative classical mathematics as a logic-enriched type theory. In: TYPES 2006 (2006) (submitted)

[BAN89]   Burrows, M., Abadi, M., Needham, R.: A logic of authentication. Proc. of the Royal Society of London 426, 233–271 (1989)

[C+86]   Constable, R., et al.: Implementing Mathematics with the NuPRL Proof Development System. Prentice-Hall, Englewood Cliffs (1986)

[CH88]   Coquand, T., Huet, G.: The calculus of constructions. Information and Computation 76(2/3) (1988)

[CL01]   Callaghan, P.C., Luo, Z.: An implementation of typed LF with coercive subtyping and universes. J. of Automated Reasoning 27(1), 3–27 (2001)

[Coq04]   The Coq Development Team. The Coq Proof Assistant Reference Manual (Version 8.0), INRIA (2004)

[Fef00]   Feferman, S.: The significance of Hermann Weyl's Das Kontinuum. In: Hendricks, V., et al. (eds.) Proof Theory (2000)

[Fef05]   Feferman, S.: Predicativity. In: Shapiro, S. (ed.) The Oxford Handbook of Philosophy of Mathematics and Logic, Oxford Univ Press, Oxford (2005)

[GA06]   Gambino, N., Aczel, P.: The generalised type-theoretic interpretation of constructive set theory. J. of Symbolic Logic 71(1), 67–103 (2006)

[Gon05]   Gonthier, G.: A computer checked proof of the four colour theorem (2005)

[HHP93]   Harper, R., Honsell, F., Plotkin, G.: A framework for defining logics. Journal of the Association for Computing Machinery 40(1), 143–184 (1993)

[Low96]   Lowe, G.: Breaking and fixing the Needham-Schroeder public-key protocol using CSP and FDR. In: Margaria, T., Steffen, B. (eds.) TACAS 1996. LNCS, vol. 1055, Springer, Heidelberg (1996)

[LP92]   Luo, Z., Pollack, R.: LEGO Proof Development System: User's Manual. LFCS Report ECS-LFCS-92-211, Dept of Computer Science, Univ of Edinburgh (1992)

[Luo94]   Luo, Z.: Computation and Reasoning: A Type Theory for Computer Science. Oxford University Press, Oxford (1994)

[Luo03]   Luo, Z.: PAL$^+$: a lambda-free logical framework. Journal of Functional Programming 13(2), 317–338 (2003)

[ML84]   Martin-Löf, P.: Intuitionistic Type Theory. Bibliopolis (1984)

[MN94]   Magnusson, L., Nordström, B.: The ALF proof editor and its proof engine. In: Barendregt, H., Nipkow, T. (eds.) TYPES 1993. LNCS, vol. 806, Springer, Heidelberg (1994)

[NPS90]   Nordström, B., Petersson, K., Smith, J.: Programming in Martin-Löf's Type Theory: An Introduction. Oxford University Press, Oxford (1990)

[NS78]   Needham, R., Schroeder, M.: Using encryption for authentication in large networks of computers. Comm. of the ACM 21(12), 993–999 (1978)

[Pau94]   Paulson, L.: Isabelle: a generic theorem prover. LNCS, vol. 828. Springer, Heidelberg (1994)

[Pau98]   Paulson, L.: The inductive approach to verifying cryptographic protocols. Journal of Computer Security 6, 85–128 (1998)

[Pau99]   Paulson, L.: Proving security protocols correct. In: LICS (1999)

[Sim99]   Simpson, S.: Subsystems of Second-Order Arithmetic. Springer, Heidelberg (1999)

[Smi88]   Smith, J.: The independence of Peano's fourth axiom from Martin-Löf's type theory without universes. Journal of Symbolic Logic 53(3) (1988)

[Wey18]   Weyl, H.: The Continuum: a critical examination of the foundation of analysis. Dover Publ., (English translation of Das Kontinuum, 1918) (1994)

On Completeness of Logical Relations for Monadic Types[*]

Sławomir Lasota[1],[**], David Nowak[2], and Yu Zhang[3],[***]

[1] Institute of Informatics, Warsaw University, Warszawa, Poland
[2] RCIS, National Institute of Advanced Industrial Science and Technology, Tokyo, Japan
[3] Project Everest, INRIA Sophia-Antipolis, France

Abstract. Software security can be ensured by specifying and verifying security properties of software using formal methods with strong theoretical bases. In particular, programs can be modeled in the framework of lambda-calculi, and interesting properties can be expressed formally by contextual equivalence (a.k.a. observational equivalence). Furthermore, imperative features, which exist in most real-life software, can be nicely expressed in the so-called computational lambda-calculus. Contextual equivalence is difficult to prove directly, but we can often use logical relations as a tool to establish it in lambda-calculi. We have already defined logical relations for the computational lambda-calculus in previous work. We devote this paper to the study of their completeness w.r.t. contextual equivalence in the computational lambda-calculus.

1 Introduction

Contextual Equivalence. Two programs are contextually equivalent (a.k.a. observationally equivalent) if they have the same observable behavior, i.e. an outsider cannot distinguish them. Interesting properties of programs can be expressed using the notion of contextual equivalence. For example, to prove that a program does not leak a secret, such as the secret key used by an ATM to communicate with the bank, it is sufficient to prove that if we change the secret, the observable behavior will not change [13,3,14]: whatever experiment a customer makes with the ATM, he or she cannot guess information about the secret key by observing the reaction of the ATM. Another example is to specify functional properties by contextual equivalence. For example, if sorted is a function which checks that a list is sorted and sort is a function which sorts a list, then, for all list l, you want the expression sorted(sort(l)) to be contextually equivalent to the expression true. Finally, in the context of parameterized verification, contextual equivalence allows the verification for all instantiations of the parameter to be reduced to the verification for a finite number of instantiations (See e.g. [5] where logical relations are one of the essential ingredients).

[*] Partially supported by the RNTL project Prouvé, the ACI Sécurité Informatique Rossignol, the ACI jeunes chercheurs "Sécurité informatique, protocoles cryptographiques et détection d'intrusions", and the ACI Cryptologie "PSI-Robuste".

[**] Partially supported by the Polish KBN grant No. 4 T11C 042 25 and by the European Community Research Training Network *Games*. This work was performed in part during the author's stay at LSV.

[***] This work was mainly done when the author was a PhD student under an MENRT grant on ACI Cryptologie funding, École Doctorale Sciences Pratiques (Cachan).

M. Okada and I. Satoh (Eds.): ASIAN 2006, LNCS 4435, pp. 223–230, 2007.
© Springer-Verlag Berlin Heidelberg 2007

Logical Relations. While contextual equivalence is difficult to prove directly because of the universal quantification over contexts, logical relations [11,6] are powerful tools that allow us to deduce contextual equivalence in typed λ-calculi. With the aid of the so-called Basic Lemma, one can easily prove that logical relations are sound w.r.t. contextual equivalence. However, completeness of logical relations is much more difficult to achieve: usually we can only show the completeness of logical relations for types up to first order.

The computational λ-calculus [8] has proved useful to define various notions of computations on top of the λ-calculus, using monadic types. Logical relations for monadic types can be derived by the construction defined in [2] where soundness of logical relations is guaranteed. However, monadic types introduce new difficulties. In particular, contextual equivalence becomes subtler due to the different semantics of different monads: equivalent programs in one monad are not necessarily equivalent in another! This accordingly makes completeness of logical relations more difficult to achieve in the computational λ-calculus. In particular the usual proofs of completeness up to first order do not go through.

Contributions. We propose in this paper a notion of contextual equivalence for the computational λ-calculus. Logical relations for this language are defined according to the general derivation in [2]. We then explore the completeness and we prove that for the partial computation monad, the exception monad and the state transformer monad, logical relations are still complete up to first-order types. In the case of the non-determinism monad, we need to restrict ourselves to a subset of first-order types.

Not like previous work on using logical relations to study contextual equivalence in models with computational effects [12,10,9], most of which focus on computations with local states, our work in this paper is based on a more general framework for describing computations, namely the computational λ-calculus. In particular, very different forms of computations like non-determinism are studied, not just those for local states.

Note that all proofs that are omitted in this short paper, can be found in the full version [4].

2   Logical Relations for the Simply Typed λ-Calculus

Let $\lambda^\rightarrow$ be a simple version of typed λ-calculus with only base types b (booleans, integers, etc.) and function types $\tau \rightarrow \tau'$. Terms consist of variables, constants, abstractions and applications. Notations and typing rules are as usual. We consider the set theoretical semantics of $\lambda^\rightarrow$. A Γ-*environment* ρ is a map such that, for every $x : \tau$ in Γ, $\rho(x)$ is an element of $[\![\tau]\!]$. Let t be a term such that $\Gamma \vdash t : \tau$ is derivable. The denotation of t, w.r.t. a Γ-environment ρ, is given as usual by an element $[\![t]\!]\rho$ of $[\![\tau]\!]$. We write $[\![t]\!]$ instead of $[\![t]\!]\rho$ when ρ is irrelevant, e.g., when t is a closed term. When given a value $a \in [\![\tau]\!]$, we say that it is *definable* if and only if there exists a closed term t such that $\vdash t : \tau$ is derivable and $a = [\![t]\!]$.

Let **Obs** be a subset of base types, called *observation types*, such as booleans, integers, etc. A *context* $\mathbb{C}$ is a term such that $x : \tau \vdash \mathbb{C} : o$ is derivable, where o is an observation type. We spell the standard notion of *contextual equivalence* in a denotational setting: two elements a_1 and a_2 of $[\![\tau]\!]$, are *contextually equivalent* (written as

$a_1 \approx_\tau a_2$), if and only if for any context $\mathbb{C}$ such that $x : \tau \vdash \mathbb{C} : o$ ($o \in \textbf{Obs}$) is derivable, $[\![\mathbb{C}]\!][x := a_1] = [\![\mathbb{C}]\!][x := a_2]$. We say that two closed terms t_1 and t_2 of the same type τ are *contextually equivalent* whenever $[\![t_1]\!] \approx_\tau [\![t_2]\!]$. We also define a relation $\sim_\tau$: for every pair of values $a_1, a_2 \in [\![\tau]\!]$, $a_1 \sim_\tau a_2$ if and only if a_1, a_2 are definable and $a_1 \approx_\tau a_2$.

Essentially, a (binary) *logical relation* [6] is a family $(\mathcal{R}_\tau)_{\tau \text{ type}}$ of relations, one for each type τ, on $[\![\tau]\!]$ such that related functions map related arguments to related results. More formally, it is a family $(\mathcal{R}_\tau)_{\tau \text{ type}}$ of relations such that for every $f_1, f_2 \in [\![\tau \to \tau']\!]$,

$$f_1 \, \mathcal{R}_{\tau \to \tau'} \, f_2 \iff \forall a_1, a_2 \in [\![\tau]\!] . \, a_1 \, \mathcal{R}_\tau \, a_2 \implies f_1(a_1) \, \mathcal{R}_{\tau'} \, f_2(a_2)$$

There is no constraint on relations at base types. In $\lambda^\to$, once the relations at base types are fixed, the above condition forces $(\mathcal{R}_\tau)_{\tau \text{ type}}$ to be uniquely determined by induction on types.

A so-called *Basic Lemma* comes along with logical relations since Plotkin's work [11]. It states that if $\Gamma \vdash t : \tau$ is derivable, ρ_1, ρ_2 are two related Γ-environments, and every constant is related to itself, then $[\![t]\!]\rho_1 \, \mathcal{R}_\tau \, [\![t]\!]\rho_2$. Here two Γ-environments ρ_1, ρ_2 are related by the logical relation, if and only if $\rho_1(x) \, \mathcal{R}_\tau \, \rho_2(x)$ for every $x : \tau$ in Γ. Basic Lemma is crucial for proving various properties using logical relations [6]. In the case of establishing contextual equivalence, it implies that, for every logical relation $(\mathcal{R}_\tau)_{\tau \text{ type}}$ such that $\mathcal{R}_o$ is the equality for every observation type o, logically related values are necessarily contextually equivalent, i.e., $\mathcal{R}_\tau \subseteq \approx_\tau$ for any type τ.

Completeness states the inverse: a logical relation $(\mathcal{R}_\tau)_{\tau \text{ type}}$ is *complete* if every contextually equivalent values are related by this logical relation, i.e., $\approx_\tau \subseteq \mathcal{R}_\tau$ for every type τ. Completeness for logical relations is hard to achieve, even in a simple version of λ-calculus like $\lambda^\to$. Usually we are only able to prove completeness for types up to first order (the order of types is defined inductively: $\textbf{ord}(b) = 0$ for any base type b; $\textbf{ord}(\tau \to \tau') = \max(\textbf{ord}(\tau) + 1, \textbf{ord}(\tau'))$ for function types). The following proposition states the completeness of logical relations in $\lambda^\to$, for types up to first order:

Proposition 1. *There exists a logical relation* $(\mathcal{R}_\tau)_{\tau \text{ type}}$ *for* $\lambda^\to$, *with partial equality on observation types, such that if* $\vdash t_1 : \tau$ *and* $\vdash t_2 : \tau$ *are derivable, for any type* τ *up to first order,* $t_1 \approx_\tau t_2 \implies [\![t_1]\!] \, \mathcal{R}_\tau \, [\![t_2]\!]$.

3 Logical Relations for the Computational λ-Calculus

3.1 The Computational λ-Calculus λ_{Comp}

Moggi's computational λ-calculus has proved a nice framework for expressing various forms of side effects (exceptions, non-determinism, etc.) [8]. The computational λ-calculus, denoted by λ_{Comp}, extends $\lambda^\to$ with a unary type constructor T: $\mathsf{T}\tau$ denotes the type of computations which return values of type τ. It also introduces two extra term constructs $\mathtt{val}(t)$ and $\mathtt{let}\ x \Leftarrow t\ \mathtt{in}\ t'$, representing respectively the trivial computation and the sequential computation, with the typing rules:

$$\frac{\Gamma \vdash t : \tau}{\Gamma \vdash \mathtt{val}(t) : \mathsf{T}\tau} \qquad\qquad \frac{\Gamma \vdash t : \mathsf{T}\tau \quad \Gamma, x : \tau \vdash t' : \mathsf{T}\tau'}{\Gamma \vdash \mathtt{let}\ x \Leftarrow t\ \mathtt{in}\ t' : \mathsf{T}\tau'}$$

Moggi also builds a categorical model for the computational λ-calculus, using the notion of monads [8]. We shall focus on Moggi's monads defined over the category Set of sets and functions. For instance, the non-determinism monad is defined by $[\![T\tau]\!] = \mathbb{P}_{\text{fin}}([\![\tau]\!])$, with

$$[\![\text{val}(t)]\!]\rho = \{[\![t]\!]\rho\},$$

$$[\![\text{let } x \Leftarrow t_1 \text{ in } t_2]\!]\rho = \bigcup_{a \in [\![t_1]\!]\rho} [\![t_2]\!]\rho[x := a].$$

In the rest of this paper, we shall restrict ourselves to four concrete monads: partial computations, exceptions, state transformers and non-determinism. Definitions of these monads can be found in [8,4]. We write λ_{Comp}^{PESN} for the particular version of λ_{Comp} where the monad is restricted to be one of these four monads.

The computational λ-calculus is strongly normalizing [1]. In fact, every term of a monadic type can be written in the following βc-normal-η-long form, w.r.t. the βc-reduction rules and η-equalities in [1] (see the proof in the full version [4]):

$$\text{let } x_1 \Leftarrow d_1 u_{11} \cdots u_{1k_1} \text{ in } \cdots \text{let } x_n \Leftarrow d_n u_{n1} \cdots u_{nk_n} \text{ in } \text{val}(u),$$

where $n = 0, 1, 2, \ldots$, every d_i ($1 \leq i \leq n$) is either a constant or a variable, u and u_{ij} ($1 \leq i \leq n, 1 \leq j \leq k_j$) are all βc-normal terms or βc-normal-η-long terms (of monadic types).

As argued in [3], the standard notion of contextual equivalence does not fit in the setting of the computational λ-calculus. In order to define contextual equivalence for λ_{Comp}, we have to consider contexts $\mathbb{C}$ of type To (o is an observation type), not of type o. Indeed, contexts should be allowed to do some computations: if they were of type o, they could only return values. In particular, a context $\mathbb{C}$ such that $x : T\tau \vdash \mathbb{C} : o$ is derivable, meant to observe computations of type τ, cannot observe anything, because the typing rule for the let construct only allows us to use computations to build other computations, never values. Taking this into account, we get the following definition:

Definition 1 (Contextual equivalence for λ_{Comp}). *In λ_{Comp}, two values $a_1, a_2 \in [\![\tau]\!]$ are* contextually equivalent, *written as $a_1 \approx_\tau a_2$, if and only if, for all observable types $o \in \mathbf{Obs}$ and contexts $\mathbb{C}$ such that $x : \tau \vdash \mathbb{C} : To$ is derivable, $[\![\mathbb{C}]\!][x := a_1] = [\![\mathbb{C}]\!][x := a_2]$. Two closed terms t_1 and t_2 of type τ are contextually equivalent if and only if $[\![t_1]\!] \approx_\tau [\![t_2]\!]$. We use the same notation*

3.2 Logical Relations for λ_{Comp}

A uniform framework for defining logical relations relies on the categorical notion of subscones [7], and a natural extension of logical relations able to deal with monadic types was introduced in [2]. The construction consists in lifting the CCC structure and the strong monad from the categorical model to the subscone. We reformulate this construction in the category Set. The subscone is the category whose objects are binary relations $(A, B, R \subseteq A \times B)$ where A and B are sets; and a morphism between two objects $(A, B, R \subseteq A \times B)$ and $(A', B', R' \subseteq A' \times B')$ is a pair of functions $(f : A \to A', g : B \to B')$ preserving relations, i.e. $a \, R \, b \Rightarrow f(a) \, R' \, g(b)$.

The lifting of the CCC structure gives rise to the standard logical relations given in Section 2 and the lifting of the strong monad will give rise to relations for monadic types. We write $\tilde{T}$ for the lifting of the strong monad T. Given a relation $R \subseteq A \times B$ and two computations $a \in TA$ and $b \in TB$, $(a, b) \in \tilde{T}(R)$ if and only if there exists a computation $c \in T(R)$ (i.e. c computes pairs in R) such that $a = T\pi_1(c)$ and $b = T\pi_2(c)$. The standard definition of logical relation for the simply typed λ-calculus $(c_1, c_2) \in \mathcal{R}_{T\tau} \iff (c_1, c_2) \in \tilde{T}(\mathcal{R}_\tau)$. This construction guarantees that Basic Lemma always holds provided that every constant is related to itself [2]. A list of instantiations of the above definition in concrete monads is also given in [2]. For instance, the logical relation for the non-determinism monad is defined by:

$$c_1 \; \mathcal{R}_{T\tau} \; c_2 \Leftrightarrow (\forall a_1 \in c_1.\; \exists a_2 \in c_2.\; a_1 \; \mathcal{R}_\tau \; a_2) \; \& \; (\forall a_2 \in c_2.\; \exists a_1 \in c_1.\; a_1 \; \mathcal{R}_\tau \; a_2).$$

Definitions of logical relations for other monads in λ_{Comp}^{PESN} can be found in [4].

We restrict our attention to logical relations $(\mathcal{R}_\tau)_{\tau \text{ type}}$ such that, for any observation type $o \in \mathbf{Obs}$, $\mathcal{R}_{To}$ is a partial equality. Such relations are called *observational* in the rest of the paper.

Theorem 1 (Soundness of logical relations in λ_{Comp}). *If $(\mathcal{R}_\tau)_{\tau \text{ type}}$ is an observational logical relation, then $\mathcal{R}_\tau \subseteq \approx_\tau$ for every type τ.*

3.3   Toward a Proof on Completeness of Logical Relations for λ_{Comp}

Completeness of logical relations for λ_{Comp} is much subtler than in $\lambda^\rightarrow$ due to the introduction of monadic types. We were expecting to find a general proof following the general construction defined in [2]. However, this turns out extremely difficult although it might not be impossible with certain restrictions, on types for example. The difficulty arises mainly from the different semantics for different forms of computations, which actually do not ensure that equivalent programs in one monad are necessarily equivalent in another. Consider two programs in λ_{Comp}: let $x \Leftarrow t_1$ in let $y \Leftarrow t_2$ in val(x) and let $y \Leftarrow t_2$ in let $x \Leftarrow t_1$ in val(x), where both t_1 and t_2 are closed term. We can conclude that they are equivalent in the non-determinism monad — they return the same set of possible results of t_1, no matter what results t_2 produces, but this is not the case in, e.g., the exception monad when t_1 and t_2 throw different exceptions.

Being with such an obstacle, we shall switch our effort to case studies in Section 4 and we explore the completeness of logical relations for a list of common monads, precisely, all the monads in λ_{Comp}^{PESN}. But, let us sketch out here a general structure for proving completeness of logical relations in λ_{Comp}. In particular, our study is still restricted to first-order types, which, in λ_{Comp}, are defined by the grammar: $\tau^1 ::= b \mid T\tau^1 \mid b \rightarrow \tau^1$, where b ranges over the set of base types.

We aim at finding an observational logical relation $(\mathcal{R}_\tau)_{\tau \text{ type}}$ such that if $\vdash t_1 : \tau$ and $\vdash t_2 : \tau$ are derivable and $t_1 \approx_\tau t_2$, for any type τ up to first order, then $[\![t_1]\!] \; \mathcal{R}_\tau \; [\![t_2]\!]$. Or briefly, $\sim_\tau \; \subseteq \; \mathcal{R}_\tau$, where $\sim_\tau$ is the relation defined in Section 2. As in the proof of Proposition 1, the logical relation $(\mathcal{R}_\tau)_{\tau \text{ type}}$ will be induced by $\mathcal{R}_b = \sim_b$, for any base type b. Then how to prove the completeness for an arbitrary monad T?

Note that we should also check that the logical relation $(\mathcal{R}_\tau)_{\tau\ \text{type}}$, induced by $\mathcal{R}_b = \sim_b$, is observational, i.e., a partial equality on To, for any observable type o. Consider any pair $(a, b) \in \mathcal{R}_{To} = \tilde{T}(\mathcal{R}_o)$. By definition of the lifted monad $\tilde{T}$, there exists a computation $c \in T\mathcal{R}_o$ such that $a = T\pi_1(c)$ and $b = T\pi_2(c)$. But $\mathcal{R}_o = \sim_o \subseteq \mathrm{id}_{[\![o]\!]}$, hence the two projections $\pi_1, \pi_2 : \mathcal{R}_o \to [\![o]\!]$ are the same function, $\pi_1 = \pi_2$, and consequently $a = T\pi_1(c) = T\pi_2(c) = b$. This proves that $\mathcal{R}_{To}$ is a partial equality.

As usual, the proof of completeness would go by induction over τ, to show $\sim_\tau \subseteq \mathcal{R}_\tau$ for each first-order type τ. Cases $\tau = b$ and $\tau = b \to \tau'$ go identically as in $\lambda^\to$. The only difficult case is $\tau = T\tau'$, i.e., $(\star)$ $\sim_\tau \subseteq \mathcal{R}_\tau \implies \sim_{T\tau} \subseteq \mathcal{R}_{T\tau}$. We did not find any general way to show $(\star)$ for an arbitrary monad. Instead, in the next section we prove it by cases, for all the monads in λ^{PESN}_{Comp} except the non-determinism monad. The non-determinism monad is an exceptional case where we do not have completeness for all first-order types but a subset of them. This will be studied separately in Section 4.3.

At the heart of the difficulty of showing $(\star)$ we find an issue of definability at monadic types in the set-theoretical model. We write def_τ for the subset of definable elements in $[\![\tau]\!]$, and we eventually show that the relation between $\mathrm{def}_{T\tau}$ and def_τ can be shortly spelled-out $(\star\star)$: $\mathrm{def}_{T\tau} \subseteq T\mathrm{def}_\tau$, for all the monads we consider in this paper. This is a crucial argument for proving completeness of logical relations for monadic types, but to show $(\star\star)$, we need different proofs for different monads. This is detailed in Section 4.1.

4   Completeness of Logical Relations for Monadic Types

4.1   Definability in the Set-Theoretical Model of λ^{PESN}_{Comp}

As we have seen in $\lambda^\to$, definability is involved largely in the proof of completeness of logical relations (for first-order types). This is also the case in λ_{Comp} and it apparently needs more concern due to the introduction of monadic types.

Despite we did not find a general proof for $(\star\star)$ it does hold for all the concrete monads in λ^{PESN}_{Comp}. To state it formally, let us first define a predicate $\mathcal{P}_\tau$ on elements of $[\![\tau]\!]$, by induction on types: $\mathcal{P}_b = \mathrm{def}_b$, for every base type b; $\mathcal{P}_{T\tau} = T(\mathrm{def}_\tau \cap \mathcal{P}_\tau)$; $\mathcal{P}_{\tau\to\tau'} = \{f \in \mathcal{P}_{\tau\to\tau'} \mid \forall a \in \mathrm{def}_\tau, f(a) \in \mathcal{P}_{\tau'}\}$. We say that a constant c (of type τ) is logical if and only if τ is a base type or $[\![c]\!] \in \mathcal{P}_\tau$. We then require that λ^{PESCN}_{Comp} contains only logical constants. Note that this restriction is valid because the predicates $\mathcal{P}_{T\tau}$ and $\mathcal{P}_{\tau\to\tau'}$ depend only on definability at type τ. Some typical logical constants for monads in λ^{PESN}_{Comp} are as follows:

- Partial computation: a constant Ω_τ of type $T\tau$, for every τ. Ω_τ denotes the non-termination, so $[\![\Omega_\tau]\!] = \bot$.
- Exception: a constant $\mathtt{raise}^e_\tau$ of type $T\tau$ for every type τ and every exception $e \in E$. $\mathtt{raise}^e_\tau$ does nothing but raises the exception e, so $[\![\mathtt{raise}^e_\tau]\!] = e$.
- State transformer: a constant $\mathtt{update}_s$ of type $T\mathsf{unit}$ for every state $s \in St$, where unit is the base type which contains only a dummy value $*$. $\mathtt{update}_s$ simply changes the current state to s, so for any $s' \in St$, $[\![\mathtt{update}_s]\!](s') = (*, s)$.
- Non-determinism: a constant $+_\tau$ of type $\tau \to \tau \to T\tau$ for every non-monadic type τ. $+_\tau$ takes two arguments and returns randomly one of them — it introduces the non-determinism, so for any $a_1, a_2 \in [\![\tau]\!]$, $[\![+_\tau]\!](a_1, a_2) = \{a_1, a_2\}$.

We assume in the rest of this paper that the above constants are present in λ_{Comp}^{PESN}. It is clear that each of these constants is related to itself.

Note that $\mathcal{P}_\tau$ being a predicate on elements of $[\![\tau]\!]$ is equivalent to say that $\mathcal{P}_\tau$ can be seen as subset of $[\![\tau]\!]$, but in the case of monadic types, $\mathcal{P}_{T\tau}$ (i.e., $T(\text{def}_\tau \cap \mathcal{P}_\tau)$) is not necessary a subset of $[\![T\tau]\!]$ (i.e., $T[\![\tau]\!]$). Fortunately, we prove that all the monads in λ_{Comp}^{PESN} preserves inclusions, which ensures that the predicate $\mathcal{P}$ is well-defined:

Proposition 2. *All the monads in λ_{Comp}^{PESN} preserve inclusions: $A \subseteq B \Rightarrow TA \subseteq TB$.*

Introducing such a constraint on constants is mainly for proving $(\star\star)$. In fact, we can prove that the denotation of every closed βc-normal-η-long computation term t (of type $T\tau$), in λ_{Comp}^{PESN} with logical constants, is an element of $T\text{def}_\tau$, i.e., $[\![t]\!] \subseteq T\text{def}_\tau$ (see [4] for details).

Proposition 3. $\text{def}_{T\tau} \subseteq T\text{def}_\tau$ *holds in the set-theoretical model of λ_{Comp}^{PESN} with logical constants.*

4.2 Completeness of Logical Relations in λ_{Comp}^{PES} for First-Order Types

We prove $(\star)$ in this section for the partial computation monad, the exception monad, the state monad and the continuation monad. We write λ_{Comp}^{PES} for λ_{Comp} where the monad is restricted to one of these four monads.

Proofs depend typically on the particular semantics of every form of computation, but a common technique is used frequently: given two definable but non-related elements of $[\![T\tau]\!]$, one can find a context to distinguish the programs (of type $T\tau$) that define the two given elements, and such a context is usually built based on another context that can distinguish programs of type τ.

Theorem 2. *In λ_{Comp}^{PES}, if all constants are logical and in particular, if the constant update_s is present for the state transformer monad, then logical relations are complete up to first-order types, in the strong sense that there exists an observational logical relation $(\mathcal{R}_\tau)_{\tau\ type}$ such that for any closed terms t_1, t_2 of any type τ^1 up to first order, if $t_1 \approx_{\tau^1} t_2$, then $[\![t_1]\!] \mathcal{R}_{\tau^1} [\![t_2]\!]$.*

4.3 Completeness of Logical Relations for the Non-determinism Monad

The non-determinism monad is an interesting case: the completeness of logical relations for this monad does not hold for all first-order types! To state it, consider the following two programs of a first-order type that break the completeness of logical relations:

$$\vdash \text{val}(\lambda x.(\text{true} +_{\text{bool}} \text{false})) : T(\text{bool} \to T\text{bool}),$$
$$\vdash \lambda x.\text{val}(\text{true}) +_{\text{bool}\to T\text{bool}} \lambda x.(\text{true} +_{\text{bool}} \text{false}) : T(\text{bool} \to T\text{bool}).$$

Recall the logical constant $+_\tau$ of type $\tau \to \tau \to T\tau$: $[\![+_\tau]\!](a_1, a_2) = \{a_1, a_2\}$ for every $a_1, a_2 \in [\![\tau]\!]$. The two programs are contextually equivalent: what contexts can do is to apply the functions to some arguments and observe the results. But no matter how many time we apply these two functions, we always get the same set of possible values ($\{\text{true}, \text{false}\}$), so there is no way to distinguish them with a context.

Recall the logical relation for non-determinism monad in Section 3.2. Clearly the denotations of the above two programs are not related by that relation because the function $[\![\lambda x.\mathtt{val}(\mathtt{true})]\!]$ from the second program is not related to the function in the first.

However, if we assume that for every non-observable base type b, there is an equality test constant $\mathtt{test}_b : b \to b \to \mathtt{bool}$ (clearly, $\mathcal{P}(\mathtt{test}_b)$ holds), logical relations for the non-determinism monad are then complete for a set of *weak first-order types*: $\tau_w^1 ::= b \mid Tb \mid b \to \tau_w^1$. Compared to all types up to first order, weak first-order types do not contain monadic types of functions, so it immediately excludes the two programs in the above counterexample.

Theorem 3. *Logical relations for the non-determinism monad are complete up to weak first-order types. in the strong sense that there exists an observational logical relation $(\mathcal{R}_\tau)_{\tau \text{ type}}$ such that for any closed terms t_1, t_2 of a weak first-order type τ_w^1, if $t_1 \approx_{\tau_w^1} t_2$, then $[\![t_1]\!] \mathcal{R}_{\tau_w^1} [\![t_2]\!]$.*

References

1. Benton, P.N., Bierman, G.M., de Paiva, V.C.V.: Computational types from a logical perspective. J. Functional Programming 8(2), 177–193 (1998)
2. Goubault-Larrecq, J., Lasota, S., Nowak, D.: Logical relations for monadic types. In: Bradfield, J.C. (ed.) CSL 2002 and EACSL 2002. LNCS, vol. 2471, pp. 553–568. Springer, Heidelberg (2002)
3. Goubault-Larrecq, J., Lasota, S., Nowak, D., Zhang, Y.: Complete lax logical relations for cryptographic lambda-calculi. In: Marcinkowski, J., Tarlecki, A. (eds.) CSL 2004. LNCS, vol. 3210, pp. 400–414. Springer, Heidelberg (2004)
4. Lasota, S., Nowak, D., Zhang, Y.: On completeness of logical relations for monadic types. Research Report cs.LO/0612106, arXiv (2006)
5. Lazić, R., Nowak, D.: A unifying approach to data-independence. In: Palamidessi, C. (ed.) CONCUR 2000. LNCS, vol. 1877, pp. 581–595. Springer, Heidelberg (2000)
6. Mitchell, J.C.: Foundations of Programming Languages. MIT Press, Cambridge (1996)
7. Mitchell, J.C., Scedrov, A.: Notes on sconing and relators. In: Martini, S., Börger, E., Kleine Büning, H., Jäger, G., Richter, M.M. (eds.) CSL 1992. LNCS, vol. 702, pp. 352–378. Springer, Heidelberg (1993)
8. Moggi, E.: Notions of computation and monads. Information and Computation 93(1), 55–92 (1991)
9. O'Hearn, P.W., Tennent, R.D.: Parametricity and local variables. J. ACM 42(3), 658–709 (1995)
10. Pitts, A., Stark, I.: Operational reasoning for functions with local state. In: Higher Order Operational Techniques in Semantics, pp. 227–273. Cambridge University Press, Cambridge (1998)
11. Plotkin, G.D.: Lambda-definability in the full type hierarchy. In: To H. B. Curry: Essays on Combinatory Logic, Lambda Calculus and Formalism, pp. 363–373. Academic Press, London (1980)
12. Sieber, K.: Full abstraction for the second order subset of an algol-like language. Theoretical Computer Science 168(1), 155–212 (1996)
13. Sumii, E., Pierce, B.C.: Logical relations for encryption. J. Computer Security 11(4), 521–554 (2003)
14. Zhang, Y.: Cryptographic logical relations. Ph. d. dissertation, ENS Cachan, France (2005)

A Spatial Logical Characterisation of Context Bisimulation[*]

Zining Cao

Department of Computer Science and Engineering
Nanjing University of Aero. & Astro., Nanjing 210016, P.R. China
caozn@nuaa.edu.cn

Abstract. In this paper, we present a spatial logic for higher order π-calculus. In order to prove that the induced logical equivalence coincides with context bisimulation, we present some new bisimulations, and prove the equivalence between these new bisimulations and context bisimulation. Furthermore, we present a variant of this spatial logic and prove that it also provides a logical characterisation of context bisimulation.

1 Introduction

Higher order π-calculus was proposed and studied intensively in Sangiorgi's dissertation [9]. In higher order π-calculus, processes and abstractions over processes of arbitrarily high order, can be communicated. Some interesting equivalences for higher order π-calculus, such as barbed equivalence, context bisimulation and normal bisimulation, were presented in [9]. Barbed equivalence can be regarded as a uniform definition of bisimulation for a variety of concurrent calculi. Context bisimulation is a very intuitive definition of bisimulation for higher order π-calculus, but it is heavy to handle, due to the appearance of universal quantifications in its definition. In the definition of normal bisimulation, all universal quantifications disappeared, therefore normal bisimulation is a very economic characterisation of bisimulation for higher order π-calculus. The coincidence between the three equivalences was proven [1,5,8,9].

Spatial logic was presented in [3]. Spatial logic extends classical logic with connectives to reason about the structure of the processes. The additional connectives belong to two families. Intensional operators allow one to inspect the structure of the process. A formula $A_1 | A_2$ is satisfied whenever we can split the process into two parts satisfying the corresponding subformula A_i, $i = 1, 2$. In presence of restriction in the underlying model, a process P satisfies formula $n \circledR A$ if we can write P as $(\nu n) P'$ with P' satisfying A. Finally, formula 0 is only satisfied by the inaction process. Connectives $|$ and $\circledR$ come with adjunct operators, called guarantee ($\triangleright$) and hiding ($\oslash$) respectively, that allow one to extend the process being observed. In this sense, these can be called contextual operators. P satisfies $A_1 \triangleright A_2$ whenever the spatial composition (using $|$) of P

---

[*] This work was supported by the National Natural Science Foundation of China under Grant 60473036.

M. Okada and I. Satoh (Eds.): ASIAN 2006, LNCS 4435, pp. 231–239, 2007.
© Springer-Verlag Berlin Heidelberg 2007

with any process satisfying A_1 satisfies A_2, and P satisfies $A \oslash n$ if $(\nu n)P$ satisfies A. Some spatial logics have an operator for fresh name quantification [2].

Existing spatial logics for concurrency are intensional [7], in the sense that they induce an equivalence that coincides with structural congruence, which is much finer than bisimilarity. In [4], Hirschkoff studied an extensional spatial logic. This logic only has spatial composition adjunct ($\triangleright$), revelation adjunct ($\oslash$), a simple temporal modality ($\langle \rangle$), and an operator for fresh name quantification. For π-calculus, this extensional spatial logic was proven to induce the same separative power as strong early bisimilarity.

There are lots of works of spatial logics for π-calculus and *Mobile Ambients*. But as far as we know, there is no spatial logic for higher order π-calculus up to now. In this paper, we present a spatial logic for higher order π-calculus, called L, which comprises a barb detecting predicate $\downarrow_\mu$, a temporal modality $\langle \rangle$ and a spatial composition adjunct $\triangleright$. We show that the equivalence induced by spatial logic coincides with context bisimulation. To establish this result, our strategy is to first give a simpler bisimulation which is equivalent to context bisimulation, and then present a logical charaterisation for this simpler bisimulation. Consequently, this logic is also a charaterisation for context bisimulation. Similar to [4], we exploit the characterisation of context bisimulation in the terms of barbed equivalence. However in the definition of barbed equivalence, testing context is an arbitrary process. It is difficult to give the logical characterisation of barbed equivalence directly. Therefore we first give a variant of normal bisimulation, $\sim_{nor}$, where in the case of higher order output action, we only need to test the remainder process by some kind of finite processes. Then we give a similar variant of contextual barbed bisimulation, $\sim_{Nb}$, where process need to be tested only with some special finite processes. The bisimulations $\sim_{nor}$ and $\sim_{Nb}$ are proven to coincide with strong context bisimulation. Furthermore, we prove that L is a characterisation of $\sim_{Nb}$. Thus L is a logic charaterisation of context bisimulation. Finally, since $\downarrow_\mu$ is not a basic operator in the traditional spatial logic, we present a variant of L, named SL, which does not have $\downarrow_\mu$, but contains $\langle \rangle$, $\triangleright$ and $\oslash$. We prove that SL induces an equivalence that coincides with context bisimulation. Thus SL is also a logic charaterisation of context bisimulation. This paper is organized as follows: In Section 2 we briefly review higher order π-calculus. In Section 3, we present some new bisimulations and give the equivalence between these bisimulations and context bisimulation. In Section 4, we give a spatial logic for context bisimulation, and prove that the logical induced equivalence coincides with context bisimulation. The paper is concluded in Section 5.

2   Higher Order π-Calculus

2.1   Syntax and Labelled Transition System

In this section we briefly recall the syntax and labelled transition system of the higher order π-calculus. Similar to [8], we only focus on a second-order fragment of the higher order π-calculus, i.e., there is no abstraction in this fragment.

We assume a set Na of names, ranged over by $a, b, c, l, m, n, ...$ and a set Var of process variables, ranged over by $X, Y, Z, U, ...$ We use $E, F, P, Q, ...$ to stand for processes. Pr denotes the set of all processes. We give the grammar for the higher order π-calculus processes as follows:

$P ::= 0 \mid U \mid \tau.P \mid l.P \mid \bar{l}.P \mid a(U).P \mid \bar{a}\langle P_1\rangle.P_2 \mid P_1|P_2 \mid (\nu a)P \mid !P$, here l, $a \in Na$, $U \in Var$.

In each process of the form $(\nu y)P$ the occurrence of y is bound within the scope of P. An occurrence of y in a process is said to be free iff it does not lie within the scope of a bound occurrence of y. The set of names occurring free in P is denoted $fn(P)$. An occurrence of a name in a process is said to be bound if it is not free, we write the set of bound names as $bn(P)$. $n(P)$ denotes the set of names of P, i.e., $n(P) = fn(P) \cup bn(P)$. The definition of substitution in process terms may involve renaming of bound names when necessary to avoid name capture. Higher order input prefix $x(U).P$ binds all free occurrences of U in P. The set of variables occurring free in P is denoted $fv(P)$. We write the set of bound variables as $bv(P)$. A process is closed if it has no free variable; it is open if it may have free variables. Pr^c is the set of all closed processes. Processes P and Q are α-convertible, $P \equiv_\alpha Q$, if Q can be obtained from P by a finite number of changes of bound names and variables. The set of names $\{b_1, ..., b_n\}$ can be abbreviated as $\tilde{b}$.

The operational semantics of higher order processes is given in Table 1. We have omitted the symmetric cases of the parallelism and communication rules.

$$ALP : \frac{P \xrightarrow{\alpha} P'}{Q \xrightarrow{\alpha} Q'} P \equiv_\alpha Q, P' \equiv_\alpha Q' \qquad TAU : \tau.P \xrightarrow{\tau} P$$

$$OUT1 : \bar{l}.P \xrightarrow{\bar{l}} P \qquad IN1 : l.P \xrightarrow{l} P$$

$$OUT2 : \bar{a}\langle E\rangle.P \xrightarrow{\bar{a}\langle E\rangle} P \qquad IN2 : a(U).P \xrightarrow{a\langle E\rangle} P\{E/U\}$$

$$PAR : \frac{P \xrightarrow{\alpha} P'}{P|Q \xrightarrow{\alpha} P'|Q} bn(\alpha) \cap fn(Q) = \emptyset$$

$$COM1 : \frac{P \xrightarrow{\bar{l}} P' \quad Q \xrightarrow{l} Q'}{P|Q \xrightarrow{\tau} P'|Q'}$$

$$COM2 : \frac{P \xrightarrow{(\nu\tilde{b})\bar{a}\langle E\rangle} P' \quad Q \xrightarrow{a\langle E\rangle} Q'}{P|Q \xrightarrow{\tau} (\nu\tilde{b})(P'|Q')} \tilde{b} \cap fn(Q) = \emptyset$$

$$RES : \frac{P \xrightarrow{\alpha} P'}{(\nu a)P \xrightarrow{\alpha} (\nu a)P'} a \notin n(\alpha) \qquad REP : \frac{P|!P \xrightarrow{\alpha} P'}{!P \xrightarrow{\alpha} P'}$$

$$OPEN : \frac{P \xrightarrow{(\nu\tilde{c})\bar{a}\langle E\rangle} P'}{(\nu b)P \xrightarrow{(\nu b,\tilde{c})\bar{a}\langle E\rangle} P'} a \neq b, \ b \in fn(E) - \tilde{c}$$

Table1

2.2   Bisimulations in Higher Order π-Calculus

Context bisimulation and normal bisimulation were presented in [9,8] to describe the behavioral equivalences for higher order π-calculus. Let us review the definition of these bisimulations. In the following, we abbreviate $P\{E/U\}$ as $P\langle E\rangle$.

Definition 1. A symmetric relation $R \subseteq Pr^c \times Pr^c$ is a strong context bisimulation if $P\ R\ Q$ implies:

(1) whenever $P \xrightarrow{\alpha} P'$, there exists Q' such that $Q \xrightarrow{\alpha} Q'$, here α is not a higher order action, and $P'\ R\ Q'$;

(2) whenever $P \xrightarrow{a\langle E\rangle} P'$, there exists Q' such that $Q \xrightarrow{a\langle E\rangle} Q'$ and $P'\ R\ Q'$;

(3) whenever $P \xrightarrow{(\nu\widetilde{b})\overline{a}\langle E\rangle} P'$, there exist Q', F, $\widetilde{c}$ such that $Q \xrightarrow{(\nu\widetilde{c})\overline{a}\langle F\rangle} Q'$ and for all $C(U)$ with $fn(C(U)) \cap \{\widetilde{b},\widetilde{c}\} = \emptyset$, $(\nu\widetilde{b})(P'|C\langle E\rangle)\ R\ (\nu\widetilde{c})(Q'|C\langle F\rangle)$. Here $C(U)$ represents a process containing a unique free variable U.

We write $P \sim_{Ct} Q$ if P and Q are strongly context bisimilar.

Distinguished from context bisimulation, normal bisimulation does not have universal quantifications in the clauses of its definition. In the following, a name is called fresh in a statement if it is different from any other name occurring in the processes of the statement.

Definition 2. A symmetric relation $R \subseteq Pr^c \times Pr^c$ is a strong normal bisimulation if $P\ R\ Q$ implies:

(1) whenever $P \xrightarrow{\alpha} P'$, there exists Q' such that $Q \xrightarrow{\alpha} Q'$, here α is not a higher order action, and $P'\ R\ Q'$;

(2) whenever $P \xrightarrow{a\langle\overline{m}.0\rangle} P'$, there exists Q' such that $Q \xrightarrow{a\langle\overline{m}.0\rangle} Q'$ and $P'\ R\ Q'$, here m is a fresh name;

(3) whenever $P \xrightarrow{(\nu\widetilde{b})\overline{a}\langle E\rangle} P'$, there exist Q', F, $\widetilde{c}$ such that $Q \xrightarrow{(\nu\widetilde{c})\overline{a}\langle F\rangle} Q'$ and $(\nu\widetilde{b})(P'|!m.E)\ R\ (\nu\widetilde{c})(Q'|!m.F)$, here m is a fresh name.

We write $P \sim_{Nr} Q$ if P and Q are strongly normal bisimilar.

In [9], barbed equivalence was presented as a uniform definition of bisimulation for first order π-calculus and higher order π-calculus. In [5], a variant of barbed equivalence, called contextual equivalence, was presented.

Definition 3. For each name or co-name μ, the observability predicate $\downarrow_\mu$ is defined by

(1) $P \downarrow_l$ if there exists P' such that $P \xrightarrow{l} P'$;

(2) $P \downarrow_{\overline{l}}$ if there exists P' such that $P \xrightarrow{\overline{l}} P'$;

(3) $P \downarrow_a$ if there exist E, P' such that $P \xrightarrow{a\langle E\rangle} P'$;

(4) $P \downarrow_{\overline{a}}$ if there exist $\widetilde{b}, E, P'$ such that $P \xrightarrow{(\nu\widetilde{b})\overline{a}\langle E\rangle} P'$.

Definition 4. A symmetric relation $R \subseteq Pr^c \times Pr^c$ is a strong contextual equivalence if $P\ R\ Q$ implies:

(1) $P|C\ R\ Q|C$ for any C;

(2) whenever $P \xrightarrow{\tau} P'$ there exists Q' such that $Q \xrightarrow{\tau} Q'$ and $P'\ R\ Q'$;

(3) $P \downarrow_\mu$ implies $Q \downarrow_\mu$.

We write $P \sim_{Ba} Q$ if P and Q are strongly contextual equivalent.

3   Variants of Bisimulations

In this section, we present some new bisimulations, and prove that they are equivalent to context bismulation. These results are used to give a logical characterisation of $\sim_{Ct}$.

3.1   Variant of Normal Bisimulation

Now we first give a variant of normal bisimulation, where parallel composition of finitary copies is used as a limit form of replication. We prove it coincides with normal bisimulation. In the following, we write $\Pi_k P$ to denote the parallel composition of k copies of P, i.e., $\Pi_k P \overset{def}{=} P|\Pi_{k-1}P$ and $\Pi_0 P \overset{def}{=} 0$. For example, $\Pi_3 P$ represents $P|P|P$.

Definition 5. A symmetric relation $R \subseteq Pr^c \times Pr^c$ is a strong limit normal bisimulation if $P\ R\ Q$ implies:

(1) whenever $P \overset{\alpha}{\longrightarrow} P'$, there exists Q' such that $Q \overset{\alpha}{\longrightarrow} Q'$, here α is not a higher order action, and $P'\ R\ Q'$;

(2) whenever $P \overset{a\langle \widetilde{m}.0\rangle}{\longrightarrow} P'$, there exists Q' such that $Q \overset{a\langle \widetilde{m}.0\rangle}{\longrightarrow} Q'$ and $P'\ R\ Q'$, here m is a fresh name;

(3) whenever $P \overset{(\nu \widetilde{b})\overline{a}\langle E\rangle}{\longrightarrow} P'$, there exist Q', F, $\widetilde{c}$ such that $Q \overset{(\nu \widetilde{c})\overline{a}\langle F\rangle}{\longrightarrow} Q'$ and $(\nu \widetilde{b})(P'|\Pi_k m.E)\ R\ (\nu \widetilde{c})(Q'|\Pi_k m.F)$ for all $k \in N = \{0, 1, 2, ...\}$, here m is a fresh name.

We write $P \sim_{nor} Q$ if P and Q are strongly limit normal bisimilar.

Now we study the equivalence between $\sim_{Ct}$, $\sim_{Nr}$ and $\sim_{nor}$.

Lemma 1. For any $P, Q \in Pr^c$, $P \sim_{Ct} Q \Rightarrow P \sim_{nor} Q$.

Lemma 2. For any $P, Q \in Pr^c$, $P \sim_{nor} Q \Rightarrow P \sim_{Nr} Q$.

By the equivalence between $\sim_{Ct}$ and $\sim_{Nr}$ [1], $P \sim_{Nr} Q \Leftrightarrow P \sim_{Ct} Q$. Furthermore, by Lemmas 1 and 2, we have that the proposition holds.

Proposition 1. For any $P, Q \in Pr^c$, $P \sim_{Ct} Q \Leftrightarrow P \sim_{nor} Q \Leftrightarrow P \sim_{Nr} Q$.

3.2   Variant of Barbed Equivalence

In [4], the logical characterisation of strong early bisimulation was exploited in terms of strong barbed equivalence. The extensional spatial logic [4] was proven to capture strong barbed equivalence firstly, then since strong early bisimulation coincides with strong barbed equivalence, this spatial logic is also a logical characterisation of strong early bisimulation. But this proof strategy seems difficult to apply directly in the case of higher order π-calculus. To give a spatial logical characterisation of $\sim_{Ct}$, we will give a simpler version of barbed equivalence. The following bisimulation is a variant of $\sim_{Ba}$, where testing contexts are some special processes.

Definition 6. A symmetric relation $R \subseteq Pr^c \times Pr^c$ is a strong normal barbed equivalence if $P\ R\ Q$ implies:

(1) $P|C \ R \ Q|C$ for any C in the form of $\overline{n}.0$, $l.n.0$, $\overline{l}.n.0$, $\overline{a}\langle\overline{m}.0\rangle.n.0$ and $a(U).\Pi_k m.U$, where m, n are fresh names, and k is an arbitrary natural number;

(2) whenever $P \xrightarrow{\tau} P'$ there exists Q' such that $Q \xrightarrow{\tau} Q'$ and $P' \ R \ Q'$;

(3) if $P \downarrow_\mu$, then also $Q \downarrow_\mu$.

We write $P \sim_{Nb} Q$ if P and Q are strongly normal barbed equivalent.

It is worth to note that all testing contexts in the above definition are finite processes. Hence it is possible to give the characteristic formulas for these testing contexts. The following proposition states that $\sim_{nor}$ coincides with $\sim_{Nb}$.

Proposition 2. For any $P, Q \in Pr^c$, $P \sim_{nor} Q \Leftrightarrow P \sim_{Nb} Q$.

Now by Propositions 1 and 2, we can give the following main proposition.

Proposition 3. For any $P, Q \in Pr^c$, $P \sim_{Ct} Q \Leftrightarrow P \sim_{nor} Q \Leftrightarrow P \sim_{Nr} Q \Leftrightarrow P \sim_{Nb} Q \Leftrightarrow P \sim_{Ba} Q$.

In fact, the definition of $\sim_{nor}$ and $\sim_{Nb}$ can be generalized to the weak versions: $\approx_{nor}$ and $\approx_{Nb}$. The following proposition on weak bisimulations can also be proved: $P \approx_{Ct} Q \Leftrightarrow P \approx_{nor} Q \Leftrightarrow P \approx_{Nr} Q \Leftrightarrow P \approx_{Nb} Q \Leftrightarrow P \approx_{Ba} Q$.

4   A Logic for Context Bisimulation

In this section, we present a logic to reason about higher order π-calculus. The induced logical equivalence will be proven to coincide with context bisimulation.

4.1   Syntax and Semantics of Logic L

Now we introduce a spatial logic called L.

Definition 7. Syntax of logic
$$A ::= \downarrow_l \ | \ \downarrow_{\overline{l}} \ | \ \downarrow_a \ | \ \downarrow_{\overline{a}} \ | \ \neg A \ | \ A_1 \wedge A_2 \ | \ \langle\rangle A \ | \ A_1 \triangleright A_2,$$ here l is a first order name, and a is a higher order name.

Definition 8. Semantics of logic

(1) $P \models \downarrow_\mu$ iff $P \downarrow_\mu$, here μ is in the form of $l, \overline{l}, a$ and $\overline{a}$;

(2) $P \models \neg A$ iff $P \not\models A$;

(3) $P \models A_1 \wedge A_2$ iff $P \models A_1$ and $P \models A_2$;

(4) $P \models \langle\rangle A$ iff $\exists P'. \ P \xrightarrow{\tau} P'$ and $P' \models A$;

(5) $P \models A_1 \triangleright A_2$ iff $\forall Q. \ Q \models A_1$ implies $P|Q \models A_2$.

The priority of the logic operators are given from the highest to the lowest: $\neg, \langle\rangle, \triangleright, \wedge$.

Definition 9. P and Q are logically equivalent with respect to L, written $P =_L Q$, iff for any formula A, $P \models A$ iff $Q \models A$.

4.2 L is a Logical Characterisation of $\sim_{Ct}$

In this section we prove the equivalence between $\sim_{Nb}$ and $=_L$. Since $\sim_{Nb}$ coincides with $\sim_{Ct}$, we have the equivalence between $\sim_{Ct}$ and $=_L$.

The following proposition can be proved by structural induction on A that whenever $P \sim_{Nb} Q$ and $P \models A$, we have $Q \models A$.

Proposition 4. For any $P, Q \in Pr^c$, $P \sim_{Nb} Q$ implies $P =_L Q$.

To prove the converse proposition, we need the following definition, which gives the characteristic formulas for the testing contexts in the definition of $\sim_{Nb}$.

Definition 10

(1) $F_0 \overset{def}{=} []\bot \wedge ([]\bot \rhd []\bot)$, here $[]B \overset{def}{=} \neg\langle\rangle\neg B$, $\bot \overset{def}{=} A \wedge \neg A$;

(2) $F_{ch(\mu)} \overset{def}{=} \downarrow_\mu \wedge []\bot \wedge ([]\bot \succ \langle\rangle F_0)$, here $B \succ C \overset{def}{=} \neg(B \rhd \neg C)$;

(3) $F_{l.0} \overset{def}{=} F_{ch(l)}$;

(4) $F_{\bar{l}.0} \overset{def}{=} F_{ch(\bar{l})}$;

(5) $F_{a(U).0} \overset{def}{=} F_{ch(a)} \wedge (F_{ch(\bar{a})} \rhd \langle\rangle F_0)$;

(6) $F_{\bar{a}\langle 0\rangle.0} \overset{def}{=} F_{ch(\bar{a})} \wedge (F_{ch(a)} \rhd \langle\rangle F_0)$;

(7) $F_{\bar{a}\langle \bar{n}.0\rangle.0} \overset{def}{=} F_{ch(\bar{a})} \wedge (F_{ch(a)} \succ \langle\rangle F_{\bar{n}.0})$;

(8) $F_{a(U).U} \overset{def}{=} F_{ch(a)} \wedge (F_{\bar{a}\langle \bar{n}.0\rangle.0} \rhd \langle\rangle F_{\bar{n}.0})$;

(9) $F_{m.n.0} \overset{def}{=} \neg \downarrow_n \wedge (F_{\bar{m}.0} \rhd \langle\rangle F_{n.0})$;

(10) $F_{\bar{m}.n.0} \overset{def}{=} \neg \downarrow_n \wedge (F_{m.0} \rhd \langle\rangle F_{n.0})$;

(11) $F_{\bar{m}.0|n.0} \overset{def}{=} (F_{m.0} \rhd \langle\rangle F_{n.0}) \wedge (F_{\bar{n}.0} \rhd \langle\rangle F_{\bar{m}.0})$;

(12) $F_{\bar{a}\langle \bar{m}.0\rangle.n.0} \overset{def}{=} \neg \downarrow_n \wedge (F_{a(U).U} \rhd \langle\rangle F_{\bar{m}.0|n.0}) \wedge (F_{a(U).0} \rhd \langle\rangle F_{n.0})$;

(13) $F_{\Pi_k \bar{n}.0} \overset{def}{=} F_{n.0} \rhd \langle\rangle F_{\Pi_{k-1}\bar{n}.0}$, here $k > 1$; $F_{\Pi_0 \bar{n}.0} \overset{def}{=} F_0$, $F_{\Pi_1 \bar{n}.0} \overset{def}{=} F_{\bar{n}.0}$;

(14) $F_{\Pi_k m.0} \overset{def}{=} F_{\bar{m}.0} \rhd \langle\rangle F_{\Pi_{k-1} m.0}$, here $k > 1$; $F_{\Pi_0 m.0} \overset{def}{=} F_0$, $F_{\Pi_1 m.0} \overset{def}{=} F_{m.0}$;

(15) $F_{\Pi_k m.\bar{n}.0} \overset{def}{=} \neg \downarrow_{\bar{n}} \wedge ((F_{\bar{m}.0} \rhd \langle\rangle)^k F_{\Pi_k \bar{n}.0}) \wedge (F_{\bar{m}.0} \rhd \langle\rangle(F_{n.0} \rhd \langle\rangle F_{\Pi_{k-1} m.\bar{n}.0}))$,

here $(B \rhd \langle\rangle)^i C \overset{def}{=} B \rhd (\langle\rangle(B \rhd \langle\rangle)^{i-1} C)$, $(B \rhd \langle\rangle)^1 C \overset{def}{=} B \rhd \langle\rangle C$, $F_{\Pi_0 m.\bar{n}.0} \overset{def}{=} F_0$;

(16) $F_{a(U).\Pi_k m.U} \overset{def}{=} \neg \downarrow_m \wedge (F_{\bar{a}\langle 0\rangle.0} \rhd \langle\rangle F_{\Pi_k m.0}) \wedge (F_{\bar{a}\langle \bar{n}.0\rangle.0} \rhd \langle\rangle F_{\Pi_k m.\bar{n}.0})$.

Lemma 3. $D \models F_C \Leftrightarrow C \sim_{Ct} D$, here C is in the form of $\bar{n}.0$, $l.n.0$, $\bar{l}.n.0$, $\bar{a}\langle \bar{m}.0\rangle.n.0$ and $a(U).\Pi_k m.U$, where k is an arbitrary natural number.

By Lemma 3, we get the following proposition.

Proposition 5. For any $P, Q \in Pr^c$, $P =_L Q$ implies $P \sim_{Nb} Q$.

By Propositions 3, 4 and 5, we get the following proposition, which states that L captures $\sim_{Ct}$.

Proposition 6. For any $P, Q \in Pr^c$, $P \sim_{Ct} Q \Leftrightarrow P =_L Q$.

4.3   A Variant of L

We have proven that $\sim_{Ct}$ coincides with $=_L$, but formula $\downarrow_\mu$ in L is not a basic formula in the traditional spatial logic. Thus we turn to seek a variant of spatial logical characterisation of $\sim_{Ct}$. In the following we consider a variant of L, called SL, in which we remove $\downarrow_\mu$ and add $\downarrow_{in}$, $\downarrow_{out}$ and a spatial connective

$\oslash$. Intuitively, P satisfies $\downarrow_{in}$ if P can communicate with other processes by an input channel, and P satisfies $\downarrow_{out}$ if P can communicate with other processes by an output channel. We show that $\downarrow_{\mu}$ can be defined by using $\downarrow_{in}$, $\downarrow_{out}$ and $\oslash$, then it is clear that SL is a spatial logical characterisation of $\sim_{Ct}$.

Definition 11. Syntax and semantics of SL

Formulas of SL are defined by the following grammar:
$$A ::= \downarrow_{in} \mid \downarrow_{out} \mid \neg A \mid A_1 \wedge A_2 \mid \langle\rangle A \mid A_1 \triangleright A_2 \mid A \oslash n$$
Semantics of SL is similar to L except that the definition of $\downarrow_{\mu}$ is eliminated and the definitions of $\downarrow_{in}$, $\downarrow_{out}$ and $\oslash$ are added as follows:

$P \models \downarrow_{in}$ iff $P \downarrow_{\mu}$ where μ is in the form of l or a;

$P \models \downarrow_{out}$ iff $P \downarrow_{\mu}$ where μ is in the form of $\bar{l}$ or $\bar{a}$;

$P \models A \oslash n$ iff $(\nu n)P \models A$.

We abbreviate $A \oslash n_1 \oslash n_2 \oslash ... \oslash n_k$ as $A \oslash \tilde{n}$, here $\tilde{n} = \{n_1, n_2, ..., n_k\}$.

Definition 12. P and Q are logically equivalent with respect to SL, written $P =_{SL} Q$, iff for any formula A, $P \models A$ iff $Q \models A$.

Lemma 4. (1) $P \models \downarrow_{\mu} \Leftrightarrow P \models \downarrow_{in} \oslash \tilde{m} \wedge (\neg \downarrow_{in}) \oslash \tilde{m} \oslash \mu$, here μ is in the form of l or a, $\tilde{m} = fn(P) - \{\mu\}$;

(2) $P \models \downarrow_{\mu} \Leftrightarrow P \models \downarrow_{out} \oslash \tilde{m} \wedge (\neg \downarrow_{out}) \oslash \tilde{m} \oslash \bar{\mu}$, here μ is in the form of $\bar{l}$ or $\bar{a}$, $\bar{\mu} = l$ if $\mu = \bar{l}$, $\bar{\mu} = a$ if $\mu = \bar{a}$, and $\tilde{m} = fn(P) - \{\bar{\mu}\}$.

By Lemma 3, Lemma 4 and Proposition 6, we can give the equivalence between $\sim_{Ct}$ and $=_{SL}$.

Proposition 7. For any $P, Q \in Pr^c$, $P \sim_{Ct} Q \Leftrightarrow P =_{SL} Q$.

5   Conclusions

In this paper, we have defined a logic L, which comprises some spatial operators. We shown that the induced logical equivalence coincides with context bisimulation for higher order π-calculus. As far as we know, this is the first spatial logical characterisation of context bisimulation. To prove that $=_L$ coincides with $\sim_{Ct}$, we present two simplified notions of observable equivalence on higher order processes named $\sim_{nor}$ and $\sim_{Nb}$. The notions of $\sim_{nor}$ and $\sim_{Nb}$, apart from its proof technical importance, also seem to be of conceptual value for other higher order process calculi.

References

1. Cao, Z.: More on bisimulations for higher-order π-calculus. In: Aceto, L., Ingólfsdóttir, A. (eds.) FOSSACS 2006 and ETAPS 2006. LNCS, vol. 3921, pp. 63–78. Springer, Heidelberg (2006)
2. Caires, L., Cardelli, L.: A Spatial Logic for Concurrency (Part II). Theoretical Computer Science 322(3), 517–565 (2004)
3. Caires, L., Cardelli, L.: A Spatial Logic for Concurrency (Part I). Information and Computation 186(2), 194–235 (2003)

4. Hirschkoff, D.: An Extensional Spatial Logic for Mobile Processes. In: Gardner, P., Yoshida, N. (eds.) CONCUR 2004. LNCS, vol. 3170, pp. 325–339. Springer, Heidelberg (2004)

5. Jeffrey, A., Rathke, J.: for higher-order π-calculus revisited. Logical Methods in Computer Science 1(1:4), 1–22 (2005)

6. Milner, R., Parrow, J., Walker, D.: Modal logics for mobile processes. Theoretical Computer Science 114(1), 149–171 (1993)

7. Sangiorgi, D.: Extensionality and Intensionality of the Ambient Logic. In: Proc. of the 28th POPL, pp. 4–17. ACM Press, New York (2001)

8. Sangiorgi, D.: Bisimulation in higher-order calculi. Information and Computation 131(2) (1996)

9. Sangiorgi, D.: Expressing mobility in process algebras: first-order and higher-order paradigms. Ph.D thesis, University of Einburgh (1992)

Information Hiding in the Join Calculus

Qin Ma[1] and Luc Maranget[2]

[1] OFFIS, Escherweg 2, 26121 Oldenburg, Germany
Qin.Ma@offis.de
[2] INRIA-Rocquencourt, BP 105, 78153 Le Chesnay Cedex, France
Luc.Maranget@inria.fr

Abstract. We aim to provide information hiding support in concurrent object-oriented programming languages. We study this issue both at the object level and the class level, in the context of an object-oriented extension of Join— a process calculus in the tradition of the π-calculus.

In this extended abstract, we focus on the class level and design a new hiding operation on classes. The purpose of this operation is to prevent part of parent classes from being visible in client (inheriting) classes. We define its formal semantics in terms of α-converting hidden names to fresh names, and its typing in terms of eliminating hidden names from class types.

1 Introduction

Object-oriented concepts are often claimed to handle concurrent systems better. On one hand, objects, exchanging messages while managing their internal states in a private fashion, model a practical view of concurrent systems. On the other hand, classes, supporting modular and incremental development, provide an effective way of controlling concurrent system complexity. Numerous fundamental studies such as [6,11] proposed calculi that combine objects and concurrency. By contrast, combining classes and concurrency faces the well-known obstacle of *inheritance anomalies* [9,10], *i.e.*, traditional overriding mechanism from sequential settings falls short in handling synchronization behavior reuse during inheritance. Recently, Fournet *et al.* have proposed a promising solution to this problem [5]. The main idea is to extend the Join calculus [3] with objects and classes, and more importantly to design a novel class operation for both behavioral and synchronization inheritance, called *selective refinement*.

However, Fournet *et al.*'s model still suffers from several limitations, mainly in typing. Briefly, their type system is counter-intuitive and significantly restricts the power of selective refinement. In prior work [7], we tackled this problem by designing a new type system. We mainly enriched class types with complete synchronization behavior to exploit the full expressiveness of selective refinement. However, doing so inevitably impaired the other dual role of class types, *i.e.* abstraction. More specifically, it was unlikely for two different classes to possess the same type. How we can regain abstraction becomes a subsequent interesting question. We manage to achieve this goal by enabling programmers with *information hiding* capability in this paper.

M. Okada and I. Satoh (Eds.): ASIAN 2006, LNCS 4435, pp. 240–247, 2007.
© Springer-Verlag Berlin Heidelberg 2007

Information hiding by itself is already a key issue in large-scale programming. Generally, information hiding allows programmers to decide what to export in the interface (which we assimilate to types) of an implementation. This principle brings advantages, such as removing irrelevant details from interfaces and protecting critical details of the implementation. As regards objects, one can easily hide some components by declaring them to be *private*, as Fournet *et al.* and many others do. These private components do not appear in object interfaces. By contrast, information hiding in classes is more involved, especially in the presence of synchronization inheritance. The difficulty resides in that synchronization introduces certain type dependency among names, while carelessly hiding some of them would result in unsafe typing. We are aware of no work on this issue. Specifically, if we classify users of a class into two categories: *object users* who create objects from the class; and *inheritance users* who derive new class definitions by inheriting the class, the simple privacy policy applies solely to object users while always leaving full access to inheritance users.

We address the issue of information hiding towards inheritance users in this paper. We do so by introducing a new explicit hiding operation in the class language. This amounts to significant changes in both the semantics and the typing of class operations. Theoretically, hiding a name in a class can be expressed as quantifying it existentially. In practice, we α-convert hidden names to fresh names in the operational semantics and remove hidden names from class types in typing. We believe that our proposal achieves a reasonable balance of semantical simplicity and expressiveness, and that it yields a practical level of abstraction in class types, while preserving safety. Moreover, our surprisingly simple idea of hiding by α-conversion should apply equally well to other class-based systems, provided they rely on structural typing as we do.

In this short paper, we focus on intuition, while making available a complementary technical report [8] for complete formalism.

2   Classes, Objects, and Hiding

Basic class definition consists of a *join definition* and an (optional) **init** process, called *initializer* (analog to *constructors* or *makers* in other languages). As an example, we define the following class for one-place buffers:

```
class c_buffer =
    put(n,r) & Empty() ▷ r.reply() & this.Some(n)
  or get(r) & Some(n) ▷ r.reply(n) & this.Empty()
  init this.Empty()
```

and instantiate an object from it:

```
obj buffer = c_buffer
```

Similar to Join, four *channels* are collectively defined in this example and arranged in two *reaction rules* disjunctively connected by **or**. We use the two channels **put** and **get** for the two possible operations, and the two channels **Empty** or **Some** for the two possible states of a one-place buffer, namely, being empty or full. We here follow Fournet *et al.*'s convention to express privacy: channels with capitalized names are *private*; they can be accessed only through recursive self references; and the privacy policy is enforced statically.

Each reaction rule consists of a *join pattern* and a *guarded process*, separated by ▷. Join patterns specify the synchronization among channels. Namely, only if there are messages pending on all the channels in a given pattern, the object can react by consuming the messages and triggering the guarded process. As a result, this one-place buffer behaves as expected: the (optional) **init** process initializes the buffer as empty; we then can put a value when it is empty, or alternatively retrieve the stored value when it is full.

By contrast with Join— whose values are channels, objects now become the values of the calculus. As an important consequence, channel names are no longer governed by the usual rules of lexical scoping (objects names are). Channel names can be seen as global, as method names are in any simple object calculi. From now on, channel names are called *labels*.

The basic operation of our calculus is asynchronous message sending, but expressed in object-oriented dot notation, such as in process r.reply(n), which stands for "send message n to the channel reply of object r". Also note that we use the keyword **this** for recursive self references, while other references are handled through object names. Compared with the design in [5], this modification significantly simplifies the privacy control in object semantics.

2.1 Inheritance and Hiding

Inheritance is basically performed by using, *i.e.* computing with, parent classes in derived classes. At the moment, all labels defined in a class are visible during inheritance. However, this complete knowledge of class behavior may not be necessary for building a new class by inheritance. Moreover, exposing full details during inheritance sometimes puts program safety at risk, and designers of parent classes may legitimately wish to restrict the view of inheritance users.

As an example, an inheritance user may attempt to extend the class c_buffer with a new channel put2 for putting two elements:

class c_put2_buffer = c_buffer
  or put2(n,m,r) & Empty() ▷ r.reply() & this.(Some(n) & Some(m))

Unfortunately, this naïve implementation breaks the invariant of a one-place buffer. More specifically, the put2 attempt, once it succeeds, sends two messages on channel Some in parallel. Semantically, this means turning a one-place buffer into an invalid state where two values are stored simultaneously.

In order to protect classes from (deliberate or accidental) integrity-violating inheritance, we introduce a new operation on classes to hide critical channels. We reach a more robust definition using hiding:

class c_hidden_buffer = c_buffer **hide** {Empty, Some}

The hiding clause **hide** {Empty, Some} hides the critical channels Empty and Some. They are now absent from the class type and become inaccessible during inheritance. As a result, the previous invariant-violating definition of channel put2 will be rejected by a "name unbound" static error. Nevertheless, programmers can still supplement one-place buffers with a put2 operation as follows:

```
class c_put2_buffer_bis = c_hidden_buffer
  or put2(n,m,r) ▷ class c_join =
                    reply() & Next() ▷ r.reply()
                    or reply() & Start() ▷ this.Next()
                    init this.Start() in
                    obj k = c_join in this.(put(n,k) & put(m,k))
```

In the code above, the (inner) class c_join serves the purpose of consuming two acknowledgments from the previous one-place buffer and of acknowledging the success of the put2 operation to the appropriate object r. One may remark that the order in which values n and m are stored remains unspecified.

2.2 Hiding Only Private Channels

We here restrict our hiding mechanism only to private channels. Such a decision originates in the problems between hiding public channels and supporting advanced features, such as *selftype* (also known as *mytype*) and *binary methods* [1]. As observed in [13,2], these two aspects do not trivially get along without endangering type soundness. More specifically, a problem manifests itself when selftype is assumed outside the class and we hide a public channel afterwards. As an example, consider the following class definitions.

```
class c_0 = f(x) ▷ x.b(1)
class c_1 = a() ▷ obj x = c_0 in x.f(this)
           or b(n) ▷ out.print_int(n)
```

Channel f of class c_0 expects an object with a channel b of type integer. This condition is satisfied when typing the guarded process of channel a in class c_1, because the self object **this** does have a channel b of type integer. However, later inheritance may hide the channel b (in class c_2), and then define a new channel also named b but with a different type string (in class c_3).

```
class c_2 = c_1 hide {b}
class c_3 = c_2 or b(s) ▷ out.print_string(s)
```

Apparently, although the above code is typed correctly, the following process will cause a runtime type error: providing an integer when a string is expected.

```
obj o = c_3 in o.a()
```

A simple solution adopted in the community is not to support both. Following OCaml, we choose to support the notion of selftype and limit hiding to private channels. By contrast, Fisher and Reppy in their work for MOBY [2] choose the reverse: not to provide selftype and instead provide complete control over class-member visibility. Nevertheless, a more comprehensive solution is still possible [13], however, more complicated as well.

3   The Semantics of Hiding

Class semantics is expressed as the rewriting of class-terms, while object semantics by the means of reflexive chemical machines [3]. Class reductions always terminate and produce *class normal forms*, which are basically object definitions, plus an (optional) initializer, plus a a list of abstract labels. In cases where the latter is empty (which can be statically controlled by our type systems), objects can be created from such class definitions in normal form. Hence, our evaluation mode is a stratified one: first rewrite classes to object definitions; then feed the resulting term and an initial input into a chemical abstract machine.

How to hide labels? The semantics of hiding in classes is governed by two concerns. On one hand, hidden labels disappear. For instance, redefining a new label homonymous to a previously hidden label yields a totally new label. On the other hand, hidden labels still exist. For instance, objects created by instantiating the class `c_hidden_buffer` from Sect. 2.1 must somehow possess labels to encode the state of a one-place buffer.

The formal evaluation rule for hiding appears as follows:

$$\text{Eval-Hide} \quad \frac{\Gamma \vDash C \Downarrow_C C_v \quad (f_i \text{ defined in } C_v, h_i \text{ fresh})^{i \in I}}{\Gamma + (c \mapsto C_v \{h_i / f_i{}^{i \in I}\}_{\mathcal{H}}) \vDash P \Downarrow_P P_v}{\Gamma \vDash \textbf{class } c = C \textbf{ hide } \{f_i{}^{i \in I}\} \textbf{ in } P \Downarrow_P P_v}$$

The above inference rule is part of the class reduction semantics (see [8]). Judgments express the reduction of classes to class normal forms, under an environment Γ that binds class names to class normal forms (call-by-value semantics).

Hiding applies only to class normal forms (C_v), and only at class binding time. The hiding procedure $\{h_i / f_i{}^{i \in I}\}_{\mathcal{H}}$ is implemented by α-converting the hidden channels $\{f_i{}^{i \in I}\}$ to fresh labels $\{h_i{}^{i \in I}\}$, whose definition is without surprise. Such a semantics makes sense because labels are *not* scoped. The α-conversion should apply to both definition occurrences (in join patterns) and reference occurrences (in guarded processes and in the **init** process) of the hidden labels in the normal form. Thanks to the restriction to only hide private labels, the recursive self references in the normal form already include *all* the reference occurrences of hidden labels. Moreover, we do not rename under nested object definitions because they re-bind **this**. To give some intuition, the normal form of class `c_hidden_buffer` from Sect. 2.1 looks as follows:

```
class c_hidden_buffer =
    get(r) & Some'(n) ▷ r.reply(n) & this.Empty'()
  or put(n,r) & Empty'() ▷ r.reply() & this.Some'(n)
  init this.Empty'()
```

Here, we assume **Empty'** and **Some'** to be the two fresh labels that replace **Empty** and **Some** respectively.

This design meets the two concerns described at the beginning of this section: on one hand, freshness guarantees hidden names not to be visible during inheritance; on the other hand, hidden names are still present in class normal forms but under fresh identities.

4   The Typing of Hiding

4.1   Class Types and Object Types, Catching Up

Types are automatically inferred. Following our prior work [7], a class type consists of three parts, written $\zeta(\rho)B^W$, where B lists the set of channels, defined or declared in the class, paired with the types of the messages they accept, and W reflects how defined channels are synchronized, *i.e.* the structure of the join patterns in the corresponding class normal form. The row type ρ collects the public label-type pairs from B for the type of objects created from this class. To avoid repetition, in concrete syntax, ρ is usually incorporated in B that is enclosed between **object** and **end**, as in the type of class c_buffer from Sect. 2:

> **class** c_buffer: **object**
>> **label** get: ([reply: (θ); ϱ]); **label** put: $(\theta, [reply: (); \varrho'])$;
>> **label** Some: (θ); **label** Empty: ();
> **end** $W = \{\{get, Some\}, \{put, Empty\}\}$

We see that messages conveyed by channels are polyadic. The type of a channel carrying k objects of types $\tau_1, \ldots, \tau_k$ is written $(\tau_1, \ldots, \tau_k)$. Object types are always enclosed in square brackets. The type of objects of this class is:

> [get: ([reply: (θ); ϱ]); put: $(\theta, [reply: (); \varrho'])$]

Channels Some and Empty do not show up because they are private. Finally, W is organized as a set of sets of labels. Two labels appear in the same member set of W if and only if they are synchronized in one join pattern.

Following ML type systems, polymorphism is parametric polymorphism, obtained essentially by generalizing free type variables. However, such generalization is controlled for object types. More specifically, any type variables that are shared by synchronized channels should not be generalized. Detailed rationale for doing so is discussed in all kinds of Join typing papers, such as [7,4]. The basic reason is for type safety. As an example, type variable θ should not be polymorphic in the object type above, because following the class type it is shared by two synchronized channels get and Some (*i.e.* appearing in the same member set of W). Otherwise, its two occurrence in get and put could then be instantiated independently as, for instance, integer and string. This then would result in a runtime type error: attempting to retrieve a string when an integer is present. By contrast, θ is safely generalized in the class type, which allows us to create two objects from it, one dealing with integers, and the other with strings. The two trailing row variables ϱ, ϱ' are both generalizable. They can be instantiated as more label-type pairs, thus introducing a useful degree of subtyping polymorphism by structure.

4.2   How to Type Hiding: Ideas

The most straightforward idea is to remove hidden names from class types. As a consequence, class `c_hidden_buffer` from Sect. 2.1 has type:

class c_hidden_buffer: object
    label get: ([reply: (θ); ϱ]); **label** put: $(\theta,$[reply: (); ϱ']);
  end $W = \{\{get\}, \{put\}\}$

The two hidden channels Some and Empty are eliminated from both the B list and W. Unfortunately, such a naïve elimination has a side-effect, which may endanger safe polymorphism in the corresponding object type. Plainly, the non-generalizable type variable θ has now falsely become generalizable, because according to this class type, the only two channels that share θ are not synchronized (*i.e.* get and put coming from two different member sets of W).

To tackle the problem, we then decide to keep track of such *dangerous type variables* caused by hiding in class types, called V. More precisely, before eliminating, we first record all the non-generalizable type variables of hidden names in V. For this example, the type of class `c_hidden_buffer` then evolves to:

class c_hidden_buffer: object
    label get: ([reply: (θ); ϱ]); **label** put: $(\theta,$[reply: (); ϱ']);
  end $W = \{\{get\}, \{put\}\}$ $V = \{\theta\}$

Right before hiding, the type variables in a hidden channel are of two kinds: non-generalizable or generalizable. The modification above solves perfectly the problem of losing information about non-generalizable ones. If type variables that are generalizable before hiding would always be kept so, we here already reach a working way of typing hiding. Unfortunately, it is not the case. Some generalizable type variables of hidden channels may later become non-generalizable during inheritance, even though the channels are already hidden. Consider the following class definition in which channel Ch' is hidden:

class $c_1 = a(x) \triangleright 0$ **or** $b(y)$ & $Ch'(n_1, n_2) \triangleright$ **this.**$(a(n_1)$ & $b(n_2))$

The corresponding class type is:

class c_1**: object label** a: (θ); **label** b: (θ') **end** $W = \{\{a\},\{b\}\}$ $V = \{\theta'\}$

The hidden channel Ch' is of type (θ, θ'). According to the definition, θ' is non-generalizable (because shared by the synchronized channel b) thus is put in V. By contrast, θ is generalizable. However, the following inheritance of class c_1 easily convert θ into non-generalizable:

class $c_2 =$ **match** c_1 **with** $b(y) \Rightarrow b(y)$ & $d(z) \triangleright$ **this.**$a(z)$ **end**

This selective refinement operation mainly replaces "b(y)" by "b(y) & d(z)" in join patterns and composes the corresponding guarded processes with "**this.**a(z)" in parallel. As a consequence, class c_2 has the following normal form:

class $c_{v2} = a(x) \triangleright 0$
    or $b(y)$ & $d(z)$ & $Ch'(n_1, n_2) \triangleright$ **this.**$(a(n_1)$ & $b(n_2)$ & $a(z))$

The new channel d is of type (θ). It synchronizes and shares θ with Ch'. However it is already too late to update the non-generalizable information to reflect this, because hidden names are already eliminated from class types thus out of control of the type system. A simple solution we adopt is to treat already all the free type variable of hidden names as dangerous, non-generalizable and generalizable, in case the non-generalizable ones increase. To sum up, the final type of class c_1 is:

class c_1: object label a: (θ); **label b:** (θ') **end** $W = \{\{a\},\{b\}\}$ $V = \{\theta,\theta'\}$

Formal discussion of the type system appears in the complementary technical report [8], including statement and proof of a *"soundness"* theorem.

5   Conclusion

We have achieved significant improvements over the original design of Fournet *et al.* [5]: in [7] as regards the class system expressiveness, and in this paper as regards visibility control, type abstraction, and simplification of runtime semantics. We claim that these improvements yield a calculus mature enough to act as the model of a full-scale implementation.

References

1. Bruce, K., Cardelli, L., Castagna, G., Leavens, G.T., Pierce, B.: On binary methods. Theory and Practice of Object Systems 1(3), 221–242 (1995)
2. Fisher, K., Reppy, J.: The design of a class mechanism for MOBY. In: Proceedings of PLDI 1999, pp.37–49 (1999)
3. Fournet, C., Gonthier, G.: The reflexive chemical abstract machine and the join-calculus. In: Proceedings of POPL 1996, pp. 372–385 (1996)
4. Fournet, C., Maranget, L., Laneve, C., Rémy, D.: Implicit typing à la ML for the join-calculus. In: Proceedings of CONCUR 1997, pp. 196–212 (1997)
5. Fournet, C., Maranget, L., Laneve, C., Rémy, D.: Inheritance in the join calculus. Journal of Logic and Algebraic Programming 57(1-2), 23–69 (2003)
6. Gordon, A.D., Hankin, P.D.: A concurrent object calculus: reduction and typing. In: Proceedings of HLCL 1998, pp. 248–264 (1998)
7. Ma, Q., Maranget, L.: Expressive synchronization types for inheritance in the join calculus. In: Proceedings of APLAS 2003, pp. 20–36 (2003)
8. Ma, Q., Maranget, L.: Information hiding, inheritance and concurrency. Inria Rocquencourt Research Report RR-5631 (2005)
9. Matsuoka, S., Yonezawa, A.: Analysis of inheritance anomaly in object-oriented concurrent programming languages. In: Research Directions in Concurrent Object-Oriented Programming, pp. 107–150. MIT Press, Cambridge (1993)
10. Milicia, G., Sassone, V.: The inheritance anomaly: ten years after. In: Proceedings of SAC 1996, pp. 1267–1274 (2004)
11. Odersky, M.: Functional nets. In: Proceedings of ESOP 2000, pp. 1–25 (2000)
12. Riecke, J.G., Stone, C.A.: Privacy via subsumption. Information and Computation 172(1), 2–28 (2002)
13. Vouillon, J.: Combining subsumption and binary methods: an object calculus with views. In: Proceedings of POPL 2001, pp. 290–303 (2001)

Modeling Urgency in Component-Based Real-Time Systems

Nguyen Van Tang[1], Dang Van Hung[2], and Mizuhito Ogawa[1]

[1] Japan Advanced Institute of Science and Technology
{tang_nguyen, mizuhito}@jaist.ac.jp
[2] United Nation University, International Institute for Software Technology
dvh@iist.unu.edu

Abstract. A component-based realtime system is a simple model for the server-client relation with time constraints. This paper presents an efficient algorithm, called a *blackbox testing algorithm*, for detecting the emptiness of a component-based realtime system. This algorithm was originally proposed in [5], but with a certain flaw. We improve it and correct the flaw by using urgency [2] of transitions.

Keywords: Component Software, Duration Automata, Automatic Verification, Real-time Systems, Model Checking.

1 Introduction

The architectural design for embedded systems often relies on specification of the interface of components only, without accessing their internal behaviors. Based on this observation, a simple model for component-based real-time systems based on duration automata was proposed in [5]. A duration automaton does not have clock variables like a time automaton [1], but simply has an upper bound and a lower bound for each transition. A component-based real-time system is defined as a system consisting of a host, which is a general duration automaton, and several components which are duration automata with certain restrictions. A component-based real-time system can be regarded as a timed automaton, thus its emptiness is PSPACE-complete.

This paper presents an efficient algorithm for detecting the emptiness, called a *blackbox testing algorithm*. This algorithm was originally proposed in [5], but with certain flaws. We improve it and correct these flaws by using urgency of transitions, which was firstly introduced by Bornot et. al. [2] as a technique for choosing time deadline condition in complex system specifications.

2 Duration Automata

Duration automata was firstly introduced in [3] for modeling simple real-time systems. A duration automaton is a finite automaton in which each transition must occur in an associated time interval. Let $\mathbb{R}^+$ be the set of non-negative real numbers, and let $Intv = \{[l, u] \mid l \in \mathbb{R}^+, u \in \mathbb{R}^+ \cup \{\infty\}\}$.

M. Okada and I. Satoh (Eds.): ASIAN 2006, LNCS 4435, pp. 248–255, 2007.
© Springer-Verlag Berlin Heidelberg 2007

Definition 1. *A duration automaton is a tuple $M = \langle S, \tilde{\Sigma}, q, R, F \rangle$, where*

1. *S is a finite set of states,*
2. *$\tilde{\Sigma}$ is alphabet of actions,*
3. *$q \in S$ is the initial state,*
4. *$R \subseteq S \times \tilde{\Sigma} \times Intv \times S$ is timed transition relation, and*
5. *$F \subseteq S$ is the set of final states.*

Each element of M is referred by $S(M)$, $\tilde{\Sigma}(M)$, $R(M)$, $q(M)$, and $F(M)$, respectively. An untimed automaton $untimed(M)$ is obtained by forgetting time constraints, i.e., replacing R with $untimed(R) = \{(s, a, s') | (s, a, [l, u], s') \in R\}$. As in standard terminology,

- A *configuration* of M is a pair $(s, d) \in S \times \mathbb{R}^+$.
- The *initial configuration* of M is $(q, 0)$.
- An *acceptance configuration* of M is a configuration (s, d) where $s \in F$.

A duration automaton is equivalent to a timed automata with a single clock such that each transition resets it. A configuration (s, d) is regarded as a state s with a clock d.

- A transition of M on configurations is either a *time transition* $(s, d) \xrightarrow{\delta} (s, d + \delta)$ or a *discrete transition* $(s, d) \xrightarrow{\delta} \xrightarrow{a} (s', 0)$ where $a \in \tilde{\Sigma}$, $\delta \geq 0$, $l \leq d + \delta \leq u$, and $(s, a, [l, u], s') \in R$.
- A (possibly empty) sequence $w = (a_1, t_1)...(a_k, t_k) \in (\tilde{\Sigma} \times \mathbb{R}^+)^*$ is a *timed word* of M if and only if there is a run $(s_0, 0) \xrightarrow{\delta_1} \xrightarrow{a_1} (s_1, 0) \xrightarrow{\delta_2} \xrightarrow{a_2} ... \xrightarrow{\delta_k} \xrightarrow{a_k} (s_k, 0)$ such that $s_0 = q$, $s_k \in F$, $t_1 = \delta_1$ and $t_{i+1} - t_i = \delta_{i+1}$ for $1 \leq i \leq k-1$.

Theorem 1. *Duration automata is closed under union, intersection and complementation. Decision problems for duration automata are decidable.*

Proof. (Sketch) For a given duration automaton M, one can reduce M to a finite automaton M'. We first list the endpoints of intervals (lower and upper bounds of intervals) of transitions in M as an increasing sequence, say, $0 = p_0 < p_1 < p_2... < p_n < \infty$. This is possible because the number of transitions of M is finite. Secondly, we define the set of basic intervals $BI = \{[p_0, p_1], ..., [p_{n-1}, p_n], [p_n, \infty)\}$. Since each interval appeared in a transition of M is the union of certain basic intervals. So, each transition of M can be divided into several ones. For instance, $(s, a, [p_0, p_2], s')$ can be divided into $(s, a, [p_0, p_1], s')$ and $(s, a, [p_1, p_2], s')$. We now construct a finite automaton M' such that $S(M') = S(M)$, $F(M') = F(M)$, the input alphabet of M' is $\tilde{\Sigma}(M') = \tilde{\Sigma}(M) \times BI$. Let $(s, (a, [p_i, p_{i+1}]), s') \in R(M')$ if $(s, a, [p_i, p_{i+1}], s') \in R(M)$. Clearly, M' accepts a word $(a_1, [l_1, u_1])...(a_n, [l_n, u_n])$ if and only if M accepts the timed word $(a_1, t_1)...(a_n, t_n)$, where $t_0 = 0$ and $(l_i \leq t_i - t_{i-1} \leq u_i)$ for $1 \leq i \leq n$. Thus, the emptiness and the closure properties of duration automata are reduced to that of finite automata, respectively. $\square$

3   Synchronized Composition Systems

Duration interface automata is duration automata in which the input alphabet $\tilde{\Sigma}$ is decomposed into pairwise disjoint alphabets Σ, Δ and ∇, which correspond to internal, input and output actions, respectively.

Definition 2. *A* host *is a duration interface automaton. A* component *is a duration interface automaton* $X = \langle S, \Sigma \cup \Delta \cup \nabla, q, R, F \rangle$ *that satisfies:*

- $\Sigma = \emptyset$ *(i.e., no "explicit" internal actions).*
- $(s, a, [l, u], s') \in R \wedge a \in \Delta$ *implies* $l = 0 \wedge u = \infty$ *(i.e., an input can occur anytime).*
- $(s, a, [l, u], s') \in R \wedge a \in \nabla$ *implies* $u = \infty$ *(i.e., when an output is ready, it can be sent at any time afterward).*

Definition 3. *A* synchronized composition system $Sys = \langle M, X_1, \cdots, X_k \rangle$ *consists of a single host M and components $X_1, \cdots, X_k$ such that $\tilde{\Sigma}(X_i) \cap \tilde{\Sigma}(X_j) = \emptyset$ for each $i \neq j$, $\Sigma(M) \cap \tilde{\Sigma}(X_i) = \emptyset$ for each i, $\Delta(M) = \bigcup_{i=1}^{k} \nabla(X_k)$, $\nabla(M) = \bigcup_{i=1}^{k} \Delta(X_k)$, and*

- *The set of configurations is* $\{((s_0, d_0), (s_1, d_1), \cdots, (s_k, d_k)) \mid s_0 \in S(M), s_1 \in S(X_1), \cdots, s_k \in S(X_k), d_i \in \mathbb{R}^+\}.$
- *A transition is* $((s_0, d_0), (s_1, d_1), .., (s_k, d_k)) \xrightarrow{\delta} \xrightarrow{a} ((s_0', d_0'), (s_1', d_1'), .., (s_k', d_k'))$ *for $\delta \geq 0$ and $a \in \bigcup_{i=1}^{k} \tilde{\Sigma}(X_i)$, if there exists i with $1 \leq i \leq k$ such that*
  - $a \in \tilde{\Sigma}(X_i)$,
  - $l_0 \leq d_0 + \delta \leq u_0$ *and* $l_i \leq d_i + \delta \leq u_i$ *(called* synchronization condition*) for* $(s_i, a, [l_i, u_i], s_i') \in R(X_i)$ *and* $(s_0, a, [l_0, u_0], s_0') \in R(M)$,
  - $d_0' = d_i' = 0$, *and*
  - $(s_j', d_j') = (s_j, d_j + \delta)$ *for* $j \neq 0, i$.
- *A run is a sequence of transitions that starts from the initial configuration* $((q(M), 0), (q(X_1), 0), \cdots, (q(x_k), 0)).$
- *A timed word* $(a_1, t_1) \cdots (a_k, t_k)$ *with* $t_1 = \delta_1$ *and* $t_{i+1} = t_i + \delta_{i+1}$ *is accepted if there is a run* $((q(M), 0), (q(X_1), 0), \cdots, (q(x_k), 0)) \xrightarrow{\delta_1} \xrightarrow{a_1} \cdots \xrightarrow{\delta_k} \xrightarrow{a_k} ((s_0, d_0), (s_1, d_1), .., (s_k, d_k))$ *with* $s_0 \in F(M), s_1 \in F(X_1), \cdots, s_k \in F(X_k).$

Theorem 2. *A* synchronized composition system $Sys = \langle M, X_1, \cdots, X_k \rangle$ *is a timed automaton with $k+1$ clocks such that each transition with a time constraint $l_i \leq d_i \leq u_i$ on a clock d_i will reset d_i to 0.*

Proof. (Sketch) Let $\mathcal{C}$ be the set of time constraints $[l_j, u_j]$ appearing in a host M and components X_i. Note that $l_j, u_j \in \mathbb{R}^+$. Assume that we can choose $\mathcal{C}'$ (a digitization of $\mathbb{C}$) consisting of rational time constraints $[l_j', u_j']$ such that there is a run of Sys if and only if there is a run of Sys', where Sys' is obtained replacing each $[l_j, u_j]$ with its digitization $[l_j', u_j']$. Then, the proof has done.

Let $rat(\mathcal{C})$ be the set of rational numbers appearing in $\mathcal{C}$ and let m be a common multiplier of dominators of positive elements in $rat(\mathcal{C})$. Let $irr(\mathcal{C})$ be the set of irrational numbers appearing in $\mathcal{C}$ and let $lin(\mathcal{C})$ be the set of all possible linear combinations of $irr(\mathcal{C})$ with natural numbers (i.e., $lin(\mathcal{C}) = \{n_1\alpha_1 + \cdots + n_l\alpha_l \mid n_j \in \mathbb{N}, \alpha_j \in irr(\mathcal{C})\}$). Assume that (α, β) is the pair such that $\alpha \in irr(\mathcal{C})$, $\beta \in lin(\mathcal{C})$, and $\epsilon_{\alpha,\beta} = \frac{\alpha}{\beta} - [\frac{\alpha}{\beta}] > 0$. Since a pair (α, β) with $\alpha \in irr(\mathcal{C})$, $\beta \in lin(\mathcal{C})$, and $\beta < \alpha$ is finitely many, (α, β) with $\epsilon_{\alpha,\beta}$ to be the least exists. We choose a sufficient large multiplier $\bar{m}$ of m such that $\frac{1}{\bar{m}} < min(\frac{\epsilon_{\alpha,\beta}}{2}, \frac{1-\epsilon_{\alpha,\beta}}{2})$, and set $l'_j = \frac{[\bar{m}l_j]}{\bar{m}}$ and $u'_j = \frac{[\bar{m}u_j]}{\bar{m}}$ for each $l_j, u_j \in \mathcal{C}$. $\qquad\square$

Example 1. Fig. 3 shows a simple synchronized composition system $Sys = \langle X_1, X_2 \rangle$ and its corresponding timed automaton $\mathcal{A}$.

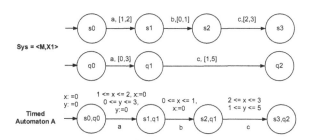

Fig. 1. Synchronized Composition System as a Timed Automaton

From Theorem 2, the emptiness problem of a component-based realtime system is decidable. However, its complexity is expensive, i.e., PSPACE-complete [1] after digitization of time constraints.

4   Component-Based Realtime Systems

Definition 4. *A component X is* input/output deterministic *if*

- *for $a \in \Delta(X)$, $(s, a, [0, \infty), s'), (s, a, [0, \infty), s") \in R(X)$ implies $s" = s'$ (input determinism), and*
- *for $b \in \nabla(X)$ and $b' \in \nabla(X) \cup \Delta(X)$, $(s, b, [l, \infty), s'), (s, b', [l', u'], s") \in R(X)$ implies $s" = s'$, $l' = l$, $u' = \infty$, and $b' = b$ (output determinism).*

A synchronized composition system $Sys = \langle M, X_1, \cdots, X_k \rangle$ is a component-based realtime system [5] if each component X_i is input/output deterministic.

Definition 5. *We borrow notations from Definition 3. In a component-based system $Sys = \langle M, X_1, \cdots, X_k \rangle$, a transition $((s_0, d_0), (s_1, d_1), .., (s_k, d_k)) \xrightarrow{\delta} \xrightarrow{a} ((s'_0, d'_0), (s'_1, d'_1), .., (s'_k, d'_k))$ is* urgent *if δ is the minimum among synchronization conditions of all possible transitions from $((s_0, d_0), (s_1, d_1), .., (s_k, d_k))$, and* delayable *otherwise. We also say a corresponding transition $(s_0, a, [l_0, u_0], s'_0) \in R(M)$ of a host is* urgent, *and* delayable *otherwise.*

Definition 6. *Let* $w = (a_1, t_1) \cdots (a_k, t_k)$ *and let* $a_i \in A$. *For* $B \subseteq A$, *the projection* $w|_B$ *is the subsequence of* w *obtained by filtering each element* (a_j, t_j) *with* $a_j \in B$. *For* $a_j \in B$, (a_h, t_h) *is a* local predecessor *of* (a_j, t_j) *wrt* B, *if* $a_h \in B$, $h < j$, *and* $a_i \notin B$ *for each* i *with* $h < i < j$.

Definition 7. *Let* $Sys = \langle M, X_1, \cdots, X_k \rangle$ *be a component-based real-time system. For a timed word* $w = (a_1, t_1)...(a_n, t_n)$, *let* $a_j \in \nabla(X_i)$ *and let* (a_h, t_h) *be the local predecessor of* (a_j, t_j) *wrt* $\tilde{\Sigma}(X_i)$. *For* $(s', a_j, [d_j, \infty), s'') \in R(X_i)$ *with*

$$q(X_i) \xrightarrow{untime(w|_{\tilde{\Sigma}(X_i)})} s' \text{ in } untimed(X_i), \ d_j \text{ is the minimum delay at } (a_j, t_j).$$

Definition 8. *A consecutive sequence of transitions* $(s_{i-1}, a_i, [l_i, u_i], s_i) \in R(M)$ ($i = 1, \cdots, n$) *is called an* accepted sequence of transitions *of the host* M *if* $s_0 = q(M)$ *and* $s_n \in F(M)$.

Note that such a minimum delay is well-defined, since each component in Sys is input/output deterministic. Let r be the number of states of M, and let m is the maximal number of states of components $X_j, j \leq k$. Let P be the length of the longest path (number of transitions) from the initial state to a final state of M in which any cycle is not repeated more than $r * m^k$ times. The next theorem reduces the emptiness of a whole component-base realtime system to that of its host under certain conditions.

Theorem 3. *Let* $Sys = \langle M, X_1, \cdots, X_k \rangle$ *be a component-based realtime system. There is an accepted timed word of* Sys *if and only if there are an accepted sequence of transitions of the host* M $\sigma = (s_0, a_1, [l_1, u_1], s_1)(s_1, a_2, [l_2, u_2], s_3)...$ $(s_{n-1}, a_n, [l_n, u_n], s_n)$ *with the length* $n \leq P$, *and a real number sequence* $0 = t_0 \leq t_1 \leq \cdots \leq t_n$ *satisfying following conditions:*

- *$w_i = a_1 a_2 ... a_n|_{\tilde{\Sigma}(X_i)}$ is accepted by* untimed(X_i) *for each* i *with* $1 \leq i \leq k$,
- *$l_i \leq t_i - t_{i-1} \leq u_i$ for all* i *with* $1 \leq i \leq n$,
- *When* $a_j \in \nabla(X_i)$, *let* (a_h, t_h) *be the local predecessor of* (a_j, t_j) *wrt* $\tilde{\Sigma}(X_i)$ *and let* d_j *be the minimum delay at* (a_j, t_j). *Then,*
  - *$t_j - t_h \geq d_j$, and*
  - *if the transition* $(s_{j-1}, a_j, [l_j, u_j], s_j)$ *is urgent,* $t_j = min \{t \mid t - t_h \geq d_j \wedge l_j \leq t - t_{j-1} \leq u_j\}$.

Proof. (Sketch) If the assumption in Theorem holds, we can inductively construct an accepted behavior of Sys $\sigma' = c_0 \xrightarrow{\delta_1} \xrightarrow{a_1} \cdots \xrightarrow{\delta_n} \xrightarrow{a_n} c_n$, where $t_1 = \delta_1$, and $t_i = \Sigma_{j=1}^{i}$. It is clear that $(a_1, t_1)(a_2, t_2)...(a_n, t_n)$ is a accepted timed word of Sys. Now, we only have to prove the bound P in "only if" part. Assume that a timed word $w = (a_1, t_1) \cdots (a_n, t_n)$ is accepted by Sys. Timed word w is inductively computed by constructing an accepted sequence of transitions $\phi = (s_0, a_1, [l_1, u_1], s_1)(s_1, a_2, [l_2, u_2], s_3) \cdots (s_{n-1}, a_n, [l_n, u_n], s_n)$ of the host M. If $n \leq P$, the proof is done. If $n > P$, then ϕ must include at least a cycle c with more than $r * m^k$ repetitions. By the pumping lemma like argument, we can find a shorter accepted sequence of transitions of M that satisfies all the conditions in the Theorem.   □

In the next section, the blackbox testing algorithm will be presented by searching an accepted sequence of the host M satisfying the conditions in Theorem 3 up to the length P.

5 Checking Emptiness of Component-Based Realtime Systems

The emptiness problem for a system plays a key role in checking the safety. An algorithm for checking the emptiness of a component-based system using black box testing was originally proposed in [5]. However, there is a flaw such that a component-based realtime system is empty, whereas the algorithm in [5] reports that the system is not empty. For instance, consider the following simple example.

Example 2. Let $Sys = \langle M, X \rangle$ where M is a host and X is a component.

- $M = \langle \{s_0, s_1, s_1'\}, \{a\}, s_0, \{(s_0, a, [2, 4], s_1), (s_0, a, [5, 10], s_1')\}, \{s_1'\}\rangle$.
- $X = \langle \{q_0, q_1\}, \{a\}, q_0, \{(q_0, a, [3, \infty), q_1)\}, \{q_1\}\rangle$.

In [5], the state (s_1', q_1) is regarded as a successor of (s_0, q_0). But, (s_1', q_1) is not reachable from (s_0, q_0). This is due to the fact that Sys has already changed from (s_0, q_0) to (s_1, q_1) at some point in the time interval [3,4].

To deal with this problem, we introduce urgency for transitions to specify time deadline condition of configurations. For the emptiness problem, we first use the **BlackboxTest** algorithm proposed in [5] for solving membership for a component. Secondly, we construct Algorithm 1 to compute time deadline condition of a given configuration. Lastly, with the aid of Algorithm 1 and Theorem 3, we construct Algorithm 2 to check the emptiness of a component-based system using black box testing.

Definition 9. *1. For a sequence of transitions ϕ, let $label(\phi)$ denote the sequence of the labels corresponding to ϕ.*
  2. For a given prefix of a generated sequence of transitions $\sigma = e_1 e_2 ... e_n$, where $e_i = (s_{i-1}, a_i, [l_i, u_i], s_i) \in R(M)$ $(i = 1..n)$. Time deadline of s_n by action a along σ, denoted by $deadline_\sigma(s_n, a)$, is the maximal value δ such that $(s_n, 0) \xrightarrow{\delta} (s_n, \delta)$ and M must change to another state at time δ.

ALGORITHM 1. **Deadline$_\sigma(s_n, a)$**: (Check the conditions (2) and (3) of Theorem 3)

Input: A prefix-generated sequence $\sigma = e_1 e_2 ... e_n$
Output: $deadline_\sigma(s_n, a)$.
Method:

1. Compute the set $R(s_n, a) := \{e \mid e = (s_n, a, [l, u], s) \in R(M)\}$.
2. $deadline := \infty$. For $j \leq k$ let m_j be the largest index of σ such that $a_{m_j} \in \bar{\Sigma}(X_j)$ if it exists, otherwise, set $m_j = 0$. For each $e = (s_n, a, [l, u], s) \in R(s_n, a)$.

(a) If $a \in \triangle(X_j) \cup \Sigma(M)$, if **BlackboxTest**$(X_j, label(\sigma)|_{\tilde{\Sigma}(X_j)})=$ "yes" and $u < deadline$ then $deadline := u$.

(b) If $a \in \nabla(X_j)$. If **BlackboxTest**$(X_j, label(\sigma)|_{\tilde{\Sigma}(X_j)}) =$ "yes", let d be the value of d_{X_j}.

    – **Case 1: e is delayable.** If $t_n - t_{m_j} + u \geq d$ and $u < deadline$ then $deadline := u$.

    – **Case 2: e is urgent.**

        • If $t_n - t_{m_j} + l \leq d \leq t_n - t_{m_j} + u$ and $d - (t_n - t_{m_j}) < deadline$ then $deadline := d - (t_n - t_{m_j})$.

        • If $t_n - t_{m_j} + l \geq d$ and $l < deadline$ then $deadline := l$.

3. **return** Delainey;

With the aid of the Algorithm 1, the emptiness of a component-based real-time system can be solved by the following testing procedure.

ALGORITHM 2. **Non-Emptiness(Sys):** (Check all conditions of Theorem 3)

Input: Component-based real-time system $Sys = \langle M, X_1, \cdots, X_k \rangle$
Output: "Yes" if the set of timed words of Sys is not empty, "No" otherwise.
Method:

1. Compute P. Generate all accepted sequences of transitions of M with length less than P.

2. Check on-the-fly whether any prefix of a generated sequence satisfies the conditions of Theorem 3. This can be done by:
   For each prefix of a generated sequence of transitions $\sigma = e_1...e_{n-1}$, where $e_i = (s_{i-1}, a_i, [l_i, u_i], s_i)$ for each i with $1 \leq i \leq n-1$. Suppose that $t_0, t_1, ...t_n$ are inductively computed in advance. For $j \leq k$ let m_j be the largest index of σ such that $a_{m_j} \in \tilde{\Sigma}(X_j)$ if it exists, otherwise, let $m_j = 0$. For each transition $e_n = (s_{n-1}, a_n, [l, u], s)$ of the host M starting from s_{n-1}. Compute $deadline_\sigma(s_{n-1}, a_n)$ using Algorithm 1. If $l \leq deadline_\sigma(s_{n-1}, a_n)$ then:

   (a) If $a_n \in \triangle(X_j)$, then if: **BlackboxTest**$(X_j, label(\sigma)|_{\tilde{\Sigma}(X_j)}) =$ "no", σe_n does not satisfy the conditions of Theorem 3. Otherwise, $\sigma := \sigma e_n$, $m_j := n$. If e_n is delayable then $t_n := t_{n-1} + u$. If e_n is urgent then $t_n := t_{n-1} + l$.

   (b) If $a_n \in \nabla(X_j)$.
   If **BlackboxTest** $(X_j, label(\sigma)|_{\tilde{\Sigma}(X_j)}) =$ "yes", let d be the value of d_{X_j}.
   Case 1: If e_n is delayable
      i. If $t_{n-1} - t_{m_j} + u < d$: then σe_n does not satisfy the conditions of Theorem 3.
      ii. If $t_{n-1} - t_{m_j} + u \geq d$: then $\sigma := \sigma e_n$, $m_j := n$, $t_n := t_{n-1} + u$.
   Case 2: If e_n is urgent
      i. If $t_{n-1} - t_{m_j} + u < d$ then σe_n does not satisfy the conditions of Theorem 3.
      ii. If $(t_{n-1} - t_{m_j} + l) < d \leq (t_{n-1} - t_{m_j} + u)$ then the conditions of Theorem 3 are satisfied; update $\sigma := \sigma e_n$, $t_n := t_{m_j} + d$, $m_j := n$.

iii. If $t_{n-1} - t_{m_j} + l \geq d$ then update $\sigma := \sigma e_n$, $t_n := t_{n-1} + l$, $m_j := n$.
If **BlackboxTest**$(X_j, label(\sigma)|_{\tilde{\Sigma}(X_j)})$ ="no", the conditions of Theorem 3 are not satisfied.

   (c) If $a_n \in \Sigma(M)$ then $\sigma := \sigma e_n$, $t_n := t_{n-1} + u$.

3. If a generated sequence satisfying the conditions of Theorem 3 is found, return "Yes". Otherwise, return "No".

The complexity for the worst cases of this algorithm is $O(P^2 * K^{P+1})$, where $K = |\tilde{\Sigma}(M)|$ is the size of the alphabet of the system Sys. Unlike the complexity of checking the emptiness for timed automata, this complexity does not depend on the size of the constants occurring in the time intervals for the transitions.

6 Conclusion

This paper presented an efficient algorithm for detecting the emptiness, called a *blackbox testing algorithm*. This algorithm was originally proposed in [5], but with a certain flaw. We improved and corrected it by using urgency of transitions, which was firstly introduced by Bornot et. al. [2] as a technique for choosing time deadline condition in complex system specifications. The urgency enables us to compute the deadline of an accepted behavior of a system using Algorithm 2.

Currently, the algorithm covers checking emptiness only. With the urgency, we can describe a property in Timed Computation Tree Logic (TCTL), such as $\phi \implies F_{\leq t} \psi$. The next step is to give an efficient checking algorithm for such TCTL properties of a component-based realtime system.

Acknowledgments

This research is supported by the 21st Century COE "Verifiable and Evolvable e-Society" funded by Japanese Ministry of Education, Culture, Sports, Science and Technology.

References

1. Alur, R., Dill, D.L.: A Theory of Timed Automata. Theoretical Computer Science 126, 183–235 (1994)
2. Bornot, S., Sifakis, J., Tripakis, S.: Modeling urgency in timed systems. In: de Roever, W.-P., Langmaack, H., Pnueli, A. (eds.) COMPOS 1997. LNCS, vol. 1536, pp. 103–129. Springer, Heidelberg (1998)
3. Chaochen, Z.: Linear Duration Invariants. In: Formal Techniques in Real-Time and Fault-Tolerant Systems. LNCS, vol. 963, pp. 86–109. Springer, Heidelberg (1994)
4. Dang, Z., Xie, G.: CTL model-checking for systems with unspecified finite state components. In: SAVCBS 2004, ACM SIGSOFT 2004/FSE-12, pp. 32–38 (2004)
5. Van Hung, D., Vu Anh, B.: Model Checking Real-time Component Based Systems with Blackbox Testing. In: IEEE proceeding of RTCSA 2005, pp. 76–79, Hong Kong, (August 2005)

Maintaining Data Consistency of XML Databases Using Verification Techniques

Khandoker Asadul Islam and Yoshimichi Watanabe

University of Yamanashi, Kofu, Yamanashi 400-8511, Japan
{asad, nabe}@s.cs.yamanashi.ac.jp

Abstract. XML document is a very popular way to transfer data between databases because of its simplicity of structure and text based data storage. In some typical implementation scenarios where XML document is used to transfer data as XML database, it is necessary to check the consistency of the data at destination. If users are responsible for storing and transferring the document, there is a possibility of data manipulation. In this paper, we propose to apply data verification techniques including checksum and hash algorithms for data verification of XML document. As an advantage, we show that we not only can check the document's authenticity, but also we can identify the specific modified portions of the document. We discuss many popular checksum techniques and secured hash algorithms applied to XML document and compare their efficiency on data verification in the scenarios of the XML data transfer.

Keywords: XML Database, Verification.

1 Introduction

Nowadays XML[1] document are gaining popularity for a standard method of transmitting data through telecommunication or storage. From the several uses of XML document in data transfer, data transmission between two different or same relational databases is generally done. Also, XML document is used to store extracted information from any databases for later use. It is necessary to check the consistency of data stored as an XML document. Applying digital signature[2] is a standard to maintain and checks the authenticity of XML document. Digital signature ensures that the document is the same as the original document send by the sender, so that any changes done between sender and receiver can be detected. For protecting data from malicious users, encryption[3] of data can also be used. In the scenario of digital signature, digest of the whole document is used for the signature. The hash algorithms used are Message Digest (MD4), MD5, Secure Hash Algorithm 1 (SHA-1), SHA-256, SHA-384, SHA-512, and so on. Any change to the document invariably produces a different hash result when the same hash function is used. Thus comparing the digests at sending and receiving time at destination, we can detect whether the document has changed or not. The efficiency of digital signature depends on the hash algorithm used to generate digest. The digest is independent to the position of data, that

M. Okada and I. Satoh (Eds.): ASIAN 2006, LNCS 4435, pp. 256–263, 2007.
© Springer-Verlag Berlin Heidelberg 2007

is, the changed digest does not give us any information about the position of the change in the document.

In this paper, we experiment various data verification techniques on typical XML documents that are used for data transfer. The data verification techniques include checksum algorithms and one-way hash algorithms. Also, we propose a procedure of using these techniques on XML document so that not only we maintain the data consistency, but also we can detect the area of change. By successfully implementing the technique, we can detect and use only the correct information from a transferred XML document, even if the document is changed.

2   Verification Techniques on XML Database

In general, the XML documents used for transferring data from databases are very simple and record oriented. Thus, this kind of documents can be easily recognized and converted to a data table. In this paper, we consider XML databases that can be easily transferred to a records oriented database and vice versa. We specify some typical data transformation scenarios and discuss how our approach of verification techniques can help on data verifications.

2.1   Typical Scenarios

XML is a very popular language used to transfer data because it is stored in basic text format that is readable to all. The simplex feature of storing XML data leads a problem of modification. Consider a scenario where there is a need of easy transfer to a set of data (records) from one database to another database. The two databases are maybe same or different. An XML document is used for the data transfer. At the sender side, the sender prepares an XML document with the selected desired data and sends it directly by transmission media (Internet, mail attachment etc.) or saves it in any storage media (CD, Flash Drives etc.) to send it manually. At the destination side, the receiver gets the file and there need to insert the data into the database.

In the scenario in Fig. 1, after preparing the XML document with the selected data, there could be a possibility of being modified before sending or any modification done in the sending process.

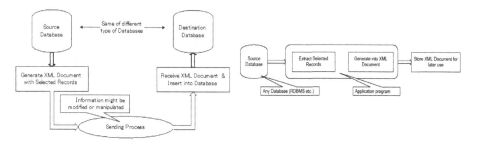

Fig. 1. Typical scenario of data transfer   **Fig. 2.** Typical scenario of data store

The same kind of data modification could arise in the situation where we store some selected data for later use in XML format shown in Fig. 2. The resultant data may be a result of complex time consuming query. To run the query, again for all, would be a very inconvenient rather than to run the query for only small number of data.

2.2   Process of Applying Verification Techniques

In the process of data verification, we will generate a digest of whole document. The algorithm for generating the digest could be the popular checksum algorithms and the hash algorithms. We will discuss on the algorithms later in this paper. This digest will append with the main document. For security purposes, the digest will be encrypted using a private key (public key cryptography techniques). Before using the document, the process will generate the digest using the same algorithm and compare the digest with the string of the document after decrypting it. Figure 3 describes the whole process.

Generating the Document Digest. As our objective is to detect errors in document and in specific records, we use each and every record's digest as a reference of that record. The idea behind this is that if any record has changed then its corresponding digest also has changed and we can detect that record.

In proposed technique, the digest of the document is composed by the digest of each record. Since we are using XML documents build from general databases, the records could be easily identifiable. Let's consider an XML document X. We assume that total number of records in X is n and the records are R_1, R_2, R_3, $\cdots$, and R_n. Let be D is the function of generating record's digest. The digest of R_1, $D_1 = D(R_1)$, digest of R_2, $D_2 = D(R_2)$ and so on. Concatenating all the record's digest we will get the document's digest. So, the document's digest D_X = $D_1 + D_2 + \cdots + D_n = D(R_1) + D(R_2) + \cdots + D(R_n)$, where "+" means the concatenation of strings. In order to get the digest of whole XML document, we detect each and every record from the whole document, prepare the string by serially concatenating the digest of each record, and append the string to the XML document.

Consider an XML document of size x (in bytes), the number of records $= n$, the average size of record $= r$, and the size of header information $= c$. Then, $x = c + r * n$. Now, on that document we will generate the digest. The length of each record's digest depends on the algorithm used. In case of using MD5, the length will be 14 bytes. Similarly for CRC the length is 4 bytes and for SHA256 the length is 32 bytes. Let be the digest size $= d$. Thus, the digest for the XML document $= d * n$. After appending the digest to the main document, the size of the document would be $x' = c + (r + d) * n$. The percentage increment of size with respect to original document, $P = (d * n) * 100/(c + r * n)$. The size of c is very small rather than $r * n$. Thus, we can conclude, $P = d * 100/r$. If $d = r$ (individual record's digest is equal to the average size of the record),

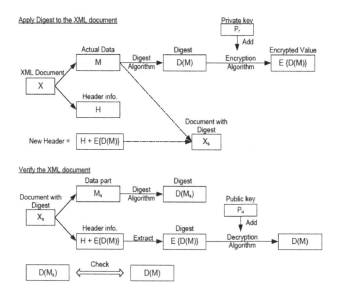

Fig. 3. Apply verification techniques

the size of the document will increase 100%. In actual case, it is effective when $d \ll s$. Single character checksum is best considering the size of the document. For single character algorithm, $d = 1$, thus the file increases by n bytes only.

Appending the Checksum to the Document. The digest of the document can append to the document as comments or processing instruction of XML. Processing instruction(PI) is an escape hatch to provide information to an application. Like comments, they are not contents part of the XML document, but the XML processor is required to pass them to an application. PI has the form ⟨?name pidata⟩. The "name", called as the PI target, identifies the PI to the application. Application should process only the targets it recognizes and ignores all other PIs. Any data that follows the PI target is optional, and it is for the application that recognizes the target. The name used in PIs may be declared as notations in order to formally identify them[5].

We append the digest string to the document as a PI. Note that, this digest can be used as digest in digital signature.

Process of Finding Modified Records. After receiving the document or at the time of use from any storage, the testing application will generate the digest string from the document with the same algorithm used previously. It is necessary to match the generated string with the string coming along with the document.

While checking the two strings we first check the length. If the generated string has the same length with the string appended in document then we will check each record's digest (for multiple character digest of each record we have to consider a block of characters of digest length) serially. If any digest of the generated string is different, then we conclude the record for which the digest was generated is modified, since the position of the digest in the whole document's digest string is in serial of the records in the document. By removing the modified records we will finally get correct records only.

When the length is not same, there were inserted or removed any records. This will be a critical problem to find out the correct one. We can check the document from beginning and from last, and get the corrected ones. Pair-wise alignment techniques can be applied for this problem. The pair-wise alignment is the problem of comparing two sequences while allowing certain mismatches between them. Alignment of two sequences S and T is obtained by inserting some gaps '_' into S and T so that the similarity score between the two resulting sequences becomes maximal as a whole[4]. For example, given two sequences ACGCTTTG and CATGTAT, one possible alignment would be:

$$A\ C\ \_\ \_\ G\ C\ T\ T\ G$$
$$\_\ C\ A\ T\ G\ \_\ T\ A\ T\ \_$$

The alignment can efficiently be computed with dynamic programming technique. Given a sequence $S_1, \cdots, S_m$ of text blocks of an H-document and a sequence $T_1, \cdots, T_n$ of a T-document, after computing the similarity score of all pairs (S_i, T_j), we can compute the alignment of two sequences $S_1, \cdots, S_m$ and $T_1, \cdots, T_n$ based on the computing similarity score.

2.3   Algorithms Used for Digest

In this paper we consider three categories of algorithm for generating digest. First is parity scheme, we experiment with the very simple single character checksum algorithm. Second is the CRC algorithm as sophisticated redundancy check and third are MD5 and SHA256 as one-way hash functions.

The length of Digest for CRC is 4 bytes. For the size perspective, this is very effective. If we consider the average length of record is 100, then the size increment in case of CRC will be 4%. Also, the algorithm takes minimum time than other algorithms. But it is possible of getting two same digest value for two different documents, thus although this is effective in terms of size, we will not get 100% accuracy in all times.

In case of 100% accuracy, we have to use the hash functions. Here we consider two most popular one-way hash algorithms: MD5 and SHA256. However, collisions (generating same digest for two different messages) already found for MD5, but for SHA256 we still not get any collisions[5]. The time required for these two algorithms is almost same. The length of digest for SHA256 is 32 bytes, whereas the length of digest for MD5 is 14 bytes. Thus, for document of average record size 100 bytes, size increment would be 14% for MD5 and 32% for SHA256. For 100% accuracy, SHA256 is most effective. If we use this algorithm, the size of the document will increase considerably.

3 Experiments

Among the various checksum and hash algorithms we took CRC, MD5 and SHA256 algorithms. From the test document, we first detect each record. We use SAX[6] to parse the document for fast processing. The final digest of the document is generated by concatenating each record's digest. We run the experiment on a computer with 3 GHz Pentium 4 CPU and 1 GB memory.

Table 1 shows the test results on applying CRC, MD5 and SHA256 algorithms applied to three different sized XML document for generating the digest. The time is the digest generating time in millisecond. Size is the total digest size in bytes.

Table 1. Digest generating time and size of the digest

XML documents		Algorithms		
		CRC	MD5	SHA256
1 MB File	Time	125	222	218
	Size	18,520	74,080	148,160
2 MB File	Time	281	468	453
	Size	37,052	148,208	296,416
5 MB File	Time	687	1,140	1,109
	Size	92,652	370,608	741,216

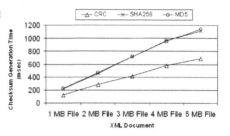

Fig. 4. Time require for generating digest

Using CRC is not only faster than MD5 and SHA256, it generates the digest very smaller than the others. From the graph in Fig. 4 we notice that the time required for MD5 and SHA256 is almost same, although the size of the digest for SHA256 is more than double than the size for MD5.

Considering each record's digest, we can take the digest from the whole document. However, in that case we cannot detect specific erroneous records. In the process of applying digital signature, the digest used is generated from the whole document and the algorithm used most commonly MD5, SHA etc. Although we cannot detect erroneous records by taking the digest of whole document, in our test we compare the time for both the process; a) time to generate digest direct from the whole document (direct method) and b) time to generate the digest from each record's digest. The test result is shown in Fig. 5.

Another part of our test is to try to detect errors in document and in specific records. In this case we also consider simple single character checksum algorithm for generating digest. We prepared for the documents by adding randomly generated characters, removing characters from random positions and replacing characters with randomly generated characters. After each time modification we try to detect the whether the procedures can detect the errors or not. We did the random test of 1,200,000 times. As a result of the test, the single character algorithm is 99.98% accurate, whereas the SHA256 and MD5 are 100% accurate.

After manipulating a record by replacing characters with randomly generated characters, removing characters from randomly and adding random characters,

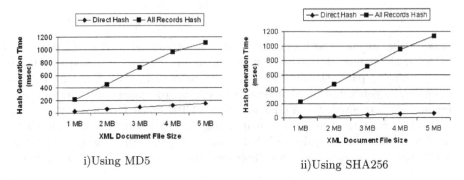

i)Using MD5   ii)Using SHA256

Fig. 5. Generating times of hash values from whole document and from individual record

we will try to detect the specific records by the proposed checksum technique. We did the random test of 1,200,000 times. As a result of the test, the accuracy of single character algorithm is 99.2%, whereas the SHA256 and MD5 are 100%.

4 Evaluation

In addition of data verification, one of our main objectives is to detect errors of a specific portion of an XML document. For easily identification and division of portions of an XML document, we use database style XML document and take each record as a small portion of the document. We propose to use digest of the document from each record's digest for the data verification process, since it will help us finding specific erroneous records when any error occurs. This digest is appended to the document directly through PI and public-key cryptography. We test our proposed technique for detecting errors in document with algorithm ranged from single character checksum to one-way cryptographic hash. We compare the algorithm is in various ways. In our proposed technique, time and size are big factors.

We have shown that, the size mainly depends on the algorithm used and the average size of record. For providing 100% accuracy, we have to use one-way hash functions, and SHA256 is most reliable. But using these functions, the size increment of the document is high. However, for a very secured and confidential data (financial records etc.), hash functions should be used.

Similar to the case of size, cryptographic hash algorithms also took more times. At the time of preparing the document, the process have to parse the whole document, get each record, generate each records digest and then result the final digest for the document. At the time of checking the document, the process again generates the digest from the whole document, extracts the digest coming along with the document and compares to find errors.

Now, we define some symbols as follows.

GCS - Time to generate the digest (including document parsing)
AC - Time to add the digest to the document

EC - Time to extract the digest coming along with the document
COMP - Time to compare two digests.

At source side, the digest is generated, appended to the document and make the document ready to transfer or store. At destination side, the document is checked before use or before inserting into the database. The time needed for these tasks is as follows.

Time required for at the source side: GCS + AC.
Time required at the destination side: EC + GCS + COMP.

Our experiment shows the time required to generate the digest. Similar to the scenarios shown in Fig. 1 and 2, the time and size factors will not degrade the performance and efficiency of the system. Thus, this process gives us an opportunity to protect our sophisticated data from malicious users even if the user manually handles the data transferring processes.

5   Conclusion

As the use of XML document in transferring data, the need for data consistency checking also increasing. Applying digital signature ensures authorization for the document. In this paper we propose a process of detecting errors in not only document but also specific records in an XML document. By applying sophisticated checksums or cryptographic hash functions, we can implement our proposed technique on secured information. So, if very few records are affected upon sending the database, at the destination we can just detect the corrected records and ignore modified records rather receive the whole document again. And we can request the modified records only. The proposed procedure is tested with a single-character checksum formula, the random test results 99.2% success. With the cryptographic one-way hash functions (MD5, SHA256 etc.) our test results 100% accuracy and correctness. Further research can be on try to produce a 100% accurate result giving formula with small length digest.

References

1. Bray, T., Paoli, J., Sperberg, C.M.: Extensible markup language (XML) 1.0 W3C Recommendation (1998), http://www.w3c.org/TR/REC-xml
2. Bartel, M., Boyer, J., Fox, B., LaMacchia, B., Simon, E.: XML-Signature Syntax and Processing W3C recommendation (2002)
3. Imamura, T., Dillaway, B., Simon, E.: XML Encryption Syntax and Processing W3C Recommendation (2002)
4. Umehara, M., Iwanuma, K., Nabeshima, H.: A Case-Based Recognition of Semantic Structures in HTML Documents - An Automated Transformation from HTML to XML. In: Proceedings of Third International Conference of Intelligent Data Engineering and Automated Learning, Manchester, pp. 141–147 (2002)
5. Ducharme, B.: XSLT, Comments and Processing Instructions (2000), http://www.xml.com
6. David Megginson: SAX (Simple API for XML) (2000), http://www.saxproject.org

An Operational Semantics of Program Dependence Graphs for Unstructured Programs

Souhei Ito, Shigeki Hagihara, and Naoki Yonezaki

Tokyo Institute of Technology

Abstract. The program dependence graph (PDG) represents data and control dependences between statements in a program. The PDG is a useful intermediate representation for compiler code optimizations, because compiler code optimizations mostly rely on data and control dependence information. However, the validity of optimization methods based on PDGs has not been well studied. In order to justify optimization based on PDGs, it is necessary to introduce a formal semantics of PDGs. This paper presents an operational semantics of PDGs corresponding to programs which have an unstructured control flow. Our PDG semantics is equivalent to sequential program semantics in the sense that a CFG and the corresponding PDG perform the same computation.

1 Introduction

The program dependence graph (PDG) [5] is an intermediate program representation which has statements represented as nodes, and data and control dependences represented as edges. The PDG is a useful intermediate representation for compiler code optimizations, because these optimizations mostly rely on data and control dependence information [4,5]. Many optimizations can be performed simply using PDGs, and incremental data flow update is also directly available by this approach. Therefore, compiler code optimizations can be performed more efficiently on PDGs than on control flow graphs (CFGs). There are several algorithms of code optimizations based on PDGs [11,5,1].

Although the PDG is an appropriate representation for many compiler code optimizations, the validity of optimization methods based on PDGs has not been well studied. In order to justify optimization methods based on PDGs, it is necessary to introduce a formal semantics of the PDG. Several previous studies have considered a formal semantics of PDGs [6,2,8,3]. However, they treated only structured programs, which have restricted branches and loops of the form (**if** *e* **then** ... **else** ...) and (**while** *e* ...) respectively. These studies are not sufficient to justify the rectitude of compiler code optimization methods based on them, since intermediate programs appearing in code optimization processes might have unstructured control flow.

This paper presents an operational semantics of PDGs corresponding to programs which have unstructured control flow. Our PDG semantics is equivalent to CFG semantics in the sense that a CFG and the corresponding PDG perform the same computations.

M. Okada and I. Satoh (Eds.): ASIAN 2006, LNCS 4435, pp. 264–271, 2007.
© Springer-Verlag Berlin Heidelberg 2007

This paper is organized as follows: Section 2 introduces CFGs as a program representation. In Section 3, the PDG is introduced. In Section 4, we define the operational semantics of PDGs, and the notion of deterministic PDG. Deterministic PDG is the class of PDGs whose any computation starting from the same initial state yields the same result. Our PDG semantics is equivalent to sequential program semantics in the sense that a CFG and the corresponding PDG perform the same computation. The final section offers some conclusions, and discusses future directions.

2   Control Flow Graphs

We consider the CFG as a representation of programs. A CFG is a pair (N, E) of a set N of nodes and a set $E \subseteq N \times N$ of edges. The nodes of a CFG are labeled by statements, and the edges of a CFG represent control flow of a program. We only consider two types of statements, an assignment statement $(x := e)$ and a conditional statement $(\text{if } e)$. Assignment statements have exactly one successor and Conditional statements have exactly two successors. Edges from a conditional statement are labeled differently, either with true or false. A CFG has a unique start node and a unique end node. The start node has no predecessor, while the end node has no successor. Any node in a CFG is reachable from the start node.

An operational semantics of CFGs can be introduced naturally.

3   Program Dependence Graphs

A program dependence graph is a quintuple (N, C, F, L, D), where N is a set of nodes, and C, F, L and D are sets of edges. These edge sets represent four types of dependences, i.e. control dependence, loop independent data dependence, loop carried data dependence, and def-order dependence respectively.

For the definition of control dependence, we adopt the one called "weak control dependence" in [7] since the standard definition of control dependence is not sufficient to define the operational semantics of PDGs. The definition of def-order dependence is the same as the one used in [6].

To define loop independent and carried data dependence, the formal definition of loops must be introduced. We first give it.

Definition 1 (Loops, back edges). *Let G be a directed graph. A* loop *is a maximal strongly connected region in G. A* back edge *of a loop is an edge contained in the loop whose target node has an incoming edge from outside of the loop. We define the sequence $G_0, G_1, G_2, \ldots$ as $G_0 = G$ and G_{i+1} is obtained by removing all back edges in G_i. Loops in G are the union of loops in $G_0, G_1, G_2, \ldots$.*

We now define loop independent data dependences and loop carried data dependences.

Definition 2 (Data dependences). *Let G be a CFG. Let s and t be nodes in G. The definition at node s reaches t if there exists a variable w such that s defines w, t uses w, and there exists a path in G from s to t such that no node except s on that path defines w. We call such a path a* reaching path *from node s to t. The node t is* data dependent *on s if the definition at s reaches t. There is a* loop independent data dependence *from s to t if i) t is data dependent on s, and s and t are not both contained in the same loop, or ii) if both s and t are contained in the same loop, there exists a reaching path from s to t which does not contain any back edge of the loop. There is a* loop carried data dependence *from s to t if both s and t are contained in the same loop, there exists a reaching path from s to t which contains a back edge of the loop, and there is no loop-independent data dependence from s to t.*

Let $G = (N, E)$ be a CFG. The PDG corresponding to G has the node set $N \cup \{entry\}$, where *entry* is the extra node which is the root node of control dependences. According to dependence types, each edge set C, F, L and D contains ordered pairs of nodes such that one is dependent on the other. Note that $(entry, n) \in C$ iff there is no node on which n is control dependent. We call the subgraph (N, C) of PDG (N, C, F, L, D) the control dependence graph (CDG) for the PDG.

We may write $c(s, t), f(s, t), l(s, t)$ and $d(s, t)$ to denote that (s, t) is an element of C, F, L and D respectively. Moreover, we sometimes write $ct(s, t)$ and $cf(s, t)$ to distinguish true control dependences and false control dependences in C respectively, and $f_x(s, t)$ and $l_x(s, t)$ to specify the depending variable. A node t is true (false) dependent on a node s iff t is control dependent on s and t is reachable from s's true (false) successor.

4   An Operational Semantics of the PDG

In this section, we present an operational semantics of the PDG. The basic idea is to define states in runs of PDGs as *state = avail × econf* where *avail* is a set of functions that take a node and a variable and return a value. We do not require global stores since an execution of a statement affects only nodes which are dependent on it.

The set *econf* is a set of functions that take an edge and return the state of the edge. Functions in *econf* indicate whether nodes are executable or not. For example, if n is an `if` statement and the expression is evaluated to **T** then its outgoing *ct*-edges are "activated" and outgoing *cf*-edges are "inactivated." Whether a node is executable or not is determined by the states of its incoming edges. *econf* is used to represent a configuration of edges in executions of PDGs.

To define the operational semantics of the PDG, we introduce the following definitions on PDGs:

Definition 3 (Looping edges). *Let $G = (N, C, F, L, D)$ be a PDG and $G_C = (N, C)$ be the CDG of G. Let R be a loop in G_C. Suppose $ct(p, q)$ (resp. $cf(p, q)$) is a back edge of R. We define* looping edges *of R to be all the ct-edges (resp. cf-edges) from p.*

Definition 4. *Let $G = (N, C, F, L, D)$ be a PDG. We define $\widehat{C}$ to be the set obtained by removing looping edges from C.*

Definition 5 (Subgraphs). *Let $G = (N, C, F, L, D)$ be a PDG and $p \in N$. We define $G(p) = (N', C', F', L', D')$ to be the* subgraph *of a node p where*

$$N' = \{n \mid \exists q.c(p, q) \in C \wedge n \text{ is } \widehat{C}\text{-reachable from } q\}$$

and $C' = C \cap (N' \times N')$. F', L' and D' are obtained in similar way.

$G(p)$ is a subgraph of G consisting of nodes which are reachable from C-successors of p without passing through looping edges. Note that $c(p, q)$ may be a looping edge. Similarly, we define $G_T(p)$ (resp. $G_F(p)$) consists of node which are reachable from ct-successors (resp. cf-successors) of p without passing through looping edges.

Intuitively, $G(p)$ is a graph with the nodes which are reachable from p's successors without passing through back edges in the corresponding CFG, and $G_T(p)$ is a graph with the nodes which are reachable from p's true successor without passing through back edges in the corresponding CFG.

Now we give the definition of the operational semantics of the PDG:

Definition 6. *The elements* avail *and* econf *are elements of the sets of functions* avail *and* econf *respectively, which are defined as follows:*

$$avail = N \times var \longrightarrow val$$
$$econf = C \oplus F \oplus L \oplus D \longrightarrow \{chk, unchk, act, inact\},$$

where $\oplus$ is the direct sum.

The expression evaluation is given by the function $\mathcal{E} : N \times exp \longrightarrow avail \longrightarrow val$.

A state is an element of state $= avail \times econf$.

A C-edge has three possible states, $\{unchk, act, inact\}$. F, L and D-edges take one of two possible states, $\{chk, unchk\}$. Intuitively, $unchk$ means that the dependence imposed by an edge has not yet been satisfied. The state act means that the source node of a ct-edge (resp. cf-edge) has been evaluated to **T** (resp. **F**), and the target node is ready to execute. The state $inact$ means that the source node of the ct-edge (resp. cf-edge) is evaluated to **F** (resp. **T**). If all incoming C-edges are $inact$, the node becomes unexecutable. The state chk means that the source node of an edge has been executed, or became unexecutable.

Definition 7 (Executable nodes). *We define the following predicates. Let $s = (av, ec)$ where $av \in avail$ and $ec \in econf$, and n is a node.*

$$condC(s, n) \stackrel{\text{def}}{=} \exists c(p, n) \in C.ec(c(p, n)) = act$$
$$\wedge \forall q \in G(n).q \neq n \Rightarrow \forall c(r, q) \in C.ec(c(r, q)) \neq act$$
$$condF(s, n) \stackrel{\text{def}}{=} \forall f(p, n) \in F.ec(f(p, n)) = chk$$
$$condL(s, n) \stackrel{\text{def}}{=} \forall l(n, p) \in L.n \neq p \Rightarrow ec(l(n, p)) = chk$$
$$condD(s, n) \stackrel{\text{def}}{=} \forall d(p, n) \in D.ec(d(p, n)) = chk.$$

We write $condCFLD(s,n)$ to represent $condC(s,n) \land condF(s,n) \land condL(s,n) \land condD(s,n)$.

We define the function $Next : state \longrightarrow 2^N$ by

$$Next(s) = \{n \mid condCFLD(s,n)\}.$$

$Next(s)$ thus represents a set of executable nodes at a state s.

Definition 8 (Update function of avails). *We define the function $udav :$ $N \times avail \longrightarrow avail$ as follows:*

$$udav(n, av) = \begin{cases} av[(p,x) \mapsto \mathcal{E}(n,e)av : (n,p) \in F \oplus L] & \text{if } n = (x := e) \\ av & \text{otherwise} \end{cases},$$

where $av[(p,x) \mapsto v : (n,p) \in S]$ is the same as av except that it maps (p,x) to v for all p such that $(n,p) \in S$.

Definition 9 (Update function of econfs). *We define the function $udec :$ $N \times state \longrightarrow econf$ is defined as $udec(n,(av,ec)) = ec'$, where ec' is determined according to n, av and ec as follows:*

- *n is any type.*
  - *$ec'(c(p,n)) := inact$, if $c(p,n) \in C$.*
  - *$ec'(l(p,n)) := chk$, if $l(p,n) \in L$.*
- *$n = (x := e)$.*
  - *$ec'((n,p)) := chk$, if $(n,p) \in F \oplus D$.*
- *$n = (\mathtt{if}\ e)$ and $\mathcal{E}(n,e)av = \mathbf{T}$.*
  - *$ec'(ct(n,p)) := act$, if $ct(n,p) \in C$.*
  - *$ec'((q,r)) := unchk$, if for $q \in G_T(n) - \{n\}$, $r \in G_T(n)$ and $(q,r) \in C \oplus F \oplus D$.*
  - *$ec'(l(r,q)) := unchk$, if $q \in G_T(n)$, $r \in G_T(n)$ and $l(r,q) \in L$.*
  - *$ec'(cf(n,p)) := inact$, if $cf(n,p) \in C$.*
  - *$ec'((q,r)) := inact$, if $q \in G_F(n) - G_T(n)$ and $(q,r) \in C$.*
  - *$ec'((q,r)) := chk$, if $q \in G_F(n) - G_T(n)$ and $(q,r) \in F \oplus D$.*
  - *$ec'(l(r,q)) := chk$, if $q \in G_F(n) - G_T(n)$ and $(r,q) \in L$.*
- *$n = (\mathtt{if}\ e)$ and $\mathcal{E}(n,e)av = \mathbf{F}$. Similar to the case of $\mathcal{E}(n,e)av = \mathbf{T}$. Exchange ct for cf and $G_T(n)$ for $G_F(n)$.*

ec and ec' are the same except for edges changed above.

Definition 10 (Operational semantics of the PDG). *Let $G = (N,C,F,L,D)$ be a PDG. A run of G is a sequence of states $s_0 \xrightarrow{n_0} s_1 \xrightarrow{n_1} \ldots$, where $s_i \in state$ and $n_i \in N$. Let $s_i = (av_i, ec_i)$, where av_0 is a given initial avail and ec_0 is an initial econf which satisfies the following conditions,*

$$\forall (p,q) \in C.ec_0((p,q)) = \begin{cases} act & \text{if } p = entry \\ unchk & \text{otherwise} \end{cases},$$

$$\forall (p,q) \in F \oplus L \oplus D.ec_0((p,q)) = unchk.$$

n_i and s_{i+1} is determined as follows.

$$s_i \xrightarrow{n_i} s_{i+1} \overset{def}{\iff} n_i \in Next(s_i) \wedge av_{i+1} = udav(n_i, av_i) \wedge ec_{i+1} = udec(n_i, s_i).$$

Runs of PDGs are finite or infinite. If a run is finite and the last state is s, then $Next(s) = \emptyset$.

The intuitive meaning of the above definitions is as follows. The first conjunct of $condC$ says that there exists an activated incoming C-edge. This means that some condition which controls the execution of the node must hold. The second conjunct prohibits the iteration of a loop when executable nodes still remain in the loop, because the function $udec$ changes the states of all the edges from the subgraph of the executed node to $unchk$.

$condF$ says that all F-predecessors should either have been executed or have become unexecutable. $condD$ is similar to $condF$.

Unlike $condF$ and $condD$, $condL$ says that all L-*successors* should either have been executed or have become unexecutable. This reflects the fact that there is a loop carried data dependence from s to t means the definition of s is used at t in the next iteration of the loop, thus t should be executed before s in the same iteration.

Runs of a PDG starting from the same initial state are not unique. However, if G is a deterministic PDG (dPDG) defined below, all runs of G starting from the same initial state have the same last state.

Before defining deterministic PDGs, we define the notion of *minimal common ancestors* (mca).

Definition 11 (Minimal common ancestors). *Let $G = (N, C, F, L, D)$ be a PDG. The* minimal common ancestors *of p and q are common ancestors of p and q in (N, C) from which no common ancestor of p and q is reachable. We write $mca(p, q)$ to represent a set of minimal common ancestors of p and q.*

Definition 12 (Deterministic PDGs). *PDG $G = (N, C, F, L, D)$ is deterministic if it satisfies the following three conditions:*

1. $(p, n) \in \widehat{C} \wedge (q, n) \in \widehat{C}$ *implies* $\forall r \in mca(p, q).\forall Q \in \{\mathbf{T}, \mathbf{F}\}.\{p, q\} \not\subseteq G_Q(r)$.
2. $f_x(p, u) \in F \wedge f_x(q, u) \in F \wedge \exists r \in mca(p, q).\exists Q \in \{\mathbf{T}, \mathbf{F}\}.\{p, q\} \subseteq G_Q(r)$ *implies* $d(p, q) \in D \vee d(q, p) \in D$.
3. *Let* $f(p, q) \in F$ *and R be a loop in (N, C). If $\exists r \in R.p \in G(r)$ then $\exists r' \in R.q \in G(r')$.*

Condition 1 says that if n is control dependent on both p and q then p and q cannot be executable on the same condition. Condition 2 says that if p and q define the same variable, have the same F-successor, and can be executable on the same condition, then there should exists def-order dependence between p and q. Condition 3 says that if there exists a data dependence from p to q, and p is control dependent on a node in a loop, then q should be control dependent on a node in that loop.

The followings are important properties of dPDGs.

Theorem 1. *A PDG constructed from a CFG is deterministic.*

Theorem 2. *Let G be a dPDG and s be a state on a run of G. If there exists a finite run of length m from s, all runs from s have length m and have the same last state.*

For an infinite run of CFG, there is the same executing sequence of the corresponding PDG.

The converse of Theorem 1 does not hold. Theorem 2 means the determinicity of dPDGs. This is proved by induction on m.

Our PDG semantics is equivalent to CFG semantics, i.e. a CFG and the corresponding PDG performs the same computations. This follows from two facts: i) a run of CFG is also a run of PDG, ii) PDGs constructed from CFGs are deterministic (therefore, all runs starting from the same initial state have the same result). We do not present the detail argument for lack of space.

5 Conclusion and Future Directions

We presented an operational semantics of PDGs corresponding to unstructured programs, which are inevitable in the intermediate steps on code optimization. We defined deterministic PDGs which have the important property that finite runs of dPDGs starting from the same initial state have the same last state. We have the equivalence of CFG operational semantics and PDG operational semantics. That is, a CFG and the corresponding PDG perform the same computation.

Our PDG representation is simple and does not contain aliasing, arrays, and procedure calls. Developing a semantics for PDGs containing such features will be important issues. For this purpose, we need to choose (or devise, if necessary) a PDG representation containing such features.

After optimizations have been performed on PDGs, sequential programs must be generated from optimized PDGs. Some algorithms translating PDGs to sequential programs have been proposed [9,10,12]. If an optimized PDG has no corresponding CFG, node duplication and predicate addition is necessary. The correctness of such modifications have not been proved formally. We can ensure that such modifications do not change the meaning of PDGs according to the present PDG semantics.

Another challenge is to show the equivalence of the parallel program semantics and the PDG semantics. This would enables us to reason and construct translation algorithms from PDGs to parallel programs.

We believe that our PDG semantics establishes a theoretical basis for optimizing compilers operating on PDGs.

Acknowledgements

We thank the Software Research Group in Tokyo Institute of Technology for discussions about this work, and the 21th Century COE-LKR Program for its financial support.

References

1. Baxter, W., III Bauer, H.R.: The program dependence graph and vectorization. In: Proceedings of the 16th ACM SIGPLAN-SIGACT symposium on Principles of programming languages, pp. 1–11. ACM Press, New York (1989)
2. Cartwright, E., Felleisen, M.: The semantics of program dependence. In: Proceedings of the ACM SIGPLAN 1989 Conference on Programming language design and implementation, pp. 13–27. ACM Press, New York (1989)
3. Das, M.: Partial evaluation using dependence graphs. PhD thesis, Supervisor-Thomas W. Reps (1998)
4. Ferrante, J., Ottenstein, K.J.: A program form based on data dependency in predicate regions. In: Principles of Programming Languages, pp. 217–236 (1983)
5. Ferrante, J., Ottenstein, K.J., Warren, J.D.: The program dependence graph and its use in optimization. ACM Transactions on Programming Languages and Systems 9(3), 319–349 (1987)
6. Parsons-Selke, R.: A rewriting semantics for program dependence graphs. In: Proceedings of the 16th ACM SIGPLAN-SIGACT symposium on Principles of programming languages, pp. 12–24. ACM Press, New York (1989)
7. Podgurski, A., Clarke, L.A.: A formal model of program dependences and its implications for software testing, debugging, and maintenance. IEEE Transactions on Software Engineering 16(9), 965–979 (1990)
8. Ramalingam, G., Reps, T.: Semantics of program representation graphs. Technical Report CS-TR-1989-900 (1989)
9. Simons, B., Alpern, D., Ferrante, J.: A foundation for sequentializing parallel code. In: SPAA 1990. Proceedings of the second annual ACM symposium on Parallel algorithms and architectures, pp. 350–359. ACM Press, New York (1990)
10. Steensgaard, B.: Sequentializing program dependence graphs for irreducible programs. Technical Report MSR-TR-93-14, Redmond, WA (1993)
11. Warren, J.: A hierarchical basis for reordering transformations. In: Proceedings of the 11th ACM SIGACT-SIGPLAN symposium on Principles of programming languages, pp. 272–282. ACM Press, New York (1984)
12. Zeng, J., Soviani, C., Edwards, S.A.: Generating fast code from concurrent program dependence graphs. In: LCTES 2004. Proceedings of the 2004 ACM SIGPLAN/SIGBED conference on Languages, compilers, and tools for embedded systems, pp. 175–181. ACM Press, New York (2004)

Combination of Abstractions in the ASTRÉE Static Analyzer*

Patrick Cousot [2], Radhia Cousot [1], Jérôme Feret [2], Laurent Mauborgne [2],
Antoine Miné [2], David Monniaux [1,2], and Xavier Rival [2]

[1] Centre National de la Recherche Scientifique (CNRS)
[2] École Normale Supérieure, Paris, France
Firstname.Lastname@ens.fr
http://www.astree.ens.fr/

Abstract. We describe the structure of the abstract domains in the
ASTRÉE static analyzer, their modular organization into a hierarchical
network, their cooperation to over-approximate the conjunction/reduced
product of different abstractions and to ensure termination using collab-
orative widenings and narrowings. This separation of the abstraction into
a combination of cooperative abstract domains makes ASTRÉE extensible, an essential feature to cope with false alarms and ultimately provide
sound formal verification of the absence of runtime errors in very large
software.

1 Introduction

ASTRÉE is a static program analyzer based on abstract interpretation [1,2] which
is aimed at proving automatically the absence of run time errors in programs written in a subset of the C programming language. It has been applied successfully
to large embedded control/command safety-critical real-time software generated
automatically from synchronous specifications, producing correctness proofs for
complex software without any false alarm, within only a few hours of computation
on personal computers [3,4,5,6]. More recently [7], it has been extended to handle
other kinds of embedded software, some of which are hand-written.

ASTRÉE was designed using:
- a syntax-directed representation of the program control flow (functions, block
  structures);
- functional representation of abstract environments with sharing [3], for memory and time efficiency, and limited support for analysis parallelization [8];
- basic abstract domains, tracking variables independently (integer and floating-
  point intervals [9] using staged widenings);
- relational abstract domains tracking dependencies between variables
  - symbolic computation and linearization of expressions [10],
  - packed octagons [11],

---

* This work was supported in part by the French exploratory project ASTRÉE of the
Réseau National de recherche et d'innovation en Technologies Logicielles (RNTL).

M. Okada and I. Satoh (Eds.): ASIAN 2006, LNCS 4435, pp. 272–300, 2007.
© Springer-Verlag Berlin Heidelberg 2007

- application-aware domains (such as the ellipsoid abstract domain for digital filters [12] or the arithmetic-geometric progression abstract domain [13], e.g. to bound potentially diverging computations);
- abstract domains tracking dependencies between boolean variables and other variables (boolean partitioning domain [4]), or the history of control flow branches and values along the execution trace (trace partitioning [14]);
- a memory abstract domain [4] recently extended to cope with unions and pointer arithmetics [7].

Contrary to many program analysis systems, ASTRÉE does not have separate phases for pointer/aliasing analysis and arithmetic analysis.

To adjust the cost/precision ratio of the analysis, some of the abstract domains are parametrized (e.g. maximal height of decision trees) and applied locally (e.g. to variables packs [4]) according to local directives automatically inserted by the analyzer[1].

The abstract domains communicate as an approximate reduced product [15] to organize the cooperation between abstract domains and allow for a modular design and refinement of the abstraction used by ASTRÉE. In this paper we describe how abstract domains are organized and do cooperate.

This modular design allows abstract domains to be turned on and off by runtime options, easy addition of new domains, and the suppression of older domains that have been superseded by newer ones (such as the clock domain [3], now superseded by the arithmetic-geometric progression abstract domain [5]). Finally, it allows the addition of new reductions / communications between existing domains. ASTRÉE is therefore an extensible abstract interpreter, an essential feature to cope with false alarms and ultimately reach zero false alarm.

ASTRÉE is programmed mostly in OCaml [16] (apart from the octagon domain library [17] and some platform-specific dependencies, e.g. to control the rounding behavior of the FPU). It is currently approximately 80 000 lines long.

2   Handling False Alarms

As all abstract interpretation-based static program analyzers, ASTRÉE may be subject to *false alarms*; that is, it may report potential bugs that happen in no possible concrete execution, because of the over-approximation of program behaviors entailed by abstractions. Thus, when ASTRÉE raises an alarm, it may be a true alarm, due to a runtime error appearing at least in one program execution, but it may also be a false alarm due to excessive over-approximation.

This is the case of all automatic sound formal methods which, because of undecidability and in absence of human interaction, must be incomplete, and hence, in many cases, either exhaust time or space resources or terminate with false alarms.

---

[1] These directives can also be inserted manually, but such intervention of end-users must be avoided, in particular for programs subject to long-term modifications.

2.1 Different Classes of Alarms

We distinguish between three classes of alarms:

1. Conditions that necessarily terminate the execution in the concrete world. Such is the case, for instance, of floating-point exceptions (invalid operations, overflows, etc.) if traps are activated, and also integer divisions by zero. We issue a warning and consider that the incorrect execution has stopped at the point of the error. The analyzer will continue by taking into account only the executions that did not trigger the run-time error.
2. Conditions that are defined to be incorrect with respect to the C specification or user requirements, but that do not terminate the execution and for which it is possible to supply a sound semantics for the outcome. For instance, overflows over signed integers will simply result in some signed integer. We issue a warning, but do not consider that the executions meeting the warning condition have stopped. The user may examine each such warning and determine if the condition signaled is really harmful (for instance, the user may decide to ignore some integer arithmetic overflows). If it is not, the user may safely ignore the warning.
3. Conditions that are defined to be incorrect with respect to the C specification, that may or may not terminate the execution when they are encountered, but for which it is next to impossible to provide a sound semantics for the remainder of the execution. They are handled by the analyzer as the first kind of alarms. The rest of the section is devoted to this third category as it deserves some explanation.

Some operations, such as pointer arithmetics across memory blocks or memory accesses out of bounds, are considered "undefined behaviors" or "implementation defined behaviors" by the specification of the C programming language [18]. They often result in no immediate runtime crash; but may result in e.g. memory corruptions, with consequences such as erratic behaviors or crashes much later.

For such conditions, ASTRÉE considers that execution stops with an error when the first undefined behavior occurs (and signals an alarm at this point). Its operational semantics thus coincides exactly with actual program executions only if there is no (false or true) alarm of the third kind.

If such alarms are raised, particularly those related to memory safety, then the analysis will not flag all possible runtime errors, i.e. not those arising from traces that have done some "undefined" memory or pointer manipulation. In this event, it is insufficient to analyze these warnings and show that the "undefined" behavior is actually defined in a harmless way for platform-specific reasons (as one would do for the second class of alarms). Rather, one has to either reach *zero* alarm of the third class, or prove by other means that their preconditions are not met in the concrete.

Our experience shows that industrial programmers often use constructs that are nonstandard with respect to the C specification [18, 6.3.2.3], but have well-defined behaviors on the target platform, such as converting a 32-bit pointer into an integer, and then back into a pointer. Thus, we have tried to reduce the third category of warnings as much as possible and, in agreement with our end-users, defined a more precise yet platform- and even application domain-specific semantics that turns most of them into either correct statements, or warnings of the second class. In several instances, it required us to adapt our concrete semantics and develop specific abstractions (e.g. the memory abstraction of [7] to cope with some situations where pointers are manipulated using integer arithmetics).

2.2 Causes of False Alarms

There are several possible causes of false alarms:
- The abstract transformers are not the best possible, in which case the algorithm can be improved in the corresponding abstract domain, if this improvement is not algorithmically too expensive.

Example 1. Consider the following program:

```
y=x; z=sqrt(x*y+3);
```

Starting from $x \in [-3, 7]$, a simple interval analysis will derive $y \in [-3, 7]$, then $x.y \in [-21, 49]$, $x.y + 3 \in [-18, 52]$ and we flag a false alarm on `sqrt`: square root of a negative number. However, we can solve this issue with a minor alteration: when computing the interval for a product $x.y$, we issue a request to the reduced product (see Sect. 6.3) and ask whether x and y are provably equal; if they are, compute the interval for x^2, that is, $[0, 49]$. We thus improve the precision at a very minor cost.

A more general approach would be to compute polynomials or other expressions symbolically and extract minimal and maximal values depending on the range of their variables, but this would be more complex and more costly, and we have not found a need for this so far.   □

- The automated parametrization (e.g. variable packing) fails to guess that some relation is important and, in order to save time, artificially limits a relational abstract domain to an inappropriate level of precision. In this case one must improve or adapt the pattern-matched program schemata.

Example 2. Our first heuristics for reducing the cost of relational domains was to relate together only variables that appear simultaneously in an assignment or test. It prevents proving that $x \leq 21$ at the end of the following program:

```
x=10; for (i=0;i<=10;i++) x++;
```

despite the ability of the octagon domain to infer the necessary inductive invariant $x - i = 10$, simply because no octagon will hold both x and i. The problem was solved by considering octagon packs relating variables that act likely as counters (i.e. are incremented or decremented within the same loop).   □

- The widening in the fixpoint approximation iteration strategy overshoots the most imprecise invariant allowing the proof of absence of runtime errors, in which case we must revise the widening. This can be very hard since at the limit only a precise infinite iteration might be able to compute the proper abstract invariant. In that case, it might be better to design a more refined abstract domain.

– The choice of a precise abstract transformer is not always the best. Indeed, our goal is to find a precise post-fixpoint: it can happen that a more relaxed abstract transformer helps the extrapolation process. In short, it is better to jump straight up to the limit, rather than try to be precise at each iteration, then fail to converge quickly and have to resort to interval widening techniques, which will in the end yield a poorer result.

When considering arithmetic-geometric progressions [13], choosing the most precise abstract transformer is not appropriate at all: it would give no more information than the interval domain.

– The current combination of abstract domains is inexpressive i.e. indispensable local inductive invariants are not expressible in the abstract. In that case a new abstract domain must be added to the reduced product (e.g. filters, arithmetic-geometric progressions).

When a new abstract domain is introduced, a communication and reduction process is used so that the other abstract domains can benefit from the information computed by the new one, as described in Sect. 5.2. This may, but should not, have effects on the enforcement of convergence by widening as discussed in Sect. 7. The modular integration of new abstract domains allows coping with variations between the various families of software successfully analyzed by ASTRÉE.

3 General Structure of Astrée

When ASTRÉE was designed, we knew that the first simple attempt with interval analysis could not be sufficient to achieve a precise analysis on the industrial software we were given. From the beginning, we had in mind the process of refinement which consists in finding the origin of false alarms and improving the information generated by the analysis by a modular extension. It is the reason why we developed ASTRÉE in a modular way, as permitted by the abstract interpretation theory.

ASTRÉE can be roughly decomposed into 4 parts:

1. a front-end, very similar to that of a compiler,
2. simple independent analyses,
3. an invariant computation mixing many interdependent analyses,
4. invariant checking and alarm reporting.

The first phase is pretty standard and did not change much during the evolution of ASTRÉE. An intermediate code is produced, typed and annotated, and then simple program transformations are applied, such as constant propagation. The transformations we implemented aim at reducing the complexity of the subsequent analyses. One important aspect is the elimination of useless variables (e.g. after constant propagation) as the size of the invariants depends directly on the number of variables.

The second phase consists in simple independent analyses, producing information useful for the subsequent invariant computation, such as variable dependencies. It implements automatic parametrization strategies, such as the octagon packing strategy [11] or the trace partitioning strategy [14].

The third phase is the most important and also the most demanding. It consists in an iterator which follows the control flow of the program and gives orders (abstract transfer directives) to modules representing information about the program. Each of these modules is what we call an abstract domain, and each of them collects some specialized information about the iteration sequence leading to the invariants of the program ASTRÉE analyzes. Such abstract domains can deal with the trace approximation [14], the shape of the data structures and memory [7], or the numerical values occurring during the program execution. The way these abstract domains are designed independently and then interact to produce precise information about the program invariant is crucial to achieve a fast and precise abstract interpreter.

4 Abstract Domains

4.1 Interfaces, Properties, and Abstractions

An abstract domain collects properties about the potential computations of a program. In ASTRÉE, the abstract interpreter follows the control flow of the program; thus, our abstract domain collects some properties about the computations of the program reaching the current program point.

The design of our abstract domains fits with [2], that is:

- We abstract sets of execution traces, not mere sets of reachable states.
- An abstract domain is not necessarily a lattice, and may not even need a preorder.
- We do not define a Galois connection, but only a concretization function; that is, concrete properties may lack a most precise abstraction.
- Abstract transformers are not necessarily monotonic with respect to the information preorder induced by the concretization; that is, it may happen that a more precise abstract precondition is transformed into a less precise abstract postcondition.

The elements of the concrete domain D are sets of *trace fragments*.[2] A trace fragment is a sequence of one or more pairs (p, s) where p is a program point and s is a memory state. All our abstractions will take the following view of a set of execution traces $(p_1, s_1), \ldots, (p_n, s_n)$:

- only final states so that p_n is the current program point of the analysis are considered;
- the final memory state s_n is abstracted quite precisely;

---

[2] In fact, it consists in sets of trace fragments collected for the *direct flow* (normal program executions) and the pending branching flows (**break**, **continue**, forward **goto**). In this paper, we shall ignore the latter for the sake of simplicity.

- the strict prefix $(p_1, s_1), \ldots, (p_{n-1}, s_{n-1})$ is abstracted more coarsely; the trace partitioning domain keeps a sequence of program points p_k of interest (e.g. those related to if-then-else or loop branches) as well as the value of a few selected variables from s_k at given program points.

An abstract domain is a set $D^\sharp$ of abstract properties of trace fragments. Each abstract property $a \in D^\sharp$ is related to the set of concrete trace fragments that satisfy this property through a concretization function $\gamma_{D^\sharp} : D^\sharp \to D$. We consider different kinds of information:

- Some abstract properties define the mapping between structured C variables and the abstract scalar variables manipulated by most abstract domains. In particular, it handles the case where overlapping sequences of bytes are manipulated as scalar variables of possibly different types (e.g. through union types or pointer casts) and frees the other domains from the burden of coping with byte-level aliases and considering the binary memory representation of variables. This structural abstraction [7] is fully dynamic because, in our model of concrete executions, the pattern of data accesses is a run-time property that is not restricted by static typing.
- Some abstract properties constrain abstract variables: they may be non relational properties (such as a range for each variable) or relational properties (such as restricted linear relations, as in octagons; restricted polynomial relations, as in ellipsoids; restricted non-polynomial relations, as in arithmetic-geometric progressions).
- Some abstract properties may be guarded by constraints about some variables (as in boolean partitioning or by properties on the computation traces that have led to the current state (as in trace partitioning).

We do not assume that an abstract domain has a lattice structure. However, we suppose that it is provided with primitives to simulate the computation of the concrete semantics at the abstract level. This way, for any concrete n-ary primitive $F : D^n \to D$, we have a sound abstraction $F_{D^\sharp} : (D^\sharp)^n \to D^\sharp$ that satisfies: for any abstract properties $a_i \in D^\sharp$, $F((\gamma_{D^\sharp}(a_i))_{1 \le i \le n}) \subseteq \gamma_{D^\sharp}(F_{D^\sharp}((a_i)_{1 \le i \le n}))$. However, we do not assume $F_{D^\sharp}$ to be the most precise transformer that satisfy this property. These primitives not only update memory states, but also the information about the computation paths that lead to these memory states.

To ensure the termination of our analysis, the abstract domain is provided with extrapolation operators: the bottom element $\bot \in D^\sharp$ is the basis of abstract iterations, the widening operator $\nabla_{D^\sharp} \in D^\sharp \times D^\sharp \to D^\sharp$ is used to speed up the iterates (it may discard some information), and the narrowing operator $\triangle_{D^\sharp} \in D^\sharp \times D^\sharp \to D^\sharp$ is used to refine the iterates (after an imprecise extrapolation). We require no property whatsoever about the bottom element $\bot$. The widening operator (resp. the narrowing operator) is a sound abstraction of the union set operator (resp. the meet set operator): this way, for any pair $(a, b) \in D^\sharp \times D^\sharp$ of abstract properties, we require that $\gamma_{D^\sharp}(a) \cup \gamma_{D^\sharp}(b) \subseteq \gamma_{D^\sharp}(a \nabla_{D^\sharp} b)$ and $\gamma_{D^\sharp}(a) \cap \gamma_{D^\sharp}(b) \subseteq \gamma_{D^\sharp}(a \triangle_{D^\sharp} b)$. Moreover, both widening and narrowing operators ensure the convergence of iterates, which means that for any sequence $(x_n) \in (D^\sharp)^{\mathbb{N}}$, the sequence (x_n^∇) (resp. $(x_n^\triangle)$) defined as $x_0^\nabla = x_0$ (resp. $x_0^\triangle = x_0$) and $x_{n+1}^\nabla =$

$x_n^\triangledown \triangledown_{D^\sharp} x_{n+1}$ (resp. $x_{n+1}^\triangle = x_n^\triangle \triangle_{D^\sharp} x_{n+1}$) is ultimately stationary. More details are given about the usage of the widening in Sect. 7 and about the usage of the narrowing in Sect. 8.

Although we do not require abstract domains to be provided with an abstract order, there always exist a so-called information preorder $\sqsubseteq^\sharp$ induced by the concretization function: $a \sqsubseteq^\sharp b \iff \gamma_{D^\sharp}(a) \subseteq \gamma_{D^\sharp}(b)$. This preorder has little use in a practical analyzer as it is often computationally expensive and sometimes not even computable. Moreover, although all abstract transfer functions are abstractions of monotonic concrete transfer functions, they are often not monotonic with respect to the information preorder.

- The first cause of non monotonicity is nested loops. Internal loops may be analyzed using widening operators, and the abstraction of the least fixpoint obtained is in general not monotonic with respect to loop precondition.

Example 3. Consider an interval analysis of the following program, using the standard widening [9]:

```
x=0;
while(random()) {
    x=x+1;
    if (random()) x=y
    if (x==10) x=0; }
```

If we know at the beginning that $y \in [0, 9]$, then we immediately obtain the invariant $x \in [0, 9]$. Suppose however that we know the more precise property $y = 0$, then our analysis gives $x \in [0, +\infty[$. Thus, a more precise precondition yields a far worse outcome. □

- Another cause is transfer functions making use of additional information that, in fact, produce a less precise result.

Example 4. Such is for instance the case of the interval domain [9] helped by the symbolic computation domain [10]. Consider the following example, depending on whether we use the rewrite rule $j \mapsto i + 1$ arising from the assignment j=i+1:

Code	Symbolic computation	Less precise symbolic
`int i, j=i+1;`	$j \mapsto i+1$	NOTHING
`int k=j+1;`	$j \mapsto i+1, k \mapsto j+1 \mapsto i+2$	$k \mapsto j+1$
`if (j > 0) {`		
`    l=k;`	$j \mapsto i+1, k \mapsto i+2, l \mapsto i+2$	$k \mapsto j+1, l \mapsto j+1$
`}`		

By default, our symbolic computation domain performs all possible rewrites, thus we try to reduce the intervals using $k \mapsto i+2$, which yields no additional precision. However, with the less precise third column, we have $k \mapsto j+1$, and since we have the interval information $j \in [1, +\infty[$ we conclude that $k \in [2, +\infty[$. □

– Finally, some abstract domains are implemented using floating-point as over-approximations of an "ideal" abstract domain and this may introduce non-monotonicity.

Example 5. The octagon abstract domain uses a propagation scheme based on an incremental Floyd–Warshall shortest-path-closure algorithm to infer and refine constraints. On reals or rationals, this propagation is both sound and complete; in particular, the outcome does not depend on the order of the variables. On floating-point numbers, soundness can be achieved easily by rounding all computations towards $+\infty$ (as only upper bounds are manipulated). However, the propagation is no longer complete and different variable orderings give incomparable sound approximations of the most precise result. Starting from the same precondition, but two different internal encodings, and applying the same transfer function, we can obtain slightly different postconditions, hence the non-monotonicity.   □

4.2   Comparison with Predicate Abstraction

Constraint messages (Sect. 5) and abstract properties are, essentially, *predicates* over the set of traces that we abstract. However, our analysis is not what is usually referred to as *predicate abstraction* [19].

Predicate abstraction generally refers to the following approach:

– one considers a (small) finite, given, set S of predicates; each predicate $p \in S$ has a semantics $[\![p]\!]$ in terms of possible program or variable states (thus, the predicate x < 5 will include all program states where variable x is less than 5); in the simplest case, predicates simply reflect the value of the boolean variables in the program;
– one computes abstract states as subsets S' of S, such that $[\![S']\!] = \bigcap_{p \in S'} [\![p]\!]$;
– transformers over these abstract states may be defined using an automatic theorem prover;
– once transformers are defined, the program is reduced to a boolean program and a model checker is used;
– if one cannot prove the desired property, and a fake "counterexample" is obtained the analysis is insufficiently precise; additional predicates have to be added, often generated through a process of automatic refinement based on the examination of the fake counterexample.

Differences with predicate abstraction are as follows:

– Our analyses do not consider a priori a small set of predicates, but rather operate on *parametric* predicates [20]. That is, where predicate abstraction considers different predicates x < 4, x < 5, etc., our analysis considers a generic predicate x $< C$ and tries to adjust C.
– We do not use an automatic theorem prover to generate the program transformers. We could perhaps do so, provided that the theorem prover is capable of handling efficiently our parametric predicates; obviously, it is more difficult to generate transformers over parametric predicates, perhaps with some measure of optimality of the result of the transformer, than to decide or even

semi-decide whether a particular ground predicate ensues from a program construct in the context of some particular ground predicates. However, such automated generation of parametric transfer functions is itself a research issue.

– We do not use automatic refinement techniques in the sense of adding new predicates and starting the analysis again. However, if our analysis fails to find an invariant, then we extrapolate the invariant "candidates" through *widening* techniques.

4.3 Domain Constructors

Some of the abstract domains used in ASTRÉE are based on similar algebraic constructs or are parametrized by the choice of an underlying abstract domain. In order to factor code and allow easy parametrization, we defined domain *constructors* [21] that are naturally implemented as OCaml functors [16], while abstract domains are OCaml modules.

Non-relational Lifting Functor. Some abstract domains used in ASTRÉE are *non-relational*; that is, they abstract the values of each scalar abstract variable separately. For instance, we have the following abstractions for scalar values:

– integer intervals with thresholds;
– floating-point intervals with thresholds;
– integer congruences.

We *lift* these abstractions to non-relational domains on multiple variables by considering abstract environments mapping each variable to an abstract value. As described in [3], environments are implemented using balanced binary trees, which allows a fast abstract union operator in $O(m \log n)$, where n is the total number of variables and m the number of variables that differ in the two environment arguments, instead of $O(n)$ for a plain array. This pays off in the kind of code we analyze, where the number of if-then-else as well as the number of variables are linear in the size $|P|$ of the program, but then and else branches have a small size. We obtain a combined cost for the meet operation at the end of all if-then-else in $O(|P| \log |P|)$ instead of $O(|P|^2)$. The same optimization is used for other binary operators, e.g. widening.

Packed Relational Lifting Functor. A similar system is used for relational domains (such as the octagon abstract domain: the set of abstract variables is partitioned[3] into *packs* of bounded size. All the variables in a pack are related together by an instance of the relational domain, but not with variables in other packs. Each transfer function only modifies a small set of packs, while abstract unions operate point-wisely on packs. The lifting of a standard relational domain

---

[3] Actually we consider a covering where one variable may appear in several packs. This is useful when a single variable is used in different contexts. However, to maintain an almost linear cost, no information flows between packs sharing variables.

to a packed domain is similar to the non-relational lifting. The resulting domain enjoys the same almost-linear asymptotic cost, assuming a bound on the size of the packs.

Trace Partitioning. Most abstract domains deal with scalar values and data structures, thus, memory states of the program. However, it is sometimes necessary to distinguish between values according to the history of the computation.

Example 6. Consider the following implementation of a piecewise linear function:

```
if (x < tx[0] || x > tx[N]) fail();
for (i=0; i<N-1; i++)
    if (x <= tx[i+1]) break;
return ty[i]+(ty[i+1]-ty[i])*(x-tx[i])/(tx[i+1]-tx[i]);
```

where tx and ty are constant arrays of size N+1, and tx is increasing. The plain interval domain would show a warning for division by zero, since it will compute the least upper bound of all tx[i+1] for all values of i, the same for tx[i], and the two would overlap. Precise analysis thus seems to require inferring complex relationships between i, tx[i], and ty[i] and handling affine functions.

However, the interval domain can find the most precise result provided that we partition the last assignment with respect to the number of iterations before exiting the loop. This is semantically equivalent to analyzing the following code:

```
if (x < tx[0] || x > tx[N])
    fail();
if (x < tx[1])
    return ty[0]+(ty[1]-ty[0])*(x-tx[0])/(tx[1]-tx[0]);
else if (x < tx[2])
    return ty[1]+(ty[2]-ty[1])*(x-tx[1])/(tx[2]-tx[1]);
else ...
else
    return ty[N-1]+(ty[N]-ty[N-1])*(x-tx[N-1])/(tx[N]-tx[N-1]);
```

□

Trace partitioning [14] is a functor parametrized by two abstractions: an abstraction of the history of former memory and control states (e.g. a sub-sequence of branches taken), and an abstraction of the current memory state. Abstract elements are maps and are implemented as trees: each path corresponds to a different control history and each leaf contains the corresponding memory state. This makes it easy to dynamically adjust the precision of history abstractions by simply splitting leaves and folding sub-trees, which is exactly what ASTRÉE does, driven by heuristics that achieve a trade-off between cost and precision.

Boolean Partitioning. An alternate way of partitioning is to distinguish between the possible values of a subset of the variables with respect to the value of one or more boolean variables.

Example 7. Consider the following code that stores an arithmetic condition in a boolean for future use[4]:

```
b = x < 5;
/* unrelated computations */
if (b) x = 5;
```

In order to prove that $x \geq 5$ at the end, one should distinguish between the case where b is true and where it is false, at least for the information concerning x.

$\square$

Partitioned abstract elements are implemented as decision diagrams [4, 2.6.4], i.e. trees with boolean variables at internal nodes and abstract memory states at the leaves, with opportunistic sharing of equivalent sub-trees. Thus, the boolean partitioning domain it is a functor parametrized by the choice of an abstraction of memory states. As for relational domains, almost-linear cost is achieved by only partitioning small, bounded sets of arithmetic variables with respect to small, bounded sets of booleans. Thus, it also reuses the packing functor.

Abstract Product. In general, the abstract domain used by the analyzer is formed of the partially reduced product of several abstract domains. Reduction is implemented through a network of communication channels, as explained in the following section. We use a binary product functor that takes two domains and implements communications between them. It returns a new domain that can be used as argument of any functor, including the product functor itself. Thus, a full network of domains can be constructed using several product applications. As the binary product multiplexes communication channels, every domain in the resulting network can communicate with every other one.

5   Network of Domains

5.1   Hierarchies

ASTRÉE handles very heterogeneous kinds of abstract properties. Each class of abstract properties is gathered inside a small, independent abstract domain. Domains are fitted with all the primitives needed to handle their particular class of abstract properties. Nevertheless, ASTRÉE is not a neutral product of separate abstract domains (which would be equivalent to running separate analyses); it organizes an active collaboration between them.

We use the binary product functor to gather several abstract domains together into a hierarchy and form a reduced product. The product is not commutative because it sets which abstract domain will be processed before the others. As a consequence, the domains that are computed first may communicate partial results to others that have not yet started their own computations. When a

---

[4] This kind of code, where the definition and the use of b are far apart, appears frequently in automatically generated programs (e.g. compiled from graphical languages *à la* Simulink).

domain $D_1^\sharp$ is computed before domain $D_2^\sharp$, we say that $D_1^\sharp$ is an *underlying* domain of the domain $D_2^\sharp$. By construction, being an underlying domain is an acyclic relation (see Fig. 1).

The argument of a unary functor, such as the trace or boolean partitioning domain, may also be an abstract domain constructed by applying the binary product functor. As a consequence, there are generally several hierarchies at work in an analysis. Each unary functor spawning a hierarchy will be called a *root*. Roots have a special role in the communication between domains, as we will see in Sects. 5.3–5.4.

Example 8. Fig. 1 is a small but realistic hierarchy used in ASTRÉE. Its main root is the trace partitioning domain. The boolean partitioning domain is used to spawn a simpler sub-hierarchy. In the example, variable ranges can be partitioned with respect to the value of some boolean variables, while octagon invariants cannot. Also note that the interval domain is the most underlying domain in both hierarchy, hence the first evaluated. On the one hand, it is the least precise, and so, the one most likely to benefit from refinement by other domains. On the other hand, it is the only one to handle all C constructs, and so, provides a base information we can always resort to.   □

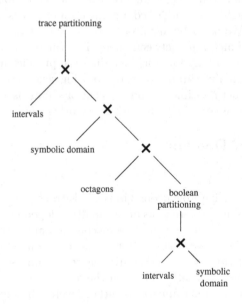

Fig. 1. Example hierarchy

5.2   Communication Channels

Domains communicate abstract properties to each other. For that purpose, we introduce a particular abstract domain of messages. This domain is defined as a set $IO^\sharp$ of abstract properties and by a concretization $\gamma_{IO^\sharp} : IO^\sharp \to D$ that maps any such abstract property to the set of concrete trace fragments that satisfy this property.

Each regular abstract domain $(D^\sharp, \gamma_{D^\sharp})$ is fitted with a primitive EXTRACT$_{D^\sharp}$: $D^\sharp \times IO^\sharp \to IO^\sharp$ that it can use to emit some constraints on communicating channels. In the expression $io' = $ EXTRACT$_{D^\sharp}(c, io)$, the message io denotes the contents of the channel before the constraint is emitted, the abstract element c denotes an abstract element in the domain $D^\sharp$, and the message io' denotes the contents of the channel enriched with constraints extracted from c (hence the name EXTRACT). This way, we require that $\gamma_{D^\sharp}(c) \cap \gamma_{IO^\sharp}(io) \subseteq \gamma_{IO^\sharp}($EXTRACT$_{D^\sharp}(c, io))$.

Conversely, each abstract domain $(D^\sharp, \gamma_{D^\sharp})$ has a primitive REFINE$_{D^\sharp}$: $D^\sharp \times IO^\sharp \to D^\sharp$ allowing the reception of constraints from a communication channel. In the expression $c' = $ REFINE$_{D^\sharp}(c, io)$, the abstract element c' is a refinement (hence the name REFINE) of the abstract element c having taken into account the constraints denoted by the contents io of the channel. We require that $\gamma_{D^\sharp}(c) \cap \gamma_{IO^\sharp}(io) \subseteq \gamma_{D^\sharp}($REFINE$_{D^\sharp}(c, io))$.

In the following subsections, we introduce some communicating channels between domains. We distinguish between two kinds of communications:

1. a domain may ask whether a more precise constraint is available; the channel used is then called an *input* channel (Sect. 5.3);
2. a domain may decide to communicate some of its constraints to other domains in order to refine them, in which case the channel used is called an *output* channel (Sect. 5.4).

Note that the abstract domain $IO^\sharp$ of messages does not need to be the same for input and output channels. In ASTRÉE, they are indeed different and implemented using different data-structures (a product type for the input, and a sum type for output). This means that we actually have two versions of REFINE$_{D^\sharp}$ and EXTRACT$_{D^\sharp}$.

5.3 Input Channels

Input channels provide information on both the postcondition being computed and the precondition computed in the last computation step. A domain $D^\sharp$ may update the contents of the postcondition channel at the end of its own computation (using EXTRACT$_{D^\sharp}$). It may read the pre-condition information from all domains, but may only access post-condition constraints that have already been computed by another domain (triggered before itself in the hierarchy). At the end of a computation step, the network root collects the contents of the channel and makes it available to all domains as the precondition of the next step.

The contents of the channel is implemented as a *functional record type*. Each field denotes a particular class of properties in $IO^\sharp$. For each field, there is a default value $\top$ which corresponds to the absence of information (when no domain has filled the field yet). To avoid useless computations, we rely on lazy evaluation: each field is a function that is evaluated only if/when required. To update a closure f, a domain replaces it with a new closure f'. When applied, the new closure f' may or may not evaluate f. Moreover, we use memoization to avoid computing the same information several times.

The advantage of this design is that adding a new kind of input communication between two domains is straightforward. First, we add a field in the signature of the channel and we update the default value of the channel contents. Then, we modify the primitive EXTRACT$_{D^\sharp}$ of the domain $D^\sharp$ that provides this information. Last, we update the primitives that use this information. The code for the other domains that do not generate nor use this information does not require any modification.

5.4   Output Channels

Output channels are used when a domain wants to send a message to others. There are two output channels:

- The first one is used to refine the computation just performed by the underlying domains; we call it the *oriented output channel*.
- The second one broadcasts a message to be used by all domains (including those that have not performed their computation yet); we call it the *broadcast output channel*.

A domain $D^\sharp$ may send messages (using EXTRACT$_{D^\sharp}$) and fetch messages to use them (using REFINE$_{D^\sharp}$). In the case of oriented outputs, the contents of the channel is simply handed from one domain to the next by the product functor so that it can be directly used, refined, or both; then, the (possibly updated) contents is forwarded to all the underlying domains. In the case of broadcast outputs, the channel is only updated during the network evaluation; no domain may use its contents. Then, once the root of the network is reached, the contents of the channel is sent to all domains using REFINE$_{D^\sharp}$ primitives, so that domains have the opportunity to use (and even refine further) the information.

The contents of an output channel is implemented as a list of constraints. Constraints are implemented with a *sum type*, where each summand is a different kind of constraints. After each computation, each domain collects a list of constraints from each output channel. The primitive REFINE$_{D^\sharp}$ scans the list and refines the abstract properties accordingly. It may also generate new constraints to be communicated to other domains but, to avoid infinite loops, we only allow REFINE$_{D^\sharp}$ to use the oriented output channel, not the broadcast one.

From the point of view of analyzer maintenance, this design is very convenient since it makes the addition of a new kind of output communication between two domains easy. First, we add a summand in the signature of the output constraints. Then, we modify the domain that outputs the constraints. Last, we update the primitive EXTRACT$_{D^\sharp}$ in the domain $D^\sharp$ that wishes to receive the constraint. The other domains do not require any modification: they will simply ignore the new information, which is safe.

6   Domain Cooperation

Abstract computations are made under assumptions about pre/postconditions. Indeed, any n-ary concrete transfer function $F \in D^n \to D$ is simulated by an abstraction $F_{D^\sharp} \in (D^\sharp \times IO^\sharp)^n \times IO^\sharp \to D^\sharp$. The abstract element $a_0 = F_{D^\sharp}((a_i, io_i)_{1 \le i \le n}, io_0)$ should be understood as: compute in the abstract the image of F, knowing that each argument a_i satisfies the constraints in io_i, and that the result a_0 satisfies the constraints in io_0. This gives the following soundness criterion: if there exists some $(c_i)_{0 \le i \le n} \in D^n$ such that

- $c_i \in \gamma_{D^\sharp}(a_i)$, for any i such that $1 \le i \le n$,
- $c_i \in \gamma_{IO^\sharp}(io_i)$, for any i such that $0 \le i \le n$,
- $c_0 \in F((c_i)_{1 \le i \le n})$.

then we must have $c_0 \in \gamma_{D^\sharp}(F_{D^\sharp}((a_i, io_i)_{1 \le i \le n}, io_0))$.

We now distinguish between several cases of collaboration. Some domains may be used to refine the abstract properties of other domains. This kind of reduction boils down to replacing an abstract operation $F_{D^\sharp}((a_i)_{1 \le i \le n}))$ with a refined counterpart $\rho_0(F_{D^\sharp}((\rho_i(a_i, io_i))_{1 \le i \le n}), io_0)$ such that, for any integer i such that $0 \le i \le n$, ρ_i is a sound abstraction of the meet: $(\gamma_{D^\sharp} \circ \rho_i)(a_i, io_i) \supseteq \gamma_{D^\sharp}(a_i) \cap \gamma_{IO^\sharp}(io_i)$. Whenever $i > 0$, the reduction $\rho_i : D^\sharp \times IO^\sharp \to D^\sharp$ is used to refine the precondition: this kind of refinement is discussed in Sect. 6.1. The reduction $\rho_0 : D^\sharp \times IO^\sharp \to D^\sharp$ is used to refine the postcondition: this kind of refinement is discussed in Sect. 6.2.

In ASTRÉE, this is not the only way the domains may collaborate. We also perform some refinement of abstract transformers that cannot be expressed as merely refining abstract states. This is discussed in Sect. 6.3.

6.1   Precondition Refinement

Some domains refine abstract states before they are fed to their abstract transformers. This is made possible thanks to the input channel as it makes the information that has been computed by all domains accessible to any domain. Since the abstract interpretation of the program follows the control flow graph, the abstract computation of the properties that are valid at a given iteration and just before interpreting an instruction are fully computed before the abstract interpretation of the instruction begins.

This kind of reductions is used whenever the domain is a partial mapping from some tuples of variables to parametric constraints (as in the filters domain or the arithmetic-geometric progressions domain). In such domains, the support (i.e. the set of tuples that are mapped to a constraint) changes during the iteration. Whenever both arguments of a binary operator do not have the same support or whenever a unary abstract transformer needs a given constraint to be precise, the domain uses the input channel to synthesize missing constraints.

Example 9. The ellipsoid domain can simulate an assignment of the form $X = a.Y + b.Z + t$ by mapping a constraint of the form $Y^2 - a.Y.Z - b.Z^2 \le k^2$ to

a constraint of the form $X^2 - a.X.Y - b.Y^2 \leq (f(k))^2$. When this constraint is missing, the ellipsoid domain synthesizes an ellipse using interval constraints about the variables Y and Z, and a possible equality relation between Y and Z.
□

6.2   Postcondition Refinement

Domains may collaborate to refine the result of an abstract transformer. There are two cases: the refinement is initiated either by the domain that has computed the information, or by the domain that misses the information.

A first use is when a domain synthesizes a very useful information and propagates it to its underlying domains using the oriented output channel[5]. For instance, many domains can infer interval information and use the oriented output channel to inform the interval domain of their discoveries.

Example 10. Consider the following code fragment computing an absolute value:

```
X=Y;
if (X<0) X=-Y;
if (X<100) { ...Y... }
```

The interval domain does not track the relationship between X and Y and so cannot prove that, in the last then block, $Y \in [-100, 100]$. However, the octagon domain can (see [11, §5.2]). Suppose now that the interval domain is underlying with respect to the octagon one, thus allowing the later to refine the result of the former through an oriented output channel (this is always the case in practice). After each assignment or test, the octagon domain gathers the variables that had their value updated (for tests, this includes all the variables appearing in the expression; for assignments, only the left-value is considered) and extracts their range in all octagons by projection. Each range is then compared to the one computed by the underlying domains (using the input channel on the postcondition). When the one computed from the octagon domain is more precise, it is output to the oriented output channel. When it is not, no interval constraint is output. This may happen because some modified variables do not appear in any octagon, or the expression has been so aggressively abstracted (due to floating-point arithmetics [22] or non-linearity [10]) that the interval domain performs better.
□

A second use is when a domain cannot synthesize a precise constraint, and so, asks for other domains to generate it. A first way to receive constraints from underlying domains is to use the input channel.

Example 11. In some cases, the octagon domain is not able to compute the effect of a transfer function at all. Consider, for instance, the assignment X=Y on an octagon containing X but not Y. In that case, the octagon domain relies on the

---

[5] Although a domain may use the broadcast output channel to propagate information to underlying domains, this has not been used in ASTRÉE until now. The broadcast channel has a more specific use, illustrated in Ex. 12.

underlying interval domain to give it the actual range of X in the postcondition. To compute the effect of the assignment, the domain first forgets all constraints about X (are they may no longer hold in the postcondition), and then adds range constraints gathered from the input channel for the postcondition.   □

Alternatively, a domain may use the broadcast output channel to request some information about some variables. The root of the network will propagate this message to all domains. Each domain will then try and compute some constraints over the given variables and communicate them using the oriented output channel. This is more powerful because all domains participate in the refinement, but also more costly.

It is important to note that we cannot rely solely on precise domains to initiate communications towards less precise ones. Suppose, for instance, that we wish an unstable constraint to be refined by a precise and stable constraint after some widening application. Because of our systematic optimization of binary operations (which is key to the scalability of ASTRÉE, see Sect. 4.3), stable constraints are not even looked at during widening application. As a consequence, the precise and stable constraint has no opportunity to initiate the communication and it is up to the unstable one to ask for help.

Example 12. The widening of the interval domain checks for the stability of variable ranges. When it detects that some variable range is not stable, it enlarges it. It also sends a broadcast message to the root of the network and informs it of the precision loss. As a consequence, each domain will collects all the information it has on the variable and try to infer a range information. When successful, this process issues a "refine range" message that is acknowledged by the interval domain.   □

6.3   Abstract Transformer Refinement

Some refinements cannot be expressed as state refinements: domains actually collaborate to set up their abstract transformers.

First, some domains require expressions to be presented with a given level of abstraction. In such cases, a domain may ask its underlying domains to abstract an expression. This kind of communication is ensured by the input channel.

Example 13. Most abstract domains are purely numerical abstract domains that abstract sets of points in a vector space $\mathbb{R}^n$. They require expressions to be arithmetic expressions over some finite set of scalar variables. However, C expressions also allow structured variables (such as arrays or structures) as well as pointers. A specific domain [7] is devoted to abstracting the memory into a set of independent scalar cells. It is its responsibility to evaluate array and structure accesses, pointer dereferences, and translate C expressions into arithmetic ones.

In order to do this, it abstracts information on the layout of the memory, as well as information on the memory blocks pointed to by pointers. However, it relies on the underlying numerical domains to abstract the contents of integer and floating-point variables, as well as pointer offsets (viewed as integers). For instance, it may ask the underlying domain for the value of some array index in the current precondition. The case of complex expressions with several levels of indirections is solved by structural induction and spawns many communications.

Another example is pointer arithmetics, which is simply translated into integer arithmetics on offsets, to be evaluated by underlying numerical domains. It is important to note that pointer and value analyses are performed at the same time and that expressions are transformed on-the-fly given the abstraction of the precondition currently available in the network of domains.   □

Example 14. Most relational domains are based on real arithmetic, because it enjoys convenient properties (e.g. associativity, distributivity). However, concrete programs use floating-point operations that violate those. Thus, we use a linearization domain [22] to soundly translate floating-point arithmetics into real arithmetics. This may decrease the precision because perfectly deterministic but highly non-linear rounding errors are abstracted into non deterministic intervals. But, it outputs simple linear forms with interval coefficients and real semantics that can be fed directly to numerical domains, even relational ones.[6]   □

Note that some domains require precise information that is lost by linearization or array access resolution. Thus, each domain should be allowed to interpret expressions at the level of abstraction it chooses (possibly in a dynamic way).

Example 15. The floating-point interval domain bounds tightly each floating-point operation, enabling us to analyze $x < y$ differently from $x \leq y$. The small non deterministic rounding errors introduced by the linearization would, however, make this impossible.   □

Example 16. When interpreting an expression of the form A[i]+B[i], where both A and B are arrays and i is an integer, there may be an invariant about the expression A[i]+B[i] for any i within the bounds of the arrays A and B. This invariant is lost when resolving array accesses. If we want abstract domains to use this invariant, we have to give them the opportunity to access expressions before array access resolution. Another solution is partitioning, but that may be too impractical or too costly.   □

Abstract domains may use more precise abstract transformers whenever some properties are satisfied. There are two cases. In the first case, a special-purpose domain is used to check whether the properties hold and inform other domains using the broadcast output channel.

---

[6] Interestingly, in relational numerical abstract domains, algorithms are usually proved on real numbers, but the implementation is done using floating-point numbers, and soundness is achieved using rounding towards $\pm\infty$ as appropriate. Thus, there exists a real abstract semantics $[\![e]\!]_{\mathbb{R}}^{\sharp}$ and an over-approximation thereof using floating-point numbers $[\![e]\!]_{F}^{\sharp}$. Let us call $[\![e]\!]_{F}$ the concrete semantics over floating-point values and $[\![e]\!]_{\mathbb{R}}$ the over-approximation using real numbers and intervals for rounding errors, we have a tower of semantics: $[\![e]\!]_{F} \sqsubseteq [\![e]\!]_{\mathbb{R}} \sqsubseteq [\![e]\!]_{\mathbb{R}}^{\sharp} \sqsubseteq [\![e]\!]_{F}^{\sharp}$.

Example 17. Consider the following code:

```
volatile float vI;
void main () {
   float I, O = 0, R, OLD;
   while (1) {
      I = vI;
      OLD = O; R = I - OLD; O = I;
      if (R <= -0.2) { O = OLD - 0.2; }
      else if (0.2 <= R) { O = OLD + 0.2; }
   }
}
```

An input stream (denoted by the variable I) is modified by a rate limiter that bounds the difference between two successive outputs by the value 0.2. The variable OLD denotes the last output; the variable R is the difference between the new input and the last output; the variable O denotes the output stream.

When a rate limiter is involved in a complex dependence cycle, it is crucial that the arithmetic-progression domain be able to compute precise abstract properties all along the cycle. A specific domain collects the guards in "if-then-else" statements. When both guards not(R <= -0.2) and not(0.2 <= R) are satisfied, it checks (using the input channel) in the symbolic domain that both R matches I-OLD and O matches I (in floating-point arithmetics). Then, it warns the arithmetic-geometric progression domains that the absolute value of the variable O is less than the expression $|(1+\varepsilon_1)\text{OLD}+0.2+\varepsilon_2|$, where the floating-point numbers ε_1 and ε_2 model rounding errors and are computed automatically.   □

In the second case, a domain may check that a special property holds using the input channel and performing abstract pattern matching over the concrete instruction it is currently abstracting. We have already seen in Ex. 1 that some transformers can be made more precise if they apply a special case when two variables are provably equal. In Ex. 18, we describe a more complex example.

Example 18. Digital filtering domains perform computations only when they discover that a variable X is equal to a linear combination of several other variables (the number of variables depends on the class of the filter). There are several trade-offs for detecting this property. The less generic way is to perform pattern matching of expressions in assignments (using a variety of abstraction levels for expressions: floating-point expressions, linearized expressions, etc.). This solution is very fragile: if a filter iteration is not computed using a single assignment (but, e.g. a loop scanning a parameter array), it is not discovered. It would be possible, but maybe costly, to collect the desired properties in a specially-designed abstract domain. Our solution is in-between those: we use the symbolic domain. Abstract pattern matching takes a pattern and an expression, and tries to unify them by replacing expression variables with the floating-point expression they are equal to in the symbolic domain. This collaboration uses the input channel.   □

Finally, some abstract domains provide several implementations for an abstract transformer and rely on strategies to select which one should be used, depending on constraints computed by other domains.

Example 19. In arithmetic-geometric progression domains, a pair of elements may lack a least upper bound. We have implemented three ways to compute a bound: the first one favors the right argument, the second one favors the left argument, whereas the third one is a trade-off. The selection between the three strategies depends not only on the arithmetic-geometric constraints, but also on the dependency graph among variables and on the range of involved variables, which can be fetched from the input channel of the precondition.   □

6.4   Reduction After Widenings

Special care should be taken when refining an extrapolation operator. Although it is always safe to refine its right argument; refining its left argument or its output may break the extrapolation process. Indeed, the standard assumption required to ensure the termination of the widening iterates (Sect. 4.1 and [1]) may not be applicable anymore. As a consequence, the analyzer may loop forever.

In ASTRÉE, we reduce the output of the extrapolation operator using the broadcast output channel, as in Ex. 12. We also refine the left argument of widenings when a constraint is missing, as in Ex. 9. Nevertheless, these kinds of refinements follow the hierarchic structure of domain networks, which prevents cyclic reductions. We ensure the termination of ASTRÉE by strengthening the definition of the widening.

7   Widenings

7.1   Framework

We use widenings to abstract the computation of post-fixpoints in a finite amount of time [1]. Formally, let D be a concrete domain and $D^\sharp$ be an abstract domain related via a concretization map $\gamma_{D^\sharp} \in D^\sharp \to D$. A widening operator $\nabla_{D^\sharp}$ over an abstract domain $D^\sharp$ is a mapping in $D^\sharp \times D^\sharp \to D^\sharp$ such that [23, Lect. 18]:

- $\forall a, b \in D^\sharp,\ \gamma_{D^\sharp}(b) \subseteq \gamma_{D^\sharp}(a \nabla_{D^\sharp} b)$;   (W$_1$)
- for all (a_i), the sequence (a_i^∇) defined as $a_0^\nabla = a_0$ and $a_{n+1}^\nabla =$ (W$_2$) $a_n^\nabla \nabla_{D^\sharp} a_{n+1}$ is ultimately stationary.

The second property implies that the widening relation $\to$ that is defined as $a \to b$ if and only if there exists c such that $a \nabla_{D^\sharp} c = b$ is well founded. Nevertheless, there may be no relation between the information preorder $\sqsubseteq^\sharp$ (defined as $a \sqsubseteq^\sharp b$ if and only if $\gamma_{D^\sharp}(a) \subseteq \gamma_{D^\sharp}(b)$) and the relation $\to$.

Least fixpoint approximation is performed in the following way. Let F be a monotonic map in $D \to D$ and $F_{D^\sharp} : D^\sharp \to D^\sharp$ be an abstraction of F satisfying $\forall a \in D^\sharp,\ (F \circ \gamma_{D^\sharp})(a) \subseteq (\gamma_{D^\sharp} \circ F_{D^\sharp})(a)$. The abstract operation $F_{D^\sharp}$ needs not be monotonic with respect to the information preorder $\sqsubseteq^\sharp$. The abstract upward iteration (x_n^∇) of $F_{D^\sharp}$ is defined as $x_0^\nabla = \bot$ and $x_{n+1}^\nabla = x_n^\nabla \nabla_{D^\sharp} F_{D^\sharp}(x_n^\nabla)$.

The sequence $(x_n^\triangledown)$ is ultimately stationary and we denote its limit by l. The following lemma ensures that the limit of the abstract upward iteration is a post-fixpoint abstraction of the map F:

Lemma 1. *We have* $F(\gamma_{D^\sharp}(l)) \subseteq \gamma_{D^\sharp}(l)$.

Proof. l is the limit of the upward-iteration, so $l = l \triangledown_{D^\sharp} F_{D^\sharp}(l)$. By (W_1), we obtain: $\gamma_{D^\sharp}(F_{D^\sharp}(l)) \subseteq \gamma_{D^\sharp}(l)$. By soundness of $F_{D^\sharp}$, we also have $F(\gamma_{D^\sharp}(l)) \subseteq \gamma_{D^\sharp}(F_{D^\sharp}(l))$. So $F(\gamma_{D^\sharp}(l)) \subseteq \gamma_{D^\sharp}(l)$.   □

The fact that the information preorder $\sqsubseteq^\sharp$ and the widening relation $\rightarrow$ are not assumed to be related limits the usage of the widening far too much for our need. Indeed, as explained in Sect. 7.2, we would like to refine the abstract properties after a widening step. Moreover, as explained in Sect. 7.3, we would like to refrain from widening abstract properties at every iterate. Doing these carelessly could break the termination of the widening process. Thus, in Sect. 7.4, we strengthen the definition of the widening to safely allow these manipulations.

7.2 Reduction of Widenings

The interval abstract domain is in many ways the "base" abstract domain. Most of the properties that we check are properties of bounds, directly expressed in the interval domain; also, while for each variable we keep an interval, we do not necessarily keep the other kinds of abstract properties. However, the interval domain, by default, applies simple preset widening thresholds (enriched with constants encountered in comparisons). In order to prevent the intervals from being widened too much, which would result in false alarms, it is necessary to reduce them using more refined abstract properties. Thus, most numerical domains reduce the intervals after widening.

However, care must be taken not to reduce too much after a widening in order not to break the termination property of the widening. A classical example is the closure operation in the octagon abstract domain, which can be considered a reduction between separate domains, each considering only a couple of variables: if one applies the classical widening operation on octagons followed by closure (reduction), then termination is no longer ensured (e.g. see [11, Fig. 25–26]).

An alternate approach would be to modify the abstract transformers, refining both its inputs and output, instead of modifying the widening. We denote by $\rho : D^\sharp \rightarrow D^\sharp$ our reduction function (i.e. it satisfies $\forall a \in D^\sharp, \gamma_{D^\sharp}(a) \subseteq \gamma_{D^\sharp}(\rho(a))$). We can define the two following sequences:

$$\begin{cases} u_0 = \bot, \\ u_{n+1} = \rho(u_n \triangledown_{D^\sharp}(\rho(F_{D^\sharp}(u_n)))); \end{cases} \qquad \begin{cases} v_0 = \bot, \\ v_{n+1} = v_n \triangledown_{D^\sharp}(\rho(F_{D^\sharp}(\rho(v_n)))). \end{cases}$$

In ASTRÉE, we compute the sequence (u_n), whereas the alternate strategy implements the sequence (v_n). The sequence (v_n) is ultimately stationary even without strengthening the definition of the widening. But the sequence (u_n) can be computed more easily, while taking benefit of functional data-structures (i.e.

balanced trees). Moreover, the sequence (u_n) provides a modular definition for the widening operator of reduced product domains.

Lemma 2. *The limit $\bar{u}$ of (u_i) (resp. $\bar{v}$ of (v_i)) satisfies* $\mathrm{F}(\gamma_{D^\sharp}(\bar{u})) \subseteq \gamma_{D^\sharp}(\bar{u})$ *(resp. $\mathrm{F}(\gamma_{D^\sharp}(\bar{v})) \subseteq \gamma_{D^\sharp}(\bar{v})$).*

Proof. For the limit $\bar{u}$ of (u_i), we have $\bar{u} = \rho(\bar{u}\nabla_{D^\sharp}(\rho(\mathrm{F}_{D^\sharp}(\bar{u}))))$ so $\gamma_{D^\sharp}(\bar{u}) = \gamma_{D^\sharp}(\rho(\bar{u}\nabla_{D^\sharp}(\rho(\mathrm{F}_{D^\sharp}(\bar{u})))))$ whence $\gamma_{D^\sharp}(\bar{u}\nabla_{D^\sharp}(\rho(\mathrm{F}_{D^\sharp}(\bar{u})))) \subseteq \gamma_{D^\sharp}(\bar{u})$ by soundness of the reduction ρ. By (W_1), $\gamma_{D^\sharp}(\rho(\mathrm{F}_{D^\sharp}(\bar{u}))) \subseteq \gamma_{D^\sharp}(\bar{u})$, whence $\gamma_{D^\sharp}(\mathrm{F}_{D^\sharp}(\bar{u})) \subseteq \gamma_{D^\sharp}(\bar{u})$ by soundness of ρ and so $\mathrm{F}(\gamma_{D^\sharp}(\bar{u})) \subseteq \gamma_{D^\sharp}(\bar{u})$ by soundness of $\mathrm{F}_{D^\sharp}$. Similarly $\bar{v} = \bar{v}\nabla_{D^\sharp}(\rho(\mathrm{F}_{D^\sharp}(\rho(\bar{v}))))$ implies $\gamma_{D^\sharp}(\bar{v}) = \gamma_{D^\sharp}(\bar{v}\nabla_{D^\sharp}(\rho(\mathrm{F}_{D^\sharp}(\rho(\bar{v})))))$ so $\gamma_{D^\sharp}(\bar{v}) \supseteq \gamma_{D^\sharp}(\rho(\mathrm{F}_{D^\sharp}(\rho(\bar{v})))) \supseteq \gamma_{D^\sharp}(\mathrm{F}_{D^\sharp}(\rho(\bar{v}))) \supseteq \mathrm{F}(\gamma_{D^\sharp}(\bar{v}))$ by (W_1) and soundness of ρ and $\mathrm{F}_{D^\sharp}$. □

Due to the non-monotonic behavior of the widening (especially with respect to the second argument), it seems difficult to compare the theoretical accuracy of the two approaches.

7.3 Delaying Strategies

Premature widenings may result in excessive over-approximation. This is particularly true when the first few iterations of the system perform some kind of initialization and do not give a good insight on the regular behavior of the loop. We therefore delay the application of the widening, replacing it with a mere abstract union, until a specified iteration, and start extrapolating afterwards.

Unfortunately, this is not sufficient and we may want to interleave unions and widenings even after the first iteration with widening. Consider the following example:

Example 20.

```
while (1) {
    X := Y + b;
    Y := a*X + c;
}
```

The sequence of assignments is equivalent to Y := a*X + d (with $d = c + a.b$), and so a widening with thresholds should find a stable interval. But if we perform a widening with thresholds at each step, each time we widen Y, X is increased to a value surpassing the threshold for Y, and so X is widened to the next stage, which in turn increases Y further and the next widening stage increases the value of Y. This eventually results in $\top$ abstract values for X and Y. We can see, however, that if we replace the widening with a union at every other step, X and Y will stabilize to the smallest threshold larger than their respective concrete bound. □

Our previous approach was the following: we first do N_0 iterations with unions on all abstract domains, then we do widenings unless a variable which was not stable becomes stable (this is the case of Y here when the threshold is big enough). We add a fairness condition to avoid livelocks in case for each iteration there exists a variable that becomes stable. Unfortunately, with large programs this strategy gives the following behavior: we never do widenings until the fairness condition is taken into account, then we do widenings at each iteration. So we fail in certifying our example.

The following approach supersedes the previous one: Each abstract property (or set of abstract properties) is fitted with a freshness indicator. At each iteration, the freshness indicator of unstable abstract properties is incremented. For each abstract property, the choice between taking the union or the widening among two consecutive iterates is determined according to the freshness indicator: each domain is fitted with a piece-wise affine function, which determines how often it is widened according to the freshness indicator of the abstract property.

7.4   Enforcing Termination

Both reductions (Sect. 7.2) and delayed widenings (Sect. 7.3) may break the termination of the extrapolation process. Even intersecting the abstract iterates with a constant abstract property (i.e. a weak form of reduction) may break the termination of the extrapolation process.

Example 21. We consider the set $D^\sharp$ of all parts of the interval $[0; 1]$ containing both 0 and 1. We want to extrapolate the iterates of the function f that inserts in a set S each rational $\frac{1}{2^{n+1}}$ whenever $\frac{1}{2^n}$ is in S (e.g. $f(S) = \{S \cup \{\frac{1}{2^{n+1}} \mid \frac{1}{2^n} \in S\})$. We define both $\cap$ and $\cup$ as the classical set operators. We define $\nabla_{D^\sharp}$ as: $a \nabla_{D^\sharp} b = \rho(a, a \cup b)$ where $\rho(a, b)$ is obtained by making the convex union of several connected components of b until there are fewer connected components than in a, and fewer than five connected components. It is obvious that $\nabla_{D^\sharp}$ is a widening, since along the abstract iterates the number of connected components decreases until it reaches 1, and the interval $[0; 1]$ is the only element with one connected component. Then:

1. The sequence:
$$\begin{cases} u_0 = \{0; 1\}, \\ u_{2n+1} = u_{2n} \cup f(u_{2n}), \\ u_{2n} = u_{2n-1} \nabla_{D^\sharp} f(u_{2n-1}), \end{cases}$$

   is not ultimately stationary.
   Indeed, we have $u_{2n} = \{0\} \cup [\frac{1}{2^{2n}}; 1]$ and $u_{2n+1} = \{0; \frac{1}{2^{2n+1}}\} \cup [\frac{1}{2^{2n}}; 1]$.
2. The sequence:
$$\begin{cases} u_0 = \{0; 1\}, \\ u_{n+1} = (u_n \nabla_{D^\sharp} f(u_n)) \cap \{0; 1; \frac{1}{2^k} \mid k > 0\}, \end{cases}$$

   is not ultimately stationary.
   Indeed, we have $u_n = f^n(u_0)$.   □

We solve this problem in two steps. First we strengthen the definition of the widenings, so that we can both delay the widening steps, and intersect the iterates with a constant value, without loosing the convergence of abstract iterates. Then, we restrict the kind of reductions that can be made after a widening step.

Strengthened Definition. To solve our problem, we require that the widening relation $\to$ and the information preorder $\sqsubseteq^\sharp$ are strongly related. We suppose that the abstract domain can be written as a finite product of totally ordered sets $(D_i^\sharp, \sqsubseteq_i^\sharp)_{i \in I}$. Moreover, we suppose that each sub-domain $D_i^\sharp$ is fitted with a widening operator ∇_i such that:

- for any $a, b \in D_i^\sharp$, we have both $a \sqsubseteq_i^\sharp a \nabla_i b$ and $b \sqsubseteq_i^\sharp a \nabla_i b$,   (W$'_1$)
- and the relation $\to'_i$ defined as: "for any $a, d \in D_i^\sharp$, $a \to_i d$ if and   (W$'_2$)
  only if there exist $b, c \in D_i^\sharp$ such that $a \sqsubseteq_i^\sharp b$ and $d = b \nabla_i c$" is
  well-founded.

In the following theorem, we want to extrapolate the iterates of a mapping $F_{D^\sharp}$. Each iterate is intersected with the abstract property $(\rho_i)_{i \in I} \in D^\sharp$ (we recall that $D^\sharp = \prod_{i \in I} D_i^\sharp$). The sequence $((b_i)_n)$ of boolean families denotes the delaying strategy of the widening.

Theorem 1. *Let $F_{D^\sharp} \in D^\sharp \to D^\sharp$ be a map. Let $(\rho_i)_{i \in I} \in D^\sharp$ be a finite family of abstract elements. Let $((b_i)_n) \in (\{false; true\}^I)^\mathbb{N}$ be a family of booleans such that for any $i \in I$, the sequence $((b_i)_n)_{n \in \mathbb{N}}$ takes the value true an unbounded number of times. We write $\bot = (\bot_i)_{i \in I}$.*

Then, the sequence:

$$
\begin{cases}
(w_i)_0 = \bot_i, \\
u_{n+1} = F_{D^\sharp}(w_n), \\
(v_i)_{n+1} = \begin{cases} \max_{\sqsubseteq_i^\sharp}((w_i)_n, (u_i)_{n+1}) & \text{whenever } (b_i)_n = false, \\ (w_i)_n \nabla_i (u_i)_{n+1} & \text{otherwise}, \end{cases} \\
(w_i)_{n+1} = \min_{\sqsubseteq_i^\sharp}((v_i)_{n+1}, \rho_i),
\end{cases}
$$

is ultimately stationary and sound.

Proof. Let i be an element of I. It is easy to see that sequence (w_i) is increasing. Moreover,

1. In the case where for any $n \in \mathbb{N}$, $(w_i)_n = (v_i)_n$, we introduce a sequence $(j_n) \in \mathbb{N}^\mathbb{N}$ such that $(b_i)_{j_n}$ is *true* for any $n \in \mathbb{N}$ (a such sequence exists by assumption). Then, we have $(w_i)_{j_n} \to_i (w_i)_{j_{n+1}}$. Since $\to_i$ is well founded, $(w_i)_{j_n}$ is ultimately stationary.
2. Otherwise, the sequence (w_i) is ultimately equal to the value ρ_i.

For the limits $\bar{u}$, $\bar{v}$, and $\bar{w}$ of $((u_i)_n)_{n \in \mathbb{N}}$, $((v_i)_n)_{n \in \mathbb{N}}$, and $((w_i)_n)_{n \in \mathbb{N}}$, we have $\bar{u} = F_{D^\sharp}(\bar{w})$, $\gamma_{D^\sharp}(\bar{v}) \supseteq \gamma_{D^\sharp}(\bar{u})$, $\gamma_{D^\sharp}(\bar{v}) \supseteq \gamma_{D^\sharp}(\bar{w})$ (by $\gamma_{D_i^\sharp}(\max_{\sqsubseteq_i^\sharp}(a, b)) \supseteq \gamma_{D_i^\sharp}(a) \cup \gamma_{D_i^\sharp}(b)$ or (W$'_1$)) and $\bar{w} \sqsubseteq^\sharp \bar{v}$ so $\gamma_{D^\sharp}(\bar{v}) = \gamma_{D^\sharp}(\bar{w}) \supseteq \gamma_{D^\sharp}(\bar{u}) = \gamma_{D^\sharp}(F_{D^\sharp}(\bar{w})) \supseteq F(\gamma_{D^\sharp}(\bar{w}))$ proving soundness. $\square$

This definition is satisfied by the widening with thresholds, which is applied to each single abstract constraint in all our domains.

Example 22. The widening $W = A \triangledown_{D^\sharp} B$ of two octagons [11] is performed point-wisely: given a constraint $\pm X \pm Y \leq c$ in A and $\pm X \pm Y \leq d$ in B with the same left member, we set the bound of the corresponding constraint in W to c if $c \geq d$, and to the next threshold greater than d if $d \geq c$. In order to gain precision, we may replace some widening application with a so-called *pre-widening* which sets this bound to $\max(c, d)$ instead. Note that contrary to the abstract union, our pre-widening does not apply constraint propagation to its argument, and thus, is less precise. Indeed, [11, Fig. 25–26] shows that mixing the widening (that tends to loosen bounds) with constraint propagation (that tends to refine bounds) breaks the convergence of the iterates. Mixing widenings with unions would have the same ill-effect. However, we can prove that mixing widenings with pre-widenings enforces termination by viewing the octagon domain as a finite product of totally ordered sets: there is one set for each left member $\pm X \pm Y$ of octagonal constraint; all sets are simply the set of reals with the standard order $\leq$; each set corresponds to the possible upper bounds of a single left member.   □

Restricting Reduction. Then, we must avoid cyclic reductions between components of the product domain. For that purpose, we use the hierarchical structure of the domain network: after a widening step, a domain can only refine its underlying domains. This ensures the termination of the analysis: the abstract iterates in the abstract domains that are at the top of the hierarchy are ultimately stationary. Once the abstract properties in the domains that are above one domain are stable, the reduction of abstract properties in this domain can be seen as an intersection with a constant abstract property. Thus, its abstract iterates are ultimately stationary.

8   Narrowings

The widening jumps above the abstraction of the concrete least fixpoint. Then, the result may be refined using downward iterations thanks to a narrowing operator. The ASTRÉE analyzer takes as parameter the number of downward iterations to compute.

Decreasing iterations raise several issues. The main problem is that the use of downward iterations may make the checking of the fact that we have computed an abstraction of the concrete least fixpoint much harder for an external procedure. Although, by construction, the limit of these decreasing iterations is indeed an abstraction of a concrete post-fixpoint, it may be hard to check *in the abstract* (i.e. without resorting to a more concrete, and thus costly, decision procedure). Performing this check instead of relying on the correctness of a complex iteration scheme is desirable to add confidence in the result of the analysis.

8.1   Frameworks

A narrowing operator $\triangle_{D^\sharp}$ over an abstract domain $D^\sharp$ [1] is a mapping in $D^\sharp \times D^\sharp \to D^\sharp$ such that: $\forall a, b \in D^\sharp, \gamma_{D^\sharp}(a) \cap \gamma_{D^\sharp}(b) \subseteq \gamma_{D^\sharp}(a \triangle_{D^\sharp} b)$. We require no termination criterion since, in ASTRÉE, the number of downward iterations is bounded by some user-chosen constant.

Given any $x \in D^\sharp$ (in practice $x = l$ is the limit of the upward iterations), the downward iteration $(x_n^\triangle)$ of $F_{D^\sharp}$ from x is defined as $x_0^\triangle = x$ and $x_{n+1}^\triangle = x_n^\triangle \triangle_{D^\sharp} F_{D^\sharp}(x_n^\triangle)$. In the following, we consider $F \in D \to D$ a monotonic function and $F_{D^\sharp}$ an abstraction of F (i.e. we have $\forall a \in D^\sharp$, $F(\gamma_{D^\sharp}(a)) \subseteq \gamma_{D^\sharp}(F_{D^\sharp}(a))$). We want to prove that downward iterates preserve abstractions of concrete post-fixpoints.

Theorem 2. *If there exists a concrete element $a \in D$ such that $F(a) \subseteq a$ and $a \subseteq \gamma_{D^\sharp}(x)$ then, for any integer $n \in \mathbb{N}$, there exists a concrete element $a' \in D$ such that $F(a') \subseteq a'$ and $a' \subseteq \gamma_{D^\sharp}(x_n^\triangle)$.*

First, we prove the following lemmas:

Lemma 3. *For any $a \in D$ and $x \in D^\sharp$, $a \subseteq \gamma_{D^\sharp}(x) \implies a \cap F(a) \subseteq \gamma_{D^\sharp}(x \triangle_{D^\sharp} F_{D^\sharp}(x))$.*

Proof. Let $a \in D$ and $x \in D^\sharp$ such that $a \subseteq \gamma_{D^\sharp}(x)$. Since F is monotonic, we have $F(a) \subseteq F(\gamma_{D^\sharp}(x))$. Then by soundness of $F_{D^\sharp}$, we have $F(\gamma_{D^\sharp}(x)) \subseteq \gamma_{D^\sharp}(F_{D^\sharp}(x))$. Thus $F(a) \subseteq \gamma_{D^\sharp}(F_{D^\sharp}(x))$. So $a \cap F(a) \subseteq \gamma_{D^\sharp}(x) \cap \gamma_{D^\sharp}(F_{D^\sharp}(x))$. By definition of the narrowing operator, we have $\gamma_{D^\sharp}(x) \cap \gamma_{D^\sharp}(F_{D^\sharp}(x)) \subseteq \gamma_{D^\sharp}(x \triangle_{D^\sharp} F_{D^\sharp}(x))$. We conclude that $a \cap F(a) \subseteq \gamma_{D^\sharp}(x \triangle_{D^\sharp} F_{D^\sharp}(x))$. □

Lemma 4. *For any $a \in D$, $F(a) \subseteq a \implies F(F(a) \cap a) \subseteq F(a) \cap a$.*

Proof. Let $a \in D$ such that $F(a) \subseteq a$. Since F is monotonic, we have $F(F(a)) \subseteq F(a)$. Moreover, we have $F(a) \cap a = F(a)$. We conclude that $F(F(a) \cap a) = F(F(a)) \subseteq F(a) = F(a) \cap a$. □

Then, Thm. 2 can easily be proved by induction on $n \in \mathbb{N}$ with $a' = F(a) \cap a$.

8.2 Practical Aspects

One may be satisfied by the fact that downward iteration provides, by construction, an abstraction of the concrete post-fixpoint (**Th. 2**). Nevertheless, we could expect more such as improvement $\gamma_{D^\sharp}(a \triangle_{D^\sharp} b) \subseteq \gamma_{D^\sharp}(a)$ [1]. Moreover, termination tests (for upward iterations) are performed using a decidable relation $\sqsubseteq^\sharp$ such that $a \sqsubseteq^\sharp b$ implies $\gamma_{D^\sharp}(a) \subseteq \gamma_{D^\sharp}(b)$ (but which is not necessarily a preorder). Then, by definition, the limit l of upward iterates of the abstract operation $F_{D^\sharp}$ satisfies $F_{D^\sharp}(l) \sqsubseteq^\sharp l$. But there is no reason for the downward iterates to satisfy this property (even if $a \sqsubseteq^\sharp b \iff \gamma_{D^\sharp}(a) \subseteq \gamma_{D^\sharp}(b)$), because the abstract operation $F_{D^\sharp}$ is in practice not monotonic with respect to $\sqsubseteq^\sharp$.

To solve this problem, whenever downward iterations provide an abstract property that is not a post-fixpoint of $F_{D^\sharp}$ (with respect to our $\sqsubseteq^\sharp$), we start upward iterations again. And then, downward iterations again. To get a finite analysis, we only "rebound" a fixed number of times. For our last try, we do not perform downward iterations, so that we get a checkable post-fixpoint of $F_{D^\sharp}$.

9   Conclusion and Further Challenges

ASTRÉE has shown to be easily extensible. Our early successes have incited our industrial partners to try and apply the analyzer to classes of programs for which it was not designed. It was thus necessary to improve domains or create new ones without a complete overhaul of the system. As with any major software endeavor, our experience is that dependencies should be limited and orthogonality encouraged; one abstract domain should be able to perform correctly (if sometimes suboptimally) if another one is not present, or has been modified.

We have targeted applications where the objective is a sound result of zero false alarms. This is very different from some other (commercial or academic) static analyzers whose objective is to find bugs. While the two approaches share common tools, they differ in that bug finding does not need to be sound (some real errors may be ignored) while a high degree of completeness (few false alarms) is expected on a variety of programs. A bug finder should thus probably ignore constructs that it fails to "understand" properly (for instance, writes through a pointer possibly aliased to many variables because of over-approximation). A program verification tool such as ASTRÉE does not have that luxury, and this is why we claim that such programs should often contain domain-specific abstractions, capable of addressing constructs, structures and algorithms that generic abstraction do not "understand". The consequence for the designer of the analysis is that it should be easy to plug new abstractions at any level.

So far, ASTRÉE has been targeted towards single-threaded programs. However, we have already implemented analyses for a restricted class of parallel programs, and we expect to consider wider classes (e.g. multi-threaded code in shared-memory systems). Our memory abstraction is currently a simple non-relational one, but we expect that more precise analyses (e.g. shape analysis and separation properties) will be necessary to tackle programs featuring dynamic manipulations of memory. One difficulty will be our stringent efficiency constraints, since we consider large programs. The other will be to achieve zero false alarms.

References

1. Cousot, P., Cousot, R.: Abstract interpretation: a unified lattice model for static analysis of programs by construction or approximation of fixpoints. In: 4th ACM POPL, pp. 238–252 (1977)
2. Cousot, P., Cousot, R.: Abstract interpretation frameworks. Journal of Logic and Computation 2, 511–547 (1992)
3. Blanchet, B., Cousot, P., Cousot, R., Feret, J., Mauborgne, L., Miné, A., Monniaux, D., Rival, X.: Design and implementation of a special-purpose static program analyzer for safety-critical real-time embedded software, invited chapter. In: Mogensen, T., Schmidt, D., Sudborough, I. (eds.) The Essence of Computation. LNCS, vol. 2566, pp. 85–108. Springer, Heidelberg (2002)
4. Blanchet, B., Cousot, P., Cousot, R., Feret, J., Mauborgne, L., Miné, A., Monniaux, D., Rival, X.: A static analyzer for large safety-critical software. In: Proc. ACM SIGPLAN '2003 Conf, PLDI, San Diego, pp. 196–207. ACM Press, New York (2003)

5. Cousot, P., Cousot, R., Feret, J., Mauborgne, L., Miné, A., Monniaux, D., Rival, X.: The ASTRÉE analyzer. In: Sagiv, M. (ed.) Proc. 14th ESOP '2005, Edinburgh, 4–8 Apr. 2005. LNCS 3444, pp. 21–30. Springer, Heidelberg (2005)

6. Mauborgne, L.: ASTRÉE: Verification of absence of run-time error. In: Jacquart, P. (ed.) Building the Information Society, pp. 385–392. Kluwer Academic Publishers, Dordrecht (2004)

7. Miné, A.: Field-sensitive value analysis of embedded C programs with union types and pointer arithmetics. In: Proc. LCTES 2006. Ottawa, Ontario, Canada, 14–16 June 2006, pp. 54–63. ACM Press, New York (2006)

8. Monniaux, D.: The parallel implementation of the ASTRÉE static analyzer. In: Yi, K. (ed.) APLAS 2005. LNCS, vol. 3780, Springer, Heidelberg (2005)

9. Cousot, P., Cousot, R.: Static determination of dynamic properties of programs. In: Proceedings of the Second International Symposium on Programming, Paris, France, Dunod, Paris, France, pp. 106–130 (1976)

10. Miné, A.: Symbolic methods to enhance the precision of numerical abstract domains. In: Emerson, E.A., Namjoshi, K.S. (eds.) VMCAI 2006. LNCS, vol. 3855, pp. 348–363. Springer, Heidelberg (2005)

11. Miné, A.: The octagon abstract domain. Higher-Order and Symbolic Computation 19, 31–100 (2006)

12. Feret, J.: Static analysis of digital filters. In: Schmidt, D. (ed.) ESOP 2004. LNCS, vol. 2986, pp. 33–48. Springer, Heidelberg (2004)

13. Feret, J.: The arithmetic-geometric progression abstract domain. In: Cousot, R. (ed.) VMCAI 2005. LNCS, vol. 3385, pp. 2–58. Springer, Heidelberg (2005)

14. Mauborgne, L., Rival, X.: Trace partitioning in abstract interpretation based static analyzers. In: Sagiv, M. (ed.) ESOP 2005. LNCS, vol. 3444, pp. 21–30. Springer, Heidelberg (2005)

15. Cousot, P., Cousot, R.: Systematic design of program analysis frameworks. In: 6th ACM POPL, pp. 269–282 (1979)

16. Leroy, X., Doligez, D., Garrigue, J., Rémy, D., Vouillon, J.: The Objective Caml system, documentation and user's manual (release 3.06). Technical report, INRIA, Rocquencourt, France (2002)

17. Miné, A.: The octagon abstract domain library (2006), www.di.ens.fr/~mine/oct/

18. ANSI/ISO: Programming languages – C. (1999) Standard ISO/IEC 9899:1999(E)

19. Henzinger, T.A., Jhala, R., Majumdar, R., Sutre, G.: Software verification with BLAST. In: Ball, T., Rajamani, S.K. (eds.) Model Checking Software. LNCS, vol. 2648, pp. 235–239. Springer, Heidelberg (2003)

20. Cousot, P.: Verification by abstract interpretation, invited chapter. In: Dershowitz, N. (ed.) Verification: Theory and Practice. LNCS, vol. 2772, pp. 243–268. Springer, Heidelberg (2004)

21. Cousot, P.: The calculational design of a generic abstract interpreter, invited chapter. In: Broy, M., Steinbrüggen, R. (eds.) Calculational System Design. NATO Science Series, Series F: Computer and Systems Sciences, vol. 173, pp. 421–505. IOS Press, Amsterdam (1999)

22. Miné, A.: Relational abstract domains for the detection of floating-point run-time errors. In: Schmidt, D. (ed.) ESOP 2004. LNCS, vol. 2986, pp. 3–17. Springer, Heidelberg (2004)

23. Cousot, P.: MIT course 16.399: Abstract Interpretation (2005), http://web.mit.edu/afs/athena.mit.edu/course/16/16.399/www/

Proving Noninterference by a Fully Complete Translation to the Simply Typed λ-Calculus

Naokata Shikuma and Atsushi Igarashi

Graduate School of Informatics, Kyoto University
{naokata,igarashi}@kuis.kyoto-u.ac.jp

Abstract. Tse and Zdancewic have formalized the notion of noninterference for Abadi et al.'s DCC in terms of logical relations and given a proof by reduction to parametricity of System F. Unfortunately, their proof contains errors in a key lemma that their translation from DCC to System F preserves the logical relations defined for both calculi. We prove noninterference for a variant of DCC by reduction to the basic lemma of a logical relation for the simply typed λ-calculus, using a *fully complete* translation to the simply typed λ-calculus. Full completeness plays an important role in showing preservation of the two logical relations through the translation.

1 Introduction

Background. Dependency analysis is a family of static program analyses to trace dependencies between inputs and outputs of a given program. For example, information flow analysis [3], binding-time analysis [8], and call tracking [16] are its instances. One of the most important correctness criteria of the dependency analysis is called *noninterference* [5], which roughly means that, for any pair of program inputs that are equivalent from the viewpoint of an observer at some security level, the outputs are also equivalent for the observer. Various techniques for type-based dependency analyses have been proposed, especially, in the context of language-based security [15].

Abadi et al. proposed a unifying framework called *dependency core calculus* (DCC) [1] for type-based dependency analyses for higher-order functional languages, and showed noninterference for several type systems of concrete dependency analyses by embedding them into DCC.

Recently, Tse and Zdancewic formalized this property for DCC by using a syntactic *logical relation* [9]—a family of type-indexed relations, defined by induction on types, over programs—as the equivalence relation for inputs and outputs, thereby generalizing the notion of noninterference to higher-order programs. They also gave a proof of noninterference by reducing it to the parametricity theorem [14, 18], which was also formalized in terms of syntactic logical relations, of System F [13, 4]. Their technical development is summarized as follows:

M. Okada and I. Satoh (Eds.): ASIAN 2006, LNCS 4435, pp. 301–315, 2007.
© Springer-Verlag Berlin Heidelberg 2007

1. Define a translation from DCC to System F;
2. Prove, by induction on the structure of types, that the translation is both sound and complete—that is, it preserves the logical relations in the sense that

$$e_1 \approx_D e_2 : t \iff f(e_1) \approx_F f(e_2) : f(t)$$

where t is a DCC type, f is the translation from DCC to System F and $\approx_D$ and $\approx_F$ represent the logical relations for DCC and System F, respectively; and
3. Prove noninterference by reduction to the parametricity theorem of System F, using the sound and complete translation above.

Unfortunately, in the second step, their proof contains an error, which we will briefly explain here. First note that, for function types $t_1 \to t_2$, the logical relations are defined by: $e_1 \approx_x e_2 : t_1 \to t_2$ if and only if, for any $e'_1 \approx_x e'_2 : t_1$, $e_1 e'_1 \approx_x e_2 e'_2 : t_2$ (x stands for either D or F) and that the type translation is homomorphic for function types, namely $f(t_1 \to t_2) = f(t_1) \to f(t_2)$. Then, consider the case where t is a function type $t_1 \to t_2$. To show the left-to-right direction, we must show that $f(e_1) M_1 \approx_F f(e_2) M_2 : f(t_2)$ for any $M_1 \approx_F M_2 :$ $f(t_1)$, from the assumption $e_1 \approx_D e_2 : t_1 \to t_2$, but we get stuck because there is no applicable induction hypothesis. If the translation were *full* [6] (or surjective), M_1 and M_2 would be of the forms $f(e'_1)$ and $f(e'_2)$, making it possible to apply an induction hypothesis, and the whole proof would go through. Their translation, however, turns out *not* to be full; we have actually found a counterexample for the preservation of the equivalence from the failure of the fullness (see Section 5 for more details). So, although interesting, this indirect proof method fails at least for the combination of DCC and System F.

Our Contributions. In this paper, we prove noninterference by Tse and Zdancewic's method in a slightly different setting: In order to obtain a fully complete translation, we change the source language to what we call Sealing Calculus ($\lambda^{[]}$), which is a subset of extended DCC of Tse and Zdancewic [17], and use a simpler target language, namely the simply typed λ-calculus $\lambda^\to$. Then, the basic lemma for a logical relation of $\lambda^\to$ is used in place of the parametricity theorem. Our technical contributions can be summarized as follows:

- Development of a sound and fully complete translation from $\lambda^{[]}$ to $\lambda^\to$; and
- A proof of the noninterference theorem of $\lambda^{[]}$ by reducing to the basic lemma of $\lambda^\to$ with the translation.

The existence of a fully complete translation means that $\lambda^{[]}$ provides syntax that is rich enough to express every denotation in the model (that is, $\lambda^\to$). Thus, this result suggests that the extension of DCC proposed by Tse and Zdancewic is really an improvement over DCC, for which the previously proposed translation is not full.

Structure of the Paper. The rest of the paper is organized as follows. Section 2 introduces $\lambda^{[]}$ with its syntax, type system, reduction, and logical relations and then the statement of the noninterference theorem. Section 3 introduces $\lambda^\to$ and defines a translation from $\lambda^{[]}$ to $\lambda^\to$ and its inverse. In Section 4, we complete our proof of noninterference by reducing it to the basic lemma of logical relations for $\lambda^\to$. Finally, Section 5 discusses related work and Section 6 gives concluding remarks.

2   Sealing Calculus

In this section, we define $\lambda^{[]}$, which is a simply typed λ-calculus extended with the notion of sealing. We write $[e]_a$ for sealing e by authority a; the sealed value can be extracted by unsealing e^a, whose result must not be leaked to anyone without the authority a. Authorities represent rights to access confidential data; so the power set of authorities naturally forms security levels, which are ordered by inclusion. To keep track of dependency by a type system, information on the authority used for sealing is attached to types of sealing $[t]_a$; furthermore, type judgments, written $\Gamma; \ell \vdash e : t$, are augmented by a level $\ell = \{a_1, \ldots, a_n\}$, which is also called a protection context elsewhere [17]. This judgment means that the value of e has type t as usual and, moreover, cannot be leaked to levels that lack some of the authorities in ℓ.

2.1   Syntax

Let $\mathcal{A}$ be the countable set of *authorities*, and ranged over by a (possibly with subscripts). The metavariable ℓ ranges over *levels*, which are finite subsets of authorities. The metavariables x, y, and z (possibly with subscripts) range over the denumerable set of *variables*. Then, the types and terms of $\lambda^{[]}$ are defined as follows.

Definition 1 (Types). *The set of types, ranged over by t, t', t_1, t_2, $\ldots$, is defined as follows:*

$$t ::= unit \mid t \to t \mid t \times t \mid t + t \mid [t]_a$$

We call $[t]_a$ a sealed value type.

Definition 2 (Terms). *The set of terms, ranged over by e, e', e_1, e_2, $\ldots$, is defined as follows:*

$$e ::= x \mid () \mid \lambda x{:}t.\, e \mid e\, e \mid \langle e, e \rangle \mid \pi_1(e) \mid \pi_2(e) \mid \iota_1(e) \mid \iota_2(e)$$
$$\mid (\mathbf{case}\ e\ \mathbf{of}\ \iota_1(x_1).e_1 \mid \iota_2(x_2).e_2) \mid [e]_a \mid e^a$$

Terms of $\lambda^{[]}$ include the unit value, pairing, projection, injection, and case analysis as well as λ-abstraction and applications. As usual, x is bound in $\lambda x{:}t.\,e$ and x_1 and x_2 are bound in e_1 and e_2 of $(\mathbf{case}\ e_0\ \mathbf{of}\ \iota_1(x_1).e_1 \mid \iota_2(x_2).e_2)$, respectively. We say, for $[e]_a$, e is *sealed at* a, and call $[e]_a$ and e^a $(a\text{-})sealing\ term$ and $(a\text{-})unsealing\ term$, respectively. In this paper, α-conversions are defined in a customary manner and implicit α-conversions are assumed to make all the bound variables distinct from other (bound and free) variables.

2.2   Type System

As mentioned above, the form of type judgement of $\lambda^{[]}$ is $\Gamma ; \ell \vdash e : t$, where Γ is a (finite) mapping from variables to types. This judgement is read as "e is given type t at level ℓ under context Γ." Since the computation of e depends on authorities in ℓ, any information on its value should not be leaked to any other level ℓ', which is not a superset of ℓ.

The typing rules of $\lambda^{[]}$ are given as follows:

$$\frac{x : t \in \Gamma}{\Gamma ; \ell \vdash x : t} \qquad \Gamma ; \ell \vdash () : unit \qquad \frac{\Gamma , x : t_1 ; \ell \vdash e : t_2}{\Gamma ; \ell \vdash \lambda x{:}t.e : t_1 \rightarrow t_2}$$

$$\frac{\Gamma ; \ell \vdash e : t_1 \rightarrow t_2 \qquad \Gamma ; \ell \vdash e' : t_1}{\Gamma ; \ell \vdash e e' : t_2} \qquad \frac{\Gamma ; \ell \vdash e_1 : t_1 \qquad \Gamma ; \ell \vdash e_2 : t_2}{\Gamma ; \ell \vdash \langle e_1, e_2 \rangle : t_1 \times t_2}$$

$$\frac{\Gamma ; \ell \vdash e : t_1 \times t_2 \qquad i \in \{1, 2\}}{\Gamma ; \ell \vdash \pi_i(e) : t_i} \qquad \frac{\Gamma ; \ell \vdash e : t \qquad i \in \{1, 2\}}{\Gamma ; \ell \vdash \iota_i(e) : t_1 + t_2}$$

$$\frac{\Gamma ; \ell \vdash e : t_1 + t_2 \qquad \Gamma , x_1 : t_1 ; \ell \vdash e_1 : t \qquad \Gamma , x_2 : t_2 ; \ell \vdash e_2 : t}{\Gamma ; \ell \vdash (\mathbf{case}\, e\, \mathbf{of}\, \iota_1(x_1).e_1 \mid \iota_2(x_2).e_2) : t}$$

$$\frac{\Gamma ; \ell \cup \{a\} \vdash e : t}{\Gamma ; \ell \vdash [e]_a : [t]_a} \qquad \frac{\Gamma ; \ell \vdash e : [t]_a \qquad a \in \ell}{\Gamma ; \ell \vdash e^a : t}$$

All the rules but the last two are standard. The (second last) rule for sealing means that, by sealing with a, it is legal to leak $[e]_a$ to a level without a: at such a level, e cannot be unsealed, as is shown in the (last) rule for unsealing.

2.3   Reduction

The reduction relation for $\lambda^{[]}$ is written $e \longrightarrow e'$ and given as the least compatible relation closed by the following rules:

$$(\lambda x{:}t.\, e_1)\, e_2 \longrightarrow [e_2/x]e_1 \qquad \pi_i(\langle e_1, e_2 \rangle) \longrightarrow e_i$$
$$(\mathbf{case}\, \iota_i(e)\, \mathbf{of}\, \iota_1(x_1).e_1 \mid \iota_2(x_2).e_2) \longrightarrow [e/x_i]e_i \qquad ([e]_a)^a \longrightarrow e$$

We write $[e/x]$ for a capture-avoiding substitution of e for the free occurrences of variable x. All rules are straightforward. The last rule says that the term sealed by a is opened by the same authority. In what follows, we use v for normal forms.

2.4   Basic Properties

We list the basic properties of $\lambda^{[]}$. The first lemma below means that, if e is permitted at some level, then it is permitted also at a higher level.

Lemma 1 (Level Weakening). *If $\Gamma ; \ell \vdash e : t$, then $\Gamma ; \ell \cup \{a\} \vdash e : t$, and the derivations of these judgements have the same size.*

The following three theorems are standard.

Theorem 1 (Subject Reduction). *If $\Gamma ; \ell \vdash e : t$ and $e \longrightarrow e'$, then $\Gamma ; \ell \vdash e' : t$.*

Theorem 2 (Strong Normalization). *If $\Gamma; \ell \vdash e : t$, then e is strongly normalizing.*

Theorem 3 (Church-Rosser Property). *If $\Gamma; \ell \vdash e : t$ and $e \longrightarrow^* e_1$ and $e \longrightarrow^* e_2$, then there exists a term e' such that $e_i \longrightarrow^* e'$ ($i = 1, 2$).*

2.5 Logical Relation and Noninterference

Now we define logical relations to express equivalence of terms from the viewpoint of an observer at some level, and then state the noninterference theorem. To take level information into account, the logical relations (for close terms and normal forms) are indexed by levels as well as types. $e_1 \approx_\ell e_2 : t$ means that closed terms e_1 and e_2 of type t are logically related at level ℓ. Similarly, $v_1 \sim_\ell v_2 : t$ means that closed normal forms v_1 and v_2 of t, are logically related at ℓ. We assume $\cdot; \ell \vdash e_i : t$ and $\cdot; \ell \vdash v_i : t$ for $i = 1, 2$ (we write $\cdot$ for the empty context).

Definition 3 (Logical Relations for $\lambda^{[]}$). *The relations $v_1 \sim_\ell v_2 : t$ and $e_1 \approx_\ell e_2 : t$ are defined by the following rules:*

$$\frac{}{() \sim_\ell () : unit} \qquad \frac{\forall (e_1 \approx_\ell e_2 : t_1). \, v_1 \, e_1 \approx_\ell v_2 \, e_2 : t_2}{v_1 \sim_\ell v_2 : t_1 \rightarrow t_2} \qquad \frac{v_{11} \sim_\ell v_{21} : t_1 \qquad v_{12} \sim_\ell v_{22} : t_2}{\langle v_{11}, v_{12} \rangle \sim_\ell \langle v_{21}, v_{22} \rangle : t_1 \times t_2}$$

$$\frac{v_1 \sim_\ell v_2 : t_i \qquad i \in \{1, 2\}}{\iota_i(v_1) \sim_\ell \iota_i(v_2) : t_1 + t_2} \qquad \frac{v_1 \sim_\ell v_2 : t \qquad a \in \ell}{[v_1]_a \sim_\ell [v_2]_a : [t]_a} \qquad \frac{a \notin \ell}{[v_1]_a \sim_\ell [v_2]_a : [t]_a}$$

$$\frac{e_1 \longrightarrow^* v_1 \qquad e_2 \longrightarrow^* v_2 \qquad v_1 \sim_\ell v_2 : t}{e_1 \approx_\ell e_2 : t}$$

Most rules are standard. There are two rules for $[v_1]_a \sim_\ell [v_2]_a : [t]_a$. When $a \in \ell$, an observer at ℓ can examine v_i by unsealing $[v_i]_a$ ($i = 1, 2$), so only when its contents are equivalent, these sealing terms are equivalent. Otherwise, the observer cannot distinguish them at all and those terms are always regarded equivalent.

We use γ to represent a simultaneous substitution of terms for variables and write $\gamma_1 \approx_\ell \gamma_2 : \Gamma$ if $dom(\gamma_1) = dom(\gamma_2) = dom(\Gamma)$ and $\gamma_1(x) \approx_\ell \gamma_2(x) : \Gamma(x)$ for any $x \in dom(\gamma_1)$. Then, the noninterference theorem is stated as follows:

Theorem 4 (Noninterference). *If $\Gamma; \ell \vdash e : t$ and $\gamma_1 \approx_\ell \gamma_2 : \Gamma$, then $\gamma_1(e) \approx_\ell \gamma_2(e) : t$.*

As mentioned in the introduction, noninterference means that, for any pair of program inputs that are equivalent from the viewpoint of an observer at some security level, the outputs are also equivalent for the observer. Here, substitutions γ_1 and γ_2 play roles of equivalent inputs to program e. So, this property guarantees the correctness of the type system as a dependency analysis.

Although we could give a direct proof of this theorem by induction on the derivation of $\Gamma; \ell \vdash e : t$ rather easily, we show an indirect proof that reduces the property to a corresponding property in $\lambda^\rightarrow$, namely the basic lemma of logical relations.

3 Translation

In this section, we define a formal translation from $\lambda^{[]}$ to the simply typed λ-calculus $\lambda^\rightarrow$ and its inverse. Both translations are shown to preserve typing. We start with reviewing $\lambda^\rightarrow$ briefly with logical relations for it.

3.1 $\lambda^\rightarrow$

$\lambda^\rightarrow$ introduced here is a standard one with unit, base, function, product, and sum types. We assume that base types, written α_a ($a \in \mathcal{A}$), have one-to-one correspondence with authorities. We use metavariables M for terms and A for types. The syntax of $\lambda^\rightarrow$ is given as follows:

$$A ::= \alpha \mid unit \mid A \rightarrow A \mid A \times A \mid A + A$$
$$M ::= x \mid () \mid \lambda x\!:\!A.\,M \mid M\,M \mid \langle M, M \rangle \mid \pi_i(M) \mid \iota_i(M)$$
$$\mid (\textbf{case } M \textbf{ of } \iota_1(x_1).M \mid \iota_2(x_2).M)$$

The form of type judgement of $\lambda^\rightarrow$ is $\Delta \vdash M : A$, where Δ is a (finite) mapping from variables to $\lambda^\rightarrow$ types. For brevity, we omit typing rules, which are completely standard. The reduction of $\lambda^\rightarrow$ terms consists of standard β-reduction and the following commutative conversion.

$$\frac{(x_1, x_2 \notin FV(M'))}{(\textbf{case } M \textbf{ of } \iota_1(x_1).M_1 \mid \iota_2(x_2).M_2)\,M' \longrightarrow \textbf{case } M \textbf{ of } \iota_1(x_1).M_1\,M' \mid \iota_2(x_2).M_2\,M'}$$

$$\frac{(i \in \{1,2\})}{\pi_i(\textbf{case } M \textbf{ of } \iota_1(x_1).M_1 \mid \iota_2(x_2).M_2) \longrightarrow \textbf{case } M \textbf{ of } \iota_1(x_1).\pi_i(M_1) \mid \iota_2(x_2).\pi_i(M_2)}$$

$$\frac{(x_1, x_2 \notin FV(M_1') \cup FV(M_2'))}{\textbf{case } (\textbf{case } M \textbf{ of } \iota_1(x_1).M_1 \mid \iota_2(x_2).M_2) \textbf{ of } \iota_1(y_1).M_1' \mid \iota_2(y_2).M_2'}$$
$$\longrightarrow \textbf{case } M \textbf{ of } \iota_1(x_1).(\textbf{case } M_1 \textbf{ of } \iota_1(y_1).M_1' \mid \iota_2(y_2).M_2')$$
$$\mid \iota_2(x_2).(\textbf{case } M_2 \textbf{ of } \iota_1(y_1).M_1' \mid \iota_2(y_2).M_2')$$

Here, we write $FV(M)$ for the set of free variables in M. In what follows, we use V for normal forms.

The resulting calculus (with commutative conversion) satisfies the standard properties of subject reduction, Church-Rosser, and strong normalization [2]. We say (the type derivation $\Delta \vdash M : A$ of) a term satisfies the subformula property when any type in the derivation is a subexpression of either A or a type occurring in Δ. Then, any well typed term can reduce to the one that satisfies the subformula property as in the theorem below, which makes it easy to ensure the fullness of the translation.

Theorem 5 (Subformula Property). *If $\Delta \vdash M : A$, then there exists a normal form V such that $M \longrightarrow^* V$ and $\Delta \vdash V : A$, which satisfies the subformula property.*

Remark 1. Commutative conversion is necessary for the above theorem to hold. Without commutative conversion,

$$\lambda x : unit + unit. \, ((\textbf{case } x \textbf{ of } \iota_1(x_1).\lambda y : unit. \, () \mid \iota_2(x_2).\lambda y : unit. \, ())) \, ()$$

of type $unit + unit \rightarrow unit$ would be a norml form, which does not satisfy the subformula property, because a subterm $\lambda y : unit. \, ()$ has type $unit \rightarrow unit$, which does not occur in $unit + unit \rightarrow unit$. This theorem also requires full reduction, which allows any redex (even under λ) to reduce.

3.2   Logical Relation for $\lambda^{\rightarrow}$

We define syntactic logical relations for $\lambda^{\rightarrow}$ in the standard manner. As for $\lambda^{[]}$, there are relations for terms and normal forms, written $\Delta \vdash M_1 \approx M_2 : A$ (read "terms M_1 and M_2 of type A are logically related under context Δ") and $\Delta \vdash V_1 \sim V_2 : A$ (read similarly), respectively. We assume that $\Delta \vdash M_i : A$ and $\Delta \vdash V_i : A$ for $i = 1, 2$.

Definition 4 (Logical Relations for $\lambda^{\rightarrow}$). *The relations* $\Delta \vdash M_1 \approx M_2 : A$ *and* $\Delta \vdash V_1 \sim V_2 : A$ *are the least relation closed under the following rules:*

$$\Delta \vdash () \sim () : unit \quad \Delta \vdash V_1 \sim V_2 : \alpha_a \quad \frac{\Delta \vdash V_{11} \sim V_{21} : A_1 \qquad \Delta \vdash V_{12} \sim V_{22} : A_2}{\Delta \vdash \langle V_{11}, V_{12} \rangle \sim \langle V_{21}, V_{22} \rangle : A_1 \times A_2}$$

$$\frac{\Delta \vdash V_1 \sim V_2 : A_i \qquad i \in \{1, 2\}}{\Delta \vdash \iota_i(V_1) \sim \iota_i(V_2) : A_1 + A_2} \quad \frac{\forall (\Delta \vdash M_1 \approx M_2 : A_1). \, \Delta \vdash V_1 \, M_1 \approx V_2 \, M_2 : A_2}{\Delta \vdash V_1 \sim V_2 : A_1 \rightarrow A_2}$$

$$\frac{M_1 \longrightarrow^* V_1 \qquad M_2 \longrightarrow^* V_2 \qquad \Delta \vdash V_1 \sim V_2 : A}{\Delta \vdash M_1 \approx M_2 : A}$$

We write δ for a simultaneous substitution of $(\lambda^{\rightarrow})$ terms for variables and $\Delta' \vdash \delta_1 \approx \delta_2 : \Delta$ if $dom(\delta_1) = dom(\delta_2) = dom(\Delta)$ and for any $x \in dom(\delta_1)$, $\Delta' \vdash \delta_1(x) \approx \delta_2(x) : \Delta(x)$. Then, the basic lemma is as follows:

Lemma 2 (Basic Lemma). *If* $\Delta \vdash M : A$ *and* $\Delta' \vdash \delta_1 \approx \delta_2 : \Delta$, *then* $\Delta' \vdash \delta_1(M) \approx \delta_2(M) : A$.

Proof. By induction on the derivation of $\Delta \vdash M : A$.

Remark 2. Although the above logical relation for $\lambda^{\rightarrow}$ are not reflexive in general (for example $x : A + A \not\vdash x \approx x : A + A$), we have $\Delta \vdash M \approx M : A$ if all the types in Δ are base types α_a. This is derived from Lemma 2 and the fact that $\Delta \vdash x \approx x : \Delta(x)$ if $\Delta(x) = \alpha_a$, by definition.

3.3   From $\lambda^{[]}$ To $\lambda^{\rightarrow}$

We define the translation of $\lambda^{[]}$ to $\lambda^{\rightarrow}$. One of the main ideas of the translation is to translate sealing of type $[t]_a$ to a function from the base type α_a, which corresponds to a. The sealed value can be extracted by passing a term of α_a as an argument. Intuitively, the term of α_a serves as a "key" to unseal.

Definition 5 (Translation of Types and Contexts). $(\cdot)^\dagger$ *is a function from* $\lambda^{[]}$ *types to* $\lambda^\rightarrow$ *type, defined by:*

$$unit^\dagger = unit \qquad (t_1 \text{ op } t_2)^\dagger = t_1^\dagger \text{ op } t_2^\dagger \qquad ([t]_a)^\dagger = \alpha_a \rightarrow t^\dagger$$

where **op** *stands for* $\rightarrow, \times,$ *or* $+$. $(\cdot)^\dagger$ *is extended pointwise to contexts by:* $\Gamma^\dagger = \{x : t^\dagger \mid x : t \in \Gamma\}$.

The translation to $\lambda^\rightarrow$ is represented by $\Gamma; \sigma \vdash e : t \searrow M$, read "$\lambda^{[]}$ term e of type t is translated to M under Γ and σ," where σ is an injective finite map from authorities to variables. We assume that the range of σ and the domain of Γ are disjoint.

Definition 6 (Translation of Terms). *The relation* $\Gamma; \sigma \vdash e : t \searrow M$ *is defined as the least relation closed under the following rules:*

$$\Gamma; \sigma \vdash x : t \searrow x \qquad \Gamma; \sigma \vdash () : unit \searrow () \qquad \frac{\Gamma, x : t_1; \sigma \vdash e : t_2 \searrow M}{\Gamma; \sigma \vdash \lambda x {:} t_1. e : t_1 \rightarrow t_2 \searrow \lambda x {:} t_1^\dagger. M}$$

$$\frac{\Gamma; \sigma \vdash e : t_1 \rightarrow t_2 \searrow M \qquad \Gamma; \sigma \vdash e' : t_1 \searrow M'}{\Gamma; \sigma \vdash e\,e' : t_2 \searrow M\,M'} \qquad \frac{\Gamma; \sigma \vdash e_1 : t_1 \searrow M_1 \qquad \Gamma; \sigma \vdash e_2 : t_2 \searrow M_2}{\Gamma; \sigma \vdash \langle e_1, e_2 \rangle : t_1 \times t_2 \searrow \langle M_1, M_2 \rangle}$$

$$\frac{\Gamma; \sigma \vdash e : t_1 \times t_2 \searrow M \qquad i \in \{1, 2\}}{\Gamma; \sigma \vdash \pi_i(e) : t_i \searrow \pi_i(M)} \qquad \frac{\Gamma; \sigma \vdash e : t_i \searrow M \qquad i \in \{1, 2\}}{\Gamma; \sigma \vdash \iota_i(e) : t_1 + t_2 \searrow \iota_i(M)}$$

$$\frac{\Gamma; \sigma \vdash e : t_1 + t_2 \searrow M \qquad \Gamma, x_1 : t_1; \sigma \vdash e_1 : t \searrow M_1 \qquad \Gamma, x_2 : t_2; \sigma \vdash e_2 : t \searrow M_2}{\Gamma; \sigma \vdash (\text{case } e \text{ of } \iota_1(x_1).e_1 \mid \iota_2(x_2).e_2) : t \searrow (\text{case } M \text{ of } \iota_1(x_1).M_1 \mid \iota_2(x_2).M_2)}$$

$$\frac{\Gamma; \sigma\{a \mapsto k\} \vdash e : t \searrow M \qquad k \text{ fresh or } k = \sigma(a)}{\Gamma; \sigma \vdash [e]_a : [t]_a \searrow \lambda k {:} \alpha_a. M} \qquad \frac{\Gamma; \sigma \vdash e : [t]_a \searrow M}{\Gamma; \sigma \vdash e^a : t \searrow M\,\sigma(a)}$$

Here, we write $\sigma\{a \mapsto k\}$ *for a mapping from* $dom(\sigma) \cup \{a\}$ *to variables defined by:* $\sigma\{a \mapsto k\}(a) = k$; *and* $\sigma\{a \mapsto k\}(a') = \sigma(a')$ *if* $a \neq a'$.

The translation of terms is easily derived from the translation rules for types. Here, the mapping σ, whose domain represents the level at which the SDC term is typed, records correspondence between authorities and variables that are used as keys. In the last rule, a key to open the sealing is retrieved from σ—if e is well typed at the level represented by $dom(\sigma)$, then a should be in the domain of σ. Then, well typed $\lambda^{[]}$ terms can be translated to well typed $\lambda^\rightarrow$ terms as in the theorem below. Here, we write $\sigma^\dagger$ for a context defined by: $\{\sigma(a) : \alpha_a \mid a \in dom(\sigma)\}$.

Theorem 6 (Translation Preserves Typing). *If* $\Gamma; \ell \vdash e : t$ *and* $dom(\sigma) = \ell$, *then there exists a* $\lambda^\rightarrow$ *term* M *such that* $\Gamma; \sigma \vdash e : t \searrow M$, *and that* $\Gamma^\dagger, \sigma^\dagger \vdash M : t^\dagger$.

Proof. By induction on the derivation of $\Gamma; \ell \vdash e : t$.

3.4 From $\lambda^\rightarrow$ To $\lambda^{[]}$

We define the inverse translation, represented by $\Gamma; \sigma \vdash M \nearrow e : t$. It is read "$\lambda^\rightarrow$ term M of type $t^\dagger$ under $\Gamma^\dagger$ and $\sigma^\dagger$ is translated back to a $\lambda^{[]}$ term e."

Definition 7 (Inverse Translation). *The relation* $\Gamma;\sigma \vdash M \nearrow e : t$ *is defined as the least relation closed by the following rules:*

$$\Gamma;\sigma \vdash x \nearrow x : t \qquad \Gamma;\sigma \vdash () \nearrow () : unit \qquad \frac{\Gamma, x : t_1;\sigma \vdash M \nearrow e : t_2}{\Gamma;\sigma \vdash \lambda x{:}t_1^\dagger.M \nearrow \lambda x{:}t_1.e : t_1 \rightarrow t_2}$$

$$\frac{\begin{array}{c}\Gamma;\sigma \vdash M \nearrow e : t_1 \rightarrow t_2 \\ \Gamma;\sigma \vdash M' \nearrow e' : t_1\end{array}}{\Gamma;\sigma \vdash M\,M' \nearrow e\,e' : t_2} \qquad \frac{\begin{array}{c}\Gamma;\sigma \vdash M_1 \nearrow e_1 : t_1 \\ \Gamma;\sigma \vdash M_2 \nearrow e_2 : t_2\end{array}}{\Gamma;\sigma \vdash \langle M_1, M_2\rangle \nearrow \langle e_1, e_2\rangle : t_1 \times t_2}$$

$$\frac{\Gamma;\sigma \vdash M \nearrow e : t_1 \times t_2 \quad i \in \{1, 2\}}{\Gamma;\sigma \vdash \pi_i(M) \nearrow \pi_i(e) : t_i} \qquad \frac{\Gamma;\sigma \vdash M \nearrow e : t_i \quad i \in \{1, 2\}}{\Gamma;\sigma \vdash \iota_i(M) \nearrow \iota_i(e) : t_1 + t_2}$$

$$\frac{\Gamma;\sigma \vdash M \nearrow e : t_1 + t_2 \quad \Gamma, x_1 : t_1;\sigma \vdash M_1 \nearrow e_1 : t \quad \Gamma, x_2 : t_2;\sigma \vdash M_2 \nearrow e_2 : t}{\Gamma;\sigma \vdash (\text{case } M \text{ of } \iota_1(x_1).M_1 \mid \iota_2(x_2).M_2) \nearrow (\text{case } e \text{ of } \iota_1(x_1).e_1 \mid \iota_2(x_2).e_2) : t}$$

$$\frac{\begin{array}{c}a \notin dom(\sigma) \\ \Gamma;\sigma\{a \mapsto k\} \vdash M \nearrow e : t\end{array}}{\Gamma;\sigma \vdash \lambda k{:}\alpha_a.\,M \nearrow [e]_a : [t]_a} \qquad \frac{\begin{array}{c}a \in dom(\sigma) \\ \Gamma;\sigma\{a \mapsto k\} \vdash [k/\sigma(a)]M \nearrow e : t\end{array}}{\Gamma;\sigma \vdash \lambda k{:}\alpha_a.\,M \nearrow [e]_a : [t]_a}$$

$$\frac{\Gamma;\sigma \vdash M \nearrow e : [t]_a \quad \Gamma^\dagger, \sigma^\dagger \vdash M' : \alpha_a}{\Gamma;\sigma \vdash M\,M' \nearrow e^a : t}$$

The second to last rule says that some occurrences of keys for a can be abstracted as long as the $\lambda^{[\,]}$ term after sealing is still at the same level ($dom(\sigma) = dom(\sigma\{a \mapsto k\})$). Note that even if $\Gamma^\dagger, \sigma^\dagger \vdash M : t^\dagger$, the inverse translation of M is *not* always possible. However, we can give a sufficient condition for the inverse translation to exist and show the inverse translation also preserves typing:

Theorem 7 (Inverse Translation Preserves Typing). *If the derivation of* $\Gamma^\dagger, \sigma^\dagger \vdash M : t^\dagger$ *satisfies the subformula property, then there exists a* $\lambda^{[\,]}$ *term* e *such that* $\Gamma;\sigma \vdash M \nearrow e : t$ *and* $\Gamma; dom(\sigma) \vdash e : t$.

Proof. By induction on the derivation of $\Gamma^\dagger, \sigma^\dagger \vdash M : t^\dagger$.

Remark 3. In the above theorem, the subformula property gives a sufficient condition to exclude "junk" terms such as $(\lambda x{:}\alpha_a \rightarrow \alpha_a.\,())(\lambda k{:}\alpha_a.\,k)$. Since $\lambda k{:}\alpha_a.\,k$ has type $\alpha_a \rightarrow \alpha_a$, no rules of inverse translation can be applied and the inverse translation will fail. Its derivation, however, does not satisfy the subformula property, so this is not a counterexample for the theorem above. (Its normal form can be translated back to a $\lambda^{[\,]}$ term.)

4   Proof of Noninterference Via Preservation of Logical Relations

In this section, we give an indirect proof of the noninterference theorem, which is obtained as an easy corollary of the theorem that the translation is sound and complete, that is, the logical relation for $\lambda^{[\,]}$ is preserved by translation to $\lambda^\rightarrow$. The properties we would expect are

If $e_1 \approx_{dom(\sigma)} e_2 : t$ and $\cdot; \sigma \vdash e_i : t \searrow M_i$ for $(i = 1, 2)$, then $\sigma^\dagger \vdash M_1 \approx M_2 : t^\dagger$,

and its converse

If $\cdot; \sigma \vdash e_i : t \searrow M_i$ for $(i = 1, 2)$ and $\sigma^\dagger \vdash M_1 \approx M_2 : t^\dagger$, then $e_1 \approx_{dom(\sigma)} e_2 : t$.

It is not very easy, however, to prove them directly because logical relations are defined by induction on types whereas the translations are not. Thus, following Tse and Zdancewic [17], we introduce another logical relation (called *logical correspondence*) $e \approx_\sigma M : t$ over terms of $\lambda^{[]}$ and $\lambda^\rightarrow$, then prove that it includes (the graphs of) the translations of both directions (Theorems 9 and 10). Then, after showing that the logical correspondence is full (Corollary 1), we finally prove preservation of logical relations by logical correspondence and reduce the noninterference theorem to the basic lemma (Lemma 2).

4.1   Logical Correspondence and Its Fullness

Definition 8 (Logical Correspondence). *The relations* $e \approx_\sigma M : t$ *and* $v \leadsto_\sigma V : t$, *where we assume that* $\Gamma; \ell \vdash e : t$ *and* $\Gamma; \ell \vdash v : t$ *and* $\Delta \vdash M : A$ *and* $\Delta \vdash V : A$, *are defined as the least relation closed under the following rules:*

$$() \leadsto_\sigma () : unit \qquad \frac{\forall(e \approx_\sigma M : t_1). v\, e \approx_\sigma V\, M : t_2}{v \leadsto_\sigma V : t_1 \to t_2} \qquad \frac{v_1 \leadsto_\sigma V_1 : t_1 \quad v_2 \leadsto_\sigma V_2 : t_2}{\langle v_1, v_2 \rangle \leadsto_\sigma \langle V_1, V_2 \rangle : t_1 \times t_2}$$

$$\frac{v \leadsto_\sigma V : t_i \quad i \in \{1, 2\}}{\iota_i(v) \leadsto_\sigma \iota_i(V) : t_1 + t_2} \qquad \frac{\forall(\sigma^\dagger \vdash M : \alpha_a). v \approx_\sigma V\, M : t}{[v]_a \leadsto_\sigma V : [t]_a}$$

$$\frac{e \longrightarrow^* v \qquad M \longrightarrow^* V \qquad v \leadsto_\sigma V : t}{e \approx_\sigma M : t}$$

Intuitively, $e \approx_\sigma M : t$ means that e and M exhibit the same behavior from the viewpoint of an observer at $dom(\sigma)$. The rule for $[t]_a$ expresses the fact that the existence of well-typed M of α_a under $\sigma^\dagger$ is equivalent to the existence of the authority a in $dom(\sigma)$. In other words, if a is not in $dom(\sigma)$, the premise is vacuously true, representing that the observer cannot distinguish anything.

Theorem 8 below shows that the logical correspondences are closed under the composition with the logical relation in $\lambda^\rightarrow$.

Theorem 8. *If* $e \approx_\sigma M_1 : t$ *and* $\sigma^\dagger \vdash M_1 \approx M_2 : t^\dagger$, *then* $e \approx_\sigma M_2 : t$.

Proof. By induction on the structure of t, using Remark 2 in the case where $t = [t']_a$.

The next theorem shows that these logical correspondences include the graphs of the translation to $\lambda^\rightarrow$. We write $\gamma \approx_\sigma \delta : \Gamma$ if $dom(\gamma) = dom(\delta) = dom(\Gamma)$ and $\gamma(x) \approx_\sigma \delta(x) : \Gamma(x)$ for any $x \in dom(\Gamma)$.

Theorem 9 (Inclusion of Translation). *If* $\Gamma; \sigma \vdash e : t \searrow M$ *and* $\gamma \approx_\sigma \delta : \Gamma$, *then* $\gamma(e) \approx_\sigma \delta(M) : t$.

Proof. By induction on the size of the derivation of $\Gamma; \sigma \vdash e : t \searrow M$.

It is slightly harder to show that the logical correspondence includes the graphs of the inverse translation, since the inverse translation is *not* quite a (right) inverse of the translation to $\lambda^{\rightarrow}$: The inverse translation followed by the forward translation may yield a term different from the original. For example, we can derive

$$x : [t]_a; \{a \mapsto k_1\} \vdash \lambda k_2 . \alpha_a . x \, k_1 \nearrow [x^a]_a : [t]_a$$

and

$$x : [t]_a; \{a \mapsto k_1\} \vdash [x^a]_a : [t]_a \searrow \lambda k_2' . \alpha_a . x \, k_2' .$$

Fortunately, the difference is only slight: They differ only in subterms of base types α_a and are in fact logically related. To identify terms only with this kind of differences, we introduce a (typed) equivalence relation $\Delta \vdash M_1 \equiv M_2 : A$, which is shown to be included in the logical relation.

Definition 9. *The relation* $\Delta \vdash M_1 \equiv M_2 : A$ *is defined as the least relation closed under the rules below:*

$$\frac{\Delta \vdash M : A}{\Delta \vdash M \equiv M : A} \qquad \frac{\Delta \vdash M_1 \equiv M_2 : A}{\Delta \vdash M_2 \equiv M_1 : A} \qquad \frac{\Delta \vdash M_1 : \alpha_a \quad \Delta \vdash M_2 : \alpha_a}{\Delta \vdash M_1 \equiv M_2 : \alpha_a}$$

$$\frac{\Delta \vdash M_1 \equiv M_2 : A \quad \Delta \vdash M_2 \equiv M_3 : A}{\Delta \vdash M_1 \equiv M_3 : A} \qquad \frac{\Delta \vdash M_1 \equiv M_2 : A \quad \Delta' \vdash \mathcal{C}[M_1] : A'}{\Delta' \vdash \mathcal{C}[M_1] \equiv \mathcal{C}[M_2] : A'}$$

where $\mathcal{C}$ *ranges over* term contexts, *which are defined by:*

$$\mathcal{C} ::= [\,] \mid \lambda x{:}A.\mathcal{C} \mid \mathcal{C} \, M \mid M \, \mathcal{C} \mid \langle \mathcal{C}, M \rangle \mid \langle M, \mathcal{C} \rangle \mid \pi_i(\mathcal{C}) \mid \iota_i(\mathcal{C})$$
$$\mid (\mathbf{case}\, \mathcal{C}\, \mathbf{of}\, \iota_1(x_1).M \mid \iota_2(x_2).M) \mid (\mathbf{case}\, M\, \mathbf{of}\, \iota_1(x_1).\mathcal{C} \mid \iota_2(x_2).M)$$
$$\mid (\mathbf{case}\, M\, \mathbf{of}\, \iota_1(x_1).M \mid \iota_2(x_2).\mathcal{C})$$

As mentioned above, the inverse translation followed by the translation yields a different term but it is still related by $\equiv$, which is included by the logical relation:

Lemma 3. *If* $\Gamma; \sigma \vdash M \nearrow e : t$ *and* $\Gamma; \sigma \vdash e : t \searrow M'$, *then* $\Gamma^\dagger, \sigma^\dagger \vdash M \equiv M' : t^\dagger$.

Proof. By induction on $\Gamma; \sigma \vdash M \nearrow e : t$.

Lemma 4. *If* $\Delta \vdash M_1 \equiv M_2 : A$ *and* $\Delta' \vdash \delta_1 \approx \delta_2 : \Delta$, *then* $\Delta' \vdash \delta_1(M_1) \approx \delta_2(M_2) : A$.

Proof. By induction on the derivation of $\Delta \vdash M_1 \equiv M_2 : A$.

Then, we can show the following theorem:

Theorem 10 (Inclusion of Inverse Translation). *If* $\Gamma; \sigma \vdash M \nearrow e : t$ *and* $\gamma \approx\!\!\!\!\gg_\sigma \delta : \Gamma$, *then* $\gamma(e) \approx\!\!\!\!\gg_\sigma \delta(M) : t$.

Proof. By Theorem 6, there exists M' such that $\Gamma; \sigma \vdash e : t \searrow M'$. Then, by Lemma 3, $\Gamma^\dagger, \sigma^\dagger \vdash M \equiv M' : t^\dagger$. Since $\sigma^\dagger \vdash \delta \approx \delta : \Gamma^\dagger$ (using Remark 2), $\sigma^\dagger \vdash \delta(M) \approx \delta(M') : t^\dagger$ by Lemma 4. Then, by Theorem 9, $\gamma(e) \approx\!\!\!\!\gg_\sigma \delta(M') : t$ and, by Theorem 8 and the symmetricity of the logical relation, $\gamma(e) \approx\!\!\!\!\gg_\sigma \delta(M) : t$.

As a corollary, the logical correspondences is shown to be full.

Corollary 1 (Fullness of Logical Correspondences). *If* $\sigma^\dagger \vdash M : t^\dagger$, *then there exists a* $\lambda^{[]}$ *term* e *such that* $e \approx\!\!\!\!\gg_\sigma M : t$.

Proof. By Theorems 5, 7, and 10.

4.2   Preservation of Logical Relations

By using the logical correspondence introduced above, we prove that the logical relations are preserved by the logical correspondence.

Theorem 11 (Preservation of Equivalences).

1. *If* $e_1 \approx_{dom(\sigma)} e_2 : t$ *and* $e_i \approx\!\!\!\!\gg_\sigma M_i : t$ $(i = 1, 2)$, *then* $\sigma^\dagger \vdash M_1 \approx M_2 : t^\dagger$.
2. *Conversely, if* $e_i \approx\!\!\!\!\gg_\sigma M_i : t$ *for* $(i = 1, 2)$ *and* $\sigma^\dagger \vdash M_1 \approx M_2 : t^\dagger$, *then* $e_1 \approx_{dom(\sigma)} e_2 : t$.

Proof. We prove both simultaneously by induction on the structure of t. We show only the main cases:

Case 1 $(t = t_1 \rightarrow t_2)$. To show (1), take arbitrary M'_1 and M'_2 such that $\sigma^\dagger \vdash M'_1 \approx M'_2 : t^\dagger_1$. By the fullness (Corollary 1), there exist e'_i such that $e'_i \approx\!\!\!\!\gg_\sigma M'_i : t_1$ $(i = 1, 2)$, and by the induction hypothesis (2) for t_1, we have $e'_1 \approx_{dom(\sigma)} e'_2 : t_1$. Then, by definition, there exist v_i, V_i $(i = 1, 2)$ such that $e_i \longrightarrow^* v_i$ and $M_i \longrightarrow^* V_i$ and $v_i e'_i \approx\!\!\!\!\gg_\sigma V_i M'_i : t_2$ for $(i = 1, 2)$, and $v_1 e'_1 \approx_{dom(\sigma)} v_2 e'_2 : t_2$. Applying the induction hypothesis (1) for t_2 to them, $\sigma^\dagger \vdash V_1 M'_1 \approx V_2 M'_2 : t^\dagger_2$. So we have $\sigma^\dagger \vdash V_1 \sim V_2 : t^\dagger_1 \rightarrow t^\dagger_2$, and hence $\sigma^\dagger \vdash M_1 \approx M_2 : t^\dagger_1 \rightarrow t^\dagger_2$. The statement (2) can be shown similarly, *without* the fullness.

Case 2 $(t = [t_1]_a)$. To show (2), we have two subcases: $a \in dom(\sigma)$ or not. If $a \in dom(\sigma)$, then, by definition, $\sigma^\dagger \vdash \sigma(a) \approx \sigma(a) : \alpha_a$. Also, by definition, there exist v_i, V_i $(i = 1, 2)$ such that $e_i \longrightarrow^* [v_i]_a$ and $M_i \longrightarrow^* V_i$ and $v_i \approx\!\!\!\!\gg_\sigma V_i \sigma(a) : t_1$ for $(i = 1, 2)$, and $\sigma^\dagger \vdash V_1 \sigma(a) \approx V_2 \sigma(a) : t^\dagger_1$. Applying the induction hypothesis (2) for t_1, we have $v_1 \approx_{dom(\sigma)} v_2 : t_1$, which is equivalent to $v_1 \sim_{dom(\sigma)} v_2 : t_1$, so $e_1 \approx_{dom(\sigma)} e_2 : [t_1]_a$. The case $a \notin \ell$ is trivial. Showing (1) is easy.

4.3   Noninterference

Then, we prove the noninterference theorem by reducing it to Lemma 2.

Corollary 2 (Noninterference). *If $\Gamma ; \ell \vdash e : t$ and $\gamma_1 \approx_\ell \gamma_2 : \Gamma$, then $\gamma_1(e) \approx_\ell \gamma_2(e) : t$.*

Proof. Choose an arbitrary σ such that $dom(\sigma) = \ell$ and $ran(\sigma) \cap dom(\Gamma) = \emptyset$. By Theorem 6, $\Gamma ; \sigma \vdash e : t \searrow M$ and $\Gamma^\dagger, \sigma^\dagger \vdash M : t^\dagger$ for some M. Similarly, for any $x \in dom(\gamma_i)$ ($i = 1, 2$), there exists M_{xi} such that $\cdot ; \sigma \vdash \gamma_i(x) : \Gamma(x) \searrow M_{xi}$ and $\Gamma^\dagger, \sigma^\dagger \vdash M_{xi} : (\Gamma(x))^\dagger$. Define δ_i ($i = 1, 2$) as a simultaneous substitution such that $dom(\delta_i) = dom(\gamma_i)$ and $\delta_i(x) = M_{xi}$ for $x \in dom(\delta_i)$. Then, by Theorem 9, $\gamma_i \approx_\sigma \delta_i : \Gamma$ for ($i = 1, 2$) and so $\gamma_i(e) \approx_\sigma \delta_i(M) : t$ for ($i = 1, 2$). By applying Theorem 11(1) to the assumption $\gamma_1 \approx_\ell \gamma_2 : \Gamma$, we have $\sigma^\dagger \vdash \delta_1 \approx \delta_2 : \Gamma^\dagger$. Thus, by Lemma 2 (with Remark 2), $\sigma^\dagger \vdash \delta_1(M) \approx \delta_2(M) : t^\dagger$. Finally, by Theorem 11(2), $\gamma_1(e) \approx_\ell \gamma_2(e) : t$.

5   Related Work

Proofs of Noninterference. There are many ways to prove noninterference theorems for type-based dependency analyses for higher-order languages. For example, Heintze and Riecke [7] and Abadi et al. [1] showed the noninterference theorem for SLam by using denotational semantics. Pottier and Simonet [12] proved it for Core ML with non-standard operational semantics. Moreover, Miyamoto and Igarashi [10], in the study of a modal typed calculus $\lambda_s^\square$, showed that the noninterference theorem for certain types can be easily proved only by using simple nondeterministic reduction system. In comparison with these proofs, the proof technique presented in this paper might seem overwhelming to show only noninterference; nevertheless, we believe it is still interesting since the translation shows that the notion of dependency can be captured only in terms of simple types.

Fullness in DCC. As we mentioned in the introduction, the translation from DCC to System F given by Tse and Zdancewic is not full. Here, we explain the reason, after quickly reviewing DCC. DCC [1] is an extension of a computational λ-calculus [11] and uses monads (indexed by a security level) for sealing. Roughly speaking, a monadic type $T_\ell\, t$, the monadic unit $\eta_\ell\, e$, and the bind operation bind $x = e_1$ in e_2 correspond to types for sealing, sealing terms, and unsealing terms. A type judgment of DCC lacks a level; instead, the notion of protected types is introduced to prevent information leakage and plays a key role in the typing rule for bind:

$$\frac{\Gamma \vdash e_1 : T_\ell\, t_1 \qquad \Gamma, x : t_1 \vdash e_2 : t_2 \qquad t_2 \text{ is protected at } \ell}{\Gamma \vdash \text{bind } x = e_1 \text{ in } e_2 : t_2}$$

Intuitively, "t is protected at ℓ" means that observers only at level ℓ (or higher) can obtain some bits of information by using the value of t. For example, $T_\ell\, t$

and $T_\ell\, t_1 \times T_\ell\, t_2$ and $t \to T_\ell\, t'$ are all protected at ℓ but $T_\ell\, t_1 + T_\ell\, t_2$ is not (see Abadi et al. [1] for the precise definition). So, this rule ensures that the value of the whole term cannot be examined at unrelated levels. However, bind is restrictive in the sense that η_ℓ must be placed within the scope of x to make t_2 protected. For example, the term $\lambda y : T_\ell$ bool.bind $x = y$ in $\eta_\ell\, x$ is given type $(T_\ell\, \text{bool}) \to (T_\ell\, \text{bool})$ while $\lambda y : T_\ell$ bool.η_ℓ (bind $x = y$ in x) cannot.

In fact, this restriction is a source of the failure of fullness of the translation by Tse and Zdancewic. Consider the DCC type $T_\ell((T_\ell\, \text{bool}) \to \text{bool})$, which is translated to $\alpha_\ell \to ((\alpha_\ell \to \text{bool}) \to \text{bool})$. Then, any DCC terms of the first type is equivalent to (sealed) constant functions $\eta_\ell(\lambda x : T_\ell\, \text{bool}.c)$ where c is either true or false. In System F, however, there is a term $\lambda k : \alpha_\ell.\lambda f : \alpha_\ell \to$ bool.fk of the translated type and it would correspond to an *ill typed* DCC term $\eta_\ell(\lambda y : T_\ell\, \text{bool}.\text{bind } x = y \text{ in } x)$. From this, we can show their translation does not preserve the logical relations. In fact,

$$\lambda f.\text{bind } f' = f \text{ in } \eta_\ell\ (f'\ (\eta_\ell\ \text{true}))$$

and

$$\lambda f.\text{bind } f' = f \text{ in } \eta_\ell\ (f'\ (\eta_\ell\ \text{false}))$$

are logically related at the type $(T_\ell((T_\ell\, \text{bool}) \to \text{bool})) \to (T_\ell\, \text{bool})$ and ℓ since, in DCC, all we can pass to these functions are the constant functions above. Their translations, however, are not because, in System F, applying them to the term $\lambda k : \alpha_\ell.\lambda f : \alpha_\ell \to \text{bool}.fk$ above will distinguish them.

Tse and Zdancewic's Extended DCC. Interestingly, Tse and Zdancewic also noticed this restriction of DCC and proposed an extension of (a pure fragment of) DCC by introducing the notion of protection contexts in type judgments. This extension allows terms like $\lambda y : T_\ell\, \text{bool}.\eta_\ell(\text{bind } x = y \text{ in } x)$ and $\eta_\ell(\lambda y : T_\ell\, \text{bool}.\text{bind } x = y \text{ in } x)$ to be well typed. Our $\lambda^{[]}$ can be considered a simplification of this extension by dropping the notion of protected types completely while leaving protection contexts (namely, levels in type judgments). We also dropped the lattice structure of security levels in DCC and now call them authorities. We believe that a similar result can be shown when the set of authorities is equipped with such a structure.

6   Conclusion

We have formalized noninterference for a typed λ-calculus $\lambda^{[]}$ by logical relations and proved by reducing it to the basic lemma of logical relation for $\lambda^{\to}$ through a translation of $\lambda^{[]}$ to $\lambda^{\to}$. Our translation is sound and fully complete and, as a result, the image of the translation is a complete representation, which captures dependency of $\lambda^{[]}$ with typeability in $\lambda^{\to}$.

Acknowledgements. Comments from anonymous referees helped up improve the final presentation. We thank Masahito Hasegawa, Eijiro Sumii, Stephen Tse, and Steve Zdancewic for discussions on this subject. This work is supported in part by Grant-in-Aid for Scientific Research (B) No. 17300003.

References

[1] Abadi, M., Banerjee, A., Heintze, N., Riecke, J.G.: A core calculus of dependency. In: POPL 1999. Proceedings of 26th ACM SIGPLAN-SIGACT Symposium on Principles of Programming Languages, pp. 147–160. ACM Press, New York (1999)

[2] de Groote, P.: On the strong normalisation of intuitionistic natural deduction with permutative-conversions. Information and Computation 178, 441–464 (2002)

[3] Denning, D.E., Denning, P.J.: Certification of programs for secure information flow. Communications of the ACM 20(7), 504–513 (1977)

[4] Girard, J.-Y Interprétation fonctionelle et élimination des coupures de l'arithmétique d'ordre supérieur. PhD thesis, Université Paris VII, A summary appeared in the Proceedings of the Second Scandinavian Logic Symposium Fenstad, J.E. (eds.). (pp. 63–92), North-Holland (1971)

[5] Goguen, J., Meseguer, J.: Security policies and security models. In: Proceedings of IEEE Symposium on Security and Privacy, pp. 11–20 (1982)

[6] Hasegawa, M.: Girard translation and logical predicates. Journal of Functional Programming 10(1), 77–89 (2000)

[7] Heintze, N., Riecke, J.G.: The SLam calculus: programming with secrecy and integrity. In: POPL 1998. Proceedings of ACM SIGPLAN-SIGACT Symposium on Principles of Programming Languages, pp. 365–377 (1998)

[8] Jones, N.D., Gomard, C.K., Sestoft, P.: Partial Evaluation and Automatic Program Generation. Prentice-Hall, Englewood Cliffs (1993)

[9] Mitchell, J.C.: Foundations for Programming Languages. The MIT Press, Cambridge (1996)

[10] Miyamoto, K., Igarashi, A.: A modal foundation for secure information flow. In: FCS 2004. Proceedings of Workshop on Foundations of Computer Security, pp. 187–203 (June 2004)

[11] Moggi, E.: Notions of computation and monads. Information and Computation 1, 55–92 (1991)

[12] Pottier, F., Simonet, V.: Information flow inference for ML. ACM Transactions on Programming Languages and Systems 25(1), 117–158 (2003)

[13] Reynolds, J.: Towards a theory of type structure. In: Robinet, B. (ed.) Programming Symposium. LNCS, vol. 19, pp. 408–425. Springer, Heidelberg (1974)

[14] Reynolds, J.C.: Types, abstraction and parametric polymorphism. In: IFIP Congress, pp. 513–523 (1983)

[15] Sabelfeld, A., Myers, A.C.: Language-based information-flow security. IEEE Journal On Selected Areas In Communications 21(1), 5–19 (2003)

[16] Tang, Y.M., Jouvelot, P.: Effect systems with subtyping. In: PEPM 1995. Proceedings of ACM Symposium on Partial Evaluation and Semantics-Based Program Manipulation, pp. 45–53 (1995)

[17] Tse, S., Zdancewic, S.: Translating dependency into parametricity. In: ICFP 2004. Proceedings of 9th ACM International Conference on Functional Programming, pp. 115–125. ACM Press, New York (2004)

[18] Wadler, P.: Theorems for free. In: FPCA 1989. Proceedings 4th Int.Conf. on Funct. Prog. Languages and Computer Arch. pp. 347–359. ACM Press, New York (1989)

Formalization of CTL* in Calculus of Inductive Constructions*

Ming-Hsien Tsai[1,2] and Bow-Yaw Wang[1,**]

[1] Institute of Information Science
Academia Sinica, Taiwan
[2] Department of Information Management
National Taiwan University, Taiwan

Abstract. A modular formalization of the branching time temporal logic CTL* is presented. Our formalization subsumes prior formalizations of propositional linear temporal logic (PTL) and computation tree logic (CTL). Moreover, the modularity allows to instantiate our formalization for different formal security models. Validity of axioms and soundness of inference rules in axiomatizations of PTL, UB, CTL, and CTL* are discussed as well.

1 Introduction

The management of digital objects in modern information systems has become very sophisticated during past years. In digital rights management, for instance, a digital content may be accessible exclusively for a fixed period of time; if the contract is expired or the content is currently in use, no access will be allowed. Since traditional static usage control models could not express the dynamic authorizations found in these applications, temporal logics are introduced in recent models [19].

The introduction of temporal logics nevertheless induces new problems. Because of the complexity in the semantics of temporal operators, users often have difficulties in writing correct requirements or verifying them. Moreover, specifications of real-world usage control systems are rather complicated. Whether one can analyze such temporal specifications correctly by hand is not without questions.

One way to help users manage complicated specifications is to mechanize the process. Indeed, fully automated approaches such as model checking are able to analyze models against temporal logic specifications without user intervention. But the expressiveness of formal security models deviates from the simplicity of computation models in algorithmic approaches; various capability and computability issues are subsequently arisen in fully automated techniques.

---

* The work is partly supported by NSC grands 95-3114-P-001-002-Y02, 95-2221-E-001-024-MY3, and the project SISARL of Academia Sinica.
** Part of the the work was done during the second author visited to the project ProVal supported by INRIA Futurs.

M. Okada and I. Satoh (Eds.): ASIAN 2006, LNCS 4435, pp. 316–330, 2007.
© Springer-Verlag Berlin Heidelberg 2007

In order to have expressive models and circumvent undecidability, semi-automated approaches such as proof checking are used. In semi-automated techniques, usage control models and their temporal logic specifications are formulated in proof assistants. Security amounts to the entailment of respective temporal logic specification. Since each step of the proof is checked by the proof assistant, the correctness of analysis is therefore ensured.

But formulations of models and their specifications require domain knowledge about formal models, temporal logics, and proof assistants. Inappropriate formulations may result in ineffective or even faulty analysis. In this paper, we address the formulation problem of temporal logics in the proof assistant COQ. Specifically, the branching time temporal logic CTL* is formalized in Calculus of Inductive Constructions. We identify assumptions in formal models and modularize our formalization based on these assumptions. Users will be able to instantiate our formalization as long as their formal models conform to the identified assumptions.

The branching time temporal logic CTL* is a proper super class of the propositional linear temporal logic (PTL) and the computation tree logic (CTL). Prior formalizations of PTL and CTL are therefore subsumed by the present work. The expressiveness of CTL* gives users more freedom to specify the requirements of their security models. To the best of our knowledge, ours is the first formalization of CTL* in any proof assistant. Moreover, we have used the formalization to establish the validity of 31 (out of 33) axiom schemata, and the soundness of 8 (out of 10) inference rules in four complete axiomatizations of various temporal logics.

The modularity distinguishes our formalization from others as well. We identify assumptions needed in the formalization of CTL* and formally specify them in a COQ module type. The formalization of CTL* is carried out in a functor from modules of the aforementioned module type. Subsequently, any formalization of security models can instantiate our CTL* formalization, provided it is of the proper module type. In domains with versatile characteristics such as security analysis, our modular formalization greatly reduces the adoption effort.

The branching-time temporal logic μ-calculus has been formalized in Coq [10,16], LEGO [18], and ACL2 [8] with different intentions. A formalization of PTL can be found in Coq [3,2]. The temporal logic of actions TLA [7] has been formalized in Isabelle [9]. A shallow embedding of CTL is also available [1]. None of these formalizations admits both state and path formulae. Although μ-calculus is more expressive than CTL*, it is not accessible to practitioners due to its arcane syntax and semantics. CTL*, on the other hand, is an accessible generalization of both PTL and CTL. We feel our CTL* formalization would be more useful in practice.

The paper is structured as follows. A brief review of the syntax and semantics of CTL* is given in Section 2. Section 3 identifies assumptions in our formalization of Kripke structures. Based on these assumptions, we formalize paths and CTL* in Section 4 and 5 respectively. The validity of axiom schemata and the soundness of inference rules are discussed in Section 6. Finally, Section 7 concludes the paper and highlights future works.

2   Preliminaries

Let AP be the set of *atomic propositions*. The *syntax* of CTL* is defined as follows [4].

(S0) If p is an atomic proposition, p is a state formula;
(S1) If p and q are state formulae, $p \wedge q$ and $\neg p$ are state formulae;
(S2) If f is a path formula, $\mathbf{A}f$ and $\mathbf{E}f$ are state formulae;
(P0) If p is a state formula, p is a path formula;
(P1) If f and g are path formulae, $f \wedge g$ and $\neg f$ are path formulae;
(P2) If f and g are path formulae, $\mathbf{X}f$ and $f\mathbf{U}g$ are path formulae.

A *Kripke structure* $K = (S, \rightarrow, L)$ consists of a set of *states* S, a total *transition relation* $\rightarrow \subseteq S \times S$, and a labeling function $L : S \rightarrow 2^{AP}$. A *path* π in K is an infinite sequence of states $s_0 s_1 \cdots s_n \cdots$ such that $s_i \rightarrow s_{i+1}$ for all $i \geq 0$. We use the notations $\pi(i) = s_i$ and $\pi_i = s_i s_{i+1} \cdots$ to denote the *i-th state* and the *i-th suffix* of the path π respectively. Note that $\pi = \pi_0$. The *semantics* of a CTL* formula is defined as follows.

$K, s \models P$ if $P \in L(s)$, where $P \in AP$
$K, s \models \neg p$ if not $K, s \models p$
$K, s \models p \wedge q$ if $K, s \models p$ and $K, s \models q$
$K, s \models \mathbf{A}f$ if $K, \pi \models f$ for all π with $\pi(0) = s$
$K, s \models \mathbf{E}f$ if $K, \pi \models f$ for some π with $\pi(0) = s$
$K, \pi \models p$ if $K, \pi(0) \models p$
$K, \pi \models \neg f$ if not $K, \pi \models f$
$K, \pi \models f \wedge g$ if $K, \pi \models f$ and $K, \pi \models g$
$K, \pi \models \mathbf{X}f$ if $K, \pi_1 \models f$
$K, \pi \models f\mathbf{U}g$ if there is a k such that $K, \pi_k \models g$ and $K, \pi_j \models f$ for all $0 \leq j < k$

We will use $p, q, r, \ldots$ for state formulae, $f, g, h, \ldots$ for path formulae, and $\phi, \psi, \ldots$ for CTL* formulae. Derived operators such as $\phi \vee \psi \equiv \neg(\neg\phi \wedge \neg\psi)$, $\phi \Rightarrow \psi \equiv \neg\phi \vee \psi$, $\phi \Leftrightarrow \psi \equiv (\phi \Rightarrow \psi) \wedge (\psi \Rightarrow \phi)$, $\mathbf{F}f \equiv true\mathbf{U}f$, and $\mathbf{G}f \equiv \neg\mathbf{F}\neg f$ are also used. The operators $\mathbf{A}$ and $\mathbf{E}$ are called *path quantifiers*; $\mathbf{X}$, $\mathbf{U}$, $\mathbf{F}$, and $\mathbf{G}$ are *linear temporal operators*.

Both propositional linear temporal logic (PTL) and computational tree logic (CTL) are proper subclasses of CTL*. PTL formulae are constructed by the rules (P0) to (P2) where atomic propositions are the only state formulae. CTL consists of state formulae with the restriction that all linear temporal operators are prefixed by path quantifiers. That is, only the temporal operators $\mathbf{AX}$, $\mathbf{AG}$, $\mathbf{AF}$, $\mathbf{AU}$, $\mathbf{EX}$, $\mathbf{EG}$, $\mathbf{EF}$, and $\mathbf{EU}$ are allowed. The system UB is a subclass of CTL, where only the temporal operators $\mathbf{AX}$, $\mathbf{AG}$, $\mathbf{AF}$, $\mathbf{EX}$, $\mathbf{EG}$, and $\mathbf{EF}$, are allowed.

Observe that all subformulae of a PTL formula are themselves PTL formulae, and PTL formulae in turn are path formulae. A formalization of pure path formulae suffices for PTL. Similarly, a formalization of pure state formulae would be sufficient for CTL. In comparison, the formalization of CTL* is greatly complicated by admitting both state and path formulae. The techniques found in [14,12,13,16,8,10] are therefore not directly applicable.

3   Kripke Structures

One distinguished feature of our formalization is the use of COQ module system. When this research was initiated, our goal was to build a unified verification framework in COQ [17]. In addition to the temporal logic CTL*, we also formalize a model specification language in our framework. It is but natural to use Kripke structures as the interface between both formalizations. Our formalization of CTL* therefore assumes an abstract interface of Kripke structures. This can be done by the following module type definition.

```
Module Type KRIPKE .
  Parameter st : Set .
  Prarmeter succ : st -> st -> Prop .
  ...
End KRIPKE .
```

Two parameters are assumed in the module type KRIPKE. The set st and the predicate succ formalize the set of states and the transition relation in a Kripke structure respectively. To formalize the totality of the transition relation, one might add the following requirement in the module type KRIPKE.[1]

Axiom totality_alt : forall s : st, exists s' : st, succ s s' .

However, Calculus of Inductive Constructions does not allow the state *s'* to be extracted from the axiom *totality_alt* lest inconsistency would incur. We therefore formalize the totality by the inductive type post and the axiom totality.

```
Inductive post (s : st) : Set :=
  | post_intro (s' : st) : succ s s' -> post s .
Axiom totality : forall s : st, post s .
```

For any state s, the set post s contains elements of the form post_intro s' where s and s' satisfy the transition relation succ. The axiom totality simply states that the set post s is not empty for all state s.

When a concrete Kripke structure is available, our formalization of CTL* can be instantiated to analyze properties on the Kripke structure. Note that the semantics of a CTL* formula varies from different Kripke structures. Each instantiation of our CTL* theory gives a specialized interpretation of formulae in the given Kripke structure.

---

[1] The keyword Axiom is perhaps a little misleading. These "axioms" need be established in module definitions; they do not hold automatically.

4 Paths

A path in a Kripke structure is an infinite state sequence where successive states satisfy the transition relation. Several formalizations of paths can be found in literature. In [11], a path is a function of type `nat -> st`, while [14,3,2] use coinductive data types. Although the coinductive formalization admits partiality and is therefore more general than the functional one [14], we feel that the benefit of generality would be better left for users to decide. Hence, we would rather not commit to a particular formalization of paths in our CTL* formalization. Since it is inessential to know exactly how paths are formalized, we can exploit the CoQ module system to isolate the formalization of paths from their interface. Consider the following interface of paths.

```
Module Type PATH .
  Parameters st path : Set .
  Parameter succ : st -> st -> Prop .
  Parameter hd : path -> st .
  Parameter tl : path -> path .
  Parameter cons : forall (s : st) (pi : path), succ s (hd pi) -> path .
  ...
End PATH .
```

The parameters `st` and `succ` inherit from a concrete `KRIPKE` module. Paths are formalized as the set `path`. The parameters `hd` and `tl` retrieve the head and tail of a path respectively. Additionally, the parameter `cons` constructs a new path from a state and a path, provided that the state and the head of the path satisfy the transition relation.

Of course, the typing information alone does not entail the intended semantics. It is rather easy to impose semantic requirements on the parameters in the CoQ module system. For instance, we enforce the following semantic constraints in the module type `PATH`.

```
  Axiom hd_cons : forall (s : st) (pi : path) (H : succ s (hd pi)),
    hd (cons s pi H) = s .
  Axiom tl_cons : forall (s : st) (pi : path) (H : succ s (hd pi)),
    tl (cons s pi H) = pi .
  Axiom pi_succ : forall pi : path, succ (hd pi) (hd (tl pi)) .
```

The axioms `hd_cons` and `tl_cons` specify the relations among the parameters `hd`, `tl`, and `cons`. The axiom `pi_succ` states that the first and the second states of any path satisfy the transition relation.

Another useful fact in our formalization is that each state has a path from it. More formally, we have the following axiom in the module type `PATH`.

```
Axiom ex_path : forall s : st, exists pi : path, hd pi = s .
```

Due to the totality of the transition relation in the underlying Kripke structure, one would expect the axiom `ex_path` in any reasonable formalization of paths. Indeed, the axiom will be handy when we prove the validity of axiom schemata in axiomatizations of various temporal logics in Section 6.

Our modular formalization of paths is a functor which takes modules of type KRIPKE and generates a module of type PATH. Furthermore, the generated module shares the formalizations of states (st) and the transition relation (succ) with the input module.

```
Module Path (KS : KRIPKE) : PATH with Definition st := KS.st
                                  with Definition succ := KS.succ .
  . . .
End Path .
```

Similar to [14,3,2], our formalization of paths is based on coinductive data types. We start with the conventional coinductive definition of lazy lists.

```
CoInductive stream : Set := scons : st -> stream -> stream .
Definition shd (str : stream) : st := match str with scons s _ => s end .
```

A stream is simply an infinite sequence of states. The constructor scons takes a state and a stream to create a stream. The function shd retrieves the head of a stream. Unlike paths, there is no restriction on successive states in a stream. To assert the transition relation succ on successive states, the following coinductively defined predicate on streams is used.

```
CoInductive is_path : stream -> Prop :=
  | path_intro (s : st) (str : stream) :
    succ s (shd str) -> is_path str -> is_path (scons s str) .
```

To check if the stream (scons s str) is a path, it suffices to verify that

1. the state s and the head of str (shd str) satisfies the transition relation succ; and
2. the stream str is indeed a path.

Note that our definitions of stream and is_path are coinductive. In comparison, streams are defined by domain equations in [14]. The coinductively defined type is_path becomes a function on the stream domain.[2]

```
Fixpoint is_path_p (str : stream) : Prop :=
  match str with scons s tl => succ s (shd tl) /\ is_path_p tl end .
```

But the function is_path_p should be evaluated lazily. Special care must be taken to define it over the stream domain. Coinductive defined types in Calculus of Constructions greatly simplify our formalization. We therefore prefer our purely coinductive formalization.

It is now easy to define the set path as follows.

```
Definition path : Set := { str : stream | is_path str } .
```

---

[2] It is noted that the definition is ill-formed because stream is not an inductive type.

The set `path` consists of streams satisfying the predicate `is_path`. The function `hd` can now be defined.

```
Definition hd (pi : path) : st := let (str, _) := pi in shd str .
```

Since a path `pi` is merely a tuple of a stream `str` and its proof of "pathness," the head of `pi` can be computed by invoking the auxiliary function `shd`. Other parameters are defined similarly.

To finish the definition of the functor `Path`, we have to establish the axioms `hd_cons`, `tl_cons`, `pi_succ`, and `ex_path` with our definitions of `hd`, `tl`, and `cons`. Except for `ex_path`, all proofs are rather straightforward. The proof of `ex_path` requires the *decomposition lemma* in [2] and essentially defines a stream from any given state coinductively.

5   CTL*

Recall that CTL* formulae consist of two types of formulae: state and path formulae describe properties about states and paths respectively. In our formalization of CTL*, state and path formulae are of type `st -> Prop` and `path -> Prop` respectively, where `st` and `path` in turn inherit from modules of type `PATH`. An atomic proposition specifies properties about states and is thus of type `st -> Prop`.

```
Module CTLS (Path : PATH) .
  Definition st := Path.st .
  Definition path := Path.path .

  Definition atomic_proposition : Type := st -> Prop .
  Definition st_formula : Type := st -> Prop .
  Definition path_formula : Type := path -> Prop .
  ...
End CTLS .
```

Since a state formula is also a path formula, we define the function `st2path` to coerce state formulae.

```
Definition st2path (p : st_formula) : path_formula :=
  fun (pi : path) => p (Path.hd pi) .
Coercion st2path : st_formula >-> path_formula .
```

To help users construct CTL* formulae, we formalize each linear temporal operator and path quantifier in CTL* as an inductively defined type in Calculus of Inductive Constructions. Each CTL* formula is therefore a type expression in our formalization. To prove a CTL* formula amounts to building a term of the corresponding type expression by constructors of respective inductively defined types.

5.1   State Formulae

Given a state formula p, its negation corresponds to the type expression neg_s p. To construct a proof of its negation, it suffices to find a proof of ~ p s for any state s.

```
Inductive neg_s (p : st_formula) : st_formula :=
  | neg_s_intro : forall s : st, ~ p s -> neg_s p s .
```

Observe that the inductively defined type neg_s p is of sort st_formula as well. It can thus be used to construct more complicated type expressions. For instance, the corresponding type expression for the CTL* formula $\neg\neg p$ is neg_s neg_s p. The following notation for the type expression neg_s p is defined for convenience.

```
Notation "! p" := (neg_s p) (at level 75, right associativity) .
```

Henceforth, we will write ! p for the type corresponding to the formula $\neg p$. Other logical operators can be formalized similarly. We use the notations p && q, p || q, p ==> q, and p <==> q for the corresponding type expressions for the formulae $p \wedge q$, $p \vee q$, $p \Rightarrow q$, and $p \Leftrightarrow q$ respectively.

It is as easy to formalize path quantifiers in CTL* as well. For instance, proving the state formula $\mathbf{A}f$ on the state s is to demonstrate that all paths π from s satisfy f. Hence the following type is used for the state formula $\mathbf{A}f$.

```
Inductive A (f : path_formula) : st_formula :=
  | A_intro : forall s : st,
    (forall pi : path, s = Path.hd pi -> f pi) -> A f s .
```

We will use the notations A f and E f for the type expressions of the formulae $\mathbf{A}f$ and $\mathbf{E}f$ respectively.

5.2   Path Formulae

Logical operators for path formulae are similar to those of state formulae. The inductively defined type and_p f g, for instance, formalizes the conjunction of path formulae f and g.

```
Inductive and_p (f g : path_formula) : path_formula :=
  | and_p_intro : forall pi : path, f pi /\ g pi -> and_p f g pi .
```

The notations '! f, f '&& g, f '|| g, f '==> g, and f '<==> g are used for the negation, conjunction, disjunction, implication, and logical equivalence respectively. Note that the back quote (') distinguishes from the corresponding types for state formulae.

Our formalization of linear temporal operators essentially follows those of PTL in [3,2]. Instead of using streams as in prior formalizations, our formalization is based on paths in Kripke structures.

In order to show that a path π satisfies the path formula $\mathbf{X}f$, it is necessary to show that the tail of π satisfies the formula f. Thus, the inductively defined type X f is as follows.

```
Inductive X (f : path_formula) : path_formula :=
  | X_intro : forall pi : path, f (Path.tl pi) -> X f pi .
```

Now consider the path formula $\mathbf{G}f$. The path π satisfies $\mathbf{G}f$ if it satisfies f *and* its tail satisfies $\mathbf{G}f$. Note that a proof term of π satisfying $\mathbf{G}f$ is infinite for π is infinite. We therefore use a coinductively defined type G f for the formula $\mathbf{G}f$.

```
CoInductive G (f : path_formula) : path_formula :=
  | G_intro : forall pi : path, f pi -> G f (Path.tl pi) -> G f pi .
```

For the path formula $\mathbf{F}f$, there are two ways to demonstrate the path π satisfying the formula. If π satisfies f, we are done. Otherwise, the tail of π must satisfy $\mathbf{F}f$. Therefore, a proof term of type F f is built by the constructors F0_intro and F_intro inductively.

```
Inductive F (f : path_formula) : path_formula :=
  | F0_intro : forall pi : path, f pi -> F f pi
  | F_intro  : forall pi : path, F f (Path.tl pi) -> F f pi .
```

The definition of the type U f g is similar to F f. To show the path π satisfying $f\mathbf{U}g$ is to show that π satisfies g, *or* it satisfies f and its tail satisfies $f\mathbf{U}g$.

```
Inductive U (f g : path_formula) : path_formula :=
  | U0_intro : forall pi : path, g pi -> U f g pi
  | U_intro  : forall pi : path, f pi -> U f g (Path.tl pi) -> U f g pi .
```

We will write X f, G f, F f, and f U g for the corresponding type expressions of formulae $\mathbf{X}f$, $\mathbf{G}f$, $\mathbf{F}f$, and $f\mathbf{U}g$ respectively. Observe that derived temporal operators are also formalized. They allow us to carry out formal proofs more intuitively.

To compare with the formalizations in [3,2], recall that a stream is an infinite sequence of states. There is no restriction imposed on successive states in a stream. A path, on the other hand, is a stream satisfying the co-inductively defined predicate is_path; successive states in a path satisfy the transition relation succ. Hence the computation of the underlying Kripke structure is implicit in our formalization.

In contrast, a stream filter path_filter : stream -> Prop is needed in statements about paths to witness the transition relation of the underlying computation model in [3,2]. For instance, the following axiom states that the state formula fair holds infinitely often along all paths from s.

```
Axiom fairness : forall (s : st) (str : stream),
    s = shd str -> path_filter str -> (G F fair) str .
```

Since there is only one implicit universal path quantifier in any PTL formula, adding path_filter does not incur too much overhead in [3,2]. However, it becomes rather cumbersome for CTL* where nested path quantifiers are allowed. Moreover, the proofs in prior formalizations would move between streams and paths for each path quantifier, even though paths are in fact of the main interest. Our formalization, on the other hand, is solely based on paths. Users do not see any reference to streams and can focus on key concepts in the our formalization.

6 Examples

With the formalization of CTL* in Section 5, we are able to prove validity of axiom schemata and soundness of inference rules in axiomatizations of temporal logics. Since PTL and CTL are subclasses of CTL*, restrictions of our CTL* formalization suffice for the proofs of respective theorems in their axiomatizations. It is unnecessary to have formal proofs in different formalizations. Moreover, all axiom schemata and inference rules in our modular formalization can be instantiated for different security models. In the following sections, we discuss the validity and soundness of axiom schemata and inference rules in axiomatizations of PTL, UB, CTL, and CTL* respectively.

6.1 PTL

Figure 1 shows the axiomatization of PTL in [6]. For each axiom schema, we would like to show it is indeed valid in our formalization. We say a PTL formula f is *valid* (denoted by $\models f$) if $K, \pi \models f$ for any Kripke structure K and path π. An *instance* of an axiom schema Ψ is a PTL formula obtained by substituting all variables in Ψ with PTL formulae. For instance, suppose $P \in AP$. Then $\mathbf{X}\neg\mathbf{G}P \Leftrightarrow \neg\mathbf{X}\mathbf{G}P$ is an instance of the axiom schema $(ax1)$. We say an axiom schema Ψ is *valid* if all instances of Ψ are valid.

To show the validity of the axiom schema $(ax2)$ in Figure 1, we first formalize the validity of path formulae as follows.

```
Definition model_p (f : path_formula) := forall pi : path, f pi .
Notation "'|= f" := (model_p f) (at level 100, no associativity) .
```

$$(ax1) \vdash \mathbf{X}\neg f \Leftrightarrow \neg\mathbf{X}f$$
$$(ax2) \vdash \mathbf{X}(f \Rightarrow g) \Rightarrow (\mathbf{X}f \Rightarrow \mathbf{X}g)$$
$$(ax3) \vdash \mathbf{G}f \Rightarrow (f \wedge \mathbf{X}\mathbf{G}f)$$
$$(mp) \ \frac{\vdash f \quad \vdash f \Rightarrow g}{\vdash g}$$
$$(nex) \ \frac{\vdash f}{\vdash \mathbf{X}f} \qquad (ind) \ \frac{\vdash f \Rightarrow g \quad \vdash f \Rightarrow \mathbf{X}f}{\vdash f \Rightarrow \mathbf{G}g}$$

Fig. 1. An Axiomatization of PTL

It is now straightforward to state the validity of each axiom schema. For example, the validity of the axiom schema $(ax2)$ is as follows.

```
Theorem ax2 : forall f g : path_formula,
  '|= (X (f '==> g)) '==> (X f) '==> (X g) .
```

The soundness of inference rules can be similarly formalized. The theorem ind, for instance, formalizes the soundness of the rule (ind).

```
Theorem ind : forall f g : path_formula,
  ('|= f '==> g) /\ ('|= f '==> X f) -> ('|= f '==> G g) .
```

Note that the theorem ax2 is in fact more general than the validity of axiom schema ($ax2$) in the pure PTL setting. The theorem states that the axiom schema ($ax2$) is valid not only for all PTL formulae, but also all path formulae in CTL*.[3] Similarly, the theorem ind is more general than the soundness of inference rule (ind). The proofs of validity and soundness are carried out in the default COQ environment. We are able to prove the validity of all axiom schemata and the soundness of all inference rules in Figure 1 with our formalization.

6.2   UB

As for the PTL axiomatization, we would like to prove the validity and soundness theorems of the axiomatization of UB in Figure 2 formally. Specifically, we say a state formula p is *valid* if $K, s \vdash p$ for any Kripke structure K and state s. An axiom schema is *valid* if all its instances are valid. The validity of state formulae is formalized as follows.

```
Definition model_s (p : st_formula) := forall s : st, p s .
Notation "|= p" := (model_s p) (at level 100, no associativity) .
```

$$(A1) \vdash \mathbf{AG}(p \Rightarrow q) \Rightarrow (\mathbf{AG}p \Rightarrow \mathbf{AG}q)$$
$$(A2) \vdash \mathbf{AX}(p \Rightarrow q) \Rightarrow (\mathbf{AX}p \Rightarrow \mathbf{AX}q)$$
$$(A3) \vdash \mathbf{AG}p \Rightarrow \mathbf{AX}p \wedge \mathbf{AXAG}p$$
$$(A4) \vdash \mathbf{AG}(p \Rightarrow \mathbf{AX}p) \Rightarrow (p \Rightarrow \mathbf{AG}p)$$
$$(E1) \vdash \mathbf{AG}(p \Rightarrow q) \Rightarrow (\mathbf{EG}p \Rightarrow \mathbf{EG}q)$$
$$(E2) \vdash \mathbf{EG}p \Rightarrow p \wedge \mathbf{EXEG}p$$
$$(E3) \vdash \mathbf{AG}p \Rightarrow \mathbf{EG}p$$
$$(E4) \vdash \mathbf{AG}(p \Rightarrow \mathbf{EX}p) \Rightarrow (p \Rightarrow \mathbf{EG}p)$$
$$(R1) \frac{\vdash p \quad \vdash p \Rightarrow q}{\vdash q} \qquad (R2) \frac{\vdash p}{\vdash \mathbf{AG}p}$$

Fig. 2. An Axiomatization of UB

The validity of the axiom schemata and the soundness of inference rules are formalized similarly. For instance, the validity of axiom schema ($A3$) is stated in the following theorem.

```
Theorem A3 : forall p : st_formula, |= (A G p) ==> (A X p && A X A G p) .
```

As in PTL, the theorem A3 is more general than the validity of the axiom schema ($A3$) in the pure UB setting. Unlike PTL, however, the proofs of validity and soundness require switching between state and path formulae. Since our

---

[3] As an anonymous reviewer points to us, it is even valid for path predicates which are not expressible in CTL* because of the shallow embedding.

formalization is in fact for CTL*, each temporal operator in a UB formula has to be decomposed as a path quantifier followed by a linear temporal operator. Consider the validity of the axiom schema (E3).

```
Theorem E3 : forall p : st_formula, |= (A G p) ==> (E G p) .
```

A simple proof is to demonstrate a path from any given state satisfying **AG**p and show it indeed satisfies **G**p. We therefore use the axiom Path.ex_path to construct an arbitrary path from the given state, and show that the path is indeed a witness of **G**p by the assumption **AG**p.

We are able to prove the soundness of all inference rules in Figure 2 formally. We also establish the validity of all axiom schemata but (E4) in Calculus of Inductive Construction. To explain the difficulty in proving the validity of (E4), recall its formulation.

```
Theorem E4 : forall p : st_formula, |= (A G (p ==> E X p)) ==> p ==> E G p .
```

One possible proof of E4 is to construct a path satisfying **G**p. But eliminating the assumption A G (p ==> E X p) of sort Prop is not allowed in the construction of paths of sort Set. Alternatively, we fail to demonstrate the existence of a path satisfying **G**p in classical logic. The assumption suggests that any path can be modified to admit p in one more state. But the existence of a path satisfying **G**p in the limit eludes us. Currently, we do not know how to prove it with the present formalization.

6.3   CTL

The axiomatization of CTL in [5,4] is shown in Figure 3. The validity and soundness of axiom schemata and inference rules follow the same style in Section 6.2. The proof techniques used in the previous section are carried over without difficulties. Indeed, the axiomatization of UB in Figure 2 can be obtained from the axiomatization of CTL in Figure 3 [5]. It is not surprising to prove the validity

$$(Ax1) \vdash \mathbf{EF}p \Leftrightarrow \mathbf{E}[true\mathbf{U}p]$$
$$(Ax2) \vdash \mathbf{AF}p \Leftrightarrow \mathbf{A}[true\mathbf{U}p]$$
$$(Ax3) \vdash \mathbf{EX}(p \vee q) \Leftrightarrow \mathbf{EX}p \vee \mathbf{EX}q$$
$$(Ax4) \vdash \mathbf{AX}p \Leftrightarrow \neg\mathbf{EX}\neg p$$
$$(Ax5) \vdash \mathbf{E}(p\mathbf{U}q) \Leftrightarrow q \vee (p \wedge \mathbf{EXE}(p\mathbf{U}q))$$
$$(Ax6) \vdash \mathbf{A}(p\mathbf{U}q) \Leftrightarrow q \vee (p \wedge \mathbf{AXA}(p\mathbf{U}q))$$
$$(Ax7) \vdash \mathbf{EX}true \wedge \mathbf{AX}true$$

$$(R1)\ \frac{\vdash p \Rightarrow q}{\vdash \mathbf{EX}p \Rightarrow \mathbf{EX}q} \qquad\qquad (R2)\ \frac{\vdash r \Rightarrow (\neg q \wedge \mathbf{EX}r)}{\vdash r \Rightarrow \neg\mathbf{A}(p\mathbf{U}q)}$$

$$(R3)\ \frac{\vdash r \Rightarrow [\neg q \wedge \mathbf{AX}(r \vee \neg\mathbf{E}(p\mathbf{U}q))]}{\vdash r \Rightarrow \neg\mathbf{E}(p\mathbf{U}q)} \qquad (R4)\ \frac{\vdash p \quad \vdash p \Rightarrow q}{\vdash q}$$

Fig. 3. An Axiomatization of CTL

and soundness of axiom schemata and inference rules for CTL by generalizing the proof techniques used for UB.

We have succeeded in proving the validity of all axiom schemata in Figure 3. Unlike the proofs for the system UB, classical reasoning is used in a couple of axiom schemata. Specifically, contraposition and De Morgan's law are used in the proofs of ($Ax4$) and ($Ax6$) respectively. As for the soundness of inference rules, an obstacle similar to the axiom schema ($E4$) in UB is encountered in the inference rule ($R2$). For other inference rules, we are able to prove their soundness formally.

6.4   CTL*

Figure 4 shows the sound and complete axiomatization of CTL* in [15]. The side condition C in the axiom schema (AA) is syntactic and somewhat complicated. It requires pairwise inconsistency of atomic propositions in finite sets, and a function choosing atomic propositions to hold at the next state along a path (Definition 4 in [15]).

Unlike the axiomatizations in previous sections, both path and state formulae are present. The validity of path formulae is used in the axiom schemata ($C1$) to ($C8$), ($C11$), and ($C15$). The axiom schemata ($C9$), ($C10$), and ($C12$) to ($C14$) are valid as state formulae. Their formal proofs can be carried out in our formalization of CTL*. Prior formalizations, in comparison, would not even be able to formulate axiom schemata ($C12$) nor ($C15$). A CTL* formalization is therefore needed in establishing validity of axiom schemata formally.

Except the axiom schemata (LC), we have proved the validity of all axiom schemata in Figure 4. The axiom schema (LC) is another generalization of the axiom schema ($E4$) in UB and the inference rule ($R3$) in CTL. The side condition

$$(C1) \vdash \mathbf{F}\neg\neg f \Leftrightarrow \mathbf{F}f$$
$$(C2) \vdash \mathbf{G}(f \Rightarrow g) \Rightarrow (\mathbf{G}f \Rightarrow \mathbf{G}g)$$
$$(C3) \vdash \mathbf{G}f \Rightarrow (f \wedge \mathbf{X}f \wedge \mathbf{X}\mathbf{G}f)$$
$$(C4) \vdash \mathbf{X}\neg f \Leftrightarrow \neg\mathbf{X}f$$
$$(C5) \vdash \mathbf{X}(f \Rightarrow g) \Rightarrow (\mathbf{X}f \Rightarrow \mathbf{X}g)$$
$$(C6) \vdash \mathbf{G}(f \Rightarrow \mathbf{X}f) \Rightarrow (f \Rightarrow \mathbf{G}f)$$
$$(C7) \vdash (f\mathbf{U}g) \Leftrightarrow (g \vee (f \wedge \mathbf{X}(f\mathbf{U}g)))$$
$$(C8) \vdash (f\mathbf{U}g) \Rightarrow \mathbf{F}g$$
$$(C9) \vdash \mathbf{A}(f \Rightarrow g) \Rightarrow (\mathbf{A}f \Rightarrow \mathbf{A}g)$$
$$(C10) \vdash \mathbf{A}f \Rightarrow \mathbf{A}\mathbf{A}f \qquad (C11) \vdash \mathbf{A}f \Rightarrow f$$
$$(C12) \vdash f \Rightarrow \mathbf{A}\mathbf{E}f \qquad (C13) \vdash \mathbf{A}\neg f \Leftrightarrow \neg\mathbf{E}f$$
$$(C14) \vdash p \Rightarrow \mathbf{A}p \qquad (C15) \vdash \mathbf{A}\mathbf{X}f \Rightarrow \mathbf{X}\mathbf{A}f$$
$$(LC) \vdash \mathbf{A}\mathbf{G}(\mathbf{E}f \Rightarrow \mathbf{E}\mathbf{X}((\mathbf{E}g)\mathbf{U}(\mathbf{E}f))) \Rightarrow (\mathbf{E}f \Rightarrow \mathbf{E}\mathbf{G}((\mathbf{E}g)\mathbf{U}(\mathbf{E}f)))$$
$$(AA) \frac{\vdash \theta \Rightarrow \psi}{\vdash \psi} \; C$$

Fig. 4. An Axiomatization of CTL*

C in the inference rule (AA) is too complicated to formulate in our current formalization. The other axiom schemata but $(C1)$ are proved in the default CoQ environment. The axiom schema $(C1)$, apparently, requires classical reasoning and is proved by importing the Classical theory.

7   Conclusion and Future Work

A modular formalization of CTL* is presented in the paper. The formalization subsumes prior works of PTL and CTL. We have succeeded in proving validity and soundness of an axiomatization of PTL formally. For the branching-time temporal logics UB, CTL, and CTL*, almost all validity of axiom schemata and soundness of inference rules have also been established in the new formalization. Furthermore, the modularity of our formalization allows to be instantiated for different security models, provided they satisfy certain assumptions. Theorems proved in this paper are reusable in any instantiation.

One possible way to resolve the difficulties in the validity of the axiom schemata $(E4)$ in UB, (LC) in CTL*, and the soundness of the inference rule $(R3)$ in CTL is by *strong specification* [2]. We are working on a new formalization based on strong specification to address the problem. For the syntactic side condition of the inference rule (AA) in CTL*, a formalization with syntactic representations of CTL* formulae would be necessary. A generalized version of the deep embedding of CTL* in [17] could be useful in formulating the side condition in (AA).

Acknowledgment. We would like to thank Yih-Kuen Tsay and anonymous reviewers for their constructive comments in improving the paper.

References

1. Bauer, G.: Some properties of CTL. Technische Universität München, Isabelle/Isar document (2001)
2. Bertot, Y., Castéran, P.: Interactive Theorem Proving and Program Development – Coq'Art: The Calculus of Inductive Constructions. In: Texts in Theoretical Computer Science, Springer, Heidelberg (2004)
3. Coupet-Grimal, S.: An axiomatization of linear temporal logic in the calculus of inductive constructions. Logic and Computation 13(6), 801–813 (2003)
4. Emerson, E.: Temporal and modal logic. In: van Leeuwen, J. (ed.) Handbook of Theoretical Computer Science, vol. B, pp. 995–1072. Elsevier Science Publishers (1990)
5. Emerson, E., Halpern, J.: Decision procedures and expressiveness in the temporal logic of branching time. Journal of Computer and System Sciences 30, 1–24 (1985)
6. Kröger, F.: Temporal Logic of Programs. Springer, Heidelberg (1987)
7. Lamport, L.: The temporal logic of actions. ACM Transactions on Programming Languages and Systems 16(3), 872–923 (1994)
8. Manolios, P.: Mu-calculus model-checking. In: Computer-Aided Reasoning: ACL2 Case Studies, pp. 93–111. Kluwer Academic Publishers, Dordrecht (2000)

9. Merz, S.: Isabelle/TLA. Technische Universität München, Isabelle/Isar document (1998)
10. Miculan, M.: On the formalization of the modal μ-calculus in the calculus of inductive constructions. Information and Computation 164(1), 199–231 (2001)
11. Müller, O., Nipkow, T.: Combining model checking and deduction for I/O-automata. In: Brinksma, E., Steffen, B., Cleaveland, W.R., Larsen, K.G., Margaria, T. (eds.) TACAS 1995. LNCS, vol. 1019, pp. 1–16. Springer, Heidelberg (1995)
12. Müller, O.: I/O automata and beyond - temporal logic and abstraction in Isabelle. In: Grundy, J., Newey, M. (eds.) Theorem Proving in Higher Order Logics. LNCS, vol. 1479, pp. 331–348. Springer, Heidelberg (1998)
13. Müller, O.: A Verification Environment for I/O Automata Based on Formalized Meta-Theory. PhD thesis, Technische Universität München (1998)
14. Müller, O., Nipkow, T.: Traces of I/O automata in Isabelle/HOLCF. In: Bidoit, M., Dauchet, M. (eds.) CAAP 1997, FASE 1997, and TAPSOFT 1997. LNCS, vol. 1214, pp. 580–595. Springer, Heidelberg (1997)
15. Reynolds, M.: An axiomatization of full computation tree logic. Journal of Symbolic Logic 66(3), 1011–1057 (2001)
16. Sprenger, C.: A verified model checker for the modal μ-calculus in Coq. In: Steffen, B. (ed.) ETAPS 1998 and TACAS 1998. LNCS, vol. 1384, pp. 167–183. Springer, Heidelberg (1998)
17. Tsai, M.H., Wang, B.Y.: Modular formalization of reactive modules and CTL* in Coq. submitted for publication (2006)
18. Yu, S., Luo, Z.: Implementing a model checker for LEGO. In: Fitzgerald, J., Jones, C.B., Lucas, P. (eds.) FME 1997. LNCS, vol. 1313, pp. 442–458. Springer, Heidelberg (1997)
19. Zhang, X., Parisi-Presicce, F., Sandhu, R.: Formal model and policy specification of usage control. ACM Transactions on Information and System Security 8(4), 351–387 (2005)

Inferring Disjunctive Postconditions

Corneliu Popeea and Wei-Ngan Chin

Department of Computer Science, National University of Singapore
{corneliu,chinwn}@comp.nus.edu.sg

Abstract. Polyhedral analysis [9] is an abstract interpretation used for automatic discovery of invariant linear inequalities among numerical variables of a program. Convexity of this abstract domain allows efficient analysis but also loses precision via convex-hull and widening operators. To selectively recover the loss of precision, sets of polyhedra (disjunctive elements) may be used to capture more precise invariants. However a balance must be struck between precision and cost.

We introduce the notion of affinity to characterize how closely related is a pair of polyhedra. Finding related elements in the polyhedron (base) domain allows the formulation of precise hull and widening operators lifted to the disjunctive (powerset extension of the) polyhedron domain. We have implemented a modular static analyzer based on the disjunctive polyhedral analysis where the relational domain and the proposed operators can progressively enhance precision at a reasonable cost.

1   Introduction

Abstract interpretation [7, 8] is a technique for approximating a basic analysis, with a refined analysis that sacrifices precision for speed. Abstract interpretation relates the two analyses using a Galois connection between the two corresponding property lattices. The framework of abstract interpretation has been used to automatically discover program invariants. For example, numerical invariants can be discovered by using numerical abstract domains like the interval domain [6] or the polyhedron domain [9]. Such convex domains are efficient and their elements represent conjunctions of linear inequality constraints.

Abstract domains can be designed incrementally based on other abstract domains. The powerset extension of an abstract domain [8, 12] refines the abstract domain by adding elements that allow disjunctions to be represented precisely. Unfortunately, analyses using powerset domains can be exponentially more expensive compared to analyses on the base domain. One well-known approach to control the number of disjuncts during analysis is to use a powerset domain where the number of disjuncts is syntactically bounded. In this setting, the challenge is to find appropriate disjuncts that can be merged without (evident) losses in precision. Recently, a technique for disjunctive static analysis has been proposed and implemented [24]. The analysis is formulated for a generic numerical domain and an heuristic function based on the Hausdorff distance is used to merge related disjuncts. Besides combining related disjuncts, another difficulty

M. Okada and I. Satoh (Eds.): ASIAN 2006, LNCS 4435, pp. 331–345, 2007.
© Springer-Verlag Berlin Heidelberg 2007

in designing a disjunctive abstract domain is to define a precise and convergent widening operator.

In this paper, we develop a novel technique for *selective hulling* to obtain precise fixed points via disjunctive inference. Our framework uses a fixed point algorithm guided by an affinity measure to find and combine disjuncts that are related. We also develop a precise widening operator on the powerset domain by using a similar affinity measure. We have built a prototype system to show the utility of the inferred postconditions and the potential for tradeoff between precision and analysis cost.

This paper is organized as follows: an overview of our method with a running example is presented in Sect. 2. Section 3 introduces our source language and a set of reasoning rules that collect a (possibly recursive) constraint abstraction from each method/loop to be analyzed. Those recursive constraint abstractions are subjected to the disjunctive fixed point analysis based on selective hulling and widening as described in Sect. 4. Our implementation and experimental results are presented in Sect. 5. Section 6 presents related work, while Sect. 7 concludes.

2   Overview

To provide an overview of our method, we will consider the following example. This program computes the index l of a specific element in an array of size N. The array contents has been abstracted out and only the updates to the index variables l and x have been retained. The call to the method *randBool* abstracts whether the current element indexed by x is found to satisfy the search criterion. Whenever the criterion is satisfied, the index variable l is updated, as well as the boolean

```
x:=0;upd:=False;
while (x < N) do {
  if (randBool()) then {
    l:=x;upd:=True
  } else { () };
  x:=x+1 }
```

flag *upd*. An assertion at the end of the loop could check that, whenever an element has been found (*upd=true*), its index l is a valid index of the array ($0 \leq l < N$). The aim of our static analysis is to infer disjunctive invariants that can help prove such properties.

A static analysis can be formulated as a *state-based* analysis: guided by the program state at the beginning of the loop, it computes the loop postcondition as a program state approximation [9, 13, 24]. As an alternative, our method is related to *trace-based* analysis [4] and computes the loop summary as a transition from the prestate (before the loop) to the poststate (after the loop body).

Our analysis is formulated in two stages. Firstly, it collects a constraint abstraction from the method/loop body to be analyzed. This abstraction can be viewed as an intermediate form and is related to the constraint abstraction introduced in [14]. As a second step, an iterating process will find the fixed point for the constraint abstraction function.

For the running example, the constraint abstraction named *wh* represents the input-output relation between the loop prestate (in terms of X, the unprimed variables x, N, l, upd) and the loop poststate (in terms of X', the primed variables x', N', l', upd').

$$wh(X, X') :- \;((nochange(X) \wedge x'{<}N')\circ_{\{l,upd\}}$$
$$(l'{=}x \wedge upd'{=}1 \vee nochange(l, upd))\circ_{\{x\}}$$
$$(x'{=}x{+}1)\circ_X wh(X, X'))$$
$$\vee\;(nochange(X) \wedge x'{\geq}N')$$

The *nochange* operator is a special transition where original and primed variables are made equal: $nochange(\{\}) =_{df} \mathtt{true}$; $nochange(\{x\}\cup X) =_{df} (x'{=}x)\wedge nochange(X)$. The composition operator $(\phi_1 \circ_W \phi_2)$ is left-associative and composes the input-output relations ϕ_1 and ϕ_2 updating W variables as specified by ϕ_2 formula. Formally, given ϕ_1, ϕ_2, and the set of variables to be updated $X{=}\{x_1, \ldots, x_n\}$, the composition operator $\circ_X$ is defined as:

$$\phi_1 \circ_X \phi_2 =_{df} \exists\, r_1..r_n \cdot \rho_1\,\phi_1 \wedge \rho_2\,\phi_2$$
$$\text{where } r_1, \ldots, r_n \text{ are fresh variables; } \rho_1 = [x'_i \mapsto r_i]_{i=1}^n$$
$$; \rho_2 = [x_i \mapsto r_i]_{i=1}^n$$

Note that ρ_1 and ρ_2 are substitutions that link each latest value of x'_i in ϕ_1 with the corresponding initial value x_i in ϕ_2 via a fresh variable r_i.

With these two operators, the effects of the loop sub-expressions are composed to obtain the effect of the entire loop body. The 1st line of the constraint abstraction corresponds to the loop test that is satisfied. The 2nd line stands for the body of the conditional expression from the loop. Note that the boolean constants *False* and *True* are modeled as integers 0 and 1. The 3rd line represents the assignment that increments x by 1 composed with the effect of subsequent loop iterations (the occurrence of the wh constraint abstraction). The 4th and last line stands for the possibility that the loop test is not satisfied.

After some simplifications, the constraint abstraction reduces to:

$$wh(X, X') :- \exists X_1 \cdot (\; (x_1{=}x{+}1 \wedge N_1{=}N \wedge l_1{=}x \wedge upd_1{=}1 \wedge wh(X_1, X'))$$
$$\vee\; (x_1{=}x{+}1 \wedge N_1{=}N \wedge l_1{=}l \wedge upd_1{=}upd \wedge wh(X_1, X'))$$
$$\vee\; (x'{=}x \wedge N'{=}N \wedge l'{=}l \wedge upd'{=}upd \wedge x'{\geq}N'))$$

where X_1 denotes the local variables (x_1, N_1, l_1, upd_1).

The analysis goal is then to compute a fixed point approximation for the constraint abstraction function. This function takes as argument a transition depending on X, X' and its result is also expressed as a transition dependent on the same variables. Both transitions can either be approximated by polyhedra or, more precisely, by sets of polyhedra. The first case is akin to the polyhedral analysis from [9] and is reviewed next. For the second case, we will use our running example to show how to compute a disjunctive loop postcondition.

2.1   Computing Fixed Points in the Polyhedron Abstract Domain

We briefly review the method based on Kleene's fixed point iteration applied to the polyhedron abstract domain. Let $(\mathcal{L}, \leq)$ be a complete lattice, and denote by $(\mathcal{P}, \Rightarrow)$ the lattice of polyhedra. We write $\bot$ for its least element (in $\mathcal{P}$, the empty polyhedron or its representation, the formula false), and $\top$ for its greatest element (in $\mathcal{P}$, the entire n-dimensional space or its representation, the formula true). The meet and join operations in the lattice of polyhedra are, respectively, the set intersection and the convex polyhedral hull, the latter being denoted by $\oplus$. A function f that is a self-map of a complete lattice is monotone if $x \leq y$ implies $f(x) \leq f(y)$. In particular, the constraint abstraction functions derived by our analysis are monotone self-maps of the (powerset) polyhedra lattice.

The least fixed point of a monotone function f can be obtained by computing the ascending chain $f_0 = \perp$, $f_{n+1} = f(f_n)$, with $n \geq 0$. If the chain becomes stationary, i.e., if $f_m = f_{m+1}$ for some m, then f_m is the least fixed point of f. In the case of a lattice infinite in height (as the lattice of polyhedra), an ascending chain may be infinite, and a widening operator must be used to ensure convergence. A widening operator ∇ is a binary operator to ensure that the iteration sequence $f_0 = \perp$, $f_{k+1} = f(f_k)$ followed by $f_{n+1} = f_n \nabla f(f_n)$, with $n > k$, converges. In this case, the limit of the sequence is known as a *post fixed point* of f. A post fixed point is a sound approximation of the least fixed point, and the criterion to verify that x is a post fixed point for f is that $x \geq f(x)$. For the polyhedron domain, the standard widening operator was introduced in [9]. Intuitively, the result of the widening $\phi_1 \nabla \phi_2$ is obtained by removing from ϕ_1 those conjuncts that are not satisfied by the next iteration ϕ_2.

For our running example, the fixed point iteration starts with the least element of the abstract domain represented by the *false* formula. The first approximation wh_1 is a transition formula that considers that the loop test fails and the loop body is never executed:

$$wh_1 :- (x'=x \wedge N'=N \wedge l'=l \wedge upd'=upd \wedge x' \geq N')$$

The next iteration is a three-disjunct formula that cannot be represented in the polyhedron domain. An approximation for the disjunctive formula is computed using the convex hull operator. A disjunctive formula can be viewed as a set of disjuncts: $\phi = \vee_{i=1}^n d_i = \{d_i\}_{i=1}^n$. Operators on these disjuncts could be used either infixed or prefixed. For example, given $\phi = d_1 \vee d_2$ then $\oplus \phi = \oplus \{d_1, d_2\} = d_1 \oplus d_2$.

$$
\begin{aligned}
wh_2 :- \ & (x'=x+1 \wedge N'=N \wedge l'=x \wedge upd'=1 \wedge x' \geq N') \\
& \vee (x'=x+1 \wedge N'=N \wedge l'=l \wedge upd'=upd \wedge x' \geq N') \\
& \vee (x'=x \wedge N'=N \wedge l'=l \wedge upd'=upd \wedge x' \geq N') \\
wh_2' :- \ & \oplus wh_2 = (x \leq x' \leq x+1 \wedge N'=N \wedge x' \geq N) \\
wh_3' :- \ & \oplus wh_3 = (x \leq x' \leq x+2 \wedge N'=N \wedge x' \geq N)
\end{aligned}
$$

The iterating sequence will not converge since the inequality $x' \leq x$ will be translated at the following iterations into $x' \leq x+1$, $x' \leq x+2$ and so on. Convergence is ensured by the widening operator which simplifies as follows:

$$wh_3'' :- wh_2' \nabla wh_3' = (x \leq x' \wedge N'=N \wedge x' \geq N)$$

This result proves to be a post fixed point for the wh function. However, the result is rather imprecise as it does not capture any information about the value of l or the flag upd at the end of the loop. Intuitively, such information was present in wh_2 and wh_3, but approximated by the convex hull operator to obtain wh_2' and wh_3'. Next, we outline a method to compute disjunctive fixed points able to capture this kind of information.

2.2 Computing Fixed Points in a Disjunctive Abstract Domain

The two ingredients that we use to compute disjunctive fixed points are counterparts to the convex hull and widening operators from the conjunctive case. Both operators ensure a bound on the number of disjuncts allowed in the formulae.

We first propose a *selective hull* operator $\oplus_m$ parameterized by a constant m that takes as argument a disjunctive formula and collapses these disjuncts into a result with at most m disjuncts. The crux of this operator is an affinity measure to choose the two most related (affine) disjuncts from a disjunctive formula. Formally, given $\phi = \vee_{i=1}^n d_i$, and let d_i, d_j be the most related disjuncts as determined by their affinity, we define the selective hull operator as follows:

$$\oplus_m \phi =_{df} if\ n \leq m\ then\ \phi$$
$$else\ \oplus_m (\phi \setminus \{d_i, d_j\} \cup \{d_i \oplus d_j\})$$

Note that the convex hull operator from the polyhedron domain $\oplus$ is equivalent to $\oplus_1$ since it reduces its disjunctive argument to a conjunctive formula with one disjunct. The affinity function aims to quantify how close is the approximation $d_1 \oplus d_2$ from the disjunctive formula $d_1 \vee d_2$. Intuitively, it works by counting the number of inequalities (planes in the n-dimensional space) from the disjunctive formula that are preserved in the approximation $d_1 \oplus d_2$. Since it counts the number of inequalities (relations between variables), the affinity function is able to handle the relational information captured by the formulae in the polyhedron domain.

As an example, consider wh_2 and wh_3 obtained previously. The results of selective hull with m=3 the bound on the number of disjuncts are as follows:

$wh_2''' :- \oplus_3 wh_2 = wh_2$
$wh_3''' :- \oplus_3 wh_3 = (x \leq x' \leq x+2 \wedge N'=N \wedge x \leq l' \leq x+2 \wedge upd'=1 \wedge x+2 \geq N)$
$\qquad \vee (x \leq x' \leq x+2 \wedge N'=N \wedge l'=l \wedge upd'=upd \wedge x+2 \geq N)$
$\qquad \vee (x'=x \wedge N'=N \wedge l'=l \wedge upd'=upd \wedge x \geq N)$

The second operator needed in the disjunctive abstract domain is a widening operator. We propose a similar affinity measure to find related disjuncts for pairwise widening. For the two disjunctive formulae $wh_2''' = (d_1 \vee d_2 \vee d_3)$ and $wh_3''' = (e_1 \vee e_2 \vee e_3)$, the most affine pairs will distribute the widening operator:

$wh_2''' \nabla_3 wh_3''' :- (d_1 \vee d_2 \vee d_3) \nabla_3 (e_1 \vee e_2 \vee e_3) = (d_1 \nabla e_1) \vee (d_2 \nabla e_3) \vee (d_3 \nabla e_3)$
$\qquad = (x'=N \wedge N'=N \wedge x \leq l' \leq N \wedge upd'=1)$
$\qquad \vee (x'=N \wedge N'=N \wedge l'=l \wedge upd'=upd \wedge x \leq N)$
$\qquad \vee (x'=x \wedge N'=N \wedge l'=l \wedge upd'=upd \wedge x > N)$

This result proves to be a post fixed point for the wh function in the powerset domain. The first disjunct captures the updates to the variable l, thus l' can safely be used as an index for the array of size N. The last two disjuncts capture the cases where, either the loop was executed but the *then* branch of the conditional has never been taken ($x{\leq}N \wedge upd'{=}upd$), or the loop has not been executed ($x{>}N$).

Note that our disjunctive fixed point computation works not only for loops, but also for general recursion. Our analysis also supports mutual recursion where fixed points are computed simultaneously for multiple constraint abstraction functions.

Since the computed fixed point represents a transition, the analysis does not rely on a fixed initial state and can be implemented in a modular fashion. While modular analysis may expose more disjuncts (because no information is assumed about the initial state) and benefits more from our approach, disjunctive analysis has been shown to be also useful for global static analyses [13, 24].

3   Forward Reasoning Rules

We propose a set of forward reasoning rules for collecting a constraint abstraction for each method/loop. Some primitive methods may lack a method body and be given instead a formula ϕ: the given formula may include a safety precondition (for example, bound checks for array operations), or simply represent the input-output relation (for primitive numerical operations like *add* or *multiply*). The reasoning process is modular, starting with the methods at the bottom of the call graph.

For simplicity, we shall use an imperative language with minimal features, as given in Fig. 1. We use *meth* for method declaration, t for type, and e for expression. This language is expression-oriented and uses a normalised form for which only variables are allowed as arguments to a method call or a conditional test. A preprocessor can transform arbitrarily

$$
\begin{array}{ll}
P & ::= meth^* \\
meth & ::= t\ mn\ (([\mathbf{ref}]\ t\ v)^*)\ \mathbf{where}\ \phi\ \{e\} \\
t & ::= \mathbf{bool}\ |\ \mathbf{int}\ |\ \mathbf{void} \\
k & ::= \mathbf{true}\ |\ \mathbf{false}\ |\ k^{\mathbf{int}}\ |\ () \\
e & ::= v\ |\ k\ |\ v{:=}e\ |\ e_1;e_2\ |\ mn(v^*)\ |\ t\ v\ ;\ e \\
 & \quad |\ \mathbf{if}\ v\ \mathbf{then}\ e_1\ \mathbf{else}\ e_2\ |\ \mathbf{while}\ v\ \mathbf{do}\ e \\
\phi & ::= s_1{=}s_2\ |\ s_1{\leq}s_2\ |\ \phi_1{\wedge}\phi_2\ |\ \phi_1{\vee}\phi_2\ |\ \exists v{\cdot}\phi \\
s & ::= k^{\mathbf{int}}\ |\ v\ |\ v'\ |\ k^{\mathbf{int}} * s\ |\ s_1 + s_2
\end{array}
$$

Fig. 1. Simple imperative language

nested arguments to this core language form. Pass-by-reference parameters are declared for each method via the **ref** keyword, while the other parameters from $\{v^*\}$ are passed-by-value. For simplicity, we disallow aliasing amongst pass-by-reference parameters. This restriction is easily enforced in our simple language by ensuring that such arguments at each call site are distinct variables.

The constraint language defined by ϕ is based on Presburger arithmetic. Our framework can accommodate either a richer sublanguage for better expressivity or a more restricted sublanguage (e.g. weakly relational difference constraints [20]) for better performance. We shall assume that a type-checker exists to ensure that expressions and constraints used in a program are well-typed.

The rule [**METH**] associates each method mn with a constraint abstraction of the same name. Namely, $mn(v^*, w^*) :- \phi$, where v^* covers the input parameters,

$$
\begin{array}{cc}
\underline{[\textbf{CONST}]} & \underline{[\textbf{VAR}]} \\
\dfrac{\phi_1 = (\phi \wedge \textbf{res}=k)}{\vdash \{\phi\}\, k\, \{\phi_1\}} & \dfrac{\phi_1 = (\phi \wedge \textbf{res}=v')}{\vdash \{\phi\}\, v\, \{\phi_1\}}
\end{array}
\qquad
\underline{[\textbf{ASSIGN}]} \\[2mm]
\dfrac{\vdash \{\phi\}\, e\, \{\phi_1\} \quad \phi_2 = \exists \textbf{res}\cdot(\phi_1 \circ_{\{v\}} v'=\textbf{res})}{\vdash \{\phi\}\, v{:=}e\, \{\phi_2\}}
$$

$$
\underline{[\textbf{IF}]} \qquad\qquad \underline{[\textbf{SEQ}]}
$$

$$
\underline{[\textbf{BLK}]} \qquad
\dfrac{\vdash \{\phi \wedge v'=1\}\, e_1\, \{\phi_1\}}{\vdash \{\phi \wedge v'=0\}\, e_2\, \{\phi_2\}} \qquad
\dfrac{\vdash \{\phi\}\, e_1\, \{\phi_1\}}{\vdash \{\exists \textbf{res}\cdot\phi_1\}\, e_2\, \{\phi_2\}}
$$

$$
\dfrac{\vdash \{\phi\}\, e\, \{\phi_1\}}{\vdash \{\phi\}\, t\ v;\ e\, \{\exists v'\cdot\phi_1\}} \qquad
\dfrac{}{\vdash \{\phi\}\, \textbf{if}\ v\ \textbf{then}\ e_1\ \textbf{else}\ e_2\, \{\phi_1 \vee \phi_2\}} \qquad
\dfrac{}{\vdash \{\phi\}\, e_1; e_2\, \{\phi_2\}}
$$

$$
\underline{[\textbf{CALL}]} \qquad\qquad \underline{[\textbf{WHILE}]}
$$

$$
\begin{array}{c}
W = \{v_i\}_{i=1}^{m-1} \quad distinct(W) \\
t_0\ mn((\textbf{ref}\ t_i\ v_i)_{i=1}^{m-1}, (t_i\ v_i)_{i=m}^{n}) \\
\textbf{where}\ \phi_{po}\ \{...\}
\end{array}
\qquad
\begin{array}{c}
X = freevars(v,e) \quad \vdash \{nochange(X) \wedge v'=1\}\, e\, \{\phi_1\} \\
\phi_2 = (\phi_1 \circ_X wh(X,X')) \vee (nochange(X) \wedge v'=0) \\
Q = \{wh(X,X') :\text{-}\ \phi_2\} \quad \phi_{po} = fix(Q)
\end{array}
$$

$$
\dfrac{}{\vdash \{\phi\}\, mn(v_1..v_n)\, \{\phi \circ_W \phi_{po}\}} \qquad
\dfrac{}{\vdash \{\phi\}\, \textbf{while}\ v\ \textbf{do}\ e\, \{\phi \circ_X \phi_{po}\} \Rightarrow \phi_{po}}
$$

Fig. 2. Forward reasoning rules

while w^* covers the method's output **res** and the primed variables from pass-by-reference parameters. The fixed point analysis outlined in the previous section is invoked by $fix(Q)$ and returns ϕ_{po}, the input-output relation of the method. To derive suitable postconditions, we shall subject each method declaration to the following rule:

$$
\underline{[\textbf{METH}]}
$$

$$
\dfrac{\begin{array}{c} W = \{v_i\}_{i=1}^{n} \quad V = \{v_i'\}_{i=m}^{n} \quad \vdash \{nochange(W)\}\, e\, \{\phi\} \\ X = \{v_1,..,v_n, \textbf{res}, v_1',..,v_{m-1}'\} \quad Q = \{mn(X) :\text{-}\ \exists V\cdot\phi\} \quad \phi_{po} = fix(Q) \end{array}}{\vdash t_0\ mn((\textbf{ref}\ t_i\ v_i)_{i=1}^{m-1}, (t_i\ v_i)_{i=m}^{n})\ \textbf{where}\ mn(X)\{e\} \Rightarrow \phi_{po}}
$$

The inference uses a set of Hoare-style forward reasoning rules of the form $\vdash \{\phi_1\}\, e\, \{\phi_2\}$. Given a transition ϕ_1 from the beginning of the current method/loop to the prestate before e's evaluation, the judgement will derive ϕ_2, a transition from the beginning of the current method/loop to the poststate after e's evaluation. A special variable **res** is used to denote the result of method declaration as well as that of the current expression under program analysis.

In Fig. 2, the [**ASSIGN**] rule captures imperative updates with the help of the prime notation. The [**SEQ**] rule captures flow-sensitivity, while the [**IF**] rule captures path-sensitivity. The [**CALL**] rule accumulates the effect of the callee postcondition using $\phi \circ_W \phi_{po}$. This rule postpones the checking of the callee precondition to a later stage. The two rules [**METH**] and [**WHILE**] compute a postcondition (indicated to the right of the $\Rightarrow$ operator) which will be inserted in the code and used subsequently in the verification rules. The result of these rules is a definition for each constraint abstraction. As an example, consider:

```
void mnA(ref int x, int n) where (mnA(x,n,x'))
  { if x>n then x:=x-1;mnA(x,n) else () }
```

After applying the forward reasoning rules, we obtain the following constraint abstraction:

$$mnA(x, n, x') :- (x{>}n{\wedge}(\exists x1{\cdot}x1{=}x{-}1{\wedge}mnA(x1, n, x'))){\vee}(x{\leq}n{\wedge}x'{=}x)$$

Note that the forward rules can be used to capture the postcondition of any recursive method, not just for tail-recursive loops. For example, consider the following recursive method:

$$int\ mnB(int\ x)\ where\ (mnB(x, res))\ \{\ if\ x{\leq}0\ then\ 1\ else\ x{:}{=}x{-}1; 2{+}mnB(x)\ \}$$

Applying forward reasoning rules will yield the following constraint abstraction:

$$mnB(x, res) :- (x{\leq}0{\wedge}res{=}1){\vee}(x{>}0{\wedge}(\exists x1, r1{\cdot}x1{=}x{-}1{\wedge}mnB(x1, r1){\wedge}res{=}2{+}r1))$$

The next step is to apply fixed point analysis on each *recursive* constraint abstraction. By applying disjunctive fixed point analysis, we can obtain:

$$mnB(x, res) :- (x{\leq}0{\wedge}res{=}1){\vee}(x{\geq}0{\wedge}res{=}2{*}x{+}1)$$

Once a closed-form formula has been derived, we shall return to checking the validity of preconditions that were previously skipped. The rules for verifying preconditions are similar to the forward rules for postcondition inference, with the exception of three rules, namely:

$$\frac{\begin{array}{c} t_0\ mn((\text{ref}\ t_i\ v_i)_{i=1}^{m-1}, (t_i\ v_i)_{i=m}^{n})\ \textbf{where}\ \phi_{po} \\ W{=}\{v_i\}_{i=1}^{m-1} \quad Z{=}\{\text{res}, v_1', .., v_{m-1}'\} \\ \phi_{pr}{=}\exists Z{\cdot}\phi_{po} \quad \phi \implies [v_i{\mapsto}v_i']_{i=1}^{n}\phi_{pr} \end{array}}{\vdash \{\phi\}\ mn(v_1..v_n)\ \{\phi \circ_W \phi_{po}\}} \quad [\textbf{VERIFY\,–\,CALL}]$$

$$\frac{\begin{array}{c} X = \textit{freevars}(v,e) \quad \rho = X{\mapsto}X' \\ \phi_{pr} = \exists X'{\cdot}\phi_2 \quad \phi \implies \rho\phi_{pr} \\ \vdash \{\phi{\wedge}\rho\phi_{pr}\}\ e\ \{\phi'\} \end{array}}{\vdash \{\phi\}\,\textbf{while}\ v\ \textbf{do}\ e\ \textbf{where}\ \phi_2\ \{\phi \circ_X \phi_2\}} \quad [\textbf{VERIFY\,–\,WHILE}]$$

$$\frac{W{=}\{v_i\}_{i=1}^{n} \quad Z{=}\{\text{res}, v_1', .., v_{m-1}'\} \\ \phi_{pr}{=}\exists Z{\cdot}\phi_{po} \quad \vdash \{\phi_{pr}{\wedge}\textit{nochange}(W)\}\ e\ \{\phi\}}{\vdash t_0\ mn((\text{ref}\ t_i\ v_i)_{i=1}^{m-1}, (t_i\ v_i)_{i=m}^{n})\ \textbf{where}\ \phi_{po}\ \{e\}} \quad [\textbf{VERIFY\,–\,METH}]$$

The [**VERIFY–CALL**] rule checks that the precondition of each method call can be verified as *statically safe* by the current program state. If it cannot be proven statically safe, a run-time test will be inserted prior to the call site to guarantee the safety of the precondition during program execution. The precondition derived for recursive methods is meant to be also satisfied recursively. The [**VERIFY–METH**] rule ensures that each of its callees is either statically safe or has a runtime test inserted. The [**VERIFY–WHILE**] rule uses X to denote the free variables appearing in the loop body; the substitution ρ maps the unprimed to primed variables. This rule uses the loop formula ϕ_2 to compute a precondition ϕ_{pr} necessary for the correct execution of the loop body. The precondition is checked for satisfiability using ϕ, the state at the beginning of the loop. We refer to this new set of rules as *forward verification* rules. We define a special class of *totally-safe* programs, as follows:

Definition 1 (Totally-Safe Program). *A method is said to be* totally-safe *if the precondition derived from all calls in its method's body can be verified as statically safe. A program is* totally-safe *if all its methods are totally-safe.*

For each totally-safe program, we can guarantee that it never encounters any runtime error due to unsatisfied preconditions.

4 Computing Disjunctive Fixed Points

Classical fixed point analysis technique in the polyhedron domain [9] attempts to obtain a conjunctive formula result with the help of convex-hull and widening operators. A challenge for disjunctive fixed point inference is to apply *selective hulling* on closely related disjuncts whenever needed.

In this paper, we propose a qualitative measure called *affinity* to determine the suitability of two formulae for hulling. In order to obtain the affinity between two terms ϕ_1 and ϕ_2, we have to compute two main expressions (i) $\phi_{hull} = \phi_1 \oplus \phi_2$ and (ii) $\phi_{diff} = \phi_{hull} \wedge \neg(\phi_1 \vee \phi_2)$. Furthermore, we also require a heuristic function *heur* that indicates how closely related is the approximation $\phi_1 \oplus \phi_2$ from the original formula $\phi_1 \vee \phi_2$. With this, we can formally define the affinity measure using:

Definition 2 (Affinity Measure). *Given a function heur that returns a value in the range 1..99, the affinity measure can be defined as:*
$$affin(\phi_1, \phi_2) =_{df} \text{if } \phi_{diff}=\texttt{false then } 100$$
$$\text{else if } \phi_{hull}=\texttt{true then } 0$$
$$\text{else } heur(\phi_1, \phi_2)$$

The precise extreme (100) indicates that the convex-hull operation is exact without any loss of precision. The imprecise extreme (0) indicates that the convex-hull operation is inexact and yields the weakest possible formula `true`. In between these two extremes, we will use an affinity measure to indicate the closeness of the two terms by returning a value in the range 1..99.

Selective Hull Based on Planar Affinity. The planar affinity measure computes the fraction of planes from the geometrical representation of the original formula that are preserved in the hulled approximation:

Definition 3 (Planar Affinity Measure). *Given two disjuncts ϕ_1, ϕ_2 and the convex-hull approximation $\phi_{hull} = \phi_1 \oplus \phi_2$, we first define the set of conjuncts mset=$\{c \in (\phi_1 \cup \phi_2) \mid \phi_{hull} \Longrightarrow c\}$. The planar affinity measure is shown below:*
$$p\text{-}heur(\phi_1, \phi_2)=_{df}(|mset|/|\phi_1 \cup \phi_2| * 98) + 1$$

The denominator $|\phi_1 \cup \phi_2|$ represents the number of planes corresponding to the original formulae (from both polyhedra ϕ_1 and ϕ_2). Some of these planes are approximated by the hulling process, while others are preserved in the approximation ϕ_{hull}. The number of preserved planes is represented by the cardinality of *mset* and indicates the suitability of the two disjuncts for hulling.

As an example, consider the following disjunctive formula:
$$\phi = (x \leq 0 \wedge x'=x) \vee (x=1 \wedge x'=0) \vee (x=2 \wedge x'=0)$$

Firstly, the three disjuncts (denoted respectively by d_1, d_2 and d_3) are converted to a minimal form. As with other operators on polyhedra (e.g. the standard widening operator from [15]), the minimal form requires that no redundant conjuncts are present and, furthermore, each equality constraint is broken into two corresponding inequalities as follows:
$$d_1 = (x \leq 0 \wedge x' \geq x \wedge x' \leq x)$$
$$d_2 = (x \geq 1 \wedge x \leq 1 \wedge x' \geq 0 \wedge x' \leq 0)$$
$$d_3 = (x \geq 2 \wedge x \leq 2 \wedge x' \geq 0 \wedge x' \leq 0)$$

We compute three affinity values, one for each pair of disjuncts from ϕ. Note that the cardinality of the set of conjuncts $(\phi_1 \cup \phi_2)$ is considered after removing duplicate conjuncts that appear both in ϕ_1 and ϕ_2.

$d_1 \oplus d_2 = (x' \leq x \wedge x' \leq 0 \wedge x' \leq x-1)$ $mset(d_1, d_2) = \{x' \leq x, x \leq 1, x' \leq 0\}$
$\qquad\qquad\qquad\qquad\qquad\qquad\qquad$ $p\text{-}heur(d_1, d_2) = 3/7 * 98 + 1 = 43$

$d_1 \oplus d_3 = (x' \leq x \wedge x' \leq 0 \wedge x' \leq x-2)$ $mset(d_1, d_3) = \{x' \leq x, x \leq 2, x' \leq 0\}$
$\qquad\qquad\qquad\qquad\qquad\qquad\qquad$ $p\text{-}heur(d_1, d_3) = 3/7 * 98 + 1 = 43$

$d_2 \oplus d_3 = (x \geq 1 \wedge x \leq 2 \wedge x' \leq 0 \wedge x' \leq 0)$ $mset(d_2, d_3) = \{x \geq 1, x \leq 2, x' \leq 0, x' \leq 0\}$
$\qquad\qquad\qquad\qquad\qquad\qquad\qquad$ $p\text{-}heur(d_2, d_3) = 4/6 * 98 + 1 = 66$

Based on these affinities, the most related pair of disjuncts is $\{d_2, d_3\}$. The result for selective hull of ϕ will therefore capture a precise relation between x and x':

$$\oplus_2 \phi = \oplus_2 \{d_1, d_2 \oplus d_3\} = (x \leq 0 \wedge x' = x) \vee (x \geq 1 \wedge x \leq 2 \wedge x' = 0)$$

Selective Hull Based on Hausdorff Distance. Related to our affinity measure, Sankaranarayanan et al [24] have recently introduced a heuristic function that uses the Hausdorff distance to measure the distance between the geometrical representations of two disjuncts.

The Hausdorff distance is a commonly used measure of distance between two sets. Given two polyhedra, P and Q, their Hausdorff distance can be defined as: $h\text{-}heur(P, Q) =_{df} max_{x \in P}\{min_{y \in Q}\{d(x, y)\}\}$ where $d(x, y)$ is the Euclidian distance between two points x and y. This heuristic was deemed as hard to compute in [24] and, as an alternative, a range-based Hausdorff heuristic was used.

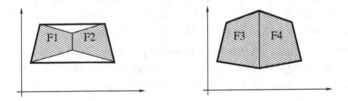

Fig. 3. Pairs of disjuncts with similar Hausdorff distance

Because it reduces the information about variables to non-relational ranges, we can argue that a range-based heuristic is less suitable for a relational abstract domain like the polyhedron domain. Furthermore, we present an intuitive argument why such a distance based heuristic is less appropriate. The pairs of disjuncts $\{F1, F2\}$ and $\{F3, F4\}$ from Fig. 3 may have similar $h\text{-}heur$ values; on the other hand, the affinity based on $p\text{-}heur$ precisely indicates that the second pair $\{F3, F4\}$ is more suited for hulling. In the Sect. 5, we compare these two heuristic functions when inferring postconditions for a suite of benchmark programs.

4.1   Powerset Widening Operator

The standard widening operator for the convex polyhedron domain was introduced in [9]. For disjunctive fixed point inference, a (powerset) widening operator for sets of polyhedra is required. Given two disjunctive formulae ϕ_1 and ϕ_2, the challenge is to find pairs of related disjuncts $\{d_i, e_i\}$ ($d_i \in \phi_1$, $e_i \in \phi_2$) such that the result of widening d_i wrt e_i is as precise as possible.

For this purpose, Bagnara et al [1] introduced a framework to lift a widening operator over a base domain to a widening operator over its powerset domain. The strategy used by the powerset widening based on a connector starts by joining (connecting) elements in ϕ_2 to ensure that each such connected element approximates some element from ϕ_1. Secondly, it chooses related pairs $\{d_i, e_i\}$ based on the logical implication relation, where $d_i \Rightarrow e_i$. Mostly concerned with convergence guarantees for widening operators, the framework from [1] does not give a recipe for defining connector operators able to find related disjuncts. Later, the generic widening operator definition was instantiated for disjunctive polyhedral analysis by Gulavani et al in [13]. However, their proposal uses a connector operator that relies on the ability to find one minimal element from a set of polyhedra. In general, the most precise result cannot be guaranteed by a deterministic algorithm, since the polyhedron domain is partially ordered. To overcome this problem, we propose an affinity measure to find related disjuncts for pairwise widening.

The strategy that we adopt for widening is to choose related pairs $\{d_i, e_i\}$ based on their affinity. After pairwise widening, we subject the result to a selective hull operation provided it contains more disjuncts than ϕ_1. In general, there may be more disjuncts in ϕ_2 than in ϕ_1. A reason for non-convergence of the powerset widening operator is that some element from ϕ_2 is not involved in any widening computation and included unchanged in the result. Our operator (similar to the connector-based widening) distributes each disjunct from the arguments ϕ_1 and ϕ_2 in a widening computation and thus ensures convergence.

Formally, given two disjunctive formulae $\phi_1 = \bigvee_{i=1}^{m} d_i$ and $\phi_2 = \bigvee_{i=1}^{n} e_i$, we define a powerset widening operator ∇_m as follows: $\phi_1 \nabla_m \phi_2 = \oplus_m \{d_i \nabla e_i | d_i \in \phi_1, e_i \in \phi_2\}$, where d_i is the best match for widening e_i as found by the *widen_affin* measure. Similar to the affinity from Def. 2, the widen-affinity aims to find related disjuncts, but proceeds by indicating how closely related is the approximation $\phi_1 \nabla \phi_2$ from the original formula ϕ_1.

$$widen\_affin(\phi_1, \phi_2) = \text{if } (\phi_1 \nabla \phi_2) \wedge \neg \phi_1 = \texttt{false then } 100$$
$$\text{else if } (\phi_1 \nabla \phi_2) = \texttt{true then } 0$$
$$\text{else } heur(\phi_1, \phi_2)$$

The planar affinity measure from Def. 3 can be used for widening, provided we redefine *mset* to relate ϕ_1, ϕ_2 with the approximation $\phi_{widen} = \phi_1 \nabla \phi_2$ as follows:
$$mset = \{c \in (\phi_1 \cup \phi_2) | \phi_{widen} \Rightarrow c\}$$

5   Experiments

We have implemented the proposed inference mechanisms with the goal of analyzing imperative programs. Our implementation includes a pre-processing phase to convert each C-like input program to our core language. The entire prototype system was built using Glasgow Haskell compiler [16] extended with the Omega constraint solving library [23]. Our test platform was a Pentium 3.0 GHz system with 2GBytes main memory, running Fedora 4.

Benchmark Programs	Source (lines)	Recursive constraints	m=1 (secs)	m=2		m=3		m=4		m=5	
				(secs)	post	(secs)	post	(secs)	post	(secs)	post
binary search	31	1	0.44	1.02	1	-	-	-	-	-	-
bubble sort	39	2	0.78	0.89	1	-	-	-	-	-	-
init array	5	1	0.17	0.24	1	-	-	-	-	-	-
merge sort	58	3	1.42	3.39	3	3.76	1	3.91	1	4.48	1
queens	39	2	1.89	2.41	2	2.48	1	-	-	-	-
quick sort	43	2	0.63	1.51	2	1.70	1	-	-	-	-
FFT	336	9	8.24	10.17	5	11.62	3	11.90	1	12.15	1
LU Decomp.	191	10	10.27	13.41	8	14.44	3	-	-	-	-
SOR	84	5	1.46	2.41	3	3.49	1	3.64	1	-	-
Linpack	903	25	28.14	33.23	20	35.04	2	-	-	-	-

Fig. 4. Statistics for postcondition inference. Timings include precondition verification. ("-" signifies a time or post similar to those from the immediate lower value of m).

We tested our system on a set of small programs with challenging recursion, and also the Scimark and Linpack benchmark suites [21, 10]. Figure 4 summarizes the statistics obtained for each program. To quantify the analysis complexity of the benchmark programs, we counted the program size (column 2) and also the number of recursive methods and loops present in each program (column 3).

The main objective for building this prototype was to certify that the disjunctive analysis can be fully automated and that it gives more precise results compared to a conjunctive analysis. To this end, we experimented with different bounds on the number m of disjuncts allowed during fixed point analysis. For each value of m, we measured the analysis time and the number of methods for which the postcondition was *more precise* than using $(m-1)$ disjuncts. For each analyzed program, we detected a *bound* on the value of m: increasing m over this bound does not yield more precision for the formulae. The analysis time remains constant for cases where m is bigger than this bound, therefore the values beyond these bounds are marked with "-". Capturing a precise postcondition for algorithms like binary search, bubble sort, or init array was done with a value of m equal to 2. We found that queens and quick sort require 3 disjuncts, while merge sort can be inferred by making use of 5 disjuncts.

We also evaluated the usefulness of the disjunctive fixed point inference for static array bound check elimination. The results are summarized in the Fig. 5. Column 2 presents the total number of checks (counted statically) that are present in the original programs. Columns 3 and 5 present the number of checks that cannot be proved safe by using conjunctive analysis ($m=1$) and, respectively, disjunctive analysis with $m=5$ and planar affinity. For comparison, column 4 shows results of analysis using the Hausdorff distance heuristic, where the number of checks not proven is greater than using planar affinity.

Using the planar affinity, the two programs bubble sort and init array were proven totally safe with 2-disjunctive analysis. Merge sort and SOR exploited the precision of 4-disjunctive analysis for total check elimination. Even if not all the checks could be proven safe for queens, quick sort, FFT, LU and Linpack benchmarks, the number of potentially unsafe checks decreased gradually, for analyses with higher values of m. As a matter of fact, our focus in this paper was to infer precise postconditions and we relied on a simple mechanism to derive preconditions. To eliminate more checks, we could employ the technique of [3] which is powerful enough to derive sufficient preconditions and eliminate

Benchmark Programs	Static Chks.	Conj. m=1	Haus. m=5	Plan. m=5
binary search	2	2	2	2
bubble sort	12	3	0	0
init array	2	2	0	0
merge sort	24	9	4	0
queens	8	4	2	2
quick sort	20	5	5	1
FFT	62	17	12	5
LU Decomp.	82	42	9	4
SOR	32	15	2	0
Linpack	166	92	65	52

Fig. 5. Statistics for check elimination

all checks in this set of benchmarks [26]. However, we stress that, either kind of prederivation we use, disjunctive analysis is needed for better check elimination.

In general, analysis with higher values for m has the potential of inferring more precise formulae. The downside is that computing the affinities of m disjuncts is an operation with quadratic complexity in terms of m and may become too expensive for higher values of m. In practice, we found that the case ($m=3$) computes formulae sufficiently precise, with a reasonable inference time.

6   Related Work

Our analysis is potentially useful for software verification and for static analyses based on numerical abstract domains.

Program verification may be performed by generating verification conditions, where their validity implies that the program satisfies its safety assertions. Verification condition generators assume that loop invariants are present in the code, either annotated by the user or inferred automatically. Methods for loop invariant inference include the induction-iteration approach [25] and approaches based on predicate abstraction [11, 17]. Leino and Logozzo [18] designed a loop invariant computation that can be invoked on demand when an assertion from the analyzed program fails. The invariant that is inferred satisfies only a subset of the program's executions on which the assertion is encountered. Comparatively, our method infers a disjunctive formula that is valid for all the program's executions, with each disjunct covering some related execution paths. We achieve this modularly, regardless of any subsequent assertions. Thus, our results can be directly used in the inter-procedural setting.

Partitioning of the abstract domain was first introduced in [5]. Recently, Mauborgne and Rival [19] have given strategies for partition creation and demonstrated their feasibility through their use in ASTRÉE static analyzer [2]. Like them, we make the choice of which disjunctions to keep at analysis time. However, the partitioning criterion is different. In their case, the control flow is used to choose which disjunctions to keep. Specifically, a token representing some conditions on the execution flow is attached to a disjunct, and formulae with similar tokens are hulled together. In our case, the partitioning criterion is based on a property of the disjuncts themselves, with the affinity measure aiming to hull together the most closely related disjuncts.

Various abstract numerical domains have been developed for static analysis based on abstract interpretation. The form of invariants to be discovered is determined by the chosen numerical domain: from the interval domain that is able to discover relations of the form ($\pm x \leq c$), to the lattice of polyhedra that represents invariants of the form ($a_1 x_1 + .. + a_n x_n \leq c$), all these abstract domains represent conjunctions of linear inequalities. Our pre/post analysis is formalised in a manner that is independent of the abstract domain used. It can therefore readily benefit from advances in constraint solving techniques for these numerical domains.

7 Conclusion

We have proposed a new method for inferring disjunctive postconditions. Our approach is based on the notion of selective hulling as a means to implement adjustable precision in our analysis. We introduced a simple but novel concept called affinity and showed that planar affinity is superior to a recently introduced method based on Hausdorff distance. We have built a prototype system for disjunctive inference and have proven its correctness in the technical report [22]. Our experiments demonstrate the utility of the disjunctive postconditions for proving a class of runtime checks safe at compile-time, and the potential for tradeoff between precision and analysis cost.

Acknowledgements. This work benefited much from research discussions with Siau-Cheng Khoo and Dana Xu from an earlier project on array bounds inference. The authors would like to acknowledge two donation grants from Microsoft Singapore and Microsoft Research Asia, and the support of A*STAR research grant R-252-000-233-305.

References

[1] Bagnara, R., Hill, P.M., Zaffanella, E.: Widening operators for powerset domains. In: Steffen, B., Levi, G. (eds.) VMCAI 2004. LNCS, vol. 2937, pp. 135–148. Springer, Heidelberg (2004)

[2] Blanchet, B., Cousot, P., Cousot, R., Feret, J., Mauborgne, L., Miné, A., Monniaux, D., Rival, X.: A static analyzer for large safety-critical software. In: PLDI, pp. 196–207 (2003)

[3] Chin, W.-N., Khoo, S.-C., Xu, D.N.: Deriving pre-conditions for array bound check elimination. In: Danvy, O., Filinski, A. (eds.) PADO 2001. LNCS, vol. 2053, pp. 2–24. Springer, Heidelberg (2001)

[4] Colby, C., Lee, P.: Trace-based program analysis. In: POPL, pp. 195–207 (1996)

[5] Cousot, P.: Semantic foundations of program analysis. In: Program Flow Analysis: Theory and Applications (1981)

[6] Cousot, P., Cousot, R.: Static determination of dynamic properties of programs. In: Proceedings of the Second International Symposium on Programming, pp. 106–130 (1976)

[7] Cousot, P., Cousot, R.: Abstract interpretation: A unified lattice model for static analysis of programs by construction or approximation of fixpoints. In: POPL, pp. 238–252 (1977)

[8] Cousot, P., Cousot, R.: Systematic design of program analysis frameworks. In: POPL, pp. 269–282 (1979)

[9] Cousot, P., Halbwachs, N.: Automatic discovery of linear restraints among variables of a program. In: POPL, pp. 84–96 (1978)

[10] Dongarra, J., Luszczek, P., Petitet, A.: The Linpack benchmark: past, present and future. Concurrency and Computation: Practice and Experience 15(9), 803–820 (2003)

[11] Flanagan, C., Qadeer, S.: Predicate abstraction for software verification. In: POPL, pp. 191–202 (2002)

[12] Giacobazzi, R., Ranzato, F.: Optimal domains for disjunctive abstract intepretation. Sci. Comput. Program 32(1-3), 177–210 (1998)

[13] Bhargav, S., Gulavani, B.S., Rajamani, S.K.: Counterexample driven refinement for abstract interpretation. In: Hermanns, H., Palsberg, J. (eds.) TACAS 2006 and ETAPS 2006. LNCS, vol. 3920, Springer, Heidelberg (2006)

[14] Gustavsson, J., Svenningsson, J.: Constraint abstractions. In: PADO, pp. 63–83 (2001)

[15] Halbwachs, N.: Détermination Automatique de Relations Linéaires Vérifiées par les Variables d'un Programme. Thèse de 3ème cycle d'informatique, Université scientifique et médicale de Grenoble, Grenoble, France (March 1979)

[16] Simon, L., Jones, P., et al.: Glasgow Haskell Compiler, http://www.haskell.org/ghc

[17] Shuvendu, K., Lahiri, S.K., Bryant, R.E.: Indexed predicate discovery for unbounded system verification. In: Alur, R., Peled, D.A. (eds.) CAV 2004. LNCS, vol. 3114, pp. 135–147. Springer, Heidelberg (2004)

[18] Rustan, K., Leino, M., Logozzo, F.: Loop invariants on demand. In: Yi, K. (ed.) APLAS 2005. LNCS, vol. 3780, pp. 119–134. Springer, Heidelberg (2005)

[19] Mauborgne, L., Rival, X.: Trace partitioning in abstract interpretation based static analyzers. In: Sagiv, M. (ed.) ESOP 2005. LNCS, vol. 3444, pp. 5–20. Springer, Heidelberg (2005)

[20] Miné, A.: A new numerical abstract domain based on difference-bound matrices. In: Danvy, O., Filinski, A. (eds.) PADO 2001. LNCS, vol. 2053, pp. 155–172. Springer, Heidelberg (2001)

[21] National Institue of Standards and Technology. Java SciMark benchmark for scientific computing, http://math.nist.gov/scimark2/

[22] Popeea, C., Chin, W.-N.: Inferring disjunctive postconditions. Technical report. http://www.comp.nus.edu.sg/$^\sim$corneliu/research/disjunctive.tr.pdf

[23] Pugh, W.: The Omega test: A fast practical integer programming algorithm for dependence analysis. Communications of the ACM 8, 102–114 (1992)

[24] Sankaranarayanan, S., Ivancic, F., Shlyakhter, I., Gupta, A.: Static analysis in disjunctive numerical domains. In: Yi, K. (ed.) SAS 2006. LNCS, vol. 4134, Springer, Heidelberg (2006)

[25] Suzuki, N., Ishihata, K.: Implementation of an array bound checker. In: POPL, pp. 132–143 (1977)

[26] Xu, D.N., Popeea, C., Khoo, S.-C., Chin, W.-N.: A modular type inference and specializer for array bound checks elimination (under preparation). Technical report, http://www.comp.nus.edu.sg/$^\sim$corneliu/research/array.pdf

An Approach to Formal Verification of Arithmetic Functions in Assembly

Reynald Affeldt[1] and Nicolas Marti[2]

[1] Research Center for Information Security,
National Institute of Advanced Industrial Science and Technology
[2] Department of Computer Science, University of Tokyo

Abstract. It is customary to write performance-critical parts of arithmetic functions in assembly: this enables finely-tuned algorithms that use specialized processor instructions. However, such optimizations make formal verification of arithmetic functions technically challenging, mainly because of many bit-level manipulations of data. In this paper, we propose an approach for formal verification of arithmetic functions in assembly. It consists in the implementation in the Coq proof assistant of (1) a Hoare logic for assembly programs augmented with loops and (2) a certified translator to ready-to-run assembly with jumps. To properly handle formal verification of bit-level manipulations of data, we propose an original encoding of machine integers. For concreteness, we use the SmartMIPS assembly language, an extension of the MIPS instruction set for smartcards, and we explain the formal verification of an optimized implementation of the Montgomery multiplication, a de facto-standard for the implementation of many cryptosystems.

1 Introduction

It is customary to write performance-critical parts of arithmetic functions in assembly: this enables finely-tuned algorithms that use specialized processor instructions. However, such optimizations make formal verification of arithmetic functions technically challenging. Indeed, the best algorithms for arithmetic functions usually rely on bit-level manipulations of data, whose properties can be tricky to figure out, especially when it comes to signed integers. But also, the usage of non-standard specialized processor instructions often calls for adequate adjustments of standard handbook algorithms, that may endanger the correctness of the algorithm itself. For these reasons, it is important to provide a concrete way to formally verify such assembly code.

In this paper, we propose an approach for formal verification of arithmetic functions in assembly. Our approach is in two steps. It consists in providing in the Coq proof assistant [3] a certified implementation of (1) a Hoare logic for assembly programs augmented with loops and (2) a certified translator to ready-to-run assembly with jumps. We favor this two-steps approach because a Hoare logic for while-programs is more familiar-looking than non-standard Hoare logics for programs with jumps (such as [12,13]).

M. Okada and I. Satoh (Eds.): ASIAN 2006, LNCS 4435, pp. 346–360, 2007.
© Springer-Verlag Berlin Heidelberg 2007

The Hoare logic we encode enables verification of assembly programs that manipulate machine integers and bounded memory. To cope with machine integers, we implement a library where integers are represented as lists of bits interpreted as unsigned or signed in two's complement notation. This library enables faithful modeling of the hardware circuitry. To cope with bounded memory, we encode the *separation logic* [6] variant of Hoare logic, that extends traditional Hoare logic with a native notion of mutable memory; because we use machine integers to access memory, the accessible range of addresses is natively bounded.

The certified translator ensures that assembled programs behave like the verified programs. Concretely, it injects structured programs (programs with loops) into the more general set of programs with jumps; the correctness of this translation is formally proved in Coq.

For concreteness, we use the SmartMIPS assembly language, an application-specific extension of the MIPS32 4Km processor core that extends the core instruction set with instructions to enhance cryptographic computations and improve the performance of virtual machines [5].

To validate our approach, we show how to formally verify several arithmetic functions, including in particular an optimized implementation of the Montgomery multiplication [2], a de facto-standard for the implementation of many cryptosystems. This verification requires bit-level predicates to specify the usage of carries and overflow flags, for which our Hoare logic turns out to be well-suited.

This paper is organized as follows. In Sect. 2, we explain how we encode machine-integers arithmetic in Coq. In Sect. 3, we explain how we encode separation logic for a subset of SmartMIPS. In Sect. 4, we explain the formal verification of the Montgomery multiplication. In Sect. 5, we explain how to extract ready-to-run SmartMIPS programs from our verifications. In Sect. 6, we review related work. In Sect. 7, we conclude and comment on future work.

2   Machine-Integers Arithmetic

Formal verification of arithmetic functions is usually done w.r.t. high-level mathematical specifications. However, at the level of assembly code, many arithmetic properties of instructions depend on the finiteness of registers and on the physical representation of data. For example, the (signed) integer "-1" appears to be larger than any unsigned (and therefore positive) integer; some instructions trap on integer overflow while others do not, etc. Overlooking such problems often leads to security breaches, most famously integer-overflow bugs (see [11] for illustrations). It is therefore important to provide formal means to define the semantics of instructions together with lemmas that capture their properties in terms of mathematical (i.e., unbounded) integers.

Our approach to encode machine-integers arithmetic is to closely model the hardware circuitry using lists of bits (booleans) to represent the contents of registers and recursive functions to represent the operations on registers. We choose this approach because it is easy to extend with new, specialized instructions, compared to encoding machine integers with, say, sign-magnitude integers modulo.

Example: Hardware Arithmetic Operations We model the hardware addition as a recursive function that does bitwise comparisons and carry propagation:

```
Inductive bit : Set := o : bit | i : bit.
(* addition with LSB first *)
Fixpoint add_lst' (a b:list bit) (carry:bit) : list bit :=
  match (a, b) with
      (o :: a', o :: b') => carry :: add_lst' a' b' o
    | (i :: a', i :: b') => carry :: add_lst' a' b' i
    | (_ :: a', _ :: b') => match carry with
      o => i :: add_lst' a' b' o | i => o :: add_lst' a' b' i end
    | _ => nil
  end.
(* addition with MSB first *)
Definition add_lst a b carry := rev (add_lst' (rev a) (rev b) carry).
```

Most computers distinguish between unsigned integers and signed integers in two's complement notation. The negation of a signed integer is defined using ones' complement and addition:

```
(* bit complement *)
Definition cplt b := match b with i => o | o => i end.
(* ones' complement *)
Fixpoint cplt1 (lst:list bit) : list bit :=
  match lst with nil => nil | hd :: tl => cplt hd :: cplt1 tl end.
(* two's complement *)
Definition cplt2 lst :=
  add_lst (cplt1 lst) (zero_extend_lst (length lst - 1) (i::nil)) o.
```

Using the addition, we further modeled the unsigned multiplication; using two's complement, we further modeled the signed multiplication, and so on.

Physical constraints and implementation choices make hardware arithmetic operations peculiar. Because of the finiteness of registers, they actually implement arithmetic modulo. A list of bits (an:: .. . ::a0) is interpreted as $(a_n \ldots a_0)_2$, the encoding in base 2 of a mathematical integer; but depending on the context, this integer is unsigned, in which case its decimal value is $a_n 2^n + \ldots + a_0$, or signed in two's complement notation, in which case its decimal value is $-a_n 2^n + a_{n-1} 2^{n-1} + \ldots + a_0$. It is customary for assembly code to rely on properties of arithmetic modulo (e.g., to detect overflows) and to freely mix unsigned and signed integers (e.g., to access memory). Precise characterization of the properties of the hardware arithmetic operations w.r.t. their mathematical counterpart is therefore a must-have for formal verification of assembly code.

Example: Overflow Properties of Addition Let us note [[lst]]u (resp. [[lst]]s) the decimal value of the list of bits lst seen as an unsigned (resp. signed) integer. In Coq, these notations are implemented as recursive functions from lists of bits to mathematical integers. The hardware addition behaves like the mathematical addition only when non-overflow conditions are met:

Lemma add_lst_nat : $\forall$ n a b, length a = n $\rightarrow$ length b = n $\rightarrow$
0 $\leq$ [[a]]u + [[b]]u < 2^^n $\rightarrow$ [[add_lst a b o]]u = [[a]]u + [[b]]u.

Lemma add_lst_Z : forall n a b, length a = S n $\rightarrow$ length b = S n $\rightarrow$
-2^^n $\leq$ [[a]]s + [[b]]s < 2^^n $\rightarrow$ [[add_lst a b o]]s = [[a]]s + [[b]]s.

We proved further lemmas that capture the overflow properties of the hardware addition when overflow conditions are *not* met, the correctness of subtraction and multiplications, the relations between unsigned and signed integers, etc.

Because a processor usually manipulates machine integers of different sizes (e.g., to represent constants or contents of special registers such as accumulators), it is cumbersome to use directly lists of bits: the conditions about their lengths clutter formal verification. To simplify our development, we encapsulate all the functions modeling the hardware circuitry and the lemmas capturing their properties in a Coq module that provides an abstract type for machine integers. This abstract type is parameterized by the length of the underlying list of bits: Parameter int : nat $\rightarrow$ Set. This makes the relation between the lengths of the input and the output of operations explicit in the type of hardware operations.

Technically, this abstract type is implemented using dependent pairs: a machine integer of length n is a dependent pair whose first projection is a list of bits lst and whose second projection is the proof that its length is equal to n: Inductive int (n:nat) : Set := mk_int : $\forall$ (lst:list bit), length lst = n $\rightarrow$ int n. An excerpt of the interface of the resulting module is given below:

```
Parameter add : ∀ n, int n → int n → int n.
Notation "a ⊕ b" := (add a b).
Parameter u2Z : ∀ n, int n → Z.   (* lists of bits as unsigned *)
Parameter s2Z : ∀ n, int n → Z.   (* lists of bits as signed *)
Parameter add_u2Z : ∀ n (a b:int n), u2Z a + u2Z b < 2^^n →
  u2Z (a ⊕ b) = u2Z a + u2Z b.
Parameter add_s2Z : ∀ n (a b:int (S n)), -2^^n ≤ s2Z a + s2Z b < 2^^n →
  s2Z (a ⊕ b) = s2Z a + s2Z b.
Parameter Z2u : ∀ n, Z → int n.
Parameter Z2s : ∀ n, Z → int n.
```

Z2u n z (resp. Z2s n z) builds an unsigned (resp. a signed) machine integer of decimal value z and length n (if possible). These two constructors are used to defined constants, such as: Definition four32 := Z2u 32 4.

3   A Hoare Logic for SmartMIPS

In this section, we encode a Hoare logic for a subset of SmartMIPS [5]. For this purpose, the module for machine-integer arithmetic introduced in the previous section is important: it enables faithful encoding of the semantics of arithmetic instructions that trap on overflow and the semantics of memory accesses, that are restricted to finite memory. The subset of SmartMIPS we consider consists of structured programs, i.e., programs whose syntax only allows for sequences and while-loops. Hereafter, we call WhileSMIPS this subset. In Sect. 5, we will certify a translator that injects WhileSMIPS programs into the set of SmartMIPS programs with jumps, that can be directly assembled and run. We favor this two-steps approach is that a Hoare logic for while-programs is more familiar-looking than non-standard Hoare logics for programs with jumps (such as [12,13]).

3.1   States

The state of a SmartMIPS processor is modeled as a tuple of a store of general-purpose registers, a store of control registers, an integer multiplier, and a heap (the mutable memory):

```
Definition state := gpr.store * cp0.store * multiplier.m * heap.h.
```

The module `gpr` is a map from the type `gp_reg` of general-purpose registers to (32-bit) words, the module `cp0` is a map from the type `cp0_reg` of control registers, and `heap` is a map from natural numbers to words. We restrict ourselves to a word-addressable heap because it is all we need for arithmetic functions (see Sect. 4). The module for heap is implemented using a module for finite maps developed in previous work [16]. Let us comment more in detail on the implementation of the `multiplier` module, that makes an extensive use of our module for machine integers.

The SmartMIPS multiplier is a set of registers called ACX, HI, and LO that has been designed to enhance cryptographic computations. HI and LO are 32 bits long; ACX is only known to be at least 8 bits long. We implement the multiplier as an abstract data type m with three lookup functions `acx`, `hi`, and `lo` that return respectively a machine integer of length at least 8 bits and machine integers of length 32. Here follows the corresponding excerpt of the module interface:

```
Parameter acx_size : nat.
Parameter acx_size_min : 8 ≤ acx_size.
Parameter m : Set.
Parameter acx : m → int acx_size.
Parameter lo : m → int 32.
Parameter hi : m → int 32.
Parameter utoZ : m → Z. (* multiplier as an unsigned *)
```

The SmartMIPS instruction set features special instructions to take advantage of the SmartMIPS multiplier. For illustration, let us explain the encoding of the `mflhxu` instruction, that is often used in arithmetic functions: it performs a division of the multiplier by $\beta = 2^{32}$, whose remainder is put in a general-purpose register and whose quotient is left in the multiplier. The corresponding hardware circuitry is essentially a shift: it puts the contents of LO into some general-purpose register, puts the contents of HI into LO, and zeroes ACX. Here is how we model this operation:

```
Definition mflhxu_op m := let (acx', hi') := (acx m, hi m) in
  (Z2u acx_size 0, (zero_extend 24 acx', hi')).
```

What is important for verification is the properties of `mflhxu` w.r.t. the decimal value of the multiplier. Such properties can be derived as lemmas from the definition of `mflhxu_op`. For example, the decimal values of the multiplier before and after `mflhxu` are related as follows (`Zbeta n` stands for $\beta^n = 2^{32n}$):

```
Lemma mflhxu_utoZ : ∀ m, utoZ m = utoZ (mflhxu_op m) * Zbeta 1 + u2Z (lo m).
```

3.2 Axiomatic Semantics

The syntax of WhileSMIPS programs is encoded as the inductive type `cmd`:

```
Definition immediate := int 16.
Inductive cmd : Set :=
  | add : gp_reg → gp_reg → gp_reg → cmd
  | addi : gp_reg → gp_reg → immediate → cmd
  | addiu : gp_reg → gp_reg → immediate → cmd
  | addu : gp_reg → gp_reg → gp_reg → cmd
  | lw : gp_reg → immediate → gp_reg → cmd
  | lwxs : gp_reg → gp_reg → gp_reg → cmd
  | maddu : gp_reg → gp_reg → cmd
  | mflhxu : gp_reg → cmd
  | sw : gp_reg → immediate → gp_reg → cmd
  | seq : cmd → cmd → cmd
  | ifte_beq : gp_reg → gp_reg → cmd → cmd → cmd
  | while_bne : gp_reg → gp_reg → cmd → cmd
  ...
```

Except for control-flow commands (`seq`, `ifte_beq`, `while_bne`, etc.), the type constructors have the same names as their SmartMIPS counterparts. As usual with MIPS, instructions with suffix "u" do not trap on overflow and instructions with prefix "m" use the multiplier. In the excerpt above, SmartMIPS-specific instructions include `lwxs`, that loads words using scaled indexed addressing, and `maddu` and `mflhxu`, that use the ACX register.

The assertion language is an instance of separation logic [6], an extension of Hoare logic with a native notion of heap. We choose separation logic because it is a general solution to represent mutable data structures such as arrays, that are used to represent multi-precision integers in arithmetic functions.

Assertions are encoded as truth-functions from states to `Prop`, the type of predicates in Coq (this technique of encoding is called *shallow embedding*):

```
Definition assert := gpr.store → cp0.store → multiplier.m → heap.h → Prop.
```

Using this type, one can easily encode any first-order predicate. For example, the predicate that is true when variables x and y have the same contents is encoded as follows (`lookup` is a function provided by the interface of stores):

```
Definition x_EQ_y (x y : gp_reg) : assert :=
  fun s _ _ _ => gpr.lookup x s = gpr.lookup y s.
```

To encode separating connectives, we use a module for heaps. In the following, we omit the definitions of heap-related functions: their names and notations are self-explanatory and details can be found in [16]. First, we introduce a language for expressions used in separating connectives:

```
Inductive expr : Set :=
  var_e : gp_reg → expr | int_e : int 32 → expr | add_e : expr → expr → expr | ...
```

In this language, variables are registers and constants are (32-bit) words. Given an expression e and a store s, the function eval returns the value of the expression e in store s.

The *mapsto* connective e1 ↦ e2 holds in a state with a store s and a singleton heap with address eval e1 s and contents eval e2 s:

```
Definition mapsto (e e':expr) : assert := fun s _ _ h =>
  ∃ p, u2Z (eval e s) = 4 * p ∧ h = heap.singleton p (eval e' s).
Notation "e1 ↦ e2" := (mapsto e1 e2).
```

The *separating conjunction* P * Q holds in a state whose heap can be divided into two disjoint heaps such that P and Q hold:

```
Definition sep_con (P Q:assert) : assert := fun s s' m h =>
  ∃ h1, ∃ h2, h1 ⊥ h2 ∧ h = h1 ∪ h2 ∧ P s s' m h1 ∧ Q s s' m h2.
Notation "P * Q" := (sep_con P Q).
```

In practice, the separating conjunction provides a concise way to express that two data structures reside in disjoint parts of the heap.

Using the separating conjunction, the mapsto connective can be generalized to arrays of words: (e ⇰ a::b::...) holds in a state whose heap contains a list of contiguous words a, b, ... starting at address eval e s:

```
Fixpoint mapstos (e:expr) (lst:list (int 32)) : assert :=
  match lst with
    | nil => empty_heap
    | hd::tl => (e ↦ int_e hd) * (mapstos (add_e e (int_e four32)) tl)
  end.
Notation "e ⇰ lst" := (mapstos e lst).
```

Hoare triples are encoded as an inductive relation {{ P }} c {{ Q }} (notation for semax P c Q) between commands and pre/post-conditions encoded as assertions. For illustration, here follows the implementation of the Hoare triples for the commands add and lw:

```
Inductive semax : assert → cmd → assert → Prop :=
| semax_add: ∀ Q rd rs rt,
  {{ update_store_add rd rs rt Q }} add rd rs rt {{ Q }}
| semax_lw : ∀ P rt offset base,
  {{ lookup_heap_lw rt offset base P }} lw rt offset base {{ P }}
| ...
```

In the preconditions, update_store_add and lookup_heap_lw are predicate transformers. The effect of executing add rd rs rt is to update the contents of the register rd with the result of the operation (vrs ⊕ vrt) (where vrs and vrt are the contents of the registers rs and rt), provided the addition in two's complement does not overflow:

```
Definition update_store_add rd rs rt P : assert := fun s s' m h =>
  - 2^^31 ≤  s2Z (gpr.lookup rs s) + s2Z (gpr.lookup rt s) < 2^^31 →
  P (gpr.update rd (gpr.lookup rs s ⊕ gpr.lookup rt s) s) s' m h.
```

The function `lookup_heap_lw` checks that the access is word-aligned and the cell-contents specified:

```
Definition lookup_heap_lw rt offset base P : assert := fun s s' m h =>
  ∃ p, u2Z (gpr.lookup base s ⊕ sign_extend offset) = 4 * p ∧
  ∃ z, heap.lookup p h = Some z ∧ P (gpr.update rt z s) s' m h.
```

4 Application to Multi-precision Arithmetic

Using our encoding of Hoare logic for SmartMIPS, we have written, specified, and verified several SmartMIPS implementations of multi-precision arithmetic functions in Coq. In this section, we give an overview of our experiments with a detailed account of the formal verification of the Montgomery multiplication.

4.1 Specification of Multi-precision Arithmetic Functions

Multi-precision Integers We encode multi-precision integers as lists of machine integers stored in memory (using the $\mapsto$ connective defined in Sect. 3.2). In the following, `Nth i A` represents the ith element of the list `A` of machine integers. The interpretation of a multi-precision integer as a mathematical integer is provided by a recursive function: `Sum k A` represents the decimal value of the k first words of the list `A` of machine integers (least significant word first) interpreted as unsigned. The fact that the length of multi-precision integers is explicit is important to write loop invariants, that often talk about "partial" multi-precision integers, to represent the decimal values of partial products for example.

Arithmetic Relations Thanks to shallow encoding and our lemmas that relate machine integers to their decimal values, we can reuse predicates and functions from the standard Coq library. In the following, `a == b [[n]]` is the Coq version of $a \equiv b[n]$.

4.2 Formal Verification of the Montgomery Multiplication

The Montgomery multiplication [2] is a modular multiplication. Given three k-word integers X, Y, and M such that

$$\text{Sum k X} < \text{Sum k M} \land \text{Sum k Y} < \text{Sum k M} \tag{1}$$

the Montgomery multiplication computes a k+1-word integer Z such that

$$\text{Zbeta k} * \text{Sum (k+1) Z} == \text{Sum k X} * \text{Sum k Y} [[\text{Sum k M}]] \tag{2}$$

The advantage of the Montgomery multiplication is that it does not require a multi-precision division, but uses less-expensive shifts instead. The price to pay is the parasite factor `Zbeta k` whose elimination requires a second pass.

The implementation of the Montgomery multiplication we deal with (Fig. 1) is the so-called "Finely Integrated Operand Scanning" (FIOS) variant [4]. Intuitively, it resembles the classical algorithm for multi-precision multiplication: it has two nested loops, the inner-loop incrementally computes partial products (modulo) that are successively added by the outer-loop. These partial products modulo are computed in such a way that the least significant word is always zero, thus guaranteeing that the final result will fit in k+1 words of storage. For this to be possible, the Montgomery multiplication requires the pre-computation of the modular inverse alpha of the least significant word of the modulus:

$$\text{u2Z (Nth 0 M) * u2Z alpha == -1 [[Zbeta 1]]} \tag{3}$$

```
Definition montgomery
  k alpha x y z m j i
  X Y M Z one zero quot C t s :=

  addiu one zero one16;
  addiu C zero zero16;
  addiu i zero zero16;
  while_bne i k (
    lwxs X i x;
    lw Y zero16 y;
    lw Z zero16 z;
    multu X Y;
    lw M zero16 m;
    maddu Z one;
    mflo t;
    mfhi s;
    multu t alpha;
    addiu j zero one16;
    mflo quot;
    mthi s;
    mtlo t;
```
```
    maddu quot M;
    mflhxu Z;
    addiu t z zero16;
    while_bne j k (
      lwxs Y j y;
      lwxs Z j z;
      maddu X Y;
      lwxs M j m;
      maddu Z one;
      maddu quot M;
      addiu j j one16;
      mflhxu Z;
      addiu t t four16;
      sw Z mfour16 t
    );
    maddu C one;
    mflhxu Z;
    addiu i i one16;
    sw Z zero16 t;
    mflhxu C
  ).
```

Fig. 1. The Montgomery Multiplication in WhileSMIPS

The SmartMIPS architecture is well-suited to the implementation of the FIOS variant of the Montgomery multiplication because the addition performed in the inner-loop (that adds two products of 32-bits integers) fits in the integer multiplier (of size greater than 72 bits).

The formal Hoare triple that specifies the Montgomery multiplication is displayed in Fig. 2. The hypotheses HX, HY, and Halpha correspond to the input-conditions (1) and (3), as explained above. Other hypotheses are technical: they prevent overflows and enforce alignments (similar-looking conditions are abbreviated by "..."). The output-condition (2) appears in the post-condition; observe that the k+1th word of storage is provided by the register C. The existence in memory of input-words and output-words is specified by the separation logic formula.

Formal verification of the Montgomery multiplication is done by forward reasoning. Let us comment on two key aspects of this verification.

Let A be the value of the multiplier before entering the inner-loop and $A\%n$ the remainder of the division of A by $2^{\frown}n$. The Montgomery multiplication computes quot = $((A\%32) \odot \text{alpha})\%32$ and adds quot $\odot$ M0 to the multiplier ($\odot$ is the unsigned multiplication, definition not displayed in this paper). The lemma

```
Lemma montgomery_specif : ∀ nk (Hk: 0 < nk) nx ny nm nz
  (Hnx: 4 * nx + 4 * nk < Zbeta 1) (Hny: ...) (Hnm: ...) (Hnz: ...)
  X Y M (Hx: length X = nk) (Hy: ...) (Hm: ...)
  (HX: Sum nk X < Sum nk M) (HY: Sum nk Y < Sum nk M)
  vx vy vm vz (Hvx: u2Z vx = 4 * nx) (Hvy: ...) (Hvm: ...) (Hvz: ...)
  valpha (Halpha: u2Z (Nth 0 M) * u2Z valpha == -1 [[ Zbeta 1 ]]),

  {{ fun s s' m_ h => ∃ Z,
     length Z = nk ∧ list_of_zeros Z ∧
     gpr.lookup x s = vx ∧ gpr.lookup y s = vy ∧
     gpr.lookup z s = vz ∧ gpr.lookup m s = vm ∧
     u2Z (gpr.lookup k s) = nk ∧ gpr.lookup alpha s = valpha ∧
     (var_e x ↦ X) * (var_e y ↦ Y) * (var_e z ↦ Z) * (var_e m ↦ M) s s' m_ h ∧
     multiplier.is_null m_ }}

  montgomery k alpha x y z m j i X_ Y_ M_ Z_ one gpr_zero quot C t s

  {{ fun s s' m_ h => ∃ Z, length Z = nk ∧
     (var_e x ↦ X) * (var_e y ↦ Y) * (var_e z ↦ Z) * (var_e m ↦ M) s s' m_ h ∧
     Zbeta nk * Sum (nk+1) (Z ++ gpr.lookup C s :: nil) ==
       Sum nk X * Sum nk Y [[ Sum nk M ]] ∧
     Sum (nk+1) (Z ++ gpr.lookup C s :: nil) < 2 * Sum nk M }}.
```

Fig. 2. Formal Specification of the Montgomery Multiplication

below captures the fact that the resulting multiplier is a multiple of β, and thus the least significant word of the partial product is always zero:

```
Import multiplier.
Lemma montgomery_lemma : ∀ alpha M0 (A:int 64) m,
  u2Z M0 * u2Z alpha == -1 [[Zbeta 1]] → utoZ m < Zbeta 2 → utoZ m = u2Z A →
  lo (maddu_op (((A % 32 ⊙ alpha) % 32) ⊙ M0) m) = zero32.
```

As usual, the heart of the verification is to produce the right invariant for the inner-loop. In the case of the FIOS variant of the Montgomery multiplication, the difficulty comes from the fact that the zeroed word of storage is used to "shift-in" the second least-significant word (LSW) of the partial product. More precisely, at the jth iteration of the inner-loop, the algorithm uses the jth LSW of the current partial product to compute the $j-1^{\text{th}}$ LSW of the new partial product. To write this invariant, we use a function for "multi-precision integers with a hole". Multi-precision integers with a hole are like multi-precision integers except that there is one word that we ignore in computing the represented value:

```
Definition Sum_hole l len hole (lst:list (int l)) :=
  Sum (len - 1) (del_nth hole lst).
```

Using this function, the relation between the multiplier and the multi-precision integers in memory is written:

```
Zbeta (ni + 1) * Sum_hole (nk + 1) (nj - 1) (Z ++ gpr.lookup C s :: nil) +
  multiplier.utoZ m * Zbeta (ni + nj) ==
Sum ni X * Sum nk Y + Sum nj Y * u2Z (nth ni X zero32) * Zbeta ni +
  Sum nj M * u2Z (gpr.lookup quot s) * Zbeta ni [[ Sum nk M ]]
```

where ni, nj, and nk are the contents of the i, j, and k registers, and s is the current store of general-purpose registers.

4.3 Experimental Results

Besides the Montgomery multiplication, we have verified SmartMIPS implementations of several classical algorithms for multi-precision arithmetic. The code is available online [17]; the table below summarizes the sizes of programs and proof scripts. For proof scripts, we distinguish between the number of lines used to write assertions (all pre/post-conditions, including intermediate forward-reasoning steps) and the number of lines used for proof construction (calls to Coq tactics, including custom tactics, and application of lemmas).

Multi-precision function	Number of asm instructions	Size of proof scripts (lines)		
		total	assertions (ratio)	individual steps (average)
addition	11	835	203 (24%)	632 (57)
subtraction	22	1473	340 (23%)	1133 (52)
multiplication	20	1634	413 (25%)	1221 (61)
Montgomery	37	3881	955 (25%)	2926 (79)

Although assertions occupy around 24% of the proof scripts, this is not a nuisance because they only change a little from one reasoning step to the other, and it anyway helps to understand the verification. Appropriate tactics for forward reasoning could get rid of this overhead.

In average, each atomic Hoare triple is proved with 62 Coq commands. Some parts are inherently difficult because of low-level manipulations of multi-precision integers, that require many syntactic manipulations of goals and hypotheses and are difficult to automate satisfactorily. Yet, many parts of proof scripts are repetitive (trivial goals, obvious rewriting, etc.) and we already have a good deal of small-scale custom tactics. As a mid-term goal, we think it should be possible and desirable to use no more than 20 Coq commands per reasoning step.

5 Program Extraction

In this section, we explain how to safely extract ready-to-run SmartMIPS programs from our Coq verifications. In Sect. 3.2, we have defined an axiomatic semantics for WhileSMIPS, a subset of structured SmartMIPS programs. Though it is sufficient to specify and verify arithmetic functions and many other programs, we cannot directly assemble and run verified programs: we first need to translate them into the set of SmartMIPS programs with jumps, and ensure that this translation is correct. For this purpose, we equip both WhileSMIPS and SmartMIPS programs with an operational semantics.

5.1 SmartMIPS Operational Semantics

The MIPS documentation [5] gives the semantics of SmartMIPS in terms of a virtual machine that represents the processor. It has an explicit program counter and its execution is described by a small-step semantics. We encode this small-step semantics in Coq. For the sake of simplicity, we restrict ourselves to word-aligned memory accesses, we ignore exceptions and pipelining optimizations[1].

Syntax We split SmartMIPS instructions into the set of instructions that modify the state and just increment the program counter (type cmd0), and the set of instructions that only modify the control-flow (type branch). We do not display in this paper the syntax of state-modifying instructions because it is similar to cmd (Sect. 3.2), without the control-flow commands (we just suffix type constructors with "0" to distinguish them). The syntax of branching instructions is encoded as the inductive type branch:

```
Definition label := nat.
Inductive branch : Set :=
 jmp : label → branch | beq : gp_reg → gp_reg → label → branch | ...
```

jmp inconditionnally jumps to a given label, and beq, etc. conditionally jump to some label. A SmartMIPS instruction is either a cmd0 or a branch instruction (the dummy instruction no_insn below is just a technical convenience) and a SmartMIPS program is a list of instructions (without explicit structure, the positions of instructions in this list serving as labels):

```
Inductive insn : Set :=
 cmd_insn : cmd0 → insn | branch_insn : branch → insn | no_insn : insn.
Definition prog := list insn.
```

Operational Semantics. The operational semantics of cmd0 instructions is encoded as an inductive type st -- c --> st' that represents the execution of the instruction c from state st to state st'. For illustration, here follows the semantics of add:

```
Inductive exec0 : option state → cmd0 → option state → Prop :=
| exec0_add : ∀ s s' vrt vrs m h rd rs rt,
  gpr.lookup rs s = vrs → gpr.lookup rt s = vrt →
  -2^^31 ≤ s2Z vrt + s2Z vrs < 2^^31 →
  Some (s,s',m,h) -- add0 rd rs rt --> Some (gpr.update rd (vrs ⊕ vrt) s,s',m,h)
| ...
```

The operational semantics of branch instructions is encoded as an inductive type n |> (pc,st) >> c >> (pc',st') that represents the execution of the branch c from program counter pc and state st to program counter pc' and state st' (under the constraint that the destination label is smaller than n). Note that st and st' can be different when the jump destination is not valid (leading to an error state). For illustration, here follows the semantics of jmp:

```
Inductive exec_branch (max:label)
  : branch → label * option state → label * option state → Prop :=
| exec_jmp : ∀ pc st j, max ≥ j ->
  max |> (pc, Some st) >> jmp j >> (j, Some st)
| ...
```

---

[1] In MIPS, the first instruction following a conditional branching is unconditionally executed. In other words, the first instruction that is syntactically after a conditional branching is executed before. In this paper, we ignore this issue.

The operational semantics of SmartMIPS programs is encoded as an inductive type prg ||- (pc,st) --> (pc',st') that represents the execution of program prg from program counter pc and state st to program counter pc' and state st':

```
Inductive exec_asm (prg:prog)
  : label * option state → label * option state → Prop :=
| exec_asm_cmd0 : ∀ pc c st st', Nth pc prg = cmd_insn c →
  Some st -- c --> Some st' →
  prg ||-- (pc, Some st) --> (pc+1, Some st')
| exec_asm_branch : ∀ pc j st pc' st', Nth pc prg = branch_insn j →
  length prg |> (pc, Some st) >> j >> (pc', st') →
  prg ||-- (pc, Some st) --> (pc', st')
| ...
```

For the composition of instructions to be possible, this inductive type also has type constructors (not displayed here for lack of space) that express the reflexivity and transitivity of the operational semantics.

5.2   Translation from WhileSMIPS to SmartMIPS

The role of the translator is simply to translate the control-flow commands of WhileSMIPS into SmartMIPS:

```
Fixpoint translate (lbl:label) (c:cmd) : prog :=
  match c with
    | while_bne r1 r2 c => let prg := translate (lbl + 1) c in
        branch_insn (beq r1 r2 (lbl + length prg + 2)) :: prg ++
    branch_insn (jmp lbl) :: nil
    ...
  end.
```

The correctness proof of this translator consists in showing that, for any state, the final state of the execution of a WhileSMIPS progam and the final state of the execution of its translated SmartMIPS version are the same. To do this proof, we still need to equip WhileSMIPS programs with an operational semantics. The latter is encoded as a inductive type exec st c st' that represents the execution of the command c from state st to state st' (big-step operational semantics, similar to [16]). To ensure that this operational semantics agrees with the axiomatic semantics of Sect. 3.2, we show that the latter is sound and complete w.r.t. the former (formal proofs are similar to [10]). Finally, using the big-step semantics of WhileSMIPS and the small-step semantics of SmartMIPS programs, the correctness of the translator is proved by induction:

```
Lemma translate_correct: ∀ c st p c' st',
  translate (length p) c = c' →
  exec (Some st) c (Some st') →
  p ++ c' ||-- (length p, Some st) --> (length (p ++ c'), Some st').
```

6   Related Work

Much work about formal encoding of assembly languages in proof assistants has been done with application to proof-carrying code (PCC) in mind [7,8,9].

Although the encoded semantics often allows for programs with arbitrary jumps, details such as machine integers are usually not treated. This makes it difficult to reuse existing implementations of PCC frameworks to formally verify arithmetic functions, whose algorithms require bit-level specifications.

There exist other encodings of machine integers in Coq. Leroy has encoded such a library for integers modulo 2^{32} as part of the development of a certified compiler [14]. His encoding uses the relative integers of Coq (the z type) instead of lists ot bits. We found it difficult to reuse directly his implementation because the length of integers (32) is hard-wired and we needed a similar library for several lengths. Chlipala has encoded a library similar to ours but based on dependent vectors [15]. We think that our implementation based on an abstract type is more flexible than dependent vectors because it separates the issues of formal proofs and dependent types.

In this paper, we use a combination of a Hoare logic for structured Smart-MIPS with a certified translator to SmartMIPS programs with jumps. Another approach would have been to encode a (more intricate) Hoare logic for low-level programs with jumps (such as [12,13]) and to specialize it to structured programs to carry out verifications. We chose the former approach because our primary concern was the formal verification of concrete examples of arithmetic functions, whose implementations turn out to fit well in structured SmartMIPS.

7 Conclusion

In this paper, we proposed an approach to formal verification of arithmetic functions in assembly based on the combined use of a certified implementation of a Hoare logic for assembly programs with loops and a certified translator to assembly programs with jumps. This approach enables formal verification of ready-to-run assembly programs with a familiar-looking Hoare logic. At the heart of our implementation is a module for machine integers that makes it possible to prove formally the lemmas, such as overflow conditions, needed for verification of assembly programs. Using this approach, we have formally verified several arithmetic functions written in SmartMIPS assembly, including an optimized implementation of the Montgomery multiplication, a de facto-standard for the implementation of many cryptosystems.

Future Work. In order to verify more arithmetic functions, we are extending our library with a semantics for function calls and returns, and with predicates to deal with signed multi-precision integers. We also plan to encode a semantics for exceptions to enable verification of embedded systems.

Acknowledgments. This work is partially supported by the Grant in Aid of Special Coordination Funds for Promoting Science and Technology, Ministry of Education, Culture, Sports, Science and Technology, Japan. The authors are grateful to Pascal Paillier at Gemalto who provided the code of the Montgomery multiplication with detailed explanations.

References

1. Hoare, C.A.R.: An Axiomatic Basis for Computer Programming. Communications of the ACM 12(10), 576–585 (1969)
2. Montgomery, P.L.: Modular multiplication without trial division. Mathematics of Computation 44(170), 519–521 (1985)
3. Various contributors. The Coq Proof assistant. http://coq.inria.fr
4. Koc, C.K., Acar, T., Kaliski Jr, B.S.: Analyzing and Comparing Montgomery Multiplication Algorithms. IEEE Micro 16(3), 23–26 (1996)
5. MIPS Technologies. MIPS32 4KS Processor Core Family Software User's Manual MIPS Technologies, Inc., 1225 Charleston Road, Mountain View, CA 94043-1353
6. Reynolds, J.C.: Separation Logic: A Logic for Shared Mutable Data Structures. In: LICS 2002. 17th IEEE Symposium on Logic in Computer Science, pp. 55–74 (2002)
7. Hamid, N.A., Shao, Z., Trifonov, V., Monnier, S., Ni, Z.: A Syntactic Approach to Foundational Proof-Carrying Code. In: LICS 2002. 7th IEEE Symposium on Logic In Computer Science, pp. 89–100 (2002)
8. Yu, D., Hamid, N.A., Shao, Z.: Building Certified Libraries for PCC: Dynamic Storage Allocation. In: Degano, P. (ed.) ESOP 2003 and ETAPS 2003. LNCS, vol. 2618, pp. 363–379. Springer, Heidelberg (2003)
9. Hamid, N.A., Shao, Z.: Interfacing Hoare Logic and Type Systems for Foundational Proof-Carrying Code. In: Slind, K., Bunker, A., Gopalakrishnan, G.C. (eds.) TPHOLs 2004. LNCS, vol. 3223, pp. 118–135. Springer, Heidelberg (2004)
10. Weber, T.: Towards Mechanized Program Verification with Separation Logic. In: Marcinkowski, J., Tarlecki, A. (eds.) CSL 2004. LNCS, vol. 3210, Springer, Heidelberg (2004)
11. Babić, D., Musuvathi, M.: Modular Arithmetic Decision Procedure. Microsoft Research Technical Report. MSR-TR-2005-114
12. Saabas, A., Uustalu, T.: A Compositional Natural Semantics and Hoare Logic for Low-Level Languages. Electronic Notes in Theoretical Computer Science 156, 151–168 (2006)
13. Tan, G., Appel, A.W.: A Compositional Logic for Control Flow. In: Emerson, E.A., Namjoshi, K.S. (eds.) VMCAI 2006. LNCS, vol. 3855, pp. 80–94. Springer, Heidelberg (2005)
14. Leroy, X.: Formal certification of a compiler back-end, or: programming a compiler with a proof assistant. In: POPL 2006. 33rd ACM SIGPLAN-SIGACT Symposium on Principles of Programming Languages, pp. 42–65
15. Chlipala, A.J.: Modular development of certified program verifiers with a proof assistant. In: ICFP 2006. 11th ACM SIGPLAN International Conference on Functional Programming, pp. 160–171 (2006)
16. Marti, N., Affeldt, R., Yonezawa, A.: Formal Verification of the Heap Manager of an Operating System using Separation Logic. In: Liu, Z., He, J. (eds.) ICFEM 2006. LNCS, vol. 4260, pp. 400–419. Springer, Heidelberg (2006)
17. Affeldt, R., Marti, N.: An Approach to Formal Verification of Arithmetic Functions in Assembly—Proof Scripts, http://staff.aist.go.jp/reynald.affeldt/seplog/asian2006

Author Index

Lecture Notes in Computer Science

Sublibrary 1: Theoretical Computer Science and General Issues

For information about Vols. 1– 4576
please contact your bookseller or Springer

Vol. 4705: O. Gervasi, M.L. Gavrilova (Eds.), Computational Science and Its Applications – ICCSA 2007, Part I. XLIV, 1169 pages. 2007.

Vol. 4703: L. Caires, V.T. Vasconcelos (Eds.), CONCUR 2007 – Concurrency Theory. XIII, 507 pages. 2007.

Vol. 4700: C.B. Jones, Z. Liu, J. Woodcock (Eds.), Formal Methods and Hybrid Real-Time Systems. XVI, 539 pages. 2007.

Vol. 4699: B. Kågström, E. Elmroth, J. Dongarra, J. Waśniewski (Eds.), Applied Parallel Computing. XXIX, 1192 pages. 2007.

Vol. 4698: L. Arge, M. Hoffmann, E. Welzl (Eds.), Algorithms – ESA 2007. XV, 769 pages. 2007.

Vol. 4697: L. Choi, Y. Paek, S. Cho (Eds.), Advances in Computer Systems Architecture. XIII, 400 pages. 2007.

Vol. 4688: K. Li, M. Fei, G.W. Irwin, S. Ma (Eds.), Bio-Inspired Computational Intelligence and Applications. XIX, 805 pages. 2007.

Vol. 4684: L. Kang, Y. Liu, S. Zeng (Eds.), Evolvable Systems: From Biology to Hardware. XIV, 446 pages. 2007.

Vol. 4683: L. Kang, Y. Liu, S. Zeng (Eds.), Advances in Computation and Intelligence. XVII, 663 pages. 2007.

Vol. 4681: D.-S. Huang, L. Heutte, M. Loog (Eds.), Advanced Intelligent Computing Theories and Applications. XXVI, 1379 pages. 2007.

Vol. 4672: K. Li, C. Jesshope, H. Jin, J.-L. Gaudiot (Eds.), Network and Parallel Computing. XVIII, 558 pages. 2007.

Vol. 4671: V.E. Malyshkin (Ed.), Parallel Computing Technologies. XIV, 635 pages. 2007.

Vol. 4669: J.M. de Sá, L.A. Alexandre, W. Duch, D. Mandic (Eds.), Artificial Neural Networks – ICANN 2007, Part II. XXXI, 990 pages. 2007.

Vol. 4668: J.M. de Sá, L.A. Alexandre, W. Duch, D. Mandic (Eds.), Artificial Neural Networks – ICANN 2007, Part I. XXXI, 948 pages. 2007.

Vol. 4666: M.E. Davies, C.J. James, S.A. Abdallah, M.D. Plumbley (Eds.), Independent Component Analysis and Blind Signal Separation. XIX, 847 pages. 2007.

Vol. 4665: J. Hromkovič, R. Královič, M. Nunkesser, P. Widmayer (Eds.), Stochastic Algorithms: Foundations and Applications. X, 167 pages. 2007.

Vol. 4664: J. Durand-Lose, M. Margenstern (Eds.), Machines, Computations, and Universality. X, 325 pages. 2007.

Vol. 4661: U. Montanari, D. Sannella, R. Bruni (Eds.), Trustworthy Global Computing. X, 339 pages. 2007.

Vol. 4649: V. Diekert, M.V. Volkov, A. Voronkov (Eds.), Computer Science – Theory and Applications. XIII, 420 pages. 2007.

Vol. 4647: R. Martin, M.A. Sabin, J.R. Winkler (Eds.), Mathematics of Surfaces XII. IX, 509 pages. 2007.

Vol. 4646: J. Duparc, T.A. Henzinger (Eds.), Computer Science Logic. XIV, 600 pages. 2007.

Vol. 4644: N. Azémard, L. Svensson (Eds.), Integrated Circuit and System Design. XIV, 583 pages. 2007.

Vol. 4641: A.-M. Kermarrec, L. Bougé, T. Priol (Eds.), Euro-Par 2007 Parallel Processing. XXVII, 974 pages. 2007.

Vol. 4639: E. Csuhaj-Varjú, Z. Ésik (Eds.), Fundamentals of Computation Theory. XIV, 508 pages. 2007.

Vol. 4638: T. Stützle, M. Birattari, H. H. Hoos (Eds.), Engineering Stochastic Local Search Algorithms. X, 223 pages. 2007.

Vol. 4630: H.J. van den Herik, P. Ciancarini, H.H.L.M.(J.) Donkers (Eds.), Computers and Games. XII, 283 pages. 2007.

Vol. 4628: L.N. de Castro, F.J. Von Zuben, H. Knidel (Eds.), Artificial Immune Systems. XII, 438 pages. 2007.

Vol. 4627: M. Charikar, K. Jansen, O. Reingold, J.D.P. Rolim (Eds.), Approximation, Randomization, and Combinatorial Optimization. XII, 626 pages. 2007.

Vol. 4624: T. Mossakowski, U. Montanari, M. Haveraaen (Eds.), Algebra and Coalgebra in Computer Science. XI, 463 pages. 2007.

Vol. 4623: M. Collard (Ed.), Ontologies-Based Databases and Information Systems. X, 153 pages. 2007.

Vol. 4621: D. Wagner, R. Wattenhofer (Eds.), Algorithms for Sensor and Ad Hoc Networks. XIII, 415 pages. 2007.

Vol. 4619: F. Dehne, J.-R. Sack, N. Zeh (Eds.), Algorithms and Data Structures. XVI, 662 pages. 2007.

Vol. 4618: S.G. Akl, C.S. Calude, M.J. Dinneen, G. Rozenberg, H.T. Wareham (Eds.), Unconventional Computation. X, 243 pages. 2007.

Vol. 4616: A.W.M. Dress, Y. Xu, B. Zhu (Eds.), Combinatorial Optimization and Applications. XI, 390 pages. 2007.

Vol. 4614: B. Chen, M. Paterson, G. Zhang (Eds.), Combinatorics, Algorithms, Probabilistic and Experimental Methodologies. XII, 530 pages. 2007.

Vol. 4613: F.P. Preparata, Q. Fang (Eds.), Frontiers in Algorithmics. XI, 348 pages. 2007.

Vol. 4600: H. Comon-Lundh, C. Kirchner, H. Kirchner (Eds.), Rewriting, Computation and Proof. XVI, 273 pages. 2007.

Vol. 4599: S. Vassiliadis, M. Bereković, T.D. Hämäläinen (Eds.), Embedded Computer Systems: Architectures, Modeling, and Simulation. XVIII, 466 pages. 2007.

Vol. 4598: G. Lin (Ed.), Computing and Combinatorics. XII, 570 pages. 2007.

Vol. 4596: L. Arge, C. Cachin, T. Jurdziński, A. Tarlecki (Eds.), Automata, Languages and Programming. XVII, 953 pages. 2007.

Vol. 4595: D. Bošnački, S. Edelkamp (Eds.), Model Checking Software. X, 285 pages. 2007.

Vol. 4590: W. Damm, H. Hermanns (Eds.), Computer Aided Verification. XV, 562 pages. 2007.

Vol. 4588: T. Harju, J. Karhumäki, A. Lepistö (Eds.), Developments in Language Theory. XI, 423 pages. 2007.

Vol. 4583: S.R. Della Rocca (Ed.), Typed Lambda Calculi and Applications. X, 397 pages. 2007.

Vol. 4580: B. Ma, K. Zhang (Eds.), Combinatorial Pattern Matching. XII, 366 pages. 2007.